Portrait of a Castrato

This book explores the fascinating life of the most documented musician of the seventeenth century. Born in 1626 into a bourgeois family in Pistoia, Italy, Atto Melani was castrated to preserve his singing voice and soon rose to both artistic and social prominence. His extant letters not only depict the musical activities of several European centers, they reveal the real-life context of music and the musician: how a singer related to patrons and colleagues, what he thought about his profession, and the role music played in his life. Whether Atto was singing, spying, having sex, composing, or even rejecting his art, his life illustrates how music-making was always also a negotiation for power. Providing a rare glimpse of the social and political contexts of seventeenth-century music, Roger Freitas sheds light on the mechanisms that generated meaning for music, clarifying what music at this time actually was.

Roger Freitas is Associate Professor in the Department of Musicology, Eastman School of Music, University of Rochester. His writing has appeared in journals including the *Journal of Musicology, Music and Letters*, and *Opera News*. This is his first book.

New perspectives in music history and criticism

General editors: Jeffrey Kallberg, Anthony Newcomb and Ruth Solie

This series explores the conceptual frameworks that shape or have shaped the ways in which we understand music and its history, and aims to elaborate structures of explanation, interpretation, commentary, and criticism which make music intelligible and which provide a basis for argument about judgements of value. The intellectual scope of the series is broad. Some investigations will treat, for example, historiographical topics, others will apply cross-disciplinary methods to the criticism of music, and there will also be studies which consider music in its relation to society, culture, and politics. Overall, the series hopes to create a greater presence for music in the ongoing discourse among the human sciences.

Published titles

Leslie C. Dunn and Nancy A. Jones (eds.), *Embodied Voices: Representing Female Vocality in Western Culture*

Downing A. Thomas, *Music and the Origins of Language: Theories from the French Enlightenment*

Thomas S. Grey, *Wagner's Musical Prose*

Daniel K.L. Chua, *Absolute Music and the Construction of Meaning*

Adam Krims, *Rap Music and the Poetics of Identity*

Annette Richards, *The Free Fantasia and the Musical Picturesque*

Richard Will, *The Characteristic Symphony in the Age of Haydn and Beethoven*

Christopher Morris, *Reading Opera Between the Lines: Orchestral Interludes and Cultural Meaning from Wagner to Berg*

Emma Dillon, *Medieval Music-Making and the 'Roman de Fauvel'*

David Yearsley, *Bach and the Meanings of Counterpoint*

David Metzer, *Quotation and Cultural Meaning in Twentieth-Century Music*

Alexander Rehding, *Hugo Riemann and the Birth of Modern Musical Thought*

Dana Gooley, *The Virtuoso Liszt*

Bonnie Gordon, *Monteverdi's Unruly Women: The Power of Song in Early Modern Italy*

Gary Tomlinson, *The Singing of the New World: Indigenous Voice in the Era of European Contact*

Matthew Gelbart, *The Invention of "Folk Music" and "Art Music": Emerging Categories from Ossian to Wagner*

Olivia A. Bloechl, *Native American Song at the Frontiers of Early Modern Music*

Giuseppe Gerbino, *Music and the Myth of Arcadia in Renaissance Italy*

Roger Freitas, *Portrait of a Castrato: Politics, Patronage, and Music in the Life of Atto Melani*

Portrait of a Castrato

*Politics, Patronage, and Music in the
Life of Atto Melani*

Roger Freitas

CAMBRIDGE
UNIVERSITY PRESS

CAMBRIDGE UNIVERSITY PRESS

Cambridge, New York, Melbourne, Madrid, Cape Town, Singapore,
São Paulo, Delhi

Cambridge University Press
The Edinburgh Building, Cambridge CB2 8RU, UK

Published in the United States of America by Cambridge University Press,
New York

www.cambridge.org
Information on this title: www.cambridge.org/9780521885218

First published 2009

Printed in the United Kingdom at the University Press, Cambridge

A catalogue record for this publication is available from the British Library

Library of Congress Cataloguing in Publication data
Freitas, Roger.
Portrait of a castrato : politics, patronage, and music in the life of
Atto Melani / Roger Freitas.
    p.   cm. – (New perspectives in music history and criticism)
Includes bibliographical references.
ISBN 978-0-521-88521-8
1. Melani, Atto, 1626-1714.   2. Castrati – Biography.   I. Title.   II. Series.
ML420.M3497F74   2009
782.1092–dc22
[B]

2009004949

ISBN 978-0-521-88521-8 hardback

For my wonderful parents, Ron and Mickey Freitas

Contents

Figures

Tables

Plates

Library sigla and abbreviations

The following library sigla and abbreviations are used throughout this study. They are adapted from the sigla used in the *Répertoire international des sources musicales*, with additions to accommodate other sources used here.

B Belgium
  Bc Brussels, Conservatoire Royal de Musique, Bibliothèque
D Germany
  Kl Kassel, Gesamthochschul-Bibliothek, Landesbibliothek und Murhardsche Bibliothek, Musiksammlung
  Mbs Munich, Bayerische Staatsbibliothek, Musiksammlung
F France
  Pae Paris, Archives de la Ministère des Affaires Étrangères
    Pae, CP —, Corréspondence politique
    Pae, MD —, Mémoires et documents
  Pan Paris, Archives Nationales
  Pc Paris, Bibliothèque du Conservatoire National de Musique (within F Pn)
  Pm Paris, Bibliothèque Mazarine
  Pn Paris, Bibliothèque Nationale de France
GB Great Britain
  Cfm Cambridge, Fitzwilliam Museum, Department of Manuscripts and Printed Books
  Ckc Cambridge, King's College, Rowe Music Library
  Lbl London, British Library
  Och Oxford, Christ Church Library
I Italy
  Bc Bologna, Civico Museo Bibliografico Musicale
  Fas Florence, Archivio di Stato
    Fas, MdP —, Archivio Mediceo del Principato
  FEas Ferrara, Archivio di Stato
    FEas, Arch. Bent. —, Archivio Bentivoglio d'Aragona, Lettere sciolte
  Fn Florence, Biblioteca Nazionale Centrale
  MAas Mantua, Archivio di Stato
  MOas Modena, Archivio di Stato

MOe   Modena, Biblioteca Estense e Universitaria

Nc   Naples, Conservatorio di Musica S. Pietro a Maiella, Biblioteca

PS   Pistoia, Basilica di S. Zeno, Archivio Capitolare

PSas   Pistoia, Archivio di Stato

PSav   Pistoia, Archivio della Curia Vescovile

PSc   Pistoia, Biblioteca Comunale Forteguerriana

Rc   Rome, Biblioteca Casanatense

Rvat   Rome [Vatican City], Biblioteca Apostolica Vaticana

SUss   Subiaco, Monastery of Santa Scolastica

TOas   Turin, Archivio di Stato

US   United States

CHH   Chapel Hill, N.C., University of North Carolina at Chapel Hill, Music Library

LAuc   Los Angeles, University of California at Los Angeles, William Andrews Clark Memorial Library

Note on the original texts of translations

Because this project depends so heavily on correspondence, the volume of quoted material is formidable. To avoid bloating the size (and cost) of the published volume, I agreed with Cambridge University Press to place the original language of all translations on a website operated by the Press. The URL for that site is www.cambridge.org/9780521885218. The entries are organized by chapter and then by footnote number. So, for example, to find the original Italian of the passage cited by footnote 15 in chapter 2, one would go to the web page for chapter 2 and then look under note 15.

As readers will quickly discern, I have not modernized the spelling and punctuation of the original-language materials. While I recognize that such updating is standard, especially in Italian, I do not pretend to the necessary text-editing skill, especially for so large and diverse a body of material. The issues go far beyond orthography, and in several cases the actual sense of passages depends on interpretations of the intended words. Instead, I have modified the text only in the following ways: I have tacitly expanded all abbreviations when their meaning was not in doubt (as is usually the case). The only exception has been in the use of honorifics (e.g., S.A.S.ma for Sua Altezza Serenissima), which, for reasons of space, I have left abbreviated. I have converted the sometimes variable use of diacritical marks to modern practice, but I have not altered diacriticals in situations where a modern word has been written as two: for example, I convert "perche" to "perché," but leave "per che" alone. Original punctuation and capitalization have been retained.

Citations of all the letters have been simplified in the body of the text to save space. For each letter, I give the author, addressee, place of origin, and date. This information can then be compared to either Appendix A (for Atto's letters) or Appendix B (for the letters of others), where full bibliographic information is provided.

Note on the editing of musical examples

For all of the musical examples and associated texts in this volume (which appear in chapter 6), I have followed the principles I adopted in my edition of Atto Melani's cantatas, published as Atto Melani, *Complete Cantatas*, Collegium Musicum: Yale University, series 2, vol. 15 (Middleton, Wis.: A-R Editions, 2006). Please see pages 95–97 of that edition for a full statement of the methodology. Fundamentally, the edition follows a "best-text" approach rather than tracing sources back to a theoretical, composer-approved version. The specific procedures used are fairly standard, and so few additional comments are necessary. I do use four types of accidentals: (1) normal accidentals generally render all accidentals present in a source, including those considered redundant by modern standards; (2) accidentals in square brackets correct conflicts between seventeenth-century and modern usage (e.g., regarding the length of time an accidental might apply); (3) small accidentals represent purely editorial suggestions; (4) accidentals in parentheses are purely cautionary. In a slight divergence from my published edition (where brackets were used), I have employed a larger and smaller font in the bass figures to indicate original versus editorial figures, respectively. Finally, all solid slurs are original, while dotted slurs are editorial. Again, the complete edition provides fuller information.

Figures 6.1 and 6.2 present the music of Luigi Rossi and Giacomo Carissimi and so do not stem from my edition, but I have retained the same basic approach. My sources for this music are as follows:

Figure 6.1   GB Och, Mus. Ms. 949, ff. 49–54; as reproduced in Luigi Rossi, *Cantatas by Luigi Rossi c. 1597–1653*, vol. I of *The Italian Cantata in the Seventeenth Century*, ed. Francesco Luisi (New York: Garland, 1986), 5–9.

Figure 6.2   I Bc, MS X.234; as edited in Robert Rau Holzer, "Music and Poetry in Seventeenth-Century Rome: Settings of the Canzonetta and Cantata Texts of Francesco Balducci, Domenico Benigni, Francesco Melosio, and Antonio Abati" (Ph.D. diss., Univ. of Pennsylvania, 1990), 933–45.

Acknowledgements

So many people have helped me so generously in the long course of this project that I almost hesitate to try to thank them all. But the pleasure of publicly acknowledging my debts is irresistible. This project began life as a dissertation, and so I start by thanking again my advisor and (now happily) friend, Ellen Rosand: her advice and support remain very important to me. One of the advantages in working on a seventeenth-century topic is the generosity that characterizes so many scholars in the field. Right at the beginning of this project, Robert L. Weaver offered me both his encouragement and his many microfilms of Melani music and documents. During my early research trips to Florence, Jean Grundy Fanelli shared much of her experience in the libraries of Tuscany as well as kind hospitality at her home. Over the years, Margaret Murata has offered all sorts of valuable advice and has helped me locate many missing bits of information: her heart must drop every time she finds another of my emails in her inbox with "just a quick question." Beth Glixon has generously notified me whenever she ran across a useful reference in her Venetian archival explorations, and more recently Valeria De Lucca has done the same while scouring the Colonna materials. During his long stays in Italy, my colleague and friend James Leve alerted me to a number of documents he found during his own work and cheerfully looked things up for me. More recently, I want to thank my department chair Patrick Macey for his (very) patient support of my work and his always helpful suggestions. And for assistance in a number of different ways I express my gratitude to Jennifer Brown, Ralph Locke, Kimberlyn Montford, and Massimiliano Sala.

I am especially in the debt of a circle of friends and associates who have offered their advice about translations. Anything worthy about the translations in this book is owed to the help of Mauro Calcagno, Sergio Parussa, Pietro Moretti, Thomas DiPiero, and Timothy Scheie. The remaining shortcomings are mine alone.

For this project, I have depended heavily on the good will and assistance of librarians and archivists, and so I am happy to be able to thank the directors and staffs of the following institutions in which I conducted research; although not all these libraries are represented in the text, the work I did in them was essential: the Archivio di Stato, Biblioteca Nazionale Centrale, and Biblioteca Mediceo-Laurenziana in Florence; the Biblioteca Forteguerriana and Archivio di Stato in Pistoia; the Archivio di Stato and Biblioteca Estense in Modena; the Archivio di Stato in Mantua; the Archivio di Stato in Lucca; the (former) Civico Museo Bibliografico-Musicale in Bologna; the Archivio di Stato in Turin; the Archivio di Stato, Biblioteca Casanatense, Biblioteca della Accademia dei Lincei, and Archivio Doria-Pamphili in Rome; the Biblioteca Apostolica Vaticana at the Vatican; the British Library in London; and, finally, the Bibliothèque Nationale, Bibliothèque Mazarine, Archives Nationales, and Archives de la Ministère des Affaires Étrangères in Paris.

Finally, I am pleased to acknowledge the following financial awards, which either directly or indirectly supported my work: two pre-dissertation fellowships from the Andrew W. Mellon Foundation; a fellowship (funding a junior leave) from the National Endowment for the Humanities; a fellowship from the American Academy in Rome; a subvention from the Donna Cardamone Jackson Publication Endowment Fund of the American Musicological Society; and support from my home institution, the Eastman School of Music, University of Rochester, in the form of leave time, the support of the Professional Development Committee, and a Provost's "first-book" subvention.

Introduction

In an age that prized extravagance, Atto Melani led a life that may itself seem an object of wonder. Born in 1626 into a bourgeois family in the Tuscan town of Pistoia, northwest of Florence, Atto was the second of seven brothers, all to become musicians, and the first of four to be castrated for the sake of his beautiful voice.[1] By the age of fifteen he seems already to have been working for Prince Mattias de' Medici, brother of the grand duke of Tuscany. Within a few years, Mattias loaned his singer to the court of France, where in the 1640s Atto first rose to prominence. On the one hand, his singing won him the favor of the queen regent Anne of Austria, mother of the young Louis XIV; on the other, his taste for political intrigue attracted the attention of Cardinal Mazarin, the queen's formidable first minister. This blend of music and politics set the tone for much of Atto's career.

Over the next fifteen years Atto in fact engineered a remarkable self-metamorphosis, from professional singer to gentleman diplomat. Early in his career, he performed whatever was commanded of him, from the title role of Luigi Rossi's historic *Orfeo* to the tiny female part of La Primavera in a one-off Mantuan spectacular. But as his ambitions grew, he became increasingly concerned about prestige. He realized that, as long as he continued to sing, especially publicly, he limited his social standing. And so, though a castrato, he adopted the unlikely posture of a talented musical amateur. When he ran into trouble, he lied, temporized, and played one patron off another, all in an attempt to shape his career and control his image. At a time when most singers were treated like servants, Atto sought the kind of professional independence that vocalists would regularly enjoy only in the following century.

He also began looking more seriously to non-musical activities for his success, particularly the fields of diplomacy and espionage. His efforts in fact involved him in many of the important political events of his day: he carried on clandestine negotiations in Bavaria preceding the 1657 Diet of Frankfurt; he accompanied Mazarin to the final conference and ceremonies for the

---

[1] Throughout this study I refer to Atto by his first name. While this intimate usage might at first seem odd, the specificity is demanded by the number of Melani family members who will appear. The practice is also historical, with "Signor Atto" as a common form of address. Also, as figure 1.1 (page 21) shows, Atto had two sisters as well, both born after all the boys. He rarely mentions his sisters in his correspondence, and so unfortunately they play little role in this study.

Peace of the Pyrenees (1659); he assisted in the marriage arrangements between Grand Prince Cosimo III of Tuscany and Princess Marguerite-Louise D'Orléans (1661); and he even contributed to the election of his *concittadino* and friend Giulio Rospigliosi as Pope Clement IX (1667). Such endeavors boosted Atto's reputation on the European political scene, and he became a genuine resource for a number of leaders.

Atto's efforts demanded extensive correspondence, and indeed much of his life must have been spent writing letters, thousands of which have been preserved. He kept the courts of Tuscany, Mantua, Modena, Rome, Turin, and Paris informed about the internal affairs and even military strategies of the others. Such reporting could be dangerous: when his letters turned up among the papers of Nicolas Fouquet, Louis XIV's condemned *surintendant des finances*, Atto suffered eighteen years of banishment from France. Usually, however, his diplomacy earned him gratitude and reward: Louis XIV made him a gentleman of his chamber and titular abbot of a monastery in Normandy; the Republic of Venice and the city of Bologna granted him patrician status; and a long list of nobles bestowed valuable gifts. In the end, it was Atto's diplomatic service, rather than his musical talent, that supplied the wealth and honor essential to his social ambitions: indeed, shortly after his death in 1714, his family was elevated to the Tuscan nobility.

The first scholar to explore Atto's life, Alessandro Ademollo (1826–91), was pursuing interests in theatrical history that eventually led him to write a short article on the Melani family. His insights were expanded by the archival work of Henry Prunières (1886–1942) and, most importantly, by Robert Lamar Weaver, whose crucial article from 1977 has enabled all subsequent research.[2] Thus, the biographical outline above has been known for some time, and Atto's correspondence has been recognized as a fount of data. But Atto's life itself – the most highly documented of any seventeenth-century musician – has never been thoroughly explored. Given the richness of sources, one may legitimately ask why, and whether the neglect is justifiable.

Certainly the conventions of biography itself have played some role. A typical study – whether of Monteverdi, Louis XIV, or George Washington – presupposes the importance of the subject: one takes as given that his (or very

---

[2] A[lessandro] Ademollo, "Un campanaio e la sua famiglia," *Fanfulla della Domenica*, 30 December 1883, 2–3; Henry Prunières, *L'opéra italien en France avant Lulli*, Bibliothèque de l'Institut Français de Florence (Université de Grenoble) ser. 1, Collection d'histoire et de linguistique française et italienne comparées, no. 3 (Paris: Honoré Champion, 1913); Robert Lamar Weaver, "Materiali per le biografie dei fratelli Melani," *Rivista italiana di musicologia* 12 (1977): 252–95. Another scholar who has made extensive use of Atto's correspondence is Lorenzo Bianconi, for example in his *Music in the Seventeenth Century*, trans. David Bryant (Cambridge: Cambridge University Press, 1987), originally published as *Il Seicento* (Turin: E.D.T., 1982).

occasionally her) accomplishments merit a consideration of the personality behind them, an exploration of the "how" and "why" behind the "what." In music history, the "accomplishments" that matter are compositions, and Atto's are few and lack influence. Further, although he was a prominent singer, he was not the "first" anything (as Anna Renzi has been called the "first diva"), nor did he partner with a composer and so influence works in that way (like Isabella Colbran with Rossini). In traditional terms, then, Atto Melani is simply not important; he is not one of the heroes of music history awaiting his eulogy.

In recent decades, of course, alternatives to this "great man" paradigm have emerged. Indeed, the field of feminist studies has established biographical models specifically for the *un*important subject. As Ruth Solie explains, "feminist practice has been somewhat less interested in those certifications [of greatness] and more interested in what the lives of women have to tell us about felicitous ways of navigating treacherous waters – about what we might call, at the risk of flippancy, the diversity of successful kangaroo lives."[3] Solie draws the term *kangaroo* from the self-reflections of Emily Dickinson, signifying women whose aspirations and achievements have left them feeling alien in their societies. This sort of biographical subject offers an exemplum of resistance, someone whose evasion of social forces helps establish the boundaries for existence within a society, the kind of life that could be lived. At first glance, the abnormal figure of the castrato would seem well suited to this model. But, as I hope to show, Atto's physical state rarely hindered him in his diverse endeavors, and he certainly betrays little consciousness of handicap. He moved through society much like any other man of his class. And so if Atto is not a hero, neither is he a kangaroo.

What he *is* – to stay with figurative labels – is a specimen. As an individual his historical significance may be limited, but he represents a historically significant group: castrato singers – or more generally, musicians – of the mid to late seventeenth century. That assertion probably demands some support, for past scholars have tended to judge Atto's life as too unusual, too varied, to be illuminating of others. Indeed, Atto's only sporadic references to music and his essential abandonment of the field later in life have led many to bemoan rather than investigate his career. As Henry Prunières complains,

[In later life] he no longer speaks of anything but political and diplomatic negotiations, and one could despair of ever learning what the old musician – who had been intimately acquainted with Luigi Rossi, Cavalli, and without doubt also Carissimi and Cesti – thought of French opera, of Lully, Campra, Destouches. From 1661, Atto disappeared from the history of music.[4]

---

[3] Ruth Solie, "Changing the Subject," *Current Musicology* 53 (1993): 58.
[4] Prunières, *L'opéra*, 274.

Alessandro Ademollo likewise grumbles that "in Florence [Atto] was occupied with art and musical things; but unfortunately they wanted him back in Paris, and politics reclaimed him."[5] Defending the nobility of art, these writers portrayed the worldly interests of Atto and his family as contamination, undermining any musical significance. Still today, as Jean Grundy Fanelli writes, "it is generally assumed that the Melani family was a phenomenon apart."[6]

Of course scholars now recognize the conventionality of careers that integrated artistic, political, and social endeavors. Like the artists Peter Paul Rubens and Gianlorenzo Bernini, more than a few contemporary musicians exploited a wide range of skills in the competition for advancement that characterized courtly life.[7] In his study of singers, Sergio Durante declares outright that in the early *Seicento* "the aspiration to integrate individuals and families into the court system characterizes singers socially … [F]rom musical aristocracy, [they] aspire to become aristocracy *tout court*."[8]

Any number of examples can illustrate the point, including Atto's slightly older contemporary, the castrato Marc'Antonio Pasqualini (1614–91). Born into an apparently large and poor family, Pasqualini found his way by the age of fifteen onto the payroll of Cardinal Antonio Barberini, nephew of Pope Urban VIII. The singer rapidly became Barberini's favorite and convinced the cardinal to declare him "gentleman of the chamber," from which position he controlled access to his patron. Soon, Pasqualini began adopting his superiors' behavior, refusing, for example, to cede precedence to bona fide aristocrats. By the summer of 1641, observers were complaining that "the boy's insolence has become unbearable," but they also admitted that "without [Pasqualini], one can do nothing" to win the cardinal's favor.[9] The volatility

---

5 Ademollo, "Un campanaio," 2.

6 Jean Grundy Fanelli, "Castrato Singers from Pistoia, 1575–1660," *Civiltà musicale*, no. 40 (May–August 2000): 47. Fanelli herself argues *against* this idea.

7 On Rubens, see Marie-Anne Lescourret, *Rubens: A Double Life*, trans. Elfreda Powell (Chicago: Ivan R. Dee, 1993), originally published as *Rubens* ([Paris]: J.C. Lattès, 1990). On Bernini, see Robert Enggass, foreword to *The Life of Bernini*, by Filippo Baldinucci, trans. Catherine Enggass (University Park, Penn.: Pennsylvania State University Press, 1966), xvii, originally published as *Vita del Cavaliere Gio. Lorenzo Bernini* (Florence: V. Vangelisti, 1682).

8 Sergio Durante, "Il cantante," in *Il sistema produttivo e le sue competenze*, vol. IV of *Storia dell'opera italiana*, ed. Lorenzo Bianconi and Giorgio Pestelli, Biblioteca di cultura musicale (Turin: E.D.T. Musica, 1987), 352 and 354. These passages are translated in their entirety (and somewhat differently) in Sergio Durante, "The Opera Singer," in *Opera Production and Its Resources*, ed. Lorenzo Bianconi and Giorgio Pestelli, trans. Lydia G. Cochrane, The History of Italian Opera, part 2, "Systems," vol. 4 (Chicago and London: University of Chicago Press, 1998), 348 and 350. See also the important study by John Rosselli on this subject, "From Princely Service to the Open Market: Singers of Italian Opera and Their Patrons, 1600–1850," *Cambridge Opera Journal* 1 (1989): 1–32.

9 Georges Dethan, *The Young Mazarin*, trans. Stanley Baron (London: Thames and Hudson, 1977), 64, originally published as *Mazarin et ses amis* (Paris: Berger-Levrault, 1968). Dethan gives no citations for these quotes but notes that the first statement was made by Cardinal Alessandro Bichi.

of the situation eventually forced Barberini to abandon his protégé, but not before engineering a prestigious canonicate for Pasqualini at the church of Santa Maria Maggiore.[10]

The case of Leonora Baroni (1611–70) is similar. Born to the celebrated singer Adriana Basile, Leonora's chamber performances – as well as her impeccable manners and conversation – earned her numerous devotees among the nobility of Rome until she became an important figure in Roman society. Prunières even suggests that it was she who helped the young Giulio Mazzarini become *maestro di camera* to Antonio Barberini, thus launching Mazarin's meteoric career. In 1644, Mazarin again looked to Leonora for help: specifically, he asked that she come to Paris, both to satisfy the queen regent's taste for Italian music, at which she succeeded, and to report the Spanish strategy for the conclave following Urban VIII's death. As the lover of Camillo Pamphili, himself nephew of the Spanish candidate, Leonora was well informed. Unfortunately, when she returned to Rome after the election of Innocent X Pamphili, she discovered that one of her letters to the French contender, Giulio Cesare Sacchetti, had been intercepted. Instead of occupying the pinnacle of society, she found herself entirely out of favor. Undaunted, Leonora simply waited for the next pope, who turned out to be Clement IX Rospigliosi, a man who admired her talents and restored her prestige.[11]

To the foregoing examples one could add the cases of three more castrati: Francesco (Cecchino) de Castris, whose relationship to Grand Prince Ferdinando de' Medici was as intimate as that of Pasqualini with Antonio Barberini; Domenico Melani (no relation to Atto), who after years of service abroad returned, ennobled, to his native Florence as a wealthy philanthropist; and Angelini Bontempi, who, in addition to his singing, became an official historian at the court of Dresden.[12] Taken together, these vignettes confirm that Atto's fusion of music and politics indeed epitomized the careers of

---

[10] The above material on Pasqualini is based on the following sources: Margaret Murata, "Pasqualini, Marc' Antonio," in *The New Grove Dictionary of Opera* (New York: Grove's Dictionaries of Music, 1992), III:902; Dethan, *The Young Mazarin*, 63–64; Prunières, *L'opéra*, 89–90; Henry Prunières, "Les musiciens du Cardinal Antonio Barberini," in *Mélanges de musicologie offerts a M. Lionel de la Laurencie*, Publications de la Société Française de Musicologie, ser. 2, vols. 3–4 (Paris: La Société Française de Musicologie / E. Droz, 1933), 121; Rosselli, "From Princely Service," 5.

[11] The above is based on Prunières, *L'opéra*, 41–55, 65.

[12] The material on De Castris is based on Harold Acton, *The Last Medici* (London: Faber and Faber, 1932), 186, 199, 215; and Warren Kirkendale, *The Court Musicians in Florence During the Principate of the Medici: With a Reconstruction of the Artistic Establishment*, "Historiae musicae cultores" biblioteca, no. 61 (Florence: Olschki, 1993), 437–46. On Domenico Melani, Weaver, "Materiali," 262n; and John Walter Hill, "Oratory Music in Florence, III: The Confraternities from 1655 to 1785," *Acta musicologica* 58 (1986): 139–40. On Bontempi, John Rosselli, "The Castrati as a Professional Group and a Social Phenomenon, 1550–1850," *Acta musicologica* 60 (1988): 169.

many seventeenth-century singers; if his case goes a little further in this direction than others, he is just an outstanding specimen of the type.

And so a study of his life opens a window on the broader world of seventeenth-century music and musicians. Through his letters one glimpses daily musical life in several of the European centers he frequented. More importantly, one observes the social context of the musician, the real-life aspects of music-making: what a singer thought about his profession, what his patrons thought about his services, how he related to those patrons, and how he related to other musicians and contemporaries generally. Ultimately, Atto's life demonstrates the inextricability of seventeenth-century music and politics, with politics understood both narrowly as the interaction between forces of governance and broadly as "the total complex of relations between people living in society."[13] That is, Atto's life portrays music not so much as an artistic event as a social or even political activity. Of course this perspective on *Seicento* art is not new. But Atto's biography furnishes a uniquely rich case study: it sheds light on the quotidian mechanisms that generated meaning for this music and thereby linked it to expressions of power. In the end, Atto helps clarify what music in seventeenth-century Europe actually *was*, what it signified to its producers and consumers. Even were his life's story not so fascinating in itself, it would be well worth the trouble of telling.

Exactly *how* to tell that story is a thorny question, for, truthfully speaking, the entire enterprise of musical biography has a bad reputation. Notwithstanding foundational studies by Spitta (on Bach), Chrysander (on Handel), and Thayer (on Beethoven), Guido Adler's influential vision of *Musikwissenschaft* relegated "biographical studies of musicians" to ancillary status, inferior to style history, paleography, aesthetics, and even pedagogy.[14] For Adler, the appropriate subject of musical research was the work itself and only secondarily the individuals who created or performed it. That tension between "work-centered" and "people-centered" approaches has of course endured. Quarrels between "music theory" and "music history," "positivism" and "criticism," "old musicology" and "new musicology" all engage this debate about musical autonomy versus social context. In the narrower field of biography, that debate plays out in the classic bifurcation of "life" and "works" and arguments about what one sphere of inquiry may reveal about the other.

---

[13] Merriam-Webster Online, s.v. "Politics," www.m-w.com/dictionary/politics (accessed November 21, 2005).

[14] See Guido Adler, "Umfang, Methode und Ziel der Musikwissenschaft" in *Music in European Thought, 1851–1912*, ed. Bojan Bujić, trans. Martin Cooper, Cambridge Readings in the Literature of Music (Cambridge: Cambridge University Press, 1988), 348–55, originally published in *Vierteljahrsschrift für Musikwissenschaft* 1 (1885): 5–8, 15–20.

Because the majority of musical biographies examine composers, defining this relationship is crucial and in fact the subject of much debate.[15] But because Atto was not primarily a composer (and will not be treated as one), such considerations are less urgent here.

Further, because he is more important as a specimen than an individual, I hope to temper the "essentializing" tendencies for which biographies of all types are regularly censured. In her insightful essay, "The Writing of Biography," the historian Elisabeth Young-Bruehl details many ways the biographer can be enticed into constructing the *essence* of a person and so positing a falsely consistent personality.[16] The musicologist Jolanta T. Pekacz likewise complains that "musical biography typically develops in a way similar to a realistic novel: a coherent, unified voice claiming to present the truth about a life; omniscient narration, repeating themes and symbols; and linear chronological presentation of events provide readers with the illusion of totality and closure."[17] The biographies these writers critique endeavor to explore the mind of the subject and so elucidate that person's actions or achievements. I too will posit reasons for many of Atto's exploits and so touch on the nature of his personality, but a deep understanding of his inner life – his motivating "essence" – is not my aim.

Indeed, it would be exceedingly difficult – perhaps even perverse – to probe the psyche of a subject who never acknowledges it himself. Atto certainly shows emotions in his letters, and his undeclared motives can often be surmised. But unlike correspondents and diarists of later centuries, his writings are virtually devoid of self-contemplation. Only once, for example, does he make even a passing remark about his physical state, what would now seem the defining fact of his identity. When faced with adversity, he does often display self-pity, bemoaning his fate, but that dramatic gesture seems a play for sympathy: like a staged lament, it shows but a fictive interiority. Indeed, through all his letters, Atto's inner life remains astonishingly opaque; he dons many masks, but we are left wondering what lies behind. Perhaps a psychoanalyst could eventually decipher something more profound, but then again one might mistrust the application of Freudian theory to *Seicento* subjectivity. In any case, the portrait promised by my title will be just that,

---

[15]   Maynard Solomon, among others, has written lucidly and provocatively on the subject: "Thoughts on Biography," in *Beethoven Essays* (Cambridge, Mass., and London: Harvard University Press, 1988), 101–15. An important consideration of these issues is Jolanta T. Pekacz, "Memory, History and Meaning: Musical Biography and Its Discontents," *Journal of Musicological Research* 23 (2004): 39–80.

[16]   Elisabeth Young-Bruehl, "The Writing of Biography," in *Mind and the Body Politic* (New York and London: Routledge, Chapman and Hall / Routledge, 1989), 125–37.

[17]   Pekacz, "Memory," 42.

a representation focusing on observable attributes, in this case, Atto's words and actions. His consciousness I leave to the reader to infer.

I also hope to mitigate the essentializing impulse by disrupting the standard "omniscient narration" and "linear chronological presentation." I doubt that the genre of biography can ever wholly escape chronology or the need for constructing a narrative. But, in the organization of this study, I try to balance the chronicling of Atto's life with essays that consider a particular feature of that life. The former chapters tend to draw heavily on documents while the latter use just a handful to initiate the discussion. Indeed, the second type usually wrestles with questions for which conclusive answers are impossible, such as the parental rationale for castration, the sexual significance of the castrato, and the function of composition in Atto's career. The irregular succession of these two modes foregrounds, I hope, the role of interpretation here and the impossibility of both certainty and objectivity.

Indeed, the opening chapter, dealing with Atto's youth, requires some of the most extensive speculation in the study. Without the letters generated by his later travels, narrative is not possible. Instead, the chapter considers the motivation of Atto's parents in their decision to castrate four of their sons. Based on the status of the Melani family, the local conditions in Pistoia, and contemporary familial customs, I conclude that Atto's parents were not in fact sacrificing sons in the hopes of financial gain, an oft-cited justification for the practice; rather, they were engaging in – and initiating their sons into – the subtler economy of patronage. This more dignified, if not entirely selfless, explanation may shed light on the objectives of other parents of castrati as well as on attitudes toward these singers at the time.

Chapter 2, which deals with the first part of Atto's singing career (1638–53), specifically addresses the links between music and power. As Atto became a cultural commodity in the relationship between France and Tuscany, he fulfilled political needs on several levels: he earned favor for Mattias de' Medici (and indeed the whole Medici regime) from the monarchy of France; he helped cement Cardinal Mazarin's relationship with the ruling queen mother, Anne of Austria; and he himself won gratitude from all parties. Each of the political figures exploited music – or in this case, one musician – to satisfy a yet more powerful figure. While this function of the arts has been much studied, Atto's activities also expose the less familiar processes by which musicians might likewise exploit their noble patrons. Any servant would of course expect remuneration from his masters, and Atto was handsomely paid. But instead of merely serving the Medici, he worked to acquire additional patrons, converting each new singing assignment into an expansion of personal support. (See table 0.1 for a chart of European rulers during Atto's lifetime.) Because Atto could not sing for all these rulers simultaneously, he began serving

Table 0.1 *Important rulers of Europe during the lifetime of Atto Melani*

	Tuscany (grand dukes) (de' Medici)	Rome (popes)	Mantua (dukes) (Gonzaga)	Modena (dukes) (d'Este)	Turin (dukes) (Savoy)	Paris (kings) (Bourbon)	Empire (emperors) (Habsburg)
1626	Ferdinando II (1621–70)	Gregory XV (1621–23)	Vincenzo II (1626–27) Carlo I Gonzaga-Nevers (1627–37)	Cesare (1597–1628)	Carlo Emanuele I (1580–1630)	Louis XIII (1610–43)	Ferdinand II (1619–37)
1628		Urban VIII (1628–44)		Alfonso III (1628–29) Francesco I (1629–58)			
1630					Vittorio Amedeo I (1630–37)		
1632							
1634							
1636			Carlo II (1637–65)		Francesco Giacinto (1637–38)		Ferdinand III (1637–57)
1638					Carlo Emanuele II (1638–75)		
1640							
1642						Louis XIV (1643–1715)	
1644		Innocent X (1644–55)					
1646							
1648							
1650							
1652							

Table 0.1 (*cont.*)

	Tuscany (grand dukes) (de' Medici)	Rome (popes)	Mantua (dukes) (Gonzaga)	Modena (dukes) (d'Este)	Turin (dukes) (Savoy)	Paris (kings) (Bourbon)	Empire (emperors) (Habsburg)
1654		Alexander VII (1655–67)					
1656							
1658				Alfonso IV (1658–62)			Leopold I (1658–1705)
1660							
1662				Franceso II (1662–94)			
1664			Carlo III (1665–1708)				
1666		Clement IX (1667–69)					
1668							
1670	Cosimo III (1670–1723)	Clement X (1670–76)					
1672							
1674					Vittorio Amedeo II (1675–1732)		
1676		Innocent XI (1676–89)					
1678							
1680							
1682							
1684							
1686							

1688

Alexander VIII
(1689–91)

1690

Innocent XII
(1691–1700)

1692

1694

Rainaldo III
(1694–1737)

1696

1698

1700

Clement XI
(1700–21)

1702

1704

Josef I
(1705–11)

1706

1708

[Habsburg control, 1708]

1710

Charles VI
(1711–40)

1712

1714

them with a new skill, one to which his travels (and character) particularly adapted him: the gathering and reporting of news, or, espionage. And when the interests of these different patrons began to conflict, Atto made his first efforts to manipulate them so as to maximize his own rewards. Indeed, this chapter demonstrates the varied uses to which strong patrons and talented clients could put one another and argues that for both parties every musical experience was tinged with questions of power.

Chapter 3 traces a change in Atto's self-perception and goals that occurred at the height of his musical abilities. From 1653 to 1655, the singer was nearly always traveling: to Innsbruck to sing in that city's first Venetian-style opera, to Regensburg to perform privately for Emperor Ferdinand III, to Rome to serenade Giovan Carlo de' Medici and Queen Christina of Sweden, and to Turin to entertain the court of Savoy. At some point, Atto began to appreciate a close relationship between musical performance and personal prestige: specifically, he recognized that some performance situations carried a stigma that could hinder social advancement. And so he began trying to withdraw from all but the most well-regarded venues. Although a castrato, he tried to behave like a gentleman amateur, conduct-ing his life by the rules of privilege that governed the aristocracy. Such a pretense required the cooperation of his patrons, and, when they sometimes proved unwilling, he readily tried to deceive and control them. In Atto's view, the character of every performance implied something about the status and favor of the performer.

During the spring and summer of 1653, a series of letters from Atto to Duke Carlo II of Mantua strongly implies a sexual link between the two. From this starting point, chapter 4 considers the vexed question of the castrato's sexuality. While little direct evidence remains of Atto's own expe-riences, recent scholarship in the history of sexuality – together with other contemporary and modern information – can suggest the sexual framework within which someone like Atto would have understood himself and been understood by his contemporaries. In fact, much testimony links the castrato to the prepubescent youth, a figure often represented in art and literature as an object of desire by both men and women. Lacking the truly "masculine" quality of abstinence, both the youth and the castrato – much like women – were considered prone to the enticements of love. For this reason, I argue, the castrato often played amorous roles in seventeenth-century operas: he was a theatrical exaggeration of the relevant social stereotype, the effeminate lover. Such an image must also have affected the private lives of these singers: to their contemporaries, seventeenth-century castrati represented not the bizarre characters they began to seem in later periods, but rather figures more or less familiar from everyday life. This acquaintance may in turn shed light on many of Atto's activities, particularly his participation in court life and his involvement in the erotically charged genre of chamber music.

During the years covered in chapter 5, 1656 to 1671, Atto showed an astonishing determination to withdraw from the field of music in favor of diplomacy. As mentioned, he had already recognized the social limitations of a performing career. That perception, reinforced by the rich rewards his diplomacy delivered, led him for the first time to state openly his intent to renounce music. Not surprisingly, he found the transition difficult: in fact, his political risk-taking eventually led to a catastrophic disgrace and his aforementioned banishment from France. Even in his darkest moments, however, Atto never seems to have contemplated the more secure, less prestigious life of a musician or music teacher. Instead, he simply waited for a change of fortune, which came dramatically with the election of Pope Clement IX. During this pontiff's short reign, Atto vigorously reinserted himself into the life of the papal court and laid the foundations for the rest of his career. By the early 1670s the transformation was complete: most of the patrons who had known Atto primarily as a singer had died off, and he now worked exclusively in the diplomatic sphere. This chapter demonstrates, then, not only how difficult was the sort of social advancement Atto attempted, but also how important it could seem. Indeed, this castrato clearly viewed music less as a fine art than as a social vehicle, to be exploited and abandoned as needed.

In chapter 6, I argue that one of the ways Atto used music to his advantage was through the writing of cantatas, that genre of vocal chamber music that dominated aristocratic entertainment in seventeenth-century Italy. To understand why Atto wrote such works, only fifteen of which are today attributable to him, I reexamine many aspects of the genre, including its poetic style, subject matter, musical conventions, and performance contexts. With this background, close readings of Atto's pieces can reveal more about his compositional goals. Hardly slapdash efforts, his cantatas show careful construction and artistry, along with a particular search for striking effects. Indeed this taste for *bizzarria*, which Atto pursues more consistently than some of his contemporaries, seems an attempt to impress patrons with his wit and sophistication. In other words, Atto's musical works bear traces of his broader efforts to distinguish himself socially. This chapter, then, suggests not only how a musician's compositions could affect his life – by earning him a living and attracting patrons – but also how a musician's life – especially his social ambitions – could affect the character of his compositions.

As Prunières complained, the subject of music almost entirely disappears from Atto's correspondence after about 1670. The last chapter, then, provides an overview of Atto's remaining forty-four years, exactly the last half of his life. During this period he and his family finally achieve their aims, with Atto becoming a respected figure at the French court and his nephews rising up the social ladder. More surprisingly, he occasionally finds himself again involved in music in these later years, especially in the effort to recruit young castrati for the French royal chapel. The elderly castrato also eventually comes to terms with the role that music played in his own life, even lamenting that his nephews were not trained in the art. Indeed, those nephews demonstrate little sympathy with their uncle's career: in both their official and personal documents, they never mention music among Atto's many accomplishments. Theirs is an attitude more characteristic of the eighteenth century and indeed more intelligible today: they obscure their uncle's embarrassing mutilation to stress his respectable accomplishments. What Atto's life illustrates so richly, however, is the older mentality of the *Seicento*, when a castrato could both imagine and achieve the life of a gentleman courtier.

1 ❧ Creating a castrato

In a traditional biography, one might well begin with the story of the subject's youth, considering his or her parents, family life, education, and early training. Even without a Freudian methodology, such experiences would presumably shed light on the subject's later life and accomplishments. For better or worse, such an approach is not possible with Atto Melani. Simply too little can be determined about his early years, and most of that material appeared already decades ago in the work of Robert Lamar Weaver, whose studies of the Melani family both inspired and enabled my research.[1] Rather than contriving a narrative, then, I begin this study by considering one fundamental issue of Atto's childhood, or, more accurately, the one issue that we today identify as fundamental in the youth of any castrato: his parents' decision to emasculate him.

That decision surely places such parents among the most difficult historical figures to comprehend, cut off from our empathy. The motivations usually posited for their choice – financial stability or advancement – only increase the problem: no matter how deep their poverty, we can little identify with people who, in John Rosselli's blunt phrase, "gamble[d] a son's virility on success," whether as star singer or workaday church chorister.[2] But I believe the issue is more complex than usually represented, even in Rosselli's balanced study. While financial concerns certainly played a key role for some families at some times and places, other forces also shaped these decisions. And here, I think, Atto's case proves valuable. The slim evidence about his youth, read in the light of local customs, suggests a more nuanced interpretation. That interpretation offers, if not full access to the parental mentality, at least richer and more culturally specific insight into the origins of one castrato, and so perhaps others. The essence of that insight, as I will argue in

---

[1] The most succinct presentation is Robert Lamar Weaver, "Materiali per le biografie dei fratelli Melani," *Rivista italiana di musicologia* 12 (1977): 252–95. But other important information appears in other publications by Weaver, including "Florentine Comic Operas of the Seventeenth Century" (Ph.D. diss., University of North Carolina, Chapel Hill, 1958); "*Il Girello*, a 17th-Century Burlesque Opera," *Quadrivium* 12.2 (1971): 141–63; Introduction to *Cantatas by Alessandro Melani 1639–1703, Atto Melani 1627–1714*, vol. XI of *The Italian Cantata in the Seventeenth Century* (New York: Garland, 1986).

[2] John Rosselli, "The Castrati as a Professional Group and a Social Phenomenon, 1550–1850," *Acta musicologica* 60 (1988): 179. For a good summary of this issue, see 149–56.

this chapter, is that Atto's parents were stimulated less by economic forces per se than by the subtler economy of patronage.

Paterfamilias

The subject of patronage in the early modern period figures crucially throughout this inquiry; indeed, it was the most important social reality of Atto's life. Scholars have much studied and theorized the institution in recent decades, and the work of Sharon Kettering, Ronald Weissman, and others informs many of the following pages.[3] Whereas thirty years ago patronage tended to be viewed – especially in the arts – as "the audience for which, and the processes through which, cultural artefacts were produced," today it is generally understood to represent a much broader practice.[4] Patronage was (and still is) a method of influencing the actions of others, that is, wielding power. Summarizing the character of early modern patronage, particularly within Mediterranean cultures, Weissman articulates five key characteristics: (1) the patron and client enjoy unequal power and/or resources; (2) the relationship is long-term, but not legally defined; (3) the relationship is multipurpose; (4) the patron provides not just protection, but rather a wide range of favors; and (5) the relationship adheres to a philosophy that stands outside official social morality.[5] For the present purposes, the most important of these points is the first. As Sharon Kettering notes, patrons were those in a position, either politically or financially, to grant rewards to clients who followed their orders, "providing them with offices, arranging profitable marriages, finding places for their children, helping them with lawsuits or tax problems," and so forth.[6] Clients, for their part, offered loyalty and obedience in exchange: they supported their patrons' projects and carried out their orders. Patrons who could offer greater and rarer benefits naturally attracted more numerous and influential clients; these clients in turn acted as patrons to their own circle of clients, and so on. Such pyramids of client relationships formed the primary mechanism by which the sovereign, at the apex, could control large numbers of subjects.[7]

---

[3] Ronald Weissman, "Taking Patronage Seriously: Mediterranean Values and Renaissance Society," in *Patronage, Art, and Society in Renaissance Italy*, ed. F. W. Kent and Patricia Simons (Canberra [Australia]: Humanities Research Centre; Oxford: Clarendon Press, 1987), 25–45. Sharon Kettering, *Patrons, Brokers, and Clients in Seventeenth-Century France* (New York: Oxford University Press, 1986).

[4] Weissman, "Taking Patronage Seriously," 26.   [5] Ibid., 25–26.   [6] Kettering, *Patrons*, 3.

[7] The above is based on ibid., 1–5, and Henry Kamen, "The Statesman," in *Baroque Personae*, ed. Rosario Villari, trans. Lydia G. Cochrane (Chicago: University of Chicago Press, 1995), 18, originally published as *L'uomo barocco*, Storia e Società (Rome: Laterza, 1991).

Of course, the originary model for these bonds was the link between a son and his strong but protective *pater*. At the simplest level, almost any father–son relationship would satisfy most of Weissman's aforementioned criteria, being a long-term, multipurpose arrangement predicated on an imbalance of power. Yet, as I shall argue here, the familial interactions of Atto's experience replicate Weissman's model even more clearly and help explain the motivations of his parents, who patronized as much as reared their children.

Bringing those parents to light is in fact rather difficult. At the opening of his foundational article on the Melani clan, Robert Weaver asserts that "their ascent, completed in the course of three generations, from the status of commoners in a small provincial town to the ranks of the Tuscan nobility suggests a well-contrived plan."[8] Certainly the Melani advancement was calculated, as observations throughout this study will confirm, but the actual extent of that advancement – dependent on the social rank from which they began – remains unclear. How "common" were they? Unfortunately, little is known of the Melani ancestors beyond their names. Atto's grandfather was called Santi Melani and his great-grandfather Antonio, or perhaps Raffaello (the sources disagree).[9] All these Melani forefathers seem to have lived in Pistoia.

Toward the end of his life, Atto further muddied the waters by fabricating a more glorious ancestry for himself. An eighteenth-century inventory of the Melani household records an inscription near a portrait of a certain Biagio del Melano. Around the year 1400 this Biagio supposedly governed the fortress of Monte Petroso in the region of Romagna. Having distinguished himself in battle, he came with some of his followers "to live in Pistoia, and they built a village, afterwards called Borgo Melano, that was [later] enclosed in the gardens of the nuns of Sala. From this Biagio, the Melani family of Pistoia had its beginning."[10] That this story originated with Atto is confirmed a late letter in which he reveals his source: he asks his brother "to find out where this fortress is that Machiavelli speaks of in his History of the Republic and whether there is some estate or castle that may be called 'del Melano.' I am certain that our family name comes from this Biagio del Melano."[11]

---

[8] Weaver, "Materiali," 252.   [9] See ibid., 254–56.

[10] I Fn, MS Tordi 350, f. 20. Weaver ("Materiali," 263n) gives the date of November 12, 1785 for the inventory and names Michele Sozzifanti as its executor. The manuscript Tordi 350, however, is a book into which many important documents of the Melani family were copied, the inventory being only the first of these. Weaver has taken his information from the last document of the collection, one unrelated to the inventory. Although the first ten folios of the inventory are missing, thereby somewhat obscuring its date, this inventory in fact constitutes the first of a series for various Melani properties, all dated May 1, 1782 and conducted by Michele Pini, "capo maestro muratore fiorentino." Thus, the date May 1, 1782 seems reasonable for this first record as well.

[11] Atto to Filippo Melani, from Paris, July 14, 1698.

Machiavelli indeed mentions a man by this name who fought at Monte Petroso, but the point of Machiavelli's tale is to praise the valor of Biagio, who, with his fortress surrounded and burning, chose to die gloriously in the flames rather than withdraw.[12] Although he threw his two children to safety, Machiavelli's Biagio did not survive to see Pistoia and is an implausible progenitor.

Concerning later generations, the documents provide more concrete information. Atto's father, Domenico Melani (1588–1648), held two positions under the bishop of Pistoia, who was at that time Alessandro Caccia, a member of the Florentine nobility: Domenico first served as litter-bearer (*lettighiere*) to the bishop himself, and later as bell-ringer (*campanaro*, or *campanaio*) of the bishop's Cathedral of S. Zeno. How Domenico became *lettighiere* is unknown, as is the length of his tenure: his position is simply mentioned in an eighteenth-century manuscript history of prominent families.[13] The position of *campanaio* seems to have come to him through his father-in-law, Mariotto Giovanelli, who held the post from at least March of 1621, when he appears in the documents of the cathedral. Domenico married Mariotto's daughter Camilla not long thereafter; at some point in the ensuing years Domenico assumed Mariotto's position.[14]

The difficulty is to decipher what these positions actually reveal about Domenico and his social standing. Weaver suggested that the two appointments were honorary, indications of the bishop's high regard; I assumed the same in my own earlier work.[15] But further research and newly available documents have complicated the picture. In Francesco Liberati's *Il perfetto maestro di casa* (first published in 1658) – a systematic account of the household of a prince or cardinal – "the litter-bearer, or mule-driver" is described as someone responsible for hauling his master's goods. The "litter" (*lettica*) is not a couch for the bishop's transport, but a cart strong enough to

---

[12] Niccolò Machiavelli, *Istorie fiorentine*, in *Tutte le opere*, [ed. Mario Martelli] ([Florence]: Sansoni, 1971; Intratext CT, 2007), book 4, section 12, www.intratext.com/IXT/ITA1109/_P8Y.HTM.

[13] Tommaso Caramelli, "Alberi genealogici delle famiglie nobili e civili della città di Pistoia"; as cited in Weaver, "Florentine Comic Operas," 173.

[14] I have not been able to find the wedding date of the Melani parents. But given Camilla's regular and numerous pregnancies (see Weaver, "Materiali," 256), and assuming that the first child was not conceived before the marriage (Mariotto, b. February 24, 1622, died in infancy), the latest possible date for their wedding would fall sometime in May 1621. Weaver (257) assumed that a mention of Domenico in the cathedral records of 1624 indicated that he had by then taken over Mariotto Giovanelli's position, but that reference in fact gives Domenico no title. The first definitive mention I have found of Domenico as *campanaro* does not appear until January 27, 1633 (in I PS, L-68, f. 25s, transcribed in Alfredo Pacini, ed., *La chiesa pistoiese e la sua cattedrale nel tempo: Repertorio di documenti* [Pistoia: Editrice CRT, 1994], IV:275).

[15] Weaver, "Florentine Comic Operas," 173; Roger Freitas, "*Un Atto d'ingegno*: A Castrato in the Seventeenth Century" (Ph.D. diss., Yale Univ., 1998), 24–26.

carry five hundred pounds of freight. The litter-bearer is expected to feed and care for the mules, wash the dust and mud off the litter, and keep track of the master's transported possessions.[16] Such labor implies low status, of course, and Liberati mentions no honorary or supervisory form of the job: the litter-bearer reports directly to the *maestro di casa*. It seems difficult to imagine how someone in this position could have become, as Weaver suggests, a "close confidant" of the bishop.

The status of a bell-ringer is even trickier to assess. In fact, Tomaso Garzoni's *La piazza universale di tutte le professioni del mondo* (1589) lists the *campanaro* among the various metal-workers, one who casts bells rather than ringing them.[17] Other sources suggest that *campanari* could hold combined duties. The accounts of the cathedral of Pistoia also produce conflicting impressions. On the one hand, a payment in 1589 of over six *lire* was made to a "maestro Agnolo, campanaio" for a brass faucet, which he apparently made.[18] On the other hand, the following year, the chapter made an extra payment of four *lire* to "Camillo, *campanaio* … for having sounded [the bells] many times for the creation and death of two popes": this *campanaio*, at least, was involved in the ringing.[19] Domenico Melani seems to have served more as a ringer than a foundry-man: when during his tenure one of the bells needed repair, payment was made to "certain French masters"; Domenico himself received extra pay only for extraordinary ringing duties.[20] Any supplementation must have been welcome, given that in 1640 Domenico's annual salary stood at thirty-seven bushels of grain.[21] Again, the Melani father emerges as more of a laborer than a man of privilege.

Nevertheless, it remains possible that Domenico's titles denoted *responsibilities* rather than actual work. A study of the history of bell-ringing in Bologna, for example, notes that the title "campanèr" could refer to the "màster," "who teaches and directs the team of bell-ringers."[22] Just as *maestri*

---

[16] Francesco Liberati, *Il perfetto maestro di casa*, rev. edn. (Rome: Bernabò, 1668), I:112–15.

[17] Tomaso Garzoni, *La piazza universale di tutte le professioni del mondo*, ed. Giovanni Battista Bronzini, Biblioteca di "Lares," monographs, n.s. vol. 49 (Florence: Leo S. Olschki, 1996), I:701–3; based on the edition from Venice: G.B. Somasco, 1589.

[18] I PS, L-25 (M-49), f. 183d; as transcribed in Pacini, *La chiesa*, IV:53. The payment was for 6 *lire*, 6 *soldi*, 8 *denari*.

[19] The citation, dated December 14, 1590, comes from I PS, H-263, f. 18s; as transcribed in Pacini, *La chiesa*, IV:58. The popes referred to are Sixtus V, who died in August 1590, Urban VII who was elected in September 1590 but died eight days later, and Gregory XIV, who was elected in December.

[20] The bell repair, in 1635, is described in I PS, C-50, p. 321; as transcribed in Pacini, *La chiesa*, IV:279–80. The extra payment to Domenico took place in 1638, for a new requirement to ring the bell every day at around 9 a.m. (I PS, C-50, p. 327; Pacini, IV:291).

[21] I PS, L-75, f. 32s, March 12, 1640; as transcribed in Pacini, *La chiesa*, IV:229.

[22] Fabio Foresti, "Il lessico della campana e del suono 'alla bolognese,'" in *Campanili e campane di Bologna e del Bolognese*, ed. Mario Fanti (Bologna: Grafis Edizioni, 1992), 263, 267.

di cappella were often expected to pay the boys in their charge from their own salaries, Domenico's remuneration could just possibly have covered subordinates who actually did the work. Another option surfaces in the civic records of sixteenth-century Parma: two payments for bell-ringing were made on the same day, one, "to the municipal *campanaro* for the residence of the lords, sixteen *lire*," and another, "to master Cristofano Scarzanino for ringing the bells and maintaining the ropes, ten lire."[23] This wording suggests that the titular *campanaro*, whatever his duties, did not in fact ring bells.

Implausible as these scenarios may seem, they are worth considering, for it is difficult to square the image of Domenico as laborer with the lofty roster of godparents (*padrini*) that he and his wife assembled for their children.[24] Already for their first son Jacopo in 1623, the parents secured as godmother Laura Rospigliosi, who came from one of Pistoia's most powerful families.[25] Jacopo's godfather, Mariotto Cellesi, belonged to an equally imposing clan, whose line and titles endured until just a few years ago.[26] The honor roll continued for the other Melani children, as figure 1.1 illustrates: the Sozzifanti, Pappagalli, Baldinotti, Panciatichi, and Ricasoli all belonged to the Pistoiese nobility.[27]

Yet the significance of these *padrini* remains murky, especially since historians of early modern Tuscany do not agree on the social significance of godparenthood itself. Some scholars hold that the elite typically sought godparents among the lower classes, even the peasantry, as a way of binding the populace to the interests of the powerful. Others assert that godparents usually came from the same social sphere as the family, with friends and neighbors the usual candidates. Still others argue, most relevantly for this

---

[23] *Capitoli della magnifica città di Parma* (Parma: Seth de Viothis, 1555), quoted in Gaspare Nello Vetro, *Dizionario della musica e dei musicisti dei territori del Ducato di Parma e Piacenza*, Istituzione Casa della Musica, http://biblioteche2.comune.parma.it/dm/449.htm (accessed May 25, 2007).

[24] Weaver first notes the significance of the *padrini* in his "Florentine Comic Operas," 175, and develops the subject further in "*Il Girello*," 149.

[25] I have been unable to find the name Laura Rospigliosi in any of the genealogies or histories of the family. The document that lists her as Jacopo's godmother (I Fn, Tordi 133; cited in Weaver, "Materiali," 255) identifies her as the daughter of Francesco Rospigliosi. Francesco, whose exact dates are unknown, was the son of Giovanni (1545–1614), and although surviving records only attribute male children to Francesco (Giovanni, Domenico, and Jacopo), those records may well omit any daughter(s). Francesco's children would generally have been born around the turn of the century, putting this inferred Laura at a plausible age to serve as godparent. See Davide Shamà, ed. "Genealogie delle famiglie nobili italiane," www.sardimpex.com (accessed December 2, 2007).

[26] The Contessa Marcella Amati-Cellesi (d. 2002) lived at the impressive family Villa La Màgia near the village of Quarrata, outside Pistoia. She was very kind in her support of this project.

[27] All these families can be found in the "*Libro d'oro*" for the city of Pistoia, published as Bruno Casini, *I "libri d'oro" delle città di Pistoia, Prato e Pescia*, Biblioteca de "Le Apuane," no. 12 (Massa-Uliveti: Edizioni del Centro Culturale Apuano, 1988).

Source: Information drawn from Robert Lamar Weaver, "Materiali per le biografie dei fratelli Melani," *Rivista italiana di musicologia* 12 (1977): 256, updated from additional sources.

Figure 1.1 The Melani family tree

case, that "among the nobility, and possibly among those directly dependent on them like household servants," "godparents were habitually chosen from people of higher status than natural parents."[28] As a servant to the bishop of Pistoia, Domenico seems to have followed this last model and linked his family to an array of noble sponsors. Unfortunately, the insight reveals less about Domenico's status than one would hope, for the three paradigms are not mutually exclusive. Was Domenico a respectable gentleman just sidling up to the godparents' own social level, or was he a laborer whose social betters agreed to stand for his humble children? Until contemporary godparenthood is better understood, the answer remains unclear.

Whatever Domenico's status, he and his family certainly behaved according to contemporary norms for the bourgeoisie. By definition, this class was essentially urban and of at least moderate affluence: members usually owned a house or other civic real estate. They also tended to be conservative: rather than risking assets on trade or entrepreneurship, as their ancestors had, the *Seicento* bourgeois increasingly invested in rural property or government debt. Their goal was to live entirely off their investments and so emulate the idleness of the aristocracy.[29] Indeed, most members harbored social ambitions, seeking – in the historian Franco Valsecchi's words – "to merge and blend into the noble classes when their accumulated honors and riches permit[ted] the acquisition of a title."[30] This profile fits the Melani well. They owned a house in Pistoia that served as the fixed hub of the family for generations.[31] As soon as the most successful member, Atto himself, began

---

[28] On the first view, Louis Haas, *The Renaissance Man and His Children: Childbirth and Early Childhood in Florence 1300–1600* (New York: St. Martin's Press, 1998), 76; Haas is here citing the work of Christiane Klapisch-Zuber, "Parenti, amici, vicini: Il territorio urbano d'una famiglia mercantile nel XV secolo," *Quaderni storici* 33 (1976): 972. On the idea of godparents as equals, again Haas, 72–73. On the second view, John Bossy, "Godparenthood: The Fortunes of a Social Institution in Early Modern Christianity," in *Religion and Society in Early Modern Europe 1500–1800*, ed. Kaspar von Greyerz (London: The German Historical Institute / George Allen & Unwin, 1984), 196. Strangely, Bossy makes this statement only as a concession in his more general argument that godparenthood was *not* used as a form of patronage. The case of the Melani family would seem to contradict that idea. Haas too takes an ambivalent position on the question. At one point (76) he writes that "Florentines rarely chose coparents whose social status was much above their own." Elsewhere (82), though, he asserts that "parents sought glory in the [baptism] ceremony and influential godparents."

[29] The above is based on James S. Amelang, "The Bourgeois," in *Baroque Personae*, ed. Rosario Villari, trans. Lydia G. Cochrane (Chicago: University of Chicago Press, 1995), 314–17 and 330, originally published as *L'uomo barocco*, Storia e Società (Rome: Laterza, 1991).

[30] Franco Valsecchi, *L'Italia nel Seicento e nel Settecento*, vol. VI of *Società e costume: Panorama di storia sociale e tecnologica* (Turin: U.T.E.T., 1967), 262.

[31] There is no evidence that the family ever moved, from Domenico's time through the beginning of the nineteenth century (and perhaps later). Attempts to identify the actual house have been only partially successful. From a codicil to the will of Atto's brother Jacopo, one learns that the home is "nel Corso contigua alla Chiesa, e monasterio di S. Lucia di Pistoia" (I-PSc, Raccolta

earning real money, he invested in country estates (see chapter 7). And Atto's successes in serving the aristocracy – his "accumulated honors and riches" – finally raised the standing of his clan. Certainly Domenico instilled in his family the kind of aspiration to social advancement that marked the *borghesia* generally.

Perhaps the first extant sign of these ambitions, and Domenico's first clear act of patronage toward his children, is his sons' enrollment in the cathedral school or *scuola eugeniana* of Pistoia. The musicologist Osvaldo Gambassi has greatly illuminated both the general tradition of these *scuole* and the activities of the particular Pistoiese institution. Aimed at training poor boys for the ecclesiastical life, the *scuole* were established in many Italian cities in the early fifteenth century with the support of the eponymous Pope Eugene IV (reg. 1431–47). The boys learned to read and write Latin *ad Donatum* (to the level of the fourth-century grammarian Aelius Donatus) and to read music and sing well enough to perform plainchant. Selected by the bishop and chapter, entering boys were supposed to be between ten and fifteen years old, "suited to study and capable at singing"; they lived at home and attended school each day. From the beginning, the school in Pistoia had two teachers: a *maestro di grammatica* and a *maestro di canto*. In 1556, the position of *maestro di cappella* was added, with the responsibility of forming a choir of the best singers to serve the cathedral. While all students continued to learn *canto fermo*, the boys of the *cappella* now undertook more complex music (*canto figurato*). According to later records, these students eventually learned to sing difficult masses and madrigals at sight, and the most talented even received lessons in composition (*contrappunto*).[32]

As table 1.1 shows, all of the Melani boys sang in the *cappella*, most from the age of ten; consequently, they must also have attended the *scuola* (even if enrollment records are lacking). But if the objective of the *scuola* was to

Chiappelli 14, fascicle "Carte varie riguardanti affari legali della famiglia Melani"). Further, from Gaetano Beani, ed., *La chiesa pistoiese dalla sua origine ai tempi nostri: Appunti storici* (Pistoia: Fratelli Bracali, 1883), 196–97, it emerges that the monastery of S. Lucia was suppressed in 1783 but was eventually incorporated into what is today the Conservatorio S. Giovanni Battista, in Corso Antonio Gramsci. In fact, truly contiguous with the part of this structure that was once S. Lucia is a narrow old house of three stories, identified as no. 33 Corso Gramsci. Whether this actual structure represents the Melani home is unclear: the location, however, seems likely.

32   The above is based on Osvaldo Gambassi, *"Pueri cantores" nelle cattedrali d'Italia tra medioevo e età moderna: Le scuole eugeniane: Scuole di canto annesse alle cappelle musicali*, "Historiae Musicae Cultores" Biblioteca, no. 80 (Florence: Leo S. Olschki, 1997), 61n, 89–97. Atto, at least, seems to have received a somewhat broader education than mandated for the *scuola*: during his first trip to France in 1644 (at the age of eighteen), he showed no signs of struggling with the French language (in contrast to his later experiences in Germany – see his letter to Mattias, from Regensburg ["Ratisbon"], July 14, 1653). And in his maturity he authored a number of histories of events, reportedly "in elegante forma," showing a command of style sometimes also evident in his letters (V[ittorio] Capponi, *Biografia pistoiese* … [Pistoia: Rossetti, 1878], 272).

Table 1.1 *Membership of Melani brothers as singers in the choir of the Cathedral of S. Zeno, Pistoia*

Name	Born	Years in choir	Ages
Jacopo	1623	1633–45	10–22
Atto	1626	1636–43	10–17
Francesco Maria (Filippo)	1628	1639–41	11–13
Jacinto	1631	1648–49	17–18
Bartolomeo	1634	1642–54	8–20
Vincenzo	1637	1647–52	10–15
Alessandro	1639	1649–60	10–21

Source: Information from Franco Baggiani, "I maestri di cappella nella cattedrale di Pistoia," *Bollettino storico pistoiese*, 3d ser., 21 (1986): 53.

educate poor children for a life in the Church, then the matriculation of all seven Melani boys requires explanation, given the school's enrollment of only twenty or thirty students in total.[33] The situation smells of favoritism, presumably on the part of Domenico's employer, the bishop. The litter-bearer likely exploited his connections to win his sons the rare commodity of an education, a worthy act of patronage. Whether the Melani were suitably "poor" again remains unknown: the bishop could certainly have exempted a favored, well-to-do family from this requirement. Then again, Domenico chose not to send his boys to the more prestigious – and expensive – *collegio dei nobili* recently established in Pistoia by the Jesuits, even though it offered a surer path to success.[34] In either case, Domenico seems to have pulled some strings on behalf of his children.

The membership of all the boys in the *cappella* also raises the question of musical talent. In his important early article on the family, the musicologist Alessandro Ademollo suggested that the brothers' involvement in music

---

[33] When the *scuola* was established, the number of students was set at twelve, ten natives of Pistoia and two of nearby Prato; in 1515, ten more positions were created, supported by a gift of land from the bishop (Gambassi, *"Pueri,"* 89, 94). I am assuming no major expansion of the school in the succeeding years, especially given that the documents record no major expansion of the facilities.

[34] Jean Grundy Fanelli, "La musica patrocinata dai Rospigliosi: Il Collegio dei Nobili," *Bollettino storico pistoiese*, ser. 3, 31 (1996): 114–18, points out that the Jesuit order established their school in 1635. Although it initially focused on Latin grammar, it soon expanded to include instruction on playing and singing music (among other subjects). This school, however, required the steep fee of five ducats per month; indeed, as a *collegio dei nobili*, it catered to the elite of Pistoia. Although its presence in the city is interesting – especially because it was "protected" by the Rospigliosi family – there is no evidence that any of the Melani children attended. On these *collegi* as tools of advancement, Valsecchi (*L'Italia*, 102) notes that "in [the Jesuits'] hands were the greater and better colleges, to which flocked the sons of the nobles and of those who, in the upper bourgeoisie, sought to assimilate themselves to the nobility."

might have stemmed from the bell-ringing job of their father and maternal grandfather.[35] But clearly that work (not to mention the duties of litter-bearer) involved little musical skill, and nothing suggests the boys enjoyed a musical patrimony. Yet, remarkably, nearly all of them joined the *cappella* immediately upon entering the *scuola* (if the minimum age to enter the school remained ten years). Perhaps the *maestro di cappella*, Pompeo Manzini, recognized special talent in Jacopo and then pursued the boy's brothers to enhance the choir. A more pecuniary explanation is also possible. The records of the chapter show that members of the *cappella* – unlike the rest of the students – received pay for their services, with the greatest earnings going to the trained treble voices. The annual distribution on March 12, 1640 tells the story: Francesco Melani, who was only eleven, received two bushels of grain; Jacopo, then sixteen and presumably already a tenor, eight bushels; and Atto, almost fourteen (and surely already castrated), fourteen bushels.[36] In any case, it is unlikely that Domenico initially planned for his sons to go into music. Given his background, his more probable goal was to assure their general schooling and at the same time introduce them to the cathedral activities that constituted his world.

Quickly, however, the question of musical careers must have surfaced, for the decision to castrate cannot long have followed Atto's entry into the choir at the age of ten. Unfortunately (though not surprisingly), no documentation survives regarding Atto's surgery, nor that of any of his brothers. For indeed, Domenico ultimately had four of his sons castrated: Atto, Franceso Maria (later called Filippo), Bartolomeo, and Vincenzo. Presumably it was Manzini, the *maestro*, who first broached the subject. Jacopo, as eldest, would not have been considered, regardless of talent: his role was to carry on the family line.[37] And so Atto was the first. The procedure itself was considered rather mild for the period, requiring around two weeks of recuperation.[38] Indeed, as Giuseppe Gerbino has demonstrated, castration was a common surgery

---

[35] A[lessandro] Ademollo, "Un campanaio e la sua famiglia," *Fanfulla della Domenica*, December 30, 1883, 2.

[36] I PS, L-75, f. 32s; as cited in Pacini, *La chiesa*, IV:303. Although this is the only relevant pay record for the Melani boys, another record on March 14, 1600 reads "A Mario di ser Giovanni Montopoli, staia quattro di grano per sua provisione, per essere soprano della nostra cappella" (I PS, L-35 [M-61], f. 35s; as cited in Pacini, IV:124).

[37] As will be seen, circumstances eventually forced that function onto the fourth son, Jacinto, who inherited his father's position as bell-ringer (see chapter 7). In her "Famiglie di cantanti pistoiesi nel secolo XVII," *Bullettino storico pistoiese*, ser. 3, vol. 34 (1999), 106–7, Jean Grundy Fanelli suggests that Jacopo too was likely castrated, since families normally only allowed one son – in this case, Jacinto – to carry on the line. But when Jacopo entered the *cappella* at the age of ten, his three brothers were aged seven, five, and two. Given the child mortality of the period, it seems very unlikely the parents would have chosen to entrust the future of their clan to the two-year-old.

[38] Rosselli, "The Castrati," 151.

(involving only the testicles), used more often to treat diseases – everything from hernia to gout to epilepsy – than to preserve voices.[39] In some later cases, as research has shown, impoverished parents entered into apprenticeship contracts with singing teachers to help pay for such surgeries: the agreements stipulate how much the teacher will pay, how he will be remunerated for his instruction, and what financial claims everyone will have on the boy.[40] Again, no such contracts have been found for the Melani, who in any case were born before the heyday of such agreements. Certainly the very flexible career that Atto later pursued could not have developed had he owed years of wages to a mentor.

The question of castration

More interesting than *how* these four surgeries took place is *why*, which is of course the central question of this chapter. The real secret to understanding Domenico's radical decision to castrate four of his sons is understanding that from his perspective the decision was not radical at all. As the foregoing has suggested, financial desperation was an unlikely motive. Domenico Melani enjoyed, if not yet high social or economic standing, at least lofty contacts, and he himself owned urban property. He was helping his children ascend by the very normal method of arranging their education and social connections. He was not a man forced into an extreme act. Instead, as I shall try to show, castration appeared to Domenico another reasonable step in the patronage of his children, consistent with his orchestration of their education. In both cases, he was equipping them with uncommon skills that could appeal to future patrons. Oddly enough, to Domenico these surgeries may have seemed the most natural, even inevitable, course of action.

A crucial point of distinction between modern culture and that of the early *Seicento* is the nature of the family itself. According to social historians, relationships within early modern Italian families – especially urban families of middle to high status – differed strikingly from current Western norms.[41] In the place of modern intimacy, relationships exhibited the sort of formality

---

[39] Giuseppe Gerbino, "The Quest for the Castrato Voice: Castrati in Renaissance Italy," *Studi musicali* 33 (2004): 340, 348.

[40] The above is based on Rosselli, "The Castrati," 151–56, and G.L. Masetti Zannini, "Virtù e crudezza: Scolari di canto e famiglie tra rinascimento e barocco," *Strenna dei romanisti* 41 (1980): 332–41 *passim.*

[41] The following discussion is based primarily on Marzio Barbagli, *Sotto lo stesso tetto: Mutamenti della famiglia in Italia dal XV al XX secolo*, Saggi, no. 267 (Bologna: Il Mulino, 1984), *passim* (but especially 23–24, 241, 270–71, 309–10), who considers and summarizes much of the preceding literature on the subject.

and distance typical of most contemporary interactions. Absolute authority rested with the male head of the household. Husband and wife, often joined through exigencies of economics and social ambition, passed much of their time apart, with members of their own sex.[42] Children spent their earliest years in the care of nurses, employed to ease the burden of child-rearing. Contact between parent and child was limited: one contemporary writer refers approvingly to "some who employ the practice of not admitting their children into the paternal presence until they are well-bred and mannered."[43] Too tender or immoderate an expression of affection was thought by some to undermine authority: young children needed to learn above all to respect their parents; loving them, at least in the modern sentimental fashion, was of secondary importance. At around the age of ten, the children were typically separated from their nurses and sent to pass the latter years of their maturation with other families, either learning a trade in the traditional system of apprenticeship or, if noble, serving in a peer household. The Melani children entered the *scuola* at this time.

Instead of nurturing each child, ambitious parents focused on the status of the family as a whole, on the dynasty. They aimed to achieve a higher social position for the "house," not necessarily for each member of it. Central to this project was the principle of the indivisible inheritance. Parents knew that if they parceled out their assets to all the children, the family would never accumulate wealth and standing. Accordingly, one male child, usually the eldest, was designated sole inheritor of the family's titles and fortune, leaving his siblings in less secure circumstances.[44] Daughters who could offer a good dowry might ascend the social ladder through marriage; otherwise, they typically found themselves in convents. Younger sons could learn a trade, but because labor implied lower status, such careers arrested advancement.[45] Military service – as the traditional province of the nobility – was more acceptable, as were careers in law or positions in the court bureaucracy.

But the most common consequence of the indivisible inheritance was the imposition of a "'sacred' or 'profane' celibacy" on the younger sons and daughters of the family.[46] Even among those children destined to marry, the

---

[42] Domenico's reasons for marrying Camilla Giovanelli are unknown, but his assumption of her father's position suggests that economics may have been at least one consideration.

[43] Giovanni Maria Memmo, *Dialogo nel quale dopo alcune filosofiche dispute, si forma un perfetto prencipe, et una perfetta repubblica, e parimente un senatore, un cittadino, un soldato, et un mercatante* (Venice: Gabriele Giolito de' Ferrari, 1659), 22, quoted in Barbagli, *Sotto lo stesso tetto*, 309.

[44] The above is based on Valsecchi, *L'Italia*, 122; D[onald] H. Pennington, *Europe in the Seventeenth Century*, A General History of Europe, 2nd edn. (London: Longman, 1989), 106–8; and Barbagli, *Sotto lo stesso tetto*, 240–41.

[45] Pennington, *Europe*, 107.   [46] Barbagli, *Sotto lo stesso tetto*, 240. Also, Valsecchi, *L'Italia*, 122.

appeal of wedded life seems to have been on the wane. Eric Cochrane has reported on the ambivalence of many educated Florentine men toward the institution of matrimony: even if the bride brought a sizable dowry, married life was usually judged to be more expensive than bachelor existence. By Cochrane's estimation, the average age of a man at the time of marriage in the early *Seicento* was over twenty-nine, and that age increased as the century wore on.[47] However, most men who chose celibacy – or rather, who had it chosen for them as part of their parents' strategy – did so within the structure of the Church. As the historian Gaetano Imbert puts it, "the younger sons, reduced to living on a miserable allowance called a *piatto*, preferred the peace and refinements of the monastic state to the traffic of commerce, then despised, and to the severities of the military."[48] New convents and monasteries were built; new monastic orders were created; and the overall number of religious soared, both as an absolute number and as a percentage of the population.[49] For many, monastic life represented the most respectable and desirable "career path" available. An important result of familial strategizing, then, was this widespread renunciation of sexual activity (of the licit sort, at least), a practice that surely forms part of the context for castration.

Similarly important, contemporary attitudes about piety and spirituality differed significantly from those of today. The early decades of the *Seicento* were still influenced by the religious zeal of the Council of Trent. While in fact many prelates did not abandon their luxurious lifestyles, traditional paths of asceticism and renunciation received new prestige, enhancing the appeal of monastic life. But more extreme practices also appeared. For example, flagellation made a comeback (after its zenith in the fourteenth century), largely under the influence of the powerful Jesuit order. Reports also tell of hermit monks who chose to live without shelter high in the Apennines, exposing themselves to the elements.[50] It was a period when mortification of the flesh earned admiration.

Indeed, certain passages of the Bible, if read literally, appear to sanction even the radical step of castration. In the well-known parallel texts of Matthew 18:8–9 and Mark 9:43–48, the faithful are encouraged to sever any offending part of their body, it being "better to enter into the kingdom of God with one eye than to keep both eyes and be thrown into hell."[51] Christ

---

[47] Eric Cochrane, *Florence in the Forgotten Centuries 1527–1800: A History of Florence and the Florentines in the Age of the Grand Dukes* (Chicago: University of Chicago Press, 1973), 278.

[48] Gaetano Imbert, *La vita fiorentina nel Seicento secondo memorie sincrone (1644–1670)* (Florence: R. Bemporad e Figlio, 1906), 173.

[49] Rosselli, "The Castrati," 172–73.

[50] Imbert, *La vita*, 174–75. Rosselli, "The Castrati" (151), also mentions the importance of asceticism.

[51] Mark 9:47 (Revised English Bible).

himself speaks approvingly of eunuchs in a number of places, including Matthew 19:12: "For there are eunuchs who have been so from birth, and there are eunuchs who have been made eunuchs by others, and there are eunuchs who have made themselves eunuchs for the sake of the kingdom of heaven."[52] But perhaps the most powerful reference comes from the book of Isaiah: "The eunuchs who keep my sabbaths, who choose to do my will and hold fast to my covenant, will receive from me something better than sons and daughters, a memorial and a name in my house and within my walls; I shall give them everlasting renown, an imperishable name."[53] In a society that witnessed and approved extremes of asceticism, some may well have seen castration as an act of devotion.

In fact, the Catholic Church at this time neither sanctioned nor censured castration definitively. As John Rosselli has noted, the practice, when conducted for purely artistic purposes, was generally considered to be forbidden. Yet a number of dissenting theologians still held that the benefit to the community outweighed the damage to the individual, one even opining that "a boy's throat was more valuable to him than his testicles."[54] Pope Clement VIII (reg. 1592–1605) went so far as to proclaim the creation of castrati for church choirs *ad honorem Dei*.[55] At best, the Church was sending mixed messages.

Of course, it was the Church's need for high male voices that directly fueled the practice. Strictly interpreting Paul's command for female silence, the Church did not allow women to sing in its liturgy; boys and falsettists were found to be problematic, for both musical and practical reasons.[56] As Rosselli has noted, until the latter half of the eighteenth century, virtually all castrati seem to have been intended primarily for church service: their earliest teachers were almost invariably connected to ecclesiastical institutions, and the relative infrequency of opera productions (outside Venice) meant that few could hope for a career on the stage. Although more is known about the few operatic stars of the period (because their careers left more historical traces), the vast majority of castrati in the seventeenth century rarely sang outside the ecclesiastical setting.[57] Thus, castrating a son at this time would nearly always have meant dedicating him to a life of service in the Church.

---

[52] New Revised Standard Version. It is this passage that supposedly inspired the early Christian scholar Origen to castrate himself.

[53] Isaiah 56:3–4 (Revised English Bible).

[54] Rosselli, "The Castrati," 151; the final opinion is credited to the Theatine Zaccaria Pasqualino in 1641 (Rosselli gives no further citation).

[55] Enid Rhodes Peschel and Richard E. Peschel, "Medicine and Music: The Castrati in Opera," *Opera Quarterly* 4, no. 4 (1987): 21. Anthony Milner, "The Sacred Capons," *Musical Times* 114 (1973): 250–52, gives a brief but useful overview of castrato participation in church music.

[56] Rosselli, "The Castrati," 147–48.   [57] The above is based on ibid., 160–63.

Finally, Pistoia itself seems to have been an important center for the production of castrati in Italy. Indeed, the number of prominent singers emanating from the city appears out of all proportion to its size. Jean Grundy Fanelli has investigated many of these figures, including the important early pioneer Onofrio Gualfreducci, who came from a lofty Pistoiese family. One of the earliest Italian castrato members of the Cappella Sistina (1577–87; and, earlier, the Cappella Giulia, 1575–77), Gualfreducci returned to Tuscany to serve the Medici and sang in the Florentine *intermedi* of 1589.[58] Other early castrati include Niccolò Bartolini (*fl.* 1570s), who probably studied with Giulio Caccini, and Luca Salvadori (d. 1639), who served the Bentivoglio family in Ferrara and is mentioned by Monteverdi in 1623.[59]

But perhaps the most important case is that of Felice Cancellieri (1603–48). Born into the most storied family of Pistoia, he was nevertheless castrated and spent his youth in Germany singing for the Emperors Matthias and Ferdinand II.[60] When he returned to Pistoia around 1635, he soon set about improving the musical life of his city, particularly in the churches, and took on the unusual double-role of patron and singer. For example, he not only helped finance the performances of a new Oratorian society, but also acted as its principal soloist. Similarly, he served one term as *priore* of the *Compagnia di S. Cecilia*, whose purpose was to enhance the celebration of the saint's feast; unlike the previous aristocratic priors (including Bartolomeo Rospigliosi), he himself starred in the musical presentations. He also formed and patronized the musical and literary *Accademia dei Risvegliati*.[61] Felice's unusual situation is significant. Certainly the noble Cancellieri family had nothing to gain by castrating one of its sons: professional singing, like any trade, would normally have sullied the aristocracy.[62] In this case, at least, one struggles to find a motivation other than piety: marked for the traditional religious celibacy of cadets (he in fact became a priest), Monsignor

[58] Fanelli, "Famiglie," 104n; Gerbino, "The Quest," 321–22, 348n. Gualfreducci sang Cavalieri's "Godi turba mortale" in the *intermedi*.

[59] On Bartolini, Fanelli, "Famiglie," 104. On Salvadori, Rosselli, "The Castrati," 169. The text of Monteverdi's letter, along with a convincing argument for its date, can be found in Paolo Fabbri, "Inediti monteverdiana," *Rivista italiana di musicologia* 15 (1980): 76.

[60] In the thirteenth and fourteenth centuries, the struggles between the Cancellieri and Panciatichi for control of Pistoia eventually involved factions in Florence (the Blacks and Whites, through which conflict Dante was exiled) and resulted in a civil war between the two families (1499–1502). See David Herlihy, *Medieval and Renaissance Pistoia: The Social History of an Italian Town, 1200–1430* (New Haven, Conn.: Yale University Press, 1967), 201–7.

[61] The material on Cancellieri is based on Jean Grundy Fanelli, "Un animatore della vita musicale pistoiese del Seicento: Monsignore Felice Cancellieri, sopranista," *Bullettino storico pistoiese*, ser. 3, 24 (1989): 53–62 *passim*. Cancellieri established the *Congregazione dei trentatré* at the Oratorian church of S. Filippo Neri.

[62] Note, however, that Felice's uncle, Fetonte Cancellieri, had been a singer at the cathedral, and also, Fanelli guesses, a castrato ("Un animatore," 59; "Famiglie," 104).

Cancellieri was rendered more valuable to the Church by the preservation of his voice. His subsequent prominence in Pistoia suggests the lack of stigma that his community attached to his special, perhaps even honored, condition. Treated as any other aristocratic cleric, Felice may well have stood as a model to others.[63]

For indeed, a virtual legion of castrati emerged from the next generation of Pistoiese. In addition to the four Melani brothers – Atto, Filippo, Bartolomeo, and Vincenzo – there were at least two Rivani boys (Giulio and Antonio), two Fedi (Giuseppe and Francesco Maria, both prominent in Rome), another unrelated Domenico Melani, Bartolomeo Fregosi, Antonio Rinconi, and Rafaello Azelini, all born in Pistoia in the 1620s and 1630s.[64] And the tradition continued to some degree in later decades: Stefano Frilli (*c.* 1664–1744) created the title role in Handel's *Rodrigo* (Florence, 1707), and Francesco Checcacci – another son of a bell-ringer! – led a career in the early eighteenth century, primarily in Bologna and Modena.[65] Rosselli cited Pistoia as one of those "decayed Central Italian towns" whose poor economy led to a surge in monasticism and so, by implication, castration. While the number of known castrati from Pistoia does seem high, the motivations for those numbers involve far more than economic depression.

Indeed, taken together, the foregoing observations paint the unfamiliar but perhaps not entirely unimaginable landscape against which Domenico Melani made his decisions. In a place where dynastic advancement was paramount; where celibacy – both in and out of the monastery – was common and esteemed; where religious asceticism and self-mortification were venerated; where the Catholic Church, in practical terms, conferred its blessing on "artistic" castration; and where castrati were numerous and accepted at even the highest levels of society: in this context, a socially connected and ambitious bell-ringer, client of the bishop, unexpectedly learned that his sons had promising voices. If today the equipment manager of an NFL team discovered his undersize high-school boy actually excelled as

---

[63] I would particularly like to thank Jean Grundy Fanelli for the useful conversations we had on the relationship between castration and piety. She also argues that Cancellieri played a direct role in training the Melani and Rivani boys ("Famiglie," 106) and states that Cancellieri selected some of the boys for special training ("Rivani, Antonio," *Grove Music Online*, ed. Laura Macy, www.grovemusic.com [accessed May 31, 2007]). I have seen no direct evidence of such an arrangement.

[64] Fanelli, "Un animatore," 60–61. For both the preceding paragraphs, see also Jean Grundy Fanelli, "Castrato Singers from Pistoia, 1575–1660," *Civiltà musicale* 40 (May–August 2000): 47–53. Some of the birth dates for these singers are known; for others, the period of birth can be inferred from the dates of their major debuts or from comments about them by others.

[65] Fanelli, "Famiglie," 109. On Frilli's dates, see Warren Kirkendale, *The Court Musicians in Florence During the Principate of the Medici: With a Reconstruction of the Artistic Establishment*, "Historiae musicae cultores" biblioteca, no. 61 (Florence: Olschki, 1993), 652.

a linebacker, such a father might be tempted to abuse a readily available medical treatment – today chemical rather than surgical – to help his son into a profession that tacitly encouraged the abuse.[66] While I would never suggest that castration in the *Seicento* was "just like" any modern practice, Domenico's decision may have been even less difficult than that of this hypothetical father, for Domenico probably believed his "sacrifice" both expressed his piety and served the cathedral. From the perspective of patronage, he was making his sons into highly desirable and rare commodities, and he was supplying those commodities to his benefactor. Domenico did these things not simply for economic gain: patronage was not a tit-for-tat arrangement. Rather, by imitating his town's leading family, he hoped both to curry favor at the cathedral and facilitate his sons' future success. Domenico's example, while remaining unclear in some details, suggests the complexity of motivations that underlie the decision to castrate a son. If perhaps he will never earn our sympathy, his dedication to his family at least enriches and complicates our sense of the mentalities behind the castrato practice.

---

[66] The first place I read of such a link between the practices of castration and steroids (or other sports doping) was in Silke Leopold, "'Not Sex but Pitch': Kastraten als Liebhaber – einmal *über der Gürtellinie betrachtet*," in *Provokation und Tradition: Erfahrung mit der Alten Musik*, ed. Hans-Martin Linde and Regula Rapp (Stuttgart and Weimar: Verlag J. B. Metzler, 2000), 223–24. The point seems most apt.

During the early years of his career, Atto worked vigorously to establish relationships with patrons. At a very young age he secured the powerful Prince Mattias de' Medici, and he continued to court others. His success was remarkable: a provincial singer in 1638, Atto had by 1653 constructed a web of patronage that enveloped northern Italy and France. The explanation for his behavior, and his success, is bound up with the nature and importance of patronage in the early modern period. In the previous chapter I introduced some fundamentals of this institution as scholars have recently theorized it. Those principles play an even greater role in Atto's early adulthood. Indeed, his experiences and behavior in this period both confirm and enhance many of these theories.

As described, patronage was the primary mechanism for the exercise of power in seventeenth-century Europe. At its heart were long-term relationships based on an exchange of favors between individuals of unequal power. In a world where public institutions were (by modern standards) weak or non-existent, all members of society depended on private contacts to protect and support them: in Ronald Weissman's words, "all politics, indeed all important transactions, were personalized."[1] The world divided into friends, who supported one's interests, and strangers, who did not. One either dealt exclusively with friends or, more practically, "convert[ed] all neutral relations, all necessary contacts with strangers, into ties of obligation, gratitude, and reciprocity."[2] To do this, the upper class could give gifts or grant favors; the more modest could offer services or even borrow money. The important thing was to establish a personal bond of obligation. As Sharon Kettering explains, those obligations often masqueraded as voluntary generosity (on the one hand) or personal loyalty (on the other), but "the compulsory reciprocity of the patron–client relationship was its distinguishing characteristic."[3] Each party owed something to the other.

The reciprocal nature of these obligations sheds light on Atto's particular case. In the more familiar view of patronage, the artist is an instrument of politics, and

---

[1] Ronald Weissman, "Taking Patronage Seriously: Mediterranean Values and Renaissance Society," in *Patronage, Art, and Society in Renaissance Italy*, ed. F. W. Kent and Patricia Simons (Canberra [Australia]: Humanities Research Centre; Oxford: Clarendon Press, 1987), 37.

[2] Ibid., 44.

[3] Sharon Kettering, "Gift-Giving and Patronage in Early Modern France," *French History* 2 (1988): 151.

certainly in these early years Atto's masters exploited his talents to satisfy their own supporters and so strengthen their position. But, as Weissman explains, the actual balance of power between patron and client could be complex:

> inequality may take many forms in addition to those based on the hierarchies of traditional social stratification: inequality of access to news, information, friendship networks, political connections, scarce resources, of technical skills such as literacy. Thus, a man may serve as a patron to another for reasons that have little to do with great differences in property or social status.[4]

From the beginning, Atto possessed one of Weissman's rare "technical skills": his accomplished castrato voice. The singer's travels soon brought other assets, including access to news and his own widespread contacts. So as Atto solicited patrons – those who could provide him with the money and prestige he desired – he was far from powerless, and his willingness to exercise that power, to selectively withhold his gifts, would grow over time. Thus, in addition to offering glimpses of music-making in this period, the story of Atto's early career illustrates the multiple uses to which strong patrons and talented clients could put one another. It argues that, whether one speaks of what musicians could do for rulers or what rulers could do for musicians, all musical activity was saturated with politics.

First steps

I suggested in the previous chapter that Atto's first experience of patronage came through his father Domenico. Atto likely encountered his next major benefactor upon entering the cathedral choir, the *maestro di cappella* Pompeo Manzini. I have already speculated on Manzini's role in Atto's musical education, but the young singer's appearance in Michelangelo Rossi's opera *Erminia sul Giordano* in 1638 must be understood as a more concrete result of Manzini's sponsorship. With a libretto by the local noble-man and prelate Giulio Rospigliosi, the work had first been performed in 1633 at the Barberini palace in Rome.[5] Now, in imitation of the Romans, it was given in Pistoia at the *palazzo* of Teodoro Cellesi, with further financial support from Gabriello Panciatichi. The published libretto lists the perform-ers without specifying their duties, but the placement of Manzini's name at the head suggests his central role: surely he was responsible for engaging

---

[4] Weissman, "Taking Patronage Seriously," 35.

[5] Margaret Murata, "*Erminia sul Giordano*," *Grove Music Online*, ed. Laura Macy, www.grovemusic.com (accessed July 5, 2007).

Plate 1 Mattias de' Medici (Giusto Suttermans; Galleria Palatina, Palazzo Pitti, Florence, Italy). *Reproduced by permission of Scala / Art Resource, NY.*

the large number of cathedral musicians involved, including the organist, Valerio Spada, and the young choristers Jacopo and Atto Melani (then aged fifteen and twelve respectively).[6] For Atto, the event may well have been life-changing: not only did he gain valuable stage experience, but, even though Rossi and Rospigliosi were absent, he was introduced into the "public eye." Indeed, a full report on the production went out at least to Rospigliosi (then in Rome) and probably to others.[7] Somehow – through either this opera or other work under Manzini – Atto came to the attention of Mattias de' Medici, the patron who would dominate the next three decades of his life.

Mattias (1613–67) was one of the three younger brothers of Grand Duke Ferdinando II, and like his brothers he assisted in the rule of Tuscany.[8]

---

[6] The citation of this libretto was kindly shared with me by Jean Grundy Fanelli and now appears in her book, *A Chronology of Operas, Oratorios, Operettas, Cantatas and Miscellaneous Stage Works with Music Performed in Pistoia: 1606–1943* (Bologna: Edizioni Pendragon, 1998), 26.

[7] On the report to Rospigliosi, see his reply to his brother Camillo, from Rome, February 20, 1638, I Rvat, Vat. lat. 13363, f. 7, as transcribed in Margaret Murata, *Operas for the Papal Court 1631–1668*, Studies in Musicology, no. 39 (Ann Arbor, Mich.: UMI Research Press, 1981), 251. On Rossi's presence in Ferrara at this time, see Catherine Moore, "Rossi, Michelangelo," *Grove Music Online*, ed. Laura Macy, www.grovemusic.com (accessed June 19, 2007).

[8] Their sister Anna was married to Archduke Ferdinand Karl of Innsbruck (see below).

Granted the governorship of Siena at the age of seventeen, Mattias eventually commanded all grand-ducal troops and even served as an imperial general during the Thirty Years' War. In the opinion of the art historian Stella Rudolph, these military successes have sometimes blinded scholars to "a typically Medicean appreciation for *objets de vertu* for which he is not usually credited."[9] In fact, Mattias was not only an avid supporter of painters, such as his battlefield artist *Il Borgognone*, but "hunted for men distinguished in every art."[10] During the 1640s, this quest focused particularly on singers. Indeed, recent work by Sara Mamone in the Florentine archives has uncovered just how highly music figured in the interests of the Medici brothers at this time.[11]

Atto was among the first of Mattias's prizes, already tied to the prince by early 1641. Evidence for this early date all relates to Mattias's sojourn in Venice for carnival that year. There, he enjoyed the round of parties and masked revelry for which the Serenissima was famous, and he also took in the five operas on offer, including the hugely successful opening of the Teatro Novissimo with Francesco Sacrati's *La finta pazza*. Indeed, this trip seems to have triggered Mattias's interest in Venetian opera, a genre just then establishing itself: he soon cultivated relationships not only with Sacrati but also with the Grimani family, who at that time managed both the Novissimo and the older Teatro SS. Giovanni e Paolo. When the prince decided to build his own theater in Siena in 1647, he took the latter house as a model.[12]

Sometime after the run of *La finta pazza*, an account of its lavish production was published. This *Cannocchiale [Telescope] per La finta pazza* concentrates, as the title might suggest, on the visual splendor of the event. But the author also praises individual performers, as in the following for the singer playing "Pensiero Improviso": "the youth, who was a most

[9] Stella Rudolph, "A Medici General, Prince Mattias, and His Battlefield Painter, Il Borgognone," *Studi secenteschi* 13 (1972): 185.

[10] Filippo Baldinucci, "Vita di Jacopo Cortesi," in *Notizie de' professori del disegno …* (Florence: G.B. Stecchi, 1773), XIX:160–61, quoted in ibid., 186–87.

[11] Much of the above is based on W.E. Knowles Middleton, "A Cardinalate for Prince Leopoldo de' Medici," *Studi secenteschi* 11 (1970): 168; Rudolph, "A Medici General," 183–87; and Lorenzo Bianconi and Thomas Walker, "Dalla *Finta pazza* alla *Veremonda*: Storie di Febiarmonici," *Rivista italiana di musicologia* 10 (1975): 440. Sara Mamone's work can be found in her article "Most Serene Brothers-Princes-Impresarios: Theater in Florence under the Management and Protection of Mattias, Giovan Carlo, and Leopoldo de' Medici," *Journal of Seventeenth-Century Music* 9 (2003), http://sscm-jscm.press.uiuc.edu/jscm/v9/no1/Mamone.html; and her edition of Giovan Carlo de' Medici's correspondence, *Serenissimi fratelli principi impresari: Notizie di spettacolo nei carteggi medicei: Carteggi di Giovan Carlo de' Medici e di Desiderio Montemagni suo segretario (1628–1664)*, Storia dello spettacolo: Fonti, no. 3 (Florence: Le Lettere, 2003).

[12] Much of this paragraph is drawn from Bianconi and Walker, "Dalla *Finta pazza*," 435–36, 444, and 402n. Mamone, *Serenissimi fratelli*, 86–90, reproduces Mattias's letters (along with those of his entourage) to his brother Giovan Carlo from this trip.

valorous little singer from Pistoia, began to sing so delicately that the souls of the listeners, as if drawn through the portals of the ears, raised themselves to heaven to assist in the enjoyment of such sweetness."[13] Already in 1913, Henry Prunières felt that, based on the age and provenance of the singer, he was "sans doute" one of the Melani brothers, probably the fifteen-year-old Atto.[14] A letter from Sacrati to Mattias some ten months later enriches the picture:

Because I know the delight that Your Highness takes in hearing something new, I have burned with a real desire always to write something that fully suited your taste. And because right now the demands of the current opera keep me from writing anything new, I am sending you here included a scene for two characters from this year's opera itself, which will serve only as a pastime and is not for Signor Grasseschi to learn, since it is for those from Pistoia.[15]

In other words, because Sacrati had no time to write something new, he was sending a scene he had already composed for the upcoming opera, which was *Bellerofonte*; this scene was not for the famous contralto castrato Michele Grasseschi, who was in Mattias's service, but for two singers from Pistoia. The implication is that at least one of them was a castrato, or Sacrati would not have needed to distinguish the music from Grasseschi's. Indeed, a published account of *Bellerofonte* (1642) describes the role of Melistea as sung by "a very worthy castrato from Pistoia."[16] In light of all these indications, then, it seems probable that the "cantarino" in the *Finta pazza* production of 1641 was in fact the same Pistoiese castrato to whom Sacrati sent a

---

[13] *Il cannocchiale per la finta pazza, dilineato da M[aolino] B[isaccioni] C[onte] di G[enova]* (Venice: Giovanni Battista Surian, 1641), 12, quoted in Ellen Rosand, *Opera in Seventeenth-Century Venice: The Creation of a Genre*, A Centennial Book (Berkeley: University of California Press, 1991), 415. (I use Rosand's translation from p. 96). The identification of the role comes immediately following this passage. Rosand thought Atto might have played the major role of Achille, who is later described as "un giovanetto castrato venuto da Roma" (Rosand, 415), but it seems unlikely the author would have described the same singer as being from both Pistoia and Rome.

[14] Henry Prunières, *L'opéra italien en France avant Lulli*, Bibliothèque de l'Institut Français de Florence (Université de Grenoble), ser. 1, Collection d'histoire et de linguistique française et italienne comparées, no. 3 (Paris: Honoré Champion, 1913), 73n.

[15] Francesco Sacrati to Mattias de' Medici, from Venice, November 23, 1641. This passage was quoted (with some errors) in A[lessandro] Ademollo, *I primi fasti della musica italiana a Parigi (1642–1662)* (Milan: Ricordi, [1884]), 102–3.

[16] From the "Descrittione de gli Apparati" by Giulio del Colle included in Vicenzo Nolfi, *Il Bellerofonte: Drama Musicale* ([Venice]: n.p., 1642); quoted in Robert Lamar Weaver, "Florentine Comic Operas of the Seventeenth Century" (Ph.D. diss., University of North Carolina, Chapel Hill, 1958), 178, and Rosand, *Opera*, 101. Del Colle also mentions that the role of Paristide was played by a tenor from Pistoia, a singer who could well have been Atto's elder brother, Jacopo. If so, Jacopo would have played Atto's father.

scene from *Bellerofonte* and who then actually performed in that opera the following year.

As scholarship has revealed the remarkable number of castrati from Pistoia, earlier theories about Atto as the "little singer" have receded in certainty: more than one singer could have fit the description. But on October 22, 1640, the canons of Atto's cathedral recorded the following appeal: "Jacopo and Atto Melani, musicians of the *cappella*, appeared [before us] and said they had been called to go to Venice to an academy being held there, and they requested leave, which was unanimously granted to them for all of carnival."[17] The wording is interesting. The passive construction, "they had been called," suggests the intervention of a higher authority, as does the unanimous approval of the chapter, which was rare. The reference to an "Accademia" instead of opera may indicate that the boys' doings had yet to be settled; or it could simply be a "white lie" designed to circumvent ecclesiastical hostility to the public stage. The timing alone links the request to Mattias's trip, and indeed one can imagine few other ways for Atto to have appeared in Venice, and in so glittering an event as *La finta pazza*. The prince must have brought the young singers with him on his carnival tour, both to further their training and to participate in musical projects, to hear and be heard. Certainly, such personal cultivation of talent would have been nothing unusual for Mattias and his brothers, as Mamone has shown.[18] Exactly when and how Atto first claimed Mattias's attention may never precisely be determined, but it would seem that by the autumn of 1640 – and probably for at least some time before that – the prince had assumed the young singer into his circle of artists.

For quite a while after this event, however, Atto's name still does not appear in connection with Mattias or his family. Although Alessandro Ademollo claims that Atto had become Mattias's "cantante da camera" by 1642 – not an impossibility – he offers no evidence. As mentioned, Atto probably did perform in the Venetian *Bellerofonte* of early 1642. But, for the next few years, he seems to have remained closer to home, with a focus on gaining experience and perfecting his technique. At this time, the musical life of Atto's home town revolved around four institutions: the Oratorian Congregazione di S. Filippo Neri at the church of S. Prospero; the Congregazione dei Trentatré, especially dedicated to the musical enrichment of prayer for souls in purgatory; the Compagnia di Santa Cecilia, organized to celebrate the feast day of this saint with special magnificence; and the

---

[17] I PS, A/1-18, f. 38r–v, as transcribed in Alfredo Pacini, ed., *La chiesa pistoiese e la sua cattedrale nel tempo: Repertorio di documenti* (Pistoia: Editrice CRT, 1994), IV:302. The "eleven black beans" represent a unanimous positive vote; negative votes were indicated by "*fave bianche.*"

[18] Again, see her "Most Serene Brothers" and *Serenissimi fratelli*.

Accademia dei Risvegliati, a secular club devoted to music and theater.[19] In all these organizations the noble castrato Felice Cancellieri was a leader (see chapter 1), and in nearly all Atto seems to have performed regularly. Atto often sang duets with Cancellieri at the usual Monday services of the Trentatré; he, along with his brother Jacopo, were among the earliest members of the Risvegliati; and, on the feast day of Saint Cecilia (November 22) in 1641, he was one of four castrati to assist in the celebration.[20] Again, Manzini, and perhaps Cancellieri himself, must have sponsored Atto in these activities, which offered valuable opportunities to perform before and introduce himself to the most discerning and aristocratic audiences in Pistoia.

Fully documented connections between Atto and Mattias first emerge in late 1643, perhaps not coincidentally as Atto was reaching young adulthood. In September of that year, Marchese Francesco Guicciardini of Florence sent a rather playful letter of gratitude to the prince in which he refers to some upcoming *commedie* and notes that "Signor Atto has assisted me well, and I will thank him in person."[21] What Atto actually did is unclear, but the statement shows that Mattias was keeping tabs. The first extant correspondence between the two comes from the following January. In what becomes the norm for their relationship, Atto writes back to his patron (in Siena) about his experiences while away. Having just been received in Florence by the assembled Medici clan, Atto reports, "In the evening, the [Grand Duchess Vittoria della Rovere] kept me with her for over an hour, where I sang for the Princes Giovan Carlo, Don Lorenzo and Cardinal [Carlo de' Medici, Ferdinando's uncle]; and they appeared to have had great pleasure in hearing me sing."[22] Atto also relates that he has faithfully delivered Mattias's letters and is attempting to track down some requested *ariette*. From performing for the Pistoiese nobility, Atto was now beginning to sing for the Medici themselves. This event may almost have been a sort of debut, the first time the wider family had heard Mattias's maturing castrato.

But while the family may have been impressed, Mattias's focus remained on Atto's training, as emerges from several of the singer's comments. When Giovan Carlo, Mattias's brother, called Atto to perform in Florence during

---

[19] Jean Grundy Fanelli, "Un animatore della vita musicale pistoiese del Seicento: Monsignore Felice Cancellieri, sopranista," *Bullettino storico pistoiese*, ser. 3, 24 (1989): 54–60.

[20] All three events are related in I PSc, Raccolta Chiappelli, 188, p. 127 (November 2, 1646), p. 36 (September 4, 1642), and p. 14 (November 22, 1641); all as cited in Fanelli, "Un animatore," 56, 58, and 60.

[21] Francesco Guicciardini to Mattias, from Florence, September 27, 1643.

[22] Atto to Mattias, from Florence, January 17, 1644. This letter is clearly dated 1643, but the late use of the *ab Incarnatione* dating style in Florence suggests its assignment to 1644. Ademollo ("Un campanaio e la sua famiglia," *Fanfulla della Domenica*, December 30, 1883, 2) mistakenly asserts that this letter is addressed to Atto's father.

Holy Week 1644, Atto assures his patron, "I will not neglect to study during my stay in Florence so that I can compete with the others, bring myself honor, and be victorious, if possible."[23] Likewise, the next month, when Atto accompanied Giovan Carlo to Rome for the prince's elevation to the cardinalate, Atto again refers to his own education: "This evening, after a pleasant trip, I arrived in Rome … I have not yet heard any of the *virtuosi*; I will report fully to Your Highness on the techniques that are in vogue here. And as for the Roman *virtuosi* whom Signor Orazio has recommended to me, Your Highness can be assured that I will seek to imitate them."[24] Finally, on May 22 he promises one of the prince's secretaries, "I will obey His Highness no matter how much he requires of me, and as regards his command that I study, I have the stimulus of my reputation, which is a constant motivation for me."[25]

At the age of eighteen, it seems, Atto was putting the final touches on his training, and his trip to Rome served as a kind of "finishing school" in taste and style. That Rome should have been the site of such training is hardly coincidental: through at least the first half of the century, that city was the acknowledged center of vocal artistry. The large number of church choirs, aristocratic courts, and Oratorian congregations generated great demand for skilled vocalists, a demand that was met by a number of singing "schools."[26] One of the most renowned, and the best known today, was overseen by Virgilio Mazzocchi, where young boys were given not only intense vocal training, but also instruction in grammar, keyboard skills, and music composition.[27] As Marco Marazzoli states in a letter of 1641, "all the men of this world seek to send their subjects to Rome to have them learn [singing], because the [true] school is here."[28]

---

[23] Atto to Mattias, from Florence, March 13, 1644.

[24] Atto to Mattias, from Rome, April 12, 1644. In a letter to Orazio Magalotti of March 23, 1644, Lorenzo Guicciardini, a Florentine nobleman in Rome, writes that Mattias has charged him to introduce Atto to Roman society and its musicians. Guicciardini further describes Atto and his voice: "canta assai bene, è sicurissimo nella musica, ha bella voce, trillo, disposizione … Il ragazzo è bonissimo, ben creato, hà bisogno di sentir diverse maniere, però bisogna introdurlo da i bravi cantanti e musici di Roma, che non deve andare a scola, ma sentirli e cantare ancora lui." This material appears in Silvia Bruno, "Musici e pittori tra Firenze e Roma nel secondo quarto del Seicento," *Studi secenteschi* 49 (2008): 194n.

[25] Atto to Mattias's secretary (?), from Rome, May 22, 1644. The precise addressee of this letter is not identified, but the salutation – "Ill.mo e Pron. mio Col.mo" – cannot be to the prince; I assume then it was intended for one of Mattias's secretaries.

[26] Sergio Durante, "Il cantante," in *Il sistema produttivo e le sue competenze*, vol. IV of *Storia dell'opera italiana*, ed. Lorenzo Bianconi and Giorgio Pestelli, Biblioteca di cultura musicale (Turin: E.D.T. Musica, 1987), 357.

[27] Giovanni Andrea Angelini Bontempi, *Historia musica* (Perugia: Costantini, 1695), 170, quoted in ibid., 368.

[28] From a letter partially published in Pier Maria Capponi, "L'educazione di una virtuosa nel secolo XVII," *Lo spettatore musicale* 3 (1968): 15, quoted in Durante, "Il cantante," 357.

Atto's promise to imitate the Romans suggests that he and Mattias shared
this opinion. But his clearest statement on the matter, and on his determination to succeed musically, appears in a letter to Mattias from June 4:

Famous here in Rome [are] Signor Luigi [Rossi] and Signor Marc'Antonio
[Pasqualini], the best *virtuosi* whom I have ever met, and truly there is much to be
learned. Now that I am working to polish myself, I beg Your Highness to allow me to
stay in Rome all summer, for [until now] I had not heard good [singing], and Signor
Luigi is holding an academy in his house this summer where all the best *virtuosi* of
Rome will be, and by his grace he has included me in that number. I assure you that
I will hear more on one of these days than in all the time that I have been in Rome and
will have the opportunity to learn many techniques. For the love of God, do not ask
me to break the thread [of my training] now that I am at the point of perfection, for
I want Your Highness to be able to boast of having the best singer in Italy.[29]

While Atto may never have studied at one of the formal schools, his work
with Rossi and Pasqualini suggests a thorough grounding in the fashionable
Roman style, and particularly the tradition of Roman chamber singing.

In the end, Atto's program of musical education in Pistoia and Rome
looks very much like it was managed by Mattias and his brothers, a practice
they are known to have pursued with other artists.[30] While Mattias may have
"discovered" Atto in 1641, the singer was left in Pistoia to develop his abilities
before being sent to Rome with Giovan Carlo for seasoning. The plan had the
advantage of rewarding (and further obligating) several of Mattias's Pistoiese
clients: the bishop and *maestro di cappella* enjoyed the boy's talents for
several more years (with perhaps some financial support for his education),
and the benefits to Atto and his family are obvious. But of course Atto's
training also served Mattias, not only by improving the quality of the prince's
personal entertainment, but also by increasing the value of Atto's service.
Mattias was creating (and controlling) one of the "scarce resources" that was
much in demand throughout Europe. The shrewdness of his efforts emerges
in the next stage of Atto's career.

Paris

That stage marked the expansion of Atto's experience – and patronage –
from a regional to an international level. The site was the French court, at

---

[29] Atto to Mattias, from Rome, June 4, 1644. Also quoted in Ademollo, "Un campanaio," 2.
[30] See Mamone, "Most Serene Brothers," *passim.*

Plate 2 Cardinal Jules Mazarin (Pierre Mignard; Musée Condé, Chantilly, France). *Reproduced by permission of Giraudon / Art Resource, NY.*

which he served during two extended stays between 1644 and 1649. Atto's link to France, which endured the rest of his life, resulted largely from the political needs of France's new first minister Cardinal Jules Mazarin, who assumed the position from the end of 1642. Of course, Mazarin was himself a native Italian, and Atto's activities in France are closely tied to the cardinal's tricky political situation.

Although in theory only the monarchs themselves surpassed Mazarin in authority, the cardinal often found his standing precarious. Mazarin's only reliable power base was the personal support of the queen regent, Anne of Austria.[31] Anne had first come to know the cardinal during the final illness of her husband, Louis XIII. Mazarin's ability to speak Spanish (her native tongue), his professed desire to reach a peace with her Habsburg relatives in Spain, his indefatigable work habits, and, most of all, his impartiality

---

[31] Anne took her title from her mother, called Margaret of Austria (daughter of Charles of Inner Austria [1540–90]); her father was Philip III, king of Spain.

Plate 3 Anne of Austria, with young Louis XIV (anonymous French; Chateaux de Versailles et de Trianon, Versailles, France). *Reproduced by permission of Erich Lessing / Art Resource, NY.*

regarding the internal affairs of France all attracted her. Indeed, he helped her negotiate a political minefield. Many French aristocrats had opposed Mazarin's predecessor, Cardinal Richelieu, and his policy of centralizing power in the person of the king. After Richelieu's death in December 1642 – followed five months later by that of Louis XIII – many looked forward to a reversal. Indeed, powerful factions at court – particularly those of Gaston d'Orléans and the Prince de Condé – aimed to weaken the

crown and competed to influence Anne's decisions, assuming her to be
politically incompetent. Mazarin, instead, counseled her to retain the powers
Richelieu had accumulated and promised to work solely in the interests of
her son, for whom he predicted a glorious future. As Ruth Kleinman notes in
her study of Anne, "it is small wonder that she consented to follow his lead
and came to regard him as indispensable."[32]

But Mazarin could hardly feel secure. His influence over Anne earned him
the animosity of the aristocracy; his wartime taxation schemes – unorthodox
and onerous – angered the bourgeoisie; and no one liked having an Italian as
de facto ruler. Worse, gossip about his frequent private conferences with the
queen began to create scandal. Although modern scholars have generally
rejected the idea of an affair, the rumors forced the pious Anne to distance
herself. To reinforce this all-important relationship, Mazarin sought to
become the queen's friend as well as her minister: in Kleinman's words,
"he knew that his only source of power lay in the queen's confidence, and he
set out to win her trust so completely that she would do nothing without
him."[33]

It was precisely here, in strengthening his position at court, that Mazarin
found a prominent use for the arts. With displays of artistic magnificence, he
hoped to bolster the image of the regency government and his role in it:
leaders who seemed dynamic and affluent earned greater respect, while
nothing pleased the queen more than seeing her son's glory proclaimed.[34]
Mazarin had in fact observed the political usefulness of the arts under his
former patrons in Rome, the Barberini family, as Madeleine Laurain-Portemer
eloquently explains:

The example of [Mazarin's] *"padroni"* [the Barberini] had convinced him forever
that the grandeur of a reign was not measured solely by its strength abroad [and] its
concord within, but further required the radiance of a civilization, that there was no
glory without song, without statues, without paintings, and that only the artistic

---

[32] Ruth Kleinman, *Anne of Austria: Queen of France* (Columbus, Ohio: Ohio State University Press,
1985), 172. The above paragraph is based on Kleinman, 136–54 *passim*, and Geoffrey
R.R. Treasure, *Seventeenth Century France*, 2nd edn. (London: John Murray, 1981), 215–17.

[33] Kleinman, *Anne*, 148; this paragraph is based on Kleinman, 148, 180–81, 230–32, and Henry
Kamen, "The Statesman," in *Baroque Personae*, ed. Rosario Villari, trans. Lydia G. Cochrane
(Chicago: University of Chicago Press, 1995), 14, originally published as *L'uomo barocco*, Storia e
Società, (Rome: Laterza, 1991).

[34] Regarding the political importance of sumptuous display, Peter N. Skrine, *The Baroque:
Literature and Culture in Seventeenth-Century Europe* (New York: Holmes and Meier, 1978),
1–24, but esp. 21–23; also Norbert Elias, *The Court Society*, trans. Edmund Jephcott (New York:
Pantheon, 1983), 41–65, originally published as *Die höfische Gesellschaft* (Darmstadt: Hermann
Luchterhand, 1969). On Anne's advocacy of her son, Kleinman, *Anne*, 278.

formulas in favor at Rome could give this ornament, this glamour without which the setting of life would be insipid and dull.[35]

To this end, Mazarin imported Roman painters, sculptors, carpenters, and decorators, all charged primarily with turning Mazarin's recently acquired palace into a baroque showpiece. The grandeur of this style and its novelty in France made it the appropriate means for communicating the vigor and authority of Mazarin and his government.[36]

But in addition to awing its noble audience, Mazarin's *offensive baroque* was intended to delight and captivate, most importantly the queen herself: as the cardinal was reportedly fond of saying, "he who possesses the heart possesses everything."[37] Mazarin knew of the queen's taste for theatrical productions: even during her official year of mourning she had discreetly attended performances.[38] And so he envisaged the young genre of opera as a means both "to alleviate the absence of warmth" between himself and the court and, more importantly, "to touch [Anne's] heart."[39] Prunières states plainly that "[Mazarin] saw in opera a marvelous instrument of seduction and domination," particularly as regarded the queen.[40]

In truth, Mazarin's efforts to bring Italian music to Paris had begun even before he became first minister, as Margaret Murata has closely chronicled.[41] But whereas the deaths of Richelieu and Louis XIII might have been expected to diminish these efforts, given the obligatory period of mourning, the cardinal seems to have stepped up his plans. In the fall of 1643, he renewed a charge to his agents in Italy to recruit personnel specifically for an Italian opera: the diary of the papal lawyer Teodoro Ameyden for November 28, 1643 reports "the order of Cardinal Mazarin to bring Roman musicians to

---

[35] Madeleine Laurain-Portemer, "La politique artistique de Mazarin," in *Il Cardinale Mazzarino in Francia: Colloquio italo–francese (Roma, 16–17 Maggio 1977)*, Atti dei Convegni Lincei, vol. 35 (Rome: Accademia Nazionale dei Lincei, 1977), 42: "L'exemple de ses 'padroni' l'a convaincu pour toujours que la grandeur d'un règne ne se mesure pas seulement par la puissance au dehors, la concorde au dedans, mais qu'il faut encore le rayonnement d'une civilisation, qu'il n'est pas de gloire sans mélodies, sans statues, sans peintures, et que seules les formules artistiques en faveur à Rome peuvent donner cette parure, cet éclat sans lesquels le cadre de vie serait fade et languissant." On Mazarin's early musical experiences in Rome, see Margaret Murata, "Why the First Opera Given in Paris Wasn't Roman," *Cambridge Opera Journal* 7 (1995): especially 88–93. On the Barberini exploitation of the arts, see Frederick Hammond, *Music and Spectacle in Baroque Rome* (New Haven, Conn.: Yale University Press, 1994), *passim*, but especially 1–60.

[36] The above is largely based on Laurain-Portemer, "La politique artistique," 53–55.

[37] The evocative term comes from ibid., 51. Mazarin's phrase is quoted in Prunières, *L'opéra*, 43.

[38] Kleinman, *Anne*, 184.

[39] Roger Simon, "Mazarin, la cour et l'influence italienne," in *La France et l'Italie au temps de Mazarin*, ed., Jean Serroy (Grenoble: Presses Universitaires de Grenoble, 1986), 36; and Prunières, *L'opéra*, 48.

[40] Prunières, *L'opéra*, 43. Prunières credits this observation originally to Romain Rolland.

[41] Murata, "Why the First Opera," 87–105 *passim*.

France for a *comedia* or *dramma musicale*."[42] If anything, the death of Mazarin's superiors increased his determination to import the new Italian genre.

Atto was soon caught up in these efforts. Although Mazarin's Barberini allies had been forced to flee Rome and charges of fiscal misconduct, Mazarin maintained contact with their former circle through personal agents such as Elpidio Benedetti. Given that both Luigi Rossi and Marc'Antonio Pasqualini had lately been in the employ of Antonio Barberini, and that, as we have seen, Atto worked with these musicians in the summer of 1644, it is not surprising that the young castrato quickly came to Benedetti's attention, and thence to that of Mazarin himself.[43]

With the cardinal's first requests to Prince Mattias for Atto's services, Atto entered the complicated field that Laurain-Portemer has labeled "la politique artistique."[44] Mazarin's political need for the singer has already been suggested, but the requests also introduced Atto to the politics of his native grand duchy. At this time, the Medici court, like many smaller Italian powers, was trying to thread its way between the Scylla and Charybdis of France and the Habsburg realms (Spain and the Empire). Officially, the Medici were Habsburg clients, which explains Mattias's generalship for the emperor. But to maintain independence, the grand duke also tried to appear a friend to France. The lending of artists and musicians to Mazarin represented a benign if important way of cementing political connections, and therefore security. Indeed, as Laurain-Portemer puts it, such cultural exchanges often opened "diplomatic-artistic relations … at the highest levels."[45]

Regardless of such advantages, the Medici seem to have been disinclined to let the young singer go. When in the summer of 1644 Mazarin asked Mattias for Atto's services, Mattias's siblings strongly urged refusal. Giovan Carlo, Leopoldo, and Anna all feared that, if Atto went to France, the queen would never let him return, and, as Leopoldo put it, "[singers] like Atto don't come along every day." Anna further complained she would lose her duet partner, for it seems they often sang together when Atto was in Florence. Mazarin pursued all channels, however, and eventually Mattias conceded, telling his siblings, "if we could obligate the queen and the cardinal by sending Atto, with the assurance that he would be returned in six months

---

[42]   As quoted in Ademollo, *I primi fasti*, 10.

[43]   Weaver, "Florentine Comic Operas," 179; Prunières, *L'opéra*, 59. The first letter requesting Atto's services, from Mazarin to Mattias, dates from July 6, 1644, roughly three months after Atto's arrival in Rome (see Appendix B).

[44]   Again, the useful term is borrowed from Laurain-Portemer, "La politique artistique."

[45]   Ibid., 48; the author is actually discussing here negotiations with the pope for the services of Bernini, but the point is apropos. On the loaning of artists and musicians, Weaver, "Florentine Comic Operas," 179–80; and Prunières, *L'opéra*, 58–59.

or less, I don't think there would be any harm; sometimes with a gesture that in fact is of little consequence one can gain advantage in things that are beneficial and important."[46] The chance to "obligate" the French politically outweighed aesthetic enjoyment. Atto's trip to France was not so much a friendly sharing of artistic resources, then, as the launching (or prolongation) of a patronage relationship crucial to Tuscan diplomacy.

Atto's period of training in Rome was thus cut short on October 5, 1644 when he left for Paris in the company of one of Mazarin's secretaries, Don Alessandro Fabri. They traveled north to Florence and were there joined by two other Medici protégés, Anna Francesca Costa and Atto's elder brother Jacopo. The four journeyed on to Genoa, where they departed by ship for France on October 19. Not surprisingly, Atto described this his first ocean voyage as "stravagante," though he proudly noted that he avoided becoming ill. By the middle of November, he had made his entrance into the French court.[47]

From the beginning, Atto more than fulfilled Mazarin's hopes. Since March of that year, the renowned Roman singer Leonora Baroni had been in Paris, where she had rapidly become the favorite of the queen and her court.[48] But in Atto's first letter back to Mattias, he is able to boast of his immediate success (and reveal something of French musical tastes):

Her Majesty has enjoyed my singing extraordinarily, and whoever told Your Highness that they only like cheerful arias here spoke little truth because Her Majesty enjoys only the sad ones. These are her favorites, and all the gentlemen [too] enjoy nothing but these. Hardly two evenings pass that I do not go to serve Her Majesty, and she does me a thousand honors. Music delights her so much that for four hours one must accept the idea of doing nothing else. [The same is true] for the queen of England, so that when I do not go [to serve] one, I go to the other.[49]

Two months later Atto enjoyed even greater favor, singing for the French queen daily: "here in Paris both Her Majesty and all these gentlemen do me

---

[46] Mattias to Giovan Carlo, from Siena, August 20, 1644. The earlier references in this paragraph come from other letters reproduced by Mamone, *Serenissimi fratelli*, 113–15: from Mazarin to Mattias, from Paris, July 6, 1644; and from Giovan Carlo, Anna, and Leopoldo to Mattias, from Florence, July 25, 1644.

[47] The above is based on Prunières, *L'opéra*, 59–60, 91, which is only slightly augmented by Adelmo Damerini, "La partitura de *L'Ercole in Tebe* di Jacopo Melani (1623–1676)," *Bullettino storico pistoiese* 19 (1917): 58; also, Atto's letter to Mattias, from Paris, November 22, 1644.

[48] Ademollo, *I primi fasti*, 10–13.

[49] Atto to Mattias de' Medici, from Paris, November 22, 1644. The wife of Charles I of England (and daughter of Henry IV of France), Queen Henrietta Maria, had fled England's civil war and arrived in Paris in 1644 with her sons Charles, the Prince of Wales (later Charles II), and Henry. She and her sons were fixtures at the French court at this time.

a thousand honors and favors, and I seem to be in Paradise, since every day I go to the queen, where one sees angelic faces."[50] Atto seems to have enchanted the queen as much as or more than his celebrated predecessor.

In late February 1645, Atto was involved in a performance that has led to much debate and whose nature still remains unclear. In a letter of March 10, 1645 he reports to Mattias:

> Finally the work was performed and it was very good, and Sunday Her Majesty wants to hear it again. Everyone performed his part well, and, to do honor to Your Highness, I sought not to be the last, which, thank God, I succeeded at more than I hoped. Signora Checha [Anna Francesca Costa] did very well, though [only] as far as her understanding allows.[51]

Five days later he wrote again, "Her Majesty wants the *commedia* performed after Easter, but Your Highness would need to assist my brother [Jacopo] with the authorities so that he will not lose his position" (presumably at the cathedral of Pistoia).[52] The only other notice of the event comes from the *Gazette de France*: "The 28th [of February], the king gave a dinner … In the evening there was an Italian comedy in the great hall and a ballet danced by several gentlemen of the court." Nowhere is this *commedia* identified further. Ademollo conjectured the work was a much altered version of the aforementioned *La finta pazza*, a view supported by Lorenzo Bianconi and Thomas Walker. More recently, Neal Zaslaw has championed Pier Capponi's suggestion of Marco Marazzoli's *Il giuditio della Ragione tra la Beltà e l'Affetto*, while Murata, evaluating all the earlier positions, has reasoned that the work may well not have been an opera at all.[53]

That the work was in fact a *dramma musicale* of some type seems implied by Atto's use of the word *recitare* to indicate performance – a word reserved for dramatic presentations – and by his reference to each singer's part or role (*parte*). Indeed, it would be difficult to imagine what sort of *commedia* a castrato of this period could *recitare* other than an opera (by our definition).[54] But one can feel confident about little more. For a few reasons,

---

[50] Atto to Mattias, from Paris, January 13, 1645.

[51] Atto to Mattias, from Paris, March 10, 1645.

[52] Atto to Mattias, from Paris, March 15, 1645.

[53] Ademollo, *I primi fasti*, 21–22; Bianconi and Walker, "Dalla *Finta pazza*," 398; Neal Zaslaw, "The First Opera in Paris: A Study in the Politics of Art," in *Jean-Baptiste Lully and the Music of the French Baroque: Essays in Honor of James R. Anthony*, ed. John Hadju Heyer, in collaboration with Catherine Massip, Carl B. Schmidt, and Herbert Schneider (Cambridge and New York: Cambridge University Press, 1989), 15–23; and Murata, "Why the First Opera," 103n.

[54] The *Grande Dizionario della lingua italiana*, ed. Salvatore Battaglia (Turin: U.T.E.T., 1988), s.v. "recitare," makes it clear that, when used with respect to singing, the word indicates (and indicated) a dramatic performance; several relevant attestations from the period are given.

I lean toward *La finta pazza*. Bianconi and Walker noted that one of the earliest groups of Febiarmonici (touring opera companies) had performed *Finta pazza* in Piacenza in May 1644 and then left for Paris at the request of the French queen.[55] The production in Paris could not have been on the same scale: not only was it widely ignored in accounts of public events, but one of the performances may even have taken place during Lent, requiring particular discretion. (According to Atto's letter of March 10, the queen desired to hear it again the following Sunday, presumably March 12; Ash Wednesday in 1645 fell on March 1.)[56] Zaslaw's idea of the work as a private chamber opera must be right. But I am persuaded by Murata's judgment of *Il giuditio* as a "poor [representative] of Italian opera, since the work lacks lyricism, demands no virtuoso singing, and requires good Italian … to understand its jokes and satire."[57] If Mazarin were trying to promote the genre to the French, such a work would seem an odd choice. Further, *Il giuditio* has no role for a lower male voice, which is certainly what the non-castrated Jacopo Melani possessed (see chapter 1). Murata admits, "Ademollo's proposal [of *Finta pazza*] would have been especially attractive if Atto Melani had in fact sung the role of Achile in *Finta pazza* in 1641."[58] As argued above, his participation in that performance now seems a certainty, even if he did not play Achile. With so many veterans of the Sacrati opera in Paris, Mazarin would surely have found it a sensible choice.

Whatever was presented, Mazarin disbanded his Italian company in late spring. At Atto's departure on May 10, the cardinal wrote to thank Mattias for his singer, "from whose talents the queen and all the court have received full satisfaction."[59] Indeed, the success of Atto and the other Italians, especially with the queen, spurred Mazarin to more ambitious undertakings. In the winter of 1645–46, the cardinal assembled another troupe of singers and comedians (this time without Atto) to perform (perhaps again) *La finta pazza*, this time in a more open and elaborate production.[60] Indeed, the grandeur of Giacomo Torelli's stage designs won it a triumph. The following year Mazarin went one step further and planned a newly composed opera by Luigi Rossi, the leading musician of Rome. Rossi arrived in Paris in June

---

[55] Bianconi and Walker, "Dalla *Finta pazza*," 397–98. Ademollo, *I primi fasti*, 21–22. Murata, "Why the First Opera," 103n, points out some potential problems with the report about the Febiarmonici but does not fully controvert it.

[56] Of course, no evidence exists to say whether or not such a performance took place; likewise, Atto's later comment that the queen wanted the work repeated after Easter does not indicate whether that would be the second or third performance.

[57] Murata, "Why the First Opera," 103n.   [58] Ibid.

[59] Mazarin to Mattias, from Paris?, May 10, 1645, quoted in Ademollo, *I primi fasti*, 20–21.

[60] The circumstances surrounding the production of this opera are examined in Murata, "Why the First Opera," 87–105 *passim*, but especially 103–4.

1646, escaping the papal disfavor suffered by all Barberini clients. Not surprisingly, given both Rossi's acquaintance with Atto and Atto's previous success in Paris, the young singer was soon recalled to play a major part in the project. By January 1647, less than two years after his departure, Atto was back in France.[61]

About the now-famous *Orfeo* of Francesco Buti and Luigi Rossi, there is little new to say: the definitive account remains that of Henry Prunières from 1913. It is Atto's letter of January 12, 1647 that has preserved much of what is known about the cast:

Your Highness is already familiar with the musicians who perform [the opera]: Signora Rossina [Martini], on account of the favorable letter Your Highness wrote for her to Cardinal Mazarin, has earned a role in this drama and plays Venus; Signora Checca [Costa], Euridice; Signor Marc'Antonio [Pasqualini], Aristeo; the castrato of the Bentivoglio gentlemen, a nurse; and I, Orfeo.[62]

Noteworthy is the Roman/Florentine rather than Venetian bias of the production: Rossi and Pasqualini were firmly associated with the papal city, and Buti was the secretary of Cardinal Antonio Barberini, while Martini, Costa, and Atto all served members of the Medici family.[63] *Orfeo* thus represents another part of Mazarin's promotion of the Roman baroque in Paris, indeed, the crowning jewel of his efforts.[64]

And Atto's role in those efforts continued. After the last presentation of *Orfeo*, when the other performers began to disperse, the queen wanted to hold on to Atto. On May 9, Anne and her court left for Amiens so that young Louis could participate (albeit at a distance) in the annual military campaign; Atto and his brother Jacopo came along. Soon, the queen wrote Mattias both to praise Atto and to demand, not so subtly, that his leave be extended:

I enjoy Italian music so much – now that I have heard it in its perfection – that I admit openly that you have pleased me by permitting Atto to come here. Because none of the Italians had as beautiful a voice as he, and no one's singing pleased me more, I have detained him with me in the belief that you would find this proper.[65]

---

[61] The events presented here are based primarily on Prunières, *L'opéra*, 64–96.

[62] Atto to Mattias, from Paris, January 12, 1647.   [63] Prunières, *L'opéra*, 91.

[64] This view is supported by Laurain-Portemer, "La politique artistique," 56. Although Murata, in "Why the First Opera," has shown that the earliest known opera in Paris was in fact a Venetian-flavored production, Mazarin (not surprisingly) seems to have maintained his taste for Roman products. Even Atto, although Tuscan, must have seemed virtually Roman to the French, with his connections to Rossi's circle.

[65] Anne of Austria to Mattias, from Amiens, May 24, 1647 (excerpted, with corrections, by Prunières, in his *L'opéra*, 141).

When Atto did not return to Italy with the other singers, Mattias first reacted angrily: he was planning an opera in Siena and was counting on Atto's voice. But when the prince learned of the queen's wishes, he relented.[66] Atto's singing continued to be an affair of state.

As it happened, Mattias was deprived of his singer for two more years, as Atto continued to serve the queen and her first minister.[67] All the parties involved had something to gain by this arrangement: both Mazarin and the Medici benefited by providing Anne with a service she valued, thereby subtly binding her to their interests; the Medici also enhanced their reputation by placing a living reminder of their taste and generosity at the French court; and finally Atto certainly valued the chance to establish himself at one of the most powerful courts in Europe. Yet increasingly Atto also faced a problem. The longer he stayed in Paris, the more he risked Mattias's neglect and the possibility of dismissal. Atto obviously could not provide the prince with musical services from such a distance, and, as Kettering has noted, patrons often cut off their support in this situation, when a client "lacked the potential for useful service or [was] no longer providing it."[68] Atto's letters from these years contain frequent affirmations of loyalty and pleas for orders that, more than usually obsequious, betray his anxiety:

I beg … Your Highness to continue your most benevolent favor toward me and convey your orders more often, because without these my service would be useless. At every opportunity I will exercise that service with such devoted affection that Your Highness will understand how resolute is my obedience, and you will find yourself obliged to command me more often.[69]

To "be certain of living in the memory of Your Highness," as Atto put it, he began providing whatever services he could execute, even – or especially – when he was away.[70] One of these – offered by many clients when traveling – was the acquisition of commodities unavailable at home. In his study of late

---

[66] Atto to Mattias, from Paris, October 25, 1647. On Mattias's plans to use Atto, see Mattias's letters to Giovan Carlo, from Siena, May 1 and 27, 1647.

[67] Catherine Massip, *La vie des musiciens de Paris au temps de Mazarin (1643–1661): Essai d'étude sociale*, La vie musicale en France sous les rois Bourbons, no. 24 (Paris: A. et J. Picard, 1976), 7–8, reports that in 1647 a theatrical entertainment was offered for the son of the landgrave of Hesse, who was visiting the French court. Describing the various elements of the performance, she writes, "Anne de La Barre chante de nouveau un air italien avant qu'apparaisse le Palais du Soleil et Phebus en personne représenté par Atto Melani 'qui chanta un air italien dont la beauté de sa voix avec sa conduitte admirable sembloient a qui mieux mieux se vouloir surmonter.'" Atto's appearance as Apollo, god of the sun, is interesting, especially as it prefigures the king's later adoption of that imagery.

[68] Kettering, "Gift-Giving," 144.   [69] Atto to Mattias, from Paris, November 7, 1647.

[70] The quotation comes from his letter to Mattias, from Amiens, July 25, 1647.

Medici art patronage, Edward Goldberg investigates the efforts of Paolo del Serra as an art dealer for the Medici, noting that, far from limiting himself to paintings, Serra often served as "a personalized mail order house for rich items."[71] Atto was soon performing a similar function from Paris, if on a more limited scale. In the fall of 1647, for example, at the same time as he was entertaining the queen and court, he was also roaming Paris in search of the newest, most stylish type of sword-hilt. Eventually, he found a worthy design, "esteemed here very beautiful and [in] the style that will begin to come into use, as five or six similar ones have already been made … for the king, the Prince de Condé [etc.]."[72] The following year the objective was skullcaps, of which Atto forwarded a boxful. And he spent much of this two-year period hunting down a particular kind of clock that would both chime the hours and sound an alarm bell, a project that ultimately failed because such clocks were all too big to transport.[73] Throughout his career, Atto continued to seek out not just musical scores and instruments (as one would expect), but all the trendy merchandise his patrons requested.

Soon, however, the "long-distance" service that became Atto's specialty, and served Mattias best, was the ability to gather information. In this era, rulers depended on agents at other centers of power to report on the activities, plans, health, and frame of mind of key personages. Such agents included everyone from formal ambassadors to the authors of anonymous *avvisi*, or private news sheets. Because etiquette limited the contacts of titled officials, most courts depended on the less visible figures to gather gossip, overhear conversations, and generally pass along bits of useful information. In essence, this was spying, although the meaning of that term varied: usually only enemies were "spies," while friends were "agents."[74] In fact, Atto had all the qualifications of the seventeenth-century spy, as the historian Lucien Bély details in his study of the type: the spy typically traveled widely, often under cover of another profession; he had access to sources of the newest information; he spoke multiple languages; he possessed great shrewdness and industry; and he was often someone whose morals were already suspect. "The

---

[71] Edward L. Goldberg, *Patterns in Late Medici Art Patronage* (Princeton: Princeton University Press, 1983), 59.

[72] Atto to Mattias, from Paris, November 14, 1647. The first report of his search comes in his letter to Mattias, from Paris, of October 25, 1647, where he tells of spending whole days visiting and interviewing makers and depending for advice on other servants of Mazarin. Mention of his efforts in this regard also appears in his letters of November 2, 7, and 8.

[73] For the skullcaps, Atto to Mattias, from Paris, of September 2, 1648; on the clock, October 25, 1647; November 2, 7, and 14, 1647; December 26, 1648; January 1 and February 27, 1649.

[74] Lucien Bély, *Espions et ambassadeurs au temps de Louis XIV* ([Paris]: Fayard, 1990), 51.

world of the debauchees – [themselves] sites of all types of encounters – furnished the social mix in which the spy could gather information."[75] On this last point, I will argue in chapter 4 how being a castrato would have marked Atto – rightly or wrongly – as part of this world. Although the presence of spies in all courts was an open secret, espionage could of course be dangerous: rulers frequently had the outgoing mail opened, and offenders could be charged with treason and executed. Like Atto, however, most were protected by powerful friends, and informants often received rewards valuable enough to justify the risk.[76]

Atto really seems to have had the knack for such work. Already during his first trip to Paris he learned to exploit his access to leaders and collected valuable information. On March 10, 1645, for example, he tells of managing to see a letter – surreptitiously, one presumes – addressed to Mazarin from the duke of Bavaria's first councilor; it contained the rather significant news that the duke, exhausted by the war, would encourage the emperor to accept a treaty.[77] Five days later, Atto expounds on these comments with even more detail (and even analysis), in a passage I excerpt here as an example of his work:

They deem the peace (or truce) with the empire secure, and to this effect many couriers, sent by the plenipotentiaries to this crown, bring sure hope. The Spanish are doing all they can to see that it not happen. But everything will succeed because the duke of Bavaria wants to be a friend of France, and the war, as it stands, accomplishes no more for him … Here [in Paris] they make much of Your Highness, knowing of the following that you have in Germany and that you are loved by most of the officials of the emperor, to which I myself have borne witness to these gentlemen … I advise Your Highness of this because it was discussed in the chamber of the cardinal.[78]

The subject is clearly the peace negotiations that eventually led to the Treaty of Westphalia (1648), the agreement between France and the Empire ending the Thirty Years' War. Such letters reveal that by this time Atto had not only great access to Mazarin, but also an impressive grasp of international relations.

During these first French trips, Atto positively brags about his ability to find things out. On March 23, 1647 he finishes a portion of a letter with words of caution:

---

[75] Ibid., 70. Bély describes the typical spy at 56–71.
[76] On the punishments, and protection from it, ibid., 200.
[77] Atto to Mattias, from Paris, March 10, 1645.   [78] Atto to Mattias, from Paris, March 15, 1645.

I would have the opportunity to satisfy the curiosity of Your Highness with other news, since I have dealings in places where such news is known, but believing this would annoy you, I will finish … [I also stop here because] I don't know whether the letters that I have written have been delivered faithfully, some of mine having been opened by the gentlemen that the [Florentine] Resident has in his house.[79]

After this gesture of circumspection, however, Atto continues (on a separate sheet) with a detailed report on the peace negotiations with the empire and the military plans of Spain; and he cannot seem to resist boasting that in his future reports "Your Highness will be able to believe me because what I will write you will be the truth itself, and you should be certain that I know the best things [*le più belle cose*] in France and all that is discussed not only here, but in Spain as well."[80]

Such claims pepper the singer's correspondence from these years, even though he plainly knew his letters might be opened. This recklessness underscores not only Atto's inexperience but also, I think, the depth of his concern about Mattias's favor. Being away from home for so long – and just as his skills were ripening – Atto genuinely worried about his most important patronage relationship. It is in this context that his turn to "espionage" should be viewed. Had he never taken the trips to Paris, and had his talent not moved the queen to detain him, he might never have entered the political arena, at least to the extent he did. It was his anxiety about his tie to Mattias that goaded him into the non-musical activities that would later dominate his life. The key point is that, for Atto, and presumably many others, artistic and non-artistic services performed the same function: to sustain and intensify the bond to a patron. Whether he was buying French gloves or reporting Spanish troop movements, Atto was just trying to please a master who could not then hear his voice.

But in fact Atto's attitude toward his patron was far more complex than his efforts at gratification might suggest. Although he consistently professed his desire to come home and serve Mattias in person, he actually worked to stay in France as long as possible.[81] His letter of August 14, 1648 reveals much about his intentions and is worth examining in detail. In response to what must have been another of Mattias's orders to return, he at first blames the queen for his delay:

From the letter that Your Highness was pleased to send me, I have fully comprehended the continuation of your benevolent disposition toward me, and so

---

[79] Atto to Mattias, from Paris, March 23, 1647.   [80] Ibid.

[81] His expressions of the desire to return home can be found, among other places, in his letters of July 25, 1647 and August 14, 1648.

I recognize that my obligations toward Your Highness have increased not a little. I therefore render you infinite thanks, assuring you that I am very anxious to return there to have the honor of receiving in person those favors that your generous hand is accustomed to distributing to your most devoted servants. But the fact that the court must go to Fontainebleau at the end of this month makes me despair of being able to receive permission right now to arrive there by the time Your Highness indicates, for the queen has no other entertainment than Italian music, her greatest diversion in this place. I am sure that if I ventured to ask my leave, I would receive the same indeterminate response that I had after my illness.[82]

As the letter continues, however, Atto's self-interest emerges so clearly as to impugn his earlier statement:

If Your Highness approves, I would like to maintain my service to Her Majesty, and when I must leave, to do so with her satisfaction, so as not to lose that little merit that I have acquired from the service I have so far rendered … The queen has promised to accord me the first benefice of two or three thousand francs that becomes vacant, which I have been assured of also by the cardinal. And since at Christmas I am to collect one hundred *doppie* of my pension; and since Her Majesty will make me a gift of another hundred, a favor she has done me every year; and since at that time winter will be quite advanced here and it would be difficult for me to undertake so long a voyage, being so fresh from my past illness; I humbly beg Your Highness to allow me to remain here through this whole period so that I do not lose this benefit and the favor of Her Majesty. Then, at the first chance, I will endeavor by all means to be able – with the satisfaction of the queen – to come serve Your Highness.[83]

Clearly, Atto wanted to stay in Paris to maximize the profitability of his services, which were almost certainly more lucrative than those for Mattias, and he hoped his patron would understand. But, just as clearly, he was brandishing the queen's greater power against his own prince. The repeated references to Anne's "satisfaction" subtly highlight the political risk of recalling the queen's favorite: Mattias would not want to be the one to *dis*satisfy her. In other words, Atto understood his own value and political function and here – hardly for the last time – dared manipulate a situation to his own advantage. The strategy of non-compliance, always cloaked in the language of submission, involved risk, and probably helps account for the

---

[82] Atto to Mattias, from Paris, August 14, 1648. A letter from another Tuscan in Paris at just this time (Giovan Battista Barducci to Giovan Carlo de' Medici, from Paris, August 21, 1648, as transcribed in Mamone, *Serenissimi fratelli*, 140) casts doubt on Atto's report, as the author claims that the Italian musicians "da sei mesi in qua non hanno cantato né pure una canzona alla presenza di Sua Maestà."

[83] Atto to Mattias, from Paris, August 14, 1648.

tone of anxiety in his letters, but Atto was beginning to understand how to make the complex system of patronage work to his benefit.

Whether or not he sincerely meant to return to Tuscany in the spring of 1649, as he claimed, internal French conflicts conspired to delay him further. In January 1649, Atto was caught up in the events of the first period of conflict known as the Fronde, one of the major political crises of the seventeenth century; for a moment, all his efforts to get ahead in France looked like they might unravel. The issues of this complicated civil war cannot be recapitulated here, but throughout 1648 long-standing tensions between Mazarin and the Parisian *Parlement* were approaching a boil, fueled by increased taxation and the cardinal's extravagant spending. As an Italian, a castrato, and the star of the lavish *Orfeo* production, Atto would have been an emblem of Mazarin's profligacy.[84] When the opposition took control of Paris in 1649, Atto faced a cruel reversal of fortune. Accustomed to the luxury of the cardinal's support, he now witnessed his powerful benefactor fleeing the city and found himself in danger: indeed, his colleague Torelli was imprisoned by the Parisian mob for several months. But Atto, along with Luigi Rossi, escaped with the court to Saint-Germain-en-Laye on the night of January 5, 1649. The secrecy of the move had precluded the usual preparations: the monarchs had to sleep on cots, and everyone else merely on piles of straw or in coaches.[85]

Only two letters from Atto survive from this period of exile, and, perhaps surprisingly, neither reveals any great sense of panic. The first, to Mattias on February 27, in fact begins with an apology for not being able to ship the famous clock that the prince had requested. Atto continues, rather matter-of-factly, "The siege of Paris will last longer than is believed because there are many provisions and they enter continuously, for the men who are supposed to stop a measure of them are themselves French and do not want to hurt their countrymen."[86] The only real sign of the hardships at Saint-Germain is the stationery on which these lines are written, a rough brown scrap that, Atto apologizes, "is the best we have here."[87] The second letter, from April 3,

---

[84] For example, in the famous anonymous *mazarinade* (March 11, 1651, excerpted in C[élestin] Moreau, ed., *Choix de Mazarinades* [Paris: Jules Renouard, 1853], II:241–53), the poet writes, "Ce beau, mais malheureux Orphée, | Ou, pour mieux parler, ce Morphée | Puisque tant de monde y dormit. | Ma foy, ce beau chef d'œuvre mit | En grand crédit ton Eminence, | Ou plustost ton Impertinence. | Tes Courtizannes, tes chastrez | Y furent les mieux chapitrez" (243).

[85] On this period of the Fronde, Treasure, *Seventeenth Century France*, 218–22; and Kleinman, *Anne*, 205–12. On the plight of the Italians, Prunières, *L'opéra*, 141–50, and Massip, *La vie*, 9.

[86] Atto to Mattias, from Saint-Germain-en-Laye, February 27, 1649. This observation seconds the view of historians that the blockade of Paris by the army of the Prince de Condé, which was supposed to soften the rebels, was largely ineffective (see Kleinman, *Anne*, 211–12).

[87] Atto to Mattias, from Saint-Germain-en-Laye, February 27, 1649.

again initially ignores the conflict, commencing with profuse thanks for help in obtaining a benefice. In fact, the hostilities had been resolved just two days earlier with the signing of the Peace of Rueil; in it, the queen had acquiesced to all of *Parlement*'s demands, except, importantly, the removal of Mazarin.[88] Atto does report on the festivities associated with this agreement and cannily observes that "the cardinal is established more than ever, and everyone competes to serve him, now that they see things settled to his great glory and advantage."[89] One senses Atto guessed it would turn out this way all along.[90]

With the conflict resolved, one might have expected Atto finally to take his leave and return to Tuscany, as he initially promised to do.[91] Instead, he remained with the French court, which proceeded directly to its annual military campaign against the Spanish, at this time mostly in and around Compiègne.[92] In a letter to Mattias from June 25 Atto once again requests an extension, this time barely veiling his economic motives with a reference to the summer heat:

In place of this my most humble letter, which I send to Your Highness, I thought to be there myself to offer you my devoted service and receive your orders personally. But even with all the efforts you have made, I have not been able to free myself, there not being the opportunity to receive my pensions. This is the reason that I have not been able to carry out my desire [to return], as will certainly happen at the first cool days. Since I am [already] in these lands, I hope that Your Highness will have the goodness to allow me not to leave for a period of two months, more or less, so as not to lose close to a thousand *scudi* that I am to collect. The lateness of the season precludes any hope of my being able to be there before September. In the meantime, therefore, may Your Highness consider whether I may do something for you from here, as humbly I beg you to do.[93]

Apparently, Mattias once again agreed. Not until the middle of August did the court return to Paris, and then only a month later did the queen finally, reluctantly, allow Atto to go. Her regret emerges in an interesting letter written by Mazarin on September 27 for Atto to present to the prince:

---

[88] Treasure, *Seventeenth Century France*, 221; and Kleinman, *Anne*, 211.

[89] Atto to Mattias, from Saint-Germain-en-Laye, April 3, 1649.

[90] Prunières, *L'opéra*, 148, suggests that "Mazarin employa sans doute Atto à quelque mission délicate durant la Fronde, car il semble avoir contracté envers lui une dette de reconnaisance." For evidence, he points to Mazarin's letter of thanks to Mattias, cited below. But I see no sign in that letter, or elsewhere, that Atto was serving Mazarin in this way at this time. In my view the cardinal's "debt of gratitude" much more likely resulted from Atto's musical service to the queen.

[91] Atto to Mattias, from Paris, April 3, 1649. Prunières (*L'opéra*, 147) was taken in and reports Atto did actually return.

[92] On the campaign, Kleinman, *Anne*, 212.

[93] Atto to Mattias, from Amiens, June 25, 1649.

Since the queen has given Atto permission to make a voyage there to settle the affairs of his house, I did not want to let him leave without giving him this letter of mine, with which I render Your Highness hearty thanks for the time that you deigned to entrust him to Her Majesty. She is so satisfied with Atto's service to date that she would not have permitted him to leave if first she had not been certain of his return … I know that Your Highness will always be disposed to support the wishes of Her Majesty, while you can be quite certain that my wishes will always be to serve Your Highness.[94]

The tone of the letter is remarkable: rather than apologizing for overextending Atto's stay, Mazarin cites Atto's own affairs as the sole reason for his return, a "viaggio" that is expected to be brief. Mazarin subtly bullies Mattias by again invoking the queen's "wishes." Although the prince is thanked, the cardinal almost implies that the queen has become Atto's primary patron and that she is now lending him back to Mattias. Atto had thoroughly ingratiated himself in France.

Indeed, from every perspective, his time there had been a success. For himself, he managed to establish prestigious and profitable patronage ties to the "foreign" rulers without losing his relationship to the Medici. In so doing, he had become at the age of twenty-three one of the most prominent and well-connected singers in Europe. Likewise Mazarin could not have been more pleased: during the Fronde, the cardinal's position had depended almost exclusively on the queen's good graces; her attachment to her minister's Italian singer could only have enlivened her commitment. And although Mattias may for a time have lost the pleasure of his castrato's singing, he gained back an increasingly capable political agent with advantageous connections, not to mention a more practiced and refined musician. Political exigency had launched Atto into an intricate career of singing, spying, and procuring. While the combination might seem unusual, his pursuits all aimed to provide uncommon and valuable services and thereby incline patrons to his interests. His talents in all three areas – as well as a certain daring in self-promotion – explain how he pulled it off.

Back in Italy

Over the next several years (1650–53), Mattias in fact had the opportunity to observe all his singer's talents at much closer range, as Atto served exclusively in northern Italy. Unfortunately, these years are less richly documented than the previous, presumably because Atto so often served his prince in person. Yet the surviving material does suggest a continuation of the pattern

---

[94] Mazarin to Mattias, from Paris, September 21, 1649.

established in France: Mattias would lend his singer to another ruler as a political investment and advertisement of Medici glory; Atto would win over these rulers with his vocalism and forge patronage ties of his own; and he would also keep his ears open and pass back any news he could learn. Because the formula was repeated several times, these years "at home" witnessed the greatest expansion of Atto's own patronage network. Indeed, by the end, he was corresponding directly with a number of sovereigns and their secretaries. Happily, this correspondence also sometimes offers unusual glimpses of contemporary musical entertainment.

Atto's first new assignment after leaving France came on the road home: a stopover at the court of Savoy in Turin. His activities there emerge only from letters written several years later to the duchess of Savoy, and so unfortunately the length and circumstances of the visit remain unclear.[95] But the result must have been positive, because Atto was soon pursuing the duchess's direct patronage. Kettering notes that letters requesting such relationships are typically filled with obsequious language and accompanied by a token gift.[96] Atto's letter from sometime in July 1650 certainly fits this profile, with the inclusion of several new vocal pieces from Rome (now lost):

I have taken the boldness to send [these pieces] to Your Royal Highness, carrying with me wherever I go my infinite desire always to serve Your Royal Highness and the obligation that I have to carry out that service. With this opportunity, but much more with the devotion of my spirit, I come to bow before you most humbly, begging you to keep me under your most powerful protection, since you have no servant who has greater knowledge of your benevolence or greater experience of your generous hand than I.[97]

The promise of service and request for "protection" clearly mark this letter as a patronage appeal. How the duchess responded is unknown, but Atto did remain in contact with Turin, and eventually his familiarity with the royal family paid off politically (as will appear in chapter 5).

A year later, he made precisely the same overtures to the music-loving Duke Carlo II of Mantua.[98] Sometime in early 1651 Atto spent time in Mantua serving the duke, although again, few details are known. Evidently,

---

[95] Atto to Christine of France, duchess of Savoy, from Florence, July, 1650 (exact day unknown) and November 13, 1653. The latter mentions his "felici memorie di quando mi udì in Turino quando di Francia me ne tornai in Italia."

[96] Kettering, "Gift-Giving," 138–40.

[97] Atto to Christine of France, duchess of Savoy, from Florence, July, 1650.

[98] On the duke's enthusiasm especially for vocal chamber music, Paola Besutti, "Produzione e trasmissione di cantate romane nel mezzo del Seicento," in *La musica a Roma attraverso le fonti d'archivio*, ed. Bianca Maria Antolini, Arnaldo Morelli, and Vera Vita Spagnuolo, Strumenti della ricerca musicale, no. 2 (Lucca: Libreria Musicale Italiana, in association with the Archivio di Stato di Roma and the Società Italiana di Musicologia, 1994), 137–66 *passim*.

Atto captivated the young sovereign, because Carlo soon asked that Atto return to Mantua that summer (a request the singer could not fulfill).[99] When the duke then came to Florence in August, he seems to have taken every opportunity to hear Atto, both in chamber concerts at court and more privately in his own rooms, to which a small harpsichord was brought for the purpose.[100] Before leaving, the duke again requested Atto to accompany him, this time for a month of further travels (a request that again was denied).[101] In the face of such enthusiasm, one is hardly surprised to find that already in June Atto had solicited the duke's patronage. Atto's language recalls that of his letter to the duchess of Savoy, and again his missive was accompanied by a gift:

The many favors that I received from the kindness of Your Highness while I had the honor of serving you in Mantua oblige me to continue my most humble obedience toward Your Highness, with the perpetual desire of living under your most powerful protection and of having a place among your most devoted and humble servants. I beg Your Highness to receive willingly this reverent homage that I offer to your greatness [music again, presumably] and to honor me now and then with some orders, so that I could also earn some merit with Your Highness by serving you, as I must and desire to do.[102]

Again, what might seem stock flattery is actually a bold attempt to inaugurate a relationship. As before, the duke's response is not recorded, but his continuing interest in Atto – resulting in an ever more complex rapport between the two (see later) – argues that some form of patronage bond was indeed established at this time.

In the spring of 1652, Archduke Ferdinand Karl of Innsbruck – accompanied by his wife, Anna de' Medici (Mattias's sister), and brother, Sigismund Franz – toured the courts of northern Italy.[103] Mattias seems to have sent Atto to shadow their journey. As usual, Atto sang whenever requested,

---

[99] In Atto's letter to the duke, from Florence, July 12, 1651, Atto apologizes at length for not being able to come as requested, "trovandomi impegnato in alcune feste che si vanno facendo qui questa estate." These "feste" must have included the performance at the Teatro del Cocomero in August (see below).

[100] Atto to Mattias, from Florence, August 28, 1651; the passage provides one of Atto's descriptions – if not terribly detailed – of a chamber music performance.

[101] Atto seems to have been reluctant toward this proposal, however. In his letter to Mattias, from Florence, August 28, 1651, he cites the summer heat and a previous commitment in Bologna as reasons the duke's request should be denied, as it apparently was. (The commitment in Bologna could have been a performance of Cavalli's *Giasone*, which took place at the Teatro Formagliari in December; see Corrado Ricci, *I teatri di Bologna nei secoli XVII e XVIII: Storia aneddotica* [1888; repr. Bologna: Arnaldo Forni, 1965], 332.)

[102] Atto to Duke Carlo II of Mantua, from Florence, June 12, 1651.

[103] The reason for their trip remains unclear: see Alice Grier Jarrard, "Theaters of Power: Francesco I d'Este and the Spectacle of Court Life in Modena" (Ph.D. diss., Columbia Univ., 1993), 202.

thereby exemplifying the taste and generosity of the Medici to both the visitors (imperial allies) and their various noble hosts (Italian peers and rivals). Atto reached the visiting party in Mantua around the beginning of February 1652 and then went on ahead of the group to Modena, where he was employed by Duke Francesco I d'Este in the festivities being prepared for the travelers.[104]

In a few letters, Atto includes details about these festivities, thereby enriching our historical picture of such events. The entire visit was elaborately organized, with activities scheduled each day:

This evening [Saturday, April 6] a party [*festino*] will be given for the entertainment of the archdukes at the house of a gentleman. Sunday, a *palio* will be run, and in the evening a ballet will be performed at the castle, which will serve as an introduction to a ball [*festino di ballo*]. Monday, they will go to Sassuolo [a country retreat], and that evening here in Modena they will have a feast and *commedia*. Tuesday evening the grand entertainment will be performed, and Wednesday a *palio* will be run. That evening they will make their courtesy calls, and Thursday they will depart.[105]

The central event of the week was clearly the "festa grande" of Tuesday evening, a heterogeneous production – until recently virtually forgotten – entitled *La gara delle stagioni*, with text by Count Girolamo Graziani and music (now lost) by *maestro di cappella* Giovanni Battista Crivelli.[106] Under

---

[104] On the journey of the archducal party and the duke of Modena's invitation, see Janet Southorn, *Power and Display in the Seventeenth Century: The Arts and Their Patrons in Modena and Ferrara*, Cambridge Studies in the History of Art (Cambridge: Cambridge University Press, 1988), 34; and Angelo Namias, ed., *Storia di Modena* (1894; repr., Bologna: Atesa, 1987), 370. Atto may have traveled to Mantua in the company of the duke of Modena, since the duke was certainly in Florence on January 15, 1652, when a *festa* was given in his honor (Robert Lamar Weaver and Norma Wright Weaver, *A Chronology of Music in the Florentine Theater 1590–1750*, Detroit Studies in Music Bibliography, no. 38 [Detroit: Information Coordinators, 1978], 118); the duke traveled to Mantua to invite the visitors to his own city (Namias, 370).

[105] Atto to Mattias, from Modena, April 6, 1652.

[106] Southorn, *Power*, 34, first identified this work, which is missing from the basic chronology of theater in Modena: Alessandro Gandini, *Cronistoria dei teatri di Modena dal 1539 al 1871* (Modena: Tipografia Sociale, 1873). It has since been studied by Jarrard, "Theaters." With Southorn's identification of the author of the festivities, I was able to discover in the Yale library a collection of poetry containing a previously unknown libretto of the work (being absent from Claudio Sartori, *I libretti italiani a stampa dalle origini al 1800: Catalogo analitico con 16 indici*, 7 vols. [Turin: Bertola e Locatelli Musica, 1993]), which also includes a detailed description of the event: Girolamo Graziani, *La gara delle stagioni: Torneo a cavallo*, in *Varie poesie, e prose* (Modena: Soliani, 1662), 139–91. The crediting of the music to Crivelli (Graziani, 144) represents a new attribution for that composer; it also may call into question his date of death, given by Jerome Roche and Elizabeth Roche, "Crivelli, Giovanni Battista," *New Grove Online*, www.grovemusic. com (accessed June 22, 2007), as "March 1652." Jarrard refers to an apparently earlier version of the libretto, which I have not seen: Girolamo Graziani, *La gara delle stagioni* [sic], *Torneo a cavallo rappresentato in Modana nel passaggio de' serenissimi arciduchi Ferdinando Carlo, Sigismondo Francesco d'Austria et Arciduchessa Anna di Toscana* (Modana: Soliani, 1652).

the direction of Gaspare Vigarani (with whom Atto would later work in Paris), an enormous temporary theater was constructed outdoors, oblong in shape, with two elaborately equipped stages at opposite ends. Most of the theatrical and musical events took place on these stages, while the central area was employed for processions and mock tournaments. Atto's own description of the performance is one of the most detailed to survive:

At the beginning a machine will appear representing a rocky mountain, from which, upon opening, will come forth the four seasons, who speak with Aeolus. From the four corners of the theater the four winds will enter and, flying through the air, will come to rest [one] next to each season. At the end of the action, from the other facade of the theater a scene in the clouds will open that will simulate the Temple of Janus, who, on a chariot, will descend to the ground with four horses met by four knights, who will serve as the four leaders of the squadrons, and the horses will be great steeds and very effective … I believe that it will fall to me to play Spring, and my brother [Jacopo], Janus.[107]

(Plate 4 is one of Stefano della Bella's engravings of the "mountain" with the seasons; the figure of "Primavera" stands near the top left.) The lavish event cost the duke around fifty thousand *scudi*, an amount that, as Janet Southorn notes, "bid fair to compete with the costs of war." Indeed, such "critically important forms of entertainment and propaganda" represented campaigns in a very real battle for political stability.[108] The d'Este dynasty was in a tricky position: it had lost its long-time capital of Ferrara to the papacy in 1598; further, as an ally of Habsburg Spain from 1635, it had subsequently contributed forces against the papal troops of Urban VIII, and then finally switched allegiance to France in 1647. From the perspective of the d'Este, the celebrations of 1652 – feting a branch of the Habsburg family – were meant to smooth over past conflicts and reassert the dynasty's traditional

---

[107] Atto to the duke of Mantua, from Modena, March 12, 1652. Atto's description supplements one provided by an anonymous agent of the Cardinal Legate Cibo in Ferrara, who writes of a "great machine, representing a Rock, on which is the throne of Aeolus, King of the Winds, and when he commands his ministers … the Rock will be seen to grow by 8 *braccia*, and … four corners will spread out and in the cavern will be seen the Four Seasons … who … will beg Aeolus for judgement, but he … will call the four principal winds who will fly to the Mount from the four corners of the theatre … they will call the Cavaliers to battle, guided by four animals … At the height of the battle … a Temple of Janus would open, a chariot would appear and an equestrian ballet would close the performance." (I MOas, Ferrara, busta 28, April 6, 1652, quoted and translated in Southorn, *Power*, 158n).

  Atto's letter also solves the question of whether his brother Jacopo was ever a singer. From another letter, to Mattias, from Modena, March 16, 1652, one learns that "Giacomo mio fratello" was also to take part in the Modenese festival, and, in the present letter, that this brother played the part of Janus. This evidence addresses Weaver's confusion ("Florentine Comic Operas," 181) about why Jacopo joined his brother on the trips to Paris: evidently, he sang.

[108] The two quotations come from Southorn, *Power*, 68 and 34.

Plate 4 Mount of Aeolus, from *La gara delle stagioni* (Stefano Della Bella, Metropolitan Museum of Art, The Elisha Whittelsey Collection, The Elisha Whittelsey Fund, 1962 [62.652.30]; image © The Metropolitan Museum of Art)

brilliance and authority.[109] The presence of the dukes and duchesses of Mantua and Parma only magnified the political import. Although the

---

[109] On the political maneuvering of the d'Este and the function of this celebration, see Jarrard, "Theaters," 8, 201–8. The presence of various rulers is attested in Atto's letter to Mattias, from Modena, April 6, 1652.

Medici did not attend, the participation of their talented castrato gave them a presence and indicated their support.

Atto also seems to have been under orders to collect any useful news he could learn. Soon after his arrival in Mantua, he reported on a potentially embarrassing conflict: the visiting archdukes were "very offended" at not being invited to Florence during their stay in Mantua, particularly as their travel plans prevented their coming at any other time. They were further incensed by rumors of how little they were esteemed in the Tuscan capital, rumors that fueled their annoyance with Giovan Carlo for certain unidentified impertinences and with the grand duke for not responding to one of their letters.[110] Atto also related that officials from his own city of Pistoia had invited the group for a visit in an apparent attempt to exploit the Florentine faux pas.[111] Presumably Atto was not the only Medici agent to sound these warnings, but his efforts were not wasted, for by mid-April the Austrians were making their way to Florence.

In typical fashion, Atto was at the same time trying to convert his musical labors into more lasting patronage. Indeed, as in the cases above, he followed up his service to the duke of Modena with a letter that uses all the now-familiar catchphrases:

> Although I know that I am incapable of serving Your Highness and that my boldness in bothering you with my letters is too great, the graces and favors that Your Highness accorded me when I was lucky enough to serve you personally have forever obligated me to continue my most humble obedience toward Your Highness … I gladly take the opportunity of these most holy holidays [Christmas] to reaffirm to Your Highness my most submissive servitude … hoping to find in these circumstances that your humanity is well disposed to accept this homage that I offer to your greatness. And while I beg Your Highness to find me worthy of your most powerful protection, I finish by making you a very deep bow.[112]

In May 1653 Atto seems to have renewed this request, on one day writing letters to both the duke and his secretary Count Girolamo Graziani. To the latter, Atto specifically offered his skills at information-gathering: "whenever I have the opportunity to inform His Highness of some news from here [Innsbruck], I will do so through Your Most Illustrious Lordship to allow you to have me honored with some of his commands."[113] With little prospect of

---

[110] Atto to Mattias, from Mantua, February 9, 1652.

[111] Atto to Mattias, from Mantua, March 2, 1652. Although Atto records that everyone found this invitation laughable, he begged Mattias not to reveal him as the source of the information for fear of reprisals from his fellow Pistoiese. It is unclear whether this incident helped provoke his later conflicts with his home town.

[112] Atto to Francesco II d'Este, duke of Modena, December 23, 1652. This letter also falls into the category of the "Christmas greeting," a common genre whose purpose – not unlike that of modern Christmas cards – was to help maintain relationships between distant correspondents.

[113] Atto to Count Girolamo Graziani, from Innsbruck, May 25, 1653.

returning soon to Modena, Atto depended on his non-musical talents to maintain (or initiate) the duke's support. In fact, Atto's subsequent letters to Modena do contain news and observations, suggesting that at least some sort of relationship was created.[114] By the beginning of 1653, then, Atto had established ties with the courts of Tuscany, Paris, Savoy, Mantua, and Modena. His efforts demonstrate how a sufficiently talented singer (and budding spy) could transform isolated musical services into long-term affiliations with the ruling elite, how official duties could be turned to personal advantage. Inevitably, this strategy involved promising "my most devoted and obedient service" to a range of different and sometimes opposed patrons, but the dangers of such divided loyalties did not fully emerge until later.

In the early 1650s, Atto's primary duty still lay with the Medici, and in spite of his travels, most of his activity seems to have revolved around them. The lack of correspondence from this period probably indicates that Atto spent long stretches with Mattias in Siena. For the first time, in fact, Mattias would have been able to enjoy his singer's talents on a regular basis, an arrangement that presumably helped resolve any remaining tensions between them. One imagines that Atto often provided vocal chamber music – both privately and before honored guests – and perhaps liturgical or devotional music as well, but in fact the sources divulge almost nothing about Atto's domestic duties.

The one telling exception relates to a visit that Mattias and Leopoldo made to Rome for Easter in the holy year 1650. The Medici archives preserve remarkable documentation of this trip, which introduced the young princes to the Roman aristocracy and its artistic patrimony.[115] A letter from both Medici brothers to the grand duke reveals that Atto indeed sang during the trip and conveys something of the context in which that singing could take place; for these reasons, and for its rare glimpse of contemporary life at the Vatican, the letter is worth quoting at some length:

Having arrived [in the pope's rooms], we stood with the Princes [Niccolò] Ludovisi and [Andrea] Giustiniani, and when His Holiness [Innocent X Pamphili] exited his chamber, we and the others serving him were led into the hall that contained the dais for His Holiness and another for us. Having washed his hands, with Prince Mattias giving him the napkin, he indicated to us that we should likewise wash and put on our hats, as we did. And then at a table placed at a distance of six *braccia* [three to four meters] to the right of His Holiness's table, we sat down and ate; we did so with

---

[114] Examples of his reporting appear in the letters of June 23, 1653 and August 4, 1655.
[115] See Edward L. Goldberg, *After Vasari: History, Art, and Patronage in Late Medici Florence* (Princeton: Princeton University Press, 1988), 17–19; on 185–90 Goldberg transcribes an official diary of the trip from I Fas, Misc. Med. 94, insert 5.

the obligatory respect but also with pleasure, for there was music from the best musicians of Rome, who sang cheerful motets, and we could tell from the pope's great cordiality and many signs of courtesy that he enjoyed having us in his presence. The room was full of gentlemen and prelates, along with Donna Olimpia incognito, the two nephews of the pope, and other ladies who stayed to watch until the end behind some screens [*a certe gelosie*]. When His Holiness drank for the first time, all the people knelt, and we stood upright; soon, with a smiling face he indicated to us to sit and put on our hats. Three times he made us a gift from his table: first, a soup; second, a pastry filled with some thrushes wrapped in the same pastry; and third, with a most courteous display, he presented us with some candied citrons, indicating that he wanted us to eat them. Then there was fruit, which was of all sorts, and so the meal ended. We stood up, and His Holiness washed his hands, and Prince Mattias gave him the napkin for the second time. Having blessed everyone, he ordered that our two stools be placed on his own dais and that we sit down, and after sending all the other people out, he remained to chat with us for over half an hour. After having been attended by us, he retired to his rooms, blessing us again. Because Cardinal Panzirolo was holding a banquet for Signora Donna Olimpia, the princesses, and many other ladies (who, as mentioned, had been to watch the pope eat), we went via the private stairs to His Eminence's apartment to pay our respects to those ladies, and we remained there in great merriment until they had eaten; and Atto sang with the other musicians.[116]

The last clause, which really reads like an afterthought, was indeed inserted later above the main text with a caret. I interpret it as the result of a plea by Atto to be remembered to the grand duke, with whom the singer rarely had contact. Certainly the princes did not normally name individual musicians in their accounts of this trip. And so it is difficult to imagine a motivation for mentioning Atto other than the singer's own request. In any case, the very rarity of the remark probably implies the frequency of Atto's singing, in such unexceptional events as the princes' daily *cappelle*, for example. And one can easily imagine that this pattern of service characterized the singer's time with Mattias generally: Atto's singing was such a ordinary part of the prince's routine that it left few traces.

Traces do exist of some of Atto's more theatrical assignments during this period, performances for which little or no other evidence survives. Atto recounts, for example, receiving orders from Cardinal Giovan Carlo to go to Florence with Jacopo in September 1651 to take part in a *commedia* "in via del Cocomero."[117] The production was almost certainly the inaugural effort of the Accademia degli Immobili, who, under Giovan Carlo's patronage,

---

[116] Leopoldo and Mattias de' Medici to Grand Duke Ferdinando II de' Medici, Rome, April 25, 1650.

[117] Atto to Mattias, from Florence, August 28, 1651.

had recently taken over that theater: the play, *Il Vincislago* by Annibale Bentivoglio, had musical *intermedi* composed by Domenico Anglesi.[118] Similarly, in October 1651 Atto received from Prince Leopoldo a very polite request to perform in some upcoming *intermedi* authored by Jacopo Salviati, duke of Giuliano. No record for such an event has come to light, and the intended venue also remains unclear. The language of the letter to Atto, actually written by Leopoldo's intermediary, Desiderio Montemagni, is interesting for its style, which resembles more a request by a peer than a command from a superior:

This evening Prince Leopoldo, my Lord, commanded me to write to Your Lordship, and to Signor Jacopo your brother, to find out whether it might be convenient this carnival season for you to come here to sing some *intermedi* of the Duke Salviati. If you are well disposed toward this idea, and you have no other engagements, His Highness will take care of obtaining your leave from Prince Mattias.[119]

Notwithstanding such courtesy, Atto asked Mattias to be excused, protesting that he would not be able to come serve Mattias in Siena.[120] The prince apparently refused, however, sending Atto on to Florence. On November 11, in a sign that these *intermedi* probably did take place, a sullen Atto writes his patron that they "will not be a great thing, in my judgment, and I will not take much part in them."[121]

Several letters also identify Atto's involvement in a work, otherwise undocumented, sponsored by Duke Ranuccio II Farnese of Parma and intended for the carnival season in Piacenza, 1653. Toward the end of 1652, the librettist, Paolo Emilio Fantuzzi, twice wrote to Mattias requesting first Atto and then also Jacopo for his opera, *Il ratto d'Europa*. Fantuzzi was apparently serving as impresario, and Francesco Manelli, then the duke's *maestro di cappella*, was writing the music. "Because this work is the child of my pen, [and being] ambitious that it be born under the protection of Your Highness, I come humbly to beg you to consent that your Signor Atto Melani play the leading role, which would be that of Europa."[122] When Fantuzzi later wrote about Jacopo, he hints that Mattias had already conceded Atto. And

---

[118] For the activities at the Cocomero theater, see Mamone, *Serenissimi fratelli*, xx–xxi.

[119] Desiderio Montemagni to Atto, from Florence, October 7, 1651.

[120] Atto to Mattias, from Pistoia, October 12, 1651.

[121] Atto to Mattias, from Pistoia, November 11, 1651. The evidence that Atto went to Siena is a letter of October 23, 1651 from Bernardo Castiglioni (in Florence) to Mattias that was written to be hand-delivered by Atto. For thoughts about the reasons for Atto's unhappiness, see chapter 3.

[122] Paolo Emilio Fantuzzi to Mattias, from Parma, November 28, 1652. The spelling of Fantuzzi's name here is uncertain: although all reference works indeed give it as "Fantuzzi," in the signature of this letter, as well as that from December 17, 1652, the spelling looks more like Fantucconi.

although in the end Jacopo went to serve the Grimani in Venice, there is no indication that Atto did not perform the role of Europa that winter in the theater of the Palazzo Gotico in Piacenza.[123]

Finally, in addition to these documented theatrical activities, Atto doubtless also sang in performances for which no casting information survives. As one of the top Medici artists, he would surely have participated whenever he was in town. His efforts probably included the *Celio* of May 1646, the "dramatic cantata" *Alidoro il costante* of October 1650, and the *Giostra* presented for the visit of the duke of Modena in January 1652.[124] In any case, Atto would certainly have been a familiar stage presence in and around Tuscany.

Indeed, after the enchanted years in France, coddled by a queen, Atto spent the early 1650s "earning his keep," singing for the patrons who set his career in motion. The work was not always glamorous, and clearly not always to Atto's taste, but he provided the services he owed. As in Paris, those services nearly always carried a political subtext: whether on an outdoor stage in Modena, in the private rooms of the Vatican, or in the new Cocomero theater, Atto always embodied Medici glory. Part of what one heard in his voice – regardless of text or mood – was political power, the wealth and influence that enabled the Medici "to boast of having the best singer in Italy." Indeed, Atto's performances represented a commodity in the dynasty's own patronage relationships, a gift that subtly obliged the sovereign who received it. Of course, Atto quickly found ways to turn all this exploitation to his own advantage. Even while he was consolidating his relationships in Tuscany, he continued to expand his own base of support: whenever the Medici made a gift of his talents, he translated his servitude into patronage ties. To maintain those scattered ties, he turned to espionage, or, more simply, the gathering and reporting of news, another service he could offer. From first practicing it to appease Mattias, Atto was soon passing on information to Mantua, Modena, and elsewhere. Inevitably, patrons' interests began to

---

[123] On the performance of this work in Piacenza, see Francesco Bussi, "I teatri d'opera a Piacenza prima della costruzione del Teatro Municipale (1804)," *Nuova rivista musicale italiana* 24 (1990): 460.

[124] See Weaver and Weaver, *Chronology*, 116–18. (*Celio*: libretto by Giacinto Andrea Cicognini; music by Niccolò Sapiti and G. Baglioni. *Alidoro il costante*: libretto by Antonio Malatesta; music by Domenico Anglesi.) Atto probably did not participate in the *Egisto* of May, 1646, as it was produced by the visiting Febiarmonici (see Bianconi and Walker, "Dalla *Finta pazza*," 400). He also did not take part in *La Deidamia* of January 11, 1650 (his correspondence shows him in Pistoia on January 3, and this work too was performed by a visiting troupe), nor the *Giasone* of May 15, 1650, which took place less than two weeks after he returned with Mattias and Leopoldo from Rome (around the beginning of May).

conflict, as they certainly had in France; there, for the first time, Atto dared resist Mattias's orders. Still, in these early years Atto focused primarily on attracting patrons through outstanding and varied service. Only with the passage of time – and presumably an increase of confidence – did he regularly try to manipulate patrons to his own self-serving ends. That story belongs to the following chapters.

3 ❧ In pursuit of prestige: 1653–1655

By 1653, Atto's singing had greatly elevated his status. His service to the Medici family alone had propelled him far beyond his social patrimony, the *famiglia* of Pistoia's bishop. And, through the Medici, he had performed for many other rulers, leading to further relationships: indeed, he had initiated a wide-ranging web of patronage. Fully mature, he was one of the most renowned and respected singers in Europe, launched by his art on an ascendant trajectory.

At precisely this point, however, Atto faced an obstacle: although all of his achievements grew out of and depended upon his skills as a performer, his very performances blocked real social advancement. John Rosselli has described the paradox: "in a court whose ruler had an interest (from whatever motive) in music, there were opportunities for those musically gifted to advance themselves as courtiers; but the more prominent and regular their musical performances, the more they needed to establish and maintain their courtly credentials."[1] The difficulty lay, of course, in the contemporary prejudice against labor as a means of subsistence, an attitude that effectively isolated the bourgeoisie from the highest levels of society. For all its benefits, Atto's career as a singer carried intrinsic social limitations.[2]

Faced with this dilemma, Atto adopted a typically *Seicento* tactic: detach appearance from reality. In a society that prized theatricality, the elite classes frequently behaved as if guided by the modern catchphrase, "image is everything." Noble families ruined their finances to provide themselves with the houses, clothes, carriages, and other accoutrements essential to the expression of their rank: a marquis was only a marquis if he lived like a marquis.

---

[1] John Rosselli, "From Princely Service to the Open Market: Singers of Italian Opera and Their Patrons, 1600–1850," *Cambridge Opera Journal* 1 (1989): 2.

[2] Richard Wistreich has richly investigated this issue in his excellent study, *Warrior, Courtier, Singer: Giulio Cesare Brancaccio and the Performance of Identity in the Late Renaissance* (Aldershot, Eng., and Burlington, Vt.: Ashgate: 2007), *passim*, but especially 239–51. Atto was aiming to raise the status of the entire Melani clan and not just himself. Titles such as Loreto Vittori's – Cavaliere della Milizia di Gesù Cristo – were not hereditary. Even hereditary ennoblement was tenuous in the case of castrati, since noble status often obeyed the rules of primogeniture, being lost when a male child was lacking. See M[ichael] L[accohee] Bush, *Rich Noble, Poor Noble*, vol. 2 of *The European Nobility* (Manchester and New York: Manchester University Press, 1988), 63–65 and 97–100.

Likewise, a bourgeois could only hope to ascend to the nobility if he appeared, in fact, to be living like a nobleman.[3] Accordingly, Atto often contrived to affect a station above that of his fellow musicians, to project the image of a talented gentleman instead of a mercenary professional, to behave like a real member of the society in which he moved, rather than its servant. He sought, in Rosselli's words, "to be seen to be patronised by the great, as far as possible on equal terms."[4]

The task was not easy. Constructing such an image depended to a large degree on the support of those around him: Atto could hardly feign the gentleman if others refused to treat him as one. And being a castrato – a man whose very body declared him a musical servant – could only have complicated his posing. From these difficulties, then, was born his fixation on matters of prestige, so evident during the period here under discussion. Although in reality Atto was still a very active singer – by his own testimony at the height of his powers – his desire to appear the aristocrat became a dominant motivation, a desire that would eventually lead him away from musical performance altogether.[5] Indeed, viewed in retrospect, the mid-1650s appear a watershed in Atto's life: although he still considered himself primarily a virtuoso (and so continued to comment about contemporary musical life), he began to recognize that social progress required him to rise above his profession.

Demanding center stage

Paradoxically, perhaps, one way Atto tried to distinguish himself from his fellow performers was to demand leading roles in staged works. On the surface, the tactic would seem a poor way to obscure musical servitude, but in fact Atto's own experiences suggest an interesting link between theatrical and social status. At least within courtly culture (as opposed to commercial venues), playing the lead character in a production was deemed to reflect high standing in general. At a time when the nobility might still participate in court theatricals, prominence on the stage required, and therefore signaled, social favor.[6]

---

[3] Norbert Elias, *The Court Society*, trans. Edmund Jephcott (New York: Pantheon, 1983), 53–56, originally published as *Die höfische Gesellschaft* (Darmstadt: Hermann Luchterhand, 1969).

[4] Rosselli, "From Princely Service," 3.

[5] On his vocal powers, his letter to Mattias de' Medici, from Regensburg, August 4, 1653: "non mi arricordo mai de miei giorni d'haver cantato come faccio adesso."

[6] The situation with public opera may well have differed. While in the earliest decades Venetian opera singers still depended on the favor of powerful patrons (see Rosselli, "From Princely Service," 1), they later became more independent, and therefore more obviously motivated by financial gain rather than prestige. Perhaps it is for this reason that, after his youthful appearances in the 1640s, Atto never returned to the opera houses of Venice.

Two episodes in particular demonstrate this way of thinking. The first relates to preparations in 1653 for a Florentine production of Antonio Cesti's *Alessandro vincitor di se stesso*, a work that had premiered two years earlier in Venice. Although no Tuscan performance can be documented before January 1654, planning was underway at least fifteen months earlier, when Prince Leopoldo wrote his brother Mattias to request Atto's services.[7] Although Leopoldo tags Atto to play the role of Apelle (the court painter), Leopoldo seems aware that Atto might covet the title role. To head off the possibility, Leopoldo first actually lies to Mattias, describing Apelle as "one of the two principals," when in fact the character sings only one aria; then he states outright that "Atto is not suitable to play Alessandro."[8] As Leopoldo feared, however, Atto was soon petitioning both Mattias and Alessandro Carducci (the so-called *coreografo* of the production) to be given the lead, protesting that Apelle "is composed for a contralto voice, and I sing soprano."[9] In fact, the part of Alessandro is written in the tenor clef, so Atto either was wholly uninformed or wanted to sing the role an octave higher. In any case, his complaint about range appears largely dissimulation, for he soon turns to the subject of honor:

I'm certain Your Highness will be happy to hear that at every opportunity I bring myself honor and that therefore I also try diligently to pursue all measures that can ease my path to it. The part of Apelle is not such as to bring the honor that they have perhaps written of to Your Highness, and so in the letter that I'm writing to Signor Carducci, I give good reasons for wanting to hear the role of Alessandro, for I would be unwilling to play below any other *virtuoso* in Florence if not by express command of Your Highness.[10]

Atto here first affirms honor as his highest goal and then, by implication, characterizes secondary roles as dishonorable. In the end, the matter required no solution, as Atto spent much of 1653 north of the Alps and did not, it

---

[7] Robert Lamar Weaver and Norma Wright Weaver, *A Chronology of Music in the Florentine Theater 1590–1750*, Detroit Studies in Music Bibliography, no. 38 (Detroit: Information Coordinators, 1978), 119; letter apparently from Leopoldo de' Medici to Mattias, October 25, 1652. On the identification of the hand in this letter, I am indebted to Beth Glixon.

[8] Leopoldo de' Medici to Mattias, October 25, 1652.

[9] The reference to Carducci as the *coreografo* comes in Lorenzo Bianconi and Thomas Walker, "Dalla *Finta pazza* alla *Veremonda*: Storie di Febiarmonici," *Rivista italiana di musicologia* 10 (1975): 443n. Along with his letter to Mattias, from Pistoia, November 5, 1652, Atto included a copy of his letter of the same date to Alessandro Carducci: "questa parte è composta per Voce di Contralto, et io faccio il' soprano." Strangely, Robert Lamar Weaver, in his articles on Atto in *The New Grove Dictionary of Music and Musicians*, 2nd edn, and *The New Grove Dictionary of Opera*, calls the singer an "alto castrato."

[10] Atto to Mattias, from Pistoia, November 5, 1652.

seems, take part in any eventual performance.[11] But his attitude underlines the link he perceived between stage and real life.

That attitude emerges even more explicitly seven years later during Atto's long third sojourn at the French court. Although outside the chronological boundaries of this chapter, the incident in question offers vivid and relevant testimony on the question of status. At the beginning of 1660, the wedding of Louis XIV to the infanta of Spain had just been arranged, and preparations were beginning for the festivities in Paris. Mazarin had engaged the famed Vigarani family to construct a new theater in the Tuileries garden and to build the sets for the inaugural production.[12] That work was to be an Italian opera, *Ercole amante*, with a libretto by Francesco Buti and music by Francesco Cavalli.[13]

These well-known facts form the background to a vicious dispute that arose between Atto and Buti. Atto's own account speaks for itself and, although lengthy, provides numerous clues to his views on performing, his relationship to Mazarin, the production process of an opera, and, above all, his anxiety about station. Writing to Mattias on March 1, 1660, Atto first assures his patron (as always) that he will soon comply with orders to return to Tuscany; he then continues,

the festivities that are supposed to be carried out in Paris for the marriage of His Majesty will not take place until the next carnival; if I were to perform in them, I could only leave here at the beginning of Lent next year. But to my great delight, an incident has occurred that may allow me to be with Your Highness much sooner.

It is Abate Buti who composed the poetry of the ballet and *commedia* to be performed. As there will be only a single entertainment, he planned to have a company of Romans come here, so as to lead and direct it in his own way. But

[11] As can be seen from the full list of Atto's letters in Appendix A, Atto returned to Tuscany by October 1653 and was in Florence in January 1654. His letter to the duke of Mantua from Florence on January 5, however, calls into question whether a Tuscan performance of *Alessandro* ever took place, notwithstanding the printed libretto signed January 15, 1653 *ab Inc.* (cited in Weaver and Weaver, *Chronology*, 119). The sudden illness of Innocent X put everything on hold, as all cardinals headed for Rome: "Finalmente il Papa non ha voluto che l'opera si faccia questo Carnevale, e più bella sarebbe che non morisse e che Pasquino havesse causa d'improvisare su l'andata a Roma di più Cardinali … Il signor Cardinale Giovan Carlo partì il giovedì mattina della passata settimana, e si è tralasciato affatto di applicare a queste feste, che se succedesse di sbrigarsi a S.E. in tempo, si fariano a Maggio." On this issue, see also Bianconi and Walker, "Dalla *Finta pazza*," 443n.

[12] The head of the family was Gaspare Vigarani (seventy-one years old in 1660), who had distinguished himself as an architect throughout Italy and particularly in his work for the duke of Modena. To assist him, his two sons Lodovico and Carlo were also engaged. See Henry Prunières, *L'opéra italien en France avant Lulli*, Bibliothèque de l'Institut Français de Florence (Université de Grenoble) ser. 1, Collection d'histoire et de linguistique française et italienne comparées, no. 3 (Paris: Honoré Champion, 1913), 213–14.

[13] Francesco Buti had been a secretary to Cardinal Antonio Barberini and had accompanied the cardinal to Paris in 1645. He soon became an important figure within the Italian community of artists in Paris and worked closely with Mazarin. See Prunières, *L'opéra*, 94–95.

because in this effort he was not serving His Majesty, I proposed Signor Cavalli as the composer, Signor Giovan Carlo [Rossi] to play the harp, and other *virtuosi* whom I believed to be the best, and these have been preferred to those that Buti wanted to bring. Honestly, I did not think that using these musicians rather than the others ought to matter to him very much, but later I found out that he was annoyed, for he has composed an opera, entitled *Gl'amori d'Ercole*, in which there are only six principal roles, including women, and [those for men] are all for basses and tenors, all the other characters performing in machines.

Buti was called to this city by Cardinal Mazarin to give the cardinal an idea of the entertainments that he was planning to mount. When one evening he read the poetry of the opera to the cardinal and said what characters it required, Buti reckoned me for a "machine" part, truly one of the most ordinary. The cardinal laughed at him and asked him whether he thought I would want to do it, to which Buti replied that the other parts were unsuitable for sopranos.

This was immediately reported to me by a person who had heard it that very evening from His Eminence, who was making fun of the abate. Because my temper is a little short, I could not observe the usual flatteries with Buti. Finding him one day in a large company, I asked him, with all possible respect and modesty, what part he had destined for me, since, as one of his best friends and servants, I was hoping he had treated me better than anyone else. He answered me that in his work he only needed six principal parts: two women, a bass to play the part of Hercules, a contralto to play an old woman, and two tenors for the sons of Hercules. He also said that there were many gods who performed in machines and that I could take the one I wanted.

I would go on too long if I informed Your Highness of all that followed in our conversation, but I will just say that I finished by telling him that he was a malicious man, an ignoramus, and that he did not deserve me to sing his most detestable verses. I said this to him because he gave me cause. He declared that if I had any part in his festivity he would seek to depart for Rome. Because I thought immediately that this could be a good opportunity to leave here without appearing ungrateful, I have let things run their course and have not made any attempt to undo his maliciousness. But it is quite true that from the king down to the last person at court, everyone has made Buti out to be ridiculous.

The poetry is already finished, however, and he remains firm in his vow. To make him even more obstinate, I do not look him in the face nor greet him, so that he understands the little esteem I bear him. I know that as soon as Cavalli arrives the parts will be announced so that he can compose them for the specific singers. Because I do not want a machine part and would not perform at all unless in one of the principal roles – excluding women also – I will let things run their course, and later I will use this justification to request permission to leave, since they will have no need for me.[14]

---

[14] Atto to Mattias, from Aix-en-Provence, March 1, 1660. One should note that Atto's enumeration of the principal roles does not quite match the final score: Hyllo is the only son of Hercules to appear in the work, and instead of a contralto to play an old woman, a tenor plays the part of Licco, confidant of Deinaria. Atto is correct, however, that the only treble parts are for female characters.

Atto seems to have viewed his claim on the leading role as a prerogative of social precedence: his letter alludes repeatedly to the greater intimacy that he maintained with Mazarin and the monarchs. And just as an aristocrat would vigorously and even violently defend such a prerogative – the source of so many squabbles and diplomatic disputes – Atto too could not allow Buti's perceived insult to pass without a show of condemnation. Indeed, the very magnitude of Atto's response belies the high stakes. Not only does he reject all lesser roles, he feels he can no longer remain in the country after Buti's affront: "my reputation would never allow me to play a secondary role and remain in France to watch others perform who are so much inferior to me."[15] And whether or not Atto could have called upon Mazarin and the king to force Buti's hand, as he claimed, the very idea of involving the monarch in such a dispute underscores Atto's more than professional anxiety: playing the leading role was a matter of personal honor.

Of course, Buti's real reasons for excluding Atto remain obscure. Prunières quite reasonably suggests that the librettist was just conforming to French tastes. The French aversion to castrati had been well established at least since the Fronde years of 1648–53, when Mazarin – and all things Italian – were scorned.[16] When Cavalli's *Xerse* was performed in November 1660 as a substitute for the delayed *Ercole*, the title role was in fact transposed from alto to bass. Nevertheless, Atto's version of the events should not be dismissed out of hand. The engagement of artists could certainly be a political process: Giacomo Torelli, the celebrated designer of *Orfeo* and *Le nozze di Peleo e di Teti* (1654), was passed over as architect for the new Tuileries theater largely because he had made enemies of both Buti and Jean-Baptiste Colbert; not even Mazarin's personal support could overcome the antagonism.[17] And surely Atto engendered antagonisms of his own with his ambitious and condescending personality. Even if Buti really chose to leave out a major castrato role for reasons of cultural taste, he must surely have relished the opportunity to thwart Atto, someone he probably viewed as a rival.[18] In the event, Atto actually remained in Paris for another year and

---

[15] Atto to Mattias, from Aix-en-Provence, February 28, 1660.

[16] See Prunières, *L'opéra*, 237, 148–49; Catherine Massip, *La vie des musiciens de Paris au temps de Mazarin (1643–1661): Essai d'étude sociale*, La vie musicale en France sous les rois Bourbons, no. 24 (Paris: A. & J. Picard, 1976), 9. Prunières (190) concludes that it was the use of castrati that doomed Italian opera in France. However, the reverse viewpoint also seems possible, that behind the French opposition to castrati lay the singers' inherent association with Italy. These two impulses could have operated simultaneously.

[17] Prunières, *L'opéra*, 214–15.

[18] This case makes the intriguing suggestion that – sometimes at least – the librettist, rather than the composer, chose the voice types employed in an opera. These determinations may have resulted either from the conventional associations of certain character types (low-voiced old men, tenor nurses, etc.) or from more explicit instructions. Buti seems to have served as the overall

received the honor of playing the leading castrato role (Arsamene) in *Xerse*, the *de facto* nuptial opera (see chapter 5). By the time *Ercole* finally reached the stage in February 1662, Atto had already left Paris, thereby avoiding the public humiliation that this incident clearly threatened.

Leid und Ekstase

In the spring and summer of 1653, Atto undertook a journey to several courts of the Holy Roman Empire. His resulting correspondence further illuminates both his growing concern for prestige and the correlation he saw between the hierarchies of stage and society. The trip apparently originated in a request for his services from the archduke and archduchess of Innsbruck, the former a member of the Tyrolean branch of the Habsburg dynasty.[19] As mentioned in the previous chapter, Archduke Ferdinand Karl had heard Atto sing when the court of Innsbruck had toured several Italian cities the previous year; the request for the singer's services thus fits the archduke's habit of emulating performances he witnessed in Italy.[20] Mattias was willing enough to lend his prized castrato, especially to a Habsburg ally, but the prince's motivation may have been more complex: Atto's extraordinary interest in political news during this trip – along with his determination to attend the imperial diet – hints that his charge may have been as much to spy as sing.[21] Of special interest, however, are Atto's reactions to his treatment in the various courts. In particular, his distress at the archduke and archduchess's indifference toward him further underlines the importance his gentlemanly pretensions had by then assumed.

impresario, with responsibilities beyond providing the text. His choices for this work are indeed unusual for an Italian opera of the period: the tenor role of the son of Hercules, Hyllo, is just the sort of amorous, youthful character that would typically have come under the castrato's purview (see chapter 4).

[19] The evidence appears in Atto's letter to Mattias, from Innsbruck, May 25, 1653: "Presentai a questi Ser.mi Arciduchi le lettere di V.A.S., e mostrorono [*sic*] grandissimo gusto che si fusse compiaciuta concedermeli per questo tempo." Atto uses the term *archdukes* ("arciduchi") to refer collectively to Ferdinand Karl and Sigismund Franz (who both carried the title *Erzherzog*), as well as the *Erzherzogin*, Anna de' Medici. I have retained his use of this plural in many places.

[20] Walter Senn, *Musik und Theater am Hof zu Innsbruck: Geschichte der Hofkapelle vom 15. Jahrhundert bis zu deren Auflösung in Jahre 1748* (Innsbruck: Österreichische Verlagsanstalt Innsbruck, 1954), 244.

[21] Most of Atto's letters from this period contain political information, and he often writes of his fears that his letters are being opened by the authorities (e.g., to Mattias, from Innsbruck, May 25 and July 2, 1653, and from Regensburg, August 4, 1653). Two years later, he even suggests that he risked his life on this trip to provide such information (letter to Mattias, from Rome, June 17, 1655): "il mio mestiero è differente dal novellista, et ho provato che nell tempo che sono stato in Francia et Alemagna dove ho procurato a tutto mio potere per servire al mio Principe, di farmi impiccare."

Atto arrived in Innsbruck on May 17, 1653, having been delayed briefly in Mantua by Duke Carlo II, who wanted to hear him again.[22] Almost immediately, Atto became troubled by the coolness of his reception, particularly on the part of Mattias's sister, the Archduchess Anna de' Medici: "[she] does not have that sweetness with which she used to treat her intimates, not having said even a word to me so far."[23] Almost a month later the situation had not changed, and Atto's alarm shows through his feigned nonchalance:

Still I have not had the luck to receive a single word from the archduchess. After she took to her to bed [with her pregnancy], she had other foreign *virtuosi* brought to her chamber to sing almost daily, but she always neglected to call upon Signor [Domenico] Anglesi and me. Although this brings me neither injury nor profit, I value my reputation highly and so have reflected on it, yet without figuring out the cause.[24]

Indeed, the archduchess's reasons for excluding Atto and Anglesi (an organist and composer in the Medici employ) remain obscure. But for Atto, who had enjoyed years of success in Paris, the disgrace of being ignored at this relatively provincial court became almost unbearable: "here I am dying of melancholy."[25]

Interestingly, the archduchess's attitude was quickly imitated by others at court, including Atto's fellow musicians. On 22 June, Atto reported to Mattias on the behavior of Antonio Cesti, Antonio Maria Viviani, and the other "Venetians":

Because a few Venetian musicians influence the minds of both the archduchess and archduke – for reasons I will tell Your Highness at the proper time – I have realized that they are trying to hold me back by every possible means. But because I'm truly

---

[22] The date of Atto's arrival can be determined from his letter to Mattias, from Innsbruck, May 25, 1653, while his stop in Mantua is explained in another to Mattias, from Mantua, May 9, 1653. (On the significance of this stopover in Mantua, see chapter 4.) Prunières (*L'opéra*, 187–88) and, following him, Adelmo Damerini ("La partitura de *L'Ercole in Tebe* di Jacopo Melani [1623–1676]," *Bullettino storico pistoiese* 19 [1917]: 59) suggest that Atto traveled to France briefly in 1653 before proceeding to the German states. The root of this belief is Prunières's misreading of the date on a letter to the duchess of Savoy from La Fera (La Fère) on July 27, 1657: Prunières reads 1653 instead.

[23] Atto to Mattias, from Innsbruck, May 25, 1653.

[24] Atto to Mattias, from Innsbruck, June 22, 1653.

[25] Atto to Girolamo Graziani, from Innsbruck, June 22, 1653. Domenico Anglesi's own letter to Giovan Carlo, May 27, 1653 (I Fas, MdP, filza 5322, f. 828; as transcribed in Sara Mamone, *Serenissimi fratelli principi impresari: Notizie di spettacolo nei carteggi medicei: Carteggi di Giovan Carlo de' Medici e di Desiderio Montemagni suo segretario [1628–1664]*, Storia dello spettacolo: Fonti, no. 3 [Florence: Le Lettere, 2003], 196), reports that Anglesi (at least) was initially received by the archduchess; no further letters hint at his subsequent treatment.

superior to all these things, I laugh to myself about it; for if ever I have the chance to go to the imperial court with the archduke, I hope to enlighten them all with ease.[26]

A week later, he offered his fullest account of the discord:

[After watching the daily *commedia* at around 6 p.m.], I remain in my rooms from 8 p.m. until midnight, awaiting those *virtuosi* who come from the imperial apartments to get dinner going. These *virtuosi* never have anything to talk about but the miraculous favors that they receive: among other things, Her Highness has asked her husband not take them along on the hunt but to leave them so that she may enjoy them. They have pumped my head so full of chatter that when I return to Italy I doubt I'll be able to squeeze it through the city gate of Florence. Having understood their goal, however, I try to stay so cheerful and free from all the pretension and attitude of this court that Signor Anglesi and I play at who can say sillier things.[27]

Such reports suggest that relationships among musicians imitated the hierarchy of court life generally. High standing depended not on seniority or talent, as in a guild, but rather on the favor of the sovereign(s). As in Norbert Elias's account of courtly manners, the "Venetian" musicians quickly perceived Atto's disfavor – his low "stock" – and modulated their behavior accordingly: showing respect to someone shunned by the ruler could endanger one's own position.[28] In this setting, professional success depended entirely on personal favor. Indeed, if mid-*Seicento* musicians strove to excel in their art, their motivation may have proceeded less from a desire for celebrity or (less still) a commitment to artistry, than from an aspiration to aristocratic esteem: the more refined one's skills, the more likely one was to strike the fancy of a powerful lord. Atto, of course, had often succeeded with precisely this strategy, blending vocal talent with courtly savoir-faire. And he hoped his eventual trip to the imperial court would reestablish his superiority, for if the emperor showed him favor, the coldness of the archdukes would be eclipsed.

But in June of 1653 he was still trapped in Innsbruck. With little to do, he expanded his reports to Mattias about musical life at court, reports that offer a welcome glimpse of such activity. On a personal level, Atto says that his disfavor allowed him the time to focus on practicing, so much so that "I hear

[26] Atto to Mattias, from Innsbruck, June 22, 1653.
[27] Atto to Mattias, from Innsbruck, June 29, 1653. For the conversion of times in this letter, which uses the Italian system, see Michael Talbot, "*Ore italiane*: The Reckoning of the Time of Day in Pre-Napoleonic Italy," *Italian Studies* 40 (1985): 51–62. Atto's reference to "*ora* 24" confirms that he is using the Italian system here, which placed this moment about a half-hour before sunset (variable through the year). Because sunset in Innsbruck in late June takes place around 8:30 p.m. (standard time, not daylight savings), he really seems to be eating dinner around midnight.
[28] Elias, *Court Society*, 91.

the profit of it very much."[29] But he also tells of performances, including a chamber concert held for a visiting gentleman from Bavaria (unnamed). For this event, Ferdinand Karl commanded all his singers to perform in turn, apparently in reverse order of their standing at court. Accordingly, Atto had to go first, and "they saved the best for last," although he notes with satisfaction that the visitor singled him out to sing again at the end.[30] On another occasion, Atto recounts that, although the archduchess – recovering from childbirth – could not yet attend stage works, "she enjoys hearing [chamber] singing from 6 to 10 in the evening, and the archduke plays along with these Venetian musicians in various arias to be heard by the emperor."[31] The prominence of vocal chamber music at this court is itself interesting, but more so is the archduke's participation, particularly if he really planned to perform alongside his professionals before the emperor. Such aristocratic music-making harkens back to the madrigal traditions of the previous century and surely sheds light on the aforementioned link between social and musical favor.

In fact, the archduke seems to have been deeply engaged in such music-making. Ferdinand Karl's taste for entertainments in general has long been known: his own chancellor characterized him with the words, "masks, plays, balls, and nothing else."[32] Yet Atto writes of a level of personal involvement that has never, to my knowledge, been remarked: "When Archduke Ferdinand does not go hunting, he spends the entire day with the musicians; Padre Cesti, the favorite, is there among the others … Music is performed in church every feast day, and the archduke comes to where we sing, and he himself distributes the parts and acts with such kindness and familiarity that I would not know how to express it to Your Highness."[33] Elsewhere, Atto notes that "the archduke is devoted to music and knows how to play a few sonatas on the harpsichord and viola [da gamba]. For singing, he likes Morello [Filippo Bombaglia] very much, and Padre Cesti is his god of music."[34]

---

[29] Atto to Mattias, from Innsbruck, June 29, 1653.

[30] Atto to Mattias, from Innsbruck, June 22, 1653.

[31] Atto to Mattias, from Innsbruck, June 29, 1653. The identification of "S[ua] A[ltezza]" as the archduke rather than the archduchess is admittedly uncertain, but given the overall context – and the archduke's acknowledged musical skills – the former interpretation seems likely.

[32] Franz Karl Zoller, *Geschichte und Denkwürdigkeiten der Stadt Innsbruck* (Innsbruck: Wagner, 1816), I:377, quoted in Senn, *Musik und Theater*, 244.

[33] Atto to Mattias, from Innsbruck, May 25, 1653.

[34] Atto to Duke Carlo II of Mantua, from Innsbruck, May 25, 1653. On Bombaglia, see Herbert Seifert, "Cesti and His Opera Troupe in Innsbruck and Vienna, with New Informations [*sic*] about His Last Year and His Oeuvre," in *La figura e l'opera di Antonio Cesti nel Seicento europeo: Convegno internazionale di studio, Arezzo, 26–27 aprile 2002*, ed. Mariateresa Dellaborra, Quaderni della Rivista Italiana di Musicologia, Società Italiana di Musicologia, no. 37 (Florence: Leo S. Olschki, 2003), 22–23.

Like many of the Habsburgs, including the reigning emperor Ferdinand III and later his son Leopold I, Ferdinand Karl was a patron of music with first-hand experience of the art.

Not surprisingly, then, Atto sometimes believed he could overcome the archduchess's disfavor by winning over the archduke. He took every opportunity to spend time in the archduke's presence. His letter of June 29 – again rich with detail – confirms that many of Atto's musical activities were motivated by concern for standing:

In the morning, when they do not go to the hunt, the archduke usually entertains himself until the lunch hour in the theater that he is having constructed for the *commedie*, testing both the changes of scenery and the machines with the musicians that must perform in them. I myself go there not so much to perform my part as to spend the time being seen by His Highness … After lunch, I go immediately to my rooms with my companion, Signor Anglesi, because the rooms are contiguous with those of Padre Cesti, who composed the opera. If His Highness does not go hunting, he comes to the quarters of this padre, where quite often the *virtuosi* rehearse the parts they are to play, and as they are so close, I take the opportunity to be seen by His Highness.[35]

Atto's efforts seem to have made little difference, however, and he soon realized his best chance for support remained personal service to the emperor. Originally, Atto had been ordered to accompany the archdukes on their planned journey from Innsbruck to the imperial diet in Regensburg.[36] But it soon became apparent that the archduchess's pregnancy and childbirth would postpone the journey considerably. That delay meant problems: not only would it extend his misery in Innsbruck, it would also prevent him from fulfilling a request from the queen of France to serve her during the coming winter. Atto's overall stay in Germany needed to be short to leave him time to return to Tuscany and then reach Paris before the

---

[35] Atto to Mattias, from Innsbruck, June 29, 1653.

[36] Even his first letters from Innsbruck note that he must "passar per qualche tempo alla Corte Cesarea" (Atto to Duke Francesco I of Modena, May 25, 1653 [letter 1]). Emperor Ferdinand III had called the diet both to ratify the 1648 Treaties of Westphalia and to elect and crown his eldest son, Ferdinand Maria, king of the Romans, that is, successor to the imperial throne. See Jean Bérenger, *A History of the Habsburg Empire 1273–1700*, trans. C. A. Simpson (London: Longman, 1994), 292, originally published as *Histoire de l'empire des Habsbourg* (Paris: Fayard, 1990); Charles W. Ingrao, *The Habsburg Monarchy 1618–1815*, New Approaches to European History, 2nd edn. (Cambridge: Cambridge University Press, 2000), 54–55. In fact, Atto's letter to the duke of Mantua, from Innsbruck, June 8, 1653, includes a long account of the celebrations in that court upon receiving news of the election (which took place on May 31), including the many toasts made and Ferdinand Karl's prodigious consumption of wine.

weather turned bad.[37] Thus, virtually from his arrival in Innsbruck, Atto was seeking ways to leave ahead of schedule.

He waged his efforts on two fronts, both of which involved manipulating his superiors. First, just three days after his arrival (and even before corresponding with Mattias), Atto sent a letter to Count Raimondo Montecuccoli, the Modenese-born general of the imperial army and Atto's contact at the imperial court. Although the letter merely notified the count of Atto's arrival, the gesture of writing directly to Regensburg was audacious, as it sidestepped the archduke's authority. It was as if today an army private were to write a secret letter over the head of his sergeant. In fact, the letter had its desired effect, for Montecuccoli soon answered that the emperor wanted Atto to come to Regensburg as soon as possible: "it will not be at all necessary to await the response from Florence, for the goodness of His Highness [Prince Mattias] assures me that he will happily take this opportunity to please His Majesty."[38]

Even before receiving this answer, however, Atto also began complaining to Mattias that the entire trip to Regensburg was threatened: "Nothing is spoken of the journey to the Diet, although everyone says it will happen, including the archduke himself; still, I do not consider it certain, and if we were to go, it could not be before September or October."[39] Similar comments appear in most of Atto's letters from this period, as he subtly goaded Mattias into ordering an early departure. That order finally arrived at the beginning of July, after Atto had also passed along the emperor's request. Immediately, Atto presented his prince's orders to Ferdinand Karl, who, though annoyed, granted Atto leave to go. Through all of these dealings, Atto had cleverly maneuvered, even deceived, the different powers to arrange his early release. It was a risky strategy, as he was soon to learn, but his unbridled expression of joy illuminates his desperation: "I feel so much happiness that if

[37] All Atto's letters to the duke of Modena and Girolamo Gratiani, from Innsbruck, on May 25, 1653, refer to the queen's request. The first letter to the duke gives the most detail about the Parisian project: "voglio procurare il mio ritorno in Italia per dover essere questo inverno in Francia, volendo quella Maestà far fare per il prossimo Carnevale un Balletto simile all'altro fatto questo Anno, ma con musiche italiane, e già il signor Buti Segretario del signor Cardinal Antonio [Barberini] compose le parole, ed in luogo di Luigi [Rossi] che haveva già havuto ordine di tornare in Francia per far la musica, piglieranno Marco Marazzoli." This work turned out to be *Le nozze di Peleo e di Teti*, with music not by Marazzoli but by Carlo Caproli and performed with great success at the Petit Bourbon in Paris in April and May of 1654.

[38] Atto includes a copy of Montecuccoli's letter with his own to Mattias, from Innsbruck, June 15, 1653.

[39] Atto to Mattias, from Innsbruck, May 25, 1653. In the end, Atto was correct. As Senn opined, the court of Innsbruck could hardly have made the trip to the diet at this time (Senn, *Musik und Theater*, 245): on July 14, from Regensburg, Atto reports the Innsbruck court still at least two weeks from arriving; then on September 7 he was back in Innsbruck in the presence of that court. No mention of the visit of such a large entourage appears in his correspondence.

I wrote something inappropriate in this letter, I beg Your Highness [Mattias] to pardon me, for I'm beside myself, and can say I'm leaving that country where asses fly."[40]

Departing on July 4, Atto arrived in Regensburg in the evening three days later. Almost immediately, his hopes were realized. If Innsbruck had frustrated and degraded him, Regensburg lavished him with every possible honor. Instead of lodging in a room at the palace with the other musicians, he stayed at the home of Felice Marchetti, official representative of the court of Tuscany. Instead of being harassed at mealtime by more favored singers, he was invited to dine each day with Count Montecuccoli himself. And instead of being ignored by the rulers, he was called almost immediately to their service.

In the imperial court, Atto experienced once again, as he had in Paris, the distinctive treatment he sought. Emperor Ferdinand III loved music and even possessed some skill at composition.[41] Unlike his cousin the archduke, however, the emperor seems to have held no prejudice against Atto: even at the singer's first performance – the account of which I relate for its wealth of detail – the emperor showed him great favor:

His Majesty sent word that I should be at the palace at 8:30 p.m., which I was. Since I was brought in just as he had taken his place at the table for dinner with the empress and the King of the Romans [his son], he had me sing throughout the entire length of dinner. Afterwards, when His Majesty rose from the table and went over to where the spinet was, I went up to him and, kissing his hand, presented him Your Highness's letter. I informed him of the order that you yourself had given me to present myself to His Majesty with all haste and that you considered it your great fortune that one of your servants had been judged worthy of being able to serve His Majesty.

Receiving the letter, he opened it immediately and said to me these precise words: "Signor Atto, I assure you that from the reports I received about your abilities, I figured you were most worthy, but I have found those abilities to be greater than your fame had suggested to me. I confess that Prince [Mattias] was quite right to have opposed releasing you, and you yourself can assure him that he could not have done me a greater favor. Please consent to sing two more *ariette*."

These were the words that His Majesty said to me, and having had three chairs brought near to the instrument, he had me sing another hour and a half, so that in total I sang for three hours. These gentlemen tell me that His Majesty has never indicated such approval to any other *virtuoso* who has come to these lands. His

---

[40] The above information and quotation comes from Atto's letter to Mattias, from Innsbruck, July 2, 1653.

[41] A number of his compositions, including monodic works, are published in Guido Adler, ed., *Musikalische Werke der Kaiser Ferdinand III., Leopold I. und Joseph I*, 2 vols. (Vienna: Artaria, [1892]).

Majesty has gone hunting every day, and when he has seen me, he has always fixed his eyes on me, smiling, a thing they say he has never done in public, as he always behaves with extreme gravity.[42]

These distinctions, specifically denied to other musicians, were precisely what Atto craved.

Over the next few weeks, Atto sang for the court several more times. For example, on Sunday, July 13, which was the emperor's birthday, he once again found himself the center of attention:

Yesterday, which was Sunday, His Majesty wanted to hear me in church. This redounded very much to my advantage, because some who had heard me in the chamber with a tempered voice [*voce moderata*] did not believe I could be heard in church. So yesterday morning I sang a solo motet with words appropriate to the birth of His Majesty, and at vespers I sang a very unusual [*bizzarra*] Magnificat. And then, to see whether I was singing with well-grounded technique, they had me sing very elaborate litanies for solo voice, to test a *musico*. Fortunately, I was in quite good voice; I allow that I satisfied very well for my part. The applause was [even] greater than the merit, and I hope that Your Highness will receive some report of it from others.[43]

Two weeks later, his cachet had not diminished:

Yesterday evening I sang for His Majesty, much to my good fortune, because the emperor said publicly that this last time he heard me he thought I sang even better than before. Yesterday morning at His Majesty's mass I sang a solo motet to very great applause, and during the day yesterday I won great esteem. I confess truly to Your Highness that I never remember in all my days having sung as I do now.[44]

With such success, especially with the emperor, Atto became a darling of the court. He reports that whenever it was announced he would sing, a crowd of nobility and even other singers would gather. As he tells it, "everyone competes to do me the greatest courtesies, and all these ladies favor me; truly

---

[42] Atto to Mattias, from Regensburg, July 14, 1653. Weaver misinterpreted Atto's presentation of the letter to the emperor as a clandestine act: Robert Lamar Weaver, "Materiali per le biografie dei fratelli Melani," *Rivista italiana di musicologia* 12 (1977): 260n.

[43] Atto to Mattias, from Regensburg, July 14, 1653. Later in the same letter, Atto also reports, "Cantai ancora hiermattina doppo che le loro MM.tà hebbero pranzato, et ancora hier Sera doppo la cena, havendo in quel mentre cantato conforme al solito gli altri Virtuosi di S.M." Unfortunately, I have been able to find no good candidates for the motet, Magnificat, or litany that Atto might have sung. That these were common elements of the liturgy, however, is explained by Andrew Hudsco Weaver in his study of sacred music at this court: "Piety, Politics, and Patronage: Motets at the Habsburg Court in Vienna during the Reign of Ferdinand III (1637–1657)" (Ph.D. diss., Yale Univ., 2002).

[44] Atto to Mattias, from Regensburg, August 4, 1653.

in no other place have I had so many honors and been heard with greater applause."[45] Some of his admirers, including the ambassador of Spain, requested private performances, but, exploiting his new status, Atto refused all requests unless ordered by the emperor's own representatives.[46] Indeed, Atto began behaving more like a talented amateur in the emperor's retinue than a professional performer on loan from Tuscany. The emperor encouraged this posture by presenting Atto with an expensive necklace and medallion, a gift matched on a smaller scale by the king of the Romans and the ambassador of Spain.[47] To receive gifts like a gentleman rather than be paid like a laborer just confirmed Atto's position.

On August 16, the emperor left Regensburg on a journey to the elector of Bavaria's court in Munich and thence to Augsburg. Atto decided to follow the court, both because his road back to Italy led through Munich and Innsbruck, and because he wanted to see the elector's wife, Henriette Adelaide of Savoy, whom he had come to know during an earlier stay in Turin (see chapter 2).[48] Rather than traveling with the court, however, Atto managed to join a small group of noblemen who were taking a more leisurely tour of the countryside.[49] Upon his arrival in the Bavarian capital, he reports:

I am in Munich in a party with the resident of Tuscany [Felice Marchetti], Count [Filippo] D'Elci, Count Enea Caprara, and the young Count Montecuccoli. We go around seeing and examining the highlights of this place, but we have not yet had word that we can see the garden, gallery, nor anything else of the palace here because they regard it as a holy relic; they live worse than Carthusian monks, with customs completely different from other places.[50]

[45] Ibid. Of course, Atto may have exaggerated some of these reports to impress his Italian patron, but as Mattias would have received independent accounts from other agents, the singer's statements are probably not wholly fabricated.

[46] Atto to Mattias, from Regensburg, August 16, 1653.   [47] Ibid.

[48] Atto to Christine of France, duchess of Savoy, from Florence, November 13, 1653. Henriette Adelaide seems to have been something of a kindred spirit for Atto: Fr[anz] M[ichael] Rudhart, *Geschichte der Oper am Hofe zu München* (Freising: Franz Datterer, 1865), 29, describes her as "selbst vortrefflich musikalisch gebildet (sie soll eine gute Sängerin gewesen sein und auf der Harfe und Laute meisterhaft gespielt haben)." Perhaps Atto even gave her lessons at some point. In any case, their relationship later redounded much to Atto's advantage (see chapter 5).

[49] Atto to Mattias, from Regensburg, August 11, 1653.

[50] Atto to Mattias, from Munich, August 22, 1653. Montecuccoli and his companions were in the midst of a tour of the courts and armies of Germany, the Netherlands, Italy, and Bohemia following the conclusion of the Thirty Years' War. See the *Dizionario biografico degli italiani*, s.v. "Caprara, Enea Silvio" and "D'Elci, Raniero" (Filippo's father); Luciano Tomassini, *Raimondo Montecuccoli: Capitano e scrittore* (Rome: Stato Maggiore dell'Esercito, Ufficio Storico, 1978), 23. Atto seems to have established and maintained a close relationship with Montecuccoli. A letter from the count to Atto, March 7, 1657, contains a remarkably intimate confession of the count's love interests: Raimund Montecuccoli, *Ausgewaehlte Schriften*, vol. IV, *Miscellen, Correspondenz*, ed. Alois Veltzé (Vienna: Wilhelm Braumüller, 1900), 369–70.

Indeed, Atto seems to have adopted as much as possible on this journey the lifestyle of a nobleman, in his behavior as much as the company he kept. He reveals how much he tried to avoid the appearance of a musician:

I will not sing if they simply request it, because I do not want to behave like all those who come to these German courts to be heard so as to receive a gift. Many noblemen ask me why I do not sing one evening at table and tell me that His Highness [the elector] would enjoy it. I answer them that when His Highness himself commands it of me, I will do it, as I am here only for my recreation.[51]

In fact, the elector did eventually ask Atto to perform for the court, including the visiting emperor, and Atto of course obliged, receiving from the electress one of those typical gifts, a small necklace.[52] During this period Atto remained perfectly happy to sing, to demonstrate his prodigious skills, but only if he did so in an aristocratic environment where he was treated as an equal. If the venue was small and elite, he could *appear* to be just another gentleman – like so many of the Habsburgs – who possessed musical talent.

To Atto's dismay, an obligatory return to Innsbruck soon challenged this pleasant fiction. After spending a week or so in Munich, Atto followed the imperial court to Augsburg and then traveled on his own back to the Tyrolean capital.[53] Because his services had originally been granted to the archduke, and the archduke still wanted Atto for the *feste*, Atto was forced to return. Although that project would detain him in Innsbruck through the winter (and thus prevent his return to France), Atto seems to have reached Innsbruck already resigned to the situation, buoyed perhaps by his recent triumphs.

Upon arrival, however, he found his reception shockingly cold. Ever since his precipitous departure, trouble had been brewing. While still in Regensburg, Atto had received word that "because I am performing one of the principal parts [in the entertainments at Innsbruck], it seems that His Highness had strong feelings about my leaving."[54] By the time of Atto's return, his "Venetian" adversaries had exacerbated the crisis. When his initial greeting and request for orders was ignored, Atto inquired with others and was told "of the evil services that had been done me … and that because of these, His Highness was very angry with me."[55] Atto's explanation of the predicament again sheds light on the sometimes ruthless competitiveness among musicians:

[51] Atto to Mattias, from Munich, August 22, 1653.
[52] Atto to Mattias, from Innsbruck, September 7, 1653.
[53] Atto to Mattias, from Munich, August 22, 1653.
[54] Atto to Mattias, from Regensburg, July 7, 1653.
[55] Atto to Mattias, from Innsbruck, September 7, 1653.

On two charges are founded the slanders that they have made against me, which have been led spiritedly by Padre Cesti with the assistance of these other musicians. Signor Anglesi too has not neglected to act in his usual manner, attacking me where he could, without regard even for Your Highness … The first charge by which they have greatly upset His Highness was that the emperor had not called me at all, but rather that I devised this opportunity to go there and wrote of it to Your Highness [Mattias], who, to relieve me from serving the archduke, found this pretext to send me to Regensburg.[56]

Of course, the charge that Atto had helped engineer his exit from Innsbruck is essentially true: his letter to Montecuccoli led to a personal request from the emperor that might not otherwise have transpired. The accusations continued:

The second charge is much worse than the first, for I find it more evil … For your information, I will tell Your Highness that immediately after I left Innsbruck, the archduke ordered Padre Cesti to write to Venice to have Anna Renzi come in my place, and because the first letters did not get through, they wanted to lay the blame on me, that I had had them lifted from the post; but as I had already departed, they did not stir up this rumor to any profit.

Having written very crafty letters to his correspondent in Venice, Padre Cesti learn[ed] that Signora Anna did not want to come, declaring herself engaged to go to Genoa. He finally received a letter that he immediately took to His Highness, accompanied by all those affectations to which the more astute friars are accustomed. He said that it was no wonder Signora Anna did not want to come, for His Highness would read the cause in that letter. This was the sense of it:

"Having tried by every means to discover the reasons that kept Signora Anna from coming to this service, I eventually learned that she had been dissuaded from it by the correspondents that Atto Melani maintains in Venice, for [Atto] wrote that he was going to Regensburg since the [work in Innsbruck] did not amount to much in his opinion. For this reason, she did not want to go to Innsbruck, considering it more to her profit and reputation to go to Genoa than to serve as a second choice [*per rifiuto*]."[57]

In other words, Anna Renzi's concern for her own status would not allow her to stand in for another singer, especially when the quality of the project stood in doubt. Ferdinand Karl interpreted Atto's involvement as an affront.

Atto then called upon all his cunning. After taking time to consider his defense, he confronted the archduke. First, Atto characterized the incident as the result of the personal envy and prejudice of his enemies, who wanted to "[make] me the author of an evil that is as great as my innocence"; he then

[56] Ibid.   [57] Ibid.

requested an investigation into the source of Cesti's letter, predicting that "the lie has short legs"; and he concluded by asking whether the archduke trusted more the word of his own brother-in-law (Mattias) or "the inventions of some poor wretches." Little impressed, the archduke replied only, "We will think about it a little."[58]

In the face of such a response, Atto begged Mattias for support. He asked his patron to write the archduke confirming all that Atto had said and further suggested that Mattias forward Montecuccoli's letter first requesting the singer's services. To deal with the Anna Renzi matter, Atto proposed a characteristic bit of subterfuge. He included with his letter to Mattias a counterfeit letter – similar to one he had earlier sent from Regensburg (probably that of July 7) – in which he informs Mattias about the archduke's anger at his departure and promises to return to Innsbruck as soon as the emperor releases him. "Your Highness can say that you immediately answered me that I must return to Innsbruck ... to do all that Their Highnesses commanded of me."[59] Pointing out how such a letter would prove Atto's good intentions – and thus counter the charge that he sabotaged the production – he asked Mattias to be sure to send it before he himself returned to Tuscany, "so that it not seem something I requested."[60]

Unfortunately, a lack of evidence conceals whether any of these strategies worked. That Atto left the city only days after sending his letter to Mattias and that Anna Renzi eventually did come to assume a series of leading roles may well indicate his failure.[61] Unclear too is Atto's actual culpability in these

---

[58] Ibid.   [59] Ibid.

[60] Ibid. Atto also warns Mattias that the paper on which his fake letter is written is from Munich; presumably Mattias would have to account for this discrepancy.

[61] On Renzi in Innsbruck, see Claudio Sartori, "La prima diva della lirica italiana: Anna Renzi," *Nuova rivista musicale italiana* 2 (1968): 450; Senn, *Musik und Theater*, 266. Scholars have generally accepted that the opera in which Atto had been scheduled to appear was in fact the work given with Renzi in January 1654, that is, a revised version of Cesti's 1651 Venetian *Cesare amante*, with a new occasional prologue. (See Senn, 256 and 287; Claudio Sartori, *I libretti italiani a stampa dalle origini al 1800: Catalogo analitico con 16 indici* [Turin: Bertola e Locatelli Musica, 1993], I:152, who, solving an anagram, revealed the librettist to be Dario Varottari; and Bianconi and Walker, "Dalla *Finta pazza*," 442n.) But in a letter to Mattias from Innsbruck on May 25, Atto writes, "il Padre Cesti ... veramente à fatto una bellissima musica ad una commedia che si farà, che le parole sono del Padre Predicatore di S.A. e non possono essere più belle nella loro bruttezza e cattività." This description makes the production sound like a newly composed work, with a libretto by the archduke's priest (unidentified). In another letter on the same day, this time to the duke of Mantua, Atto further notes, "l'opera che è per farsi è tutta fondata sopra la nascita del Serenissimo Principe figlio di V.A.S., Le parole sono come appunto ella mi disse, e per hora voglio procurare di mandarle qui annesso l'argumento per servirla a suo tempo delle medesime." These comments suggest, in fact, that the entire work – and not just its prologue – was related to the birth of the Mantuan prince. A letter from Domenico Anglesi to Giovan Carlo, from Innsbruck, May 27, 1663 (I Fas, MdP, filza 5322, f. 828, transcribed in Mamone, *Serenissimi fratelli*, 196), confirms Atto's report and further reveals that the work was a pastiche: "Si va

matters. He may have written of his plans to Renzi and other correspondents in Venice (above all, his brother Jacopo) without foreseeing the consequences of his remarks: one doubts he would have tried to dissuade another singer from spending the winter in Innsbruck just to reserve that duty for himself. In any case, the entire adventure in the German states highlights the powerful desire for prestige that now dominated his concerns: in his machinations to escape the disrespect of Innsbruck for the cordiality of Regensburg, Atto showed his willingness to adopt risky tactics, including overstepping his authority and deceiving his patrons. While such tactics may have backfired in Innsbruck, they succeeded in bringing him to the far more important imperial court.[62]

Frustration at home

After Innsbruck, Atto's life becomes more difficult to follow for a time. If he kept to his plans, he left that city on September 8 and traveled to Venice, where he spent several days with his brother Jacopo investigating the source of the "slander" against him.[63] The much-desired trip to Paris that winter never materialized, and in the end Atto spent the next year-and-a-half in

mettendo in ordine una commedia in musica, fatta dal padre Cesti una parte e l'altra dal Viviani, avendomi Sua Altezza onorato di servarmi il prologo da mettere in musica, dal che io non mene curavo punto per più [rispetti] e particolarmente per le parole, che sono assai ordinarie, fatte da un frate francescano della riforma, sì come anco ha fatto tutta la commedia, sì che Vostra Altezza si puole immaginare che cosa puol essere." Clearly, the work originally planned in Innsbruck was not Cesti's *Cesare amante*. Instead, when Atto left for Regensburg, Cesti and the archduke decided to mount a different opera. Cesti's earlier Venetian work fit the bill, and a new prologue could be quickly written to tie the opera to its ever more remote celebratory purpose. Anglesi confirms the switch in his letter to Giovan Carlo, from Innsbruck, December 7, 1653 (I Fas, MdP, filza 5326, f. 598r–v; Mamone, *Serenissimi fratelli*, 203): "Si aspetta il Serenissimo di Mantova per le feste di Natale con la Serenissima sua sposa, che per ciò se gli è preparando un'altra commedia, che è stata fatta in Venezia dal frate Cesti." This version of events has the benefit of not casting Atto in the role of Cleopatra (in *Cesare*), as has been suggested. The use of castrati for leading female roles seems to have been uncommon outside of Rome, and one might have expected Atto to have commented (at this point in his career) on such an unusual and potentially demeaning assignment.

[62] Weaver states that in 1653 Atto went back and forth twice between Mazarin in La Fère and the emperor in Innsbruck: Robert Lamar Weaver, "Florentine Comic Operas of the Seventeenth Century" (Ph.D. diss., University of North Carolina, Chapel Hill, 1958), 195. Weaver believes the emperor was giving shelter to important Frondeurs in his territory. Needless to say, I see no evidence that Atto could have made such trips: the documents leave no time (see Appendix A).

[63] Atto to Mattias, from Innsbruck, September 7, 1653; and to Duke Carlo II of Mantua, from Florence, October 2, 1653. The latter confirms that Atto did indeed return to Italy by way of Venice. The brother Atto mentions he will visit in his letter of September 7 is almost certainly Jacopo, as argued by Weaver, "Materiali," 265n.

Florence, often shuttling back and forth to his home in Pistoia.[64] As always, his proximity to Mattias depressed his production of letters. Still, even this more limited material offers insights of value.

For example, several of the letters shed light on musical life at mid-century at the court of Florence. These letters primarily concern preparations for the "festa teatrale" *Hipermestra*, with libretto by the Florentine physician Giovanni Andrea Moniglia and music by Francesco Cavalli. One of the few operas Cavalli did not compose for Venice, *Hipermestra* was commissioned by Cardinal Giovan Carlo de' Medici for the inauguration of the new Teatro in Via della Pergola. That theater was the project of the Accademia degli Immobili, an aristocratic association formed in 1649 under the protection of Giovan Carlo for the purpose of promoting dramatic performances. Although the production was delayed until June 1658, preparations were underway by late 1654.[65]

Atto's reports reveal an interesting and rarely discussed performance practice: the presentation of operas as chamber entertainment, presumably in "concert" style.

Today in the chamber of the cardinal [Giovan Carlo], I sang the entire *commedia*, and Prince Leopoldo was also there; and I swear to Your Highness that it is music of paradise and that one could not hear anything more beautiful. Various noble academicians were there too, among others, Count [Ferdinando] Bardi and Marchese [Filippo] Niccolini. Because [the work] was sung by other *virtuosi* at Pratolino in the chamber of the grand duchess, and then also here in Florence in the presence of the cardinal, they honored me today by praising me for having sung it much better than the others.[66]

Atto's tone here suggests that this sort of performance was not entirely unprecedented; clearly, distinguished audiences sometimes listened to operas without the magnificent trappings normally associated with the genre.[67] Such a group must have been capable of perceiving and appreciating the

---

[64] In a letter to Christine of France, duchess of Savoy, from Florence, November 13, 1653, Atto still speaks of hoping to go to Paris and so visit the duchess on the way, but his extant correspondence does not leave time for such a trip (see Appendix A). Atto uses the opportunity of this letter to confirm his ties to the duchess by reporting on his visit to the German states and particularly by giving news of the duchess's daughter, the electress of Bavaria.

[65] On this opera, Weaver and Weaver, *Chronology*, 120–23; Bianconi and Walker, "Dalla *Finta pazza*," 438–39.

[66] Atto to Mattias, from Florence, October 2, 1654. In addition, Atto writes that he would like to come to Siena to perform his part (presumably alone) for Mattias. Atto could not in fact have performed "tutta la Commedia" because by this date only the first act had arrived in Florence: see Mamone, *Serenissimi fratelli*, 229–30, 234.

[67] Mamone, *Serenissimi fratelli*, 498, excerpts a letter from Francesco Panciatichi to Desiderio Montemagni, from Florence, December 5, 1654 (I Fas, MdP, filza 1509, f. 581) reporting that "in camera di Sua Eminenza si sta cantando un atto di commedia e vi sono molti a sentirlo."

musical, poetic, and perhaps even dramatic qualities of such a work apart from its visual brilliance.

This notion receives added support from Atto's account of an episode that took place during rehearsals. At one point, Atto's aforementioned travel companion in Germany, Domenico Anglesi, proposed "correcting" certain notes in Cavalli's score. In response, "His Highness [Giovan Carlo] told him to leave them alone because perhaps they were all right and according to the intention of the composer, and [Anglesi] did not know it."[68] Such respect for the details of a score hints again at a high level of musical understanding, higher than has sometimes been allowed to *Seicento* aristocrats.[69] While many music patrons concerned themselves primarily with the political or even propagandistic capacities of the art, at least some possessed a refined musical or even musico-dramatic sensibility as well.

Atto's correspondence from this period also reveals that his fixation on social advancement was leading him to contemplate radical measures. His many triumphs in Paris and Regensburg threw into stark relief the comparative apathy of his own sovereign: he especially faulted Grand Duke Ferdinando II for only rarely supporting his applications for benefices. Feeling unappreciated, Atto expressed a surprising dissatisfaction with the Medici family and began looking to transfer his primary loyalty elsewhere.

The ecclesiastical benefice had always played a crucial role in Atto's strategies. The practice of the *commendam* – the separation of the assigned income of a church office from its clerical functions – had become a customary method of rewarding court favorites, and at the age of seventeen Atto was already pressing Mattias for help in obtaining such compensation.[70] Generally granted for life, benefices had the advantage of greater permanence than stipends from a patron: one of Atto's own justifications for his requests was "to assure myself of bread even in my old age."[71] Benefices also carried greater prestige because their disbursement was not predicated on labor. As Atto knew, the acquisition of a benefice depended largely on the advocacy of

---

[68] Atto to Mattias, from Florence, September 27, 1654.

[69] On the presumed lack of understanding on the part of noblemen, see, for example, Lorenzo Bianconi, *Music in the Seventeenth Century*, trans. David Bryant (Cambridge: Cambridge University Press, 1987), 61–64, originally published as *Il Seicento* (Turin: E.D.T., 1982).

[70] This use of the benefice began with the Concordat of 1516; see Wolfgang Müller *et al.*, *The Church in the Age of Absolutism and Enlightenment*, trans. Gunther J. Holst, vol. VI of *History of the Church* (New York: Crossroad, 1981), 7–8, originally published as *Die Kirche im Zeitalter des Absolutismus und der Aufklärung* (Freiburg: Herder, 1970). One of Atto's earliest requests comes in his letter to Mattias, from Florence, March 13, 1644, where the young singer calls attention to the imminent death of a Pistoiese priest.

[71] Atto to Mattias, from Pistoia, September 12, 1654. Rosselli, "From Princely Service," 6, remarks on the insecurity of income tied to a specific aristocrat, which "was more exposed to the hazards of war, mortality, and whim."

secular authorities, and so his usual strategy involved soliciting favorable letters from Mattias, the grand duke, and the grand duchess. To judge from Atto's own comments, his track record was poor: with a few exceptions, his letters generally convey disappointment laced with sarcasm: "one works for Holy Mary at home," or, "[I am] accustomed to making requests in [Florence] only to receive good words."[72] This grumbling may well have been a pretense, however, for in 1659 a government official in Pistoia protested that "the Melani are as juicy as a grape in benefices and offices."[73]

However justified, Atto's frustrations seem to have come to a head in the fall of 1654. He had heard of the death of a certain Prior Panciatichi and the resultant vacancy of the prior's benefice; accordingly, he had requested the usual letters of support from the Medici. Although he realized that many others would apply, he remained optimistic because, as he reminded Mattias, the grand duke had promised him support for the next vacancy.[74] But when the grand duke proved only lukewarm, Atto's confidence evaporated. In a last-ditch effort, he put forward a startling new rationale for the benefice – which he describes in great detail – involving the relocation of his entire family to Florence:

Already with my other most humble letter I told Your Highness of the response I received from the grand duke, which consisted of kind words, as usual. … The annual yield of that benefice is sixty bushels of grain and thirty barrels of wine. If I could obtain it, I would wholly abandon the city of Pistoia and have my brothers and mother come to Florence, where I would establish my house. Selling the little I have to the state, I would put the money into some businesses where I would employ those brothers of mine who had no other way of supporting themselves. Thus, I would free myself from that evil district [Pistoia] where one cannot have dealings with one person without making enemies of ten. I cannot execute this plan, my master, without a secure arrangement, because with time I could lose everything, and where in Florence a person lives with four, in Pistoia he gets by with one. The vacant benefice is not of such quality that the grand duke could think to confer it on great and qualified persons for the support of numerous attendants, and because I have never obtained a single favor from the grand duke, and because I have such a worthy goal, I do not think my requests are too bold.[75]

---

[72] On one of his successes, see his letter to Mattias, from Saint-Germain-en-Laye, April 3, 1649: "Dal Padre Filippo mio fratello ho inteso il segnalato favore che V. A. si è compiaciuta farmi di operare ch'io resti gratiato del Benefitio impetratomi dalla Generosità di V. A." On his complaints, his letters to Mattias, from Pistoia, September 29, 1645 (quoted here), and from Florence, September 27, 1654 ("essendo [io] avvezzo a chieder in questo luogho per non havere che buone parole").

[73] Lionardo Signorini to Mattias, from Pistoia, September 7, 1659: "i Melani sono Zippi come una uva di benefitii et uffitii."

[74] Atto to Mattias, from Pistoia, September 12, 1654.

[75] Atto to Mattias, from Florence, October 10, 1654. Later in this passage, Atto points out that "quando io habbia indotta la mia Casa in Firenze, Jacopo ancora ci s'impiegherà con ogni trattenimento."

This approach too failed, however, and Atto does not appear to have received this benefice; nor did he ever move his family from Pistoia.

Instead, the failure fed his dissatisfaction. Five months after the previous letter, he was exploring the possibility of transferring his loyalties to the duke of Mantua, a sovereign with whom he maintained particularly close ties (see chapter 4). A letter from March 1655 sheds light on many of his goals:

From the last letter written to me by Signor Garrachia, I learned of the kind disposition of Your Highness concerning my interests, which accord with my scant desire to remain in this region, precisely as Your Highness comprehended. This is not because I do not receive excellent treatment from my patron [Mattias], but because my goal has always been to assure myself an appropriate emolument in life, having, to this end, taken the habit [i.e., for the purpose of acquiring benefices]. Because I have not found here [in Florence] the reciprocity that I desire and that was promised me by the grand duke, I have resolved to seize the opportunities that present themselves to me, since I have been disappointed many times by the assurances made to me concerning vacant benefices. Considering that I might end up like other *virtuosi*, who in their old age find themselves without earnings, I am moved to think about the future. If I find an arrangement in ecclesiastical benefices instead of wages, I think I will withdraw from this service.

The particular inclination I have to serve Your Highness, strengthened by your kind demonstrations, obligates me to offer my service first to Your Highness, if it be assured that – may it please Your Highness – you will find a way to remunerate me in the manner I desire and thus to have me with no increase in expense, for people of advanced age find themselves possessors of benefices capable of rendering an annuity equivalent to the salary that I receive here.[76]

In other words, Atto was offering his loyalty to the duke if payment could be guaranteed in benefices equivalent to the direct salary he was then receiving; Atto further hints that, because benefices of this value were commonly held by elderly incumbents, they might soon become available. Fundamentally, then, he was trying to convert his stipend from Mattias – inherently impermanent and a mark of dependence – into a more stable and dignified form of income. In the end, Atto never did leave the Medici. But his exasperation with what he perceived as their lack of regard almost drove him to abandon the patrons who had authored his career. That he would pursue such a course – and in Florence, right under their noses – shows again Atto's willingness to gamble big on bettering his lot.

[76] Atto to Duke Carlo II of Mantua, from Florence, March 23, 1655. Already the previous year (in a letter to the duke of Mantua, from Florence, on January 5, 1654), Atto had broached the subject of becoming one of the duke's servants: "supponendomi … di potere un giorno godere l'honore di essere con più vivo carattere ascritto per suo actual Servitore." I have been unable to identify "Signor Garrachia."

Rome 1655

Not surprisingly, similar concerns about prestige dominate Atto's sojourn in Rome during the latter half of 1655. Since his first visit to that city a decade earlier, he had returned just once, accompanying Mattias and Leopoldo on a trip in April 1650 (see chapter 2). In 1655, however, Atto seems to have been called to serve the other Medici brother, Cardinal Giovan Carlo. Fabio Chigi had just been elected Pope Alexander VII on April 7, and, as the reigning Medici cardinal, Giovan Carlo wanted to impress the new pope with his power and taste. He also hoped to convince Alexander to restore to the duke of Parma some of the lands seized by Urban VIII after the War of Castro.[77]

According to his later account, Atto originally planned only a short stay in Rome.[78] After his arrival toward the end of April, his first letters back to Mattias mostly concern efforts to initiate (or revive) influential contacts and reestablish his musical reputation. In other words, he seems to have viewed the trip as a chance to broaden his search for patrons. In addition to lunching with Cardinals Giulio Rospigliosi and Girolamo Buonvisi, both of whom Atto had known from his youth, he exploited his eminence as a singer to meet many of Rome's *signori grandi*:

I have been to bow before many of these princes and cardinals who wanted to hear me, a thing I have done with extreme pleasure, having, by my good fortune, satisfied the tastes of all, or so at least they led me to believe. I have truly appreciated being in Rome at a time when many other *virtuosi* have converged here with their patrons, because, as this place represents the touchstone of merit and ability, the applause is had justly, and prejudices and criticisms remain in the head of the person alone who conceives them … If there are to be any occasions of principal feasts, I want to be heard in public also.[79]

As becomes clear in later correspondence, the phrase "in publico" refers less to a true public venue than to the upper-class congregations of certain churches. For the time being, though, these individual performances served Atto well: Buonvisi even suggested he pay his initial respects to the pope in song, "as when one sings to beg graces from God."[80]

After the initial greetings, however, Atto turned to the *conversazione* as the most frequent setting of his interactions with the elite of Rome. Like a

[77] On the Medici political hopes, Riguccio Galluzzi, *Istoria del Granducato di Toscana sotto il governo della Casa Medici* (Florence: Gaetano Cambiagi, 1781), VII:119–20. Weaver's suggestion (in "Florentine Comic Operas," 198) that Atto went primarily to perform in the celebrations for the arrival of Queen Christina of Sweden must be reconsidered, as shown below.

[78] Atto to Duke Carlo II of Mantua, from Rome, November 20, 1655.

[79] Atto to Mattias, from Rome, May 1, 1655.   [80] Ibid.

salon or soirée, such a gathering provided intellectual recreation for the socially elite and could include elegant discussions of literature, theology, and the arts; it was also frequently the site of chamber singing.[81] The following excerpt not only depicts something of this world, but also records Atto's evaluation of the state of singing and singers in Rome at this time:

I find myself daily in the most beautiful *conversazioni* with cardinals, prelates, and male and female singers, and I have the opportunity to hear the best gentlemen and ladies who sing, which can only serve to teach me something since each has some considerable qualities in his [or her] style. Rome, however, is doing very badly for male singers, with no one flourishing except Buonaventura [Argenti], who does not sing with great artifice but with naturalness and a truly very beautiful voice. The others are over the hill.

Among the women, there is a nun at [the convent of] Campo Marzo [Maria Alessandra Galvani] who is a supernatural miracle, since one could not desire qualities that she does not have. Of women who are in the city to sing, there is only a certain Angiola, called La Pollarola, who truly sings very well, having a very beautiful voice, a very tender way of singing, a trill, a good disposition, and the accents are not lost in her diction. I esteem this lady very much, and she is an honest woman; at least that is what Rome thinks of her and what she herself claims. I am persuaded of it because in the face she is quite ugly. There are many many other women who sing, and they are very beautiful, like certain ladies Cardinal [Virginio] Orsini has under his protection, but one would have more satisfaction hearing them in bed than in the chamber, which is as much as I can tell Your Highness about music.[82]

Atto's concluding comments make explicit the often implied association of female singers and courtesans. Indeed, Mattias had a reputation for "protecting" singers of this type, and Atto seems to have been on the lookout for

---

[81] For more on the *conversazione*, see chapter 6.

[82] Atto to Mattias, from Rome, May 10, 1655. The translation of *disposizione* is problematic: the word can also carry the sense of *arrangement* or *layout* and so might refer to the registration or evenness of the voice. In his treatise of 1723, however, Tosi too joins the words *voce* and *disposizione*, warning that potential singers should have "voce, e disposizione per cantare." This construction would suggest the sense of *personality* and *attitude* that I have implied here: *Opinioni de' cantori antichi e moderni o sieno Osservazioni sopra il canto figurato* (Bologna: Lelio dalla Volpe, 1723), 8.

In his *Historia della Sacra Real Maestà di Christina Alessandra Regina di Svetia, &c.* (Rome: Stamperia della Rev. Camera Apost., 1656), 291, Galeazzo Gualdo Priorato mentions the queen listening to Galvani's "angelica voce" during a visit to the convent at Campo Marzo. Presumably, Atto's nun is the same woman. He mentions her again in his letter to Mattias, from Rome, May 27, 1655: "Fa venire a Roma il serenissimo signor Cardinale [Giovan Carlo] quella fanciulla di Antonio Fanti che sta in S. Giorgio, e qui starà nell Convento di Campo Marzo dove è quella monaca che canta così divinamente et havrà occasione di apprendere molto." Unfortunately, I have not been able to identify "La Pollarola." Prunières (*L'opéra*, 177n) publishes a letter from Elpidio Benedetti to Mazarin on October 26, 1654 that seconds many of Atto's observations here.

candidates, as he admitted on November 13: "Your Highness should consider whether you want me to bring from here a few pretty Roman girls to dance the *ciaccona*."[83] The remark is a lascivious play on words, juxtaposing *romanesca* – both a popular bass formula and a Roman girl – with *ciaccona* – a dance with erotic overtones.[84] The passage suggests the sexual playfulness that could be a part of chamber singing, but it also confirms the place of music in the *conversazione*. And in this exclusive atmosphere, Atto could pursue his obsession with prestige.

His wish to perform in church was also soon satisfied. As he himself noted, music was heard by the greatest numbers of influential aristocrats during important services. On the Feast of S. Filippo Neri, May 26, he took advantage of his chance to "refresh the memory of these Romans as to my abilities" by singing a solo motet (unidentified) in the largely aristocratic church of S. Maria in Vallicella (the Chiesa Nuova). Though "all of Rome" was present, "not a breath was heard, which makes me think they were not dissatisfied with my singing."[85] Indeed, all through the month of May, Atto seems to have been content in Rome, basking in the honors he was receiving.

But at the end of the month, when he sought to depart, Giovan Carlo refused him leave: the cardinal wanted to employ Atto over the summer, in private entertainments as well as public outdoor performances of serenatas (large cantata-like works). Sponsoring such great events enhanced Giovan Carlo's own reputation, for, as Margaret Murata notes, "[the] munificence [of the nobles] in donating [to the public] the pleasures in which they themselves indulged, served in the end to exalt their position in Roman society."[86] In fact, the most usual spot for these concerts was also among the most politically charged: the Piazza di Spagna, which served as a buffer zone between the Spanish embassy and the French-controlled Chiesa della Trinità dei Monti.[87] (Atto, for his part, states that crowds gathered there

---

[83] Atto to Mattias, from Rome, November 13, 1655. On Mattias's reputation, see Bianconi and Walker, "Dalla *Finta pazza*," 440–41.

[84] On the implications of the ciaccona, Alexander Silbiger, "Chaconne," *Grove Music Online*, www.grovemusic.com (accessed October 11, 2004): "It was often condemned for its suggestive movements and mocking texts … and was said to have been invented by the devil … During the 1600s the chaconne rapidly became established as Spain's most popular dance, overshadowing its older (but equally 'immoral') rival, the *zarabanda*, with which it was often associated."

[85] Atto to Mattias, from Rome, May 27, 1655.

[86] Margaret Murata, "Il carnevale a Roma sotto Clemente IX Rospigliosi," *Rivista italiana di musicologia* 12 (1977): 97.

[87] See Arnaldo Morelli, "La musica a Roma nella seconda metà del Seicento attraverso l'archivio Cartari-Febei," in *La musica a Roma attraverso le fonti d'archivio*, ed. Bianca Maria Antolini, Arnaldo Morelli, and Vera Vita Spagnuolo, Strumenti della ricerca musicale, no. 2 (Lucca: Libreria Musicale Italiana in association with the Archivio di Stato di Roma and Società Italiana di Musicologia, 1994), 114.

simply to escape the summer heat in the relative coolness of the spot.[88]) In any case, the cardinal's political motivations may have been seconded by personal ones. A notorious womanizer, Giovan Carlo writes to Mattias, "I have been asked by a number of these ladies to retain [Atto] a little longer to have him sing this summer. With many of them here this evening, I answered that I decided to find out whether Your Highness would consent to his remaining here for the necessary period. So now I bring you their prayers, and I accompany them with my own, so as to serve these ladies."[89] Giovan Carlo may well have been planning to employ his charming singer in "serenades" of a rather intimate nature.[90]

But Atto had no interest in these duties, particularly the public *serenate*. Singing as part of a large group, before an undiscriminating and perhaps even common audience, offered no aggrandizement and would only have reinforced the image of a professional musician. Further, Atto had already made other, more profitable plans for his summer, as emerges from a later letter to the duke of Mantua:

> When I was about to take my leave of Cardinal Giovan Carlo, I was detained by His Highness, who desired my services in various *serenate* – in fact, quite lovely ones – that were performed this past summer. I knew of the journey to France that Your Highness wanted to make, and for this sole purpose I sought to hasten from here. Without your knowing anything about it, I wanted to appear before you suddenly, so as to be found worthy of admission to the company of others who have had the honor of serving you.[91]

In other words, Atto was hoping to continue to woo his best prospect for new patronage, the duke of Mantua, at the court where he had garnered the greatest prestige, Paris. Atto's situation in Rome – trapped in duties he considered beneath him and prevented from pursuing greater honors elsewhere – bitterly recalled his dilemma in Innsbruck.

---

[88] Atto to Mattias, from Rome, June 17, 1655.

[89] Giovan Carlo de' Medici to Mattias, from Rome, June 1, 1655. Atto reported the same comments by Giovan Carlo (in his letter to Mattias, from Rome, May 27, 1655): "Mi soggiunse ancora che erono state molte Dame e Prencipesse che gli havevano fatta questa istanza."

[90] On Giovan Carlo's reputation, see Harold Acton, *The Last Medici* (London: Faber and Faber, 1932), 45–49.

[91] Atto to Duke Carlo II of Mantua, from Rome, November 20, 1655. Indeed, Atto had been planning the trip to Paris at least since March 9, when he wrote of it to the duke of Mantua from Florence. The duke did in fact go to Paris, leaving Mantua on July 24 and returning on October 4. See Leonardo Mazzoldi, Renato Giusti, and Rinaldo Salvadori, eds., *Mantova: La storia*, vol. III, *Da Guglielmo III Duca alla fine della seconda guerra mondiale*, Mantova: La storia, le lettere, le arti (Mantua: Istituto Carlo D'Arco per la storia di Mantova, 1963), 182n.

Not surprisingly, he soon began intriguing to win his release, employing as before more than a little deception. As he often did, he complained about the weather, in this case, the approaching heat of summer, yet he could hardly have hoped to escape such temperatures back in Florence.[92] He professed his extreme devotion to Mattias, insisting that "four or five months of summer will seem to me a very long time to be away from Your Highness."[93] But of course Atto had remained contentedly in Paris for much longer and in fact felt little loyalty toward the Medici at this time. He begged to come defend himself against an imagined conspiracy of his enemies, but, while he certainly had rivals in Tuscany (as earlier letters reveal), this particular story lacks corroboration.[94] And he claimed to have assembled so much sensitive news that he dared report it only in person; but when in July he was finally ordered to remain in Rome, he suddenly forgot all his gossip and could think of nothing worthwhile to recount.[95] In the end, Atto was forced to stay in Rome and provide all the services requested of him: this time, dissimulation simply failed.

His tribulations only increased when later that summer he discovered Giovan Carlo's plan to retain him through the fall, to serve in the festivities for Queen Christina of Sweden. The queen had famously abdicated her throne and converted from her native Lutheranism to Catholicism. For several months she had been traveling south on a pilgrimage toward Rome, and Giovan Carlo had been named one of the two papal legates to welcome her. That position demanded a degree of magnificence and offered the chance to dazzle the prestigious guest, who was known to love music. On the surface, such an opportunity should have appealed to Atto, as it promised another illustrious contact.[96] But he soon learned that Giovan Carlo "wanted to have [the queen] hear his *virtuosi* in competition with these Roman ones."[97]

---

[92] Atto to Mattias, from Rome, May 10 and June 17, 1655. Either Atto was especially sensitive to extremes of temperature, or he used weather as a standard excuse, for such complaints appear regularly in his correspondence. He reveals a touch of humor in this regard in one of his letters from Regensburg, again asking for a speedy return home (to Mattias, August 11, 1653): "Sento però un grandissimo freddo non ostante che sia il tempo che si deve soffrire ogni maggior calore, e se hora vado ben vestito di Panno e Camiciole, bisogneria questo Inverno che tenessi un paro di materassi per riscaldarmi."

[93] Atto to Mattias, from Rome, May 27, 1655.   [94] Atto to Mattias, from Rome, June 19, 1655.

[95] On his dangerous news, Atto's letter to Mattias, from Rome, June 12, 1655. His change of attitude emerges from his letter to Mattias, from Rome, July 3, 1655: "tutto quello che sarà a mia notitia di Curioso lo parteciparò a V.A. se bene pochissime novità occorrano essendo tutta freddura e Malinconia la Città."

[96] Acton, *The Last Medici*, 45.   [97] Atto to Mattias, from Rome, October 23, 1655.

The prospect of being presented to the queen as some sort of contestant alarmed Atto. He quickly proposed instead that he return to Florence to perform for her by himself during her visit to that city:

If the queen of Sweden were not about to come to Florence, I more than anyone would beg Your Highness to let me sing for Her Majesty [here]. But as she is supposed to be coming there, it seems to me I might gain more by presenting myself to her apart from the others, and not in the commotion that will exist here.[98]

He also contended that the queen's arrival was expected to be much delayed and that her initial stay at the Vatican would further postpone entertainments.[99] Although Christina never did stop in Florence – and never seems to have planned to – by the end of October Atto's arguments finally convinced Mattias to let him come home. Yet before he could leave Giovan Carlo again intervened, arguing to Mattias the importance of the singer's services. Once more, Atto was frustrated and required to wait in Rome for his turn to perform.[100]

When he did finally sing for Christina, he was disappointed.[101] The following rather well-known passages reveal something of the character of the queen, the schedule of her entertainments, and Atto's (predictable) distaste for her brusqueness:

This queen is so impatient and voluble that I think my serving her one or two more times will suffice to convince [Giovan Carlo] to let me return to serve Your Highness [Mattias]. Two evenings each week, *accademie* of voices and instruments are performed before Her Majesty, but she cannot be there one moment without walking around, talking, or laughing, so the *virtuosi* are little satisfied with her, since they have nothing else to hope for. She behaves like that in everything she does, it sometimes being enough for her to hear the mass up to the Gospel.[102]

---

[98]   Atto to Mattias, from Rome, October 30, 1655.

[99]   Atto to Mattias, from Rome, October 26, 1655. In the event, Atto was right, for Christina's official reception in Rome did not occur until December 23: Giorgina Masson, *Queen Christina* (New York: Farrar, Straus and Giroux, 1968), 235.

[100] A letter from Giovan Carlo to Mattias, from Rome, October 30, 1655, mentions the situation: "In proposito d'Atto scrissi all'A. V. con la mia precedente, che sarebbe stato pronto ad ogni suo cenno [i.e., to return], ma le mettevo in considerazione, che alla metà di 9.bre, o poco più potrà esser qua la Regina di Svezia." This letter responds to a request from Mattias (from Siena, October 20, 1655) to send Atto back by All Saints' Day (November 1).

[101] The queen may first have heard Atto in Bracciano, shortly before her entrance to Rome. In his letter to Mattias, from Rome, November 13, 1655, Atto reports, "penso che S.A. [Giovan Carlo] habbi havuto a caro d'havermi per quella sera particolarmente che dovrà con S.M. stare a Bracciano." Indeed, the queen stayed in Bracciano just prior to making her entrance to Rome. See Gualdo Priorato, *Historia*, 225.

[102] Atto to Mattias, from Rome, January 8, 1656.

His duties fulfilled, Atto's departure was finally approved, and he sang for the queen one last time:

it being the last time, I had the fortune to find myself in so perfect a state of voice and mood that I enjoyed enormous applause. After I sang many Italian arias, Her Majesty had me sing in French and Spanish. Perhaps to hear her views, [Giovan Carlo] told Her Majesty that I would be leaving soon, and although she told him that everyone could hear he should not let me go, His Highness did not judge her interest more than ordinary.[103]

Accustomed to receiving the careful attention of the queen of France and the holy Roman emperor, Atto resented Christina's rudeness and indifference, even grumbling to Mattias about the "little attentiveness the queen has for all things."[104] Indeed, Atto's actions and attitudes throughout his eight-and-a-half months in Rome confirm his high social pretensions, higher than Christina was willing to recognize. One can be sure of his relief when on January 18, 1656 he at last left Giovan Carlo's service and headed for home.[105]

One final event epitomizes Atto's outlook on music and prestige at this stage of his life. After returning to Tuscany in January 1656, he remained at home for much of the year (leaving little documentation). But on October 15 he began another journey toward Paris, with intermediate stops at the north-Italian courts – Modena, Mantua, Parma – at which he maintained contacts.[106] Indeed, after a month-and-a-half he had only progressed as far as Moncalieri, the residence of the court of Savoy just outside Turin. He apologized to Mattias for his delay, noting that first he had been ill and then his singing had been so appreciated in Savoy that the ruling family had detained him.[107] This sort of attention still thrilled the thirty-year-old, whose report, as usual, reveals something about contemporary music-making:

I assure Your Highness that never in my life have I sung with so much pleasure, seeing the enjoyment that these princes take in it; they want to see the limit of my books, having me sing every evening for four hours or more. They made me promise to remain at their court all this winter, and the duke [Carlo Emanuele II] told me

---

[103] Atto to Mattias, from Rome, January 14, 1656.

[104] Ibid.: "haviamo [Giovan Carlo and Atto] discorso del poco applicamento, che ha questa Regina a tutte le cose."

[105] Ibid.: Atto mentions his planned departure date in this letter.

[106] Atto spent a little time at the courts of Modena, Mantua, and Parma, before continuing to Turin. See his letters to Mattias, from Florence, October 14, 1656; Parma, October 26, 1656; and Paris, January 11, 1657. For a discussion of the motivations behind this trip to Paris, see chapter 5.

[107] In the same letter quoted below (to Mattias, from Montcalier, November 30 [or 3], 1656), Atto reports that the doctors called the illness "bollittione di sangue" and bled him three times for it.

recently that, to see me perform in a *commedia*, he would quickly have to mount an *opera in musica*. Honestly, if in Paris they had not known I was already on the way, I would happily have stayed to serve His Royal Highness … He adores music, and every evening in his private apartment he likes two hours of it before dinner, having me then sing for two more hours after. Twice already I have tried to take my leave, and always I am begged to remain for two more days, so that my departure from this court will cause me infinite pain on account of the great loving kindness I receive here.[108]

In these years Atto still took great pleasure in performing, provided he was the sole focus of an admiring aristocratic audience. Only in such a configuration – where he seemed on familiar terms with the powerful – could he derive the prestige he sought. When he was asked to perform in public, to sing a secondary role, to appear as part of a group, or indeed to share the spotlight in any way with another singer, he tried to excuse himself. While still a professional musician, he strove to conduct his life by the rules of privilege that governed his superiors; indeed, he tried to affect the unlikely station of "gentleman castrato." Though he sometimes succeeded, he was often stymied and forced to pursue risky strategies of deception and manipulation. When these backfired or simply failed to work, his frustrations goaded him to risk even Mattias's protection in his search for greener pastures. Atto was indeed treading a difficult path. And its persistent obstacles seem to have affected his attitude over the next decade. For, while he continued to sing, he started to view musical performances as inherently undesirable, and he increasingly sought to interact with the nobility in more respectable, non-musical ways. As chapter 5 will show, Atto greeted the peak of his vocal career by looking to exit the musical profession altogether.

---

[108] Atto to Mattias, from Montcalier (Moncalieri), November 30 (or 3), 1656. The intriguing reference to Atto's "libri" is unfortunately never explained further in any of his letters.

4 ❧ The sexuality of the castrato*

In the spring of 1653, Atto wrote a series of remarkable letters to Carlo II, duke of Mantua. Atto had just passed through the Mantuan court on his way to Innsbruck (see chapter 3), and the stream of letters he addressed back to the duke differ strikingly in character from his earlier correspondence. The first of these, from May 25, surprises not by its subject matter – Atto complained to everyone he knew about his unhappiness in Innsbruck – but rather by its tone:

> the greatest consolation that I have in this place is thinking about the graces and favors that Your Highness was pleased to do me during my passage through Mantua … for I believe that God created you to captivate the souls of all the world, since I have not yet met a prince who compares to Your Highness in the least part, and most humbly I beg you to believe in this candor of mine, because I express it with all my heart … I pray to God that he inspire you to come here, because seeing and serving Your Highness personally would be the greatest fortune that I could have in this and any other place.[1]

In light of Atto's later more open pursuit of the duke's patronage, one might dismiss his style here as calculated rhetoric. But his manner, verging on ardor, is almost without parallel in his writings: his earlier letters to the duke are in fact quite formal, and nowhere in his extensive correspondence with Mattias de' Medici – by far his closest patron – does he express this kind of adulation.[2] Similarly, only at this time and with the duke does Atto adopt the seemingly familiar affectation of referring to himself in the third person, as

---

* The main argument, and much of the material, of this chapter appeared in my article "The Eroticism of Emasculation: Confronting the Baroque Body of the Castrato," *Journal of Musicology* 20 (2003): 196–249. The present treatment, quite naturally, focuses more on Atto's circumstances.

[1] Atto to Duke Carlo II of Mantua, from Innsbruck, May 25, 1653.

[2] After visiting the duke for the first time in the spring of 1651, Atto wrote the following, more conventionally worded solicitation of patronage to him, from Florence, June 12, 1651: "Li molti favori che io ricevei dall'humanità di V.A.S. nel tempo che io hebbi l'honore di servirla in Mantova, m'obligano a tener viva la mia humilissima osservanza verso di V.A., con desiderio perpetuo di vivere sotto la sua potentissima protetione, e di haver luogo fra i suoi più devoti et humili servitori; Suplico l'A.V.ra ricevere in grado questo riverente ossequio che io porgo alla sua grandezza, et honorarmi tal volta di qualche suo comando, perché io possa haver anche qualche merito appresso di V.A. col servirla come devo e desidero, mentre qui all'A.V.ra faccio profondissima Riverenza."

when he writes, "I hope … that you will always believe me to be that Atto who was only born into the world to live eternally … as the most devoted, humble, and indebted servant of Your Highness."[3]

Keen attention to the content of these letters confirms just how close the relationship had become between the twenty-seven-year-old castrato and twenty-three-year-old duke. On 8 June, Atto writes rather enigmatically, "I continue entertaining myself with these Italians here, and particularly with a gentleman, much my friend, called St. Boniface, who [does me] the same courtesy. I know that Your Highness knows him and that in the past you have been a devotee of this saint."[4] Atto follows this passage, curiously enough, with a report about a priest who sexually abused his male servant (to be considered below). The following week, Atto expands on his previous references but remains cryptic:

Here I pass the time in contemplation, meditating on that saint of whom you yourself were a devotee in the past, and I am incited to this devotion principally for that reason [that you were a devotee]. The greatest pleasure I have experienced in this country, however, has been for a short period of time having seen and held near me a certain little portrait … made by a painter who died in Mantua, of whom Your Highness has some memory. Truly it could not be more beautiful and elegant than it is, but it lacks all the grace and style that are possessed by the original and that are beyond all imitation.[5]

Fortunately for posterity, the duke did not understand Atto's veiled allusions, and so on July 21 Atto spelled out his meaning:

Now to return to that saint that Your Highness does not understand or does not remember, I will tell you clearly that he is a page of the archduke who did not displease you when Your Highness was in Innsbruck [winter 1651], and I received this information from a good source. The portrait was that of the duke of Mantua, my only Lord … and I affirm to Your Highness that I did not see anything in Innsbruck that gave me more pleasure than that portrait, having recognized, by comparison, that the portrait I carry engraved on my heart is more ardently sculpted.[6]

Taken together, the testimony here reveals that at different times both Atto and the duke of Mantua carried on a relationship – almost certainly sexual in nature – with the same young Italian nobleman in Innsbruck. But the style and context of the passages suggest somewhat more. Atto's language toward the duke goes well beyond normal flattery, evoking nothing so much

---

[3] Atto to Duke Carlo II of Mantua, from Florence, October 2, 1653.
[4] Atto to the duke of Mantua, from Innsbruck, June 8, 1653.
[5] Atto to the duke of Mantua, from Innsbruck, June 15, 1653.
[6] Atto to the duke of Mantua, from Regensburg ("Ratisbon"), July 21, 1653.

as contemporary lyric poetry: the lover in one of Atto's own cantatas, for example, tells his maiden, "Open my breast, O beautiful Phyllis, / for there you are sculpted by the hand of Cupid."[7] For Atto to direct this sort of amorous language at the duke, especially while revealing a shared sexual experience, strongly hints that Atto and the duke themselves carried on some sort of affair during Atto's visit in 1653.

Such an affair would certainly agree with the portrayal of Atto in a contemporary poetic satire. While accusations of homosexuality were a commonplace of vituperation, the anonymous poet's accuracy about other details of Atto's life gives one pause. Even the title of the poem shows familiarity: "On Atto Melani, Musician, Castrato of Pistoia, Son of a Bell-Ringer"; and later the author alludes to Atto's French sympathies, his conflict with his brother Jacopo, the property he purchased near Pistoia (see chapter 7), and perhaps even his role in Rossi's *Orfeo*. A couple of stanzas are enough to give the character of the poem, full of bawdy double entendre (which I have attempted to render in two translations):

So che fate mille mode	I know you wear a thousand fashions	I know you do it a thousand
nelle forme più eccellenti,	in the best styles,	ways with the best techniques,
e pur dicono le genti,	and yet people say	and yet people say
che attendete a cose sode:	you are looking for serious things:	you are looking for hard things:
et ogn'un che vi rimira	and everyone who sees you	and everyone who stares at you
per le strade andar tirato	being drawn through the streets	being stingy in the streets
sa ch'in camera serrato	knows that behind locked doors	knows that behind locked doors
v'inchinate, e sete humile	you bow and are humble.	you bend over and are humble.
Deh pensate [al campanile].	Oh think of the bell-tower.	Oh think of the bell-tower.
Ben si vede ne v'adulo	Obviously I'm not flattering you,	Obviously I'm not flattering
che seguendo il franco stile	because, to say it frankly,	you, because, after the French
la campana e il campanile	you have the bell and the bell-tower	dick, you have the bell and the
e il batocchio havete in culo:	and the clapper up your ass:	bell-tower and the clapper up
et ad onta della corda	and despite being threadbare,	your ass: in the face of
di cordelle un Milione	you crudely wear	torture/the dick you suffer
		the strappado/rough treatment
vi mettete a strapazzone	a million little ribbons	from a million little ropes/dicks
all'usanza signorile	in the noble manner.	in servicing the nobles.
Deh pensate [al campanile].[8]	Oh think of the bell-tower.	Oh think of the bell-tower.

---

[7] The passage comes from *S'io sapessi dipingere*: "Aprite, O bella Filli, il petto mio: / Ch'ivi per man' d'Amor scolpita sete!" See appendix F, as well as Atto Melani, *Complete Cantatas*, ed. Roger Freitas, Collegium Musicum: Yale University, ser. 2, vol. 15 (Middleton, Wis.: A-R Editions, 2006), xxxv–xxxvi.

[8] "Sopra Atto Melani, musico, castrato di Pistoia, figliolo d'un campanaio," I Fn, Cl.VII.359, pp. 758–59. For the full poem, see Appendix C. To render the various meanings of this text (and others that follow), I have drawn on Valter Boggione and Giovanni Casalegno, *Dizionario storico*

Portrait of a Castrato

Along with these suggestions of homosexual behavior, a number of scattered clues hint that Atto also enjoyed heterosexual relationships, or at least desire. In two of his letters (previously quoted), he reports with great satisfaction on his popularity among ladies at court, boasting at Regensburg, for example, that "all these ladies favor me [*queste dame sono tutte per me*]."[9] But the clearest evidence relates to the nieces of Cardinal Mazarin, specifically Hortense and Marie Mancini. The beautiful Hortense enjoyed the attentions of many suitors and eventually married the most ardent, the Marquis de la Meilleraye, who took the title of duke Mazarin on inheriting the cardinal's fortune. Hortense's sister Marie won the affections of young King Louis XIV himself; Louis only broke off their relationship when he was convinced of the need for a political marriage to the infanta of Spain. Mazarin promptly wedded Marie to the safely distant *contestabile* of Naples, Lorenzo Onofrio Colonna.

Hortense recounts Atto's infatuation in her memoirs. Although she never identifies him by name, her story so fits his circumstances – especially his difficulties in Paris in 1661 (discussed in chapter 5) – that no one else could be intended. The following excerpt reveals Atto's jealous reaction to Hortense's husband:

The eunuch, [Marie's] confidant, who was living without status because of her absence and because of the death of the cardinal, set out to make himself indispensable to me. But besides the fact that my disposition quite deterred me from all types of love-affairs [*intrigues*], M. Mazarin [Hortense's husband] had me watched too carefully. Enraged by this obstacle, [the eunuch] resolved to avenge himself on M. Mazarin. He had maintained quite free access to the king ever since he had been the confidant of my sister. He made great complaints to the king about the harshness with which M. Mazarin treated me; he said that he had been obliged to concern himself with this subject as a creature of the cardinal and my special servant; that M. Mazarin was jealous of everyone and above all of His Majesty and that [the duke] had me watched with extraordinary attention wherever the king (who was not even dreaming of me) might visit me; that moreover he was acting like a great minister, and that he had threatened to make all the Italians leave Paris. To all this the king answered only that if all [the eunuch] said was true, the duke Mazarin was mad.[10]

del lessico erotico italiano: Metafore, eufemismi, oscenità, doppi sensi, parole dotte e parole basse in otto secoli di letteratura italiana, Teadue, no. 762 (Milan: Tascabili degli Editori Associati, 1999).
[9] Atto to Mattias, from Regensburg, August 4, 1653. A similar comment comes in his letter to Mattias, from Rome, May 27, 1655.
[10] Hortense Mancini, *Les illustres aventurières ou Mémoires d'Hortense et de Marie Mancini*, ed. G. Doscot, Les hommes, les faits et les moeurs (Paris: Henri Jonquières, 1929), 45–46, originally published as *Mémoires de M. L. D. M. A.* (Cologne: Pierre de Marteau, 1676). My decision to translate "intrigues" as love-affairs is based not only on this common contemporary usage (see *Le Grand Robert de la Langue Française*, 2nd edn. [Paris: Le Robert, 1985], s.v. "intrigue"), but also on the sense of the passage (and the next one): from other accounts, it emerges that the highly

Elsewhere in her memoirs, Hortense states outright that Atto was attracted to her:

[Monsieur Mazarin] was not the only person I had the misfortune to please. An Italian eunuch, musician of Monsieur the Cardinal [Mazarin] [and] man of much talent, was accused of the same thing; but it is true that it was equally for my sisters and for me. He was likewise accused of being in love with the beautiful statues of the Palais Mazarin, and it surely must be that the love of this man brought misfortune, for those poor statues have been punished even more cruelly than I, although they were no more criminal.[11]

These last lines refer to the duke Mazarin's notorious destruction of Cardinal Mazarin's collection of sculpture and probably also hint at the futility Hortense saw in Atto's love. The duke, however, took seriously the threat to his wife's virtue and thus his own honor: citing the hazard, he even convinced Louis XIV to banish Atto from Paris, initiating the central crisis of Atto's career (again, see chapter 5).[12] Indeed, the fear of Atto's heterosexual desire was, from his own perspective, all too real.

Atto's interest in women is also treated by the author of the aforementioned satire. The following stanza plays on the name of a popular card game:

È di già publica fama	It's already common knowledge	It's already common knowledge
che il giocar non vi dispiaccia	that you don't mind playing,	that you don't mind gambling,
e de giochi sol vi piaccia	and of all the games, you only enjoy	and of all the games, you only enjoy
calabrache con la dama.	*calabrache* with a lady.	dropping your pants with a lady.
Meritate per tal brama	Since you do not defeat the lady	Since you do not master the lady
già che a Dama non vincete	and are the first to play,	and are the first to lose your erection
e a calar primiero sete	you deserve, for such greed,	you deserve, for that kind of passion,
nelle chiappe lo staffile.	the lash on your butt.	the dick in your butt.
Deh pensate [al campanile].[13]	Oh think of the bell-tower.	Oh think of the bell-tower.

jealous duke Mazarin had Hortense watched for precisely this reason (Bryan Bevan, *The Duchess Hortense: Cardinal Mazarin's Wanton Niece* [London: Rubicon Press, 1987], 25–26). Also, Hortense's protestation that she avoided love-affairs is risible, considering that soon after these incidents she fled her husband and passed the greater part of her life with various lovers.

[11] Hortense Mancini, *Les illustres aventurières*, 35. On the duke Mazarin's destructive spree with a sledgehammer, see Bevan, *The Duchess Hortense*, 28.

[12] See Atto to Hugues de Lionne, from Rome, August 8, 1661 (cited in Henry Prunières, *L'opéra italien en France avant Lulli*, Bibliothèque de l'Institut Français de Florence [Université de Grenoble], ser. 1, Collection d'histoire et de linquistique française et italienne comparées, no. 3 [Paris: Honoré Champion, 1913], 272), where he notes that "seulement l'injustice et le caprice de M.r Mazarrin m'aie a fair demeurer eloignés de mon Maistre [i.e., the king]." See also the discussion of this incident in chapter 5, and especially the quoted testimony of Nicolas Fouquet.

[13] Again, from I Fn, Cl.VII.359, p. 764.

Such lines hardly constitute sure evidence of sexual activity, and indeed proof of a relationship between Atto and any woman is finally lacking. Still, his attraction to some women seems to have been genuine, and many around him certainly considered it so.

Of course these observations raise many questions. What broader picture of castrato identity can be discerned from such bits of information? How should the evidence of Atto's sexual activities and interests be interpreted? And how would contemporaries, or even Atto himself, have understood the sexual life of a castrated man? Until very recently, these sorts of issues were not carefully investigated. Although the question of sex has always been linked to the figure of the castrato, "serious" scholars traditionally shunned the subject, leaving it to more popular, clichéd treatments. Even John Rosselli, who has otherwise provided the most detailed and sensible account of the castrato lifestyle, dismisses the issue in a few words: "Many [castrati] were said to have affairs, homosexual or heterosexual. We need not now rehearse most of these stories: their truth cannot be determined."[14]

More recently, though, attitudes have changed. As the study of historical sexuality has developed, and as scholars have accepted sex "as one of the major, if not the most important, forces, in shaping history," researchers have at last turned to the castrato.[15] Happily, Atto's case can contribute to such work. As the evidence above argues, he clearly participated in some sort of sexual activity: that is, Atto himself moves the question of sex to the foreground. And then, because so much is known about the rest of his life, Atto's sexual behavior appears in an unusually full context, influenced by and influencing other factors. Such an inquiry still requires some speculation, but today one can situate the evidence within an expanding picture of contemporary sexuality and so elevate that speculation to far more than guesswork. Indeed, I will argue here that the sexual side of Atto's life – and so by extrapolation the lives of his many colleagues – fit easily into the conception of sexuality common at that time. In other words, I propose that the castrato seemed to most people not some sort of monster, incomprehensible in his exoticism, but rather a familiar variant of a recognized and pervasive social type: the effeminate male. In the end, I hope, this perspective will shed light not only on Atto's life and the lives of other castrati, but also on the vast repertoire of music that they sang, a repertoire surely influenced by their character and social image.

---

[14] John Rosselli, "The Castrati as a Professional Group and a Social Phenomenon, 1550–1850," *Acta musicologica* 60 (1988): 176.

[15] The quote comes from Vern L. Bullough, *Sexual Variance in Society and History* (New York: John Wiley and Sons, 1976), vii. The important recent work is cited throughout this chapter.

The framework

A key to comprehending contemporary attitudes toward the castrato may be found in the perceptions of sexuality and the body that characterized the early modern period. For this background, I am indebted primarily to the work of Thomas Laqueur, whose groundbreaking research has traced the discontinuities in sexual attitudes between the early modern and post-Enlightenment periods.[16] He suggests that the most fundamental, and radically unfamiliar, element of the earlier viewpoint is its premise of a one-sex system. That is to say, instead of explaining male and female bodies as the two distinct forms of the human species, the early modern tradition considered man to be the more perfect manifestation of the single body that both men and women shared.[17] Key to this view was the widespread acceptance of the female genitalia as the precise inversion of the male: Stephen Greenblatt notes that "in the sixteenth and seventeenth centuries, physicians and laymen of sharply divergent schools agreed that male and female sexual organs were fully homologous."[18] The ovaries corresponded to the testicles, the uterus to the scrotum, the vagina to the penis. Sexually speaking, a woman had simply failed to develop fully: she was an inside-out, or rather, outside-in, man.[19]

The differences between the sexes lay not in the flesh, which was thought to be identical, but in the higher phenomenon of vital heat. This insensible but fundamental energy of life not only determined whether sexual organs would develop outside or inside the body, but also affected the humors and thus all aspects of one's health, character, and intelligence.[20] According to the Galenic two-seed model of conception, the level of this vital heat was established in the act of procreation. During intercourse, the hotter, thicker semen of the man was thought to combine with the cooler, thinner "ejaculate" of the woman to initiate a new life. The relative proportions of these two "seeds" determined the

---

[16] Thomas Laqueur, *Making Sex: Body and Gender from the Greeks to Freud* (Cambridge, Mass.: Harvard University Press, 1990).

[17] Laqueur examines this view in detail throughout the first four chapters of his book (ibid., 1–148), but the idea receives a clear statement at 124. Laqueur's emphasis on the "one-sex system" has been criticized as an oversimplification, a privileging of the Galenic/Hippocratic model of sex over a competing Aristotelian account: see, for example, Lorraine Datson and Katharine Park, "The Hermaphrodite and the Orders of Nature: Sexual Ambiguity in Early Modern France," in *Premodern Sexualities*, ed. Louise Fradenburg and Carla Freccero (New York: Routledge, 1996), 118–19. But even these authors suggest that the Galenic/Hippocratic view seems to have predominated from the second half of the sixteenth through at least the seventeenth centuries (121–22).

[18] Stephen Greenblatt, *Shakespearean Negotiations: The Circulation of Social Energy in Renaissance England*, The New Historicism: Studies in Cultural Poetics, vol. 4 (Berkeley: University of California Press, 1988), 79.

[19] Laqueur, *Making Sex*, 4 and 63–98.   [20] Ibid., 4.

vital heat in the embryo: if the heat were great enough, the genitals would develop "normally," outside the body; if it were less, they would remain "under-developed" and inside.[21] Thus, sexual organs themselves were not determinants of sex but rather one of many manifestations of a person's vital heat: in Laqueur's expression, "biology only record[ed] a higher truth."[22]

With respect to the castrato, the greatest significance of the one-sex model lies in its implication of a vertical, hierarchical continuum ranging from man down to woman. According to Laqueur, in the seventeenth century and before, woman was regarded as "a lesser version of man along a vertical axis of infinite gradations," while after the eighteenth century she was considered "an altogether different creature along a horizontal axis whose middle ground was largely empty."[23] Indeed, we continue to speak of the sexes as "opposite." But in the earlier period, difference in sex was more a quantitative than qualitative matter, and a well-populated middle ground between the usual sexes was broadly acknowledged: tales abounded, many treated by physicians as factual case studies, of weak men who began to lactate and strong women who suddenly grew a penis.[24]

Significantly, the most familiar inhabitant of this middle ground was the prepubescent child. Although in the womb differences in vital heat between male and female were considered great enough to determine genital formation, a man's full heat was not thought to develop until adolescence, when the bodies of boys and girls began to differentiate themselves.[25] Castrating a boy before puberty, then, did not throw his sex, in the modern sense, into question. It merely froze him within the middle ground of the sexual hierarchy: he never experienced the final burst of vital heat that would have taken him to full masculinity. Sexually speaking – and this is an essential point – the castrato would have been viewed as equivalent to the boy. In fact, he was an arrested boy: although his body would increase in size, his surgery ensured that his vital heat, and thus his physical characteristics, would remain at the less markedly masculine level of youth.

Lacking this heat, both castrati and young boys were described as *effeminate*, an important concept in this discussion.[26] Although the denotation of

---

[21] Ibid., 40; Greenblatt, *Shakespearean Negotiations*, 78; Wendy Heller, *Emblems of Eloquence: Opera and Women's Voices in Seventeenth-Century Venice* (Berkeley: University of California Press, 2003), 10.

[22] Laqueur, *Making Sex*, 16, 26.

[23] Ibid., 148. Datson and Park, "The Hermaphrodite," 122, use this continuum to explain the increased eroticization of the hermaphrodite from the middle of the sixteenth century.

[24] Laqueur, *Making Sex*, 106, 126–30.

[25] Greenblatt, *Shakespearean Negotiations*, 91; Laqueur, *Making Sex*, 101.

[26] For example, "Eunuchs … seeme to have degenerated into a womanish nature, by deficiency of heate; their smooth body and soft and shirle [i.e., shrill] voyce doe very much assimilate

the term seems to have changed little since the seventeenth century, its connotations today are quite different: whereas nowadays describing a man as "effeminate" might imply homosexual leanings, a womanish demeanor in the seventeenth century was considered rather a sign of too great a taste for *women*.[27] The 1612 dictionary of the Accademia della Crusca defines *femminacciolo*, for example, as "[a man who is] pretty in a feminine way, and who likes being among [women], effeminate."[28] Indeed, scholars such as Ann Jones and Peter Stallybrass have concluded – surprisingly to the modern sensibility – that in this period "it is 'heterosexuality' itself which is effeminating for men."[29]

To comprehend such an attitude, it helps to remember that before the Enlightenment an unbroken continuity was considered to exist between a person's physical and behavioral disposition: the vital heat and humors of one's body determined not only outward appearance (including genital sex and muscle tone) but also personality. Conversely, this vital heat could itself be affected, either by physical intervention – in the form of bleeding, medication, or indeed childhood castration – or by conduct, consorting with or behaving like people whose vital heat differed from one's own. This instability provoked real anxiety: a man who succumbed too much to the pleasures of the flesh, whose existence revolved too much around women, was considered in danger of losing his masculine nature and even physical strength.[30] By the same token, a man who presented a rather feminine

weomen." Ambroise Paré, *The Workes of Ambrose Parey*, trans. Thomas Johnson (London, 1634), 27, quoted in Ann Rosalind Jones and Peter Stallybrass, "Fetishizing Gender: Constructing the Hermaphrodite in Renaissance Europe," in *Body Guards: The Cultural Politics of Gender Ambiguity*, ed. Julia Epstein and Kristina Straub (New York: Routledge, 1991), 83.

[27] On the similarity of the denotation, the *Vocabolario degli Accademici della Crusca* (Venice: Giovanni Alberti, 1612), s.v. "effeminato," offers, "di costumi, modi, e animo femminile, dilicato [*sic*], morbido."

[28] Ibid., s.v. "femminacciolo." See also Laqueur, *Making Sex*, 123–24.

[29] Jones and Stallybrass, "Fetishizing Gender," 97.

[30] Peter Brown writes, "each man trembled forever on the brink of becoming 'womanish.' His flickering heat was an uncertain force. If it was to remain effective, its momentum had to be consciously maintained. It was never enough to be male: a man had to strive to remain 'virile.' He had to learn to exclude from his character and from the poise and temper of his body all telltale traces of 'softness' that might betray, in him, the half-formed state of a woman": *The Body and Society: Men, Women, and Sexual Renunciation in Early Christianity* (New York: Columbia University Press, 1988), 11, quoted in Jones and Stallybrass, "Fetishizing Gender," 86. And from the *Vocabolario*, s.v. "*femminacciolo*," one of the attestations offers confirmation of the connection between feminine behavior and an effeminate body: "Sapeva ben lo'ngegnoso huomo, che'l male dilettamento fa gli huomini femminaccioli, e assottiglia il corpo soggetto a carnalità." Of course, much work on this issue has been done in the field of English Renaissance theater; see, for example, Laura Levine, *Men in Women's Clothing: Anti-Theatricality and Effeminization, 1579–1642*, Cambridge Studies in Renaissance Literature and Culture, no. 5 (Cambridge: Cambridge University Press, 1994), *passim*, but neatly summarized at pp. 3–8.

demeanor – like the boy or castrato – was considered predisposed to the womanish pursuits of love.

Of course, any move toward feminine qualities carried broad social implications. In patriarchal *Seicento* society, many of the binary oppositions of life were joined to the vertical sexual axis, with the attributes deemed positive always gendered masculine.[31] Laqueur reports that contemporary scholars produced "an enormous literature that relate[d] the cold, wet humors said to dominate women's bodies to their social qualities – deceptiveness, changeability, instability – while the hot, dry humors in men supposedly account[ed] for their honor, bravery, muscle tone, and general hardness of body and spirit."[32] Women were especially condemned for having sexual appetites so voracious as to imperil the virtue of men; in Linda Austern's words, they "were associated by nature with sin, with the dark uncontrollable side of sensuality and with the loss of paradise."[33] Clusters of ideas such as masculinity-heat-virtue-perfection and, on the other hand, femininity-cold-depravity-imperfection were so firmly linked that *femininity* and *degeneracy* could function as synonyms.

Thus, the sexually overactive man who compromised his masculinity through too much sociability with women was at the same time, by diminishing his vital heat, compromising his virtue. Likewise, the male whose very appearance belied his more feminine humors – the prepubescent boy and castrato – was regarded as a highly sensual creature, wanting in the "masculine" virtues of restraint and abstinence. In Wendy Heller's useful formulation, effeminate men were simply those who had "exchange[d] Mars for Venus."[34]

Castrati were further feminized by their employment as musicians, for the practice of music itself was widely gendered female. Like women themselves, Austern notes, music "was often perceived by theoretical writers as a vain sensual delight and enemy to masculine rationality."[35] Signor Gaspar in Castiglione's *Il libro del cortegiano* warns men especially to avoid this art:

---

[31] As part of her argument about the gendering of the Monteverdi–Artusi debate, Suzanne G. Cusick produces a useful table that lays out some of these binary oppositions, demonstrating the links between femininity and a host of negative traits: "Gendering Modern Music: Thoughts on the Monteverdi–Artusi Controversy," *Journal of the American Musicological Society* 46 (1993): 4.

[32] Laqueur, *Making Sex*, 108.

[33] Linda Phyllis Austern, "'Alluring the Auditorie to Effiminacie': Music and the Idea of the Feminine in Early Modern England," *Music and Letters* 74 (1993): 346, where the author summarizes the ideas of such writers as John Knox and Joseph Swetnam. Austern's conclusions are supported by one of the attestations in the *Vocabolario*, s.v. "femmina": "Che altro è femmina, se non inchinevole amistà, fuggevole pena, necessario male, naturale tentazione, domestico pericolo, dilettevol dannaggio, natura di male dipinta di color di bene." See also Heller, *Emblems*, 32–33, 272–75 (among other places).

[34] Heller, *Emblems*, 239.   [35] Austern, "'Alluring,'" 347.

"I beleve musicke together with many other vanities is mete for women, &
paraventure for some also that have the lykeness of men, but not for them
that be men in deede: who ought not with such delicacies to womannishe
their minds."[36] Although Gaspar represents a minority view among the
interlocutors, his outlook indeed persisted: in a well-known satire on
music, the seventeenth-century painter, writer, and sometime music-lover
Salvator Rosa seconds Gaspar's position, again associating the art with
effeminate evils:

Non è virtù d' un Animo ò decoro	There is no virtue or honor for a soul
Trattar chitarre, cimbali, e leuti,	in playing guitars, cembalos, and lutes:
Nè diletto è da Re musico coro;	neither is a tuneful chorus a pleasure suitable for a king;
Ma ben d' Animi molli, e dissoluti	but rather for soft and dissolute souls,
Da persone lascive, e da impudichi,	for lascivious and lewd people,
Da spirti di piacer solo imbeuti.	for spirits imbued only with pleasure.
. . .	. . .
Sempre nel suo principio il Vizio è poco,	In its beginning, the vice [of listening to music] is always small,
Mà vi sovvenga che un incendio imenso	but remember that an immense conflagration
D' una breve favilla attrasse il fuoco.	draws its fire from a brief spark.
Creder non vuole effeminato il senso,	The effeminized mind does not want to believe
Che da questa malia cosi soave	that from this sickness, so sweet,
Possa poi derivarne un male immenso:	an immense evil can then spring.
Mà se disponga il canto à cose prave,	But the harsh end of proud Nero
Con maggiore evidenza à voi l' accenne	showed you with great clarity
Del superbo Neron l'esito grave.[37]	whether or not song inclines one to wicked things.

Some kinds of music were thought more effeminizing than others. The
worst, not surprisingly, was the music of love poetry: the madrigal and
monody. The rapidly shifting textures, dissonance, chromaticism, twisting
melodies, and elaborate ornamentation were regarded not only as imitative
of the wavering amorous mood, as Thomas Morley proposed, but also as
analogous to the deceptive, unstable character of woman herself.[38] The use of
the human voice in these genres heightened the effect, as the voice was

---

[36] Baldassare Castiglione, *The Courtyer of Count Baldessar Castilio*, trans. Thomas Hoby (London:
Wyllyam Seres, 1561), sig. 12r, quoted in Austern, "'Alluring,'" 350.

[37] Salvator Rosa, "La musica," in *Poesie e lettere edite e inedite di Salvator Rosa*, ed. G. A. Cesareo
(Naples: R. Accademia di Archeologia, Lettere e Belle Arti, 1892), I:177, 183, lines 415–20 and
598–606.

[38] Austern, "'Alluring,'" 352–53. The reference to Morley, cited here by Austern, comes from his *A
Plaine and Easie Introduction to Practicall Musicke* (London: P. Short, 1597), 172.

considered the most potently erotic instrument.[39] The puritan thinker Philip Stubbes states baldly the now tripartite nexus, woman-degeneracy-music, at which Rosa's satire already hinted:

> If you would have your sonne softe, womannishe, uncleane, smothe mouthed, affected to *baudrie, scurrilitie, filthy Rimes*, & unsemely talkying: briefly, if you would have hym, as it were transnatured into a Woman, or worse, and inclined to all kinde of Whoredom and abhomination, sett hym … to learne Musicke, and then shall you not faile your purpose.[40]

While Stubbes is an extremist, he articulates a mode of thinking then in wide circulation. And so, to many in the seventeenth century, a man whose very body marked him as a singer would have appeared acutely effeminized, surely of dubious morals and voluptuous lifestyle. The castrato physically embodied the dangers of vocalism: he was a man truly made for music.

Sex with men

The foregoing sketch of attitudes aids the interpretation of other more specific information about the sexual lives of castrati, including Atto's correspondence with the duke of Mantua. To organize the inquiry, I will defer for the moment the question of heterosexual activities and focus on the relationships between castrati and (other) men. Again, several questions arise. How might such relationships have been viewed at the time, by both the participants and their contemporaries? How were the reputations of the participants affected? And indeed, what role might such relationships have played in the general image of the castrato?

In the first place, it seems clear that sex between men – which, along with a number of other activities, went by the name of sodomy – took place fairly regularly in elite *Seicento* society. Certainly it was tolerated more than it had been in the past, especially in Italy. While all sexual acts *contra natura* remained illegal and punishable by death (a sentence that was still sometimes imposed), criminal records reveal an increasing reluctance to prosecute all but the most violent cases. Gabriele Martini attributes this change in attitude

---

[39] Winfried Schleiner, "Male Cross-Dressing and Transvestism in Renaissance Romances," *Sixteenth Century Journal* 19 (1988): 617–18; Heller, *Emblems*, 76.

[40] Philip Stubbes, *The Anatomy of Abuses* (London: Richard Iones, 1583), f. 110v, quoted in Austern, "Alluring," 350.

at least partially to the economic distress of the period, which "did not leave room for scapegoats of a moral character."[41] His study of Venice shows that by "the second half of the seventeenth century, sodomy was no longer considered a crime of public interest."[42] Likewise in Florence, the staunch persecution that had characterized the early decades of the century gave way under Grand Duke Ferdinando II (reg. 1621–70) to greater permissiveness.[43] Given that Ferdinando himself regularly participated in such activities, the change hardly surprises.[44] Although the eighteenth century was to see renewed prosecution, participation in consensual sodomy during Atto's lifetime seems to have involved less risk of scandal and disgrace than in other periods.[45]

This greater tolerance was especially true for the nobility and clergy, the classes among whom Atto, like most castrati, spent his career.[46] Traditionally, of course, the nobility had been less bound by moral standards than the rest of society, but other issues also seem to have been at work. In the first place, the educated classes learned about the homosexual practices of ancient Greece, a fact that at least one researcher feels strongly influenced contemporary predilections.[47] Further, these gentlemen would have absorbed the misogynistic view of gender relations described above: the negative taint of heterosexual sociability, with its damage to masculinity and virtue, seems to have affected sexual choices.

But perhaps the most important factor encouraging sodomy among the nobility and clergy was the principle of the indivisible inheritance, the tradition that led upper-class families to allow only their eldest sons to marry and father children (see chapter 1). For the majority of the highborn

---

[41] Gabriele Martini, *Il "vitio nefando" nella Venezia del Seicento: Aspetti sociali e repressione di giustizia*, Collana della Facoltà di Lettere e Filosofia dell'Università di Venezia *in San Sebastiano*, sezione di studi storici 2; Materiali e Ricerche, n.s., 4 (Rome: Jouvence, 1988), 91.

[42] Ibid., 90.

[43] Concerning the intolerance of early *Seicento* Florence, Luciano Marcello, "Società maschile e sodomia: Dal declino della 'polis' al principato," *Archivio storico italiano* 150 (1992): 134–35.

[44] Harold Acton, *The Last Medici* (London: Faber and Faber, 1932), 25–26. According to Acton, who appears to be depending on an anonymous "Vita di Ferdinando II, quinto Granduca di Toscana" (printed with two other works in an otherwise untitled book, ed. F. Orlando and G. Baccini, Bibliotechina Grassoccia, Capricci e curiosità letterarie inedite o rare, vol. 1 [Florence: Il "Giornale di Erudizione," 1886], I:5–36), Ferdinando II enjoyed the affections of a young page and protected known sodomites from the righteous wrath of his wife (10–13). (See also below.)

[45] On the renewed persecution of sodomites in the eighteenth century, see Randolph Trumbach, "Sex, Gender, and Sexual Identity in Modern Culture: Male Sodomy and Female Prostitution in Enlightenment London," *Journal of the History of Sexuality* 2 (1991): 186–203 *passim*; and Michael Rey, "Parisian Homosexuals Create a Lifestyle, 1700–1750: The Police Archives," trans. Robert A. Day and Robert Welch, in *'Tis Nature's Fault: Unauthorized Sexuality during the Enlightenment*, ed. Robert Purks Maccubbin (Cambridge: Cambridge University Press, 1985), 179–91 *passim*.

[46] Martini, *Il "vitio nefando"*, 110, 124, 131; Marcello, "Società," 135.   [47] Marcello, "Società," 120.

male population, sex tended to lose its traditional association with procreation: studies have shown that as these sons were increasingly denied the option of marriage – the only fully sanctioned outlet of sexual energy – unorthodox sexual practices proliferated.[48] In other words, the exigencies of dynastic ambition generated an extensive subculture of illicit sex. This subculture also turned up in ecclesiastical institutions, populated of course by many of the younger sons of noble families, men of little or no religious vocation.

Significantly, such activities carried a very different stigma than they do today. While sodomy was indeed considered sinful, it did not necessarily call one's masculinity into question. As is now well understood, seventeenth-century sodomites were not viewed as "homosexual": such an identity – not to mention the term itself – did not yet exist.[49] Instead, a broad repertoire of sexual acts was open to any sexual actor. Randolph Trumbach notes that, "before 1700, in London and at court, wild rakes such as Lord Rochester had had wives, mistresses, and boys."[50] Even the term *bisexuality* is inappropriate, as it suggests an anachronistic demarcation between male and female: in Greenblatt's words, "one consequence of the [one-sex] conceptual scheme … is an apparent homoeroticism in all sexuality."[51] Men who practiced sodomy were thus no different, no more effeminate, in their basic identities than those effeminate hedonists who demonstrated large appetites for sex in general; indeed, as I shall suggest below, some men considered their masculinity less threatened by homosexual than by heterosexual sex.

Interestingly, Duke Carlo II of Mantua himself provides an example of such catholic profligacy. As Gregorio Leti reports in his *Amori di Carlo Gonzaga, duca di Mantova*, Carlo carried on a nearly life-long affair with the Countess Margarita della Rovere, a relationship undisturbed by the duke's official marriage to Isabella Clara of Innsbruck.[52] Leti is generally sympathetic to his subject and even claims that the duke was entirely faithful to his mistress over the course of their long relationship, "quite contrary to the custom of other Princes, who delight in change."[53] But while never even

---

[48] Martini, *Il "vitio nefando"*, 99–100; Marcello, "Società," 121.

[49] See, among many other sources, Leonard Barkan, *Transuming Passion: Ganymede and the Erotics of Humanism* (Stanford: Stanford University Press, 1991), 22; and Pierre Hurteau, "Catholic Moral Discourse on Male Sodomy and Masturbation in the Seventeenth and Eighteenth Centuries," *Journal of the History of Sexuality* 4 (1993): 13.

[50] Trumbach, "Sex," 189.   [51] Greenblatt, *Shakespearean Negotiations*, 92.

[52] Gregorio Leti, *The Loves of Charles, Duke of Mantua, and of Margaret, Countess of Rovera* (Savoy: Henry Herringman, 1669), originally published as Giulio Capocoda [Gregorio Leti], *L'amore di Carlo Gonzaga, duca di Mantova, e della Contessa Margarita della Rovere* (Ragusa [Geneva]: Fabio Fabi, 1666).

[53] Ibid., 67.

hinting at homosexual behavior, Leti several times labels the duke "effeminate." He tells of one civic senator, for example, who worried that, given the duke's indulgent mother and upbringing among ladies, "the State would have but an Effeminate Prince, in which, [the senator] proved no false Prophet."[54] One of Leti's regular themes, in fact, is that the countess della Rovere's amorous ascendancy, which began in Carlo's childhood, weakened the duke's masculinity: Leti recounts that Carlo "lived in such a manner [with Margarita] that the world were almost perswaded that there had pass'd some Clandestine Marriage between them, which was the Cause of no small displeasure amongst the people who were very much afflicted to see their Prince so effeminated."[55] Margarita's potency was perhaps most keenly embodied in one *Fidelio*-like episode Leti describes: as Carlo was about to lead Spanish troops into battle, he fell ill with a fever, but Margarita, dressed as a man, rushed to his aid at the front.[56] Again, it is the duke's subordination to his mistress rather than any homosexual encounter that prompts Leti to call him effeminate.

The duke's masculinity was actually more compromised in this way than Leti knew or was prepared to reveal.[57] Scholars agree that Carlo's "immoderate lusts" and "many infidelities" were extensive: "frivolous, unbridled man of pleasure, impenitent spendthrift, Carlo II had ... given back to his court and to the city itself that luxurious way of life, that depravity, that quality of perpetual carnival that had led to the ruin of his predecessors."[58] Further, the duke seems to have participated personally in the most tainted kinds of music-making. Paola Besutti and Beth Glixon have demonstrated that, when Carlo instructed several of his courtiers to find him the best new chamber cantatas, he intended them for his own high baritone voice.[59] One of Atto's letters to the duke corroborates the point: "[the archduchess of

---

[54] Ibid., 3.

[55] Ibid., 134. The theme of the duke's weakness for Margarita is pursued throughout the book.

[56] Ibid., 151–64; concerning similar opera plots, see Heller, *Emblems*, 17–18.

[57] Toward the end of his book, Leti states openly his main theme: when Carlo II died, he was much mourned by his people, "and with reason, for set aside his Sin, which after all that can be said, proceeded from the weakness of human nature, he had all the Vertues; or to say better, in a word, he had all the qualities necessary to make a great Prince, and a great Monarch" (*The Loves*, 196). Leti's goal seems to have been to recuperate the duke's reputation, and so he only reveals the most public and undeniable indiscretions.

[58] Romolo Quazza, *Mantova attraverso i secoli* (Mantua: Tipografia editoriale de "La voce di Mantova," 1933), 218. On Carlo's lusts and infidelities, Selwyn Brinton, *The Gonzaga – Lords of Mantua* (London: Methuen and Co., 1927), 243; Quazza, *Mantova*, 218.

[59] Paola Besutti, "Produzione e trasmissione di cantate romane nel mezzo del Seicento," in *La musica a Roma attraverso le fonti d'archivio*, ed. Bianca Maria Antolini, Arnaldo Morelli, and Vera Vita Spagnuolo, Strumenti della ricerca musicale, no. 2 (Lucca: Libreria Musicale Italiana in association with the Archivio di Stato di Roma and Società Italiana di Musicologia, 1994), 139. Beth L. Glixon, "New Light on the Life and Career of Barbara Strozzi," *Musical Quarterly* 81 (1997): 323–24.

Innsbruck] asked me how Your Highness's singing had improved, and I answered her that I had found you at a level capable of performing a concert with Her Highness."[60] Besutti further believes that some of the duke's performances took place onstage, in "public."[61] Such vocal exhibitions by a male sovereign appear to have been unique to this court and surely reinforced the duke's effeminate image.

As this case suggests, it was the loss of self-mastery to a passion for women or "womanish" activities that threatened masculinity. Under this logic, sexual relations with another man incurred less risk, provided, importantly, that one always took the active role. Like so many other social exchanges, sexual acts carried hierarchical implications: active and passive roles were supposed to be fixed so that sexual and social domination corresponded.[62] The active participant needed to rank higher on the axis of masculinity than his passive partner, whatever that partner's genital sex.

This kind of thinking surely helps explain contemporary attitudes toward the most familiar member of the sexual "middle ground," the pubescent boy. As suggested above, seventeenth-century literature, art, and records of everyday life – nearly all produced by men – repeatedly characterize the boy as an object of desire, and it was his physical effeminacy that made him so. Exploring this abundant evidence can shed light on the perceptions of other, rarer, "middle-ground" creatures, like the castrato.

Winfried Schleiner observes that, in general, authors of Renaissance romances "had a predilection for very young heroes."[63] The central character of the paradigmatic *Amadis de Gaule*, for example, is described by his companion as "so young that you don't yet have any facial hair and have an appearance that will let you be taken for a beautiful girl."[64] Later, other male characters make the same observation about each other: "We are both of us still without hair on our chin."[65] Yet the very youth of these characters

---

[60] Atto to the duke of Mantua, from Innsbruck, May 25, 1653. It is unclear whether the archduchess sang or played an accompanying instrument. Atto again refers to the duke's singing in his letter to Orazio Canossa, from Paris, June 25, 1659: "Servirò l'A.S. di qualche Aria nuova, e per le voci che sono nella portata della memoria che V.E. mi ha inviata."

[61] Giuseppe Cattaneo to Francesco Tinti, from Rome, March 8, 1656, quoted in Besutti, "Produzione," 146.

[62] Barkan, *Transuming Passion*, 23.   [63] Schleiner, "Male Cross-Dressing," 618.

[64] Nicolas de Herberay, *Le huitiesme livre d'Amadis de Gaule* (Lyon: Benoist Rigaud, 1575), 525, quoted and translated in Schleiner, "Male Cross-Dressing," 608. The first known version of *Amadís de Gaula* is by Garci Ordóñez de Montalvo in 1508, but evidence suggests the material was in circulation from the late thirteenth or early fourteenth century. This romance became particularly popular in the sixteenth century, especially in France, where it served as a model for deportment and writing style and was expanded and continued by other writers.

[65] *11ᵉ livre d'Amadis de Gaule* (Lyon, 1577), fol. 62r, quoted and translated in Schleiner, "Male Cross-Dressing," 608.

seems the source of their desirability. In one instance the valiant young knight Oronce removes his armor before a duchess. The duchess had expected someone "robust and strong, because of the high degree of valor; when she saw such a delicate, rosy, and beautiful face, she was overcome not only by much wonder but also by a wonderful pleasure: and as she felt the pleasure, she fell in love as if she had never seen or hoped to see such a handsome and graceful knight."[66]

Similarly, in the first canto of Giambattista Marino's influential epic *L'Adone* (1623), the hero is described in revealing terms:

Era Adon ne l'età che la facella	Adonis was then at the age that feels
Sente d'Amor più vigorosa e viva,	the spark of love most vigorous and keen,
Ed avea dispostezza a la novella	and he was disposed to face
Acerbità de gli anni intempestiva.	the new bitterness, ill-timed to his years.
Nè su le rose de la guancia bella	Nor on the roses of his lovely cheeks
Alcun germoglio ancor d'oro fioriva;	had yet blossomed any bud of gold;
O, se pur vi spuntava ombra di pelo,	or if any shadow of hair had begun to show,
Era qual fiore in prato o stella in cielo.	it seemed like a flower in the field or star in heaven.
In bionde anella di fin or lucente	In blond ringlets of pure shining gold
Tutto si torce e si rincrespa il crine;	his hair writhed and curled,
De l'ampia fronte in maestà ridente	under which there flowed the white line
Sotto gli sorge il candido confine.	of his ample forehead in smiling majesty.
Un dolce minio, un dolce foco ardente	A sweet vermilion, a sweet burning flame,
Sparso tra vivo latte e vive brine	mingled with living milk and living frosts,
Gli tinge il viso in quel rossor, che suole	tinged his face with such a blush as
Prender la rosa infra l'aurora e 'l sole.	roses take on between dawn and daytime.
Ma chi ritrar de l'uno e l'altro ciglio	But who can paint the two stars, clear and bright,
Può le due stelle lucide serene?	of his twin brows?
Chi de le dolci labra il bel vermiglio	Who can portray the lovely scarlet of his sweet lips,
Che di vivi tesor son ricche e piene?	rich and full of fiery treasure?
O qual candor d'avorio, o qual di giglio	What whiteness of ivory or lily
La gola pareggiar ch'erge e sostiene,	can equal his throat, which raises and sustains,
Quasi colonna adamantina, accolto	like a column of adamant,
Un ciel di meraviglie in quel bel volto?	a heaven of marvels assembled in that lovely countenance?[67]

---

[66] *Le vingtiesme livre d'Amadis de Gaule*, fol. 192v, quoted and translated (without publication information) in Winfried Schleiner, "Cross-Dressing, Gender Errors, and Sexual Taboos in Renaissance Literature," in *Gender Reversals and Gender Cultures: Anthropological and Historical Perspectives*, ed. Sabrina Petra Ramet (London: Routledge, 1996), 99. Oronce is elsewhere described as "si jeune et sans poil de barbe."

[67] Canto 1, stanzas 41–43. Translation adapted from Giambattista Marino, *Adonis: Selections from L'Adone of Giambattista Marino*, trans. and intro. Harold Martin Priest (Ithaca, N.Y.: Cornell University Press, 1967), 11–12.

Far from the virile specimen the name Adonis might today invoke, Marino's paragon of male beauty stands just at the threshold of puberty, with the first hints of down on his face. The account of his long golden hair, white skin, blushing cheeks, ruby lips, clear eyes, and ivory neck could just as easily have described a woman; but here, such traits portray a boy at the age "when the spark of love feels most vigorous and ardent." In England, Shakespeare represented his own Adonis – here in Venus's words – as similarly youthful and feminine:

"Thrice fairer than myself," she thus began,
"The field's chief flower, sweet above compare;
Stain to all nymphs, more lovely than a man,
More white and red than doves or roses are:
Nature that made thee with herself at strife,
Saith that the world hath ending with thy life."[68]

Of course, representations of Adonis and his youthful brethren populate not only the field of literature but also the visual arts. Annibale Carracci's *Venus and Adonis* (1588–89), for example, shows a young hunter who seems almost the incarnation of Marino's hero, with his long golden hair, white body, and beardless, feminine face. (See plate 5.) Guercino's representation of this figure (1646), though at the point of death, is likewise boyish in appearance. Similarly, the Christian knight of Domenichino's *Rinaldo and Armida* (*c.* 1620–21) could almost be mistaken for the enchantress's handmaiden instead of her lover. (See plate 6.) Luca Giordano's *Diana and Endimion* of the late 1670s and Giovanni Battista Tiepolo's *Rinaldo Leaving Armida* of *c.* 1756–57 confirm the persistence of this boyishly effeminate ideal.

The connection of youth with love-making is promulgated most explicitly in a ceiling fresco in the Palazzo Pitti by Pietro da Cortona. (See plate 7.) Crowning the Sala di Venere, Cortona's work (1641–42) depicts Minerva carrying off a youth from the sumptuous couch of a dismayed Venus and Cupid and transporting him to the waiting arms of Hercules and Anteros (the other winged boy, holding the wreath). Venus and Cupid, of course, represent the world of sensuality and love, while Hercules stands for masculine strength, and Anteros, Cupid's virtuous counterpart, for moral or divine love. Bearing the inscription "Pallas tears the adolescent away from Venus," the message of the image is clear: when a boy passes through puberty – that is, when he becomes fully male – he should leave behind the pleasures of the

---

[68] William Shakespeare, *Venus and Adonis*, in *The Poems*, ed. F. T. Prince, 3rd edn., The Arden Edition of the Works of William Shakespeare (London: Methuen & Co.; Cambridge, Mass.: Harvard University Press, 1960), lines 7–12.

Plate 5 *Venus and Adonis* (Annibale Carracci, 1588–89; Museo del Prado, Madrid, Spain). *Reproduced by permission of Erich Lessing / Art Resource, NY.*

Plate 6 *Rinaldo and Armida* (Domenichino, ca. 1620–21; Musée du Louvre, Paris, France). *Reproduced by permission of Erich Lessing / Art Resource, NY.*

Plate 7 *Pallade strappa l'Adolescenza dalle braccia di Venere* (Pietro da Cortona, 1641–42; Palazzo Pitti, Florence, Italy). *Reproduced by permission of Alinari / Art Resource, NY.*

flesh and strive after heroic deeds and manly virtues.[69] As Malcolm Campbell points out, this painting serves as the key to the remaining frescoes in the room, which – for the benefit of maturing Medici princes – all depict ancient (adult) heroes resisting the temptations of love.[70] By implication, however, the ceiling fresco also suggests that pre-adult males may appropriately give themselves over to Venusian pleasures. One is not surprised, then, to discover that the youth here closely resembles so many of the Adonises and Rinaldos of other works: he is only just past the age of love.

Of course, the boyish lover idealized in literature and art was also the object of much real-life desire, and an important locus of that eroticization was pederasty. Most researchers agree that pederasty was practiced more or less widely throughout the early modern period and that indeed most male homosexual behavior adhered to this model.[71] Michael Rocke's comprehensive study of homosexual practices in late fifteenth-century Florence, based on the records of the Office of the Night, confirms the norm: "The 'active'

[69] The Latin inscription reads "ADOLESCENTIAM PALLAS A VENERE AVELLIT," as reported in Malcolm Campbell, *Pietro da Cortona at the Pitti Palace: A Study of the Planetary Rooms and Related Projects*, Princeton Monographs in Art and Archaeology, no. 41 (Princeton: Princeton University Press, 1977), 93.

[70] The preceding discussion of the fresco is based on Campbell, *Pietro da Cortona*, 92–93, 99.

[71] Criminal records of the period abound with reports of such transgressions, still a capital offense. See Marcello, "Società," 115–38; and Martini, *Il "vitio nefando"*, passim.

partner was usually an adult over the age of eighteen, while his companion was normally an adolescent."[72] Luciano Marcello further suggests that "the pederastic type of relationship was widespread and almost rooted in social custom … it represented a phase of life entirely within [normal] customs and the masculine sexual life."[73] Marcello notes that, when adolescents themselves reached adulthood, they normally changed roles: in Florence, gangs of maturing boys would seek out younger ones to sodomize as a kind of rite of passage, marking arrival at full masculinity.[74]

The pederastic model is perhaps most clearly expressed, indeed championed, in the writings of Antonio Rocco, a lecturer in philosophy at San Giorgio Maggiore in Venice and, importantly, a member of the Accademia degli Incogniti.[75] As Heller has shown in her ground-breaking work, the Incogniti emerged as one of the most prominent fora for the discourse on sex and gender in the first half of the seventeenth century; many of the members also, of course, played a crucial role in the evolution of opera.[76] The group had inherited a libertine ethic from its ideological mentor, Cesare Cremonini, longtime professor of Aristotelian philosophy at the University of Padua.[77] Taking a radical (and dangerous) position, Cremonini viewed nature, rather than God, as supreme; he thus denied the immortality of the soul and saw the Church as a political institution. Extending this reasoning, he logically concluded that no desire born of human nature could be contrary to nature, and thus the moral stain attaching to consensual sodomy was erased.

Rocco's *L'Alcibiade fanciullo a scola* (published no later than 1651) fully exploits Cremonini's ideas in its dialogue between a Greek tutor, Filotimo, and his young student, Alcibiade. Throughout the work Filotimo warns of the contaminating nature of sex with women and argues the naturalness and indeed superiority of pederasty. He characterizes sex with women as "most

[72] Michael Rocke, *Forbidden Friendships: Homosexuality and Male Culture in Renaissance Florence*, Studies in the History of Sexuality (New York: Oxford University Press, 1996), 94–95. The norm of the pederastic model is established generally throughout his third chapter, 87–111.

[73] Marcello, "Società," 119.

[74] Ibid., 122–24. Pederastic practices seem to have been a constant to the end of the early modern period. At the conclusion of his study, Rocke observes that, notwithstanding harsher sodomy laws instituted in 1542, the extent of pederasty seems to have remained little changed well into the seventeenth century; indeed, the 1542 laws were rarely enforced after their first decade (*Forbidden Friendships*, 234–35).

[75] On Rocco's position, and the publication date of the treatise, see Laura Coci, introduction to *L'Alcibiade fanciullo a scola*, by Antonio Rocco, ed. Laura Coci, 2nd edn., Faville, no. 22 (Rome: Salerno, 2003), 24–29.

[76] Heller, *Emblems*, 48–81 *passim*; Martini, *Il "vitio nefando"*, 106. On the Incogniti, Ellen Rosand, *Opera in Seventeenth-Century Venice: The Creation of a Genre*, A Centennial Book (Berkeley: University of California Press, 1991), especially 37–40.

[77] On the libertinism of the Incogniti and their debt to Cremonini in this regard, Martini, *Il "vitio nefando"*, 104–6; Coci, introduction, 28; and Heller, *Emblems*, 50–52.

bitter because of the fiery and poisonous excretions of her menses," the reason that "whoremongers are always unwell and detestable." To this he contrasts the axiom of a "famous doctor" that "the [sexual] use and embrace of the boy, when well moderated, is a healthful medicine."[78] In Heller's assessment of Rocco's central point, "Alcibiade's perfection consists in his possession of female beauty in a male body. Boys are thus the ideal objects for male love because they are superior to women both spiritually and physically. And the particular pleasure of boys is that they offer the possibility of enjoying feminine beauty without the necessity of congress with a woman."[79] A boy partook of enough of the feminine to be attractive to a man, but not so much as to contaminate him: the boy was socially and physically subordinate, but he also was male, and so less threatening to another man's masculinity. While Rocco's talk of feminine "contamination" may also relate to fears of venereal disease (from which boys probably represented a safer refuge), his arguments clearly participate in the widespread identification of the boy as an erotic object for men.

An incident that Atto reports in one of his later letters further illustrates this attitude. Writing to the Tuscan secretary Carlo Antonio Gondi on June 12, 1682, Atto tells of a scandal at the French court when Louis XIV discovered the homosexual activities of a large number of his nobles, leading him to expel many of them.[80] Atto's account, remarkable in its candor, includes his own assessment of such behavior:

Your Most Illustrious Lordship already knows that the subject of all conversations in Paris is a report that brought amazement and scandal concerning the behavior of some ecclesiastics with those lacking facial hair [*gente di poco pelo*]; and you know that the ladies here, no longer being courted, had to make the first move with those gentlemen who are devotees of gallantry. This gallantry had been so instilled in the young duke [*recte* count] de Vermandois [age 13] that he had become the most

[78] Antonio Rocco, *L'Alcibiade fanciullo a scola*, ed. and intro. Laura Coci, 2nd edn., Faville, no. 22 (Rome: Salerno, 2003), 82 and 84.

[79] Heller, *Emblems*, 75.

[80] This scandal is sometimes referred to as the "Confraternity of Sodomites." A sizeable group of aristocrats gathered secretly and established a sort of club, complete with charter, dedicated to homosexual sex. Members had to pledge not to have sex with women – including their wives – unless absolutely necessary, and the main goal of the group seems to have been to attract young men to be the passive objects of the older (for which a strict hierarchy of precedence was established). For further information, see Jeffrey Merrick and Bryant T. Ragan, Jr., eds., *Homosexuality in Early Modern France: A Documentary Collection* (New York and Oxford: Oxford University Press, 2001), 118–24; and Lewis C. Seifert, "Masculinity and Satires of 'Sodomites' in France, 1660–1715," *Journal of Homosexuality* 41 (2001): 40–45. Atto's reference to "ecclesiastics" does not jibe with what is known of the "confraternity," which was aristocratic; he may have been misinformed or referring to a different scandal. In any case, Atto's letter would seem to add to what is known about this affair.

lascivious of them all; so many things are said of him that they can hardly be believed. Recently, it seems [these gentlemen] were at a soiree at the house of the duke de Gramont [age 42] in Versailles, and they invited a most beautiful page of the prince de la Roche-sur-Yon [age 18] to attend, dressed as a lady. After dinner, all these youths went into a room, [and] evidently the marquis de Créquy [age 21] got to know that page, while the prince de la Roche-sur-Yon did the same thing upon the most tender buttocks of the young duke [i.e., count de Vermandois], in the presence of the entire company. They say there were others who wanted to taste the fruit but they were prevented from it by the duke de Vendôme [age 29]. The upshot is this: since these young princes and great gentlemen of court are entirely prey to lasciviousness and licentiousness, the king has been forced to dismiss them all, up to forty in number, so that now one only finds old fogies at court … The scandal is far worse than the evil itself, for after all it's not a new thing for youth to take this license, but what is more objectionable is that persons of quality, like the duke de Gramont, the chevalier de Tilladet, Monsieur Langlois [spelling unclear], and others of this rank gave the impetus and spirit to the youth[s] instead of deterring them with their protests and warning of the potential scandal.[81]

Atto essentially excuses the younger men here with the argument "boys will be boys," revealing his view of youth as erotically charged. And though Atto may in this case condemn the mature men for their involvement, his report in fact confirms the pederastic model.

At the same time, Atto's letter suggests some of the difficulties that could face men who sought sex with boys. In the first place, such boys, particularly unwilling ones, could be dangerously indiscreet. Because the courts usually considered boys blameless in sodomy cases, youths could make accusations with impunity. The historian Luciano Marcello tells of a shopkeeper in Florence who in 1625 sodomized one of his young apprentices. When the boy told his mother, she took the matter to court, more to protect the honor of her family – and thereby the marriage prospects of her eldest daughter – than to defend her son. The shopkeeper was eventually sentenced to death.[82] The French scandal Atto describes led mostly to banishments rather than

---

[81] Atto to Carlo Antonio Gondi, from Paris, June 12, 1682. In the remainder of the letter, Atto tells how this group tried to involve the dauphin, much to the anger of Louis XIV. Toward the end of the report, Atto wryly observes, "Infine non avranno più occasionne di rimpoverare ai Toscani questo Vizio, dopo quello che si vede qui." The figures mentioned in the cited passage are Louis de Bourbon, count de Vermandois (1669–83; illegitimate son of Louis XIV and Louise de la Vallière); Antoine Charles IV, third duke de Gramont (1641–1720); François Louis de Bourbon, prince de la Roche-sur-Yon (1664–1709); François-Joseph de Blanchefort, marquis de Créquy (1662–1702); Louis Joseph, duke de Vendôme (1654–1712); and Gabriel de Cassagnet, chevalier de Tilladet (d. 1690). I have been unable to learn more about Langlois, if that indeed is the correct spelling of the name.

[82] Marcello, "Società," 129–31.

executions: the nobility always enjoyed greater protection.[83] But even in the relatively permissive world of the aristocrats, pederasty could not be publicly revealed without risk.

In addition, procuring a partner could be difficult. Many boys were understandably unwilling to participate, and in frustration some men turned to violence. These violent cases, however, were precisely those that the courts were unwilling to overlook. Marcello reports one such example in which a priest was prosecuted for sodomy because he had repeatedly beaten a student to force him to submit.[84] A strikingly parallel case again emerges in Atto's own correspondence. On June 2, 1653, Atto writes the duke of Mantua from Innsbruck,

> Yesterday morning there arrived here that priest who fixes the harpsichords, and he presented the letter of Your Highness to the archduke, who immediately ordered quarters for him and everything necessary … He brought with him a very good-looking page because, having heard it said that here he did not have to behave as he did in other places, he wanted the opportunity nearby, without having to seek it elsewhere.[85]

The riddle of the last sentence is solved in Atto's letter from the following week:

> That priest whom Your Highness recommended to the archduke has brought a page here, as you will already have heard from my other letter. One evening, the page fled the house naked, announcing that the priest was not satisfied with frottage and, rather than finding relief in that, wanted to have anal sex [see note on this translation]. Because the page did not want to, the priest beat him very badly. To quiet this business, it was worked out that the priest have a suit of clothes made for him and give him a little money to send him back to Italy, as was done. But having taken up again with another page from this area, and having wanted to do the same with him, the priest gave him a number of very serious beatings, and the page announced it throughout Innsbruck, so that both incidents are known publicly at court. The priest tries to make excuses, but everything is already well known, and I believe that as soon as he has fixed some of these harpsichords he will be sent back to Italy.[86]

[83] But note the case of Jacques Chausson, a bourgeois, who unlike the aristocrats was in fact burned at the stake: Seifert, "Masculinity," 41.
[84] Marcello, "Società," 133.
[85] Atto to the duke of Mantua, from Innsbruck, June 2, 1653.
[86] Atto to the duke of Mantua, from Innsbruck, June 8, 1653. According to Boggione and Casalegno, *Dizionario*, 534–35, *tamburo* was slang for anus (based on the sounds that emerge from it), and *avere* could indicate a sexual act, particularly between active and passive partners (78). So I think the sense of the passage "non contento d'haverli sotto il tamburo in luogo di trovarvi rimedio voleva servirsene" is that the priest was not content with rubbing his penis between the boy's legs (that is, below the "drum") but in fact wanted to penetrate ("make use of") the "drum" itself.

That Atto would write of such an affair to the duke of Mantua testifies again to the intimacy of their relationship. More to the point, Atto's report reiterates many of the hazards of pederasty at this time: the boy could be unwilling, the man might resort to violence, and the boy's public complaint could ruin the man's reputation (or worse). For men interested in sodomy, the charm of boys must have been tempered by the serious dangers they presented.

To these dangers the castrato in many ways offered a solution. In the first place, castrati were chronologically adults, responsible for their actions: charges of illicit sex threatened their own reputations as much as their partners', and so they exercised greater circumspection. More fundamentally, castrati shared with boys that fusion of masculinity and femininity that lay at the heart of pederastic desire.

In fact, according to a range of evidence, contemporaries frequently regarded castrati as analogues to boys. Physically, of course, a castrato simply retained many of his boyish features well into the years of adulthood: although he might grow in height (sometimes to unusual proportions), he retained his high voice, lack of beard, and soft body. The few known portraits of castrati also suggest that they retained their boyishly round faces and full cheeks, probably a consequence of the eunuchoidism discussed below. (See plates 8 and 9.[87]) That this boyish appearance tended to affect the contemporary conception of castrati is suggested by the frequent use, well into adulthood, of diminutive nicknames for them, such as Nicolino, Senesino, Giuseppino, Marianino, and Pauluccio.[88] Atto himself apparently sometimes thought of himself in boyish terms: at the age of thirty-five, for example, he lamented after his banishment from France that he was "le plus miserable *garçon* du monde."[89]

The castrato does seem frequently to have taken the boy's role in sodomitical sex. Satirists habitually characterized such relationships – especially between castrati and the nobility – as normative. In addition to the poem

---

[87] See also the photograph of Alessandro Moreschi reproduced in Hans Fritz, *Kastratengesang: Hormonelle, konstitutionelle und pädagogische Aspekte*, Musikethnologische Sammelbände, vol. 13 (Tutzing: Hans Schneider, 1994), 116.

[88] Nicolino is Nicolò Grimaldi (1673–1732); the best-known Senesino is Francesco Bernardi (d. 1759), but at least two others were known by that nickname, Andrea Martini (1761–1819) and Giusto Ferdinando Tenducci (1735–90); Giuseppino is the castrato mentioned below in connection with Anna Maria Sardelli (identity unknown); Marianino is Mariano Nicolini (*fl.* 1731–58); Pauluccio is mentioned by the anonymous translator of [Charles Ancillon], *Eunuchism Display'd* (London: E. Curll, 1718), 30, originally published as (and expanded and slightly altered from) *Traité des eunuques* (Paris: n.p., 1707), but I have been unable to discover anything further about his identity. Other diminutive nicknames for castrati include Annibalino (Domenico Annibali, *c.* 1704–*c.* 1779), Appianino (Giuseppe Appiani, 1712–*c.* 1742), Cusanino (Giovanni Carestini, *c.* 1704–60), Gizziello (Gioacchino Conti, 1714–61), and Matteuccio (Matteo Sassani, *c.* 1667–1737).

[89] Atto to Hugues de Lionne, from Rome, October 31, 1661 (emphasis mine). See chapter 5 for details.

Plate 8 Domenico Annibali (Anton Raphael Mengs, 1744; Gemäldegalerie Alte Meister, Staatliche Kunstsammlung Dresden). *Reproduced by permission of the Staatliche Kunstsammlung Dresden; all rights reserved.*

above directed at Atto, Rosa's satire complains repeatedly about castrati offering themselves to their princes, and thereby gaining power:

Son miracoli usati entro à i palaggi,	Miracles are so customary in the palaces
Che un Musico sbarbato co i suoi vezzi	that, with his charms, a beardless *musico*
Cavalcato scavalchi anche i più saggi.[90]	by being ridden unhorses (ousts) even the most wise.

Still at the end of the eighteenth century, sexually overindulgent men were assumed to be attracted to castrati: writing in 1792, Mary Wollstonecraft complains that, for the "lustful prowler," "something more soft than women is sought for; till, in Italy and Portugal, men attend the levees of equivocal beings, to sigh for more than female languor."[91] Although these lines point to a broad change in the conception of gender – by then the castrato stands beyond, rather than between, male and female – Wollstonecraft still views the figure as sexually alluring to men.

[90] Rosa, "La musica," I:164, 173 (lines 46–48 and 307–9).

[91] Mary Wollstonecraft, *A Vindication of the Rights of Women* (1792; repr., Harmondsworth: Penguin, 1985), 249, quoted in Chloe Chard, "Effeminacy, Pleasure and the Classical Body," in *Femininity and Masculinity in Eighteenth-Century Art and Culture*, ed. Gill Perry and Michael Rossington (Manchester: Manchester University Press, 1994), 160.

Plate 9 Carlo Broschi (Farinelli) (Bartolomeo Nazzari, 1734; London, Royal College of Music). *Reproduced by permission of the Royal College of Music.*

Considering how much participants would have wanted to hide their activities, the number of documented liaisons between noblemen and castrati is surprising. Marc'Antonio Pasqualini's intimacy with Cardinal Antonio Barberini in the early 1640s is well known: contemporary testimony leaves little doubt that the cardinal's "veritable passion" extended to more than Pasqualini's beautiful voice.[92] In an even clearer case, Grand Prince Ferdinando

---

[92] The phrase comes from Prunières, *L'opéra*, 89. See also Georges Dethan, *The Young Mazarin*, trans. Stanley Baron (London: Thames and Hudson, 1977), 63–64, originally published as *Mazarin et ses amis* (Paris: Berger-Levrault, 1968). Cardinal Alessandro Bichi, among others,

128

de' Medici (1663–1713), grandson of Ferdinando II, carried on a rather open affair with the castrato Francesco (Cecchino) de Castris, who himself replaced Ferdinando's previous castrato favorite, Petrillo. De Castris too rose to a position of great influence before envy and intrigue led to his banishment.[93] One can now probably add Atto's affair with Carlo II to this list.

A well-known letter of the French gentleman Saint-Évremond from around 1685 emphasizes the connection between castrati and boys in a different way. The letter is addressed to a Monsieur Dery, a young page serving the duchess Mazarin and known for his singing. Saint-Évremond's purpose is to convince the boy to submit to castration.

I would say to you, using the whole lexicon of persuasion, that you must sweeten yourself by means of a mild operation that will assure the delicacy of your complexion for a long time and the beauty of your voice for your whole life. The money, the red coats, the little horses that you receive are not given to the son of Monsieur Dery because of his nobility; your face and your voice win them. In three or four years, alas!, you will lose the quality of both if you do not have the good sense to take care of them, and the source of all these nice things will have dried up … But you fear, you say, to be loved less by the ladies. Cease your worry: we no longer live in the age of idiots. The benefit that comes from the operation is well recognized today, and for every mistress that Monsieur Dery would have in his natural state, the sweetened Monsieur Dery will have a hundred.[94]

Not only does this letter suggest that the "mild operation" will make the boy more – rather than less – attractive to women (and presumably to men as well), but it also highlights the sense of *preservation* that surrounds the surgery: the castrato is indeed viewed as a temporally extended boy. The effect – indeed, the purpose – of castration is to preserve the boy's charms, his beautiful face and voice.[95]

complained bitterly about Pasqualini's influence over Antonio: "[Antonio's] blindness is unbelievable, and the boy's insolence has become unbearable." (Letter from Cardinal Bichi [no further information given], quoted and translated in ibid., 64.) Dethan points out in a note (178) that Bichi refers to Pasqualini with the word "ragazzo" even though the castrato was twenty-seven, another case like that in the previous paragraph. (See the introduction for more on Pasqualini.)

93 Evidence for this relationship appears in Acton, *The Last Medici*, 175–76, 186, 199, and 215; and Warren Kirkendale, *The Court Musicians in Florence During the Principate of the Medici: With a Reconstruction of the Artistic Establishment*, "Historiae musicae cultores" biblioteca, no. 61 (Florence: Olschki, 1993), 437–46.

94 Charles Marguetel de Saint Denis, Seigneur de Saint-Évremond to Monsieur Dery, 1685?, in *Lettres*, ed. René Ternois, Société des Textes Français Modernes (Paris: Librairie Marcel Didier, 1968), II:49–50. Clearly, Saint-Évremond refers here to two different people with the title "Monsieur Dery": first, he means the boy's father, and later, the boy himself.

95 Another reference to the eternal boyishness of the castrato can be found in an aria that concludes the first act of Giovanni Filippo Apolloni's libretto for *La Dori* (set by Antonio Cesti, 1657). The

That voice – if it seems not too obvious to say so – also linked the castrato to the youth. Naturally, the high vocal register was significant. But the castrato's very association with singing tied him to that realm of effeminate sensuality so much the province of the boy. Schleiner, for example, cites a recurrent episode in romances in which the singing of a cross-dressed boy is found alluring, by both women and men. That this singing never gives away the character's real sex only confirms the tender age of the heroes.[96] Similarly, in Rocco's *L'Alcibiade*, the tutor Filotimo admits that it is his young student's voice, even in speech, that most effectively enchants him: "the inestimable joy of this treasure was his angelic speech: he promptly expressed the characters of the words with a voice so gentle … that like a siren he enchanted souls with sweetness, not to deprive them of life, but to torment them, while living, with love."[97] It seems the boy's voice itself could carry erotic associations. For a castrato so regularly to flaunt this boyish attribute in public only heightened the titillation.

With the foregoing as context, then, I return to the question that initiated this discussion: how would Atto's sexual affair with the duke of Mantua have been understood? The evidence in fact suggests that, far from aberrant, it would have seemed almost predictable, a manifestation of contemporary notions about sex. Noblemen were allowed relative moral freedom; misogyny was culturally acceptable; homosexual acts did not necessarily evoke effeminacy; pederasty was widespread and endorsed by Greek tradition; sex with boys carried tangible risks; castrati mimicked boys but without those risks, and with the further attraction of their voices. Although officially proscribed, relationships between men and castrati fell within – rather than outside – recognized cultural norms. Put another way, one could almost foresee that a confirmed profligate like Carlo II would view Atto as a sexual target.

This point suggests a number of corollaries. If such relationships were predictable, sexual affairs between noblemen and castrati may well have been more frequent than has yet been revealed. Under the proper circumstances, historians may rightly suspect them. For example, a number of figures close to Atto – and in particular within the Medici family – imitated the duke of Mantua in their devotion to sensuality, both carnal and aural. As mentioned above, Grand Duke Ferdinand II is known to have enjoyed sex with boys and

---

character Bagoa is a eunuch himself, and his aria leads to a "Ballo d'Eunuchi" to conclude the act. He describes his colleagues as "you who resound (= "have sex") in musical pastimes even to the heavens and with a cheek lacking hair remain always boys" ("Voi ch'in musici trastulli / Risonate fino al Ciel, / E con guancia senza pel / Ogni dì sete fanciulli").

[96] Schleiner, "Male Cross-Dressing," 616–18, in which the author relates such a case from *11ᵉ livre d'Amadis de Gaule*, fol. 181.

[97] Rocco, *L'Alcibiade*, 45.

to have had an affair with his young page, Count Bruto della Molara.[98] Closer to Atto was the grand duke's brother, Cardinal Giovan Carlo (1611–63), who has been described as "a prelate who would not have been out of place in the *Satyricon*," given "headlong to the pleasures of Venus."[99] If no indication of homosexual activities has yet emerged, Giovan Carlo was clearly cut from the same cloth as Carlo II: contemporaries would hardly have been surprised to learn that a cardinal so enthralled by women would have on occasion also taken his pleasure with young men or, in their place, castrati. Though the evidence is lacking, the conditions are right.

The same can be said of the third Medici brother, Mattias, Atto's primary patron. Like Giovan Carlo, but without the ecclesiastical motive, Mattias never married. Such a decision was not in itself unusual: as noted, younger brothers were often denied the right to marry. But Mattias does seem to have participated in the subculture of illicit sex that has been linked to such cadets. As mentioned in chapter 3, he particularly liked to "protect" young female singers, with the understanding that they would serve him sexually as well.[100] The prince's most celebrated relationship of this type was with the notorious vocalist and courtesan Anna Maria Sardelli, whom, like Atto, Mattias supported until he died.[101] Although again no evidence indicates Mattias ever practiced sodomy, his general sexual conduct, along with his love for music, matches qualities of other noblemen who did. One begins to wonder whether Mattias's relationships to Atto and to Sardelli were more similar than has yet been recognized.

The case of Mazarin likewise raises questions. His detractors, of course, regularly portrayed him as a sodomite; even his closest supporter, the queen regent, tried to defuse the scandal of their private meetings by declaring that "Mazarin did not love women since he came from a country where other inclinations were fashionable."[102] And the cardinal did like to employ young male musicians from Italy as his *valets de chambre*, charging his agent in Rome with seeking good candidates.[103] Still, these and other bits of information have not produced a consensus among historians, who admittedly have often ignored Mazarin's personal life. For now, the question must remain open.

It is important to recognize that the pursuit of such questions produces more than historical tittle-tattle. All of the men discussed here patronized

---

[98] Acton, *The Last Medici*, 25.   [99] Ibid., 24 and 45; see also 45–48 for anecdotes of his lifestyle.

[100] Lorenzo Bianconi and Thomas Walker, "Dalla *Finta pazza* alla *Veremonda*: Storie di Febiarmonici," *Rivista italiana di musicologia* 10 (1975): 440–41.

[101] Ibid.

[102] Ruth Kleinman, *Anne of Austria: Queen of France* (Columbus, Ohio: Ohio State University Press, 1985), 166; Kleinman cites a letter for this information at F Pae, MD France 855, ff. 220–23.

[103] Prunières, *L'opéra*, 247.

music, and so their tastes and conduct certainly influenced the context of music-making, especially in private circumstances.[104] Indeed, the connection between sex and chamber music is already well understood with respect to female singers of this period: the reports surrounding Anna Maria Sardelli, Leonora Baroni, and numerous others leave no doubt that, with these ladies, musical and sexual services could coincide.[105] Atto himself insinuated that only an ugly songstress could be chaste and that some ladies were better heard "in the bed than in the chamber."[106] If, however, castrati carried a similar sexual charge, if they frequently provided more than musical services, then the ambience of all chamber singing, of chamber singing per se, may have been suffused with eroticism. Such was certainly the view of the satirists, who implied that music and sex were inseparable.[107] One begins to wonder how often a cantata served as foreplay, and, even in more decorous settings, to what degree the meaning and effect of chamber genres depended on sexual overtones.

And then, if singing and sex did often go hand in hand, how much of the access and social advantage enjoyed by some castrati derived from their vocal as opposed to sexual attractions? Again, the situation with women is better understood. Leonora Baroni, for example, exploited her affairs with Mazarin and Camillo Pamphili (see the introduction). And Anna Maria Sardelli used her many charms to secure an array of patrons, whom, like Atto, she sometimes played against one another.[108] The cases of castrato "favorites" such as Pasqualini and de Castris also seem relevant in this connection: that de Castris was the highest paid musician in the history of the Medici court may have had as much to do with Grand Prince Ferdinando's particular favor

---

[104] For a recent objection to inquiring after castrato sexuality (as well as a thoughtful consideration of the significance of the castrato onstage), see Silke Leopold, "'Not Sex but Pitch': Kastraten als Liebhaber – einmal *über* der Gürtellinie betrachtet," in *Provokation und Tradition: Erfahrung mit der Alten Musik*, ed. Hans-Martin Linde and Regula Rapp (Stuttgart and Weimar: Verlag J. B. Metzler, 2000), 219–20.

[105] Good discussions of the tendency to view female vocalists as courtesans may be found in John Rosselli, "From Princely Service to the Open Market: Singers of Italian Opera and Their Patrons, 1600–1850," *Cambridge Opera Journal* 1 (1989): 2–12 *passim*. Also, Bianconi and Walker, "Dalla *Finta pazza*," 440–44.

[106] For citations and further information, see chapter 3.

[107] In addition to the passages cited earlier in the chapter, one may consider the following from the anonymous satire "Sopra Atto Melani, Musico," 767 (see appendix C for the Italian): If you sing a song / to someone you are entreating, / what gift do you expect for it / if the same man plays it [back] to you (screws you)? / And because everyone gives you / the first blood of life [i.e., semen] / and not gold, which fades in the end, / the gift is not worthless. / Oh think of the bell-tower."

[108] Again, see Bianconi and Walker, "Dalla *Finta pazza*," 440–44; also, Sara Mamone, "Most Serene Brothers-Princes-Impresarios: Theater in Florence under the Management and Protection of Mattias, Giovan Carlo, and Leopoldo de' Medici," *Journal of Seventeenth-Century Music* 9 (2003), http://sscm-jscm.press.uiuc.edu/jscm/v9/no1/Mamone.html, section 5.

as with the singer's vocal talents.[109] And so although the evidence is slender indeed, one cannot discount the role that Atto's sexual availability may have played in his ascendance.

After so much conjecture, it is perhaps worth underscoring the dearth of secure documentation here: none of the deductions above is really unassailable, except that Atto had a particularly intimate relationship with the duke of Mantua. But, as I have tried to demonstrate, establishing the context for that relationship can legitimately fill in the picture and suggest at least plausible hypotheses about the relationships between castrati and other men. Not only does the sexual framework of the period locate the castrato in an eroticized middle ground, but evidence of contemporary habits confirms a regular role for him in a subculture of "deviant" sexuality. In both theory and practice, the castrato's physical and vocal effeminacy – that is, his arrested youth – made him desirable to certain men, usually from the elite classes. These men tended also to luxuriate in sex with women, especially the courtesan-singers who populated the musical scene. To put it simply, it seems that the men who fancied vocal music were likely also to fancy the musicians – of both sexes – who made it.

Sex with women?

Assessing the heterosexual relationships of castrati is, if possible, an even more complex task. A key question – often passed over as inappropriate to scholarship – is whether a castrato could actually "have sex" with a woman.[110] Indeed, unlike the singers' passive role in sodomy, their participation in heterosexual sex raises issues of physical function. And those issues in turn seem relevant to understanding their overall sexual reputation. Could these singers take a sexually active role? And how did that ability, or lack of it, affect listeners' perceptions of the castrati when – as they so often did – they sang of love? Particularly in an era when performers never completely disappeared into their characters, physical reality would seem pertinent to dramatic impression.[111] Thus, a frank investigation of that reality promises

---

[109] Kirkendale, *The Court Musicians*, 437.
[110] Again, see Leopold, "'Not Sex,'" 219–20.
[111] A number of singers were actually called by the name of a character they had famously portrayed: Giovanni Francesco Grossi, for example, was known as Siface, after a role in Cavalli's *Scipione africano*. Similarly, the aforementioned Sardelli was sometimes called Campaspe, after that part in Cesti's *Alessandro*. Others have pointed out the transparency of character portrayal in baroque opera: see particularly Martha Feldman, "Magic Mirrors and the *Seria* Stage: Thoughts toward a Ritual View," *Journal of the American Musicological Society* 48 (1995): 423–84, but especially 460–72, where she argues that opera seria is designed to disallow audience absorption in the drama.

to shed light not only on the nature of relationships between women and castrati, including Atto's purported ties to the Mancini sisters, but also on the characters and roles that castrati regularly portrayed. I will argue, in fact, that the castrati were neither the prodigious lovers of legend nor asexual neuters: though handicapped, many possessed enough desire and function to be plausible as paramours, both in the chamber and on the stage.

The limited scholarship on this question would seem to offer no clear answers. On the one hand, numerous tales of the castrato's sexual escapades, particularly as related by Angus Heriot, have become familiar fare. In what was clearly intended as a popular sort of book, Heriot tells a number of spicy stories: of one castrato's assassination by his mistress's alarmed family; of another's openly sexual exploits with a Russian grand duchess; and of others' attempts to have their relationships with women sanctified by marriage.[112] Unfortunately, the reliability of Heriot's accounts – and even of his more general information – is often impossible to judge, as he cites few sources. Still, his image of the castrato as sexually potent has permeated the literature.

Ardently opposed are Enid and Richard Peschel, who have published two medically oriented articles on the physical consequences of castration. From their perspective, "the notion that various castrati had natural sex lives with women is ... a hoax."[113] The Peschels' medical posture has lent their arguments an air of authority, and their work is also regularly cited.[114] In the following paragraphs, I will attempt to reevaluate and shed light on this disagreement, to the extent that evidence permits. Not surprisingly, that evidence remains limited: one cannot expect straightforward historical testimony on so intimate a subject. And yet some relevant information is available, in the form of modern scientific research into endocrinology and historical reports on the castrati themselves.

Any basic medical dictionary tells something about the physical results of the castrato's operation.[115] The destruction of the testes before puberty

---

[112] Angus Heriot, *The Castrati in Opera* (1956; repr., New York: Da Capo Paperback, 1975), 133–34, 193, and 185–88, respectively. The castrati involved were Siface (1653–97); Velluti (Giovanni Battista Velluti, 1780–1861); and Tenducci (the aforementioned Giusto Ferdinando Tenducci, 1735–90), among others. The question of castrato marriage has recently been tackled head on by Mary E. Frandsen, "*Eunuchi conjugium*: The Marriage of a Castrato in Early Modern Germany," *Early Music History* 24 (2005): 53–124.

[113] Enid Rhodes Peschel and Richard E. Peschel, "Medicine and Music: The Castrati in Opera," *Opera Quarterly* 4, no. 4 (1987): 33; their other article is Enid Rhodes Peschel and Richard E. Peschel, "Medical Insights into the Castrati in Opera," *American Scientist* 75 (1987): 578–83.

[114] See, for example, John Rosselli, "Castrato," *Grove Music Online*, ed. Laura Macy, www.grovemusic.com (accessed July 6, 2007).

[115] As Rosselli notes ("The Castrati," 151), the procedure used in the operation is not entirely certain. Virtually the only information comes from the treatise by Ancillon (*Eunuchism*, 15–16), who was hardly a medical expert. Ancillon tells of several possible methods: the testicles could

creates the condition of eunuchoidism, in which the male secondary sexual characteristics are not expressed: the penis remains small; beard growth does not occur; axillary and pubic hair follow a female rather than male pattern, as does the distribution of body fat; and of course the larynx does not grow. In addition, the proportions of the body are sometimes upset by the lack of the hormone that arrests the growth of longer bones.[116] Many of these observations are confirmed in a 1937 study of the radical Russian Orthodox sect known as the *skopecs*, who still into the twentieth century ritually castrated themselves – sometimes prepubertally – in the pursuit of spiritual purity.[117]

The castrato's operation certainly produced infertility: on this point every source agrees. Nor could their sexual activity have been "normal," at least in comparison to intact males. The question here, however, centers on the issue of potency, that is, "the ability to respond appropriately and orgastically to sexual stimulation."[118] Unfortunately, the Peschels do not seriously address this question, dismissing the reports of castrato affairs as "fanciful tales" and "disput[ing] the claim that castration had no damaging effect on the subject's … sexual impulses."[119] For their opinions, the Peschels rely heavily on a study of sexual endocrinology from 1924.[120] Even more problematically, they conflate the ability to have sex with the ability to procreate: as evidence of Giovanni Battista Velluti's "maimed sexual condition" and inability to "consummate heterosexual love affairs," they cite a letter (reported in Heriot) in which the castrato admits he cannot conceive a child.[121] And by "sexual impulses," the Peschels seem to mean only fertility and potency, since they never investigate the issue of desire. In the end, they only succeed in confirming what is already known, that the castrati were infertile and sexually abnormal; their judgment that castrati lived entirely asexually is

either be removed through an incision, or simply caused to wither through pressure or the severing of key ducts. As a rule, the penis was not removed. All the procedures were considered relatively safe by seventeenth-century standards, requiring only about two weeks of recuperation. See also chapter 1.

[116] The above is based on the *International Dictionary of Medicine and Biology* (New York: John Wiley and Sons, 1986), s.v. "eunuchoidism." Peschel and Peschel, "Medical Insights," 582, also provide a useful summary.

[117] Ionel Florian Rapaport, *La castration rituelle: L'état mental des Skoptzy* (Paris: Lipschutz, 1937), 41–42. Information about the Skopecs, along with some disturbing photographs documenting these physical characteristics, can be found in Hans Fritz, *Kastratengesang: Hormonelle, Konstitutionelle und Pädagogische Aspekte*, Musikethnologische Sammelbände, vol. 13 (Tutzing: Hans Schneider, 1994), 24–36.

[118] The definition comes from the *International Dictionary of Medicine and Biology*, s.v. "potency – sexual potency."

[119] Peschel and Peschel, "Medical Insights," 583, 582.

[120] Alexander Lipschütz, *The Internal Secretions of the Sex Glands: The Problem of the "Puberty Gland"* (Cambridge: W. Heffer and Sons, 1924).

[121] Peschel and Peschel, "Medicine and Music," 31–32. See also their "Medical Insights," 583.

undermined by their outdated evidence and limited conception of sexuality itself.

To explore questions of sexual urge and function among the castrati, the uropathologist Meyer Melicow conducted a survey of urologic surgeons on the subject in 1983. Although the answers he received varied considerably, some areas of consensus emerged. Bilateral orchiectomy (the removal of both testes) performed between the ages of five and seven should cause permanent sterility and impotence; however, if the procedure were done later, from ages nine to twelve, the subject would not necessarily be rendered impotent, "because the interstitial cells that manufacture testosterone had probably functioned and induced erections and, once begun, erectability may have continued because of testosterone-producing cells along the [spermatic] cords and in the retro-peritoneum."[122] Of course, historical reports indicate that boys were more likely castrated at the later ages, when the quality of their voices had become apparent.[123] In sum, the survey suggested that, while certainly infertile, some castrati might have been potent.

This conclusion is seconded by the very medical text that the Peschels cite in their own arguments. The author, Alexander Lipschütz, recounts some research into the physiology of the aforementioned Russian *skopecs*. In at least one case, the researchers "observed erection in a prepubertally castrated *skopec* during the examination."[124] The report is important because it offers perhaps the most direct evidence obtainable of castrato erectability.

With such limited information about the effects of castration in humans, studies of other mammals, particularly primates, offer useful indications. One study of rhesus monkeys, in which an isolated family group was prepubertally gonadectomized, showed that such surgery did not in fact seem to discourage sexual impulses: the castrated males of the study actually showed higher rates of sexual behavior than normal, even if most of this behavior took place with other males.[125] Another study observed prepubertally castrated male rhesus monkeys in more normal monkey society, that is, mingling with sexually mature males and females. In this setting, the

[122] Meyer M. Melicow, "Castrati Singers and the Lost 'Cords,'" *Bulletin of the New York Academy of Medicine* 59 (1983): 749–54; quote, 754.

[123] Ancillon, *Eunuchism*, 39.

[124] Lipschütz, *Internal Secretions*, 12. Lipschütz is citing the study, Julius Tandler and Siegfried Grosz, "Über den Einfluβ der Kastration auf den Organismus, II., Die Skopzen," *Archiv für Entwicklungsmechanik der Organismen* 30 (1910): 236–53.

[125] The researchers interpreted this male mounting activity as an arrested form of juvenile social behavior, in which most of the males' interactions, including frequent mountings, occurred with their own sex. The above discussion is drawn from James Loy *et al.*, *The Behavior of Gonadectomized Rhesus Monkeys*, Contributions to Primatology, no. 20 (Basel: Karger, 1984), 51–72. In fact, the researchers conclude that "the 'sexless' society we hoped to produce actually contained a high degree of isosexual eroticism" (69).

castrated males in fact developed full sexual behavior, including mounting, thrusting, and the motor response associated with ejaculation (although with no release of semen).[126] From both these studies, the researchers arrived at their primary conclusions: monkeys seem to learn sexual behavior in society, and that behavior is not entirely dependent upon the hormones produced by the testes during puberty.[127]

Similar results have in fact been found for other mammals: studies of marmosets, horses, bulls, and dogs, for example, parallel the studies of monkeys above.[128] There is of course some variance between species as well as among individuals within the same species. But the animal research all seems to point in the same direction, namely, that prepubertally castrated mammals tend to retain sexual impulses and – particularly when raised in their normal society – substantial sexual function. Of course, conclusions concerning animals cannot recklessly be transferred to humans, but it is also true that monkeys, at least, are used in hormonal research precisely because of their similar physiology.[129] The information gained from their study should at least be able to suggest possibilities, and even likelihoods.

Particularly striking, then, is the prevailing agreement of these modern studies with the historical evidence, spotty and indirect as it often is. Again, the satirical poetry of the period can be helpful. Satire must always be taken with a grain of salt, of course, but comments that are incidental or even contrary to the author's intent can produce credible testimony. For example, in one poem the aforementioned Anna Maria Sardelli is depicted lamenting the forced departure of her castrato lover from Venice.[130] A recurring theme

[126] Ibid., 68, citing C. F. Bielert, "The Effects of Early Castration and Testosterone Propionate Treatment on the Development and Display of Behavior Patterns by Male Rhesus Monkeys" (Ph.D. diss., Michigan State Univ., 1974).

[127] Loy *et al.*, *Behavior*, 70, 72.

[128] A study of male marmosets notes that prepubertal castrates "are sexually very active in adulthood, frequently mounting females and making pelvic thrusting movements with the penis erect" (A. F. Dixson, "Sexual and Aggressive Behaviour of Adult Male Marmosets [*Callithrix jacchus*] Castrated Neonatally, Prepubertally, or in Adulthood," *Physiology and Behaviour* 54 [1993]: 305). Studies of horses, bulls, and even dogs present similar results: Scott W. Line, Benjamin L. Hart, and Linda Sanders, "Effect of Prepubertal Versus Postpubertal Castration on Sexual and Aggressive Behavior in Male Horses," *Journal of the American Veterinary Medical Association* 186 (1985): 250–51. Y. Folman and R. Volcani, "Copulatory Behaviour of the Prepubertally Castrated Bull," *Animal Behavior* 14 (1966): 572–73. Burney J. Le Boeuf, "Copulatory and Aggressive Behavior in the Prepubertally Castrated Dog," *Hormones and Behavior* 1 (1970): 134.

[129] Loy *et al.*, *Behavior*, 1: "Due to their phylogenetic ties, all anthropoid primates show broad similarities in anatomy, physiology and behavior – a situation which has led to the widespread use of nonhuman primates as 'models' in research into a variety of human problems."

[130] The poem's full title is "Per la partenza di un castrato amato dalla Sig.ra Anna Maria N. [backwards] Cortigiana, e cantatrice romana detta Campaspe per haver recitata quella parte con grande applauso in una commedia in musica nella città di Firenze." It appears in I Fn, Magl.

is Sardelli's foolish contentment with her impaired partner; denigrating the castrato's sexual capacity thus furthers the poet's goal. So when the author grudgingly admits some capacity – always via double entendre – his points carry greater weight. In the following passage, the conceits of money, the empty purse, and capital clearly refer to sperm, the scrotum, and the penis:

Questi cervelli insani	These lunatics (mad penises)
San, ch'io son donna liberale, e quieta,	know that I am a generous and restrained woman;
Perciò quella moneta,	and so I was satisfied to take
Mi compiacqui pigliar scarsa due grani.	just two grains of that coin.
Ma non venghino all'esca	But these tight-fisted dimwits (drops/testicles),
Del buon mercato i goccioloni avari,	who are overflowing with money,
Ch'hanno le loro a traboccar danari.	should not be tempted by my good prices.
Ah ch'avida non sono,	Oh, I am not greedy;
De miei pregi fo dono,	I make a gift of my virtues (value)
Mentre è cosa ben nota,	for it is well known
Che il mannerino amante	that I always received into my lap
Sempre raccolsi in grembo a borsa vota.	the amorous wether [gelded ram], even with his empty purse.
Non son di queste no, che fanno mescere;	I am not one of those women who make it pour out;
Anzi fui seco tale,	rather, when I was with him
Che sul suo capitale	I put my hands
Messi le mani sol per farlo crescere.[131]	on his capital only to make it grow.

In another passage, the imagery is even clearer:

L'imbroglio de coglioni	The entanglement of idiots (testicles)
Alle gioie d'amor serve d'impaccio;	in the joys of love causes trouble;
…	…
Assioma gentile,	Kind axiom
Che mi contenta a pieno;	that fully satisfies me:
In lui levato il più, s'accresce il meno.	with him, the more that's raised up (taken away), the less he grows.
Sia dunque il mio petto	Therefore, let my breast be
Continuo ricetto	a constant shelter
Di strali pungenti	from piercing arrows
Se del mio bel cupido	if, from my beautiful Cupid,
Non è pericol più, che l'arco allenti.[132]	there is no greater danger than that his bow slacken.

VII.364, ff. 289–95v. I am most grateful to James Leve for notifying me of this poem and transcribing it for me. For information on Sardelli, see Bianconi and Walker, "Dalla *Finta pazza*," 440–44. In an astonishing coincidence, the departure to which the poem refers is mentioned in a postscript to one of Atto's letters to Mattias, from Florence, October 2, 1654: "Già V.A. saprà come Giuseppino andò a Venetia e perché il fine fu di levarlo dagli Amori dell'Anna Maria adesso che quella prelibata Dama è occupata in congiungimenti di Cavaliere sbarbato (bello) e richissimo." Unfortunately, the lover's identity remains uncertain.
[131] "Per la partenza," ff. 289–95v.   [132] Ibid.

The author of this poem clearly believed that a castrato could achieve an erection: "I put my hands on his capital only to make it grow." But the danger of the "slackening bow" may suggest the fleeting nature of this condition. The poem may even hint that some sort of climax was possible: in the line, "I was satisfied to take just two grains of that coin," coin clearly represents semen.

Further evidence for a sort of impaired climax appears much earlier and in an unexpected place: a letter of 1587 from Pope Sixtus V to the papal nuncio to Spain, Cesare Speciano. In the letter, whose main purpose is to exclude castrati from marriage, the pope states that, as opposed to "true seed," the castrati "pour out a certain liquid perhaps similar to semen, although by no means suitable to generation and the cause of matrimony."[133] The castrati themselves may have been claiming the ability to ejaculate as a justification for marriage; Sixtus rejects that reasoning and, as Ute Ranke-Heinemann observes, establishes the requirement of fertility for marriage.[134]

Another glimpse of castrato sexuality emerges from two French pamphlets published in 1619, likewise dedicated to denouncing relationships between eunuchs and women.[135] One pamphlet echoes Sixtus's arguments and in the process touches on a number of relevant details:

If one cannot reach orgasm on account of the dysfunction or the excessive dispro-portion of the genital members, or if the man has none at all, he can in no way be married. Yet it would seem, according to the premises I have made, that the opposite would be true for those who have lost only their testicles, since eunuchs and castrates who retain their members would be able to orgasm with women [*jouir des femmes*], as they say. This is not so, however, for no matter how much such type of men can orgasm with women, they cannot return the favor. They are mockers and insulters

---

[133] Sixtus V to Cesare Speciano, bishop of Novara, June 22, 1587, in *Bullarum, diplomatum et privilegiorum sanctorum romanorum* …, vol. VIII (Turin: Seb. Franco and Enrico Dalmazzo, 1863), 870. For a superb study of the role of Spain in the origins of Western castrati (including further insight into this letter), see Giuseppe Gerbino, "The Quest for the Castrato Voice: Castrati in Renaissance Italy," *Studi musicali* 33 (2004): 303–57.

[134] Uta Ranke-Heinemann, *Eunuchs for the Kingdom of Heaven: Women, Sexuality and the Catholic Church*, trans. Peter Heinegg (New York: Doubleday, 1990), 250; originally published as *Eunuchen für das Himmelreich: Katholische Kirche und Sexualität* (Hamburg: Hoffmann und Campe, 1988). In fact, Sixtus allowed marriage to men suffering from sterility for unknown reasons, but not when the cause was known (251). See also Frandsen, "*Eunuchi conjugium*," 53–124 *passim*.

[135] *Arrest contre les chastrez* (Paris: n.p., 1619); *Les privileges et fidelitez des chastrez* (Paris: n.p., 1619). Both pamphlets are anonymous. Exemplars of both are held by the Beinecke Rare Book and Manuscript Library, Yale Univ. One may legitimately wonder at the early dates of these pamphlets, well before the arrival of Italian opera and its characteristic singers. Gerbino ("The Quest," 323, 331–32, 344n) highlights a number of known French castrati from the sixteenth century; his general argument for the multiple uses of the surgery is also relevant (339–41).

who have committed the crime of fraud for having represented false merchandise as genuine.[136]

Admittedly, the sense of the phrase "jouir des femmes," which I have translated as "to orgasm with women," is debatable. The first edition of the *Dictionnaire de l'Académie française* (1696) gives for "jouïr d'une femme," "La posseder charnellement."[137] Likewise earlier in this passage the phrase "parvenir à la jouissance" invokes the sense of orgasm. And so, because the author is contrasting the man who cannot orgasm (and therefore cannot marry) with the type of man under discussion, the phrase "jouir des femmes" would seem to indicate that orgasm was indeed the specific "enjoyment" that the castrato derived from women. According to this interpretation, the related discussion of the castrato's inability to "rendre la pareille" could indicate his incapability to bring a woman to orgasm or to impregnate her, the former being at this time considered necessary for the latter. His "merchandise" is fraudulent, then, because it cannot give the woman what it promises. However one explains this passage (and other interpretations are not impossible), the author does seem to believe that eunuchs who had lost only their testicles could still achieve an erection and even, perhaps, experience an orgasm.

The other pamphlet holds the sexual facility of eunuchs in somewhat lower esteem but again gives helpful details. Here, women are warned to avoid affairs with castrated men because of the inherent frustration of such unions. Women who ignore this advice are doomed to

regrets, sighs, tears, and sobs; one finds only scolding, hate, and jealousy, since what the lady desires [is] what the gentleman cannot give her … there is nothing so limp as he in the face of battle: stupidity follows cowardice, and the good fellow faints at the door, which he can only enter with his head … so weak are his loins, and he cannot keep himself up … [T]o the devil with these castrates who light the hearth-fire but cannot put it out.[138]

A close reading largely agrees with the foregoing: the castrato desires women and apparently can achieve at least a temporary erection that nevertheless "faints at the door"; it is presumably the small size of the castrato's member that prevents the entry of more than his "head"; and while he can excite a woman, he cannot bring her to orgasm and thereby "put out" that desire.

---

[136] *Arrest*, 4–5.
[137] *Le Dictionnaire de l'Académie Française* (Paris: Jean Baptiste Coignard, 1694), s.v. "jouir," www.lexilogos.com/francais_langue_dictionnaires.htm (accessed December 13, 2007).
[138] *Les privileges*, 4–5.

Interestingly, even in this tract, which is specifically aimed at discrediting the castrato's abilities, the author still admits some sexual function.[139]

Finally, the famous treatise *Eunuchism Display'd*, by the eighteenth-century historian and lawyer Charles Ancillon, concedes something more. As in the French pamphlets a century earlier, Ancillon argues that marriage is forbidden to eunuchs because they cannot father children. To strengthen his point, he rebuts a series of counterarguments, one of which holds that because some castrati can sexually satisfy women, they at least should be allowed to marry. Ancillon responds that, since "the [only] lawful Desires of a Woman are to have Children,"

it is certain that an Eunuch *can only satisfy the Desires of the Flesh*, Sensuality, Impurity, and Debauchery; and as they are not capable of Procreation, they are more proper for such criminal Commerce than perfect Man, and more esteem'd for that Reason by lewd Women, because they *can give them all the satisfaction* without running any Risk or Danger.[140]

Ancillon later acknowledges that not all eunuchs are capable of this degree of sexual activity.[141] But more than the other writers examined here, Ancillon grants that many castrati could gratify women, an ability that probably implies real function.

While again none of this evidence, scientific or historical, can be said to *prove* the nature of the castrato's sexual capacity, the general similarity of the testimony is plain. As opposed to the Peschels' conclusion that the operation

---

[139] In her recent and fascinating work on a collection of documents first published in 1685 as *Eunuchi conjugium*, Mary E. Frandsen has turned up further testimony consistent with the foregoing. This publication brought together key records surrounding the controversial marriage in 1667 of Bartolomeo Sorlisi, a castrato at the Dresden court, to Dorothea Lichtwer, stepdaughter of a local lawyer. Offering an opinion on the proposed union, the pastor of the bride's family warned, "it would soon make one or the other of these two people ill and exhausted, for in her the semen would be irritated, but (as the doctors say) not elicited" ("es würde eines das andere von disen beÿden leuthen bald ungesund machen und auffreiben, denn bey Ihr würde das *semen irritir*et, aber [wie die *Medici* rendeten] nicht *elicir*et werden"), (Hieronymus Delphinus [pseud.] [ed.], *Eunuchi conjugium: Die Capaunen-Heirath. ..*, 3rd edn. [Halle: n.p., 1718], as quoted and translated in Frandsen, "*Eunuchi conjugium*," 87). Surprisingly, Frandsen interprets this passage as attributing to Sorlisi the ability to produce semen, which nevertheless lacks generative power. The lines make more sense, I believe, if understood as referring to *Dorothea's* "seed" – an essential element in the two-seed model of procreation – which was agitated but not released; it is this buildup that causes the pastor to worry about "*putridines in matrice*" and "große Mutterbeschwerung." In other words, the passage conforms with the idea, seen above, that the castrato could excite but not satisfy a woman. A similar, later, example of this sort of evidence comes from [Ancillon], *Eunuchism*, 206–7 (see below).

[140] Ancillon, *Eunuchism*, 210, and 206–7 (emphasis mine).

[141] Ancillon, *Eunuchism*, 213. This distinction may suggest that Ancillon possessed a genuine knowledge of his subject.

"probably produced *asexual* behavior in the castrati," I would maintain that a far greater degree of desire and function is indicated.[142] The most capable could probably have had erections and something like an orgasm; others may have had lesser abilities. But even those left entirely impotent need not have lived "asexually": Casanova's memoirs tell of an orgy in Rome involving castrati who, along with the abbés present, employed the "secret des Lesbiennes."[143] One way or another, it seems clear that many of these singers were interested in and capable of sex. And surely this capacity, which seems to have been widely recognized, influenced their reputation as sensual, erotic creatures.

The implications

Such a reputation would certainly seem to have implications for interpreting the operatic characters that the castrato regularly played. As I shall discuss further below, the individual personalities of baroque opera singers always seem to have shaped the listeners' experience of them: just as today reports on the romantic lives of movie stars can influence reactions to their portrayals, so too did knowledge of – or at least assumptions about – the lives of earlier singers color audience response. And so, I believe the castrato began to assume the amorous male lead in operas at least in part because his special sexual status was found alluring and wholly appropriate to men in love. He played the lover not in spite of his physical distinctiveness but because of it. He was an exaggerated embodiment of the seductive boy and presumed devotee of sensuality; that he was also considered (probably rightly) to be sexually active only added to his appeal. A brief consideration of the use made of these singers by composers and librettists over the baroque period lends support to this hypothesis and at the same time challenges some of the modern approaches to castrato characters.

The crucial moment in operatic history came in Venice in the decades around 1650, when the many conventions of the genre actually developed.[144]

---

[142] Peschel and Peschel, "Medicine and Music," 30.
[143] [Giacomo] Casanova, *Mémoires*, ed. Robert Abirached, Bibliothèque de la Pléiade ([Paris]: Gallimard, 1959), II:797. Similarly, Todd S. Gilman cites Henry Fielding's satirical play *The Historical Register for the Year 1736* as indicating that wax dildos, called "children," were the secret to castrato sex: *The Historical Register for the Year 1736* and *Eurydice Hissed*, ed. William W. Appleton (Lincoln, Neb.: University of Nebraska Press, 1967), 24–25, quoted in Todd S. Gilman, "The Italian (Castrato) in London," in *The Work of Opera: Genre, Nationhood, and Sexual Difference*, ed. Richard Dellamora and Daniel Fischlin (New York: Columbia University Press, 1997), 57.
[144] See Rosand, *Opera*, especially 322–86.

Whereas in early Florentine and Roman opera changed-voice lovers had been customary (with some exceptions), the Venetian modifications raised the importance of the castrato as a leading man.[145] Among the key forces in this development must be counted the Accademia degli Incogniti. As seen above, Heller has shown how members of the Incogniti led the contemporary debate about gender – especially, the nature and power of women – and how this interest spilled over into their paradigmatic librettos. Of particular fascination were the so-called "exceptional" women of history and legend. Powerful figures such as Semiramis, Cleopatra, Zenobia, and Lucretia, whose behavior so differed from canonical femininity, required special explanation and thus appeared often in the academicians' discussions and operas. Seen as invading the "masculine" provinces of politics and glory, these women were thought to occupy loftier than usual positions in the sexual continuum; their humors were hotter, more manly. In Heller's words, "as long as virtue retained its association with gender, many exceptional women – whose deeds were inappropriate to their sex – would appear to be endowed with masculine characteristics."[146] And this masculinity was threatening. In the cultural imagination, the "absorption [by these women] of the masculine almost invariably resulted in the loss of stature – and masculinity – for the men with whom they were juxtaposed."[147] Contemporary gender construction was almost a zero-sum game in which the extra heat of the exceptional woman was necessarily drawn from surrounding men.[148]

Who more appropriately than the castrati, then, could have portrayed the men enthralled to such women? For example, in *L'incoronazione di Poppea* by Giovanni Francesco Busenello and (primarily) Claudio Monteverdi (1643), the two leading castrato roles, Nero and Otho, represent the two men who have lost their rational, masculine self-control and are under the powerfully feminizing influence of – that is, are in love with – Poppea, who in

---

[145] In "The Eroticism," 235–39, I examine in somewhat more detail the rise in casting castrati as lovers. See also Heller, *Emblems*, 18.

[146] Heller, *Emblems*, 17; the above is generally based on ibid., 9–18.   [147] Ibid., 17.

[148] I borrow the idea of gender as a zero-sum game from an author in a interestingly related field: Jennifer Robertson, *Takarazuka: Sexual Politics and Popular Culture in Modern Japan* (Berkeley: University of California Press, 1998), 57. The wide diffusion of this configuration in Europe is attested by a range of cultural products from the period. See Raymond B. Waddington, "The Bisexual Portrait of Francis I: Fontainebleau, Castiglione, and the Tone of Courtly Mythology," in *Playing with Gender: A Renaissance Pursuit*, ed. Jean R. Brink, Maryanne C. Horowitz, and Allison P. Coudert (Urbana: University of Illinois Press, 1991), 105–22 *passim*. Also, Sarah Colvin, *The Rhetorical Feminine: Gender and Orient on the German Stage, 1647– 1742*, Oxford Modern Languages and Literature Monographs (Oxford: Clarendon Press, 1999), 71–83. Finally, see Beth Kowaleski-Wallace, "Shunning the Bearded Kiss: Castrati and the Definition of Female Sexuality," *Prose Studies* 15 (1992): 160, where the author argues that, in Ancillon's conception, "[Semiramis's] alleged castration of men is only a metaphor for her symbolic castration of them."

this context represents all that is most dangerous in women. In *Giasone*, by Giacinto Andrea Cicognini and Francesco Cavalli (1649), it is the title character who is emasculated. Hercules opens the first act by denouncing his leader's dissipation, echoing typical attitudes about effeminacy:

Dall'oriente porge	Dawn from the east
l'alba ai mortali il suo dorato lume,	brings its golden light to mortals;
e tra lascive piume	and from his wanton pillows
avvilito Giasone ancor non sorge?	debauched Jason has not yet risen?
Come potrà costui,	How will he then,
disanimato dai notturni amplessi,	fatigued by his nocturnal embraces,
animarsi agl'assalti, alle battaglie?	sally forth to the assault or the battle?[149]

At the beginning of the opera Jason is under Medea's spell; in the final scene he abruptly transfers his love to Queen Isifile. At no time does he appear in control of his passions. In fact, his only heroic deed in the opera, the capture of the golden fleece, is accomplished as much through the magic of his sorceress lover as through any valor on his part. Not surprisingly, this love-besotted character was again assigned to a castrato. As one of the most frequently produced operas of the century, *Giasone* figured importantly in the diffusion of the Venetian genre.[150] And just as this work, and others like it, transmitted conventions like the sleep scene, the invocation, and the descending-tetrachord lament, so too, I would suggest, did it popularize the use of castrati to convey the effeminacy of men in love.

The one major operatic role unquestionably portrayed by Atto himself – Orpheus in Luigi Rossi's *Orfeo* – fits the same pattern, even though the work originated in the Roman rather than Venetian orbit. Both of the characters in love with Eurydice in this opera, Orpheus and Aristeus, were sung by castrati. Further, Orpheus is given two laments (in III.1 and III.11) and Aristeus a lament of his own (III.3) as well as a mad scene (III.4): both of these conventions are more usually associated with female characters.[151] Of course, Orpheus is the prototypical musician, and in his ability to soften

[149] The text and translation, by Derek Yeld, come from the liner notes to Francesco Cavalli, *Giasone*, cond. René Jacobs, Harmonia Mundi France 901282.84.

[150] See Rosand, *Opera*, 275–77.

[151] Susan McClary, in her "Constructions of Gender in Monteverdi's Dramatic Music," in *Feminine Endings: Music, Gender, and Sexuality* (Minneapolis: University of Minnesota Press, 1991), 46–48, notes the feminizing effect of Orfeo's laments and moments of madness already in the earlier Striggio/Monteverdi opera (where the character was portrayed by a tenor). She even suggests that this characterization "may well have precipitated a crisis in gender representation for the musical stage": "sexuality and madness … prove to be extremely problematic when enacted by male characters" (48). I might conjecture that, if such a dilemma was truly felt to exist, it may have been at least partially solved by the employment of castrati (who at the early date of Monteverdi's *Orfeo* had yet to find a regular niche for themselves in the new genre) in these effeminized operatic roles.

the soul of Pluto he reveals his dangerously effeminate powers. In fact, with respect to the Orpheus legend generally, Austern notes that in this period "the power of Orpheus over the finality of Death and over all earthly objects and beings was clearly secondary ... to the implicitly sexual and feminizing capacity of his music."[152] The alluring voice and effeminate appearance of an Atto Melani would have rendered such a figure with ease.

With the operatic reforms of the early eighteenth century, roles for castrati would seem to take on a more masculine character. In works by Metastasio and his imitators, castrato singers could portray heroic military leaders like Julius Caesar or Alexander the Great, apparently far less enslaved by their amorous passions. Indeed, Heller has spoken of a "reconstruction of operatic masculinity that was a driving force in the reform of Italian opera in the early 18th century," a "complete reworking of ... gender representation."[153] She constructs this view from the writings of several important opera critics, including Lodovico Muratori, Gian Vincenzo Gravina, Giovanni Maria Crescimbeni, and Scipione Maffei, all of whom (implicitly or explicitly) fault the genre for its effeminizing effects. She also evaluates actual librettos, with Metastasio's *Achille in Sciro* as a case study. This opera tells the story of Achilles's concealment as a woman at the court of King Lycomedes, Ulysses's ensuing ruse to recruit the hero for the Trojan War, and Achilles's anxiety over abandoning his lover Deidamia. Heller points out that, unlike earlier librettos on the subject, Metastasio's text highlights the moment when Achilles rejects his feminine disguise and, specifically, the feminine practice of singing. As she puts it, "by rejecting his skirt for armour and throwing down his lyre in favour of a sword, he abandons the ambiguity of gender that was integral to the conventions of *seicento* opera (including his own operatic representations), and so becomes an eloquent proponent of the reform of Italian opera."[154]

Metastasian heroes – including Achilles – are certainly more "masculine" than their seventeenth-century forebears, and doubtless the change owes much to contemporary discourse on gender in opera. But I would describe this change less as a "complete reworking" than as a shift of emphasis. While reform librettos may abandon obviously weak male roles, the heroes are still particularly susceptible to love: indeed, this susceptibility, which typically conflicts with the demands of duty, provokes the action of many reform operas. Although in act II, scene 8, Metastasio's Achilles forswears all things feminine – including music – in favor of war, he almost immediately

---

[152] Austern, "'Alluring,'" 351.

[153] Wendy Heller, "Reforming Achilles: Gender, *Opera seria* and the Rhetoric of the Enlightened Hero," *Early Music* 26 (1998): 567–68.

[154] Ibid., 567.

launches into another aria (II.9), in which he admits, "at the sight of her beautiful eyes alone does my heart melt."[155] Indeed, notwithstanding his decision to leave for the war, Achilles spends most of act III vacillating between his love for Deidamia, who begs him to stay, and his duty to Ulysses, who urges departure. In scene 3, Arcade, a secondary character, tellingly observes of the hero, "Behold both glory and love put to the test"; and as the scene progresses, and Achilles refuses to abandon his lady, Arcade whispers, "Love has triumphed."[156] At this point Achilles sings to his beloved a text that any of his *Seicento* predecessors could have uttered:

Tornate sereni,	Becalm yourselves,
Begli astri d'amore:	beautiful stars of love:
La speme baleni	Hope flashes
Fra il vostro dolore:	into your sorrow:
Se mesti girate,	If you turn sad,
Mi fate morir.	it will kill me.
Oh Dio! lo sapete,	Oh God! you know that
Voi soli al mio core,	you alone in my heart
Voi date e togliete	give and take away
La forza e l'ardir.[157]	strength and courage.

In discussing Giulio Strozzi's 1641 opera on the same subject (*La finta pazza*), Heller comments on the character identified as Eunuco: "The importance of the eunuch in this translation of the Achilles myth cannot be underestimated, as he mediates the space between Achilles' masculine and feminine identities, a constant reminder of the transience of gender categories, particularly on the opera stage."[158] I would make the same argument for Metastasio's own Achilles: that this character would typically have been portrayed by a eunuch (as Metastasio must have expected) ensures that Achilles's feminine side – conspicuous to the end of the opera – receives full expression.[159] Indeed, most Metastasian heroes, like Achilles, remain

---

[155] The aria is sung as a message that Nearco should take to Deidamia (Pietro Metastasio, *Tutte le opere di Pietro Metastasio*, ed. Bruno Brunelli, vol. I, I Classici Mondadori, Fondazione Borletti [Milan: A. Mondadori, 1943], 785–86): "Dille che si consoli; / Dille che m'ami; e dille / Che parti fido Achille, / Che fido tornerà. // Che a' suoi begli occhi soli / Vuo' che il mio cor si stempre; / Che l'idol mio fu sempre, / Che l'idol mio sarà."

[156] Ibid., 791 and 795.   [157] Ibid., 796–97.   [158] Heller, "Reforming Achilles," 575.

[159] Roger Covell's study of casting practices – which concentrates on Metastasio's operas, many in productions under Metastasio's supervision – confirms that such roles continued to be taken primarily by castrati: Roger Covell, "Voice Register as an Index of Age and Status in Opera Seria," in *Opera and Vivaldi*, ed. Michael Collins and Elise K. Kirk (Austin: University of Texas Press, 1984), 193–210 *passim*. It seems unlikely that Metastasio, for all his apparent concern about the problems of "effeminacy" in opera, would have imagined anything other than treble voices taking his leading male roles.

highly susceptible to love, even if they recognize the competing claims of duty: they continue to inhabit a middle ground, they "mediate the space," between amorous effeminacy and scrupulous masculinity.

The extremist operatic reformers who attempted to eliminate the amo-rous/effeminate element in opera simply did not succeed, nor can their tastes be taken as representative of contemporary audiences, for whom the soft hero must by that time have seemed normative and fitting. Perhaps the clearest expression of such an outlook comes in 1702 from the Italophile Frenchman François Raguenet in his famous *Paralele des Italiens et des François, en ce qui regarde la musique et les opera*. In a passage that articulates the general theme of this chapter, he writes,

these [castrato] voices, sweet as nightingales, are enchanting in the mouths of actors playing the part of a lover. Nothing is more touching than the expression of their pains uttered in that timbre of voice, so tender and impassioned. And in this the Italians have a great advantage over the lovers in our [French] theaters whose voices, heavy and virile, are always far less suited to the sweet words they address to their mistresses.[160]

In a similar way, but from the opposite perspective, Muratori's very com-plaints confirm that treble voices continued to "inspire undue tenderness and languor in the souls of the audience."[161] That is, these voices communi-cated precisely the "effeminate passion – love – without which," Apostolo Zeno lamented in 1730, "it appears that no plausible drama can be writ-ten."[162] I would suggest, then, that the Metastasian reforms achieved just one step in the movement toward modern "masculinity" on the lyrical stage, a movement whose next obvious step (in opera seria) came only with the elimination of the treble hero in the early nineteenth century. Throughout virtually his entire history, then, the castrato remained tied to the tempered masculinity of the lover.

To conclude this discussion, I return to Atto's life. By now I hope it is clear why he might have attracted some men and women. He certainly did little to dispel his aura of effeminacy. Admitting that he lacked "vivacity of spirit," Atto openly loathed typically masculine activities such as hunting and instead seems to have cultivated a more refined elegance: the anonymous

---

[160] [François Raguenet], *Paralele des Italiens et des François, en ce qui regarde la musique et les opera* (1702; repr., Geneva: Minkoff Reprint, 1976), 79–81.

[161] Lodovico Antonio Muratori, *Della perfetta poesia italiana spiegata* (Modena: Soliani, 1706), quoted and translated in Heller, "Reforming Achilles," 568.

[162] Apostolo Zeno, *Lettere*, 2nd edn. (Venice: Sansoni, 1785), no. 756, quoted and translated in Heller, "Reforming Achilles," 571.

satire aimed at him suggests that he adopted the most fashionable clothes, hairstyles, and makeup.[163] With similarly polished manners, he claims to have made himself into "a most perfect courtier," and his letters reveal an extreme of obsequiousness that must often have been maddening to men of a more forthright – that is, masculine – character. One can imagine repeated exchanges like Cardinal Jacopo Rospigliosi's interruption of Atto's lengthy pleasantries with an impatient "Basta Signor Atto."[164] In both appearance and behavior, it would seem, Atto fit well the pattern of the enticing effeminate.

Interestingly, the two ladies most closely tied to him, Hortense and Marie Mancini, were considered in their time dangerously strong women. (For more on their mutual history, see chapter 5.) Both were outspoken and powerful personalities. After marrying Lorenzo Onofrio Colonna, Marie became virtually the second woman of Rome, after the even more "mannish" Queen Christina of Sweden. But Marie's eventual dissatisfaction with that city and with her husband led her finally to flee back to France, a move considered both embarrassing and effeminizing for Lorenzo.[165] Hortense too fled her husband, the duke Mazarin, ostensibly to escape his mistreatment and bizarre behavior, but probably as much to conduct her many love affairs with freedom.[166] For these she earned a formidable reputation, upon which Atto himself even comments in a series of letters.[167]

In fact, the qualities of these ladies are so extraordinary as to evoke the aforementioned discourse of the Incogniti on exceptional women. To my mind, they even recall specific operatic heroines. On the one hand, Marie might be said to resemble the Dido of Giovanni Francesco Busenello's *La Didone* (Cavalli, 1641): deserted by her Aeneas (in Marie's case, Louis XIV) for political reasons, this Dido resigns herself not to death but to marrying another (Colonna). On the other hand, Hortense even more clearly corresponds to the Messalina of Francesco Maria Piccioli's *La Messalina* (Pallavicino, 1680): by reputation, at least, Hortense shared the sexual voraciousness of the wife of the Roman Emperor Claudius. In both operas, the men enamored of these women – King Iarba and Claudius – are portrayed by

---

[163] On his lack of "la vivacità dello spirito," see his letter to Mattias, from Fontainebleau, August 31, 1658; on his aversion to the hunt, his letters to the duke of Mantua, from Innsbruck, May 25, 1653 and June 8, 1653: "qui si va ogni giorno al gallo, ma spero di ritornare in Italia senza haver veduta questa caccia"; "io che non sono cacciatore." On the satire, see above and appendix C.
[164] Atto to de Lionne, from Rome, August 5, 1669.
[165] Bevan, *The Duchess Hortense*, 39–51; Claude Dulong, *Marie Mancini: La première passion de Louis XIV* (Paris: Perrin, 1993), 149–222.
[166] Bevan, *The Duchess Hortense*, 25–31.
[167] On Hortense's extra-marital affairs, ibid., 28–29 and *passim*. On Atto's comments, see for example his letter to de Lionne, from Rome, October 23, 1668 (chapter 6).

castrati.[168] To push the analogy even further, one might observe that in the relationship of Carlo II of Mantua and Margarita della Rovere, one can find all the weakness and dependence of a Nerone on his Poppea: at least as described by Leti, Margarita used her charms to dominate the duke. And there is even an Ottone in this scenario in the person of Margarita's jealous but powerless husband, the count della Rovere. If Carlo II had ever become an operatic character, he too would almost certainly have been played by a castrato.

Such parallels are more, I would suggest, than fortuitous coincidences. Strong women and weak men were stock characters not only on stage but in real life: they represented two of the implicit personae that contemporaries recognized in the world around them. The difference between street and theater was one of magnitude. Just as stage sets might idealize an architectural vista or costumes aggrandize Roman armor, so too did the castrato magnify the familiar effeminate youth. It was an age that valued artifice: the far-flung conceits of Marinistic poetry, the fantastic opulence of Jesuit church style, the extravagant rituals of court existence. Even in landscape design, as the historian Franco Valsecchi writes, "it is artifice that dominates, the search for effect … Nature is transformed, deformed; the vegetation is choked by art."[169] So too was the natural boy transformed by his deforming surgery into something deemed more compelling than Nature's own creations. And yet this change did not make him alien. Rather, theater and life so thoroughly interpenetrated in this century as to make a castrato like Atto seem just one more avatar – if especially vivid – of the erotically boyish male.

---

[168] Also interesting is that Enea in *La Didone* is *not* played by a castrato, but by a tenor: here is a man who eventually masters his passions and pursues the more masculine task of state-building.

[169] Franco Valsecchi, *L'Italia nel Seicento e nel Settecento*, vol. VI of *Società e costume: Panorama di storia sociale e tecnologica* (Turin: U.T.E.T., 1967), 23–24.

5 ❧ Disgrace and transformation: 1656–1671

As we have seen, by the mid-1650s, Atto was concerning himself increasingly over prestige and social advancement. To cultivate his image, he sought to behave and be treated like a gentleman, a musical amateur rather than professional. For a castrato, such a pose was challenging, and Atto's patrons often thwarted him. As he must have realized, his benefits hinged fundamentally on his voice; the aristocrats who fed, clothed, and paid him were hardly ready to relinquish the service on which they founded their support. In their eyes, Atto remained first and foremost a *virtuoso*, and no amount of cleverness and nerve on Atto's part could really challenge that perception.

Atto seems to have recognized this problem and, in the later 1650s, formulated his radical solution: he would give up performance altogether. The trick was how to do it without losing everything: he needed to offer another, equally valuable service. Of course, he had already demonstrated a talent for news-gathering and foreign espionage, and so not surprisingly he sought greater involvement in international politics. It was a career path with some precedent: politically savvy singers such as Marc'Antonio Pasqualini and Felice Cancellieri, as well as artists like Peter Paul Rubens, had turned increasingly to diplomacy in later life (see introduction and chapter 1).[1] The key difference is that none of these predecessors ever fully abandoned his art. Yet over the course of fifteen years, Atto did just that. The more he mediated between powerful aristocrats, the less he sang for them, so that by the early 1670s he had fully transformed himself. As a *pronotario apostolico* to Clement X and a recognized agent of France in Rome, Atto was considered a diplomat, and his musical background, rarely mentioned, played virtually no role in his endeavors.

One may legitimately ask whether tracing a singer's renunciation of music can reveal anything of interest about music history. At least in Atto's case, I believe it can, for his efforts help expose the place of music and musicians in his culture. From one angle, these years show even more clearly than before how musical relationships could fit into the broader patronage structures governing society. From another, Atto's successful makeover corroborates

---

[1] See Marie-Anne Lescourret, *Rubens: A Double Life*, trans. Elfreda Powell (Chicago: Ivan R. Dee, 1993), 104, 116–17, originally published as *Rubens* ([Paris]: J.C. Lattès, 1990).

the idea – introduced in the previous chapter – of the *Seicento* castrato as an unremarkable figure. The unifying theme of this period of Atto's life is the depth of his resolve to leave his profession: it drove him to risky conduct, sustained him through disgrace, and finally propelled him to distinction and wealth. At many points, he could have opted for the safer, more predictable life of a court or church musician. His steady refusal of those paths gauges the dishonor he now saw in musical service, even as a star singer. While vocal artistry may have earned him social entrée, real advancement depended on an equally artistic feat of retirement.

Le chant du cygne

It is hardly coincidental that Atto's last important period of vocal activity – in many ways his swan song – took place in France, specifically, during the five years following his return to that country in 1656.[2] Predictably, his obsession with prestige continued to intensify at this time. Yet because the French lyric theater – with king and courtiers on both sides of the footlights – retained its aristocratic character, Atto performed contentedly in several productions that, had they occurred elsewhere, he might have shunned. As the political situation in France began to change, however, Atto's personal blend of politics and art began to create new problems for him. And these developments, which eliminated Paris as a performance venue, surely reinforced his determination to change careers.

At first, though, all went very well. As in the previous decade, Cardinal Mazarin requested Atto's presence in Paris, hoping the singer would again charm the French sovereigns. The cardinal writes to Mattias de' Medici on January 4, 1657, "Your Highness could not have given these Majesties [Anne and Louis] a gift more precious and valued than the person of Atto Melani, who has been received in this court with particular relish … Having now heard him, Their Majesties have found him entirely to their satisfaction."[3] Atto himself reports on the enthusiasm of the royal family and, as usual, emphasizes his success: "the curiosity of the queen and of His Majesty kept me [at court] until midnight, so that I sang for over three hours on the first night. By my good fortune I have met with the approval of Their Majesties

---

[2] The precise date of Atto's return to Paris is uncertain. He writes to Mattias from Lyon on December 16, 1656 and then next from Paris on January 4, 1657. The latter letter (quoted below) does not indicate the day of arrival, but because he apologizes for not writing with the preceding post, which usually ran weekly, he probably arrived shortly before December 28.

[3] Cardinal Jules Mazarin to Mattias de' Medici, from Paris, January 4, 1657.

and His Eminence, who have said repeatedly that they find my singing much better than the last time I was in France."[4]

Contrary to Louis XIV's reputation, the teenage monarch really does seem to have enjoyed Italian music at this time. In addition to Atto's testimony, a letter of April 1656 from the composer Giovanni Francesco Tagliavacca reports that a pair of his own arias are "the two favorite songs of His Majesty, which he enjoys tremendously, especially *Amar per penare*, which the king, my master, commands to be performed continually."[5] While the self-serving goals of this statement (like Atto's) might seem to undermine its credibility, an anonymous letter from the same year offers less biased testimony: "Oh, what applause that cantata by Signor Carissimi, *Le ferite d'un cor*, has received here from the king, queen, and the entire court. They are happy because this music has surpassed all the other pieces that had satisfied in the past."[6]

That the king's primary affection and talent lay with the ballet goes without saying. Henry Prunières contends, quite reasonably, that the king enjoyed Italian music best when it was incorporated into a dance medium.[7] Atto's correspondence seems to agree:

I serve the king and queen with the keenest diligence, and to find out whether I sing better than before, they hear and see me most gladly. The queen in particular requests that I be at her *lever* every morning, so as to have me sing while she dresses and arranges her hair … and at these times the king also is present. As he takes

---

[4] Atto to Mattias, from Paris, January 4, 1657. Earlier in the same letter he apologizes for being late with his news: "Credevo di poter la settimana passata Riverire V.A. dandole parte del mio arrivo in questa Corte e di quanto mi era seguito, ma la Curiosità della Regina e di S.M., me tennero fino alla meza [*sic*] notte, havendo la prima sera, Cantato sopra tre hore."

[5] The letter of Tagliavacca dates from April 21, 1656 and is to Duke Carlo II of Mantua (I MAas, E.XV.3, busta 685, Diversi-1656, quoted and translated by Henry Prunières, *L'opéra italien en France avant Lulli*, Bibliothèque de l'Institut Français de Florence [Université de Grenoble] ser. 1, Collection d'histoire et de linguistique française et italienne comparées, no. 3 [Paris: Honoré Champion, 1913], 183–84). Atto casts Tagliavacca in a rather less positive light in a letter to Mattias, from Paris, January 11, 1657: "Tagliavacca è pessissimo di mal francese, facendolo però passare per cattarro falso."

[6] Anonymous letter of September 8, 1656 from the French court in Compiègne, as cited in Josef Loschelder, "Neue Beiträge zu einer Biographie Giacomo Carissimis," *Archiv für Musikforschung* 5 (1940): 229. Loschelder notes only that this letter appears in a *fond* in the archives of the Collegium Germanicum in Rome entitled "Carissimis Leben, wie es hätte verlaufen können." The work is the three-voice (SST) cantata *Le ferite d'un cor sono i tormenti*, as identified in Gloria Rose, compil., *Giacomo Carissimi (1605–1674)*, The Wellesley Cantata Index Series, fasc. 5 ([Wellesley, Mass.]: Wellesley College, 1966).

[7] Prunières, *L'opéra italien*, 180–81. Prunières (267) also cites an exchange in which Francesco Buti tries to convince Mazarin that such entertainments would be more appreciated by the court if they were sung in French, to which Mazarin responds that these performances are not for the court but for the king and queen, who both prefer Italian music and verse.

extraordinary delight in Italian music, he is very happy I have come to France, especially because I have arrived in time to serve him in his ballet.[8]

The ballet in question, entitled *Amour malade* (*Amor malato*), was a collaboration between Francesco Buti and the young Jean-Baptiste Lully and blended French dance and Italian singing just as the king favored.[9] The conceit of this elaborately produced work, first performed on January 17, 1657, is described in the *livret*: "After a short consultation about the sickness with which Love is afflicted, two great doctors, Time and Scorn – in the presence of Reason, who was acting as Love's escort – prescribe the diversion of a comic ballet as a remedy."[10] This trifle of a plot introduces the danced entertainment; vocal music is limited to two scenes at the beginning and end, and single short arias after each of the ten *entrées*.

Notwithstanding his recent arrival, Atto was assigned the title role. Mazarin apparently hoped to encourage the young king's project by contributing an esteemed singer. Atto's letter of January 26 describes not only his participation, but also his interaction with the king, who danced the role of Divertissement: "Here we devote ourselves to performing His Majesty's ballet, which is to be presented Sunday and Wednesday. Never again will I be able to see an entertainment in such comfort, since, portraying "Ailing Cupid," I remain in bed from beginning to end, and resting there too is His Majesty, who dances in a manner that steals everyone's heart."[11] No wonder Atto was happy: to share the same rather intimate piece of furniture with someone whose very glance signaled favor constituted real social distinction.

Atto also appeared in the entertainments surrounding the wedding of the king to Maria Teresa of Spain in 1660. The central event was planned to be Buti and Cavalli's *Ercole amante*, the work that infuriated Atto for its lack of a leading castrato role (see chapter 3). But delays in construction of the new

---

[8] Atto to Mattias, from Paris, February 2, 1657.

[9] Marie-Françoise Christout, *Le ballet de cour de Louis XIV 1643–1672: Mises en scène*, La vie musicale en France sous les rois Bourbons, no. 12 (Paris: A. et J. Picard, 1967), 82–83: Buti wrote the Italian "livret" and Isaac de Benserade the accompanying French "vers." All of the information below concerning *Amor malato* is drawn from Christout, 82–83; Prunières, *L'opéra*, 198–205; and Philippe Beaussant, *Lully, ou, Le musicien du soleil* (Paris: Gallimard/Théâtre des Champs-Elysées, 1992), 149–52.

[10] Beaussant (*Lully*, 149) quotes these lines without citation; they seem to be drawn, however, from the published *livret* (see Christout, *Le ballet de cour*, 262).

[11] Atto to Mattias, from Paris, January 26, 1657. The first part of this quotation has previously been cited by other authors (Prunières, *L'opéra*, 203; Beaussant, *Lully*, 149), but always without the concluding information about the king. The libretto of the ballet states that it was "Dansé par Sa Majesté le 17. jour de janvier 1657" (as cited in Christout, *Le ballet de cour*, 262, although in the text [82] Christout gives the date as January 20). Atto's comments in this letter would place performances on Sunday, January 21, and Wednesday, January 24.

theater forced a substitution of amusements.[12] First, Cavalli's *Xerse* was given on November 22 in a small temporary theater in the Galerie des Peintures at the Louvre.[13] *Entrées de ballets*, by Lully, were added between each act in an attempt to adapt the work for its audience. But while the dancing succeeded splendidly, the eight-hour performance – which lacked changes of scenery and breaks for meals – irritated more than impressed. To recover, Mazarin quickly ordered another work, this time a Franco-Italian ballet in the mold of *Amour malade*. The result was the aptly themed *Ballet de l'Impatience*, first performed on February 19, 1661, with an Italian text by Buti, French text by Isaac de Benserade, and music by Lully. With greater aristocratic participation and music more to French tastes, the ballet earned general approval.[14]

Atto's participation in both these works raises a number of questions about his singing at this time. First, both the libretto and score from *Xerse* indicate that Atto sang the alto-range role of Arsamene, brother of Xerxes.[15] The vocal compass of the role extends a minor third below the lowest note of Atto's own compositions (b♭), works he presumably wrote for himself.[16] Had something happened to Atto's soprano voice? Certainly castrato voices (like all voices) did sometimes deepen with age.[17] Prunières reinforces this impression by suggesting that Atto sang another alto role in the *Ballet de l'Impatience*.[18] Perhaps at the age of thirty-five the singer's voice had begun to change or deteriorate.

---

[12] In his letter to Mattias, from Paris, October 22, 1660, Atto wryly comments about the delayed *Ercole* production, "Per le feste, non sono che una, e costerà sopra 500 mila scudi, perché sono 500 mila persone che rubbano, e la sala che si fabbrica, con le scene, importerà più di 300 mila scudi."

[13] Atto writes to Mattias, from Paris, September 10, 1660, revealing that other performances of the work were at least planned: "Si dichiarò appunto hiersera il signor Cardinale, che voleva che si facesse qui nel suo palazzo, il più presto che fosse stato possibile, la commedia del Xerse, che s'imparò già per farsi in Provenza, a St. Giovanni de Lutz [Saint-Jean-de-Luz], et a Fontanablò, e che per non essersene più parlato, tutti se l'erano scordata."

[14] The above paragraph is based on Prunières, *L'opéra*, 250–55, 261; Christout, *Le ballet de cour*, 101–4; and [Isaac de] Benserade, *Ballets pour Louis XIV*, ed. Marie-Claude Canova-Green, Collection de rééditions de textes du XVIIe siècle (Toulouse: Société de Littératures Classiques; Paris: Éditions Klincksieck, 1997), II:473–74.

[15] He also apparently sang in the second *entrée de ballet*, "Des Paysans et Paysanes, chantans et dansans à l'Espagnole": his name is included in the list of performers cited in the libretto. See Fernando Liuzzi, *I musicisti in Francia*, vol. I, *Dalle origini al secolo XVII*, L'opera del genio italiano all'estero, second series (Rome: Edizioni d'arte Danesi, 1946), 199.

[16] For an edition of these works, see Atto Melani, *Complete Cantatas*, ed. Roger Freitas, Collegium Musicum: Yale University, series 2, vol. 15 (Middleton, Wis.: A-R Editions, 2006). The lowest written note for his part in Rossi's *Orfeo* is c′, which is in fact Orpheus's last note, sung as he expires; otherwise, the lowest note is d′.

[17] Peter Browe, *Zur Geschichte der Entmannung: Eine religions- und rechtsgeschlichtliche Studie* (Breslau: Müller und Seiffert, 1936), 86–91, quoted in John Rosselli, "The Castrati as a Professional Group and a Social Phenomenon, 1550–1850," *Acta musicologica* 60 (1988): 148.

[18] Prunières, *L'opéra*, 264.

I doubt this explanation, however. As several of the preceding quotations attest, Atto's auditors were at this time praising his singing as better than ever, with no mention of decline or radical change. Likewise, Atto continued to identify himself as a soprano, if indirectly: in his rant about Buti's libretto for *Ercole*, Atto charges that "through his malevolence, [Buti] has created characters inappropriate for a *soprano* voice."[19] Finally, the libretto of the second work, the *Ballet de l'Impatience*, gives only the names of performers, not their voice types, and all but a single scene of the Italian music is lost.[20] Prunières only thought Atto sang alto in the ballet because he had done so in *Xerse*.

A better justification for these events can again be found, I believe, in status, specifically in Atto's stated refusal to portray minor or female characters (again, see chapter 3).[21] With the role of Xerse transposed for baritone, the only remaining treble-range leading male part was Arsamene. In the end, Atto sang the only principal role that his voice and self-image would allow. One could perhaps argue that, were Atto still singing soprano, his role too could have been transposed. But such a transposition, by third or fourth, would have been more complicated than the simple octave shift for Xerse, particularly in the many ensemble passages. And considering the rushed nature of the production, Atto may well have been asked to adapt his accomplished technique to the music as it stood. In any case, the evidence suggests that Atto was still in command of his voice at this time.

More difficult to explain is Atto's portrayal of the quite subordinate character of L'Amante capriccioso in the *Ballet*. The featured singers in this work were Atto's fellow Pistoiese Antonio Rivani (as Amore), his own brother Filippo (La Patienza), and Anna Bergerotti (L'Impatienza).[22] Although the latter two characters would probably have been represented as female, making them uninviting to Atto, he must have bristled to see Rivani, whose abilities he had once disparaged, usurp the character of Amore in which Atto himself had recently triumphed (in *Amour malade*).[23] Interestingly, Buti

---

[19] Atto to Mattias, from Aix-en-Provence, February 28, 1660 (emphasis mine).

[20] Prunières, *L'opéra*, 262–65. Prunières reproduces the one surviving Italian scene, the "Récit des Preneurs de Tabac" in his appendix (19–26).

[21] The relevant comment comes from his letter to Mattias, from Aix-en-Provence, March 1, 1660: "perché io non voglio [cantare in] machine, e non rappresenterei in alcun modo, a meno di fare una delle principali parte, fuori anche di donne, voglio lasciar correre [le cose]."

[22] Filippo Melani was called by Mazarin from his post at the court of Archduke Sigismund of Austria at the end of 1659 to take part in the wedding festivities (Prunières, *L'opéra*, 233). As Atto's letter to Mattias, from Paris, October 22, 1660 reveals, Filippo did not like Paris at all: "non le piace punto la francia, e meno la città di Parigi." The name of Atto's role is given slightly differently in French at the beginning of the libretto: "L'amour capricieux" (Benserade, *Ballets*, II:476).

[23] Atto to Mattias, from Rome, May 1, 1655. (The context confirms that Atto is indeed speaking of Rivani's *vocal* abilities here.)

had called Rivani to Paris without Mazarin's knowledge, and Prunières suggests his motivation was to have a castrato to oppose to the Melani brothers.[24] If true, Atto's resentment must have been intense. How could he have countenanced the indignity?

Unfortunately, Atto's regular correspondence with Mattias does not survive from this period (November 1660 to May 1661), but I would offer the following conjecture. Mazarin was suffering his final illness just as this ballet was being prepared; indeed, the cardinal died (on March 9) just days before a scheduled performance at his chateau.[25] As will emerge below, the passing of Mazarin resulted in catastrophe for Atto's position in France: without his powerful protector, latent hostility erupted from many quarters. As the cardinal's potency waned, Buti may have felt free to settle old scores and demote his enemy. In this changed political terrain, Atto could no longer suppress his rival and was forced to yield to those whom he considered "so much my inferiors."[26] Whereas Atto had often exploited to his benefit the link between stage and society, especially in France, the tables were now turned. In the power struggle surrounding Mazarin's death, Atto found himself downgraded from favorite to outsider, a descent paralleled within the theatrical pecking order. Once that happened and even France ceased to be a refuge of prestige, Atto faced a crisis.

Man of action

Well before the dire events of 1661, of course, Atto had been exploring his non-musical options. Earlier chapters have recounted how Atto's artistic assignments had always been mixed up with politics and how his efforts at espionage moved him further in this direction. But in the years just prior to 1661 he saw his first opportunities to do more than simply report what he learned: he was now called to take an active role in diplomacy. Not surprisingly, perhaps, many of his early efforts faltered. But those efforts won him appreciation and, more importantly, financial and personal honors, all to

---

[24] Prunières, *L'opéra*, 244.   [25] Ibid., 266.

[26] Atto to Mattias, from Aix-en-Provence, February 28, 1660. Not surprisingly, Rivani's opinion differed completely. When he learned that Atto was scheduled to take part in *Ercole in Tebe* (G.A. Moniglia/Jacopo Melani) in Florence, he warned Cardinal Giovan Carlo, "guardi bene quello che fa, perché non ha [Atto] più voce di soprano, né di contralto, né di mezo soprano" (letter from Paris, October 22, 1660; as transcribed in Sara Mamone, *Serenissimi fratelli principi impresari: Notizie di spettacolo nei carteggi medicei: Carteggi di Giovan Carlo de' Medici e di Desiderio Montemagni suo segretario [1628–1664]*, Storia dello spettacolo: Fonti, no. 3 [Florence: Le Lettere, 2003], 347). These singers competed too intensely for this comment to be taken seriously (although the articulation of voice types is interesting).

such a degree – so much greater than his singing had achieved – that diplomacy must quickly have seemed the best path forward.

Atto's first assignment involved him in the aftermath of the death of his one-time admirer Emperor Ferdinand III on April 2, 1657. To understand Atto's role, some background is needed. For many years, the primary aim of French foreign policy had been to weaken Habsburg control over the nations ringing France. Although hostilities between France and the Empire had ceased with the signing of the Peace of Westphalia in 1648, Mazarin saw in the imperial interregnum an opportunity to further this goal. By convention the succession was voted by eight princely electors (sacred and secular), but for almost a century the dominance of the Habsburg family had made the election little more than ceremonial. But the peace treaty, which favored French interests, had undermined the image of the imperial family, and at Ferdinand's death his son Leopold, at sixteen, was still fourteen months too young to be elected. Sensing vulnerability, Mazarin nourished the hope of putting a non-Habsburg on the throne.[27]

The cardinal quickly made his case to his allies among the German states. Many of the Protestant rulers already feared encroachment from the arch-Catholic Habsburgs, and Mazarin fueled anxieties by warning that a strong Habsburg emperor might reignite the German wars. Naturally, Mazarin proposed alternative candidates. Foremost was Louis XIV himself, although the cardinal probably never expected the young king to be considered seriously. More in earnest, he suggested two German princes with French sympathies: Count Philipp-Wilhelm of Neuburg and Elector Ferdinand Maria of Bavaria. To further his designs, Mazarin sent the Maréchal Antoine III, duke de Gramont, and Hugues de Lionne as plenipotentiaries to Frankfurt, the site of the electoral college.

As the historian Adolphe Chéruel observes, Mazarin generally liked to employ clandestine tactics in addition to public ones, and it is here that the cardinal found a role for his favorite singer.[28] The elector of Bavaria was demonstrating a reluctance to accept the imperial candidacy: both his mother, the sister of the previous emperor, and his pro-Habsburg prime minister, Count Maximilian Kurtz, strongly advised against it. But the elector's wife, Henriette-Adelaide of Savoy, supported Mazarin's project, out of personal ambition if for no other reason. As we have seen, Atto's quest for patronage

---

[27] The preceding paragraph, and the following one, are based on A[dolphe] Chéruel, *Histoire de France sous le ministère de Mazarin (1651–1661)* (Paris: Hachette, 1882), III:84–87, 109–10; and Charles W. Ingrao, *The Habsburg Monarchy 1618–1815*, New Approaches to European History, 2nd edn. (Cambridge: Cambridge Univeristy Press, 2000), 54–57.

[28] Chéruel, *Histoire*, III:96: "Il [Mazarin] aimait à se servir de ces émissaires obscurs." This comment refers specifically to Atto and Blondel.

had resulted in long-standing ties with the Savoy dynasty: he first met Henriette-Adelaide in Turin in 1649, and he had visited her again during his trip through the German states in 1653.[29] Mazarin now looked to exploit his singer's contacts. At first, Atto merely launched a campaign of correspondence with the electress aimed at helping her persuade her husband to accept the nomination. None of these letters survives, but Mazarin remarks on September 2 that "it is [Signor Atto] whom I employed rather usefully to initiate negotiations with the elector of Bavaria."[30] When the elector still would not commit, Mazarin asked much more of Atto and charged him with a delicate personal mission to the Bavarian court.

On August 30, 1657, the eve of his journey, Atto wrote a letter to Mattias in which he not only confirms his prior role in the project, but indicates his special fitness:

I was once again about to travel to Germany, since … much better news arrived about the intentions and decisions of the elector of Bavaria. Because I can say I played a big role in this, the king judged me capable of furthering the ongoing plan, and of doing so with extreme secrecy, for, being far from suspicion, I can act without drawing attention to myself.[31]

Indeed, Mazarin confirms in his letter to Gramont that "if there is something to do on the Bavarian issue, you can send [Atto] there, and he will execute your orders without anyone developing suspicion."[32] Atto's reputation as a singer, in addition to his acquaintance with the electress, allowed him access to all the important figures at court.

Atto must have worked quickly, for although he seems to have arrived in Munich only in early September, Mazarin's first responses to his efforts date from the twenty-fifth of that month.[33] The cardinal's letter is interesting not only because it evaluates Atto's efforts, but also because it is one of just a few extant missives from Mazarin to Atto:

[29] Atto mentions his first visit to Turin in his letter to Christine of France, the duchess of Savoy, November 13, 1653.

[30] Mazarin to Gramont, September 2, 1657, quoted in Chéruel, *Histoire*, III:96.

[31] Atto to Mattias, from Péronne, August 30, 1657. Another reason Atto was able to carry out his mission was that the elector spoke excellent Italian (Chéruel, *Histoire*, III:87); Atto apparently never mastered German.

[32] Mazarin to Gramont, September 2, 1657, quoted in Chéruel, *Histoire*, III:96. Atto's primary duty was apparently to deliver secret letters to the elector and his wife, something the official plenipotentiaries could not do without the elector's mother or Count Kurtz finding out (see Atto's letter to the duchess of Savoy, from La Fère, August 28, 1657). His assignment seems to have become more complex as time passed.

[33] The documents do not establish Atto's precise date of arrival in Munich, but considering that he wrote from Péronne on August 30, and that Mazarin's letter to him in Munich on September 25 is a response to at least one previous letter from that city, an arrival date in early September is likely.

You will receive enclosed a long letter I am writing for you, ostensibly to the duke and duchess of Bavaria, but I will say aside to you that the spirit and zeal with which you have conducted your assigned business merits praise. But I cannot approve the facility with which you have represented your proposal as signed, with nothing else required. You do not have great experience in the affairs of the world, and so you mistake a good intention for the completed agreement and crow of triumph before the victory.[34]

As Mazarin suggests, Atto tended to exaggerate the positive results of his projects, sometimes to the point of distortion: presumably he hoped to impress his patrons by overstating his skills. The following report to the duchess of Savoy, the electress's mother, not only describes his work in Munich, but also misrepresents, as will be seen, the degree of his success:

It has been several weeks since I returned to Frankfurt from Bavaria with the responses of those electoral highnesses to His Majesty. Since the responses entirely satisfied these royal ambassadors [Gramont and de Lionne], I hope that the king himself will be very pleased with them and that the elector accepts the offers the king has made him. The elector still has not declared himself willing to accept the crown because he fears that eventually the secret would be discovered; he promises to make the final decision on this situation.

The fact that I was received into that court for every other thing [but negotiating] has given me the freedom to receive many audiences from the elector, which took place in extreme secrecy. Even so, his minister [Kurtz] is furious at not being able to figure out how His Electoral Highness has learned about things. Although [Kurtz] is now trying to impress different decisions upon the elector's mind, the principal resolution remains nailed down, and the elector – through me – agrees to it secretly with the king, having given me the message himself.[35]

In fact, despite Atto's optimism, the mission ended in failure. Already on October 20 Mazarin doubted the encouraging reports: "the more I examine Atto's undertaking, the more it seems to me that the thing is not in so good a state as first appeared, for it is impossible that the elector's responses, so just and measured, were not planned with Count Kurtz."[36] In the end, the elector's personal ambition did not overcome the advice of his ministers, who feared that challenging the Habsburgs could bring damaging reprisals.[37] Worse, Atto's subterfuge was eventually discovered, and he was duly expelled

---

[34] Mazarin to Atto, from Metz, September 25, 1657.

[35] Atto to Christine of France, duchess of Savoy, from Frankfurt, December 8, 1657.

[36] Mazarin to Hugues de Lionne and Gramont, from Metz, October 20, 1657. Atto himself reported the elector's negative position in his letter to Mazarin, from Munich, November 7, 1657, although apparently Atto had not yet given up hope.

[37] See Ingrao, *The Habsburg Monarchy*, 55–56. For his part, Atto counseled that timidity had no place in affairs of this magnitude, advice by which he himself lived (letter to Mazarin, from Frankfurt, November 27, 1657).

from Munich.[38] Contrary to his own glowing accounts, his first major diplomatic assignment failed miserably.

Yet Atto was not faulted. Mazarin understood that "however much one labors to till the sand, one cannot get it to bear fruit."[39] On December 21, after Atto had withdrawn from Munich, the cardinal comforted him: "I have seen and heard all that you accomplished while in Munich, to my entire satisfaction … I have approved your return to Frankfurt, where you can remain or return [here] as necessary; in this matter, you can follow the advice of the ambassadors, being assured in the meantime that here I would be happy to see you and there I will remember you and your service."[40]

Instead of being reprimanded, in fact, Atto received a series of rewards, the most notable of which was the post of gentleman of the chamber to Louis XIV. Atto's own report best explains the distinction:

While the court was at Calais, there opened up a post of Gentleman Servant to the King, which carries little income but much honor; whoever possesses it can resign it with a profit of ten to twelve thousand francs. I was advised to request it as a reward for my trip to Germany, since His Eminence has repeatedly said he wanted to do something for me. So I petitioned for it, being more interested in the potential honor than in the earnings, for it would have given me access to the person of the king wherever he was. But because a lady had already requested it for salary owed to her, I could not have an absolute "yes." … Meanwhile … I persisted in petitioning for some favor to distinguish me from the other *virtuosi*. Without the cardinal having anything to do with it, the queen – who is my protectress and shows great affection for me and for the furthering of my interests – arranged for the king to declare me "Gentleman Ordinary of his Chamber," and in this quality I will have admittance to court at all hours. If I can obtain the other post, I will sell it immediately.[41]

Indeed, on August 6, 1658, Atto was sworn in as a gentleman of the chamber by Louis XIV's *grand maître de la chambre*, the duke de Mortemart.[42] Further rewards followed. In the same letter, Atto goes on to say that, because this

[38] Atto to Mazarin, from Munich, November 7, 1657. In the letter to Mazarin, from Frankfurt, November 27, 1657, Atto suggests that the elector was forced to send him away almost against his will, reporting that the elector made him demonstrations of affection as well as giving a necklace with his medallion.

[39] This line, referring specifically to the situation with the elector, appears in a letter from Mazarin to Gramont, February 6, 1658, in [Jules Mazarin], *Lettres du Cardinal Mazarin pendant son ministère*, ed. G. D'Avenel (Paris: Imprimerie Nationale, 1894), VIII:296.

[40] Mazarin to Atto, from Paris, December 21, 1657.

[41] Atto to Mattias, from Paris, August 27, 1658.

[42] As indicated in a printed folio included in I PSc, Raccolta Chiappelli 64.ii. An anonymous eighteenth-century manuscript entitled "Memorie antiche" includes a "Vita dell'Abate Atto Melani" that cites the "Maréchal d'Harcourt" as the one who swore Atto in (I Fn, Rossi Cassigoli MS 268, p. 151), but as Mortemart was in fact the *grand maître* at that time, he seems the more

honor will bring little money, the queen promised he would receive additional recompense. And again, the promise was fulfilled, for shortly afterwards Atto was named abbot of the royal abbey of Beaubec in Normandy, with an accompanying annual income of 3,000 *livres*. This benefice was soon supplemented by a pension of 1,200 *livres* drawn on the bishopric of Beziers, a position held by the Tuscan representative to the French court, Pietro Bonsi.[43] To receive this ecclesiastical income, Atto was required to become a naturalized French citizen, a process he finally completed in December 1660; he had already taken minor orders.[44] From his first shaky foray into the world of diplomacy, then, Atto netted over 4,200 *livres* annually and the honor of unrestricted access to the court of France.[45]

This incident also seems to have sparked changes in Atto's self-perception, because for the first time his letters openly reveal aspirations for a non-musical career. In July 1657, for example, as he prepared for his trip to Munich, he writes Mattias, "I hope Your Highness is glad that I can now serve His Majesty in something other than music alone"; and again a month

---

likely candidate. Henri de Lorraine, count (not maréchal) d'Harcourt, was *grand écuyer* at the French court from 1643 to 1666.

[43] A degree of confusion has existed in the literature regarding Atto's French honor, most of which can be traced back to Prunières's report (*L'opéra*, 238n) that "en 1659, [Atto] avait été pourvu du bénéfice de l'abbaye de Beauhé [*sic*] en Normandie qui lui rapportait 1800 livres de revenu." As his source, Prunières cites F Pae, MD France, 933, f. 21v. This document, however, is entitled "Mémoire des expéditions qui ont ésté signées par Monsieur Colbert depuis le xvi jusques au xxixe du présent mois de Janvier 1671." In fact, the relevant entry is dated January 29, 1671 and records not 1,800 but "3m" or 3,000 *livres* in pension: in other words, this document is completely unrelated to the events of 1658. As will be shown, the 1671 payment represents part of the reinstatement of Atto's French benefits that accompanied his return to favor after the Fouquet incident. More recently, Catherine Massip, *La vie des musiciens de Paris au temps de Mazarin (1643–1661): Essai d'étude sociale*, La vie musicale en France sous les rois Bourbons, no. 24 (Paris: A. & J. Picard, 1976), 9, has mistakenly stated that Atto became Gentleman of the Chamber in 1657, one year too early. (She also mistakes the year of his disgrace as 1660 instead of 1661.)

The information presented here comes from a note to Cardinal Noailles, archbishop of Paris, in which Atto recounts the history of his benefices in France (with the aim of receiving tax exemption; F Pae, CP, Rome suppl. 10). Although the document is admittedly undated, it does mention that these benefices were rewards for his service in Germany. Atto's letter to Mattias, from Aix-en-Provence, February 28, 1660, provides a *terminus post quem non*: "spero che intanto si spediranno le bolle a Roma, del vescovado di Beziers, e che conseguentemente verrà solidata la mia pensione."

[44] For the date of his naturalization, Prunières, *L'opéra*, 238n; Prunières cites a document, Bibliothèque de la chambre des Députés, MS 340, f. 219, that I have been unable to locate. Atto had taken minor orders at least by 1655, as he notes in his letter to the duke of Mantua, from Florence, March 23, 1655 (see chapter 3).

[45] The definitive source on the constitution of the king's chamber is Mathieu Da Vinha, *Les valets de chambre de Louis XIV* (Paris: Perrin, 2004). There were twenty-six *gentilshommes ordinaires de la chambre* at a time: they served for six months and received 2,000 *livres* (apparently "little money" to Atto); the post "était encore une charge de grande confiance puisqu'ils étaient les représentants du roi dans les parlements, cours souveraines, à l'armée, en province et dans les pays étrangers" (251).

later, "however this trip ends up, I will have been very fortunate that a great king like this one and so expert a minister have judged me able to serve outside the profession of music."[46] His most definitive statement, however, comes in August of the following year. Basking in the glow of his recent honors, Atto shares a rare moment of self-reflection: "In this country, I have tried to get myself out of the rank of *musico*, and happily I have been able to do it. I am loved by all the court and acknowledged a most perfect courtier, not for the vivacity of my spirit, because I do not possess that, but for the access I have acquired with my perseverance."[47]

Indeed, he soon found a way to involve himself in diplomacy again, specifically, the final negotiations of the peace treaty between France and Spain, a pact subsequently known as the Peace of the Pyrenees (1659). Again, some background is warranted. The 1648 Treaty of Westphalia between France and the Empire purposely left unresolved the conflict with Spain, as Mazarin looked to win greater advantage through battle and negotiation. By the late 1650s, however, circumstances had changed: France had succeeded in loosening the Habsburg "noose," fashioning alliances with both Cromwell's England and the anti-Habsburg *Rheinbund*, while the Spanish had suffered a series of military defeats at the hands of both the French and the Portuguese. Both countries – one satisfied with its gains, and the other fearful of further losses – were finally ready for peace.[48]

A secret, preliminary treaty, known as the Peace of Paris, was worked out by negotiators in the spring of 1659. The remaining issues were to be solved that fall at a conference between Mazarin and his Spanish counterpart, Don Luis de Haro. To avoid complex problems of precedence, the conference was held on neutral territory, the tiny Island of the Pheasants in the middle of the River Bidassoa; that river forms the westernmost segment of the Franco–Spanish border, near the Bay of Biscay at the end of the Pyrenees mountains. Although Mazarin had expected the talks to be brief, little more than an endorsement of the Treaty of Paris, the Spanish negotiators demanded reconsideration of several points. Along with such weighty concerns as the marriage of Louis XIV to the Spanish infanta Maria-Teresa and the restoration to good graces of the Spanish-allied prince de Condé, the negotiators discussed a long-standing territorial dispute over the Italian region of Montferrato, claimed by both the duke of Mantua, who was aligned with Spain, and the house of Savoy,

---

[46] Atto to Mattias, from Sedan, July 30?, 1657; and from Péronne, August 30, 1657.
[47] Atto to Mattias, from Fontainebleau, August 31, 1658.
[48] The above paragraph is based on Geoffrey R.R. Treasure, *Seventeenth Century France*, 2nd edn. (London: John Murray, 1981), 212–13.

Plate 10 Meeting of Louis XIV and Philip IV on the Isle of the Pheasants (Gobelin tapestry after Charles Lebrun; Embassy of France, Madrid, Spain). *Reproduced by permission of Réunion des Musées Nationaux / Art Resource, NY.*

an adherent of France. It was into this controversy that Atto inserted himself.[49]

The issue appealed to him for several reasons. First, he was well positioned as an intermediary: not only had he met all the protagonists personally (except de Haro from Spain), but he accompanied Mazarin to the site of the final meetings in the Pyrenees. (Although the cardinal's reasons for bringing Atto do not clearly emerge from the documents, one can assume both his musical and diplomatic services were utilized.[50]) Atto was also probably hoping to shore up his relationship with the court of Mantua, a tie that

---

[49] The details of this dispute are too complex to rehearse here. See Basilio Cialdea, *Gli stati italiani e la pace dei Pirenei: Saggio sulla diplomazia seicentesca*, Istituto di studi storico-politici, Università di Roma-Facoltà di scienze politiche, no. 8 (Milan: A. Giuffrè, 1961), *passim*, but especially 14–21 and 260–308; Romolo Quazza, *Mantova attraverso i secoli* (Mantua: Tipografia editoriale de "La voce di Mantova," 1933), 216–19.

[50] Prunières (*L'opéra*, 236) claims that "Atto avait accompagné Mazarin à Saint-Jean de Luz [the town where the French were staying] et lui servait de secrétaire dans les conférences avec Don Louis de Haro." I find no evidence to support such extensive participation. Cialdea (*Gli stati*, 279) notes specifically that very few representatives, particularly foreigners, were allowed onto the island itself, and Atto's letters offer no convincing indications of his having been present during the conferences (although he did draw a nice map of the island: I Fas, MdP, filza 5408, ff. 586v–587). He probably remained in Saint-Jean-de-Luz with the bulk of the French contingent.

seems to have deteriorated in the preceding years: although the origin of the rift remains obscure, Atto's correspondence from the summer of 1659 repeatedly bemoans the duke's indifference toward his services.[51] By taking up the Mantuan cause, Atto was angling for a restoration of favor.

In Munich Atto had been the agent of a powerful nation, but he was now trying to broker an agreement on his own. The methods he was obliged to employ illustrate how even a singer – with enough access and wits – could carve out a diplomatic role. In one of his letters to the duke of Mantua, Atto himself articulates the part he thought he could play:

Because Your Highness is a prince, and a great prince, I will not stand here telling you what a difference it makes when one has to do everything on one's own as opposed to when things are facilitated and arranged by good courtiers, who take the opportunity to prepare the mind of the *padrone* in favor of those [gentlemen] who are to see him, negotiate with him, and seek difficult things [from him].[52]

Atto demonstrated his approach in one of his conversations with Mazarin. Knowing the cardinal's taste for extravagant festivities, Atto tried to "prepare the mind of the *padrone*" in favor of the duke of Mantua and thereby extract something useful. Atto's description, from a letter to the duke, is worth quoting at length:

The evening of the day before yesterday, I took the opportunity to apprise the cardinal of the great esteem Your Highness bears him … I had with me the libretto of the ballet with which Your Highness favored me, and I left it with him since he wanted to see it … I recounted to him the entertainments that Your Highness arranged for the empress, your sister, and for the arrival of the archdukes in Mantua, for in that city the celebrations ordered by Your Highness create a perpetual carnival. He was indeed very pleased with my narration of such beautiful spectacles, of fireworks, *commedie*, jousts, tournaments, and of the magnificence with which you received and entertained the archdukes for so many weeks …

---

[51] The following passage, from his letter to the duke of Mantua, from Saint-Jean-de-Luz, September 18, 1659, is typical. His mention of the Savoyards in this context may be significant: Atto may have appeared too friendly to the enemies of Mantua: "nel mentre V.A. m'haveva obliato e più non curava quegl'ossequij, che l'humilissima mia servitù le andava tributando, il Ser.mo Signore Duca di Savoia, e Madama Reale medesima mi honoravano spessissimo di loro lettere; Mi facevono infinite gratie e favori, e pure, quando mi son trovato in luoghi dove si è trattato e parlato della Persona et interessi di V.A., chiamo Iddio a testimonio, e lo saranno la maggior parte di questi ministri francesi, con qual tenerezza e zelo, io habbia sostenute le parti di V.A. senza riguardo alcuno." Mentions of his disfavor at Mantua also surface in his letters to Orazio Canossa, from Paris, June 25, 1659, and from Châteauneuf, July 9, 1659, and to the duke of Mantua, from Saint-Jean-de-Luz, July 31, 1659: "Sa Iddio quanto passione io havessi nella sola apprensione che V.A. mi havesse scancellato dalla sua memoria, e quante cose ho fatto per rimeritare la sua pregiatissima gratia, da me tanto ambita."

[52] Atto to the duke of Mantua, from Saint-Jean-de-Luz, September 18, 1659.

It delighted him that I could describe what little I remembered of such festivities, in light of his own plans to present festivities to mark this treaty and wedding … His Eminence ordered me to convey to Your Highness most fervent thanks for the memory and affection you bear him, and to tell you that he is among the most impassioned and true of Your Highness's servants. Because I asked whether he wanted me to give you no details about the matters to be discussed, he answered me with these very words: "Write to His Highness that if the Spanish will now and again bring their arguments, I, for my part, will facilitate things and will concur in such a way that His Highness will be satisfied."[53]

While these last words amount to little more than doublespeak (Mazarin's loyalties lay with Savoy), Atto's efforts had at least procured for the duke a positive statement from the French first minister.

By contrast, Atto could also work to engender negative feelings about those he opposed. In the Mantuan negotiations, he showed Mazarin an intercepted Savoyard letter "full of animosity against His Eminence." To increase the impact, Atto seems to have circulated the letter to all key French negotiators. This attempt to "move [the cardinal] to disdain against the author" had some effect, for shortly thereafter Atto describes Mazarin as "extremely irritated with the Savoyards."[54] Just as he had tried to incline Mazarin toward Mantua, Atto hoped to estrange him from Turin.

But beyond these subtle tactics, Atto played an active role in the negotiations. His combination of wide acquaintance and innocuous status allowed him to present the duke's case directly to the central mediators, avoiding the issues of precedence that encumbered Mantua's official representative, Count Girolamo Sannazaro. As Atto reports,

[Count Sannazzaro] trusted me with a letter of Your Highness for [the Spanish negotiator] Signor Pimentel, who at that time, as now, was receiving no one. I presented this letter, along with a few notes and details about the arguments of Your Highness against the duke of Savoy, to [Pimentel] himself. Because he is staying in the palace of the cardinal [Mazarin], where I live, I had the opportunity to speak to him on not just one, but rather on two and then three evenings and in such effective terms that he easily recognized me as one of Your Highness's most faithful and humble servants. Further, I obliged him to acknowledge the interests that the Spanish have in satisfying and supporting Your Highness, and I drew from him his word that he would be the advocate for Your Highness with Don Luis de Haro at the proper time.[55]

---

[53] Atto to the duke of Mantua, from Saint-Jean-de-Luz, July 31, 1659.

[54] These excerpts come from the two letters that discuss the offending dispatch: Atto to Orazio Canossa, from Paris, June 20 and 25, 1659.

[55] Atto to the duke of Mantua, from Saint-Jean-de-Luz, July 31, 1659.

As in Munich, Atto proved his value by gaining access where others were denied.

Also as in Munich, however, Atto's project failed. Despite his best efforts – and those of the duke's other agents – Mantua lost its bid to recover Montferrato. In the end, France benefited too much from the *status quo* of the treaty for Mazarin to risk altering it, and Spain cared too much about reaching a peace for de Haro to pursue the dispute. Atto had again taken on a doomed task, but he had also again demonstrated his utility "outside the profession of music."

In addition to the two big projects in Germany and the Pyrenees, Atto repeatedly dabbled in the specialized field of marriage arrangements. Of course, politically advantageous unions remained a high priority for the noble class in the seventeenth century, and Atto's contacts well equipped him to facilitate matches. His best-documented activities involve the marriages of Grand Prince Cosimo III of Florence to Princess Marguerite-Louise D'Orléans, and Contestabile Lorenzo Colonna of Rome to Marie Mancini.

In the case of the Medici–d'Orléans match, Atto seems simply to have facilitated the exchange of information about physical appearance, personality, and lifestyle. Like everyone else involved, Atto played down the fundamental differences in character between the sophisticated, headstrong princess and the narrow-minded, pious grand prince. While on September 3, 1660 Atto had admitted to Mattias that "this princess puts the whole court into discord with her infinite pretensions," he changed his tune the following month when negotiations commenced: "I do not believe that anything more could be desired in this princess, neither in beauty of spirit, nor of body or manners."[56] Indeed, Atto liberally employed the diplomatic tool of dissimulation, in this and other projects:

[The princess] only hears about the financial difficulties with which – according to some here – we live in Italy. I have really cheered her up by relating in great detail (at her request) how we entertain ourselves in Tuscany. I have overlooked no conceivable opportunity to stimulate her desire to come as soon as possible. I assure Your Highness that the grand prince will have the most beautiful princess in Europe.[57]

---

[56] Atto to Mattias, from Paris, September 3, 1660 and October 22, 1660.

[57] Atto to Mattias, from Paris, October 22, 1660. This description comes from late in the negotiation process. On the very day that the Florentine *residente* at Paris first approached the duke d'Orléans about a possible marriage, September 14, 1658, Atto reported the news to Mattias. Further references to the princess occur in Atto's letters of September 7, 1658; September 4 and 18, 1659; and perhaps September 3, 1660, although it is not clear which Princess d'Orléans he refers to here. Atto later also mentions the troubled marriage in his letters of April 14 and 22, 1664.

As Atto should have foreseen, Marguerite-Louise eventually found the "financial difficulties" and repressive atmosphere of the Florentine court intolerable. Creating enormous scandal, she left her husband in 1675 to return to France, where she passed the remainder of her days in and out of convents.[58]

More significant for his own future was Atto's role in the marriage arrangements of Marie Mancini. As mentioned in chapter 4, this niece of Cardinal Mazarin became in 1658 the great love of Louis XIV. They spent that summer in the particularly idyllic setting of Fontainebleau, pursuing daily entertainments and festivities. Atto's letter of September 7, 1658 paints a detailed picture of this little world, and, at the risk of a short digression, I offer an excerpt of its account. Although this particular passage repeatedly mentions Marie's older sister Olympe, a former favorite of the king, other sources confirm that at this time it was Marie who was "virtually a queen" at the French court.[59]

I will tell Your Highness how these Majesties occupy themselves each day, one day being similar to the next. The king goes to the hunt in the morning; he returns at midday. After lunch, he goes to the rooms of the Countess de Soissons [Olympe Mancini], where he gambles until it is time to go to the gardens. He gets into an open calèche [two-wheeled carriage] with that same countess and another niece of His Eminence [probably Marie], and although he sits in the back, he can hold the reins of the horses, which he directs himself. The countess sits at his right, and one or two ladies sit by the doors. The queen too has toured around many times in her open calèche, and these are now in fashion and quite numerous here: every gentleman escorts his ladies in this manner.

In the evening a comedy is given, sometimes by the French and other times by the Italians. After dinner, there is the ball, which lasts until two hours after midnight. In the evening in the gardens they get into certain boats kept in the canal of the park – four in number, all gilded and lined with brocades – and almost every evening there is singing in the boat of Their Majesties.

The queen rises at noon; at two, [she and her attendants] eat lunch; at four, she sets herself to playing the game of Rovescia, and she does not move until six. After the daily promenade, she retires to pray for an hour, and then she goes to the comedy. After this, she goes to dinner, and within a half-hour she begins to yawn and retires to

---

[58] The subject of this ill-fated marriage is a central issue in E[mmanuel] Rodocanachi, *Les infortunes d'une petite-fille d'Henri IV: Marguerite d'Orléans Grande-Duchesse de Toscanne (1645–1727)* (Paris: Ernst Flammarion, [1902?]), and is also treated throughout Harold Acton's less well documented study, *The Last Medici* (London: Faber and Faber, 1932).

[59] This observation comes from Bryan Bevan, *The Duchess Hortense: Cardinal Mazarin's Wanton Niece* (London: Rubicon Press, 1987), 15.

go to sleep at midnight. But the great devotion of Their Majesties to recreation means that only those who are within the royal party come to court; up to now, the only ladies who have been here are the nieces of His Eminence.[60]

In this gracious setting, then, Louis and Marie indulged their love. But Louis's marriage was always destined to be an affair of state, and so Mazarin soon found a more appropriate husband for Marie in Rome.[61] Atto does appear to have played some small role in the Colonna match, for at the time of his following comments (August 13, 1660) Marie would have been the only likely niece of the cardinal under discussion: "a marriage between a great prince and a niece of His Eminence [Mazarin] will perhaps take place, and because I played a big part in this arrangement, both parties have promised me a reward that, if the wedding goes through, will benefit me more than anything else I have attained in this kingdom."[62] Indeed, a wedding did go through, by proxy, in the king's chambers on April 11, 1661, coincidentally just eight days before the proxy marriage of the Princess d'Orléans in the same rooms.[63] What immediate "reward" Atto received is never disclosed, but certainly he later exploited his close ties with both Marie and her husband to benefit his position – and that of his family – in Roman society (see chapter 7).

Ultimately, however, the Colonna pairing failed as miserably as did the Medici, with the bride again fleeing back to France. In fact, Atto's attempts to arrange such matches proved no more fortunate than his other early ventures into diplomacy. Nevertheless, as with those projects, his efforts extended his reputation as a negotiator. They confirmed that, even when not singing, his services carried value, and that meant he could legitimately pursue the rewards that diplomacy offered.

---

[60]   Atto to Mattias, from Fontainebleau, September 7, 1658.

[61]   The information on Marie is taken largely from Claude Dulong, *Marie Mancini: La première passion de Louis XIV* (Paris: Perrin, 1993); and Ruth Kleinman, *Anne of Austria: Queen of France* (Columbus, Ohio: Ohio State Univeristy Press, 1985).

[62]   Atto to Mattias, from Paris, August 13, 1660. A[lessandro] Ademollo, *I primi fasti della musica italiana a Parigi (1645–1662)* (Milan: Ricordi, [1884]), 15, states that "Atto Melani in una diecina d'anni diventò francese e riuscì a far fortuna più che altro coi guadagni d'agente segreto del Mazzarino e poi del Re in maneggi e raggiri di genere diverse, cominciando dai matrimoni delle ultime Mancini." By 1660, all the "Mazarinettes" were married, except for Marie and her younger sister Hortense. In a letter just two weeks before this one (July 30, to Mattias, from Paris), Atto reported as virtually settled a marriage arrangement between Hortense and the duke d'Enghien; Atto's more circumspect comments on August 13, then, seem appropriate only to Marie. In the end, of course, he was wrong about Hortense's match; nor does he ever mention Lorenzo Colonna in connection with Marie. Still, whether effectively or not, he seems to have been involved in the marriage negotiations.

[63]   Rodocanachi, *Les infortunes*, 47.

Risks worth taking

If this new occupation promised greater rewards, it also demanded greater
risks. Much of the peril – like the opportunity – inhered in Atto's singular
position. With the allies of Spain – including Tuscany, Mantua, and the
German Habsburg territories – on one side, and those of France – Savoy,
Modena, and the *Rheinbund* states – on the other, Atto's personal circle of
patrons transgressed the political alignments of Europe. His practice of
reporting news to this circle in itself represented a violation of loyalties that
could earn the charge of espionage. And as he took a more active role in
diplomacy, such infractions became increasingly difficult to conceal. Finding
a way to please his several masters while avoiding indictments of treason
demanded fortitude and daring. Of course Atto possessed these qualities in
abundance, one might even say superabundance, for, at least in the early part
of his diplomatic career, Atto was more likely to dash out onto the tightrope
of diplomacy than patiently secure his footing. With ambition overriding
prudence, his headlong style often landed him in trouble. Those troubles
themselves tell something about his thinking at this time, for they show the
risks he was prepared to take to slough off his musical identity.

Even in simply reporting news, Atto frequently sacrificed discretion in his
attempt to please. As we have seen, he understood from the beginning the
delicate character of his letters and the consequences of their going astray,
but even as he matured he could rarely restrain his desire to impress. In the
following passage addressed to Mattias, he also reveals something of his
relationship to Louis XIV:

> I read all of your letter to His Majesty, in the presence of Maréchal Villeroy, and the
> king asked me many questions about the person of Your Highness, about your age,
> where you spent the most time, if you were married, and if you spoke French. Your
> Highness should not be surprised that I have such familiarity to speak with and
> entertain the king, because I am the gazetteer of the court, and my notices of Rome as
> well as of Piedmont and Germany are recognized as the best, and the king and queen
> are happy to hear them.[64]

Essentially, Atto is trying to inflate his importance by bragging about his
promiscuity with information. Such admissions were dangerous. If the king
had learned that Atto was circulating reports on France – like the military
information in this very letter – Atto could have been exiled or worse. The
episode also shows, of course, that whatever Louis thought of Italian musicians
he was happy enough to receive their news, an attitude surely not lost on Atto.

---

[64] Atto to Mattias, from Fontainebleau, August 31, 1658.

Atto's one shield against his blunders was the support of his patrons, particularly Mattias and Mazarin. Their forgiving assistance is suggested in an incident from the summer of 1657, when Atto's loose tongue almost ruined him. For reasons never identified, he had publicly maligned another prominent Tuscan in Paris, Abate Vittorio Siri, today known for his histories of this period in France.[65] After Siri protested the attacks to Florence, Atto received a sharp rebuke from the secretary of the grand duke:

The grand duke commands me to write you that he has received a letter from Abate Siri in which he complains that you wrongly slander his person, and the abate begs His Highness to remedy the situation. His Highness has therefore ordered me to tell you in this letter that your way of speaking and writing does not come as news to him and that the things you have said about Abate Siri, whom he esteems infinitely, are all falsehoods … and that if you do not mend your ways, the grand duke will not lack for a way to punish you. Although you are outside his dominion, you nevertheless have interests and property upon which he can vent his indignation.[66]

Siri in fact filched this letter of reproach from Atto's mail and circulated it to members of the French court, all to discredit his adversary. Atto was overmatched: assailed from all sides, he turned to his patrons, with numerous and frantic pleas. They must have come to the rescue, for the incident produced no lasting repercussions: Atto was soon back in favor in both Paris and Florence.[67]

With this sort of support, Atto's activities sometimes injured members of his family more than himself. On March 7, 1659 Atto reports, "Cardinal Mazarin told me the day before yesterday that the Spanish did not want to allow Archduke Sigismund [of Innsbruck] to bring Don Filippo with him to Flanders, solely on account of his being my brother."[68] After his work in Munich, Atto's reputation as a French agent was great enough to raise suspicion about his brother as well. Worse, when Filippo returned to Innsbruck in 1661, after two years' service on the Parisian stage, "the Archduke Sigismund, his patron, did not view him with the same confidence as before."[69] Although

---

[65] See his *Il Mercurio, ovvero, Historia de' correnti tempi*, 15 vols. (Casale: Christoforo della Casa, 1644–82); *Memorie recondite dall'anno 1601 sino al 1640*, 8 vols. (Ronco: n.p., 1677–79).

[66] Copy of a letter from Giovan Battista Gondi (*primo segretario di stato*) to Atto, from Florence (without date), included with Atto's letter to Mattias, from Sedan, July 29, 1657.

[67] The evidence for this sequence of events appears in his letters to Mattias from Sedan, July 29, and August 16; Péronne, August 30; and Munich, October 19, 1657.

[68] Atto to Mattias, from Paris, March 7, 1659.

[69] Atto to de Lionne, from Rome, August 24, 1663 (Atto is here reporting on past events). No clear evidence reports the date of Filippo's return to Innsbruck. He performed in the *Ballet de l'impatience* of early 1661, but no later records place him in Paris. He probably returned to Innsbruck shortly after the death of Mazarin, who had called him there in the first place.

Filippo continued to serve in Innsbruck until November 1665, Atto's diplomatic activities almost certainly hampered his brother's career: after Innsbruck, Filippo retreated to Tuscany where he remained the rest of his life.[70]

For Bartolomeo Melani, the price of being Atto's sibling was even higher. In late 1657, Bartolomeo was appointed a singer at the court of Munich, probably at Atto's urging (see chapter 7). However, the indignation Atto provoked at that court soon devolved upon his brother:

the letters from Germany arrived, which brought me the news that in Munich they have imprisoned my brother Bartolomeo and another youth, my countryman, by the name of Bartolomeo Fregosi, under suspicion that they assisted the electress in receiving and sending letters to the king and Cardinal Mazarin in France. This action was based on the malice of someone from that court rather than on the truth, since all the letters that were written from here passed through the hands of the confessors of those princes, according to their orders. It is quite true that everything took place against the will of Count Kurtz, who did everything possible to intercept the letters, and because in the end he was unable to lay hold of me, he seized my brother and a friend of mine.[71]

---

[70] On the return of Filippo from Innsbruck to Italy, see the letter of Antonio Cesti to Marco Faustini, from Innsbruck, November 1, 1665, in Remo Giazotto, "Nel CCC anno della morte di Antonio Cesti: Ventidue lettere ritrovate nell'Archivio di Stato di Venezia," *Nuova rivista musicale italiana* 3 (1969): 506: "Il Signor Giuseppino ottenne licenza da S. Maestà di rimpatriare come haveva sempre desiderato; partirà di questa settimana a cotesta volta in compagnia del Signor Melani e Signor Biancucci." How long Filippo remained in Venice (where Faustini was) is unclear: Robert Lamar Weaver, "Materiali per le biografie dei fratelli Melani," *Rivista italiana di musicologia* 12 (1977): 267, 271n, provides documentation of Filippo's activities in Pistoia and Florence after 1668. But clearly Filippo had previously been granted periods of leave from Innsbruck to work in Venice. Beth L. Glixon and Jonathan E. Glixon, *Inventing the Business of Opera: The Impresario and His World in Seventeenth-Century Venice*, AMS Studies in Music (Oxford: Oxford Univeristy Press, 2006), 333, report that in early 1664 Filippo sang in the opera *Rosilena* (Aureli/Volpe) at the Teatro SS. Giovanni e Paolo; this service may in fact represent a loan to the Grimani family who was then running that theater. No evidence of any later performances in Venice has emerged, so perhaps in 1665 Filippo returned promptly to Tuscany. For much of the remainder of his life he lived in Florence. He appears among the Medici salaried musicians, and he performed in a number of Florentine oratorio and opera productions. See Weaver, "Materiali," 267; Warren Kirkendale, *The Court Musicians in Florence During the Principate of the Medici: With a Reconstruction of the Artistic Establishment*, "Historiae musicae cultores" biblioteca, no. 61 (Florence: Olschki, 1993), 412–13; and John Walter Hill, "Oratory Music in Florence, II: At San Firenze in the Seventeenth and Eighteenth Centuries," *Acta musicologica* 51 (1979): 256n, 266. He also seems to have served as Atto's representative in Tuscany, presenting Atto's concerns at the Medici court; he gathered and communicated to Atto news from the Italian peninsula; and he was Atto's primary correspondent within the family.

[71] This letter (I Fas, MdP, filza 5419, f. 940) bears no date or place; however, it almost certainly dates from sometime in 1658, not long after Atto returned from Munich and Bartolomeo had begun his services there. The paper on which it is written is consistent with Atto's other letters to Mattias from Paris. On Bartolomeo Fregosi, see below.

Atto begged Mattias to request their release, and the prince apparently obliged, for at least by sometime in 1660 Bartolomeo was back at the cathedral of Pistoia.[72] His international career too was over.

In light of this fundamental dependence on his patrons, Atto's deliberate antagonism of Mattias in the fall of 1657 vividly illustrates his determination to change careers. Ordered by the prince to return from Paris, Atto politely refused, preferring – as he had in the previous decade – to pursue greater opportunities in France. Although in a letter of August 30 he acknowledges his patron's "express command" to return, he also protests the disadvantages of immediate departure, with the king and cardinal too involved in "weighty concerns" to give him any "grace or recognition." He promises to return to Italy "as soon as the court turns [from Péronne] toward Paris," but his pledge is an outright deception: he already knew he was about to embark on the mission to Munich.[73]

That Atto undertook this mission without authorization apparently infuriated the prince. Atto must have suspected that such permission would be denied: Tuscany's alignment with the Habsburgs conflicted with Mazarin's openly anti-Habsburg project. Although Atto did finally inform Mattias of his actions, after the fact, the prince took the extreme step of removing Atto from his payroll. With a whiff of exasperation, Mattias writes to Louis XIV, "I will be happy to prove my desire to obey you in the matter of Atto Melani, *musico*, when he is here with me or I know where he is."[74]

Astonishingly, Atto exhibited little concern about this turn of events. Although he informed Mazarin of the incident, he apparently did not request assistance.[75] Atto may well have viewed his dismissal as an opportunity. As discussed in chapter 3, Atto had for some years considered leaving the Medici in search of greater munificence. Now he was free to do so, as he states openly at the end of a long letter to the duchess of Savoy on December 8:

whenever I have some news worthy of your attention, I will be sure to advise you of it with complete accuracy, provided that one day I can merit to number among Your Royal Highness's true and actual servants. Prince Mattias removed me from his payroll for never having written nor informed him that, out of curiosity, I was going

---

[72]   Weaver, "Materiali," 269. Weaver's chart, from which this information is taken, indicates only the year in which Bartolomeo's name appears again among the musicians of the cathedral, not the exact date.

[73]   The foregoing quotations are extracted from Atto's letter to Mattias, from Péronne, August 30, 1657.

[74]   Notes for a letter from Mattias to Louis XIV, December 26, 1657.

[75]   Atto to Mazarin, from Frankfurt, November 27, 1657.

to Germany; and so I now have greater freedom to serve truly as a most humble, devoted, and obedient servant of Your Royal Highness.[76]

As the early months of 1658 passed, however, Atto slowly began to recognize his miscalculation. The precise reasons for the change of heart remain unclear, but Bartolomeo's incarceration could well have played a role. As a kind of peace offering, Atto began once again sending Mattias his political reports from Paris, which at first were ignored. Atto then directed his brother Jacopo to plead his case to the prince in person. By mid-summer, the conflict had been resolved and, still without coming home, Atto was reinstated to his prince's favor and payroll.[77] While Atto was willing to gamble much on the hope of advancement, he seems to have recognized his continuing need for protection. The truth of that insight would soon become alarmingly clear.

Disaster

In his book on culture and the Italian Renaissance, Peter Burke observes that "permanent service at court gave the artist a relatively high status, without the social taint of shopkeeping. It also meant relative economic security … When the prince died, however, the artist might lose everything."[78] Atto faced precisely this prospect at the death of Cardinal Mazarin in 1661. More than any other patron (including Mattias), Mazarin had advanced Atto's career, musical and otherwise: Mazarin first called him out of Tuscany, first awarded him a leading operatic role, first trained him in diplomacy. While Atto may sometimes have acted independently, he was clearly one of Mazarin's clients – in contemporary terms, his *creatura*. And although Atto was aware of the cardinal's worsening health, he surely did not foresee the coming sea-change in French politics. The misfortune that change would bring – the worst he ever suffered – highlights the dangers intrinsic to Atto's ambitions. It also shows his resolve.

The cardinal's health had certainly been deteriorating for some time, as he dealt with kidney stones, gout, breathing difficulties, and chronic blood poisoning. After the strain of the negotiations in the Pyrenees, he grew sicker

---

[76] Atto to the duchess of Savoy, from Frankfurt, December 8, 1657.

[77] This sequence of events is based on Atto's letters to Mattias, from Paris, February 15, and April 12; from Calais, June 19, and July 2, 1658. In this last letter, Atto writes, "la megliore che potessi sperare me l'ha portata le lettere che ricevo da Jacomo mio fratello, al quale rispondo perché ha da V.A. confermarli tutto ciò che già le haveva rappresentato mentre dall' medesimo verranno rese all'A.V. le più vive gratie di tanta benignità che conserva verso di me."

[78] Peter Burke, *The Italian Renaissance: Culture and Society in Italy*, 2nd edn. (Princeton: Princeton Univeristy Press, 1987), 94.

still: he was only barely able to host a celebration at his *palais* on September 9, 1660, probably the last time he heard Atto sing. The final blow came during the night of February 5, 1661 when a fire broke out in a room at the Louvre near the cardinal's sleeping quarters, the very gallery where Cavalli's *Xerse* was being prepared. Despite the efforts of the doctors and the personal attention of Louis and Anne, the shock and smoke from the blaze proved fatal, and the cardinal died on March 9.[79]

Atto was affected almost immediately. As we have seen, several members of court – both Italià and French – resented Atto's successes and social pretensions. The most outspoken of these turned out to be the young duke Mazarin, husband of Hortense Mancini, Marie's sister. As outlined in chapter 4, the duke became so jealous of Atto's familiarity with his wife that he convinced Louis XIV to expel Atto from Paris.

Confirmation of these incidents, along with a wealth of detail, emerges from a surprising contemporary source: an account of the trial of Nicolas Fouquet. Fouquet had been the *surintendant des finances* under Mazarin and one of the wealthiest and most powerful men in France. But soon after the cardinal's death he was arrested on charges of embezzlement and treason. The account, published in thirteen volumes between 1665 and 1668, records Fouquet's point-by-point rebuttal of the charges leveled during his three-year trial. Among those allegations are several that mention Atto specifically. This previously overlooked source is worth quoting at length not only for the picture it gives of Atto's dilemma, but also for its third-person witness to Atto's long relationship with the cardinal and to the duke's violent agitation. Responding to the charge that he had squandered money on Atto for personal reasons, Fouquet explains:

Atto was an Italian of the *musique du Roy*, very much favored by His Majesty and very devoted to his service; [he was also] much employed by the cardinal during his lifetime and very well known in the household of His Eminence. This man had rendered great services in Germany during the negotiations in Frankfurt. He had

---

[79] The above paragraph is based on Geoffrey R. R. Treasure, *Mazarin: The Crisis of Absolutism in France* (London and New York: Routledge, 1995), 307–8; Kleinman, *Anne of Austria*, 274–47; and Prunières, *L'opéra*, 245–47. Atto mentions the festivities at the Cardinal's palace in his letter to Mattias, from Paris, September 10, 1660: "Hieri si fece qui al Palazzo del Signore Cardinale un gran festino, essendoci venute le loro MM.tà, con la Regina e Principessa d'Inghilterra, e tutte le Principesse della Corte … S.Em.za le fece vedere il Palazzo, che è addobbato veramente in modo, che pare di entrare in un incanto. Le diede la commedia spagnola. Le fece sentire tutta la musica italiana, e le diede una cena, degna di esser veduta, sì per la dispositione, quantità, e qualità delle viande, che dei personaggi che v'intervennero." As Atto was one of the principal performers of "la musica italiana" at the French court, he must have taken part in the performances.

Plate 11 Hugues de Lionne (anonymous; Bibliothèque Nationale de France, Paris, France). *Reproduced by permission of the Bibliothèque Nationale de France.*

maintained close connections with M. de Lionne and had provided very important information, so that one could not doubt his industry nor his affection and zeal for France, and in particular for the family of the cardinal: he was then living in the Palais Mazarin.

As soon as the funeral ceremonies for the cardinal were over, the trouble began in his household. Madame Colonna [Marie Mancini] was married and left, discontent with her allotment; the heirs disagreed among themselves; the servants followed their inclinations and departed, each in his own direction; those who were living in the house were dismissed…

But of all the disputes, there was none that caused more uproar than that between the Duke Mazarin and Madame his wife [Hortense]. One need not give the details here, but, in his fury, the husband found it essential to his honor and fortune to prevent those he disliked from having any contact with Madame his wife, and he begged the king to make Atto leave not only the Palais Mazarin, but the kingdom entirely and go back to Italy. The duke craved this favor so fervently that the king wanted to know the cause of his hatred and to dissuade him from this undertaking. Faced with M. Mazarin's persistence, the king did not after all want to refuse him what he so ardently desired, and so the king made it known to Atto that he should prepare to leave; the king also led Atto to hope that His Majesty would permit him to return when the storm had calmed.

Meanwhile, Atto had recourse to M. de Lionne, from whom he asked protection. M. de Lionne witnessed the services Atto had rendered and had previously conveyed to Atto so many kind words on behalf of the cardinal that Atto wished again to have M. de Lionne vouch for him.

The Duke Mazarin learned of this and loudly condemned M. de Lionne. He said that he would thrash Atto with a truncheon wherever he came upon him, so that Atto found himself obliged to leave. But he was not able to do so for a few days, as he needed to put his little affairs in order, to buy the things necessary and sell those he could not carry. In the meantime he wanted to take cover from the threats that had been made against him but was at a loss to choose a shelter. And so he appealed to M. de Lionne, who brought him to me. De Lionne informed me of Atto's turmoil and asked me to see what I could do for him, telling me that he himself did not want to take Atto in because M. Mazarin would surely watch his house as suspect. But since Atto was not known to have any relationship with me, he could pass the requested two or three days in my house without anyone becoming aware of it.

M. de Lionne then explained to me the services that Atto had rendered, those that he was capable of rendering, the associations that he had, and that he was a man who ought to be retained for the service of the king. I offered to give Atto shelter, during which time M. de Lionne told me to settle on a secret code and exchange addresses with him for the news that he wanted to send and for the actions we wanted him to take.

… The Duke Mazarin no longer had any regard for me, so that I had no difficulty giving shelter to a servant who had been recommended to me and who asked only to be kept safe for two days to avoid an assault. And, to tell the truth, I believed that I was rendering a service to the king, and an even greater one to M. Mazarin, by eliminating the chance to mistreat a foreigner who was leaving with proofs of the king's affection.

The king commanded me to have 1,500 *livres* paid to Atto. I believe that he received one portion of 500 *livres* before his departure and that he asked that the remaining 1,000 *livres* be given to him in Rome when he arrived there, to save some money in the exchange and avoid the risk of being robbed on the roads…

He left immediately afterwards, and since that time he has written to the king personally and recounted his voyage to His Majesty. The king read us his letters in council. He addressed them to M. de Lionne and sometimes addressed the packet for M. de Lionne to me. He informed me of different things; he has sent others to M. de Lionne using the same cipher that he had left me. And he evidenced a great desire to make himself useful and to do something that could obtain his return.[80]

Among other things, this testimony serves to confirm that Atto was not forced to leave Paris because of Fouquet's ruin, as has generally been thought,

---

[80] Nicolas Fouquet, *Recueil des defenses de Mr Fouquet*, vol. VIII, *Suite de la continuation de la production de Mr Fouquet, pour servir de réponse a celle de Mr Talon sur le pretendu crime d'estat* ([Paris?]: n.p., 1666), 167–69. See appendix D for the original French of this passage.

but rather because of the resentment of Hortense's jealous husband.[81] For this reason, the setback did not immediately panic Atto: as Fouquet suggests, Atto probably assumed the exile would be brief and that the king himself would soon assume his patronage, especially after he proved his usefulness in Rome. He did not leave the country as if in disgrace, but rather joined the escort of the Princess d'Orléans, who was reluctantly making her way toward her new home in Florence. In Atto's reckoning, surely, the shift of power in France at first seemed but a temporary interruption of his successes.

Conveniently, the princess's entourage was met in Marseille by Mattias de' Medici, as representative for the grand duke.[82] Considering Atto's bouts of disobedience, their reunion could have been less than cordial. Instead, Mattias seems to have done everything in his power to support his beleaguered singer. Although the prince had not seen Atto for nearly five years, he allowed him to proceed immediately to Rome and so continue his service to France: although Atto embarked from Marseille only at the end of May 1661, he arrived in the papal city no later than the end of July (see appendix A). Further, the prince wrote ahead to his Roman contacts on Atto's behalf. The brief response from Cardinal Flavio Chigi, one of the leading men of the city, confirms Mattias's favor: "The fact that Atto Melani is a current servant of Your Highness by itself recommends him to me, so much do I desire to serve you. But seeing in Your Highness an extraordinary solicitude in his favor, I will endeavor to help him extraordinarily, and to assist him in any of his needs."[83]

At first, Mattias's help seemed to promise Atto redemption back in France. Atto quickly secured a privileged position in Rome, from which he hoped to earn the king's appreciation. On August 4, for example, Atto reported back to de Lionne, now the French foreign minister:

Cardinal Chigi had me introduced to kiss the feet of His Holiness [Pope Alexander VII] at the end of his midday meal. The pope talked to me for more than an hour. He asked me many things regarding the sickness and death of the late cardinal; about

---

[81] See, for example, Robert Lamar Weaver, introduction to *Cantatas by Alessandro Melani 1639–1703, Atto Melani 1627–1714*, vol. XI of *The Italian Cantata in the Seventeenth Century* (New York: Garland, 1986), [ix]; Robert Lamar Weaver, "Florentine Comic Operas of the Seventeenth Century" (Ph.D. diss. University of North Carolina, Chapel Hill, 1958), 321; "Melani, Atto," *Grove Music Online*, ed. Laura Macy, www.grovemusic.com (accessed June 6, 2007).

[82] Acton, *The Last Medici*, 68. In Atto's letter to Anna Maria Gonzaga, princess Palatine, from Marseille, May 25, 1661, he states outright that "Jc suis en Provence pour y voir le Prince Matthias mon entien [*sic*] maistre qui vient icy pour reccevoir madame la Princesse de Toscana." Atto may well have sung in the various entertainments provided for the princess. Acton (67–68) mentions a sung *commedia* performed for the princess in Marseille before embarkation and further serenading on board the ship. Gaetano Imbert, *La vita fiorentina nel Seicento secondo memorie sincrone (1644–1670)* (Florence: R. Bemporad e Figlio, 1906), 74, refers to another *commedia cantata* performed as part of the reception on June 12, 1661 for the princess at her arrival in Livorno.

[83] Cardinal Flavio Chigi to Mattias, from Rome, July 30, 1661.

the riches that he had left and his will; whether the king had shown much sadness at his death; and for which of you other gentlemen [de Lionne, Le Tellier, and Colbert] he had more inclination and confidence.[84]

Having established such lofty access, Atto confidently informed his Roman hosts that he would return to France at the end of October.[85]

In this same cheerful spirit, he wrote a letter to Mattias on September 3 that is remarkable for its assessment of the musical life in Rome at this time and worthy of another short digression. The first section concerns sacred music:

I am sending three motets to Your Highness, which I have chosen from among many, and still they do not entirely satisfy me. It will seem strange to Your Highness when I say that, having heard many of these *virtuose*, I have not yet heard a pair of *ariette* suitable for a gentleman, so that here music is doing very badly. I still have to go to the home of a copyist who has all the *ariette*, and at that time I will choose the newest and best ones to supply to Your Highness. In the meantime, if Signor [Ilario] Fregosi wants other motets, I will write this very day to my brother Jacinto that, at Signor Fregosi's earliest request, he give one of my books of motets to whomever Signor Fregosi desires. Those motets are beautiful and unusual and certainly will be more to Your Highness's taste than these Roman ones, which seem to me without invention and quite ordinary.[86]

The book of motets Atto mentions may have been his own compositions – certainly his boast about their quality would be typical – but no extant motets

---

[84] Atto to de Lionne, from Rome, August 8, 1661. For some time after Atto's return to Italy, he continued to correspond with de Lionne in French. He himself asked his various readers' indulgence (letter to the marquis de Pomponne, from Rome, December 22, 1671) "se nell'Ortografia farò molti errori," errors that I have preserved in my transcriptions.

[85] Atto to de Lionne, from Rome, August 8, 1661.

[86] Atto to Mattias, from Rome, September 3, 1661. In 1661, Jacinto Melani was receiving payments from the cathedral of Pistoia, presumably as a choir member (under the direction of his brother Jacopo). Jacinto had the least "musical" career of any of the brothers, instead inheriting his father's position and title, so Atto's referral to him here is somewhat surprising. In 1654 Jacinto was declared Atto's "verus et legitimus protector" in Pistoia, establishing a kind of power of attorney for Jacinto to act on Atto's behalf (I Fas, Notarile moderno, protocollo 14596, ff. 28v–29). Perhaps, then, Atto saw Jacinto as his primary contact in Pistoia at this time.
  Ilario Fregosi, an organist, was the brother of Bartolomeo Fregosi, the castrato who of course had shared a cell with Bartolomeo Melani in Munich. Since the "Signor Fregosi" of this letter seems to be supplying motets to someone else, rather than singing them himself, Ilario appears the more probable referent. Like the Melani, the Fregosi brothers were clients of the Medici from a young age. The context here suggests that Ilario bore some responsibility for sacred music under Mattias at this time (perhaps as the prince's own *maestro di cappella* in Siena). In any case, this passage probably adds to the little known about Ilario. See Jean Grundy Fanelli, "Castrato Singers from Pistoia, 1575–1660," *Civiltà musicale*, no. 40 (May–August 2000): 52. Ilario does seem to have been following the path of church musician: a letter from Stefano Panciatichi to Cardinal Giovan Carlo de' Medici, from Pistoia, October 2, 1643, asks the cardinal to support the "giovane" Ilario's bid for the post of organist in Livorno (I Fas, MdP, Filza 5345, f. 229, transcribed in Mamone, *Serenissimi fratelli*, 110).

bear his name. Atto also confirms the view of Roman sacred music as conservative, in his view, lacking sufficient "bizzarria" and "invenzione."

Atto's letter continues with a description of a particular musical event:

On one recent evening a serenata was performed in the courtyard of the Contestabile Colonna. The work, written by Carluccio del Violino [Carlo Caprioli], involved five voices, with a great many instruments. I was thinking to send it to Your Highness, but it struck me as a big nothing. One aria that was sung has caused all of Rome to talk because it seemed inappropriate to be performed under the windows of someone's wife:

A beauty who is not beautiful
Tyrannizes my heart;
She is not beautiful, but she is beautiful to me,
For I am satisfied with little beauty.

Some, however, contend that the poet wrote these little strophes by order of the contestabile in response to a statement they say was made by Prince Don Agostino [Chigi, nephew of the pope] one day in his carriage when, upon encountering the lady contestabilessa [Marie Mancini Colonna], he said that she did not seem at all beautiful to him. One of these evenings another serenata will be performed in the same courtyard, and along with the previous, I want to arrange to obtain the words of both to send to Your Highness, because in this second one there is some creativity in the *ariette*.[87]

The aria Atto quotes is in fact extant, apparently the only portion of this serenata to survive.[88] More interesting is Atto's evaluation of such works primarily by their poetry rather than their music: "creativity in the *ariette*" relates to the words rather than their setting.

Such an attitude seems particularly surprising from someone who may well have sung the work himself. Atto says nothing about his involvement, but in the manuscript collection of the poetry of Sebastiano Baldini, the text of the serenata *Vivere e non amar non è possibile* is preceded by a description of its performance:

Serenata in five [*sic*] voices: three happy lovers, three unhappy [lovers], and Momus. The serenata was composed by order of Cardinal Giovanni [Carlo] de' Medici and set to music by [Marco] Marazzoli. It was sung in three carts by the light of torches, first to the lady contestabilessa in the courtyard of her palace at SS. Apostoli, then to the ambassador of Spain. In the first cart were the three happy lovers: Atto Melani, Ciccolino [Antonio Rivani], and [Giovanni] Carpano. The three unhappy lovers were in the second carriage: Francesco and G. B. Vulpio and Isodoro Cerruti. In the third carriage: Don Francesco, the bass of the prince of Gallicano [Pompeo Colonna],

---

[87] Atto to Mattias, from Rome, September 3, 1661.
[88] The amusing text is presented on the website associated with this book, see p. xvii.

with two theorbos, two archlutes, four violins, two *violoni*, two violas, two harpsichords, and a trumpet.[89]

This description obviously matches Atto's in many ways, including the designation of the serenata as "a 5 voci" (even if seven singers were involved). It is tempting to think that *Vivere e non amar* was the second of the two serenatas Atto mentions (i.e., the one he liked). That Atto himself set at least two of Baldini's poems to music certainly hints that he found *inventione* in Baldini's work (see chapter 6). And so if Atto performed in one of these serenatas, he likely did in the other as well. At the very least, this report establishes the interval of August to October 1661 for the performance of Marazzoli's serenata, this being the only period of Atto's performing activity in Rome after the arrival of Marie Mancini Colonna.[90]

In any event, Atto's interests were soon absorbed by far more serious matters. On September 5, 1661 Nicolas Fouquet was arrested, and among his papers were discovered letters Atto had written from Rome. As Prunières observes, "Reckless Atto, confident in the fortune of the *surintendant* and counting on him to defend [Atto] against his enemies, had regularly sent [Fouquet] copies of all the diplomatic letters he addressed to the king and his secretaries."[91] This practice, along with Fouquet's order to pay Atto the 1,000 *livres* promised him, made Atto seem Fouquet's personal, clandestine agent in Rome – paid off with public funds – rather than a loyal representative of France.[92] The king felt betrayed and ordered all Atto's stipends withheld and contact ended. Fortunately for Atto (and us), de Lionne disobeyed the order and maintained a sympathetic correspondence. But he could do little: Atto had been condemned by association.

At least this is how Atto's disgrace has traditionally been explained.[93] But a closer consideration suggests a slightly different story. In the first place,

---

[89] This Italian text is taken from Giorgio Morelli, ed., *Sebastiano Baldini (1615–1685): Le poesie per musica nei codici della Biblioteca Apostolica Vaticana*, intro. Flavia Cardinale, Studi, Cataloghi e Sussidi Istituto di Bibliografia Musicale, no. 5; Progetti di ricerca bibliografica-musicale dell'IBIMUS, no. 5. (Rome: Istituto di Bibliografia Musicale, 2000), 112, where Morelli locates the text in I Rvat, Chig. L.VI.187, ff. 102–4 or ff. 150–55v. Having examined this manuscript, however, I can report that this passage is not found there. I assume, then, that it appears in the other source for the serenata text, I Rvat, Chig. L.V.153B, ff. 183–94, which I have not been able to study. I have not been able to identify further "Don Francesco."

[90] One can hardly imagine him performing publicly like this after the fortuitous events of 1667 (see below).

[91] Prunières, *L'opéra*, 272. Prunières (271–72) suggests that Atto's correspondence with Fouquet had been going on for years and was "volumineuse." As I have seen no evidence for this view in the archives (Prunières provides no citations) and find no previous mention of Fouquet in Atto's correspondence, I am inclined rather to believe Fouquet's testimony that the two only first met shortly before the singer's departure from Paris.

[92] See Fouquet, *Recueil*, VIII:165–204 *passim*.   [93] Prunières, *L'opéra*, 271–73, and see above.

most historians agree that Fouquet's arrest and trial simply offered a pretense for removing a man Louis otherwise found disagreeable. Whatever Fouquet's guilt or innocence with regard to the charges, he did nothing very unusual for government officials of his time; indeed, most of Fouquet's "abuses" had been rehearsed on a much vaster scale by Mazarin himself, a man whose memory the king always honored. Instead, as Georges Mongredien suggests, "When Louis XIV took power following Mazarin's death, with the clear intent of exercising it personally, he aimed to break not only with the tradition of the 'ministériat,' but with an entire past of political and financial disorders that had lasted a score of years, since the death of Richelieu."[94] For the king, the years of his regency were colored by the chaos of the Fronde and had to be repudiated. In the political sphere, this meant establishing a group of ministers who were loyal to himself alone. Jean Meyer suggests that Fouquet may have been aiming for Mazarin's position and that Louis found his presumptions incompatible with the idea of personal rule.[95] Fouquet's fall from favor had more to do with post-Mazarine French politics than with real concerns over finances or treason.

In the artistic sphere too, Louis broke with the past. Prunières points out that although the king had enjoyed Italian music in his youth, he now "only want[ed] to believe in the artistic superiority of the French and desire[d], as much as possible, to do without foreigners, in both his amusements and his business."[96] To his misfortune, Atto had been a part of both, and, as a castrato among the gentlemen of the king's chamber, he must have been a conspicuous – and perhaps offensive – reminder of the "excesses" of the regency. While Atto's letters to Fouquet may have contained only "simple expressions of deference and affection," as Atto's family later claimed, their discovery provided a convenient excuse to jettison another vestige of the past.[97] Certainly many figures far closer to the finance minister never came under scrutiny: upon first hearing of Fouquet's arrest, Atto's main worry was for his confidant de Lionne, who knew the accused well. Yet "His Majesty

---

[94] Georges Mongredien, *L'affaire Fouquet* ([Paris]: Hachette, 1956), 11.

[95] Jean Meyer, "Le cas Fouquet: Faut-il réhabiliter Fouquet?," in *Les années Fouquet: Politique, société, vie artistique et culturelle dans les années 1650*, ed. Chantal Grell and Klaus Malettke, Forschungen zur Geschichte der Neuzeit: Marburger Beiträge, vol. 2 (Münster: LIT, 2001), 11–33.

[96] Prunières, *L'opéra*, 268. Strictly speaking, Lully represented an exception to this rule, but the composer had so aligned himself with French musical ideals and had so pleased Louis personally with his dance music that his Italian origins were overlooked.

[97] The characterization of Atto's correspondence with Fouquet comes from a biographical sketch of the singer given in Tommaso Trenta, *Memorie per servire alla storia politica del Cardinale Francesco Buonvisi patrizio lucchese* (Lucca: Francesco Bertini, 1818), I:261. As this sketch is based on a "*vita*" written by one of Atto's nephews (which has since disappeared, along with the virtually all the rest of the Melani family documents), I consider it a rather reliable record of the Melani family position in this matter. For a full transcription, see appendix E. I have been unable to uncover the letters to Fouquet themselves.

told M. de Lionne that he need not fear this attention … assuring him of the affection and esteem that he felt for his person."[98] In the end, Atto's disgrace resulted less from connections to Fouquet himself than from association with the social order Fouquet represented.

Sometime around the middle of October, news of Atto's misfortune reached him in Rome. The gravity of the blow emerges in his letter of October 31, 1661, in which he pours out his distress to de Lionne in language as charged as the cantata poetry he knew so well:

You tell me in your last letter of October 9 that my injury is without remedy, and that *the king is forever* provoked *against me*. It is *the decree of my death* that you have drafted … Would to God that I had not loved the king so much and that I had been more attached to M. Fouquet than to him, for at least I would be punished justly for a crime I had committed … [A]t this moment I am the most miserable boy in the world, for I will never be able to console myself, as I think of the king not as a great prince, but as a person for whom I am impassioned with the greatest possible love …

My soul is not strong enough to withstand so great a misfortune. I dare to complain of it without knowing to whom to attribute such a disgrace, and although it seems to me that the king does me a great injustice, I cannot protest, for he was right to have been surprised that I exchanged letters with the *surintendant* … Yes, my poor M. de Lionne, the king has treated me justly in telling you that he was displeased with me, for the hand that drafted all those letters deserves to be cut off, but my heart is innocent and my soul has committed no error. I have always been faithful to the king, and if the king wants to be just, he should condemn the one and absolve the others, because the hand erred through an excess of love that my heart had for the king. It erred because it had too great a desire to return to him …

… [T]here is not a single word in all my letters that I cannot justify, and if the king would have the goodness to accord me this favor, which has never been denied to any criminal, have them scrutinize all my letters and have them interrogate me, for I will go to a prison to give my answers, either to be punished or to be pardoned, if I deserve it … One will never find in [Fouquet's] records that he gave me any money nor that I had been among his retainers …

To tell you now what my conduct is like, know that although I have suffered such a great misfortune, there is not a soul who knows it here from my lips, and that, from hiding it, I am destroyed in heart and soul. *I weep day and night*, as when one *has lost one's mistress*, but soon I will retire to a place of mine in the country where I *will no longer see anyone*. I leave tomorrow for there, and you will always be with me. If the good Lord does not somehow make me forget the king, my pain will be incurable or I will soon die.[99]

---

[98] Atto to Mattias, from Rome, October 1, 1661.

[99] Atto to de Lionne, from Rome, October 31, 1661. Prunières (*L'opéra*, 273n) finds the underlining in this passage "ironic," concluding that it was probably done by a derisive de Lionne. I find no support for this, as the ink of the underlining matches the rest of the letter, and in other places Atto employs underlining for particular emphasis.

Even if Atto's correspondence is regularly flamboyant, the special intensity of these lines is unmistakable. In a single blow, Atto saw vanish all the financial and political capital he had amassed in France over the previous sixteen years. Deeply humiliated, he determined to leave Rome at once, before his situation became known. (Despite his claim to have informed no one, he tells in a previous letter of confiding in Marie Mancini Colonna; they were indeed close.[100]) Atto left on November 1, just in time: according to Elpidio Benedetti, de Lionne's agent in Rome,

Signor Atto then left for Tuscany, and I was very unhappy at not being able to question him about a certain notice lately come to me from Paris that some of his letters were found among the [papers] of M. Fouquet, the contents of which did not please His Majesty. It seemed strange to me that Atto gave me no news about this. It is true that in the preceding days I noticed some changes in his mood and that he took the defense of M. Fouquet with too much passion.[101]

One can well imagine.

Atto returned to his home in Pistoia, outwardly, at least, resigned to abandoning his lofty goals. He wanted, in his words, "to be home with my relatives and to live just to reside with them, dreaming no more of anything but praying to the good Lord to pardon my sins."[102] Without the backing of the cardinal, all Atto's risky enterprises – the labor of so many years – had collapsed. Tying his fortunes to Mazarin's, he had played the dangerous game of social advancement and lost. Over a decade later, the poet Marc-Antonio Romagnesi dedicated to Atto a sonnet on the dangers of pride; given that Romagnesi had probably known Atto in Paris, the poem seems a moralizing commentary on the disaster:

Al Signor Abate Atto Melani, *Contra fortunam non satis cauta mortalitas est*	To Abate Atto Melani: "Against Fortune Mankind is Not Sufficiently Wary"
Preme con piè superbo empia Fortuna E capanne mendiche, & aurei Troni; E de l'instabil Rota al giro aduna Mille Sisifi ogn'hor, mille Issioni.	With her proud foot Fortune crushes Both beggars' huts and golden thrones; And at the turn of the fickle wheel she gathers A thousand Sisyphuses, a thousand Ixions.
Nel basso le miserie indi raguna Le ricchezze nel sommo avien che doni, Copre Codri nel'imo ombra importuna, Aureo Vello nel sommo hanno i Giasoni.	At the bottom, then, she musters the miseries; At the top, she gives riches; At the nadir, a bleak shadow covers the Codruses; At the zenith, the Jasons have their golden fleece.
Ma s'unqua oppresso il frale inclina al fondo,	But if the frail, when oppressed, tend toward the bottom,

---

100 Atto to de Lionne, from Rome, October 25, 1661.
101 Elpidio Benedetti to de Lionne, from Rome, November 8, 1661.
102 Atto to de Lionne, from Rome, October 25, 1661.

Sostener non gli è dato in rio cordoglio	They cannot sustain in cruel sorrow
Di gravi affanni intolerabil pondo.	The intolerable weight of heavy anguish.
A franger solo il ribellante orgoglio	In the stormy sea of the world,
Nel procelloso pelago del mondo	Fortune is the wave, and Virtue is the reef,
Fortuna è flutto, e la Virtute è scoglio.[103]	Whose purpose is only to break unruly pride.

Indeed, Atto now gave the appearance of retiring from the game, leaving international politics to others. Had that truly been his plan, however, one would expect to see his name reappear in the *cappella* at the cathedral of Pistoia, an institution then virtually ruled by his family. Or he might have found his way into the ranks of the Medici court musicians. Or, if his voice really were in decline, he could have served as *maestro di cappella* at some church or court.[104] But even at his lowest point, Atto did not go back to music: having surpassed that station in life, he could not endure a return. Instead, he chose a quiet semi-retirement, living perhaps on wealth and lands already acquired and hoping for a change in fortune. Notwithstanding his protestations, he never entirely abandoned his ambitions. And through his

---

[103] Marc-Antonio Romagnesi, *Poesie liriche … divise in quattro parti* (Paris: Denys Langlois, 1673), 432. The Latin quotation is taken from Quintus Curtius Rufus, *Historiam Alexandri Magni Macedonis*, 8.4.24, and serves as a warning from the narrator as Alexander enjoys his first meeting with Roxane. Regarding the mythological allusions: Sisyphus was a cruel man who offended the gods and was punished in Hades by being forced eternally to push a stone block up a steep hill, only to have it roll back down on him each time. Ixion was admitted by Zeus to Olympus but abused that privilege by trying to seduce Hera; his punishment was to be bound on a fiery wheel that rolled unceasingly. Codrus was the last king of Athens; when it was foretold that the Dorians would conquer Athens unless they killed its king, Codrus went to the Dorian camp in disguise and provoked the soldiers to kill him, thus saving his people through his own misfortune.

    Romagnesi (1633–1706) was the son of Brigida Bianchi (1613–1703), also a poet (as well as a famous *commedia dell'arte* actress and singer), who spent extended periods at the court of Paris. She was there, presumably with her son, around 1640, from 1644 to 1646, and from 1653 to her death, thus covering virtually all of Atto's time in France. Although none of Atto's extant cantatas appears to use her poetry, it seems likely that Bianchi and her son would have known Atto, as they were all Italian entertainers favored at court (especially by Anne of Austria). See Colin Timms, "Brigida Bianchi's *Poesie musicali* and Their Settings," *I quaderni della civica scuola di musica* 9, nos. 19–20 (December 1990): 19–37 *passim*, but especially 20–21; also, Émile Campardon, *Les comédiens du roi de la troupe italienne pendant les deux derniers siècles: Documents inèdits recueillis aux Archives Nationales* (Paris: Berger-Levrault, 1880), II:107. Admittedly, Romagnesi's poem was published long after Atto's disastrous year, but I can think of no other events closer to the time of publication that would fit this poem; indeed, in late 1670 Atto was allowed to return to Paris as a sign of his renewed favor (see below). More likely, this poem was an earlier work of Romagnesi's.

[104] On the Melani family's control of the musical posts at the cathedral of Pistoia, see Weaver, "Materiali," 268–70; and Franco Baggiani, "I maestri di cappella nella cattedrale di Pistoia," *Bollettino storico pistoiese*, 3rd ser., 21 (1986): 52–56. On Atto's absence from the Medici payroll, note his absence from Kirkendale, *The Court Musicians*. On older castrati as teachers and members of church choirs, Rosselli, "The Castrati," 169–72.

perseverance, characteristic daring, and plain good fortune, those ambitions were eventually fulfilled.

Salvation

The roughly five-year period after Atto's withdrawal from Rome indeed marks the low point of his life. Almost no letters from him survive for the eighteen months following his return to Tuscany. And unlike earlier periods at home, Atto gives no sign of singing for Mattias or anyone else: although such service is possible, Atto really does appear to have retired.[105] When in the spring of 1663 he reestablished contact with de Lionne, his wounds were still unhealed, and the bitterness that jumps from the page seems more than rhetorical:

Your most recent letter has been a real lifesaver for me since it revived all my spirits, which previously were so dejected and humiliated that my greatest consolation was thinking about death and the vanities of this world ... I have been in a room for weeks and months without leaving it, with no other company than a few spiritual books and histories, and I have received no less profit from the ones than relief from the others. I have finally learned that this world is a theater in which every age performs its *commedia*, and that it is not only now that in some parts of the world one may see ignorance exalted and virtue debased.[106]

In his depression, Atto spent his days reliving and chronicling past experiences. More than once he mentions writing a history of the negotiations at the Peace of the Pyrenees, a work that he sent to de Lionne for correction and that the grand duke apparently considered for publication.[107]

---

[105] Sara Mamone (*Serenissimi fratelli*, 399–400) has published a curious letter from Antonio Rivani to Giovan Carlo de' Medici, from London, March 16, 1662 (I Fas, MdP, Filza 5340, ff. 553–55v). In it, Rivani writes of his successful performances before Charles II and further reports "Sua Maestà fece un paragon del signor Atto e di me, dove essendo il detto signor Atto stato sentito da quasi tutti i presenti nel cabinetto, fu concluso e mi permetta Vostra Altezza di dirlo, che il Signor Atto meritava di esser messo nel inferno, come io in cielo." How Atto could have found his way to London at this time is baffling. Rivani's path is well documented: he arrived in Paris on November 8, 1661 to prepare for Cavalli's *Ercole amante*; after performing the opera several times, he made a rapid trip to London during Lent, arriving in mid-March and returning to Paris by mid-April. This route cannot have been Atto's: on the date Rivani first arrived in Paris, Atto had just left Rome, and, given Atto's disgrace with the king of France, he simply could not have shown his face in Paris; indeed Atto is mentioned in none of the other available correspondence surrounding Rivani. I do not mistrust Rivani's report, but Atto's presence in London cannot at this time be explained. (As to Rivani's denigration of Atto's singing, I put little stock in it: neither singer ever had a good word to say about the other.)
[106] Atto to de Lionne, from Florence, March 20, 1665.
[107] Ibid. This particular writing project is also mentioned in his letters of May 12, and October 16, 1665.

In this effort, Atto may well have been imitating his associate (and past enemy) Vittorio Siri, who published a series of such accounts. Indeed, a later biographical sketch records that "[Atto] wrote in elegant form about many curious and important dealings that passed through his hands, and these can be read in the many volumes of his memoirs."[108] Accustomed as he was to writing copious letters, and with little else to do, the role of author probably came easily. Sadly, most of these accounts are now lost.[109]

Before long, though, old habits began leading Atto back into the political arena. Residing in Florence, he began operating a sort of clearinghouse for information. He typically received news from a network of contacts close to the papal court and then summarized the material in letters to de Lionne in Paris (letters that, perhaps for de Lionne's safety, he no longer signed).[110] One of the most consequential exchanges concerned the celebrated clash in Rome on August 20, 1662 between the pope's Corsican guards and the bodyguards of the French ambassador. The result of long-standing tensions, the incident seemed to Louis XIV a personal affront, and even an apology

---

[108] This sketch was inscribed below a portrait of Atto in his home in Pistoia and is recorded in an inventory of the Melani household conducted in 1782 (I Fn, Tordi 350, pp. 61–62). Interestingly, when thirty years earlier the castrato Loreto Vittori had been exiled from Rome for his indiscretions, he too turned to writing. See Sergio Durante, "Il cantante," in *Il sistema produttivo e le sue competenze*, vol. IV of *Storia dell'opera italiana*, ed. Lorenzo Bianconi and Giorgio Pestelli, Biblioteca di cultura musicale (Turin: E.D.T./ Musica, 1987), 362.

[109] The inventory mentioned in the previous note reveals that these books, along with many others, were still in 1782 on the shelves of the bookcase in Atto's former room (see appendix H). The note that many of these manuscripts "furono stampati in Francese senza nome dell'Autore" suggests that while some of his writings may still exist, they are unlikely to be identified. Rita Monaldi and Francesco Sorti, who have published two novels with Atto as protagonist (*Imprimatur*, Omnibus [Milan: Arnaldo Mondadori, 2002] and *Secretum* [Amsterdam: De Bezige Bij, Cargo, 2005]), have also published an edition (apparently in Spanish and German translations only) of a manuscript they attribute to Atto, originally entitled "Memoires secrets contenant les evenemens plus notables des quatre derniers conclaves avec plus remarques sur la cour de Rome" (*Los secretos del cónclave* [Barcelona: Ediciones Salamandra, 2005]). Unfortunately, they provide no information on the location of this manuscript, obscuring the significance of their work and its connection to Atto.

Sergio Monaldini's publication of the Bentivoglio family's correspondence reveals another activity of Atto's during this period. (*L'orto dell'Esperidi: Musici, attori e artisti nel patrocinio della famiglia Bentivoglio [1646–1685]*, ConNotazioni no. 5 [Lucca: Libreria Musicale Italiana, 2000]). Filippo Melani writes to Ippolito Bentivoglio from Florence on August 23, 1664 that Atto can help adjust one of the parts from Antonio Cesti's opera *La magnanimità d'Alessandro* for a singer soon to perform it at the court of Innsbruck: "Atto l'aggiusterà per appunto ad suo dono, senza toccar punto il basso continuo" (203). On November 8, Atto himself confirms these dealings and offers one of his usual assessments of Cesti's gifts: "certo non vi trovo nella musica gran miracoli, anzi molte improprietà" (214).

[110] That Atto did not sign many of his letters from this period raises some questions of authorship. But having seen so many examples of his handwriting, I feel confident that I have picked out his letters from the others in the same collections, even though at times they have been misattributed in the indices.

from the cardinal nephew, delivered in person, did not appease the king. Given Atto's familiarity with the parties involved, one is hardly surprised to find that he "played not a small role in the long negotiation of the satisfactions to be given to the king," presumably as a low-level intermediary.[111] Atto certainly was in direct contact with the French ambassador, the duke de Créquy: later, in April of 1664, the duke actually spent the night at the Melani home in Pistoia, and the following year Atto wrote to Leopoldo de' Medici in support of an unspecified request from the duke.[112] Such dealings surely signal a softening of French antipathy toward Atto. Though still officially in disgrace, he was slowly rebuilding a network.

But Atto's full return to diplomacy is first marked by his reentry into papal politics. With the health of Alexander VII failing, Atto began to consider a trip to Rome, and as the news grew worse Atto increasingly reflected upon the *papabili*, the possible candidates.[113] After a year-and-a-half "keep[ing] my boots ready so I can jump on a horse," word finally came of the pope's death, and Atto tore off to Rome, arriving on May 31, 1667.[114] As before, Mattias sent out a letter of introduction to a member of the Chigi family (this time, Prince Don Mario) requesting protection and support.[115] And, as before, Atto was immediately granted meetings with some of the highest officials, including Cardinal de Retz and the new French ambassador to Rome, Charles d'Albert d'Ailly, duke de Chaulnes.[116] Gone in a flash was Atto's resigned, world-weary demeanor, replaced by his more characteristic enthusiasm: he now saw an opportunity to realize a plan he had long cultivated.

Incredible as it may seem, Atto had been scheming for years to win the papacy for Cardinal Giulio Rospigliosi. Atto's association with the Rospigliosi family, ancient members of the Pistoiese nobility, dated virtually from birth (see chapter 1), and through the years Atto seems to have maintained a special link to Giulio. In May of 1655 Atto boasted to Mattias

---

[111] Again, from Trenta's biographical sketch, *Memorie*, I:260 (see appendix E). For information on the Corsican guards incident, see Treasure, *Seventeenth Century France*, 250–51, or, for more extensive detail, Charles Gérin, *Louis XIV et le Saint-Siège* (Paris: Victoire Lecoffre, 1894), I:283–543.

[112] Atto to the duke of Mantua, from Ferrara, April 14, 1664; Atto to Leopoldo de' Medici, from Florence, February 14, 1665.

[113] Atto first mentions such a journey, to my knowledge, in his letter to de Lionne, from Florence, September 11, 1665.

[114] The quotation ("tengo pronti gli stivali per salire a Cavallo") comes from Atto's letter to de Lionne, from Florence, April 15, 1667; his arrival date in Rome is mentioned in his first letter from that city, to de Lionne, 31, May 1667.

[115] Mattias to Prince Don Mario Chigi, from Florence, May 24, 1667.

[116] Meetings with these two are mentioned in Atto's letters to de Lionne, from Rome, May 31 and June 1, 1667.

that he regularly dined with Rospigliosi, and in 1659, Giulio himself wrote a letter to the prince in support of Atto's bid for a vacant benefice in Pistoia.[117] Two years later, the bond was closer than ever: "Three evenings ago I was at one of Cardinal Rospigliosi's gardens for dinner … I swear to Your Highness, without any partiality, that since I entered society I have not met a man more accomplished in all ways than this cardinal, worthy to be adored and esteemed by all gentlemen."[118]

That Atto should be voicing such praise in 1661 is highly revealing, for by this time he had reached a critical stage in his plan. According to Atto's later account, the plan itself had begun in 1656, before Rospigliosi was made cardinal.[119] From 1644 to 1652 Archbishop Rospigliosi had served Pope Alexander VII as papal nuncio to Spain. That position brought much honor, but it also prejudiced the French against Rospigliosi, as a presumed Spanish client. According to Atto, this suspicion was particularly current in 1657 and 1658, at which time "God, through His divine plan, permitted … me to be in France so as to be able to warn [Rospigliosi] about so much slander and to defend him."[120] Atto's "defense" apparently consisted of showing the king Atto's own weekly correspondence with the now-cardinal, "full of homage and veneration toward the king."[121] By this means, Atto strove to convince Louis and his ministers of Rospigliosi's French sympathies. Over time, these efforts facilitated correspondence – and indeed later trust and friendship – between Rospigliosi and the French court, particularly de Lionne. More importantly from his own perspective, Atto positioned himself as the key liaison between the parties.

Further, in 1661 Atto specifically negotiated French support for Rospigliosi's candidacy in any forthcoming conclave. The historian Charles Gérin confirms that, "through the mediation of a former retainer of Mazarin, Atto Melani, Rospigliosi had [in 1661] indulged in a secret correspondence with the court of France, with the purpose of assuring himself, in a future conclave, the support of the king's faction."[122] At issue were the favors Rospigliosi was willing to guarantee in return for the king's backing. Eventually, the cardinal did vaguely promise that "if ever it came about [that he were elected], he would not be ungrateful to His Majesty and to those who

---

[117] Atto to Mattias, from Rome, May 1, 1655; Cardinal Giulio Rospigliosi to Mattias, from Castel Gandolfo, October 25, 1659.

[118] Atto to Mattias, from Rome, August 27, 1661 (postscript).

[119] Letter to Simon Arnauld, marquis de Pomponne, or César d'Estrées, bishop of Laon (unclear), from Rome, March 15, 1672. Rospigliosi was made cardinal on April 9, 1657.

[120] Atto to de Lionne, from Rome, April 2, 1669.

[121] From the anonymous "Vita dell'Abate Atto Melani," pp. 151–52.

[122] Gérin, *Louis XIV*, I:274–75n. See also pp. 183–85n.

had favored him."[123] But before long the reigning pope, Alexander VII, became suspicious and forced Rospigliosi to break off dealings with Paris; Atto's disgrace in the fall of 1661 likewise precluded further involvement.

This background helps explain why Atto rushed to Rome at Alexander's death in 1667: he saw the chance to bring his earlier negotiations to fruition. Although his correspondence during the critical weeks is vague, he seems to have continued to mediate between French diplomats and church figures: in his letter of June, 12 for example, he claims that the French ambassador depended on him for news from the conclave.[124] At this time Atto also corresponded with the rest of the Rospigliosi family in Pistoia, apparently assuring them that Giulio would be elected.[125]

To Atto's enormous good fortune, his prediction was right: Rospigliosi was elected pope on the evening of June 20, 1667, taking the name Clement IX. Rospigliosi had successfully appealed to the three most significant factions within the cardinalate: the Spanish endorsed him because of his successful nunciature in that country; the *squadrone volante* – the group of ostensibly independent cardinals – approved because they saw him as pious and able; and the French consented because of his past promises to them, promises that Atto had helped arrange.[126] Thus, Atto's later claims to have contributed to the election of this pope cannot be dismissed, in Robert Weaver's words, as "a nonsensical proposition": although other figures were certainly more influential, Atto had played a real part.[127] His elation, as well as self-interest, emerge clearly from his first letter to de Lionne after the election (the first Atto actually signed in years):

Let the Spanish not boast of having made the pope, much less Cardinals [Antonio] Barberini and [Flavio] Chigi, and those of the *squadrone*, because all the glory is owed to the king, and to Your Excellency. If His Holiness turns out to be grateful to France, as I hope he will, I will consider it my fortune to have cultivated and contributed for so long to the fulfillment of such a fine project. But if Your

---

[123]   Rospigliosi to de Lionne, from Rome, September 19, 1661, in Gérin, *Louis XIV*, II:183n. Confirming this negotiation, Gérin also quotes from Atto's letter to de Lionne, from Rome, October 3, 1661, and Rospigliosi's letter to de Lionne, from Rome, June 10, 1662.

[124]   Atto to de Lionne, from Rome, June 12, 1667.

[125]   The evidence is Camillo Rospigliosi's (largely illegible) response, which, although without a date, clearly comes from June 1667. After thanking Atto for his support, Camillo warns, "siamo più lontani di quello, che lei si da a credere."

[126]   Ludwig Pastor, *The History of the Popes from the Close of the Middle Ages*, trans. Ernest Graf (London: Kegan Paul, Trench, Trubner and Co., 1940), XXXI:318–19. Pastor notes (XXXI:328) that Queen Christina of Sweden also favored Rospigliosi and that she helped to persuade her confidant, Cardinal Decio Azzolini, the leader of the *squadrone*, to support him in the conclave.

[127]   The disparagement of Atto's claims comes from Weaver, in both his "Florentine Comic Operas," 176, and his "*Il Girello*, a 17th-Century Burlesque Opera," *Quadrivium* 12 (1971): 149.

Excellency does not use this opportunity to make my king – forever adored – understand that all my actions had no other object than his royal service, all my happiness will become embittered.[128]

In fact, Atto's happiness was not at all embittered, for as quickly as his status had fallen with Fouquet, it now rose with Clement IX. Only three days after the election, Atto was admitted for a private audience of over two hours with the pope. Remarkably, Clement shared with him his reflections on politics, concerns about finances, and general hopes for the future.[129] Atto immediately recognized the value of such discussions: his special access to the pope could help him in France. And so the only reward Atto requested for his efforts, which Clement openly acknowledged, was to be allowed continued free admittance to the pope's presence.[130] "'Signor Atto,' he answered me, 'we have not been able to think about anything yet, and you see how many affairs we have,' pointing to a little table covered with papers and petitions. 'When things get underway, we will see you often and with relish, for we do not believe that the papacy makes one forget one's friends.'"[131]

The pope kept his word. Clement often allowed Atto to attend him during and after meals, particularly in the interval before his afternoon siesta when the two would speak privately. On other occasions, Clement called for Atto to join him for a walk in the gardens or through a gallery of the palace: the pope seems truly to have enjoyed Atto's company. In fact, Atto was admitted nearly every time he presented himself, even up to nine times on one day.[132] He assured de Lionne that "no one will ever speak to the pope with the liberty and efficacy that I will" and bragged that "the pope sings my praises to

---

[128] Atto to de Lionne, from Rome, June 22, 1667.

[129] "Relazione dell'Udienza havuta da N.S. il dì 23 di Giugno all'ore 19," included in Atto's letter to de Lionne, from Rome, June 28, 1667. This report is also the source for the rest of the paragraph. Worth relating here simply for its charm is a story that Atto told the pope at this meeting: "trovandosi la corte di Francia in Amiens [making the date 1647 or 1649], e discorrendo quivi una sera col signor Cardinale Mazzarino sopra il di lui oroscopo che gl'haveva indovinato, tutto ciò che gl'era succeduto, dissi che ancor io speravo d'havere un giorno qualche buona sorte, venendomi predetto gran cose circa gl'anni *40* e io speravo, le dissi, che tutte le mie speranze erano fondate sopra due giulij [a type of coin, worth a fraction of a lira]. Tu farai molto poco se non hai altro capitale rispondesse il Cardinale, al che soggiunsi, che intanto il giulio presente valeva molto, e che l'altro valerebbe assai un giorno, e che a tal valuta S.Em.za haverebbe anch'essa contribuito. Sorrise il Papa."

[130] Ibid. Clement acknowledged Atto's role more than once (at least, according to Atto): see, for example, Atto's report in his letter to de Lionne, from Rome, July 5, 1667: "mi disse il Papa l'ultima volta ch'io gli parlai, che sapeva et haveva molto ben a memoria quanto io havevo cooperato alla sua Esaltazione."

[131] Atto to de Lionne (the "Relazione"), from Rome, June 28, 1667.

[132] These instances appear in various of Atto's letters to de Lionne, from Rome, from late June through August 1667.

whomever he speaks of such things. His relatives give me such a reception and treat me in such a way that all Rome thinks I'm the favorite."[133]

Such accounts might well seem the exaggerations of a courtier trying to overcome disfavor except that contemporaries also remarked on Atto's privileges. Ferdinando Raggi, a Genoese agent at the papal court, reports with jealousy, "Atto Melani ... is a castrato who formerly sang well here, in France, and in Florence. He is introduced to the pope's residence every time he desires it. He claims to have stratagems and sound judgment to assist the pope ... He is from Pistoia, bold, and apt to put his hands in everything."[134] More approvingly, the French ambassador relates that "Atto serves here perfectly well and is a great help to me, because through him I make known all that I wish to the pope and to Cardinal [Jacopo] Rospigliosi [the cardinal nephew]."[135]

It really appears that for a time at least the forty-one-year-old castrato had more access to the pontiff than just about anyone else at court, and he happily and thoroughly exploited the situation. On the one hand, Atto served France: his regular conversations with Clement offered the chance both to promote French interests within the Church and to monitor – and report back about – the state of those interests. On the other hand, he served the pope: he could offer Clement an insider's view of Louis XIV's court, the focus of much papal business.[136] And, of course, Atto was always serving himself: as he had in the past, he was working for multiple patrons, portraying himself as an indispensable negotiator. Inevitably, his conflicting loyalties drew criticism. But Atto saw himself not as some sort of double agent, but rather as a facilitator, someone who, by knowing the secrets of both sides, could mediate disputes and generally get things done. As he puts it,

my principal goal has always been to cultivate good relations between the [Quirinal] palace [seat of the pope] and the minister [de Chaulnes]; to remove difficulties and never expose the leaders to them; to tell them useful things and hide unpleasant ones. In short, I have sought to avoid making a big deal of every simple trifle and to handle the more difficult things with such skill that no one be troubled and bothered by them; in this way I have succeeded in doing everything without thrashing about (as certain zealous blusterers usually do), having made use of private *conversazioni* to intertwine weightier matters with more common things.[137]

---

[133] Atto to de Lionne, from Rome, June 28, 1667.

[134] *Fogli d'avvisi* of Ferdinando Raggi, from Rome, September 25, 1667, in A[lessandro] Ademollo, "Un campanaio e la sua famiglia," *Fanfulla della Domenica*, December 30, 1883, 3.

[135] The duke de Chaulnes to de Lionne, from Rome, January 24, 1668.

[136] On the complexities of this relationship, which turned especially on the promotion of cardinals, the Jansenist controversy, and especially the war with the Turks over Crete, see Pastor, *History*, 345–423.

[137] Atto to de Lionne, from Rome, August 28, 1668. Admittedly, whether "conversationi" here indicates "conversations" or "soirées" is not entirely clear.

Indeed, the *conversazione* was Atto's home turf, where he had spent much of his life entertaining and observing the fusion of leisure and politics. He now drew on that experience to maximize the benefits of Rospigliosi's election.

His efforts quickly paid off. Within weeks, he received confirmation of his return to Louis XIV's favor.[138] Giddy, he writes to de Lionne, "May Your Excellency now consider what pleasure is mine at seeing myself restored to the grace not only of so great a monarch, but of a king whom I have always adored like a god on earth."[139] By early December, Louis backed up his words with the reestablishment of Atto's pension, a gesture Atto recognized as "a manifest indication of my reinstatement into his royal grace."[140] After six years at the very bottom of Fortune's wheel, Atto was spun dizzily to the top.

A new reality

Unfortunately, the wheel kept spinning. After the first blush of elation, Atto found himself confronting unanticipated problems. Instead of the increased wealth he had expected, he suffered shortfalls; instead of public recognition, he found himself excluded from official positions; and instead of lasting security, he discovered his papal benefactor was sickly and unlikely to reign for long. This last misfortune, the most serious, threatened to land him in the same mess as at Mazarin's death. In response, Atto forged new alliances and redoubled his diplomatic efforts for France. In fact, this frantic burst of activity brought about the final stage of his personal transformation. By 1671, all Atto's ties to a musical past had dissolved, and he was launched – now unassailably – into the diplomatic career that would shape the rest of his life.

Atto's financial problems began not long after the papal election. His sense of his own rising status forced him to adopt the outward trappings of a gentleman: for the first time Atto speaks of renting carriages, retaining liveried servants, and purchasing his own furniture.[141] But his income did not grow with his expenses. Although a French stipend had been promised, it

---

[138] Whereas Weaver ("Florentine Comic Operas," 322) assumed that Atto had won this approval only in 1679, at the time of his definitive return to Paris, Atto's redemption in fact arrived in the summer of 1667.

[139] Atto to de Lionne, from Rome, August 9, 1667.

[140] The quotation comes from Atto's letter to de Lionne, from Rome, December 13, 1667.

[141] Regarding his need to travel by carriage, and the financial burden he represented to others, he writes in a letter to de Lionne, from Rome, January 25, 1668: "Intanto io continuo a dar spesa, et incommodo, al signor Abate Benedetti. Sono astretto d'andar cercando ogni dì Carrozze perché un galant'huomo non può andare a piedi; ne io voglio mettermi in una spesa, per fare una mascherata, senza poterla durare, ne sono così gran Signore di servire il Re, a mie spese." He speaks of the servants and the furniture in his letter to de Lionne, from Rome, March 20, 1668: "dovendo tener Servitori a Livrea, e provedermi di tutto, mi rovino affatto."

amounted to just half his pre-1661 allotment, and he had trouble collecting even that amount.[142] In March 1668 the pope granted Atto a prebend worth about 300 *scudi* from an abbey in Naples, but because Naples was a Spanish dominion and Atto's allegiances were French, he was never allowed to collect. Indeed, he repeatedly mentions a scheme – never successful – to swap benefices with Cardinal Giulio Spinola, who faced a similar problem with a Tuscan benefice repudiated by the grand duke.[143]

The greatest damage to his finances, however, resulted from the death of his old patron Mattias de' Medici in October 1667. This passing marked the close of a long chapter in Atto's life. Mattias had first nurtured Atto's talents, supported his ambitions, and forgiven his transgressions; and even if Atto's attentions in recent years had mostly turned away from Tuscany, Mattias's patronage still represented the sheltered port to which Atto could always return. Atto's sorrow at the prince's death seems to have been real: he wrote to one of his contacts in Mantua about "the grave loss I have suffered of Prince Mattias of Tuscany, my old and generous master, about whom I can say nothing to Your Excellency except that I will be inconsolable all the rest of my life."[144] But certainly a part of that sorrow related to a loss of income: Atto revealed to de Lionne that Mattias had regularly assigned him forty *ducatoni* per month whenever he was away from Tuscany, and, to his alarm, Atto saw no way to replace that income.[145]

Soon Atto became sorely frustrated with the papal city. In addition to his financial troubles, his extraordinary relationship with the pope began to cool as Atto's enemies, resentful of his favor, sought to diminish his influence. Some simply chastised Atto for daring to give Clement information and

---

[142] The relative size of the benefice from France emerges in Atto's later summary of his financial position in a letter to de Lionne, from Rome, October 29, 1669: where he originally received 200 *scudi* per month, he now was awarded only 100. (The question of what is meant by the term *scudo* in a letter from a native Tuscan to France from Rome is complex and really beside my point here; each principality had its own coinage. See Frederick Hammond, *Girolamo Frescobaldi: A Guide to Research*, Garland Composer Resource Manuals, vol. 9, Garland Reference Library of the Humanities, vol. 672 [New York: Garland, 1988], 67–71). Although Atto mentions receiving a specific payment on this benefice in a letter to de Lionne, from Rome, May 8, 1668, he still complains about not receiving the money. On May 29, 1668, Atto thanks de Lionne for an abbotship worth 2,000 francs per year, a partial restoration of Atto's income from Beaubec, as discussed above. This income is not mentioned, however, in his summary of income from 1669, leading one to doubt he ever actually received the money, at least before returning to France in 1670. Atto also mentions his French benefices in his letters to de Lionne, from Rome, February 15, March 6 and 20, May 15, and October 16, 1668.

[143] Atto mentions this benefice in his letters to de Lionne, from Rome, March 3 and 20, April 17, 1668. His letter of October 29, 1669 reveals that he never managed to receive anything.

[144] Atto to Orazio Canossa (in Mantua), from Rome, October 15, 1667.

[145] Atto discusses his financial support from Mattias in his letter to de Lionne, from Rome, October 11, 1667. The following week (October 18), Atto remarks on the poor prospects of replacing this lost income in what he characterizes as the stingy climate of Rome.

advice, a criticism Atto blithely ignored.[146] Others, however, questioned his loyalty to the pope, declaring publicly that Atto's main purpose in Rome was to report everything back to Paris. While from a certain perspective this characterization was accurate, Atto was surprised to note an abrupt change in the behavior of Clement who "no longer opens himself up to me as before on issues that regard France, persuaded, perhaps, that I take more the side of the king and of the [French] ambassador than his own."[147]

Although Atto tried hard to mask his French ties, they plainly held him back, most conspicuously in his attempt to obtain an official post. Atto believed Clement would reward his efforts with a lucrative and prestigious position. At first, he hoped to be named one of the pope's *camerieri segreti*, and he even heard positive rumors about his chances. When he was denied, the resentment he had harbored through his years of exile welled up once again in a passage – unique in his correspondence – that acknowledges his physical state: "Signor Elpidio [Benedetti] thinks that my lack of beard has perhaps been the reason His Holiness has so far overlooked me; in my view, it is perhaps to put me in the service of the cardinal nephew. But, if I must tell Your Excellency the truth, I am not without enormous bitterness at seeing all my hopes cheated after so long a service."[148] Teodoro Cellesi, a nobleman from Pistoia, offered a different and more likely explanation: as the pope tried to balance his favors between Spain and France, Atto's well-known allegiances would have made his appointment seem too great a concession to Paris.[149]

In any case, by December 1667 Atto had his sights set on the post of *segretario delle memoriali*. In light of his enormous experience with correspondence, he probably rightly considered this position "adeguato per me."[150] Yet as he was waiting for the announcement, Cardinal Jacopo Rospigliosi again warned him that his French service might hold him back. Atto's response must rank among his most outrageous flashes of insolence: "I answered that if I had not been a servant of the king [of France] … perhaps he would not have been the nephew of a pope."[151] Such behavior may or may not have exacerbated Atto's problems; in any case, he did not get the post.

Given these frustrations and Clement's obvious ill health, Atto soon began looking more exclusively to his beloved France to secure his future.

---

[146] Atto to de Lionne, from Rome, September 6, 1667.
[147] Atto to de Lionne, from Rome, September 27, 1667.
[148] Atto to de Lionne, from Rome, July 19, 1667.
[149] Atto to de Lionne, from Rome, July 5, 1667. Cavaliere Francesco Teodoro Cellesi had been the *padrino* of Atto's brother, Vincenzo Paolo (Weaver, "Materiali," 256).
[150] From his letter to de Lionne, from Rome, December 20, 1667.
[151] Atto to de Lionne, from Rome, December 13, 1667.

At this time French interests in Rome revolved largely around the promotion of politically advantageous cardinals: France, like Spain, sought to control papal elections and thus harness the resources of the Church.[152] From December of 1668, Atto involved himself deeply in these efforts. Having been granted rooms in the Quirinal palace in March, Atto found himself conveniently close to the pontiff – physically, if not now psychologically – and so once again well positioned to serve France.[153]

The instigator of these negotiations was the powerful French general Henri de la Tour d'Auvergne, viscount de Turenne, who earlier in the year had publicly converted to Catholicism. Expecting a reward for this act, Turenne demanded that his nephew, the Abbé Emmanuel-Théodose d'Albret, be promoted to the cardinalate. While he pressured the French court to support this bid, Turenne also sent a personal envoy to Rome (the Abbé Bigorre) to pursue the issue directly with the cardinal nephew. He likewise enlisted Atto's services.[154]

Atto embraced the task with his familiar mix of industry and self-interest. Within months, he had discussed the matter with some of the leading figures in the Church, including Cardinals Rospigliosi and Azzolini. At the same time, he managed to extract a promise from d'Albret with profound implications for Atto's future: if the project should succeed, Atto would serve as d'Albret's conclavist during the next papal election.[155] The long deadlock in negotiations finally broke when France agreed to contribute troops to help free the island of Crete from the Turks, a project dear to Clement.[156] When on August 5, 1669 the promotion of d'Albret was announced, a jubilant Atto reported the good news, declaring himself "fuori di me."[157]

He had good reason to be. Although he was denied the honor of bringing to Paris the *berretta* of d'Albret – now called Cardinal Bouillon – he still profited greatly: in France, he reinforced his reputation as a negotiator, and

---

[152] Pastor, *History*, XXXI:345–46, 473.

[153] News of Atto's move to the Quirinal palace – a sign, in his view, of Clement's renewed favor toward him – comes in his letter to de Lionne, from Rome, March 20, 1668.

[154] The above information comes from [Henri de la Tour d'Auvergne, vicomte de Turenne], *Lettres de Turenne extraites des Archives Rohan-Bouillon*, ed. Suzanne d'Huart, Archives Nationales, Inventaires et Documents (Ministère des Affaires Culturelles, Direction des Archives de France) (Paris: S.E.V.P.E.N., 1971), 601 and 611. A letter from Turenne to Abbé Bigorre, June 25, 1669, states, "J'ai escrit par cet ordinaire à l'abbé Melani. M. de Lionne m'a encores dit ce matin qu'il est persuadé que la voie que l'on a pris est très bonne."

[155] On d'Albret's promise, Atto's letter to de Lionne, from Rome, February 19, 1669; Atto also mentions his efforts on this project in his letters of December 18, 1668 and January 8 and 11, 1669.

[156] Pastor, *History*, XXXI:413. The military effort failed miserably: see A[nthony] D[avid] Wright, *The Early Modern Papacy: From the Council of Trent to the French Revolution, 1564–1789*, Longman History of the Papacy (Harlow: Pearson Education, Longman, 2000), 210.

[157] Atto to de Lionne, from Rome, August 5, 1669.

in Rome – with the pope's health failing – he initiated a new role for himself as official representative for the distant cardinal.[158] This link to Bouillon assured, in fact, that Atto's involvement in papal politics survived Clement IX. When the pope died on December 9, 1669, Atto did not prepare to leave the city, as many of Clement's other supporters were forced to do, but instead happily busied himself decorating Bouillon's apartments for the forthcoming conclave.[159] By the end of Clement's two-and-a-half-year reign, Atto had managed to make himself over from a personal favorite, subject to the pontiff's whim, to a fixture of the French diplomatic corps in Rome. At last, his future no longer hung on the support of a single patron.

Confirmation of this metamorphosis – and evidence of Atto's confidence – emerges from the events of the conclave of 1669–70. Soon after the assembly began on December 20, Atto demonstrated that, notwithstanding his allegiance to Bouillon and the French party, he would continue to pursue his own interests. For years, he had fostered a patronage relationship with Cardinal Girolamo Buonvisi of Lucca, and now, in the hope of great rewards, Atto nervily sought to elect his second pope.[160]

Instead of supporting the French candidate, Cardinal Pietro Vidoni, Atto went about praising Buonvisi's merits to the principals of the various factions.[161] He claimed that such leaders as Chigi and Azzolini were amenable to his plan and complained that the French party was too quickly abandoning Buonvisi, who was the best choice for France.[162] The duke de Chaulnes soon registered annoyance and then alarm at Atto's project, as the following rather entertaining note to de Lionne records:

Would you believe that the person who is troubling us is the very Abbé Melani about whom I already sent you something in the last post? As if all my orders [to him] to obey Cardinals de Retz and Bouillon have no effect, he does nothing to correct his behavior. And he is getting worse, to the point that the aforementioned cardinals are always finding him in their paths, mixed up in their business. Today [they write] me

---

[158] The issue of the *beretta* appears in a series of letters to de Lionne, from Rome, in May and early June 1669, before the promotion was announced. The later anonymous "Vita dell'Abate Atto Melani" (p. 151) claims that Atto's official position was "primo conclavista" to Bouillon.

[159] The date of December 9 for Clement IX's death is taken from Pastor, *History*, XXXI:429, although Atto reports it already in his letter to de Lionne, dated December 8. On December 17, Atto reports to de Lionne that Bouillon was assigned a good room for the conclave and that, although "non vi è stato dissegno del Bernino," the decorations have succeeded well.

[160] Already in his letter to de Lionne, from Florence, April 1, 1667, Atto writes, "quando fusse vero, che riuscire a Buonvisi d'esser Papa, non potrei se non sperarne qualche mercede, essendo egli sempre stato mio Padrone particolare."

[161] On Vidoni as the French candidate, Pastor, *History*, XXXI:433–36.

[162] Letters to de Lionne, from Rome, February 18, July 8, and August 12, 1670; the latter two letters were written after the fact and represent an analysis of the conclave.

that it would be to the honor and interest of the king to remove him. I still adopt certain expedients to avoid it, but in the end, if he persists in his conduct, I will be required to do so. There is something pleasant in his folly, which is to make Buonvisi pope, based on [Buonvisi's] nephew promising him a position. To reach this end, there is no indiscretion he will not commit ... and the worst is that to accomplish what he is proposing, he is often found at cross-purposes with us, undoing the arrangements we are making. If he does not change, I will make use of harsh remedies, after the gentle ones, which I will [first] exhaust because I know he is one of your friends. But I know even better that you reckon nothing for yourself when it involves the service of the king.[163]

De Chaulnes's complaint is interesting for what it does not say. One could imagine that, faced with a renegade castrato in the conclave, the French ambassador might have grumbled about the sheer impropriety of it all. What was this bourgeois-born musician doing in papal negotiations? Instead, de Chaulnes uses the respectful title "Abbé Melani" instead of the "Signor Atto" more common earlier, and he speaks of Atto as he would of anyone in his retinue who had impeded policy. Likewise, when de Lionne responds to de Chaulnes's complaint – agreeing to sacrifice his friend before suffering disservice to the king – he does not excuse Atto's behavior with reference to his inferior background, as Mazarin had done thirteen years before.[164] Even in their private correspondence, and even when angry, these ministers of France now give no sign that Atto might be inherently unfit for diplomacy. He is a misguided negotiator, not a presumptuous castrato.

It is precisely at this time that Atto cut all his remaining ties to music. His last recorded performance, a private entertainment for the Rospigliosi family, came on March 23, 1668.[165] Otherwise, he refers to his musical past only scornfully. For example, in efforts to regain his full French pension, he repeatedly refers to his earlier years in France as a period "when I did nothing," or "when ultimately I was not useful to the king for a single thing."[166] Although Atto is here trying to accentuate his current services, his disparagement of the past is telling. In fact, he seems to have tried to hide it. As James Amelang has shown, the desire to conceal one's inferior origins was typical of the ambitious bourgeois generally; Leonora Baroni had tried to do the same once she established herself as a lady of Rome.[167] Certainly one

---

[163] Duke de Chaulnes to de Lionne, from Rome, February 18, 1670.

[164] Copy of a letter from De Lionne to the duke de Chaulnes, from Paris (?), March 21, 1670.

[165] Reported by the Genoese agent in Rome, Ferdinando Raggi, quoted in Ademollo, "Un campanaio," 3.

[166] Atto to de Lionne, from Rome, August 31, 1669 and October 29, 1669.

[167] James S. Amelang, "The Bourgeois," in *Baroque Personae*, ed. Rosario Villari, trans. Lydia G. Cochrane (Chicago: University of Chicago Press, 1995), 321, originally published as *L'uomo*

would never suspect from Atto's correspondence at this time that he had been a musician: he ceases to report on performances he witnesses, and when on rare occasions the subject does come up, he betrays no professional expertise.[168] He also seems to have tried to quash stories about his past, as emerges from a somewhat ambiguous passage in a letter from January 3, 1668:

[I am trying to ensure that] nothing is printed that could serve as a pretext and motive to malicious men here to hold me back and hurt me, because if what Abate Bentivoglio writes me is true, it's rather mysterious, and the report comes from France rather than Rome, for here they could not know if I had performed *Amore ammalato* in the ballet of the king.[169]

In the end, Atto's "revisionism" succeeded extremely well: Vittorio Capponi, an important early historian of Pistoia, wrote a lengthy entry on Atto in his *Biografia pistoiese* without realizing his subject had been a musician, much less a castrato. Surely Atto would have been pleased.[170]

In any case, by the death of Clement IX, Atto's role on the diplomatic stage was secure, little threatened by his occasional missteps. When his gambit to elevate Buonvisi finally failed and on April 29, 1670 Emilio Altieri was elected as Pope Clement X, Atto emerged unscathed.[171] If anything, his position improved: he seems quickly to have established nearly as

    barocco, Storia e Società (Rome: Laterza, 1991). According to John Rosselli, "From Princely Service to the Open Market: Singers of Italian Opera and Their Patrons, 1600–1850," *Cambridge Opera Journal* 1 (1989): 4–5, Baroni became "annoyed when people brought up her singing days."

168 Already in 1664 Atto was attending more performances than he participated in (letters to Mattias, from Venice, February 16 and 18, 1664). His last interesting comments come from this period: having attended some of the operas of the Venetian Carnival, he writes on February 16, "Scrivo al signor Conte le poche novità che produce questa Città, che altre non sono, se non le solite Opere musicali, Commedie, e Maschere, essendo Io restato però molto scandalizato delle prime, perché certo non sono nella perfettione che ho vedute in altri tempi, bastando hora il far quattro cambiamenti di Scena, senza machine di sorte alcuna, e quelli pochi, sono ancora male dipinti, e non vanno ordinatamente." Two days later, he had somewhat kinder words, "L'opera di S[S]. Giov. e Paulo, Patrocinato dal signor Abbate Grimani, è quella che ha tutto l'applauso, perché vi sono Virtuosi di prima riga, che non possano certo oprar meglio di quello che fanno." One of Atto's few later mentions of a performance comes in his letter to de Lionne, from Rome, July 9, 1669, where he mentions that Cardinals Rospigliosi and Azzolini attended an *accademia* "che si fece di musica, e di lett[eratura] in Casa del Padre, e dei fratellli [Rospigliosi]"; Atto was not involved. On his later dabbling in music, see chapter 7.

169 Atto to de Lionne, from Rome, January 3, 1668. Atto has been speaking about reports from Holland.

170 Vittorio Capponi, *Biografia pistoiese* … (Pistoia: Rossetti, 1878), 51. Alessandro Ademollo was the first to fully reconstruct Atto's identity, in his "Un campanaio."

171 Interestingly enough, this defeat did not prompt Atto to give up his hopes for making Buonvisi pope. His continuing efforts to that end can be seen, among other places, in his letters to de Lionne, from Rome, July 29, August 19, August 26, 1670. Of course, the project never succeeded.

familiar a relationship with the new pope – a man he barely knew – as with his predecessor. In a July audience, Atto bluntly told the pope that as long as the papacy remained on good terms with France it would be loved and feared by all powers. The pope responded to this impudence not with a rebuke, but with the command to permit Atto "the same access to his rooms as enjoyed by the *camerieri segreti*, his intimates, so that he can see me more often, without uproar and consternation."[172] Additionally, Clement X finally gave Atto an official post, that of *pronotario apostolico*, and further granted him noble citizenship in the papal city of Bologna.[173]

In France too Atto's waywardness during the conclave was overlooked. After only a few months, de Lionne finally gave Atto permission to return to Paris for a visit, a favor Atto had been requesting for some time as a token of "la total mia reintegrazione."[174] When he arrived in fall 1670, he was welcomed back to court and even into the presence of Louis XIV, whom he had not seen for nine years. Indeed, Louis further brightened Atto's return with a 50 percent increase in his pension from the Abbey of Beaubec and the gift of a diamond-encrusted portrait of the king, valued at two thousand *scudi*.[175] Clearly, all past offenses had been forgiven.

[172]   Atto to de Lionne, from Rome, July 8, 1670.

[173]   This information comes from a printed sheet dated 1730 sitting loose in the back of I PSc, Raccolta Chiappelli, 64.ii. The document, essentially a resumé of Atto's accomplishments, seems to be a *memoriale* produced by Atto's nephew, Luigi Melani, to impress the Tuscan government with the accomplishments of the family. According to Johann Heinrich Bangen, *Die römische Curie, ihre gegenwärtige Zusammensetzung und ihr Geschäftsgang* (Münster: Aschendorffschen Buchhandlung, 1854), the title *pronotario apostolico*, during Atto's period, could refer to several different positions: the twelve *pronotarii participantes* bore responsibilities for the beatification and canonization processes; the *pronotarii supernumerarii ad instar participantium* were merely honorary, but retained the privileges of the *participantes*; the *pronotarii titulares* were often named by church officials other than the pope and received reduced honors. Atto probably belonged to the second category, for – as the previous passage indicated – he still seems to have retained a privileged position at the papal court.

[174]   Atto first mentions wanting to return to Paris in his letter to de Lionne, from Rome, April 2, 1669, and the subject recurs regularly thereafter. The quotation comes from his letter to de Lionne, from Rome, August 31, 1669.

[175]   Marcelle Benoit, *Musiques de cour (1661–1733): Chappelle – chambre – écurie*, La vie musicale en France sous les rois Bourbons, no. 20 (Paris: A. et J. Picard, 1971), 34, reproduces an entry from the Secrétariat de la Maison du Roi, 1671, dated January 15, 1671 and entitled "Creation de 1.000 lt de pension sur l'abbaye de Beaubec pour le Sr Melany" (F Pan, O^1 15, ff. 41v and 43). The entry confirms that at this time – i.e., during Atto's trip to Paris – the king added 1,000 *livres* to the 2,000 that had been assigned to Atto back on May 14, 1668. Payments of 1,500 *livres* were to be disbursed twice per year, the first coming only on June 24 (St. John the Baptist) 1672, the second to follow at Christmas. Atto mentions the increased benefice in his letter to Pomponne, from Rome, March 15, 1672; the increase is also recorded in F Pae, MD France, 933, f. 21v. Tommaso Trenta, who had access to now-lost Melani documents, mentions the portrait and states that it was given to Atto during this trip (see appendix E). It is mentioned again later in one of the fragments of the Melani family diary, with its arrival in Pistoia recorded sometime in 1699: I PSc, Raccolta Chiappelli, 188, loose fascicle ("1699–1700"), f. 16v: "Ritratto Gioellato viene a Pistoia."

The security of Atto's position was fully demonstrated in the fall of 1671 with the death of Hugues de Lionne on September 1. Atto's anxiety at the passing of his most loyal French supporter can be seen in the flurry of letters he addressed to the king and all the highest officials at court.[176] As Atto writes to the new foreign minister, Simon Arnauld, marquis de Pomponne, "I have lost a gentleman who loved me and who excused my defects."[177] Reassuring news came quickly: François-Michel Le Tellier, marquis de Louvois, wrote: "His Majesty has strongly approved that you continue to pass along all that you learn."[178] Pomponne was assigned as Atto's new contact, and Atto quickly returned to providing his familiar reports on – and advice about – French projects in Rome.[179] With the death of de Lionne, following the passing of Mazarin, Mattias, and Clement IX, all of Atto's patrons who had first known him as a singer were gone. He no longer depended on memories of that service to sustain him but instead made his way forward exclusively as a diplomat.

He had done it: Atto had managed the transformation. By fits and starts, he had replaced vocal performances with diplomatic ones. Where once he had sung for Louis XIV, he now wrote the king letters of political analysis and advice; where once his music had offered cover for clandestine politics, now his political influence helped him hide his musical tracks; and where once his voice had won him gold chains and trinkets, now his negotiations gained him lucrative benefices and diamond-studded portraits.[180] A beautiful castrato voice was a rare and valuable commodity, but one that ultimately stigmatized its possessor as a laborer, however skilled. For someone with Atto's ambition, music could offer just so much advantage. To win the big prize – to enter fully the upper echelon of society and reap its rewards – one's pursuits had to be more honorable. This Atto understood, and with his determination he pulled

---

[176] See the letters listed in appendix A from October 1671 to the spring of 1672. I am grateful to Valeria De Lucca for sharing with me a notice she found in the *avvisi di Roma* for September 26, 1671 that further attests to Atto's anxiety. Specifically, it shows Atto's financial concerns and also reveals that some in Rome still joked about his musical background (I Rvat, Barb. lat. 6407, f. 244): "Per la morte del Signor di Lionne segretario di Stato del Cristianissimo e che haveva fatta dar pensione a 5 o 6 soggetti habitanti in Roma, restano questi con le mosche in pugno, e particolare il Signor Atto Melani nunzio castrato d'antica fama il quale godeva 400 luigi d'oro all'anno, hora non più il soprano, ma cantava il basso."

[177] Atto to Pomponne, from Rome, November 17, 1671.

[178] François-Michel Le Tellier, marquis de Louvois, to Atto, from Paris, January 1, 1672.

[179] His primary endeavor at this time was the protracted effort to have César d'Estrées, bishop of Laon, promoted to the cardinalate; see chapter 7.

[180] As regards Atto writing to the king, his letter to Louis, from Rome, February 28, 1672, provides a fine example: he is surprisingly frank in his opinions about what the king should do, in this case with respect to papal relations. These sorts of letters proliferate as Atto ages.

off the switch, even while working for French patrons. His case makes one wonder whether a castrato's greatest social obstacle was his operation or his profession. Did being a castrato carry less of a stigma than being a musician? For Atto, at least, the answer clearly was yes. By the eighteenth century, with its cult of the natural, the same question would seem absurd. But the seventeenth century cared more about actions than identities. The castrato was just a man, unusually "effeminate" perhaps, but no more so than some other members of society. As soon as that man provided entertainment for money, however, he marked himself as bourgeois. Atto's path from 1656 to 1671 demonstrates his awareness of this reality and his striving to excel within it, to improve not only his own lifestyle, but his family's position in the world.

6 ❧ Atto Melani and the cantata

Most studies of individual musicians divide themselves between a narration of the subject's biography and an appraisal of his or her compositions – the time-honored "life-and-works" model. If the present inquiry avoids that formula, part of the explanation lies with its subject. Composition simply did not play a central role in Atto's life. Just fifteen works are now attributable to him, all examples of the Italian cantata (see table 6.1): even if one allows for the disappearance or anonymity of many pieces, writing *letters* clearly occupied far more of Atto's energies than writing music.[1] And yet these very letters – with their descriptions of lengthy and frequent private performances – suggest his extensive chamber repertoire. Even if Atto originally wrote twice as many works as now remain, the number could hardly account for all this singing. The majority of Atto's repertoire, it would seem, consisted of the works of other musicians, most likely the composers with whom he associated – Luigi Rossi, Marc'Antonio Pasqualini, and Antonio Cesti, among others.[2] The question arises, then, as to why Atto bothered to compose at all. Why not sing the works of others *all* the time, instead of just *most* of the time? What purpose did composition serve in the life of this ambitious courtier?

In one sense, the answers to these questions are practical and historical: Atto composed vocal music because professional singers at this time might be expected to do so. From Giulio Caccini and Jacopo Peri to Loreto Vittori, Barbara Strozzi and the aforementioned Pasqualini and Cesti, singers often wrote music for their own use. From this standpoint, Atto was simply conforming to a tradition, encouraged perhaps by patrons' specific requests.

But, in another sense, such an explanation does not suffice. Not every *virtuoso* wrote music, or so at least extant sources would imply. While the list

---

[1] For information on the sources of Atto's cantatas, as well as edited scores of all the works, see Atto Melani, *Complete Cantatas*, ed. Roger Freitas, Collegium Musicum: Yale University, ser. 2, vol. 15 (Middleton, Wis.: A-R Editions, 2006).

[2] Atto must regularly have trafficked in Rossi's music. In a letter to Annibale Bentivoglio (from Paris, September 17, 1655), Giovanni Bentivoglio asks that Atto send (from Rome) two works that Luigi Rossi set to Giovanni's own texts: the *Lamento d'Erminia* (*Erminia sventurata*) and an apparently lost *Entro ai fiori un angue ascosto*. See Sergio Monaldini, ed., *L'orto dell'Esperidi: Musici, attori e artisti nel patrocinio della famiglia Bentivoglio (1646–1685)*, ConNotazioni, no.5 (Lucca: Libreria Musicale Italiana, 2000), 100.

Table 6.1 *The cantatas of Atto Melani (first lines)*
(All the texts are anonymous unless indicated.)

A più sventure ancora
Fileno, idolo mio
Filli, per cui mi moro
Il tacer non fa per me
Io voglio esser infelice
La più dolente, e misera, che viva (Sebastiano Baldini)
M'abbandona la sorte
Occhi miei belli
O quanto si dolea (Sebastiano Baldini)
Ove, tra sponde d'oro
Scrivete, occhi dolenti (Francesco Melosio)
S'io sapessi dipingere
Sola tra le sue pene
Tra sponde di smeraldo
Anima, che di foco (duet)

of lesser-known singers without musical attributions is endless, even many prominent vocalists – such as the well-traveled Giuseppe Bianchi, Antonio Rivani, and Giovanni Francesco Grossi (Siface) – seem not to have composed. Some singers did, and others did not, presumably for particular reasons. More importantly, as I hope this study suggests, Atto habitually assessed his actions by their capacity to further personal aims. I know of not a single letter, even among those to his own family members, written purely for "pleasure": whether praising, pleading, cajoling, or admonishing his correspondent, Atto was all business, all the time. That his attitude toward writing music would differ seems improbable. Indeed, I will argue in this chapter that Atto composed cantatas with the same concern for status and prestige that he displayed in his other activities: at a certain point in his career, writing such works simply offered another means of advancement. Put succinctly, Atto composed music (just as he sang it) to better his social position.

To understand how writing cantatas could bring social credit requires looking at the genre from new perspectives.[3] Investigation of the cantata has

___

[3] My use of the term *cantata* requires some comment. Efforts to define this genre and its various subtypes have been extensive: see, for example, Robert Rau Holzer, "Music and Poetry in Seventeenth-Century Rome: Settings of the Canzonetta and Cantata Texts of Francesco Balducci, Domenico Benigni, Francesco Melosio, and Antonio Abati" (Ph.D. diss., University of Pennsylvania, 1990), I:226–62; Eleanor Caluori, *The Cantatas of Luigi Rossi: Analysis and Thematic Index*, Studies in Musicology, no. 41 (Ann Arbor, Mich.: University Microfilms, 1981), I:3–6 (in fact, the entire study is focused around questions of genre); Gloria Rose, "The Italian Cantata of the Baroque Period," in *Gattungen der Musik in Einzeldarstellungen: Gedenkschrift Leo Schrade*, ed. Wulf Arlt, Ernst Lichtenhahn, and Hans Oesch (Bern: Francke, 1973), 655–77 *passim*;

in general lagged behind that of its more glamorous cousin, opera: already in 1950 Nigel Fortune trenchantly observed that "opera, like a thick hedge, hides monody from the historian."[4] Piero Mioli has further cited the long-standing prejudice against *Seicento* culture generally – particularly in Italy, under the influence of Benedetto Croce's views – as a specific reason for this neglect: "the almost constantly prevailing Crocean idealism … has hindered a complete reading and provoked a general insensitivity toward a genre so bound up with its time as the *cantata da camera*."[5] Although in recent years this prejudice has begun to fade, the literature on the cantata is still dominated by studies of bibliography, genre definition, and style development, supporting Mioli's view. Indeed, the themes of social context and cultural meaning – so rich for the study of opera – have as yet been little discussed.[6] To grasp the significance of Atto's compositional activity, then, at least a preliminary inquiry into these issues is necessary.

At the most obvious level, writing cantatas could offer advancement because it provided a valuable service to patrons. As we have seen, Atto frequently sought to ingratiate himself by offering as many different services (beyond singing) as possible. In composing music, Atto demonstrated yet another rare skill, another chance to boost his value. Further, his compositions – like his political reports – could help him sustain his

Gloria Rose, "The Cantatas of Carissimi" (Ph.D. diss., Yale Univ., 1959), *passim*, but esp. 22–53; Carolyn Gianturco, "The Italian Seventeenth-Century Cantata: A Textual Approach," in *The Well-Enchanting Skill: Music, Poetry, and Drama in the Culture of the Renaissance: Essays in Honour of F. W. Sternfeld*, ed. John Caldwell, Edward Olleson, and Susan Wollenberg (Oxford: Clarendon Press, 1990), 41–51. The best historical overview of the term is provided by Holzer. My own usage, however, is more general. Along with Colin Timms, I find that, in view of the close relationships between virtually all types of vocal chamber music from this period, "there might be some merit in using the word 'cantata' as an umbrella term for the entire repertory of continuo-accompanied chamber cantatas, arias, madrigals, *canzonette*, *duetti* and the rest – as well as in its accepted, more limited sense": Colin Timms, "The Italian Cantata since 1945: Progress and Prospects," in *Cinquant'anni di produzioni e consumi della musica dell'età di Vivaldi 1947–1997*, ed. Francesco Fanna and Michael Talbot, Fondazione Giorgio Cini, Istituto Italiano Antonio Vivaldi; Studi di Musica Veneta, Quaderni Vivaldiani, no. 10 (Florence: Leo S. Olschki, 1998), 85. Unless the context indicates otherwise, then, I use the word *cantata* here in this more general way.

[4] Nigel Fortune, "Italian Secular Monody from 1600 to 1635: An Introductory Survey," *Musical Quarterly* 39 (1953): 172.

[5] Piero Mioli, "Per uno studio sulla cantata italiana del 600: L'opera di Cesti e di Stradella," in *Alessandro Stradella e Modena*, ed. Carolyn Gianturco (Modena: Teatro Comunale, 1985), 66. The history of this intellectual tradition, with important contributions by Luigi Settembrini, Francesco de Sanctis, and Benedetto Croce, is neatly summarized in Holzer, "Music and Poetry," I:11–17; and by W. Theodor Elwert, *La poesia lirica italiana del Seicento: Studio sullo stile barocco*, Saggi di "Lettere italiane," no. 10 (Florence: Leo S. Olschki, 1967), 4–13n.

[6] For an overview of the bibliography on the cantata, see Teresa M. Gialdroni, "Bibliografia della cantata da camera italiana (1620–1740 ca.)," *Le fonti musicali in Italia: Studi e ricerche* 4 (1990): 31–131; and Timms, "The Italian Cantata," 75–94. An important exception to the limitations outlined here is the first chapter of Holzer, "Music and Poetry," I:1–34, which deals with seventeenth-century Roman culture and its relationship to the cantata.

far-flung patronage network: when he mailed cantatas to his supporters, he reaffirmed his loyalty and usefulness even from afar.[7] Although patrons might not be able to hear Atto's voice, they could see and hear his music.[8]

But writing cantatas also worked to Atto's advantage on a level both more subtle and more significant. In his theorizing of musical patronage, Claudio Annibaldi distinguishes between what he calls "conventional patronage," in which a work's genre alone expresses its patron's rank and power, and "humanistic patronage," in which the music "represent[s] the rank of its élite patrons by demonstrating their artistic sensibility and connoisseurship."[9] Recognition of this "humanistic patronage" allows modern cultural analysis to expand from the oft-studied public and ceremonial works to private genres like the cantata. In both types, the patron seeks to *impress* his/her audience, but whereas in public that impression is of power and wealth, in private it is more often of taste and intelligence.[10]

To Annibaldi's insights, Atto's case adds the perspective of the composer/ performer. For if supporting fashionable works reflected well on the patron's sophistication, then actually creating such works must have brought at least some credit to the artist(s). As I will contend in the following pages, cantatas were indeed among the most fashionable and thought-provoking musical works of their time. *Pace* most critics, both the poetry and music of this genre stood at the cutting edge of contemporary tastes. Cantatas participated in the refined world of aristocratic entertainment, a world devoted to intellect and wit. By contributing to this world, by demonstrating sophistication and

---

[7] Atto to Duke Carlo II of Mantua, from Venice, March 12, 1664; and to Duchess Christine Marie of Savoy, from La Fère, July 20, 1657. (The details of these cases appear below.) These two isolated instances surely represent a more general practice.

[8] This use of cantata scores as surrogates for performance adds to the functions Margaret Murata outlines in her "Roman Cantata Scores as Traces of Musical Culture and Signs of Its Place in Society," in *Atti del XIV congresso della Società Internazionale di Musicologia: Trasmissione e recezione delle forme di cultura musicale*, vol. I, *Round Tables*, ed. Angelo Pompilio *et al.* (Turin: EDT, 1990), 272–84.

[9] Claudio Annibaldi, "Towards a Theory of Musical Patronage in the Renaissance and Baroque: The Perspective from Anthropology and Semiotics," *Recercare* 10 (1998): 174. See also his valuable "Introduzione" to *La musica e il mondo: Mecenatismo e committenza musicale in Italia tra Quattro e Settecento*, ed. Claudio Annibaldi, Polifonie: Musica e spettacolo nella storia (Bologna: Società Editrice il Mulino, 1993), 9–43.

[10] The same point is made by Fabrizio Della Seta, "I Borghese (1691–1731): La musica di una generazione," *Note d'archivio per la storia musicale*, n.s., 1 (1983): 145–46; and Peter Burke, *The Italian Renaissance: Culture and Society in Italy*, 2nd edn. (Princeton: Princeton University Press, 1987), 124–42. Della Seta's remarks are particularly pertinent: "Mi sembra necessaria una preliminare distinzione fra consumo musicale pubblico e privato; quest'ultimo destinato al diletto esclusivo del committente ed eventualmente di un ristretto numero di invitati; l'altro rivolto all'esterno, ad un pubblico assai più vasto di invitati, come ornamento di 'conversazioni' o di altri avvenimenti mondani … Questa distinzione si riflette sui prodotti musicali anche a livello di scelte stilistiche, e di questo i compositori hanno piena coscienza."

cleverness, a singer like Atto could prove his quality, his *virtù*. He could offer his patrons more than his professional, technical skills: he could reveal his noble spirit – learned, insightful, and amusing. In other words, Atto could raise his status, not only by providing a distinctive service, but more fundamentally by showing how much his character already marked him as elite.

The literary status of the cantata

Anyone familiar with the historiography of the cantata, and especially its poetry, may well be puzzled by these claims. In both literary and musicological circles, cantata poetry has long been condemned as representing the *worst* tastes of its period. In the fourth volume of his influential *Geschichte der Musik* (1878), August Wilhelm Ambros wrote,

[Cantata texts express] the conventional misery of love in phrases full of false tragic pathos or in witty conceits, faithfully repeated, that centuries before had become stock clichés, rhymed quite gracefully, expressed quite nicely, but of unspeakable dreariness. Whether the lover wails because he must part from his beloved or because [his lady] remains pitiless toward him – one always gets the same dulcet apostrophes to the incredibly beautiful and incredibly cruel object of the heart's fire, always the same proclamations and nobly stylised cries of pain, always the "io moro" or "morirò" as the ultimate cure for unending agony – always the same expression of [a] passion in whose veracity no one believes, least of all [the passion] of the poet speaking through the lover.[11]

This view of cantata poetry as insincere and unoriginal fit naturally into the then prevailing construction of *Seicento* Italy as a decadent successor to Renaissance glory. Ambros's entire passage was approvingly quoted by Eugen Schmitz in his 1914 study of the cantata, still, in its 1955 revision, the most comprehensive to date. Henry Prunières agreed: "the chief grounds for criticism [of the cantata] are the weakness, the bombast, and the bad taste of the words."[12]

Remarkably, perhaps, this attitude has changed little with time. Even so outstanding a scholar as Lorenzo Bianconi finds little of value in cantata texts:

---

[11]   August Wilhelm Ambros, *Geschichte der Musik*, vol. IV [ed. G. Nottebohm] (Leipzig: Leuckart, 1878), 189–90.

[12]   Eugen Schmitz, *Geschichte der weltlichen Solokantate* [2nd edn.] (Leipzig: Breitkopf & Härtel, 1955), 31. Henry Prunières, "The Italian Cantata of the XVII Century," *Music and Letters* 7 (1926): 126.

Much more than in the musical poetry of the previous century, the text is above all a mere pretext for musical invention … A clever but consciously trivial poetic genre, an elite musical genre for quick use … the seventeenth-century *cantata da camera* – in the historical outline of relationships between music and poetry in Italy – is important above all as a testament to the consumption (not to say the exhaustion) of an artificial and yet popularized poetic language, inured to every cleverness and yet whimsical and extravagant, which musical inspiration redeems in the brief charm of an artful and bewitching voice.[13]

Cantatas are lousy poems rescued by song.

Paradoxically, scholars of the cantata have in recent decades emphasized the importance of the poetry within these works. Indeed, the texts have been shown to govern many aspects of musical form and style: details once interpreted as compositional choices are now recognized as standard responses to poetic form (see below). As with opera, the poet, rather than the composer, seems to have dominated the genre. Given the social context of these works, such conclusions are hardly surprising: as Carolyn Gianturco asks rhetorically, "would the patron [of the cantata] and his friends, most of whom considered themselves *cognoscenti*, have enjoyed a composite art form in which the art they undoubtedly understood best – the poetry – was glossed over?"[14] But this insight exposes an inconsistency in the modern under-standing of the genre. If the poetry was so important, how could the best-educated men and women of the era have tolerated the awful verses that Bianconi and others describe?

Certainly one obstacle to understanding this poetry has been its broad characterization as Marinist, that is, in the style of Giambattista Marino (1569–1625) and his followers.[15] The term itself often carries pejorative overtones. As Theodor Elwert has observed, many older literary historians, including Croce, mistakenly labeled all Italian seventeenth-century poetry as Marinist, making *marinismo* a synonym for the decadence attributed generally to the period.[16] Musicologists too have often fallen into the trap: Gloria Rose asserts that all the poets of Carissimi's cantatas were followers of Marino and continues sardonically, "again and again we are confronted with

---

[13] Lorenzo Bianconi, "Il Cinquecento e il Seicento," in *Letteratura italiana*, vol. VI, *Teatro, musica, tradizione dei classici*, ed. Roberto Antonelli, Angelo Cicchetti, and Giorgio Inglese (Turin: Giulio Einaudi, 1986), 354–55. Interestingly, these comments come not in an article intended for other musicologists, but in a contribution to an influential text on Italian literature (under the direction of Alberto Asor Rosa).

[14] Gianturco, "The Italian Seventeenth-Century Cantata," 48.

[15] For example, ibid., 47. See also Gloria Rose, "The Cantatas of Giacomo Carissimi," *Musical Quarterly* 48 (1962): 206; and, more influentially, Rose, "The Italian Cantata," 669.

[16] Elwert, *La poesia lirica*, 98–101.

a cruel, heartless lady and her suffering, faithful lover, who nevertheless rejoices in his despair."[17] Such widespread misconceptions have provoked one literary scholar, Gianfranco Folena, to a stinging reproach: "at least from the point of view of literary texts, [musicological studies of the cantata] are generally poorly informed and sometimes give the impression of probing the ocean with a teaspoon."[18]

Seeking to escape such censure, I have turned especially to the work of W. Theodor Elwert, who – though writing forty years ago – paints a subtle and historically grounded portrait of *Seicento* lyric poetry. In the first place, Elwert reevaluates Marinism itself. One of his central points is that the baroque style in general, and Marinism specifically, adopt a posture more public and objective than intimate and personal: "Baroque poetry is not sentimental and subjective, but rather objective; it is not all confession and expression of personal and lived experiences, but instead has in the first place a social function: it wants to be decorative, representative."[19] Explaining Marino's maxim that "the goal of the poet is astonishment," Elwert suggests that this astonishment was directed primarily at the intellectual rather than the emotional register: "If Petrarch aimed to persuade the reader to sigh with him and [if] the romantic poet tends to upset him with metaphysical horrors, the baroque poet intends to bring a smile to his lips, a smile owed to the exquisite pleasure that a clever thought or a successful witticism can excite."[20] In the Marinistic style, these clever thoughts and witticisms usually take the form of metaphors, often paradoxical or hyperbolic: indeed, the metaphor was regarded as the quintessence of the style, much cherished by Marino's audience.[21] Emanuele Tesauro, a key literary theorist of the period, describes the metaphor as "the most ingenious and pointed, the most exotic and admirable, the most jovial and beneficial, the most eloquent and fertile fruit of the human intellect."[22]

---

[17] Rose, "The Cantatas of Giacomo Carissimi," 206.

[18] Gianfranco Folena, *L'italiano in Europa: Esperienze linguistiche del Settecento*, Einaudi Paperbacks, no. 139 (Turin: Giulio Einaudi, 1983), 263. Of course, I am attempting the same sort of marine exploration here, hopefully better equipped.

[19] Elwert, *La poesia lirica*, 3–4.

[20] Ibid., 20. Marino's famous dictum, "È del poeta il fin la meraviglia," comes from his "Fischiata 33" in his *La Murtoleide* (Nuremberg: Joseph Stampier, 1619), quoted in Elwert, *La poesia lirica*, 20.

[21] Elwert, *La poesia lirica*, 54–8; Alberto Asor Rosa, *La lirica del Seicento*, Letteratura italiana Laterza, no. 28 (Rome: Laterza, 1975), 7–9.

[22] Emanuele Tesauro, *Il cannocchiale aristotelico* (Turin: Gio. Sinibaldo, 1654), 179, quoted in Elwert, *La poesia lirica*, 56. For a recent example of Tesauro's theories applied productively to Marino's works, see Pierantonio Frare, "Antitesi, metafora e argutezza tra Marino e Tesauro," in *The Sense of Marino: Literature, Fine Arts and Music of the Italian Baroque*, ed. Francesco Guardiani, Literary Criticism Series, no. 5 (New York: Legas, 1994), 299–321.

In addition to the metaphor, Marino employed unusual subject matter –
often shockingly erotic or banal – to surprise and delight his readers. Elwert
emphasizes that Marino's stance toward his material is not pornographic or
perverse, as often charged, but again rather detached: he does not place
himself or the reader within the scene, but merely describes it, using an
elevated and often musical style that is wittily inconsistent with the subject:
"the virtuosity of the description becomes part of the content itself," perhaps
the most important part.[23] In Elwert's view, then, the sensibility of Marinistic
poetry hinges on this notion of depersonalized virtuosity: the oft-heard
condemnation of "insincerity" misses the point.[24]

Like many literary historians, Elwert also sketches a more complex
picture of seventeenth-century lyric poetry generally than cantata scholars
have often acknowledged.[25] Important for this discussion is the growing taste
over the course of the century for the style of Gabriello Chiabrera (1552–
1638).[26] Like Marino, Chiabrera sought to create a sense of surprise and
wonder in his works, but, instead of concentrating on startling metaphors
and unusual subject matter, he expanded the formal range of Italian lyric
poetry. For all his eccentricity, Marino usually employed the poetic forms he
had inherited from the Petrarchan tradition – sonnets, madrigals, canzoni –
all composed in the customary *endecasillabi* and *settenari* (eleven- and seven-
syllable lines, respectively).[27] But under the influence of the French poets
known as the Pleïade, as well as ancient authors like Anacreon, Pindar, and
Horace, Chiabrera introduced new poetic forms and metrical patterns to
serious Italian poetry.[28] Instead of the sonnet or madrigal, Chiabrera (in his
lyrical mode) wrote in short, freely structured strophes, usually of no more
than six lines, a stanzaic form he called the *canzonetta melica*. And instead of

---

[23] Elwert, *La poesia lirica*, 27.

[24] The label of insincerity dates back at least to Croce (as reported by Elwert, *La poesia lirica*, 48n)
and is picked up by musicologists like Rose, "The Cantatas of Giacomo Carissimi," 206. Peter N.
Skrine, a scholar of comparative literature of this period, supports Elwert's viewpoint: "Love was
seen as the point at which the senses and the spirit meet: an encounter whose enormous range
and impact could be successfully expressed by baroque poets and artists thanks to their awareness
of the fundamental distinction between the sensuous pleasures of love-making in itself and those,
more permanent and public, of language, form and colour": *The Baroque: Literature and Culture
in Seventeenth-Century Europe* (New York: Holmes and Meier, 1978), 125.

[25] See also, for example, Asor Rosa, *La lirica*; Carmine Jannaco and Martino Capucci, *Il Seicento*,
vol. VIII of *Storia letteraria d'Italia*, ed. A. Balduino, 3rd rev. edn. (Padua: Dr. Francesco Vallardi;
Piccin Nuova Libraria, 1986); and Francesco Erspamer, "Il primo Seicento" and "L'età del
barocco," in *Manuale di letteratura italiana: Storia per generi e problemi*, vol. II, *Dal Cinquecento
alla metà del Settecento*, ed. Franco Brioschi and Costanzo Di Girolamo (Turin: Bollati
Boringhieri, 1994), 225–36 and 237–49.

[26] A good discussion in English of Chiabrera's style can be found in Holzer, "Music and Poetry," 35–87.

[27] See below, however, regarding Marino's use of the *selva* for his pastoral *Idilli*.

[28] On Chiabrera's influences, see Asor Rosa, *La lirica*, 119–20.

traditional rhythmically complex verses, he often used shorter lines of even-numbered syllables, with their characteristic rhythmic lilt.[29] Likewise, Chiabrera frequently employed alliteration, assonance, and other playful sonic effects, as can be seen in the opening stanzas of the following poem from his *Maniere de' versi toscani* (1599):

Del mio sol son ricciutegli
i capegli,
non biondetti, ma brunetti;
son due rose vermigliuzze
le gotuzze,
le due labbra rubinetti.

Ma, dal dì ch'io la mirai
fin qui, mai
non mi vidi ora tranquilla:
ché d'amor non mise Amore
in quel core
né pur piccola favilla.[30]

As Elwert writes, "in the melic canzonetta [of Chiabrera] the word does nothing but sustain the melody and is completely subordinated to the principle of rhythm."[31] Just as Marino explored the metaphor, so Chiabrera concentrated on the musical possibilities of language.

The history of lyric poetry in the seventeenth century is often cast as a dialectic between these two approaches, typically characterized as "baroque" versus "classical." In the first part of the century, the followers of Marino dominated stylistic debates, but later the pendulum swung back toward the champions of Chiabrera. In spite of the latter's innovations, Chiabrera was viewed retrospectively as a disciple of such Renaissance poets as Pietro Bembo and Giovanni Della Casa, and before them, Petrarch himself. By the turn of the century, Chiabrera's more conventional subject matter and simpler language were taken as welcome signs of a rationalism and order that

---

[29] These developments of Chiabrera are summarized in Elwert, *La poesia lirica*, 108–9, and elaborated in the surrounding pages.

[30] Gabriello Chiabrera, *Maniere, scherzi e canzonette morali*, ed. Giulia Raboni, Biblioteca di scrittori italiani (Parma: Fondazione Pietro Bembo and Ugo Guanda, 1998).

[31] Elwert, *La poesia lirica*, 111. Of course, musicologists, especially Silke Leopold, have also authored some important studies on Chiabrera and his relationship to music and composers: Silke Leopold, "Chiabrera und die Monodie: Die Entwicklung der Arie," *Studi musicali* 10 (1981): 75–106; Leopold, "Al modo d'Orfeo: Dichtung und Musik im italienischen Sologesang des frühen 17. Jahrhunderts," *Analecta musicologica* 29 (1995): all; several articles collected in *La scelta della misura: Gabriello Chiabrera, L'altro fuoco del barocco italiano*, ed. Fulvio Bianchi and Paolo Russo (Genoa: Costa & Nolan, 1993).

conformed to both the resurgent Counter-Reformation spirit and the trend toward authoritarian rule.[32]

The position of cantata poetry within such a dialectic is complex, as elements from both traditions can be found. To Marino is probably owed the typically amorous, even sensual approach to much subject matter. And the irregular mixture of what we now call *versi sciolti* – unstructured passages of *endecasillabi* and *settenari* – with closed poetic units strongly resembles Marino's *selva* form, devised for his *idilli favolosi*. On the other hand, the greater weight given to the closed canzonettas, at least in cantata poetry generally, belies a deep sympathy with Chiabrera's approach, as does the simpler syntax and imagery that more often characterize the genre.

Convenient demonstrations of these competing influences can be found in Atto's own cantata texts (all available in appendix F). A rather more Marinist work is Francesco Melosio's poem for *Scrivete, occhi dolenti* (appendix F, no. 11).[33] The form of *Scrivete* resembles a much abbreviated *selva*, although the four-stanza canzonetta dominates the poem to much greater degree than it would in Marino. More strikingly, Melosio develops the extended conceit of the lover's face as a sheet of paper on which he must silently write to his lady: his eyes become the pen, his tears the ink, and his pain the poetic inspiration. Such an elaborate metaphor is certainly redolent of Marinism.

Other works more strongly evoke Chiabrera. The anonymous poem of *Occhi miei belli* exhibits a form decidedly similar to the *canzonette meliche*: its rhyme and metrical patterns (a_5 b_5 b_5 a_5 c_{11} c_{11}, with a variant at the end) closely resemble such standard Chiabreran patterns as a_8 b_8 b_8 a_8 c_8 c_8 and a_5 a_5 b_5 b_5 c_5 c_5 d_{11} d_{11}.[34] Similarly, the two arias of *Fileno, idolo mio* not only

---

[32] The above paragraph is based on Asor Rosa, *La lirica*, 135, 163–64, 181–82; Elwert, *La poesia lirica*, 102, 112–15; Holzer, "Music and Poetry," 51; and Carlo Calcaterra, "La melica italiana della seconda metà del Cinquecento al Rolli e al Metastasio," in his *Poesia e canto: Studi sulla poesia melica italiana e sulla favola per musica* (Bologna: Nicola Zanichelli, 1951), 172. See also Jannaco and Capucci's telling chapter title, "La poesia tra classicismo e concettismo" (*Il Seicento*, 177).

[33] The story of the rather unlucky career of Francesco Melosio (1608/9–1670), who worked in Rome, Venice, Ferrara, Turin, and various provincial centers, is told by Holzer, "Music and Poetry," 340–59. Holzer (400) notes that this particular poem was first published in the added "parte terza" of Iseppo Prodocimo's 1678 edition of Melosio's works (and see 349–59 for a detailed publication history of this work). Holzer's research contradicts, rather convincingly, the textual attribution to Giovanni Filippo Apolloni found in one of the sources of this cantata (F Pn, Rés. Vmf. 41 [olim H.P. 1], ff. 61–72v), an attribution reported by Robert Weaver in his catalogue of Atto's works: *Alessandro Melani (1639–1703), Atto Melani (1626–1714)*, The Wellesley Edition Cantata Index Series, fasc. 8–9 ([Wellesley, Mass.]: Wellesley College, 1972). For information on all the musical and textual attributions of Atto's cantatas, see Melani, *Complete Cantatas*, xix and 97–106.

[34] These two patterns are offered by W. Th[eodor] Elwert, *Versificazione italiana dalle origini ai giorni nostri* (Florence: Felice Le Monnier, 1973), 158; and Calcaterra, "La melica italiana," 159, respectively. For a listing of more such patterns, see Elwert, *Versificazione italiana*, 158–59.

employ stanzas of *ottonari* (finished off with *settenari* or *endecasillabi*); they also highlight the elements of alliteration and assonance so favored by Chiabrera, indicated below by bold-face and italics respectively:[35]

Vieni **s**ol, che **s**ol'ad*o*r*o*;
Vi*e*ni, **v**ieni a q*ue*sto s*e*no:
A **p**ortar **p**ace, e ristoro
Ad un'alma, che si more.
Vieni mio **s**ol, sì, sì,
A questo afflitto sen riporta il dì.
…

Hor dell'*a*lb*a* i v*a*ghi r*a*i
Già de' mont'*i*l cr*i*n *i*ndorano,
E con dolce cant'omai
Gl'augeletti il gi*o*rno *o*norano;
S*o*l'indarno il mio c*o*r si lagna, e du*o*le;
Ch'è nato il dì, e non rimira il sole.

Especially playful are repeated sounds such as "*sol* che *solo*," "cr*in in*dorano," and "gi*orno honor*ano." Further, this poem uses the more traditional diction and imagery – such as the conceit of the lover as the sun – for which Chiabrera was later praised. On the other hand, the play of metaphors and sensuality in lines such as "Come, and taste on my lips, O my heart, / the honey of love in a cup of roses" conjures Marino even in this lyrical context.[36]

In fact, the distinctively mixed nature of cantata verse fits so problemati-cally into the standard account of *Seicento* poetry that a few scholars have proposed viewing melic poetry – poetry written specifically to be set to music – as a discrete genus, a "third line" of development in the period.[37] Carlo Calcaterra already advocated such a notion fifty years ago, tracing the melic tradition from the simple, lyrical language of sixteenth-century *canzoni villanesche* through the cantata and on to the opera librettos of Metastasio.[38] More recently, several studies of Francesco De Lemene's *cantate a voce sola* have reinforced and refined Calcaterra's view. In his edition of De Lemene's *cantate*, Elvezio Canonica points out the predictable debts of the author's style to Chiabrera and Marino, especially as regards metrical variety and

---

[35] Calcaterra ("La melica italiana," 159) specifically notes Chiabrera's frequent habit of finishing off a rhythmically regular poem with one or two slower, more grave lines, particularly *endecasillabi*.

[36] "Vieni, e su labri miei gusta, o mio core, / Dentro coppa di rose il miel d'amore."

[37] The term itself comes from Maria Grazia Accorsi, introduction to *Scherzi e favole per musica*, by Francesco De Lemene, ed. Maria Grazia Accorsi, Il lapazio: Collezione di letteratura italiana moderna, no. 10 (Bologna: Mucchi, 1992), lxxxvii.

[38] Calcaterra, "La melica italiana," *passim*.

subject matter. But Canonica argues that the most striking stylistic links – confirmed by numerous intertextual allusions – go back to Petrarch, the figure he sees as the primary inspiration for this "third line":

such an enormous Petrarchan presence enters into a literary and cultural environment of poetic-linguistic renewal with an "anti-baroque" purpose, [an environment] that will find its most complete expression in the production of the members of the Arcadian Academy and which, for northern Italy, has been termed a "northern pre-Arcadia" [*prearcadia settentrionale*].[39]

Maria Grazia Accorsi defines the "third line" somewhat differently, associating it specifically with the mix of meters (polymeter) typical of melic poetry. Contrary to Canonica, she views the tradition as more "baroque" than "classical," extinguished by the metrical regularity of poets like Metastasio. She argues that

polymeter [is] typical of the seventeenth century and typical for music … part of the rehabilitation of refrain forms, i.e., of another search for novelty and variety; Polymeter is a component of baroque poetry, of the desire for the new, the unexpected, the surprising, of the idea of rhythm and music less as regularity and confirmation than as cleverness, wit, eccentricity.[40]

However the melic tradition is interpreted, these writers (with the exception of Calcaterra) continue to grant only minimal literary significance to poetry for music. More generously than most, Folena writes that "from the literary, and not musical, point of view, [the cantata] is a minor genre, a micro-genre, but under the protection of music, it had its historical foundation and importance, and also, if quite rarely, an autonomous poetic significance."[41] Such an account does not tally, I would argue, with the enormous diffusion of cantata poetry. In addition to the occasional published works by Melosio, De Lemene, and Metastasio, an immense repository of such poetry is preserved in manuscript.[42] Canonica, for example, seems hardly to realize

---

[39] Elvezio Canonica, introduction to *Raccolta di cantate a voce sola*, by Francesco De Lemene, ed. Elvezio Canonica, Biblioteca di scrittori italiani (Parma: Fondazione Pietro Bembo/Ugo Guanda, 1996), xxvii. The quoted term comes from W[alter] Binni, *L'Arcadia e il Metastasio* (Florence: La Nuova Italia, 1963), 47–93. Canonica's more general discussion of De Lemene's stylistic debts can be found in his introduction, xxviii–xxxii.

[40] Accorsi, introduction to *Scherzi e favole*, lxxxviii. Accorsi's more general views on the historiography of the melic style are found at lxxxiii–xci.

[41] Folena, *L'italiano in Europa*, 262.

[42] The papers of Sebastiano Baldini at the Biblioteca Apostolica Vaticana represent the proverbial tip of the iceberg: see Giorgio Morelli, ed., *Sebastiano Baldini (1615–1685): Le poesie per musica nei codici della Biblioteca Apostolica Vaticana*, intro. Flavia Cardinale, Studi, Cataloghi e Sussidi Istituto di Bibliografia Musicale, no. 5, Progetti di ricerca bibliografica-musicale dell'IBIMUS,

that the conclusions he draws about De Lemene's trickle of published *cantate* would apply equally to the ocean of similar unpublished works from the same period.

And that ocean was indeed vast. Cantata scores themselves preserve these poems by the thousands. Based on this quantity, in fact, Calcaterra describes melic poetry as "the most vibrant [genre] of the *Seicento*, that is, the most loved and most enjoyed."[43] But, as hinted by Folena, this poetry also led an independent existence, and the papers of the secretary and poet Sebastiano Baldini (1615–85) offer an important glimpse of this life. Preserved in thirty-seven-odd volumes in the *fondo chigiano* at the Vatican library, the papers consist primarily of poems originally written on loose sheets and small fascicles, later bound together into miscellanies.[44] The sheets seem originally to have circulated independently, and many show evidence of having been mailed. Significantly, a large proportion of the corpus exhibits the mix of *versi sciolti* and canzonettas that characterizes poetry for music.[45] Indeed, the Baldini papers, preserving a rare type of ephemera, argue for a vigorous commerce in melic poetry at this time, with writers exchanging works with their patrons and colleagues. That this commerce took place primarily in *manuscript* and not in the presses argues not for the triviality of these poems but for their status as private rather than public art.[46] And just as a singer could gain status by avoiding exposure before the public, a literary genre that circulated only privately would carry greater, not lesser, standing.

Indeed, I would argue that it was more often protectiveness than shame that deterred the publication of melic poetry. Whether, as Accorsi suggests, cantata texts were too much "[a] sign of rebellion, of irregularity, [a] search for astonishment … [a] rejection of traditional forms," or whether, according to Calcaterra and Canonica, they heralded the Arcadian reforms of the early

no. 5 (Rome: Istituto di Bibliografia Musicale, 2000). Some bibliographical control of the material has been gained through works such as the series edited by Fabio Carboni, *Incipitario della lirica italiana dei secoli XV–XX*, Studi e testi no. 297– (Rome: Biblioteca Apostolica Vaticana, 1982–). Much work remains, however.

43   Calcaterra, "La melica italiana," 107. Echoing him, Accorsi writes, "un gran parte di poeti in quegli anni … pratica poesia per musica" (introduction to *Scherzi e favole*, lxxxviii).

44   Baldini's papers ended up in the Chigi materials apparently because he willed a portion of his effects to the Chigi family, one of his patrons (ibid., 24).

45   Musical settings of only a small proportion of these works have been located. See the invaluable work by Morelli, ed., *Sebastiano Baldini*.

46   See chapter 3 for discussions of Atto's specific efforts to avoid public presentation. On the selfishness of some patrons regarding the music they commissioned, see John Walter Hill, *Roman Monody, Cantata, and Opera from the Circles around Cardinal Montalto*, Oxford Monographs on Music (Oxford: Clarendon Press, 1997), vol. I, *passim*; one clear statement comes on p. 140, a reference to "the manuscript music books that Cardinal Montalto so jealously guarded." Anthony Newcomb, *The Madrigal at Ferrara 1579–1597*, Princeton Studies in Music, no. 7 (Princeton: Princeton University Press, 1980), I:20–28, also clearly outlines the different nature of public vs. private music.

eighteenth century, the melic style may at first have been too avant-garde to be shared widely.[47] Hardly a literary backwater, cantata poetry remained the exclusive province of the elite, and indeed members of the nobility often tried their hand at the style: Rose has identified just among Giacomo Carissimi's authors Pompeo Colonna (prince of Gallicano), Count Carlo Teodoli, and even Pope Alexander VII (Fabio Chigi).[48] Only as the century wore on did melic poetry develop a "public" audience. Not until 1672, two years after the poet's death, were any of Melosio's cantatas published (among his other poems), and De Lemene only brought out his own cantata poetry, written in the 1650s and 1660s, in 1692. Of course, melic poetry reached the zenith of its esteem with the opera and cantata librettos of Metastasio, works considered then and now fully independent and masterful pieces of literature. By then, the chic melic poetry had entered the mainstream.

If the prized status of this poetry is recognized, the cantata itself appears in a different light. At the least, that status helps clarify the motivations of an Atto Melani in setting such works to music. Just as members of the nobility sought to arrogate the glory of the artists they supported, so a musician might try to enhance his reputation by working with the most stylish poetry of the day. In both cases, personal status could be derived by association, by proving one's taste and discrimination. And even if the choice of texts was not the composer's, he still showed his quality by setting them with flair, by proving his mastery of their form and character. Working with melic poetry gave Atto another way to demonstrate that he truly belonged among the company of the most educated and fashionable gentlemen of his day.

The context of reception

Of course, the cantata was not pure literature: it required a musical realization, a physical performance. To comprehend fully Atto's decision to compose – and further, how his compositions may have achieved their purpose – the context of that performance requires investigation, the atmosphere in which these works were understood and used. Such insight can suggest how individual works might have furthered Atto's goals and also how the context of the genre may have shaped his individual creations.

---

[47] Accorsi, introduction to *Scherzi e favole*, lxxxix.

[48] Rose, "The Cantatas of Giacomo Carissimi," 206. Schmitz, *Geschichte*, 29, also highlights the poetic contributions of the aristocracy.

Penetrating this environment is not easy, and it has in fact been little investigated.[49] Scholars generally agree that the genre was intended for "small and cultivated audiences," "cognoscenti who appreciated displays of erudition, technical skill … topicality and spontaneity."[50] Lorenzo Bianconi describes a particularly cerebral environment, characterizing the cantata as a product of the "interaction … between musicians, men of letters and intellectuals."[51] Instead, I would argue that, while the cantata was certainly designed for the most educated classes (to a greater degree than Venetian opera, for example), the context of the genre belongs less to the realm of "intellectuals," in the modern sense of that term, than to the more charming domain of courtly recreation. In other words, rather than appealing to men like Galileo Galilei, Athanasius Kircher, or Francesco Redi, the cantata allies itself with the witty and amorous world of aristocratic leisure.[52]

The work of recent cultural historians provides a starting point for trying to understand this world, and ultimately the place of music within it.[53] One of the most consistent themes of this work is the fundamentally performative character of the age. As the European nobility gradually abandoned its traditional warrior function during the Renaissance – and thus its ancient justification for social dominance – it relied increasingly on behavior and style as markers of superiority. The quality (or *virtù*) of aristocrats began to be judged by how they presented themselves in society, how they spoke, gestured, danced. But because these behavioral markers could be learned and imitated by pretenders, these early modern aristocrats felt less secure in their status than had their medieval forebears. With so much at stake, their social

---

[49] An apparent exception to this statement would seem to be David Merrell Bridges's "The Social Setting of *musica da camera* in Rome: 1667–1700" (Ph.D. diss., George Peabody College for Teachers, 1976). Unfortunately, the author relies too much on financial records, which tend to note payments only for exceptional musical occasions rather than more routine events like cantata performances. Bridges thus ends up discussing events of a far more public and occasional nature than his title implies.

[50] The first quotation comes from Rose, "The Italian Cantata," 672. The second comes from Colin Timms and Malcolm Boyd, "Cantata, The Italian Cantata to 1800," *Grove Music Online*, ed. Laura Macy (accessed June 7, 2005), www.grovemusic.com.

[51] Lorenzo Bianconi, *Music in the Seventeenth Century*, trans. David Bryant (Cambridge: Cambridge University Press, 1987), 87, originally published as *Il Seicento* (Turin: E.D.T., 1982).

[52] Much of the following is taken from my "Singing and Playing: The Italian Cantata and the Rage for Wit," *Music and Letters* 82 (2001): 510–20.

[53] The following is based on Frank Whigham, "Interpretation at Court: Courtesy and the Performance–Audience Dialectic," *New Literary History: A Journal of Theory and Interpretation* 14 (1983): 623–39; Amadeo Quondam, introduction to *La civil conversazione*, by Stefano Guazzo, Testi: Istituto di Studi Rinascimentali Ferrara (Bologna: Franco Cosimo Panini, 1993; first published, Venice: Enea de Alaris, 1574), I:ix–lx; Philippe Ariès, introduction to *A History of Private Life*, vol. III, *Passions of the Renaissance*, ed. Roger Chartier, trans. Arthur Goldhammer (Cambridge, Mass., and London: Harvard University Press / Belknap Press, 1989), 1–11; and Jacques Revel, "The Uses of Civility," in *A History of Private Life*, III:167–205.

interaction could take on the character of a fiercely competitive struggle, now not of arms but of fashion and manners. As Frank Whigham summarizes it,

those who would maintain their privileged position had to constitute their own fundamental difference from their ambitious inferiors, for themselves as well as for their rivals, while stifling if possible not only the latter's accomplishments but even their dreams. On the other side, those who would relocate aimed to make themselves indistinguishable from their future peers, ideally to those peers themselves.[54]

Shakespeare's maxim that "all the world's a stage" resonated powerfully in this environment: in a concrete way, status often depended on performance.[55]

And one of the most important venues for this kind of performance was the private social gathering known as the *conversazione*.[56] Hardly an escape from the pressures of personal exhibition, aristocratic leisure time was among the most scrutinized by social peers and rivals. As Norbert Elias explains,

social life at court and within court society [has] a characteristic double face. On the one hand it has the function of our own private life, to provide relaxation, amusement, conversation. At the same time it has the function of our professional life, to be the direct instrument of one's career, the medium of one's rise or fall.[57]

[54] Whigham, "Interpretation at Court," 625. In this view, Whigham is echoing Norbert Elias's earlier work on court society: "all members of the [court] society are involved in a ceaseless struggle for status and prestige" (Norbert Elias, *The Court Society*, trans. Edmund Jephcott [New York: Pantheon, 1983], originally published as *Die höfische Gesellschaft* [Darmstadt: Hermann Luchterhand, 1969], 63).

[55] The line comes from *As You Like It*, II.7.139. The prevalence of this image is explored in detail in Skrine, *The Baroque*, 1–24.

[56] In the notes to Stefano Guazzo's *La civil conversazione*, II:97, Amadeo Quondam comments on Guazzo's usage of this term: "*conversazione* indica sia lo scambio comunicativo (di parole e di gesti), che lo stesso frequentarsi, in quanto pratica socialmente codificata, consuetudine di vita tra gruppi omogenei per *status* e cultura; indica anche il gruppo stesso dei conversatori, il loro colloquiare amabile e discreto su argomenti definiti, il loro comportamento virtuoso o vizioso che sia, il loro profilare un modello di convivenza e di società." This usage is supported by the *Vocabolario degli Accademici della Crusca* (Venice: G. Alberti, 1612), which gives s.v. "conversazione," "il conversare, e la gente stessa unita, che conversa insieme."

[57] Elias, *The Court Society*, 53. Although Elias's study focuses primarily on the French court of the *ancien régime*, the situation in Italy appears to have been quite similar, as Quondam makes clear (introduction to *La civil conversazione*, I:xxxi): "La conversazione, insomma, non è tanto o soltanto una forma culturale e mondana, non riguarda tanto o soltanto la piacevolezza e la gradevolezza di motti e risposte arguti e pronti, non è soltanto o tanto il modo con cui trascorrere il tempo libero dai negozi. Guazzo è chiarissimo: la pertinenza della conversazione è al tempo stesso etica (riguarda i *buoni costumi* e le *virtù*) ed economica … Saper conversare è … una forma d'investimento: può produrre non solo *onore*, ma anche *utile*, cioè beni materiali, o comunque può rendere più sicuro il proprio *status*."

Fortunately, glimpses into this complex interchange emerge from a variety of sources, including behavior treatises, game books, and fictionalized accounts.[58]

Together these sources reveal that in the world of courtly pastimes it was the quality of wit that was most often prized and admired. Numerous demonstrations appear in Stefano Guazzo's *La civil conversazione* (1574), a fundamental behavior treatise that, in a multitude of editions and translations, remained popular well into the seventeenth century.[59] In the fourth book, Guazzo presents his model of the private gathering, at which ten participants discuss issues of refined social conduct in a way that simultaneously illustrates such conduct. Much of the conversation revolves around games designed to allow speakers to display their verbal cleverness.

One of these games illuminates the performance atmosphere with particular clarity. A gentleman of the company, Signor Ercole, is challenged to improvise a love lament addressed to one of the ladies, Signora Lelia. I quote his response at some length:

To you, most beautiful angel of Paradise, to you, wonder of the world, to you, my life, rather my death … I am conducted upon the triumphal car of Love to announce to you with this trembling and weak voice, with this little breath which I have left, my approaching death. … But because my sorrowing soul has long lodged in your royal and generous heart, I beg you as a reward for the long sufferings which loving you

---

[58] Among the behavior treatises, Baldassare Castiglione, *Il libro del cortegiano*, ed. Giulio Preti, I millenni, no. 49 (Turin: G. Einaudi, 1960; first published, Venice: Aldo Romano e Andrea d'Asola, 1528); Stefano Guazzo, *La civil conversazione*. Among the game books, Girolamo Bargagli, *Dialogo de' giuochi che nelle vegghie sanesi si usano da fare*, ed. Patrizia D'Incalci Ermini, Accademia Senese degli Intronati: Monografie di storia e letteratura senese, no. 9 (Siena: Industria Grafica Pistolesi, 1982; first published, Siena: Luca Bonetti, 1572); Innocentio Ringhieri, *Cento giuochi liberali, et d'ingegno* (Bologna: Anselmo Giaccarelli, 1551). Among the fictionalized accounts, Matteo Bandello, *Novelle*, 4 vols. (Lucca: Il Busdrago, 1554–73); Pietro Fortini, *Le giornate delle novelle de' novizi*, ed. Adriana Mauriello, 2 vols., I novellieri italiani, no. 28 (Rome: Salerno, 1988; originally manuscript, sixteenth century); Giovan Francesco Straparola, *Le piacevoli notti*, ed. Donato Pirovano, 2 vols., I novellieri italiani, no. 29 (Rome: Salerno, 2000; originally manuscript, sixteenth century). The broad agreement that exists among these works encourages a degree of confidence in their descriptions; that many of them – particularly the behavior treatises – were reprinted well into the seventeenth century also argues for a significant continuity of practice (see next note). Thomas Frederick Crane, a scholar of this material, agrees that the various descriptions probably do represent something close to actual early modern practice: *Italian Social Customs of the Sixteenth Century and Their Effect on the Literatures of Europe*, Cornell Studies in English (New Haven, Conn.: Yale University Press, 1920), 141n.

[59] In his notes to his edition of *La civil conversazione*, Amadeo Quondam lists at least thirty-four Italian editions published between 1574 and 1631; eight French editions between 1579 and 1609; six English editions between 1581 and 1788; and eight Latin editions (distributed in Northern Europe) between 1585 and 1624 (Guazzo, *La civil conversazione*, I:lxix–lxxiii). The Guazzo treatise, like most such works from the period, is of course modeled on Castiglione's *Il libro del cortegiano*, though organized more systematically.

I have kept silent, and dying I have endured until now, that you will at least not refuse to place your lips to mine and with your sweet breath force my soul back to its first abode ... And if by the will of heaven [my soul] should have to depart without further delay from the unhappy body, I shall die satisfied ... with the hope that at my departure you will say with pitiful voice and some tears:

Alma, ch'albergo havesti nel mio petto,
Habbi hor là su nel ciel degno ricetto.[60]
[Soul, which dwelt in my breast,
now may you have in heaven above a worthy shelter.]

The similarity of this passage to much cantata poetry is striking: all the traditional rhetoric – centering on the impending death of the suffering lover – is present, including the summation of sentiments in a final rhymed couplet. But more to the present point is the response from the rest of the company. Rather than being caught up in the speaker's oratory and moved to sorrow, the small audience "laughed at this lament ... and afterwards Signora Lelia replied to [Signor Ercole] with pleasing countenance: 'If I knew you were as near death as your sorrowful words indicate, I would not fail to restore your soul to you with a kiss.'"[61] The discussion then turns to an analysis of the lament's merits and faults, providing further opportunity for clever remarks. In other words, this sophisticated audience did not look to the lament for some vicarious experience of emotion, but used it rather like any other game, as a foundation for verbal display. They reacted to the speech with laughter not because it contained comic elements, but because they understood and appreciated (and were ready to critique) the devices that Signor Ercole had employed: they responded to the cleverness of his rhetoric, to his performance *as* a performance.

Eric Cochrane's study of Italian learned academies corroborates this appreciation for what might be called style over substance and confirms that it continued into the seventeenth century. He relates, for example, that the venerable literary institutions of Tuscany spent much of their time debating amorous *dubbi* similar to those of the *conversazioni*, if with more erudite responses. For example, to the inquiry of whether "the fire of love is awakened more by seeing the beloved laugh or cry," the Accademia della

---

[60] Guazzo, *La civil conversazione*, book 4, part 2, paragraph 172 (p. I:315), as quoted and translated in Crane, *Italian Social Customs*, 422–23. The final couplet almost certainly represents a quotation from a prominent Italian poet, although neither Crane nor Quondam was able to find the source: many of Guazzo's examples conclude with a motto of this sort.

[61] Crane, *Italian Social Customs*, 423; he quotes and translates here from Guazzo, *La civil conversazione*, book 4, part 2, paragraph 173 (p. I:315).

Crusca eventually settled on "laugh," "because Beatrice smiles at Dante in Paradise."[62] The academies also played a variety of more complex games, including *Sibilla* (particularly popular with the Accademia degli Apatisti). In it, a blindfolded child was brought before the academicians and asked an abstruse question; his meaningless response was then "interpreted" extemporaneously by a member, again with extensive reference to recognized authors. Even the progressive scientific academies seem not to have been immune to such tastes for wit: Jay Tribby has argued convincingly that Francesco Redi's *Osservazioni intorno alle vipere* (1664) – a work probably connected to the Accademia del Cimento – is as much a flamboyant proof of Cleopatra's means of suicide as it is a scientific investigation of poisonous snakes.[63]

As Cochrane concludes, the academies – like the *conversazioni* – focused less on the content of the material presented (as the game of *Sibilla* plainly indicates) than on the style of the delivery. "Needless to say, no one cared ... whether a smile might more easily win a lady's affection than a frown. What mattered was not the subject of the discourse, but the mere fact of its composition and recitation ... not what was said but how it was said."[64] Tribby concurs that the subject matter of such discussions was simply "booty for the display of discursive skills, points of imminent conversational departure, destination unknown."[65] Although *conversazioni* differed from the academies in various ways, lacking the relative formality and single-sex environment of the latter, their ruling tastes appear similar. As members of court society strove to display refinement and mental agility, they applied rhetorical strategies to whatever material was at hand, caring less about expressing a novel idea or sentiment than about expressing familiar ideas and sentiments with a novel turn.

In my view, the evidence strongly argues that this self-conscious cleverness, this taste for wit, constituted the native environment of the cantata. In the first place, cantatas seem to have been performed most often in the very settings described above, where wit was most prized. As mentioned, musicologists have long recognized, in a general way, that these works were normally intended for private consumption by the upper classes: seventeenth-century taxonomies of music always associate the genre with

---

[62] Eric W. Cochrane, *Tradition and Enlightenment in the Tuscan Academies 1690–1800* (Chicago: University of Chicago Press, 1961), 8. He cites an entry from the *Diario* of the academy dated January 2, 1698.

[63] Jay Tribby, "Cooking (with) Clio and Cleo: Eloquence and Experiment in Seventeenth-Century Florence," *Journal of the History of Ideas* 52 (1991), 417–39 *passim*, but especially at 432–33.

[64] Cochrane, *Tradition and Enlightenment*, 25–26.   [65] Tribby, "Cooking," 421.

chamber performance.[66] Sporadically, however, additional details have been culled from archives that confirm and elaborate on this picture, including the details I have been extracting from Atto's correspondence throughout this study.[67] At one end of the spectrum, it seems, cantatas sometimes functioned as little more than background music during meals or other activities, or even as an aid to sleep: Atto reports on singing during dinner for Emperor Ferdinand III and while Anne of Austria dressed and fixed her hair during her *lever*. Atto may even have helped Pope Clement IX drop off to sleep for his afternoon siesta, an apparently common practice satirized by Salvator Rosa: "Princes: singing is so beloved by you that sleep does not come to your brow unless it is first coaxed by song."[68] In many other cases, though, cantatas received full attention. Atto tells of the meticulous consideration given his performances by Duke Charles-Emmanuel II of Savoy, Duke Carlo II of Mantua, and even, in different situations, Anne of Austria and Emperor Ferdinand.[69] In fact, the singer's description of his performance in 1653 before the emperor is worth repeating here (in abridged form) for its unusually detailed account of a chamber setting:

Since I was brought in just as [the emperor] had taken his place at the table for dinner with the empress and the king of the Romans [his son], he had me sing throughout the entire length of dinner. Afterwards, when His Majesty rose from the table and went over to where the spinet was, I went up to him and, kissing his hand, presented him the letter of Your Highness. I inform[ed] him of the order that you yourself had given me to present myself to His Majesty with all haste, and that you had considered [it] your great fortune that one of your servants had been judged worthy of being able to serve His Majesty.

Receiving the letter, he opened it immediately and said to me these precise words: "Signor Atto, I assure you that from the information that had been given to me about your abilities, I figured that you were very valuable, but I have found [your abilities] to be greater than what [your] fame had conveyed to me. I confess that Prince [Mattias] was quite right never to want to deprive himself of your person, and you yourself can assure him that he could not have done me a greater favor. Please consent to sing two more *ariette*."

---

[66] On the various taxonomies that place the cantata under *musica cubicularis*, see Claude V. Palisca, "Marco Scacchi's Defense of Modern Music (1649)," in *Words and Music, the Scholar's View: A Medley of Problems and Solutions Compiled in Honor of A. Tillman Merritt by Sundry Hands*, ed. Laurence Berman ([Cambridge, Mass.]: Harvard Univ. Department of Music, 1972), 190–93.

[67] A rich new source of such details may be found in Hill, *Roman Monody*.

[68] Salvator Rosa, "La musica," in *Poesie e lettere edite e inedite di Salvator Rosa*, vol. I, ed. G.A. Cesareo (Naples: R. Accademia di Archeologia, Lettere e Belle Arti, 1892), lines 349–51.

[69] For documentation of Atto's reports, see chapters 3 and 5.

These were the words that His Majesty said to me, and having had three chairs brought near to the instrument, he had me sing another hour and a half, so that in total I sang for three hours.[70]

With its combination of eating, music-making, and (one senses) elegant conversation, this occasion strongly resembles the type of *conversazione* first outlined by Guazzo nearly seventy-five years earlier. Indeed, this enduring model of informal intercourse – although seldom documented *because* informal – probably represents the most usual context for vocal chamber works.

Academies too, however, have been recognized as important venues for cantatas. Owen Jander has investigated in some detail the special subgenre of the *cantata in accademia* and reports that these works, presented before the members, often provided lyric synopses of academic debates.[71] Such use is confirmed by Cochrane's aforementioned study, which describes academicians regularly critiquing new literary works – including those set to music – as a creative stimulus to the members.[72] More familiar, of course, are the literary and musical academies of Rome, particularly those associated with Queen Christina of Sweden: Atto himself reports that "two evenings a week, *accademie* of voices and instruments are given before Her Majesty."[73]

Locating cantata performance in settings that valued cleverness might itself argue for a shared playful attitude, but it is important to verify, I believe, that cantatas indeed fit into the intellectual climate of their surroundings, that presentations of vocal chamber music did not somehow stand outside the ambience of the chamber – like a modern concert, subject to a different sensibility – but rather were fully integrated into that environment. In fact, the evidence suggests a strong kinship between those refined amusements outlined above and the musical works that complemented them.

Such a link has already been proposed for an important antecedent of the cantata in the chamber venue, the polyphonic madrigal. In a paper given at the 1994 meeting of the American Musicological Society, Laura W. Macy pointed out that the interlocutors of Antonfrancesco Doni's *Dialogo della musica* (1544) "mix conversation with madrigals," and that "the singing of each madrigal is preceded by, and arises out of, some casual discussion."[74] She then compared these conditions to those in descriptions of games

---

[70] Atto to Mattias, from Regensburg, July 14, 1653 (see citation in chapter 3, note 42, page 83).

[71] Owen Jander, "The Cantata in Accademia: Music for the *Accademia de' Dissonanti* and Their Duke, Francesco II d'Este," *Rivista italiana di musicologia* 10 (1975): 519–44.

[72] Cochrane, *Tradition and Enlightenment*, 19.

[73] Atto to Mattias, from Rome, January 8, 1656. (See chapter 5.)

[74] Laura W. Macy, "The Italian Madrigal and Renaissance Games" (paper presented at the annual meeting of the American Musicological Society, Minneapolis, October 1994), 2.

intended for polite society, drawing specifically on Guazzo's treatise. She concluded that

> both Guazzo's game and Doni's madrigals arise from the conversation and give shape to it ... in both social and literary function, games and madrigals are one [and] the same activity. At the heart of both is the act of voicing language. In the madrigal, the words – the topic and its clever development – have been supplied by the poet, they form the famous madrigalian "conceit." ... In Guazzo's game ... the development of the conceit is up to the players themselves.[75]

She further noted that in some cases the participants in games were actually provided with texts written beforehand, thereby relieving somewhat the burden of ingenuity and rendering the experience of madrigals and games even more similar.[76]

Macy's conclusions receive strong support from other contemporary sources that describe musical entertainment. A number of these are nicely summarized in Thomas Crane's study of the relationships between Italian social customs and literature. As he shows, music is often incorporated into the amusements of an afternoon or evening otherwise focused primarily on the telling of stories and playing of games. In some cases, the musical content is minimal: one of the participants might have to sing a few verses as a "forfeit" for not having played well.[77] In other instances, the concertizing is extended to an hour or more.[78]

Here I will offer just a couple of examples. In Pietro Fortini's sixteenth-century "Le giornate delle novelle de' novizi," the telling of stories or *novelle* is itself presented in its social context, a format that dates back at least to Boccaccio's *Decameron*. Each day for eight days a small company of ladies and gentlemen meet in a garden to while away the hot afternoons. Crane's summary of three of these days illustrates the place of music in such a setting:

> On the Second Day ... Costanzio crowns Corintia [making her "queen" for the day], who commands Emilia to begin [telling stories]. The Second Day ... contains seven novels. When the last is ended, the queen commands Adriana to sing some canzonettas, and proposes that they should take the subject of Fortune for their rhymes.

---

[75] Ibid., 4. The connection of madrigals to games was broached previously, although in a more limited way, by James Haar in his "On Musical Games in the 16th Century," *Journal of the American Musicological Society* 15 (1962): 22–34.

[76] Macy, "The Italian Madrigal," 4.

[77] Pietro Fortini, *Le piacevoli et amorose notti de' novizi*, ed. Adriana Mauriello, 2 vols., I novellieri italiani, no. 28–2 (Rome: Salerno, 1995), 514–15, as summarized from a sixteenth-century manuscript source in Crane, *Italian Social Customs*, 315. Often, the forfeits are far more entertaining than the games themselves and seem really to be the point.

[78] Fortini, *Le piacevoli*, 414–81, as described in Crane, *Italian Social Customs*, 314.

This they do and the day is ending when they finish. Corintia crowns Emilia, who says that the story-telling will be continued next day, and since Adriana had restricted their songs to the subject of Fortune, she intends to confine the story-telling next day to "the evil life of wicked ecclesiastics." The company then breaks up …

The Fourth Day does not differ in the opening. The garden is described more fully, the company sitting under an arbour. Ipolito sings to the accompaniment of a *gravicembalo*. Then Fulgida begins her novel. At the conclusion of the twenty-eighth *novelle* [*sic*], Emilia is commanded to sing, which she does to the sound of a lute. The subject of her song is still Fortune. Ipolito is then crowned, and assigns as a topic "whatever is most pleasing to each."…

The Sixth Day is peculiar. The company meets in the garden as usual, and Fulgida addresses them and expresses her will that story-telling should be omitted that day because it is Good Friday. In order, however, not to lose the day, she commands Costanzio and Ipolito to relate a part of their ill-rewarded love, and also entertain the company with "qualche bella rima." Costanzio says he will first narrate who the lady is who makes his heart languish so, then in the second part he will express his just demands. He then proceeds to sing. After a duett between Costanzio and Ipolito, the latter begins his song, most of which is in *versi sciolti*, describing the palace of Venus, with the pictures on the walls … Costanzio replies to Ipolito, singing the praises of Fortune in *ottava rima*.[79]

Likewise, in the similar setting of Giovan Francesco Straparola's "Le piacevoli notti," the noble hostess "proposed that every evening … they should dance, and afterwards five damsels should sing a canzonetta as they liked, and each of the five on whom the lot fell should tell a story, concluding with an enigma to be solved by the company."[80] In all of these scenes, as Macy argued, singing seems to be a natural extension of other verbal activities.

One must consider, of course, whether this behavior survived into the seventeenth century, the period of the cantata. Certainly an important change in vocal chamber music did take place in the late sixteenth century. The earlier madrigal – along with the aria, villanella, and canzonetta – had regularly been performed by talented, often aristocratic, amateurs.[81] These rather simple musical styles are probably implied in the descriptions of the *conversazioni* above, with their impromptu music-making. Toward the end of the sixteenth century, however, the most progressive madrigal styles

---

[79] Fortini, *Le giornate*, I. 379–II. 373, as quoted and described in Crane, *Italian Social Customs*, 309–10.

[80] Crane, *Italian Social Customs*, 293.

[81] One source, among many, to confirm such usage is Anthony Newcomb, "Secular Polyphony in the 16th Century," in *Performance Practice: Music before 1600*, ed. Howard Mayer Brown and Stanley Sadie, The Norton/Grove Handbooks of Music (New York and London: W.W. Norton, 1989), 223; also, Newcomb, *The Madrigal at Ferrara*, I:14 and 18, gives specific examples of the simpler styles being used at least through the 1570s.

demanded the vocal skill of professionals: for these works, most aristocrats were reduced from active participation to passive listening.

Yet this change does not seem to have altered the context of the performances. In Guazzo's model *conversazione*, for example, the sole musical episode is provided by a professional who, during the course of dinner, enters the gathering, sings the praises of one of the guests, and then departs. The diners then focus on his presentation as a topic of conversation: although in this case the singer is not a member of the company, his contribution is treated as if he had been (like Signor Ercole's lament above).[82] But perhaps the most telling case is that of the *concerto delle donne* in Ferrara. As Anthony Newcomb reports, the famously skilled ensemble of the 1580s represented simply a more professional incarnation of an aristocratic trio that had preceded it. And just as the earlier ensemble had grown out of the duchess's circle of attendants – always a most natural group for leisure activities – so too the trained singers of the *concerto* were themselves given posts as ladies-in-waiting. The only difference in the new configuration was the awarding of these intimate positions on the basis of talent rather than birth.[83]

In the early seventeenth century, of course, monody began to gain precedence over the polyphonic madrigal. But, by this time, the change represented merely the substitution of one professionalized genre for another. In other words, the rise of monody need not have occasioned a revolution in performance context, and there are few indications that it did. Giovanni Maria Crescimbeni suggests this continuity when in 1702 he writes of the cantata, "this type of poetry is the invention of the seventeenth century, since in the preceding [century] madrigals and other regulated compositions served for music."[84] Eugen Schmitz makes the same point:

---

[82] Guazzo, *La civil conversazione*, book 4, part 1, paragraphs 235–245 (pp. I:289–90), as described in Crane, *Italian Social Customs*, 409–10.

[83] The above material is based on Newcomb, *The Madrigal at Ferrara*, I:7: "The first group was made up of courtiers who happened to sing, the second of singers who, because of their musical ability, were made courtiers."

[84] Following Holzer, I quote from the 1731 edition: Giovanni Maria Crescimbeni, *Commentarj ... intorno alla sua Istoria della volgar poesia* (Venice: Lorenzo Basegio, 1731), 299–300, as quoted and translated in Holzer, "Music and Poetry," 229. In connection with this observation by Crescimbeni, Paola Besutti questions whether the cantata practice should really be considered equivalent to the old *a tavolino* tradition: "Produzione e trasmissione di cantate romane nel mezzo del Seicento," in *La musica a Roma attraverso le fonti d'archivio*, ed. Bianca Maria Antolini, Arnaldo Morelli, and Vera Vita Spagnuolo, Strumenti della ricerca musicale, no. 2 (Lucca: Libreria Musicale Italiana in association with the Archivio di Stato di Roma and the Società Italiana di Musicologia, 1994), 147. As the division of sixteenth-century music into dilettante and professional categories suggests, the cantata would usually *not* have been considered part of the old participatory tradition, a tradition that probably continued to exist alongside the newer styles. The social setting, however, seems to remain similar.

it was adapted madrigals that, from the Renaissance period, first gave normal domestic and virtuosic music-making its substance. Henceforth, with the beginning of the seventeenth century, lyrical monody took the place of these compositions and gave soloistic music-making new bases … Thus, the chamber cantata at that point took the place of the polyphonic madrigal.[85]

Indeed, the fanciful titles of some early monody publications – for example, *Fuggilotio musicale* (Musical Pastime; Romano, 1613), *Recreatione armonica* (Harmonic Recreation; Anerio, 1611), and *Strali d'amore* (Arrows of Love; Boschetti, 1618) – reflect both the connection of these works to their madrigalian past, where similar titles were often used, and their design for precisely the sort of social atmosphere propounded above. This diversity of appellations only gradually gave way to the single term *cantata*: even as late as the works of Agostino Steffani (1654–1728) a chamber duet could be called a "madrigale a 2."[86]

A few excerpts from Atto's own correspondence help corroborate the continued association of vocal chamber music with the *conversazione*. Atto seems to employ this last word exclusively in Guazzo's sense of "soirée," rather than the modern "conversation," as when he comments to Mattias from Rome on July 3, 1655, "it was necessary to make many meetings and *conversationi*."[87] In his letter of May 10, 1655 (seen before in chapter 3), the usage is even less ambiguous: "I find myself daily in very beautiful *conversationi* of cardinals, prelates, *virtuosi*, and *virtuose*, and I have occasion to hear the best men and women who sing, so that [being there] can only serve to teach me something, each [of the singers] having some considerable qualities in his or her style."[88] One other comment even hints at the continued connection of vocal music to social games. In a letter to the duchess of Savoy, Atto begins, "I had sent from Florence those words to the game *Cocconetto* that I could never tell Your Royal Highness while I had the honor of serving you at Moncale [Moncalieri], wherefore I am sending them to Your Royal Highness appended here with two other canzonettas that I wrote here."[89] The proximity of Atto's discussion of a parlor game

---

[85] Schmitz, *Geschichte*, 20–21.

[86] The above material is based on ibid., 22–26. As indicated above, the best discussion of the growth of the term *cantata* may be found in Holzer, "Music and Poetry," 226–62.

[87] Atto to Mattias, from Rome, July 3, 1655. On the term *conversazione*, see note 56 above.

[88] Atto to Mattias, from Rome, May 10, 1655.

[89] Atto to Duchess Christine Marie of Savoy, from La Fère, July 20, 1657. Cocconetto was apparently a popular card game of the period: more than one poem refers to it, in somewhat lascivious tones. See, for example, the canzone "Sopra il Giuoco del Cocconetto" in I Fn, Magl. VII.364, ff. 300v–302r, as well as G[iovanni] B[attista] Ricciardi's *Rime burlesche*, ed. Ettore Toci (Livorno: Francesco Vigo, 1881), 27–30.

to his mention of the canzonetta, a frequent term for vocal chamber music, suggests once again – precisely as Macy proposed – that vocal music remained an important resource for aristocratic entertainment.

Taken together, the evidence presented here suggests, I believe, that the social context of the cantata probably did not differ radically from that of the madrigal. In other words, cantata reception seems often to have been characterized by the same self-conscious wit that dominated aristocratic gatherings throughout the early modern period. From this perspective too, it seems, writing cantatas could situate the composer in that intimate and playful sphere that captivated so many figures of power.

Lyrical constructions of love

If the spirit of elite recreation was wit, its matter – that is, its subject matter – was love. The historian Gaetano Imbert confirms that love was "the sovereign of that little world of gallantry."[90] The culture of love – its pleasures, pains, rules, and conventions – had for centuries served as the most fashionable topic of courtly discourse.[91] The short stories or *novelle* mentioned above were usually tales of love, sometimes even acted out in a semi-dramatic presentation. And the participants in a *conversazione* might improvise a love lament, present a prepared poem or speech on the subject, or focus on the traditional *questioni d'amore*. As they had for centuries, aristocrats looked to this topic as the primary "booty" for their display of discursive skills, the raw material on which they exercised their cleverness.

The topic was also, of course, the most common focus of cantatas. Like earlier madrigals, cantatas contemplate love more often than any other topic. On one level, this convention simply corroborates the link between the genre and its context: vocal chamber music was just another medium through which the social conversation about love could take place. But to penetrate fully how individual works – by Atto Melani or any composer – communicated meaning, a more detailed consideration of the realm of love itself is in order. For idealized love in the *Seicento* was a far more complex phenomenon than usually allowed. In fact, contemporary literature distinguishes a number of perspectives on the subject, each generating a cluster of recurrent themes.

The perspective on love most commonly found in cantatas involves a faithful man whose love for his lady causes him to suffer. In a valuable

---

90 Gaetano Imbert, *La vita fiorentina nel Seicento secondo memorie sincrone (1644–1670)* (Florence: R. Bemporad e Figlio, 1906), 121.

91 On the history of amorous subject matter, from the troubadours to the French Revolution, see Crane, *Italian Social Customs*, 98–158.

study of seventeenth-century love literature, Jean-Michel Pelous describes this construct of love – descended from the troubadour's *fin' amors* – as "*amour tendre*."[92] According to this doctrine, the man must love his lady unconditionally, whether or not he harbors hope of reciprocation; he must prove his worth through his constancy, discretion, and complete submission to her will. The woman, on the other hand, is expected to ignore his advances, demanding silence and unquestioning obedience. The aim is to extend the initial purity of the relationship, to somehow maintain the ideal of Platonic love by forever deferring a consummation. Of course, it is this protraction of desire that leads inevitably to suffering. In fact, the very rules of *amour tendre* serve to thwart the realization of a loving relationship, at least as we would define it today: "in the *tendre* universe, there are no happy lovers: as soon as they become engaged in the amorous adventure, the persecutions commence."[93]

Instead, the experience of becoming enthralled by love was meant to refine a man, tempering his natural ferocity and rendering him more civilized. In a passage that seconds many of my observations in chapter 4, Pelous notes that

amour tendre, by preaching obeisance and resignation to men, ends up by imposing on them a comportment traditionally attributed to the other sex … The exigencies of an art of loving where submission and sweetness are sovereign produce curiously effeminate lovers … For, [and this is] the final paradox, the "*tendre*" lovers draw the essence of their power from their very weakness.[94]

By contrast, the woman, through her resistance, commands the position of strength. Again, in Pelous's words, "it is a commonplace of the period to oppose war and love; it would be more just to say that love is to women what war is for men, a way of exteriorizing their will to power and of acquiring what both the one and the other call 'glory.'"[95] Yet the woman's power was precarious, contingent upon her consistent rejection of the lover. Were she to treat him with affection, she would lose control. In the formulation of Madeleine de Scudéry, "as soon as he is certain of being loved, he nearly

[92] Jean-Michel Pelous, *Amour précieux, amour galant (1654–1675): Essai sur la répresentation de l'amour dans la littérature et la société mondaines*, Bibliothèque française et romane, ser. C, vol. 77 (Paris: Librairie Klincksieck, 1980). While Pelous's study concerns primarily the literature of seventeenth-century France, I find his mapping of the *géographie amoureuse* helpful in conceptualizing many aspects of European love literature generally.
[93] Ibid., 46. This paragraph is based on 44–46.
[94] Ibid., 56.
[95] Ibid., 62. This observation immediately calls to mind Monteverdi's eighth book of madrigals and suggests a gendering of its two components.

ceases to be loving."[96] The oft-lamented "cruelty" of the lady is in fact essential to the maintenance of the affair.[97]

Over its long history, this traditional philosophy was examined from many points of view, which tended to fall into a range of standard topoi. I identify some of the most common here with short Italian epithets, using words that frequently appear in such poems. (1) *La bella sdegnosa*: perhaps the most straightforward representation of the *tendre* attitude emerges in poems that consider, in Calcaterra's words, "the unloved lover [who] swears that with invincible devotion he will not cease to love the beautiful lady who scorns him."[98] (2) *Amor crudele*: the speaker reveals that love alone leads to his suffering, however much that love may also soften the pain. (3) *Silenzio*: in accord with tradition, the lady demands her admirer's silence, which increases his agony. (4) *Lontananza*: the distance that separates the lovers, either because of Fate's decree or the lady's choice, inspires further expressions of anguish. (5) *Speranze bugiarde*: the lover curses the false hopes that extend his torment; he sometimes also begs the hopes, and so the pain, to continue. (6) *Lode di bellezza*: in perhaps the most upbeat topic, the man praises the lady's beauty, but the gesture usually also acknowledges (and sometimes embraces) the pain of her inevitable rejection. While this list touches on only some of the themes encountered, all are linked by the essential *tendre* belief in the nexus of beauty, love, and pain.

Opposed to *amour tendre* is an attitude that Pelous labels *amour galant*. The *galant* outlook does not in fact accept the link between pain and love and so inverts the traditional attitudes: the lover aims to be inconstant, insincere, and light-hearted. Rather than the teary seriousness of *amour tendre*, this manner is smiling, ironic, and essentially derisive of tradition. Madame de Scudéry sets forth some of the telling principles in the voice of a character from her romance *Clélie*:

One must love everyone who seems agreeable, provided that there is some indication of finding greater pleasure than pain in the conquest one thinks to make … Among women, one must certainly refrain from acting the habitual inconstant, but regardless it is never necessary to be too scrupulously faithful, for it would be better to have a thousand lovers than to have only one that lasted one's whole life.[99]

---

[96] Madeleine de Scudéry, *Clélie* (Paris: A. Courbé, 1654–60), IV:734, as quoted in Pelous, *Amour précieux*, 65.

[97] This paragraph is based on Pelous, *Amour précieux*, 53–67.

[98] Calcaterra, "La melica italiana," 108. This description is part of a list of some of what Calcaterra considers the most common themes in melic poetry.

[99] De Scudéry, *Clélie*, VI:1360–61, as quoted in Pelous, *Amour précieux*, 151–52.

Pelous attributes the rise of the *galant* position, first encountered in the salons of Paris, to a real-life change in attitudes toward love, as courtiers adopted the light-hearted sensibility they perceived in the affairs of their amorous young king, Louis XIV. But the complexity and artificiality of the traditional approach had always made it an easy target; certainly Italian satirists had for centuries launched attacks on *tendre* norms.

A perspective not represented by Pelous but certainly prevalent in cantata poetry is that of the suffering lady, particularly when abandoned or betrayed by her lover. The story of Dido and Aeneas is archetypal here: the lady laments that fate, or her lover's faithlessness, has taken him from her. Of course the female lament had a long history, with important manifestations in Ariosto's Olimpia and Bradamante, and (most relevantly) Rinuccini's Ariadne.[100] Although the link between love and pain in these cases certainly recalls the *tendre* mentality, no lady within that system could afford to admit her love. In fact, the female lament is really the inevitable consequence of breaking the *tendre* "rules": by yielding to a man, a lady makes herself vulnerable. The tradition participates in the same patriarchal fantasy that informs male complaints: if a man suffers because his lady withholds her "favor," a woman suffers when she loses the man to whom she surrendered that favor. In other words, it pains a man to be without sex; it pains a woman to be without her husband.

The subject of love is also approached from (at least) three other perspectives, each represented by a smaller segment of the literature. The comic approach differs from the *galant* in its greater ridiculousness, often involving characters normally thought unsuitable for romance (nurses, old men, hunchbacks, courtesans, etc.); dialect may also be used, lending the piece a comic coarseness. Love can also be treated from a moralizing standpoint: here the theme of *vanitas* often appears, or love is viewed in a more spiritual light. Finally, love can form part of texts that are otherwise more historical in nature, in which particular events are recounted, sometimes in semi-dramatic fashion.

The cantatas of Atto Melani: Poetry

With the preceding background, one can begin to consider Atto's specific works and their role in his life. One would like to be able to identify exactly when and for whom each cantata was written, but unfortunately the evidence

---

[100] See Leofranc Holford-Strevens, "'Her Eyes Became Two Spouts': Classical Antecedents of Renaissance Laments," *Early Music* 27 (1999): 379–93.

is far too meager. Even defining Atto's period of composition is tricky. His earliest clear reference to composing comes in a letter of July 20, 1657 to the duchess of Savoy (quoted above), to whom he sent two of his "canzonettas." The only earlier evidence is negative. As we have seen in chapter 2, he complained in 1652 about the vocal range of his role in a new opera and added, "since composing is not my profession, I did not think nor dare to alter it."[101] A comment two years earlier, again to the duchess of Savoy, strengthens the impression that Atto was not composing in the early 1650s, or at least not at a level he judged acceptable: "I was in Rome and had the opportunity to obtain from those *virtuosi* a few arias that seemed to me quite lovely, and so I emboldened myself to send them to Your Royal Highness."[102] If Atto had been writing music at this time, he surely would have sent his own works instead (or in addition). While these statements are far from conclusive, the best evidence is that Atto began composing seriously sometime between 1652 and 1657. At the other end of the timeline, his last reference to his own works comes on March 12, 1664, in a letter to the duke of Mantua (also cited above), in which Atto inquires anxiously about the duke's satisfaction with a new cantata. Given that, after the late 1660s, Atto ceased referring to music in his correspondence and indeed seems for a time to have avoided all links to the art (see chapter 5), one may reasonably conjecture that he also stopped composing at about that time. Atto's most likely period of compositional activity would thus appear to be very roughly the decade from 1655 to 1665.

Data about the patrons of Atto's works is equally sparse. Surprisingly, I have found no document testifying to Atto's writing music for any of his primary patrons, including Mattias, Mazarin, and Anne of Austria. Instead, Atto identifies only his more peripheral supporters, like the duchess of Savoy and duke of Mantua. That at various times Atto coveted the patronage of these two figures is doubtless significant. I will further speculate below that, based on internal indications, some of Atto's works were directed to Marie Mancini and/or her sister Hortense. In any event, one can hardly believe that Atto wrote nothing for Mattias or the French: the practice must have been so regular as to obviate references.

Closely connected to the issue of patronage is that of performance, and again little can be said for certain. Indeed, Atto's performance of his own works is nowhere explicitly substantiated. But considering that his apparent period of composition coincides with some of his busiest years as a singer,

---

[101] Copy of a letter to Alessandro Carducci included with Atto's letter to Mattias, from Pistoia, November 5, 1652.

[102] Atto to the duchess of Savoy, from Florence, July 1650.

one must assume that many, if not all, of his works were originally intended for his own use. Yet Atto certainly did not consider his cantatas to be his exclusive repertoire. He entrusted other singers to perform the pieces he sent to Turin and Mantua, and while he was living in Rome in 1661 he bragged that "my [*ariette*] are in such high esteem that all these *virtuose* seek them from me."[103]

With so little information from the documents, one looks to the works themselves to try to understand their significance for Atto's audience. In this endeavor, the foregoing framework of aristocratic pastimes and amorous ideologies is crucial. A consideration here of the content and style of Atto's various texts not only suggests how each work might have fit into the context of aristocratic leisure but also prompts further thoughts on the meanings and uses of specific cantatas.

As one might expect, the largest group of Atto's texts are written from the traditional viewpoint of the suffering male lover, using many of the standard *tendre* themes. The subject of *Filli, per cui mi moro*, for example, is the *bella sdegnosa* (appendix F, no. 3): "Phyllis, for whom I die, despises my weeping; and always cruel, O God, she abhors me, disdains me: and [still] I love her!" This thirty-four-line poem consists almost exclusively of *versi sciolti*, interrupted by a single four-line canzonetta. By mid-century, this structure plainly evoked the recitative lament, an operatic and chamber genre firmly established by Monteverdi's archetypal *Lamento d'Arianna*. Although the inclusion of the canzonetta complicates the traditional form, such lyrical interludes had been appearing in operatic laments from before 1650 and do not seem to have altered the identity of such a piece.[104] Indeed, this text shows few overt signs of playfulness, yet, as noted above, even such "serious" laments could in fact be employed as a form of diversion, a test of rhetorical prowess. And so a poem like *Filli per cui mi moro* might well have seemed to some auditors like one of the more artful responses in such a game.

A more obviously witty spirit can be found in Atto's three texts on the particular problem of *silenzio*, the lady's painful demand for silence: *Scrivete, occhi dolenti*; *Anima, che di foco*; and *Il tacer non fa per me*. In Melosio's *Scrivete* (as discussed above) the man begs his lady to read his silent face as if it were a declaration of love. In analyzing the poem, Robert Holzer notes that Melosio referred to the work as a *lettera amorosa*, a genre that began with

---

[103] Atto to Mattias, from Rome, September 3, 1661.

[104] On the recitative lament, see Margaret Murata, "The Recitative Soliloquy," *Journal of the American Musicological Society* 32 (1979): 45–73; also Ellen Rosand, *Opera in Seventeenth-Century Venice: The Creation of a Genre*, A Centennial Book (Berkeley: University of California Press, 1991), 362–77. Luigi Rossi's "Lagrime, dove sete" (from *Orfeo*, 1647) is a recitative lament with a concluding two-stanza canzonetta.

Ovid's *Heroïdes*, passed through late sixteenth-century imitators of the form (including Marino), and finally arrived in opera librettos generally and the lament form in particular.[105] Holzer does not mention, however, that, as with laments, the improvisation of love letters could be a social pastime, as emerges from Girolamo Bargagli's *Dialogo de' giuochi* (1572).[106] Unlike the lengthy tragic or heroic letters of the Ovidian tradition, *Scrivete* more closely follows Bargagli's advice that "love letters which by command must be dictated in companies [should be done] either in an affected way or be very witty and brief, and sometimes laconic and capricious."[107] The conceits of *Scrivete*, comparing the lover's face to paper and tears to ink, certainly qualify as "affected" and "witty," and the pun referring to the musical setting – "read, oh beautiful lady, the *notes* directed to you" – might generously be called "capricious."[108] If Melosio's poem is based on a classical genre, the style has certainly been adapted to the lighter taste of elite amusements.

The character of *Anima, che di foco* at first appears to conflict with such tastes, as it compares a lover's pain to the fires of hell. But the concluding passage of the poem is so overwrought – in both its syntax and, especially, its jumble of metaphors – that a parodic intent seems inescapable, especially in view of the last line:

Gelo, che mai si strugge;	Ice that never melts,
Fiamma, che non consuma:	flame that never consumes:
Sirti son di chi fugge	these are quicksands for whoever flees
Calma di libertà, sopra la spuma	the calm of liberty over the foam
Del vasto Egeo d'amore.	of the vast Aegean of love.
E chi, senza dolore	And whoever, without the pain
D'una giurata, e poi mentita fede,	of a promised and then betrayed faith,
Solca del cieco dio il golfo immenso;	sails the immense gulf of the blind god,
O non arde, o non crede, o non ha senso.	either does not burn, does not believe, or is out of his mind.

This lament too aims to leave its audience with a smile.

Beyond content, the very form of this group of poems contributes to the playful effect. While each presents a male complaint, none adopts the austere

---

[105] Holzer, "Music and Poetry," 272, 267–70.

[106] Crane, *Italian Social Customs*, 283, where he is summarizing material from Girolamo Bargagli, *Dialogo*, book 2, paragraphs 441–45 (pp. 214–15).

[107] Bargagli, *Dialogo*, paragraph 445 (p. 215). Translation adapted from Crane, *Italian Social Customs*, 283.

[108] Holzer ("Music and Poetry," 364–65) notes that Melosio was often criticized even during his lifetime for his fondness for extravagant wordplay, especially puns. Not uncommonly, his cantata texts refer directly to the interplay of music and poetry, as here (ibid., 400).

structure of the recitative lament, even to the degree seen in *Filli, per cui mi moro*. *Scrivete* perhaps comes closest, with two substantial passages of *versi sciolti*, but at the heart of that poem is a sixteen-line canzonetta in four quatrains that undermines the hegemony of recitative. In *Anima*, the balance is shifted even further, with canzonettas accounting for twelve of twenty-seven lines. In both poems, it seems, the author employs sufficient *versi sciolti* to gesture toward the recitative lament but allows the lyrical impulse to assume center stage.

And while that lyricism certainly mirrors the rising taste for arias evident in contemporary opera, it also seems tied – at least in chamber works – to a more playful ethos. For example, *Il tacer non fa per me* is the most lyrical of these three poems: with sixteen of twenty-four lines devoted to canzonetta text, the form owes nothing to the recitative lament. And this greater lyricism seems to cue greater verbal wit (or rather, the two features are linked). The refrain, "Being silent is not for me," itself bluntly pokes fun at the *silenzio* convention. That bluntness is underlined by the improbable euphony of "Su voci veloci" and "Dal core all'ardore" and, even more, by the ungainly reiteration of *tronco* rhymes that characterize the poem. Indeed, ten of the twenty-four lines use the same "-è" rhyme, with a remarkable three in a row at lines 18 to 20:

Rimedio si dia, si cerchi mercé;
Per chi copre il suo mal cura non v'è.
Il tacer non fa per me.

Such repetition is highly unusual in cantata poetry: in his anxiety, it seems, the speaker has briefly – and humorously – lost his creative self-control. As in all three of these texts, lyricism and wit seem to go hand in hand.

This same combination also characterizes *Io voglio esser infelice*, Atto's one text on the topic of *speranze bugiarde*. Fully thirty-one of the poem's forty-three lines are lyrical in character: an opening refrain stanza or *estriviglio* surrounds a longer stanza of *ottonari* (what Eleanor Caluori calls "envelope design") and eventually returns to round off the whole poem; the remaining verses consist of an eleven-line passage of *versi sciolti* and a two-stanza canzonetta in *senari*. Typically for this subject, the speaker curses his hopes: "I realize that in the sea of my tears, you are sirens, unfaithful seducers, and that quite often the cruel sweetness of your song kills." The ostensible seriousness of such statements is again belied by a playfulness of language – already suggested in the poem's first line – that sometimes even recalls the clever responses of verbal games. The paradoxical complaint, "I am left with nothing but the hope of not having hope" ("altro non m'avanza, / Che lo sperar di non aver speranza"), sounds a lot like the response of Guazzo's Signora Lelia above and would surely have struck its listeners as a desirable sort of play on conventional material.

Among the most lyrical of all Atto's texts are two of the most cheerful, both praising a lady's beauty: *S'io sapessi dipingere* and *Occhi miei belli*. Both poems take the form of simple canzonettas, in two and three stanzas respectively, and both seem particularly appropriate to the context of the *conversazione*.[109] In Guazzo's book 4, the characters consider in detail the power of praise in winning a lady. When members are asked to demonstrate this approach to the ladies present, one gentleman extemporizes a speech in prose, and another – more tellingly – reads a series of laudatory madrigals he had written beforehand.[110] A further variant of the "praising game" is the aforementioned case, again from Guazzo, of the professional singer who sings tributes to the hostess. Both these cantatas could fulfill such a function. In *S'io sapessi*, an artist-lover objects that only the stars are worthy to trace the image of his beloved and that Love himself has sculpted her on his heart. This last point, in fact, leads to a passage in which the poet exploits the double entendre of some words to signal a witty subtext of suffering and idolatry:

L'opra fu del suo strale;	The work was of his arrow;
altro che *Amore*	nothing but *Cupid/Love*
Non *travaglia* il mio core;	*shapes/afflicts* my heart;
…	…
Sì, sì; forza è di stella	Yes, yes; it is by means of a star
Idolatrando Amor cosa sì bella.	that *Cupid/Love makes an idol of/worships* something so beautiful.

The poet of *Occhi miei belli* accomplishes something similar through formal means. The first line of each of the poem's three stanzas states the subject of that stanza, creating a structure that encourages the listener to connect the three ideas. Thus, when "my beautiful eyes" and "[my] divine lips" are succeeded by "my dear bonds," the very construction of the poem clearly hints at the dangers beauty poses for a lover.

Opposed to the structural simplicity and lightness of these last two works is the poem *O quanto si dolea*, which treats the subject of *lontananza*. The

---

[109] Both poems, in fact, have some minor structural irregularities that complicate their forms: the two stanzas of *S'io sapessi* open with slightly different rhyme schemes (abba vs. abab), and, instead of the couplet that concludes the first two stanzas of *Occhi miei belli*, $a_{12}\ a_{11}$, the third stanza closes with three lines, $a_{11}\ b_7\ a_7$. None of these variants is sufficient, however, to alter the stanzaic character of these works.

[110] Guazzo, *La civil conversazione*, book 4, part 2, paragraphs 137–63 (pp. 307–12), as described in Crane, *Italian Social Customs*, 417–20.

author of *O quanto* is the aforementioned Sebastiano Baldini, who seems to have known Atto personally.[111] The poem is among the longest (sixty lines) and most elaborate Atto set, with three passages of *versi sciolti* preceding three canzonettas. A single refrain line, repeated just once, helps stitch the form together. In terms of content, the poem presents an ostensibly straight-forward treatment of its theme. The speaker defies both distance and time to heal his wounds of love, which he carefully guards. (Baldini titles the poem "Il costantissimo," "The Most Faithful Man.") The language of the text seems mostly serious, although the stumbling rhythm of a quatrain of

[111] The poem of this cantata appears independently among Baldini's papers in I Rvat, Chig. L.IV.94, ff. 338v–340. Unfortunately, I was unable to spend any time with this version, which contains changes in Baldini's hand, because the manuscript was removed indefinitely for preservation. The evidence for Atto's acquaintance with the poet includes the casual mention of Atto in one of Baldini's letters to Lorenzo Onofrio Colonna, from Venice, March 27 (or 29?), 1664 (I Rvat, Chig. L.VI.197, f. 91r): "[L]'aria a due è Bellissima … voglio mandarla a Cesti, e forse anche ad'Atto." Baldini also writes Atto's name, along with the names of several other singers, against certain portions of his poem *Il contrasto degli amanti* (I Rvat, Chig. L.VI.187, ff. 102–4v): apparently the poet conceived certain passages for specific singers. Finally, a poem about Atto appears in the Baldini manuscripts, although its authorship is uncertain. Flavia Cardinale (intro. to Morelli, ed., *Sebastiano Baldini*, 32) assumes it is Baldini's, even though the poem is not written in Baldini's hand and appears alongside a number of works not by him (Morelli, in fact, does not include this poem in the catalogue of Baldini's works). Still, some connection is probably indicated.

Al signor Atto Melani
1
All'hor ch'Atto sta cantando,
Nell'orecchie a gl'Uditori
Mille Gratie, mille Amori
Par che danzin festeggiando,
et i cori
fra quei piani, e fra quei forti,
Hora han vite, et hora han morti.
2
Quelle tremole gorghette,
Che per l'aria impennan l'ali
Nell'orecchie de mortali
Son d'amor tante saette.
Trionfali
Egli ha palme a tutte l'hore,
A ogni trillo acquista un core.
3
Ah che angelico è quel lusso,
C'ho in udir sì nobil canti.
Son quei labbri ciel notanti,
Donde piove un dolce influsso.
Tremolanti
N'escon voci armoniose,
Che son stelle in Ciel di rose.

versi sdruccioli (lines 45–48) and the rapid rhyme of three successive *quaternari* (lines 52–54) both temporarily undermine the gravity.

A noteworthy feature is the division of the text between two personae, a narrator and the male protagonist. Crescimbeni later characterized this combination of narrative and dramatic elements – absent in the preceding texts – as typical of the cantata in general.[112] But such a format also strongly recalls the *novelle* or story-telling entertainments that seem to have featured regularly in *conversazioni*. Indeed, in his treatise on games, Bargagli endorses such entertainments and specifies that

the one who's telling the story need not remain a simple narrator but sometimes, as if he were an actor, should speak in the character of each personage of the story ... Nor is it enough to say everything that one could say to persuade or move or frighten, but one must also accompany [the speech] with the voice, the gestures, and the pronunciation required to imitate the character in question.[113]

Such a practice seems reflected in these "semi-dramatic" cantata poems.

Perhaps the most interesting feature of *O quanto*, however, is its peculiar inconsistency of setting. While the generic pastoral name "Filli" ("Phyllis") suggests a standard Arcadian landscape, the reference in line 3 to the Tiber River complicates the issue. In this poem, it seems, the real and pastoral worlds interpenetrate. This literary gambit is not unusual for the era, and scholars have much discussed its significance with respect to other genres. Some have suggested that the intrigues and perils of life at court led to such a longing for utopian simplicity that writers conceived a hopeful merging of the two worlds. Others emphasize the artificiality of the Arcadian construct and so see pastoral writing as the natural product of urban culture. Still others have proposed that the linking of Arcadia to known landmarks – as in Honoré d'Urfé's *Astrée* – attempted to exploit an incipient sense of patriotism.[114]

But perhaps the most sophisticated reading, and ultimately the most convincing, suggests that the pastoral mode provided a conveniently oblique system of expression. Elizabeth C. Goldsmith has shown how Madame de

---

[112] Crescimbeni, *Commentarj*, 299–300, as quoted in Holzer, "Music and Poetry," 229n.

[113] Bargagli, *Dialogo*, book 2, paragraphs 489–90 (p. 225). I was led to this passage by Crane, *Italian Social Customs*, 283–84.

[114] On these various views, see Skrine, *The Baroque*, 42–49; Imbert, *La vita fiorentina*, 131–32; Elwert, *La poesia lirica*, 32–33, 38–39. See also José Antonio Maravall, *Culture of the Baroque: Analysis of a Historical Structure*, trans. Terry Cochran, Theory and History of Literature, vol. 25 (Minneapolis: University of Minnesota Press, 1986), 114, originally published as *La cultura del barroco: Un análisis de una estructura histórica*, Letras e ideas, maior, vol. 7 (Esplugues de Llobregat [Spain]: Editorial Ariel, 1975), who argues that the idealization of the countryside represented a reaction to the increased urbanization of society.

Sévigné used references to Arcadian characters in her letters to stand for real people: "by using fictive voices to communicate her own sentiments, Sévigné calls upon a literary frame to make a private anxiety into a more playful spectacle, and one which is less threatening."[115] A century earlier, Castiglione had already commented upon the frequent necessity of masking real feelings with figurative constructs: he remarks of his protagonists, for example, that, "under a variety of concealments, the participants often revealed their thoughts through allegories."[116] The incursion of Arcadia into the real world could be a sign of hidden messages, a veiled reality.

If that is true, one naturally wonders what message, if any, may lurk beneath the surface of *O quanto*. Here, of course, one can only speculate, but I think the indulgence is worthwhile. Atto is known to have mailed his cantatas to distant patrons in attempts to impress them, and certainly at different times some of the those patrons resided in Rome. Lines such as "he swore that no distance could ever make him lose his claim to faithfulness and constancy" sound not so different from the frequent protestations of loyalty that pepper his correspondence, as in the following example from Paris: "The greatest anxiety I have is finding myself deprived of Your Highness's most esteemed orders, on which depends all my happiness, for I long to make myself known – no less when nearby than when distant – as one of Your Highness's most devoted and faithful servants."[117] One could even push the conjecture further and consider who might have been a female patron of his in Rome at this time (although it is perhaps not certain that the counterpart of Filli need be a woman). By far the best prospect is Marie Mancini Colonna, who lived in Rome from 1661 to 1672. As seen in chapters 4 and 5, Atto was on intimate terms with Marie; she heard his cantatas on at least one documented occasion; and she seems to have remained Atto's confidante even later in life.[118] Further, although he joined her briefly in Rome in 1661 after both were forced to leave France, Atto resided from November of that year until May 1667 in Tuscany, "far from the lovely Tiber." (He did see her in Venice in the spring of 1664.) Finally, Baldini was himself well acquainted

---

[115] Elizabeth C. Goldsmith, *"Exclusive Conversations": The Art of Interaction in Seventeenth-Century France* (Philadelphia: University of Philadelphia Press, 1988), 128.

[116] Castiglione, *Il libro del cortegiano*, book 1, chapter 5 (p. 22). I was led to this quotation by Macy, "The Italian Madrigal," 4.

[117] Atto to Mattias, from Paris, April 27, 1657.

[118] On Marie hearing Atto's works, his letter to Duke Carlo II of Mantua, from Venice, March 12, 1664: "Vivo Impatientissimo di sapere, se quella Cantata che feci per V.A. è sortita di sua sodisfatione, perché haverei desiderato d'incontrare il gusto di V.A., così come ha piaciuto a Madama [Colonna], et a chi l'ha sentita." Marie and Atto seem to have corresponded virtually until his death. In one of Atto's letters to the French court, from Paris, March 27, 1701, he mentions receiving information on a particular issue from "Madama Colonna" (who was by that time living in Italy).

with the Colonnas, as his preserved letters to Marie's husband suggest.[119] Could Atto have appropriated Baldini's poem as an affirmation – couched in Arcadian language – of his continuing devotion to Marie? The possibility at least merits consideration.[120]

Atto's two other treatments of the *lontananza* theme both adopt the perspective of the wronged lady. *Fileno idolo mio* and *Sola tra le sue pene* share so many similarities, in fact, as to suggest a single author. In structure, both follow the pattern recitative–aria–recitative–aria, with a relatively balanced number of lines in each section: indeed, these two poems are formally the most forward-looking that Atto set, prefiguring the "RARA" structure that typified the cantata by the end of the century. The texts also exhibit similar verse patterns in their canzonettas, especially a six-line, ababcc form (*not* typical of eighteenth-century works). Both cantatas express a woman's sorrow at the distance of her lover, but the poems further share the conceit of the lover's eyes as the sun, which the lady calls back to her breast for a new dawn. Finally, the poetic diction of the two works corresponds. The emphasis on the sound of language and on verbal puns that was observed above in *Fileno* appears in *Sola* as well. The latter poem is filled with assonance in lines like "sovra corde sonore" and playful internal rhymes like "muove altrove" and "pensiero messagiero," but the climax arrives at the end of the piece, with an amusing play on the double meaning of *cara*: "And let stingy distance not deprive my eyes of a light so *dear/expensive*" ("E lontananza avara / Non tolga agli occhi miei luce sì *cara*").

The female perspective is also presented in *M'abbandona la sorte*, but in other ways this poem stands apart in Atto's oeuvre. Formally, the text is a simple canzonetta, in two stanzas of eight lines each. Based on preceding examples, one might expect this more lyrical structure to treat its subject of female abandonment with a lighter touch. Instead, the text appears thoroughly serious: "Fate abandons me and the stars [are] angered: made hostile, they hurl arrows of death against my unarmed breast. Full of anger, my heaven breathes thunderbolts, and truly abandoned, I am not guilty, but unfortunate." The lady implies that her lover (her "heaven") has abandoned her because of an alleged infidelity, which she denies. In fact, the lyricism of the poem's form is somewhat neutralized by its remarkable polymeter – $a_7 b_7$ $b_7 a_{11} c_4 c_8 d_7 d_{11}$ – as well as by its reliance on *settenari* and *endecasillabi*. No regular pattern of accents is established, even in the four- and eight-syllable

---

[119] See note 111 above.

[120] Some refinement of this conjecture might be possible when the Baldini manuscript again becomes available; his changes and marginalia sometimes contain clues to his thinking.

lines, and the irregular inflections of this canzonetta communicate a weight unusual for the genre and unique among Atto's works.[121]

Sebastiano Baldini's *La più dolente, e misera, che viva* seems at first an equally serious treatment of the same theme. The opening line suggests the hopeless outlook of the female protagonist, and the impression is confirmed by such rhetorically charged passages as the following:

And what have I done to you, O stars,
that you are so enraged against me,
so cruel and contrary,
so haughty and pitiless?
It is no great glory
to see the tears rain down from my eyes.

Although the poem never mentions a lover, one assumes a man as the source of the lady's suffering: the predominance of *versi sciolti* certainly evokes the lament tradition (much more clearly, for example, than does the form of *M'abbandona*).

Fortunately, a version of this poem is preserved among Baldini's papers, and it sheds an entirely different light on the text (appendix F, no. 6b).[122] In Baldini's copy, the poem carries a title and brief *argomento*: "*The Wretched Lady*: A very beautiful lady, being much distressed by various mishaps, gives voice to the following *recitativo*."[123] The reason for the lady's distress is finally revealed in a concluding narration, absent from Atto's version:

Thus spoke a nymph, rather, a goddess,
a goddess who, like Psyche,
because of Venus's jealousy, I think,
lived afflicted in this town and that [one]
because she was too beautiful for a mortal woman.

In the end, the lady's problem is not abandonment, but an impolitic excess of beauty. By delaying this revelation to the very last line, Baldini plays with the listener's expectations and of course drastically lightens the overall effect.

---

[121] The *ottonari* in both stanzas eschew the lilting trochaic meter typical of such lines. Line 6 presents an awkward juxtaposition of two accented syllables: "Il mio *ciel ful*mini spira"; the same effect, slightly softened, recurs in the corresponding line 14: "Pur m'opprima‿empia fortuna." See Holzer's discussion of the canzonetta as a serious genre, "Music and Poetry," 50–63. I do not find all his arguments in this section fully convincing: he occasionally conflates aspects of the canzonetta with those of the canzone, an undeniably serious genre.

[122] The poem appears in I Rvat, Chig. L.VI.187, ff. 28–29v.

[123] The use of the term *recitativo* is interesting, especially as the text includes canzonettas along with *versi sciolti*. Holzer, "Music and Poetry," 249–54, explains the varied use of this term as a genre designation at this time.

Baldini's version in fact raises a number of questions. What form of the text did Atto possess? If he in fact had something like Baldini's version, does his choice to eliminate the ending signify a desire for greater melodrama? Or could he assume that his audience (or some part of it) would know the full context of the poem and get the "joke," even if not made explicit? And did this poem refer to a specific person? I lack evidence to answer any of these questions, but for the last I would once again cautiously speculate that the "sventurata" could come from the Mancini family, this time perhaps Marie's sister Hortense. Both Hortense and Marie were widely regarded as among the most beautiful women in Europe; they also both became notorious for their public and private tribulations, often resulting from their own uncommonly independent behavior.[124] After Hortense fled her French husband in 1666 and wandered for a short period, she arrived in 1668 to live with her sister in Rome, where she stayed for four years. During this period, Atto in fact mentions Hortense (and her annoying lover) several times in his letters.[125] With both Baldini's and Atto's connections to the Mancini, one can perhaps read Baldini's text as a clever statement of sympathy for – or perhaps a satirical jab at – the "suffering" Hortense. Indeed, the Venus in this scenario could even be Marie, who, in exasperation, finally threw Hortense's lover out of the house.[126]

The last three of Atto's works depart strikingly in tone from the foregoing: instead of exploring some typically sorrowful aspect of love, they embody the more ironic ideals of Pelous's *amour galant*. In *A più sventure ancora*, *Ove tra sponde d'oro*, and *Tra sponde di smeraldo*, the traditional code of behavior is scorned in favor of insincerity and hedonism. According to Pelous, "between 1650 and 1670, statements that attack the timidity of lovers of ancient times become common currency; it is fashionable to mock their weepy slowness and the excessive submission that paralyzes them."[127] To register their derision, writers often adopted the literary forms and language of *amour*

---

[124] See, for example, Claude Dulong, *Marie Mancini: La première passion de Louis XIV* (Paris: Perrin, 1993), especially after Marie left her husband (187–372). A more chatty telling can be found in Bryan Bevan, *The Duchess Hortense: Cardinal Mazarin's Wanton Niece* (London: Rubicon Press, 1987).

[125] Atto records Hortense's arrival in Rome in his letter to Hugues de Lionne, from Rome, October 9, 1668, and further remarks, "Io la trovai bellissima al solito, e non maliconica, com'era stato supposto, ma allegra." He mentions Hortense's lover, Courbeville, in a series of letters to de Lionne from this period: October 16, 23, 30 and November 21. On October 23, he writes, "penso di sicuro che [lui] sia qualche Ministro fedele delle sue più interne passioni."

[126] Atto comments in his letter of October 30: "Disse però Madama Colonna a questo nuovo Orlando, che senza il riguardo della sorella, l'haverebbe fatto gettar dalle finestre." Dulong, *Marie Mancini*, 159–60, chronicles these incidents as well.

[127] Pelous, *Amour précieux*, 136.

tendre but in such a way as to ridicule its ideals.[128] This technique appears in all three of these works.

Both *Tra sponde di smeraldo* and *Ove tra sponde d'oro* play on the formal expectations of the recitative lament. Both begin with a long passage of *versi sciolti* in which a narrator prepares the listener for the man's outpouring of sorrow:

Tra sponde di smeraldo	*Ove tra sponde d'oro*
Between banks of emerald	Where, between banks of gold,
was running, with silvery foot,	the sand imprisoned the Ganges of India,
a noisy brook, sprung from an old rock,	having grasped the white hand
where a betrayed lover	of charming Cloris,
presented his harsh lament.	the loving sailor held her there with him;
	and showing harsh pain in his countenance,
	he said, his heart speaking through his lips:

In *Ove tra*, the lover then begins a conventional comparison between the ever-refreshed beauties of Cloris and the daily renewal of the sun. But in the last two lines of the passage he turns the comparison on its head: "if from your beautiful face the day one day departs, it will never again return." He then launches into a vigorously rhythmic canzonetta in *senari* that serves as the poem's refrain: "Oh cease such harshness, severe, proud, and haughty woman: your beauty is not eternal, nor is my pain." The remainder of the mostly lyrical text continues to develop this theme, arguing that Cloris should yield to the man's advances while she is still desirable.

In *Tra sponde di smeraldo*, the pretense of the lament is maintained much longer, in terms of both form and sense. Indeed the poem is structurally akin to *Filli, per cui mi moro*, with its long series of *versi sciolti* and single brief canzonetta; *Tra sponde* even employs a refrain line, like the standard lament. For thirty-one lines, the complaint remains serious, touching on the usual *lagrime*, *tormento*, *martire*, *dolore*, and *morte*, and the lover finishes on the verge of drowning himself in a stream. But at this point, the stream itself – the third character to speak – stops him and delivers the punch line: "Stop! Every mistress, like my waves, is inconstant." As in Baldini's version of *La più dolente*, this last-minute reversal transforms the tone of the entire poem from serious to ironic.

Perhaps the most extreme manifestation of this tactic may be found in *A più sventure ancora*, another particularly interesting text. The theme is the *donna abbandonata*, and here the parallels to the Dido story are made

---

[128] Ibid., 153–55.

explicit: as if referring to Aeneas, the lady complains, "Fortune and Fate require the faithless lover to depart"; later, the narrator reports that the lady, "driven by pain, on the nearby sand, was in the embrace of death, abandoned." But at that moment, instead of expiring, "so much rage arose in her that, out of spite, she did not turn to her death." The narrator then closes with a series of *galant* morals, concluding that "people in love say they want to die, but then repent." Ridiculing the Dido story – such a classic expression of love – only intensifies the satirical message of this sort of poem. Further, like *O quanto si dolea*, this text hints at a personal reference, as again the Tiber River inhabits the same realm as an Arcadian shepherd (Fileno). And again, perhaps, the hidden addressee could be Marie Mancini Colonna. Sometime in 1665 Marie became aware of her husband's infidelity; at about the same time, she broke off marital relations with him, in a much-publicized *separazione di letto*.[129] While the second event may or may not have resulted from the first, the line, "Learn to leave, constant lovers, whoever abandons you" seems almost prophetic of Marie's eventual flight from Rome and her husband (in 1672).[130] At the very least, Marie, raised in the *galant* atmosphere of the French court, would have been able to appreciate the cynical outlook of *A più sventure ancora*.

In fashionable melic forms, these texts of Atto's cantatas treat the very subject – love – that dominated private aristocratic leisure and even academic debate. The variety of perspectives and themes represented reflects contemporary thinking and writing on the subject, and nearly all of the texts demonstrate the taste for wit that characterizes the era. Anthony Newcomb writes that, at the end of the sixteenth century, "the qualities expected in a professional male solo singer" included that he be "not only a musician but a wit and conversationalist … [existing] somewhere between the courtier and the professional musician."[131] These poems show how, in the seventeenth century, the cantata could constitute an effective contribution for such a musical "conversationalist," especially if some works concealed personal messages. By accompanying these texts into the chamber – either in person or in spirit – Atto could appropriate something of their aura and demonstrate his stylish tastes. Of course, his primary contribution to the artwork remained the music. And so I turn now to investigate that crucial element in both its technical and significative aspects.

---

[129] Dulong, *Marie Mancini*, 154–57.
[130] For the latest thinking on Marie's rationale, see *ibid.*, 149–86; in the end, Marie may well have feared for her life.
[131] Newcomb, *The Madrigal at Ferrara*, 47.

The cantatas of Atto Melani: Music

Any attempt to locate "fashionability" in music requires audience members sensitive to musical styles and techniques, what Margaret Murata calls "historical acute listeners."[132] I have already shown, of course, that a number of Atto's patrons fall into this category, and others may have possessed similar literacy, like Mattias de' Medici and Jules Mazarin, who spent so much time and money procuring the best singers and newest pieces. Certainly music – along with many of the other arts – figured in the education of most aristocrats from this period.[133] And some of them showed a remarkable alertness to style. Duke Carlo II of Mantua, for example, favored "a certain naturalness" in his cantatas, disliking the artifices he associated with ecclesiastical music.[134] And, later in the century, Grand Prince Ferdinando de' Medici too implored his composer, Alessandro Scarlatti, to use less learned techniques.[135] Such astute patrons surely perceived a great deal about the music they heard and would have favored settings they found tasteful and fashionable.

Determining just which musical traits might have registered as "fashionable" is of course a big challenge. One might reasonably suppose, however, that such traits would have mirrored characteristics of other elite pastimes. As we have seen, the qualities of newness and surprise were particularly esteemed, especially when they could be forged out of familiar materials. Marino himself encouraged poets to "titillate the ears of the reader with the whimsy [*bizzarria*] of novelty," for which the most important guideline was "to know how to break the rules at the proper time and place."[136] I believe that the cantata – in its music as much as its poetry (and perhaps, most of all, in the relationship between the two) – aspired to an effect of *bizzarria* or

---

[132] Margaret Murata, "Scylla and Charybdis, or Steering between Form and Social Context in the Seventeenth Century," in *Explorations in Music, the Arts, and Ideas: Essays in Honor of Leonard B. Meyer*, ed. Eugene Narmour and Ruth A. Solie, Festschrift Series, no. 7 (Stuyvesant, N.Y.: Pendragon Press, 1988): 82–83. Murata uses this expression several times to refer to musicians; in this article she does not grant this status to patrons.

[133] See Stefano Lorenzetti, "'Per animare agli esercizi nobili': Esperienza musicale e identità nobiliare nei collegi di educazione," *Quaderni storici*, vol. 32, no. 95 (August 1997): 441–50.

[134] Besutti, "Produzione," 141, 142, 145.

[135] Edward J. Dent, *Alessandro Scarlatti: His Life and Works*, 2nd edn. (London: Edward Arnold, 1960), 102–3.

[136] The first quote is taken from Franco Valsecchi, *L'Italia nel Seicento e nel Settecento*, vol. VI of *Società e costume: Panorama di storia sociale e tecnologica* (Turin: U.T.E.T., 1967), 538, where no citation is given. The second comes from Giambattista Marino's letter to Girolamo Preti, from Naples, summer 1624, published in Marino's *Epistolario, seguito da lettere di altri scrittori del Seicento*, ed. Angelo Borzelli and Fausto Nicolini (Bari: Gius. Laterza & Figli, 1911–12), II:55, as quoted in Asor Rosa, *La lirica*, 6.

imaginative surprise, and this effect would have reflected well on the artistic and intellectual life of its patrons.

How can such *bizzarria* be defined? To recognize a breach of norms, one must first define those norms, the "rules" that could be broken. I will contend below that, for Atto, the governing practice was the musical style of Luigi Rossi and his circle. Not surprisingly, Atto took as his starting point the approach of the most esteemed composer of vocal chamber music at the time, and someone he knew personally. With this baseline, Atto's personal style becomes perceptible, a style that in many ways seems to reflect his specific circumstances. On the one hand, he employs some compositional devices so consistently as to suggest the limited imagination of a part-time composer, someone whose primary interests lay elsewhere. But, on the other hand, Atto's frequent and complex experimentation, particularly in the area of form, suggests a more serious artist, in pursuit of novelty. These formulaic and experimental aspects seem to converge in Atto's concern for communicating the sense of his texts: if his patrons appreciated literature, Atto made sure his music supported its effects. Indeed, in its textually oriented blend of conventional and innovative techniques, Atto's cantata style seems virtually a reflection of its intended social milieu, the aristocratic *conversazione*.

In his correspondence, Atto shows that he was familiar with many of the most prominent Italian composers of his period. After his exposure to the music of Rossi and Pasqualini at Rossi's "academies" in 1644, Atto's relationship to these two men continued for several years at least, as they all found themselves serving together at the French court. In Innsbruck in 1653, if not before, Atto came to know the music of Cesti, admiring it, even if he disliked the man himself. And he reserved some of his highest praise for the operas of Cavalli, works he performed at several points during his career (see chapters 2 and 3). Further, Atto surely knew his brother Jacopo's largely operatic output, as well as the works of a number of less prominent composers of his acquaintance, including Domenico Anglesi, Antonio Maria Viviani, and Lelio Colista.[137] Atto also consciously distinguished between opera and cantata styles: as the celebrations for Louis XIV's wedding were being prepared, he observed, "the works of Signor Cavalli are as yet more pleasing for the theater than the chamber, and there have been no great miracles from these new *virtuosi* [that Cavalli brought from Venice] because here

---

[137] Anglesi and Viviani are mentioned in chapter 3. Atto's familiarity with Colista is evidenced in a series of letters to Mattias, from Rome, in the fall of 1655 (October 2, 23; November 13, 20; December 4, 1655) in which Atto reports on attempts to procure his patron a good archlute. Colista apparently helped Atto assess the quality of the instruments.

[the patrons] have good taste and are used to hearing good singing."[138] Apparently the Venetians, so expert in opera, did not succeed so well in private.

Given Atto's experience and interests, an astonishing omission from his correspondence is the name of Giacomo Carissimi, one of the most renowned composers of the century. Atto's interactions with the Barberini and Chigi families, as well as with Queen Christina of Sweden, certainly placed him in the same orbit. Yet, as David Burrows has suggested, Carissimi seems often to have stood apart from other musicians: "Carissimi alone of his generation was not referred to familiarly [in manuscripts], and this seems to bespeak an aloofness from the Rossi circle that was, in fact, musical, as well as personal."[139] Indeed, a number of scholars have identified a fundamental stylistic division within the Roman cantata "school" between the Rossian composers – including Pasqualini and Mario Savioni – and Carissimi (and to a certain extent, Cesti).[140] A number of traits separate the styles of the two camps, but confirming Atto's loyalties requires consideration of only a few key differences.

Already in 1914, Schmitz distinguished between Rossi's contrasting recitative and aria styles and Carissimi's tendency to blend the two in a prevailing arioso.[141] Rose reaffirmed this difference in her studies of the composer, citing as Carissimi's hallmark "the similarity of [recitative and aria] styles, coupled with the smooth merging of recitative and arioso, arioso and aria."[142] A work like his *Sempre m'affligo più* well illustrates this quality: as can be seen in the schematic of table 6.2, Carissimi largely reverses reigning stylistic conventions, setting the *versi sciolti* of the refrain in aria style and the more lyrical *ottonari* as recitatives, though with an unusual degree of text repetition.[143] By contrast, Rossi tends to keep his recitative and aria styles more distinct and to observe more consistently the implications of the poetry.

Another difference between the two approaches, previously little noted, concerns musical development. Characteristic of both Carissimi's and Cesti's

---

[138] Atto to Mattias, from Paris, September 3, 1660. Earlier in the letter, Atto refers to "questi virtuosi forastieri che ha condotti il signor Cavalli da Venezia."

[139] David L. Burrows, "The Cantatas of Antonio Cesti" (Ph.D. diss., Brandeis Univ., 1961), 7.

[140] Ibid. Later (93–94), Burrows admits that Cesti's style mixes elements from both Rossi and Carissimi. Rose ("The Cantatas of Carissimi," 151) notes that some of Carissimi's style traits distinguish him from virtually all other Roman cantata composers.

[141] Schmitz, *Geschichte*, 93 and 88.

[142] Rose, "The Cantatas of Giacomo Carissimi," 215.

[143] The somewhat loose rhyme scheme of the *ottonari* sections may help explain the recitative setting, but in a work like *Ove fuggi, o mia speranza*, Carissimi shows that he sometimes did set similar sections (e.g., a_8 b_8 b_8 a_8 c_8 d_8 d_8 e_8) in aria style. He simply pays less attention to poetic cues than many of his contemporaries. On these cues, see Gianturco, "The Italian Seventeenth-Century Cantata," *passim*.

Table 6.2 *A schematic of* Sempre m'affliggo più, *as set by*
Giacomo Carissimi

Time signature[a]		Poetic form	
A° C $\frac{6}{4}$	Sempre m'affliggo più	**A**	**7t**
	In pensar che mia fede,	**b**	**7**
	Priva d'ogni mercede,	**b**	**7**
	Vuol ch'io pianga e languisca in servitù.	**a**	**11t**
	Sempre m'affliggo più.	**A**	**7t**
R	Io non chiedo al duolo aita,	c	8
	Io non bramo altro che morte	d	8
	E non vuol l'iniqua sorte	d	8
	Ch'il mio cor esca di vita.	c	8
	Dentro al fianco aspra ferita	c	8
	Mi stampò d'amor lo strale	e	8
	Ma però non è mortale,	e	8
	Ché d'un misero la piaga	f	8
	Nunzia di pene e non di morte fu.	a	11t
A° C $\frac{6}{4}$	Sempre m'affliggo più	**A**	**7t**
	In pensar che mia fede,	**b**	**7**
	Priva d'ogni mercede,	**b**	**7**
	Vuol ch'io pianga e languisca in servitù.	**a**	**11t**
	Sempre m'affliggo più.	**A**	**7t**
R	Mi rammento del gran pianto	g	8
	Che già sparse Eco sovente	h	8
	Né conforto la dolente	h	8
	D'impetrar si diede vanto.	g	8
	Tal memoria – ahi quanto, ahi quanto!	g	8
	Rende grave il mio dolore	i	8
	Mentre veggio ch'in amore	i	8
	Una intrepida costanza	j	8
	Di ritrovar pietà non ha virtù[.]	a	11t
A° C $\frac{6}{4}$	Sempre m'affliggo più	**A**	**7t**
	In pensar che mia fede,	**b**	**7**
	Priva d'ogni mercede,	**b**	**7**
	Vuol ch'io pianga e languisca in servitù.	**a**	**11t**
	Sempre m'affliggo più.	**A**	**7t**

[a] The non-standard symbols used in this table and the following may be translated as
follows:
A: aria style in aria form (time signature follows)
A°: aria style in arioso form (time signature follows)
R: recitative (the time signature is always C)

style is the process I call "block sequential repetition." In it, an entire passage, normally consisting of more than one phrase, is repeated exactly at another pitch level, usually a perfect fourth or fifth away.[144] This practice differs somewhat from Carissimi's widely recognized penchant for initiating a passage with a phrase immediately subjected to sequence, a rhetorical *exordium*.[145] Block sequential repetition involves a longer span and normally occurs in the concluding B section of an aria in standard ABB′ form: where a Rossian composer develops preceding material with small-scale segmentation, sequences, or other elaboration, Carissimi and Cesti usually just repeat the B material on a different tonal plane (see below for an example). The music of Rossi's circle, as Irving Eisley puts it, "does not yet wholly create its designs upon the structural foundations of contrasting stable tonal areas," whereas Carissimi and Cesti often indeed do employ such areas as a means of compositional elaboration.[146] I do not mean to suggest that block sequential repetition is wholly absent from Rossian works, but it rarely plays the vital role that it does with Carissimi and Cesti.

In addition to these two general stylistic differences, a smaller, "fingerprint" trait also seems to divide the two schools: Rossi and his followers employ a particular rhythmic device that I have never observed in Carissimi's cantatas.[147] Occasionally, in triple-meter passages, Rossian composers will interject one or more quadruple bars, writing a small numeral "4" above the middle of each affected measure. A good example can be seen in the aria "Amo Filli" from Rossi's *E che cantar poss'io* (figure 6.1). Here, as in most cases, the technique seems aimed to increase the metrical complexity of a triple-meter passage that might otherwise be quite regular: indeed, Rossi's

---

[144] William Holmes notes throughout his study of Cesti's *Orontea* the regularity of this practice in Cesti's style, although he gives it no special name: William Carl Holmes, "*Orontea*: A Study of Change and Development in the Libretto and the Music of Mid-Seventeenth-Century Italian Opera" (Ph.D. diss., Columbia Univ., 1968), 155, 180, 184. While Carissimi's practice of sequencing the opening phrase of a cantata has been much remarked (see next note), his use of real block sequential repetition has not. Both Caluori (*The Cantatas of Luigi Rossi*, 67) and Holzer ("Music and Poetry," 157) observe that the exact transposition of passages becomes an important compositional procedure by mid-century, although they do not distinguish between the practices of the circles around Rossi and Carissimi.

[145] Rose, "The Cantatas of Giacomo Carissimi," 212.

[146] Irving Robert Eisley, "The Secular Cantatas of Mario Savioni (1608–85)" (Ph.D. diss., University of California, Los Angeles, 1964), 149. Although Eisley is here speaking specifically of Savioni's music, he had previously agreed with Prunières's assessment of Savioni as a member of Rossi's "entourage" (55; citing Prunières, *L'opéra italien en France avant Lulli*, Bibliothèque de l'Institut Français de Florence [Université de Grenoble], ser. 1, Collection d'histoire et de linguistique française et italienne comparées, no. 3 [Paris: Honoré Champion, 1913], 46). Study of the works of the two composers seems to confirm that assessment.

[147] It does, however, occur in Cesti's cantatas.

Figure 6.1 The aria "Amo Filli" from *E che cantar poss'io* by Luigi Rossi

mixture of triple, quadruple, and hemiola measures in this aria creates moments of significant metrical ambiguity.

On the basis of these traits, then, one can confidently assign Atto's cantatas to the Rossian camp. Indeed, a comparison of Atto's *Scrivete, occhi dolenti* to a setting of the same text by Carissimi conveniently illustrates the affiliation.[148] Table 6.3 provides a schematic comparison of the opening of both works. It shows that while Atto throughout follows the traditional implications of the text in his choice of styles, Carissimi typically converts a

[148] Holzer ("Music and Poetry," 402–5) brings these concordant settings to light but makes only brief comparative remarks. *Scrivete* is the only text set by Atto for which a concordance is known. (The variances between the two versions of the poem are minor.)

Table 6.3 *A comparative schematic of the settings of* Scrivete, occhi dolenti *by Giacomo Carissimi and Atto Melani*

Carissimi Time sign.	Atto Melani Time sign.		Poetic form	
A^o C	R	Scrivete, occhi dolenti,	a	7
$A^o \frac{3}{2}$		Con inchiostro di pianto	b	7
		Sul foglio del mio volto i vostri affanni.	c	11
		Narrate i miei tormenti,	a	7
		Registrate i miei danni;	c	7
		E dite a chi no' l' crede,	d	7
	A^o C	Ch'amar tacendo ogni martire eccede.	d	11
R	R	Per un ciglio amoroso,	e	7
		Che piace ma saetta;	f	7
		Per un labbro vezoso,	e	7
		Ch'uccide, ma diletta;	f	7
		Per un seno di neve,	g	7
		Che mirar non si può senza adorarlo:	h	11
$A^o \frac{3}{2}$	$A^o \frac{3}{4}$	Ardo, piango, sospiro; e pur non parlo.	h	11
R	R	Sì, sì, tacia la lingua;	i	7
		Ma favellino i lumi.	j	7
		Dolor, tu detta i carmi; Amor, coreggi;	k	11
	A^o C	Occhi, scrivete: e tu mia vita, leggi.	k	11
A C	$A \frac{3}{8}$	Se il mio cor non sa ridire	l	8
		La caggion, che l'arde tanto;	m	8
		A caratteri di pianto	m	8
		Farò noto il mio morire.	l	8
		Segnarò per tutti i lidi	n	8
		La beltà, che m'inamora;	o	8
		E sapran l'arene ancora,	o	8
		Che tu sol, bella, m'uccidi.	n	8
		Ogni amante leggerà	p	8t
		Quest'epilogo d'amore,	q	8
		Ch'io sospiro a tutte l'ore	q	8
		La perduta libertà.	p	8t
		E perché mia vita langue,	r	8
		Chiudo il foglio sventurato;	s	8
		Sottoscritto dal mio fato,	s	8
		Sigillato col mio sangue.	r	8
R	R	Leggi, deh leggi, o bella,	t	7
		Le note a te dirette;	u	7
		E se qualche pietà nel seno ascondi,	v	11
		Con un muto rescritto	w	7
$A^o \frac{3}{2}$	$A^o \frac{3}{4}$	O di vita o di morte almen rispondi!	v	11

Figure 6.2 The aria "Ardo piango" from *Scrivete, occhi dolenti* by Giacomo Carissimi

large section of the opening *versi sciolti* into a pseudo-aria. Another telling difference appears in the two composers' settings of the single hendecasyllable "Ardo, piango, sospiro; e pur non parlo." Carissimi employs his standard block sequential repetition (figure 6.2), the first statement in G minor at measures 64–71 being immediately duplicated in C minor (followed then by

Figure 6.3 The aria "Ardo piango" from *Scrivete, occhi dolenti* by Atto Melani

a final cadence to B-flat major). At first glance, Atto's setting (figure 6.3) might seem to follow the same pattern, since the second statement of the text repeats the opening melodic contour of the first at the distance of a perfect fifth. But whereas the first phrase remains in F minor, the second modulates from C minor to G minor and is then followed by a third statement that moves from E-flat major back to C minor.[149] Although each of these three phrases begins similarly, they conclude with different melodic material and

---

[149] Here and in the discussion that follows, I use a standard (Ramellian) tonal vocabulary to describe harmonic language. I do not mean to suggest that mid-*Seicento* composers thought of their music in these terms. But the analytical tools that may serve slightly earlier repertories – e.g., modal theory and attention to mollis–durus harmonic shifts – seem of little relevance to this music, at least for the features I wish to describe. The same may be said for theories of "church

harmonic motion. This strategy of varying repetitions is much more typically Russian.[150] It seems obvious, then, that Atto's youthful studies with Rossi and Pasqualini permanently influenced his compositional style.

Viewed against his Rossian heritage, Atto's more personal idiosyncrasies begin to emerge. As suggested above, an important aspect of his style is the almost formulaic use of certain compositional gestures. One of the most striking is the descending tetrachord employed as a structural device, particularly as the opening gambit of a section. The effect can be found in many of his cantatas, in both recitatives and arias, but *Fileno, idolo mio* offers a clear example. The first two lines of this cantata are written over a bass that slowly descends in stepwise motion from tonic to dominant in the minor mode, concluding with the expected Phrygian cadence to V (figure 6.4a). The third recitative, at "Sol'indarno il mio cor," is set the same way (figure 6.4c), while the entire text of the second recit, "Ahi, che tardi Fileno?" is set to two statements – in G minor and A minor, respectively – of an abbreviated form of the tetrachord, lacking the seventh degree (figure 6.4b). The first phrase of the triple-meter passage "Vieni mio sol, sì, sì" also employs a descending tetrachord figure (figure 6.4d), as do the first two phrases of the triple-meter arioso, "Dentro coppa di rose" (figure 6.4e).

Of course, Ellen Rosand has drawn much attention to the descending tetrachord and its association with laments in Venetian opera.[151] Atto's usage, however, often appears to lack affective implications: the pattern serves purely as a structural component. In this cantata, for example, the second recitative and arioso are dominated by the tetrachord but express a hopeful, even erotic sentiment:

Ah, why do you delay, Fileno?
This breast awaits you,
which constantly prepares for you charms and pleasures;
Come, and taste on my lips, O my beloved,
the honey of love in a cup of roses.[152]

---

keys." The short, cadence-oriented phrases that typify the mid-*Seicento* usually do deploy harmonies in recognizably tonal ways, at least in the short range. And the few anomalies that appear are explained no better by any of the earlier systems than by the method I have chosen. On those earlier techniques, see especially Eric Chafe, *Monteverdi's Tonal Language* (New York: Schirmer, 1992); Gregory Barnett, "Modal Theory, Church Keys, and the Sonata at the End of the Seventeenth Century," *Journal of the American Musicological Society* 51 (1998): 245–81.

[150] Although Atto does not use the "4" sign in this particular cantata, he does employ it elsewhere in his works: e.g., *Io voglio esser infelice*, mm. 60, 63, 66; and *O quanto si dolea*, mm. 21, 28. See Atto Melani, *Complete Cantatas*, 25–26, 42.

[151] Ellen Rosand, "The Descending Tetrachord: An Emblem of Lament," *Musical Quarterly* 55 (1979): 346–59; and Rosand, *Opera in Seventeenth-Century Venice*, 369–77.

[152] Rosand also notes the sometimes erotic implications of the descending tetrachord ("Descending Tetrachord," 353n). But, as the next examples suggest, the point here is the rather haphazard variety of affects for which Atto employs the pattern.

Figure 6.4a The opening of *Fileno, idolo mio*

Figure 6.4b The recitative "Ahi, che tardi Fileno?" from *Fileno, idolo mio*

Figure 6.4c The recitative "Sol'indarno il mio cor" from *Fileno, idolo mio*

Figure 6.4d The opening of the aria "Vieni mio sol, sì, sì" from *Fileno, idolo mio*

Figure 6.4e The opening of the aria "Dentro coppa di rose" from *Fileno, idolo mio*

Elsewhere, as in the aria "Numi cieli" of *A più sventure*, the mood is more rhetorical and tragic: "Gods, heavens, spheres, stars, you who shine down on my wrongs." Indeed, the variety of texts set to the tetrachord is great, and table 6.4, which lists all movements that begin with the figure, reveals the extent of Atto's usage. He likely inherited this practice from the composers of Rossi's circle, for, unlike Carissimi or Cesti, the Rossians do periodically employ the tetrachord, if not as extensively as Atto. For him, one gets the feeling that the tetrachord offered a ready-made compositional unit, attractive, perhaps, because its strong harmonic motion never failed to generate a successful opening.

As noted, the ABB' design served as a common aria form in the seventeenth century. Atto too followed this pattern, but the details of his approach to it are consistent enough to suggest another personal formula. Table 6.5 shows a schematic of the aria "Lumi rei" (from *Filli, per cui mi moro*) that illustrates Atto's paradigm (the score appears in figure 6.5). I call it his "quatrain form" because he normally employs the pattern with a four-line aria text. One of the characteristic features of his approach is the avoidance of an authentic cadence until after all four lines of text have been presented. The midpoint of the quatrain (the end of the A section) is often punctuated with a less conclusive Phrygian cadence to the dominant of the home key.[153] The second two lines of text (the B section) then normally modulate, so that the first full cadence occurs in a contrasting tonal area. In minor keys, the goal is

---

[153] The location of this intermediate Phrygian cadence is somewhat variable according to the syntax of the text. For a contemporary presentation of a hierarchy of cadence types, see Lorenzo Penna, *Li primi albori musicali*, Bibliotheca musica bononiensis, sezione 2, no. 38 (Bologna: Arnaldo Forni, 1996; rpt. of Bologna: Giacomo Monti, 1684), 173–83.

Table 6.4 *Occurrences of the descending tetrachord at the beginning of movements in Atto's cantatas*

Cantata	Section begins	Style
Anima, che di foco	E chi, senza dolore	recit.
A più sventure ancora	A più sventure ancora	aria
	Numi, cieli	aria
Fileno, idolo mio	Fileno, idolo mio	recit.
	Vieni sol, che sol'adoro	aria
	Ahi, che tardi Fileno	recit.
	Sol'indarno	recit.
Il tacer non fa per me	Il tacer non fa per me	aria
	Nacque nel seno mio	recit.
Io voglio esser infelice	Io voglio esser infelice	aria
	Ah, speranze bugiarde	recit.
O quanto si dolea	O quanto si dolea	recit.
	Sieno pur tuoi rimedi	recit.
	Io so, che ben tu puoi	recit.
Ove, tra sponde d'oro	Ove, tra sponde d'oro	recit.
Scrivete, occhi dolenti	Scrivete, occhi dolenti	recit.
Tra sponde di smeraldo	Tra sponde di smeraldo	recit.

Table 6.5 *A schematic of "Lumi rei," from Atto's* Filli, per cui mi moro

Textual line	Cadence type[a]	Cadence point (in f)
1	2–1	C
2	P	V/f
3	7–1	f
4	X	c
3′	X	f
3′	X	b♭
4	X	b♭
3′	X	f
4	X	f
4	X	f
ritorn.	X	f

Source: Atto Melani, *Complete Cantatas*, ed. Roger Freitas, Collegium Musicum Yale University, series 2, vol. 15 (Middleton, Wis.: A-R Editions, 2006), 16–17.

[a] The cadential symbols used in this and the following tables may be translated as follows:

X: an authentic cadence

P: a Phrygian cadence

1/2: a half-cadence, with the bass moving from the first to fifth scale degrees

2–1: a dominant–tonic cadence in which the bass line progresses from the second to first scale degrees (resulting in V_4^6 [or $\frac{4}{3}$] to I)

7–1: a dominant–tonic cadence in which the bass lines progresses from the seventh to first scale degrees (resulting in V^6 to I)

Figure 6.5 The aria "Lumi rei" from *Filli, per cui mi moro*

usually the minor dominant or relative major, and in major keys, the dominant. This cadence is followed by the B section, typically composed to repetitions of the latter two textual lines. In Atto's practice, this closing material is often more motivic in character than the opening, as the case of "Lumi rei" again illustrates.

Figure 6.5 (cont.)

Può mi - rar - vi, e non__ lan - gui - re, Può mi - rar - vi, e

non__ lan - gui - re.

In fact, the specifics of Atto's quatrain form are not generally shared by his contemporaries. Instead, the cadential structures of their arias appear to vary much more frequently and to a greater degree. Tables 6.6a and 6.6b present schematics of two arias arbitrarily chosen from among Pasqualini's works. In "Cieco dio," full cadences on the tonic and minor dominant occur already at the end of the first and second lines respectively, while the quatrain closes with a cadence on the tonic; in "Io lo so," a full cadence on the subdominant occurs after the second line, which is then repeated with another full cadence on the tonic. Similarly, the opening quatrain of Rossi's *Se non corre una speranza* is given a full cadence at the end of its second, third, and fourth lines, on tonic and minor dominant (table 6.6c). These approaches are sufficiently different from Atto's usual practice, and from each other, as to support the formulaic character of Atto's usage.

The rationale behind Atto's quatrain form is not immediately apparent. Certainly, just by having a set model, the busy courtier freed himself from devising a new approach each time. But the clear division in this form between the initial straightforward declamation and the ensuing musical development may also have appealed to Atto's concern for the poetry (to be considered below). In any case, his predilection for the form is amply demonstrated by table 6.7, which records all of the arias that begin with it. I have included only those pieces that stick closely to the paradigm as I have described it: several others diverge slightly but are still guided by the model. As with the descending tetrachord, Atto seems to have followed a sort of recipe to open his arias.

Table 6.6a *A schematic of "Cieco dio" from Marc'Antonio*
Pasqualini's Sì, ch'io voglio languire

Textual line	Cadence type	Cadence point (in e)
1	X	e
2	X	b
3	1/2	V/e
4	X	e
3		
4a	1/2	V/e
4	X	e
4	X	e

Source: Marc'Antonio Pasqualini, *Cantatas by Marc'Antonio Pasqualini*
1614–1691, vol. 3 of *The Italian Cantata in the Seventeenth Century*, ed.
Margaret Murata (New York and London: Garland Publishing, 1985), 64–65.

Table 6.6b *A schematic of "Io lo so, che'l duol sopporto"*
from Marc'Antonio Pasqualini's Un infelice core

Textual line	Cadence type	Cadence point (in b)
1	P	V/e
2	X X	e b
3	P	V/G
4	X	e
4	X	E
3	X	b
4	X	b
4	X	b
ritorn.	X	b

Source: Marc'Antonio Pasqualini, *Cantatas*, 141–42.

Table 6.6c *A schematic of the opening aria of Luigi*
Rossi's Se non corre una speranza

Textual line	Cadence type	Cadence point (in g)
1		
2	X	g
3	X	d
4	X	d
4	X	B♭
3	X	g
4	X	g

Source: Luigi Rossi, *Cantatas*, 51.

Table 6.7 *Occurrences of the "quatrain form" in Atto's arias*

Cantata	Aria begins
A più sventure ancora	Numi, cieli
Fileno, idolo mio	Vieni sol, che sol'adoro
	Or dell'alba i vaghi rai
Filli, per cui mi moro	Lumi rei del mio morire
La più dolente, e misera, che viva	Da chi spero aver pietà
O quanto si dolea	Il pensier dispiega il volo
	Se, col tempo insuperabile
S'io sapessi dipingere	S'io sapessi dipingere
Tra sponde di smeraldo	Ma, se vuol crudo destino

Atto's penchant for formulas can also be seen in the recurrence of musical material in different cantatas. Of course, the broad melodic, harmonic, and rhythmic practices around mid-century were so widely shared as to constitute a common language: Murata suggests that "those materials that cross from aria to aria or move from opera to opera are the oral, or aural, elements of musical style and performance."[154] I am concerned here not with the general resemblance of many musical gestures, but rather with more exact motivic duplication. In her study of Rossi's works, Caluori records just such recurrent material, which she calls "migrating themes."[155] Although Atto's motives match none of Rossi's, the young singer may well have inherited, along with the rest of Rossi's methods, the idea of reusing particularly successful musical ingredients.

At least two passages appear to have been favorites. The first is shown in its three incarnations in figure 6.6. In essence, it is a descending sequence of $^4_2$–$^6_3$ progressions under a melody that traces the upper chord tone signified by those figures. That this passage is used to set three very different texts suggests its expressive neutrality: "let us talk no more of life"; "with [Time's] wings my sparks catch fire"; and "thus the shadows disappear." The sequential character of the configuration simply makes it useful to Atto in the developmental passages of his arias and ariosos.

By contrast, his other recurrent figure has a strong affective charge, especially as its melodic element centers on a diminished fourth. Figure 6.7 shows the different renderings of this figure, which takes essentially two forms: the first moves through scale degrees 2–♭3–♮7–1, and the second adds the fifth scale degree at the beginning: 5–2–♭3–♮7–1. Both obviously emphasize the diminished fourth between the flat third and raised seventh of

---

[154] Murata, "Scylla and Charybdis," 75.   [155] Caluori, *The Cantatas of Luigi Rossi*, 76–79.

Figure 6.6 Cases of Atto's common $^4_2$–$^6_3$ material

A più sventure ancora

ta,   No, no, non si par-li,   no, no, non si

par-li, no, no, non si par-li più di vi   -   ta,

O quanto si dolea

de; Con l'a-li sue le mie fa-vil-le,   con l'a-li sue le

mie fa-vil-le,   le mie fa-vil-le ac-cen   -   de.

Ove, tra sponde d'oro

Dop-po la not-te al fin ri-na   -

-    -   -   sce, ri-na   -   sce il dì,

Figure 6.7 Cases of Atto's common diminished-fourth motive

Filli, per cui mi moro (Tell, tell how a heart can gaze on you [and not languish])

A più sventure ancora (Rain on that soul [forces so contrary])

O quanto si dolea (The one who injures me)

Tra sponde di smeraldo (No, no, no, for one cannot suffer [pain more cruel])

the harmonic minor scale. Although the metrical configuration of the two versions varies, the fixed presence of the diminished fourth leads to consistent use with anguished texts, as shown by the translations in the figure. When Atto was faced with portraying the pain of a lover – that most common of postures – it seems he had this effective figure ready at hand.

The foregoing characteristics might be interpreted to imply that Atto expended little creativity on his cantatas, a tactic particularly understandable given his busy lifestyle. Perhaps he was just aiming to turn out standard, if unexceptional, embodiments of a Rossian heritage. Or perhaps his use of formulas is a sign of improvisation, his extant works representing little more than notated extemporizations.[156] Other aspects of the works argue against both conclusions and suggest instead that Atto devoted considerable care and imagination to his compositions.

Such care appears quite consistently, for example, in his handling of recitatives. A close examination of one, the first in *A più sventure ancora*, can ably stand for all (for the score, see figure 6.8). In the first place, Atto meticulously observes both the word and line accents of his text. Contemporary literary theorists conceived of each poetic line as having a primary accent on its penultimate syllable (if it was a normal *verso piano*) and a secondary accent somewhere else in the line, depending on the precise words used.[157] The text below shows the accents for this passage, and a comparison with Atto's setting reveals that in virtually every case the more accented syllables receive the longer note values.

A più sventure ancora,
Serberò questa vita; e la fortuna
Lieta calpesterà le mie rovine.
Forse l'empia padrona
Versa i suoi mali, e contro me l'aduna;
Perché tutte le pene abbia vicine.
Ahi, che Fileno al fine,
Filen, volgendo il piede in altra parte;
Quel traditor Fileno, oh Dio, si parte!

The few exceptions each have an expressive justification: for example, the long dotted quarter note used to set the relatively unaccented "me" of "e contro me l'aduna," (m. 11) serves to emphasize the feeling of personal persecution: "[fortune] assembles [her evils] against *me*." In a more complex case, at "tutte le pene abbia vicine" (m. 13), Atto rushes past "*pene*," the

---

[156] Murata suggests something of the typical role of improvisation in performance in "Scylla and Charybdis," 75: "In the seventeenth century … the score is not yet identical to the notion 'music.' In manuscript, the score is still very much part of an artisan's kit. It can be short-hand for obtaining a performance, or it can be an *exemplum* of a class of performance possibilities. The score is either a disposable part of the musical culture, or it is a sign of it." For evidence of improvised chamber music, see (among other places) Hill, *Roman Monody*, 121–39.

[157] Elwert, *Versificazione*, 44–50; his analysis of the usual rhythmic patterns of the different line lengths of Italian poetry follows, 52–83.

Figure 6.8 The opening recitative of Atto's *A più sventure ancora*

normal accent, to lengthen the unimportant "*ab*bia." The key to this distortion is found in the line "Quel traditor Fileno, oh Dio" (mm. 19–20),
where Atto again bypasses the main accent on "Fi*le*no" to stress "oh." The
sudden emphasis on these poetically weak syllables, achieved through a high
range and syncopated rhythm, is surely intended to evoke impassioned

declamation: the character's normal speech patterns are overwhelmed by her emotions. Indeed, occasional flawed accentuation seems regularly to serve this function in Atto's recitatives.

A number of other expressive techniques are also present. For example, the very first chord of the cantata is not the usual root position tonic but a first-inversion dominant, already creating a sense of instability. That this effect is repeated at the opening of the second and third phrases ("e la fortuna," m. 4, and "Forse l'empia," m. 8) confirms and intensifies its impact. Further, the second element of each of these three parallel phrases is articulated from the first element by a rest and a wide leap, features that at first seem inexplicable, as they interrupt syntactical units (mm. 2, 6, 10). Like the V^6 chords, however, these halting, angular lines act to project a sense of passion barely held in check: "and Fortune, happy, will trample [pause] *my ruins*!" In fact, this opening passage reaches its greatest intensity in the third of these phrases, where the c″ of the voice clashes with the B-major chord of the continuo at "Versa i suoi mali" (m. 9), and the melody presents the unusual leap of a diminished seventh at "contro me l'aduna" (m. 11). In the final line of this section, Atto creates the first climax of the piece by means of the defective accentuation observed above and by stressing the note e″ (mm. 14–15), the highest pitch so far to receive such emphasis.

In the latter half of the recitative, the intensification continues. "Ahi, che Fileno" is a veritable cry, which quickly trails off with the almost absent-minded repetition of the lover's name (mm. 16–17), an ingenious violation of the division between poetic lines (7–8). The next several measures trace a gradual rise in the vocal register to the climax at "oh Dio": c″–d″–d♯″–e″–f♯″. The rapid concluding progression up the circle of fifths from E minor to B minor and then F-sharp major at the point of greatest tension heightens the effect (mm. 19–20). Although the succeeding repetition of this text occurs at a lower pitch level, almost as if the character is now mumbling in disbelief, the harmony at the second "oh Dio," a dominant seventh in third inversion, is actually more dissonant against the voice, and the vocal leaps are wider, this time a falling major seventh followed by a rising minor ninth (mm. 20–23): this quieter anguish is more painful. Finally, at the last cadence (m. 24), the voice drops out before the continuo reaches the tonic chord, a construct that Beth Glixon calls the "delayed cadence" and notes is conventionally used to depict intense emotion.[158]

---

[158] Beth Lise Glixon, "Recitative in Seventeenth-Century Venetian Opera: Its Dramatic Function and Musical Language" (Ph.D. diss., Rutgers Univ., 1985), 92.

The dramatic and inventive gestures of this recitative illustrate not only that Atto possessed genuine compositional skill, but that he occasionally aimed to surprise and even shock his listeners. Such little jolts of stylish *bizzarria* are particularly common in Atto's harmonic practice. As an illustration, the duet *Anima, che di foco* is especially revealing because its three-part texture leaves little doubt about the desired harmonies (no examples here; see published edition). A measure of the dissonance Atto could call for appears in the last real climax of *Anima*, at the cadence to B minor in measures 181–83. The downbeat of measure 181 is unremarkable, merely a dominant with a suspended seventh; but on the next beat the soprano leaps down into a major seventh against the bass (g–f♯′) and then back up into a minor seventh against the alto (c♯′–b′). The soprano and alto then execute parallel minor sevenths, creating a downbeat in measure 182 that (with the usual bass harmonization) would consist of the pitches F♯, B, C♯, D. Even the resolution of the 4–3 suspension at the end of this measure has an added tonic anticipation (b′), ensuring that the series of dissonant harmonies stretches over a full two measures.

This passage is not unique. Another biting example appears in measure 48, as preparation for a cadence in A minor. From the D major subdominant harmony of the previous measure, the music arrives on the downbeat with the expected dominant (E major), plus suspended seventh. The second beat moves to the flat submediant (F major), but both the E and G♯ of the previous chord are retained, and in a particularly abrasive way: while the soprano voice just rearticulates its preceding e′, the alto leaps down a diminished fifth from its already dissonant seventh (d′) to an even more jarring g♯. Then, as the underlying ♭VI continues over the third beat, the alto goes further by leaping up to the octave g♯′, creating an additional clash with the soprano, now on a′. Then, as if stung, the alto quickly resolves into the soprano's note, and the cadence finishes conventionally. Another rendering of this harmonic progression can be found in measure 168. This time, the arrival of the E-major dominant on the downbeat is complicated by the alto's addition of a c♮′. As the alto tries to resolve to b on the next beat, the harmony moves to F major^7 (♭VI^7), making the resolution again dissonant. This time the b is allowed to resolve in peace (to c′), and the cadence proceeds normally. Comparable examples can be found elsewhere in this cantata and indeed throughout Atto's oeuvre, particularly in the approach to important cadences. In each instance, Atto breaks the rules of counterpoint and dissonance treatment to create quick but deliciously shocking effects.

Perhaps the most interesting aspect of Atto's approach, however, is his experimentation with form, for in these efforts he demonstrates both his

Table 6.8 *A schematic of the four strophes of the aria "Se il mio cor non sa ridire" from Atto's* Scrivete, occhi dolenti

Textual line	1	2	3	4	3	4	4	rit.
Cadence type	X	P	X	X	X	X	X	X
Cadence point (c:)	c	V/c	B♭	E♭	B♭	c	c	c
	5	6	7	8	7	8	8	rit.
	X	P	X	X	7-1	X	X	X
	c	V/c	B♭	g	B♭	c	c	c
	9	10	11	12	11	12	12	rit.
	X	P	X	X	X	X	X	X
	c	V/c	F	g	B♭	c	c	c
	13	14	15	16	15	16	16	rit.
	X	P	X	X	X	X	X	X
	c	V/c	B♭	E♭	c	c	c	c

imagination and his pursuit of the novel. The sheer variety of Atto's small output is remarkable, with cantatas ranging from simple canzonettas, to complex composite forms, to almost classic structures balancing recitatives and arias. In fifteen works he essays nearly every formal approach – conservative and progressive – then available to him. But his interests are nowhere more apparent than in his use of structures that, by mid-century standards, are more complex than they need to be. For example, when presented with a perfectly strophic aria text, a composer was only expected to write a strophic setting, an expectation that Atto indeed fulfilled in several cases.[159] But at other times he exhibits a surfeit of originality that seems specifically intended to evade predictability.

A good example is the aria "Se il mio cor non sa ridire" from *Scrivete, occhi dolenti*. Here, Atto was working with four parallel quatrains of *ottonari*, rhymed abba. A composer could easily have set all four verses to the same music; as seen above, Carissimi essentially wrote two arias, pairing the stanzas. Atto, however, responds with four similar, but not strophic, settings, an unusual approach. Table 6.8 shows a textual and harmonic schematic of the aria, while figure 6.9 gives a vertically aligned comparison of the four

---

[159] Gianturco, "The Italian Seventeenth-Century Cantata," 48. Atto's strophic responses to strophic texts include *M'abbandona la sorte* (entire canzonetta) and "Su voci veloci," from *Il tacer non fa per me*. In "Pensieri sì sì" from *Io voglio esser infelice*, he even sets imperfect strophes (with different rhyme schemes) to strophic music.

Figure 6.9 The four strophic melodies of "Se il mio cor non sa ridire" from *Scrivete, occhi dolenti* (blank measures inserted for rhythmic alignment)

melodies. As the different melodic lines and harmonic goals indicate, the technique here amounts neither to strophic repetition nor to variation. Yet so many melodic and formal elements recur that the general impression of a strophic structure remains. Strangely, Atto's habitual sensitivity to text

Figure 6.9 (cont.)

does not play a role here, as nearly every strophe presents at least one mis-accented word, and none tries to interpret its specific text.[160] Instead,

---

[160] In considering this aria, Holzer ("Music and Poetry," 405) states that Atto uses "essentially the same music for the first three quatrains," followed by "new music" for the final strophe, a procedure Holzer finds particularly appropriate to the text. Actually, each verse differs from the others by about the same degree, and none is especially matched to its text.

Figure 6.10 A comparison of bass lines in the two strophes of *S'io sapessi dipingere* (blank measures inserted for alignment)

he has simply written a pleasant minor-mode tune that, subjected to a kind of permutation, avoids monotony while respecting the poetic form. Although not deeply expressive, his approach manages to avoid the kind of mismatch between text and music that can plague a more textually specific strophic aria. (See Carissimi's second and fourth verses, for example.)

Figure 6.10 (cont.)

Atto also challenges expectations in *S'io sapessi dipingere*, which takes the form that Caluori describes as strophic binary.[161] Even though the poem is not precisely strophic (the rhyme scheme changes slightly between stanzas), the difference is so minor that Atto could have overlooked it, as in fact he did when he wrote an almost purely strophic aria for the analogous "Pensieri sì sì" from *Io voglio esser infelice*.[162] For *S'io sapessi*, Atto employs an extreme form of strophic variation. A comparison of the bass lines of the two strophes reveals that, while the succession of pitches is essentially maintained, the rhythms vary considerably (see figure 6.10). Caluori has shown that Rossi too used this technique, which Atto surely inherited, but Atto goes one step further by varying the amount of text – and therefore bass line – treated in recitative style. Atto sets lines 5 through 7 of the first stanza as recitative, but

---

[161] Caluori, *The Cantatas of Luigi Rossi*, 89–90.

[162] Gianturco ("The Seventeenth-Century Italian Cantata," 49) probably overstates her contention that "if the poetry [of an aria] is of more than one strophe or stanza but these are not symmetrical (that is, they exhibit differences of number of lines, number of syllables per line or rhyme scheme), the composer will write a non-strophic, sectional form which adheres to the poetic divisions." Although this procedure indeed appears to have been the norm, composers sometimes did in fact ignore small deviations. In addition to Atto's own work, I can cite the aria "Fuori, fuori dal mio petto" from Rossi's *Tutto cinto di ferro* (*Cantatas by Luigi Rossi c. 1597–1653*, vol. I of *The Italian Cantata in the Seventeenth Century*, ed. Francesco Luisi [New York: Garland, 1986], 103–15), which is set strophically although its rhyme scheme is abcbc // addee; a similar procedure is followed in Carissimi's "Ahi, ch'invan le voci" from *O voi che in aride ossa* (*Cantatas by Giacomo Carissimi 1605–1674*, vol. II of *The Italian Cantata in the Seventeenth Century*, ed. Günther Massenkeil [New York: Garland, 1986], 26–32), with its complex and asymmetrical pattern a_8 b_8 a_8 b_{11} c_6 d_6 d_6 c_6 e_{11} e_{11} // f_8 g_8 g_8 f_8 h_6 i_6 i_6 h_6 j_{11} j_{11} set to strophic variation form.

Table 6.9 *The two stanzas of* S'io sapessi dipingere, *showing changes of style and meter in Atto's setting*

	Stanza 1		Stanza 2
A 3	S'io sapessi dipingere,	A 3	Ma poiché non poss'io,
	Belle cose farei		Se pur voi lo volete;
	Pria te, bella cagion de' dolor miei;		Aprite, o bella Filli, il petto mio:
	In una vaga tela vorrei fingere		Ch'ivi per man d'Amor scolpita sete!
R	Ciò ch'ha di bel il ciel tutto raccolto	R	L'opra fu del suo strale; altro che Amore
	Ritrarvi nel bel volto;		Non travaglia il mio core;
	Ma non hanno i colori	A 3	E di sì bella immago
A 3	Così vivi splendori:		Vivo contento, e pago:
	No, no; solo le stelle		Sì, sì; forza è di stella
	Ponno ritrar la sù forme sì belle.		Idolatrando Amor cosa sì bella.

only lines 5 and 6 (15 and 16) of the second stanza (see the schematic in table 6.9). In both stanzas, the syntactic break comes after the sixth line, so that it is the continuation of recitative style for line 7 that seems unusual. The remarkable disruption Atto creates for the word "ma" at the beginning of line 7 (m. 32) – moving from C major to E major via a chromatic semitone in the voice and an augmented second in the bass – may explain his decision. In any case, his avoidance of what would be the easy norm is again noteworthy.

Atto takes similarly unusual approaches to strophic form in his arias "Da chi spero aver pietà" from *La più dolente, e misera, che viva* and "Lascia pur le piaghe intatte" from *O quanto si dolea*. The poetic schematics of Table 6.10a and b show that these arias have the same structure: two strophes plus a concluding couplet. This form appears to belong to a genre identified by contemporaries as the "Pindaric canzonetta," whose nature and typical musical realization Chiabrera himself described: "In Rome, the masters of the music have let us hear a *strophe* sung with one aria, and the *anti-strophe* with the same aria as well. But when the listener expected the same aria to be returned to once again for a third time, he found himself tricked, because he heard a new aria formed over the *epode*."[163] Aside from these two examples (and another in Atto's *La più dolente, e misera, che viva*, also by Baldini), I have only found one roughly contemporary text approximating this form: the aria "Noiosi pensieri," from Luigi Rossi's cantata *Mentre sorge dal mar*, although in that case three rather than two strophes precede the "epode": a_6 b_6 a_6 b_6 // c_6 d_6 d_6 c_6 // e_6 f_6 e_6 f_6 // g_{11} g_{11}.[164] Rossi seems to have followed

[163] Gabriello Chiabrera, "Il Geri: Dialogo della tessitura delle canzoni," in *Opere di Gabriello Chiabrera e lirici non marinisti*, ed. Marcello Turchi, 2nd edn. (Turin: Unione Tipografico-Editrice Torinese, 1973), 582, quoted and translated by Holzer, "Music and Poetry," 75.

[164] The cantata can be found in Luisi, ed., *The Italian Cantata*, vol. I, 21–28.

Table 6.10a *A schematic of "Da chi spero aver pietà," from Atto's* La più dolente, e misera, che viva

Time signature		Poetic form	
A C	Da chi spero aver pietà	a	8t
	Di sì barbari tormenti,	b	8
	Se congiuran gli elementi	b	8
	Per usarmi crudeltà?	a	8t
	Viver sì sventurato il cor non cura;	c	11
	Perdasi con la vita ogni sventura.	c	11
A $\frac{3}{4}$	Oh, che strana servitù	d	8t
	Vuol da me l'empia fortuna?	e	8
	Tante pene insieme aduna,	e	8
	Che non può crescerne più.	d	8t
R	Ah, perfida, ah, crudel nemica sorte!	f	11
	Dove, per minor mal, dov'è la morte?	f	11
A° $\frac{3}{4}$	No, no, che non curo aita;	g	7
	Un, che misero sia, sprezza la vita.	g	11

Table 6.10b *A schematic of "Lascia pur le piaghe intatte," from Atto's* O quanto si dolea

Time signature		Poetic form	
A 3	Lascia pur le piaghe intatte	a	8
	Per cui l'anima vien meno;	b	8
	Chi le aperse nel mio seno	b	8
	Insanabili l'ha fatte.	a	8
	È vano il tuo rimedio, il tuo conforto:	c	11
	La feritrice mia nel core io porto.	c	11
	Se di Lete il cieco oblio	d	8
	Vuoi destar contro di me,	e	8t
	Se d'amor la pura fé	e	8t
	Vuoi scacciar dal petto mio,	d	8
	Del mio sen la costanza, ah, non intendi,	f	11
	Sin l'acque dell'oblio cangia in incendi;	f	11
	E sa le forze tue schernire Amore:	g	11
	Ché quando parte il piè, non parte il core.	g	11

Chiabrera's advice, for he sets the three parallel stanzas to the same aria and then changes to recitative for the first line of the epode (and to triple-meter arioso for the second). Clearly, Atto could have set his even more "Pindaric" texts similarly, but in both cases he pursues a through-composed approach, masking the form of the poem and creating two of his most complex arias.

Figure 6.11a The aria "Da chi spero aver pietà" from *La più dolente, e misera, che viva*

Because they share so many traits, I will discuss them together. (For scores, see figures 6.11a and 6.11b.)

Both arias open with Atto's standard "quatrain form," although "Lascia pur" eliminates the B′ section and does not return to tonic at the end (m. 32), and "Da chi spero" has the added interest of a bass line that hints at ostinato.

Figure 6.11a (cont.)

Next comes the first surprise: both arias give the impression that their fifth line, in the midst of the first six-line stanza, is actually the beginning of a second strophe ("Da chi spero," m. 28, and "Lascia pur," m. 37). In both cases, a preceding ritornello for the continuo reinforces this sense of starting again. "Lascia pur" then essentially restates the opening melody, creating the effect of strophic repetition (mm. 37–40), while "Da chi spero" duplicates the

Figure 6.11a (cont.)

initial bass line, promising strophic variation (mm. 28–29). In both instances, the strophic signal is false, and the rest of the stanza continues with new material. Atto's rationale for breaking up the stanzas in this way, as well as giving deceptive signals of repetition, is not immediately apparent. He does often set the initial quatrain of a poem as a unit, although in most cases such quatrains are also poetically independent. His practice here may be a playful

Figure 6.11a (cont.)

thwarting of conventions, or it may simply be an attempt to create a recognizable signpost in what turns out to be a lengthy and intricate form. In any event, both arias mark the true end of the first stanza with a major point of articulation, emphasized by a firm return to the tonic and either a change of meter ("Da chi spero," mm. 38–39) or another continuo ritornello ("Lascia pur," mm. 67–71).

Again in striking parallel, both arias set the opening of the next stanza (beginning with the seventh line) to a freely treated descending-tetrachord ostinato. In "Da chi spero," this bass line (beginning in m. 39) is really just a variation of the aforementioned ostinato pattern (cf. mm. 24–25). Similarly, in "Lascia pur" Atto subtly introduces the ground (mm. 68–71) in the previous section: it first appears as the bass under the second poetic line (mm. 21–24) and then returns under the last statement of the sixth line

Figure 6.11b The aria, "Lascia pur le piaghe intatte" from *O quanto si dolea*

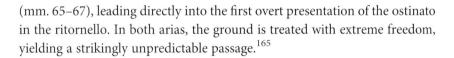

(mm. 65–67), leading directly into the first overt presentation of the ostinato in the ritornello. In both arias, the ground is treated with extreme freedom, yielding a strikingly unpredictable passage.[165]

---

[165] Caluori (*The Cantatas of Luigi Rossi*, 84) points out that extreme flexibility is also the norm when Rossi uses ostinato. Atto probably inherited this attitude, although he certainly could have written these passages more simply than he does.

Figure 6.11b (cont.)

From the end of these sections, the two arias diverge. From about the third line of the second stanza (mm. 88 ff.), "Lascia pur" begins to abandon the ground, with only a few hints of its contour occasionally affecting the bass line. At the beginning of the last two lines of the aria (m. 123), Atto employs an abrupt harmonic shift from the previously well-established tonic of D minor to C major, formally articulating these final lines. The first half of the

Figure 6.11b (cont.)

penultimate line, set to a declamatory repeated pitch, is stated twice in a
Carissimi-like sequence up a perfect fourth; the second half of the line returns
to a cadence on A minor. The last line begins with another harmonic shift,
this time a minor third away to F (the relative major of the aria tonic; m. 131),
and then the aria concludes with a long developmental section based on this
final line, including a climactic rising sequential pattern. At the very end

Figure 6.11b (cont.)

(mm. 155–60), Atto brings back the ground that he used to set lines 7 and 8, apparently to unify the work.

The conclusion of "Da chi spero" is even more unusual. Here, the free ostinato lasts only through the end of the first quatrain of the second stanza (m. 80). Then, the sudden impassioned outburst of "Ah treacherous, ah cruel, hostile fate" leads to a radical interruption of form: with an abrupt harmonic leap from tonic to V^6/vi, the singer launches into recitative, tonally centered on the submediant and filled with expressive dissonance and chromaticism (mm. 81–85). When in the penultimate line of the aria the speaker regains her self-control ("No, no, I care not for help," mm. 85–86), the harmony immediately shifts back to the tonic B-flat major, effectively isolating the preceding moment of intense passion and demonstrating, at least in this passage, Atto's use of tonal areas for dramatic purposes. The final line, which forms the *motto* of the entire cantata, is set – as in "Lascia pur" – to a lengthy triple-meter section crowned by a rising sequence (mm. 87–105). Here too one finds concern for compositional unity, for, although no specific elements from earlier in the aria return, the lilting triple meter suggests a connection to previous lyric material, and the initial octave leap of the bass and its slow descent under $^4_2$–$^6_3$ progressions recalls the very opening of the aria.

The complexity of these two pieces further supports the idea that Atto possessed the ability and, at least sometimes, the will to abandon compositional norms in favor of more daring solutions: his treatment of the foregoing strophic texts may well have struck his listeners as novel and even pleasantly *bizzarro*. Two other examples with these qualities, less tied to strophic concerns, conclude this discussion. In *Scrivete, occhi dolenti*, Atto divides the opening recitative into three sections, each marked off by arioso conclusions. Interestingly, the first and third ariosos end with the same music, lending to this long recitative an almost ternary structure that neither the sense nor form of the text suggests. Similarly, the concluding music of the second arioso – the highly affective setting of "I burn, I weep, I sigh, and yet I do not speak," surely the *motto* of this cantata – returns in a melodically varied form at the very end of the work, to the words "at least answer 'life' or 'death'!" (mm. 40–44 and 202–6). This recurrence creates both a rounding effect and a recollection of the work's central idea. Such a veiled musical allusion may again have struck Atto's more astute listeners as a clever commentary.

Even more experimental is Atto's approach to *Ove, tra sponde d'oro*. Although the poem contains twenty-one lines of *versi sciolti* (see table 6.11), Atto sets all but the first seven in aria-style passages. The work in fact becomes a study in lyricism and represents Atto's closest approach to the procedures of Carissimi. Even more interesting, however, is the particular relationship between the arioso "Tra l'umane vicende" and the following aria, "Sfioriscono gl'anni." As figure 6.12 demonstrates, the aria is actually a loose strophic variation of the arioso, an astonishing arrangement. The relationship is clearly audible because both the opening of the arioso and its later prominent sequential material are reproduced almost exactly in the aria.

Table 6.11 *A schematic of Atto's* Ove, tra sponde d'oro

Time signature				Poetic form
R	Ove, tra sponde d'oro,	a	7	
	L'indico Gange imprigionò l'arena;	b	11	
	Stretta la bianca mano	c	7	
	Della vezzosa Clori,	d	7	
	Seco fermolla consigliero amante;	e	11	
	E mostrando nel volto aspro dolore,	f	11	
	Disse sui labri suoi, parlando il core.	f	11	
A° C$^3_4$	Vedi la bella Aurora,	g	7	
	Che del vecchio Titon lascia le piume;	h	11	
	Fuga le stelle, e intanto al nuovo sole	i	11	
	Fanno cuna i ligustri, e le viole.	i	11	
A° C	Passan l'ombre così:	j	7t	
	Doppo la notte al fin rinasce il dì.	j	11t	
A° $\frac{3}{2}$	Ma dal tuo viso adorno	k	7	
	Se parte un dì, mai più ritorna il giorno.	k	11	
A C$^3_4$	Deh, lascia, severa,	**l**	**6**	
	Superba et altera,	**l**	**6**	
	Cotanto rigore:	**f**	**6**	
	Non è eterno il tuo bel, né 'l mio dolore!	**f**	**11**	
A° C	Tra l'umane vicende,	m	7	
	Nei giardin di Fortuna;	n	7	
	È rosa la bellezza:	o	7	
	Ma sol di pianto, oh Dio, beve ruggiade!	p	11	
	E quando al sol s'appressa, allora cade.	p	11	
A C	Sfioriscono gl'anni	q	6	
	Coi gigli del seno;	r	6	
	Verranno ben meno	r	6	
	A te bellezza, et a chi t'ama affanni.	q	11	
A° $\frac{3}{2}$	Così con alta legge il tempo impera.	l	11	
A C$^3_4$	Deh, lascia, severa,	**l**	**6**	
	Superba et altera,	**l**	**6**	
	Cotanto rigore:	**f**	**6**	
	Non è eterno il tuo bel, né 'l mio dolore!	**f**	**11**	

Perhaps Atto felt a need for greater organization in the long string of lyrical movements he was creating. Support for this interpretation appears at the end of the cantata poem itself, where a single *endecasillabo* ("Così con alta legge il tempo impera") creates a rhyme-link back to an earlier aria, which is then recalled. Because such lone poetic lines are so uncommon in this style, one can justifiably speculate that Atto himself added it, just so he could repeat the aria and further fortify the structure. At the same time he was

Figure 6.12 A comparison of bass lines between the arioso "Tra l'umane vicende" and aria "Sfioriscono gl'anni" from *Ove, tra sponde d'oro* (blank beats inserted for rhythmic alignment)

experimenting with unusual forms, Atto seems to have given special attention to the coherence of his works. Again, far from being a distracted dilettante, he appears to have taken pride in both his inventiveness and his craftsmanship.

In his 1686 *Osservazioni intorno alle vipere*, the Tuscan scientist and latter-day Renaissance man Francesco Redi observed that if one's skin were punctured by the fangs of a snake even up to half an hour after its death, "not all the sweet music of the famous Atto Melani, of Cavalier Cesti, or the silvery voice of Ciecolino, with as many musical instruments as the ancient and modern schools could have invented, would suffice to bring about a cure."[166] Although all three of the men Redi mentions were singers, he refers explicitly only to the voice of Ciecolino (Antonio Rivani): the "sweet music" of Melani

---

[166] Francesco Redi, *Osservazioni intorno alle vipere* (Florence: All'Insegna della Stella, 1664), 38.

and Cesti would seem to be their compositions.[167] Was Atto highly regarded as a composer? The evidence is just too slim to say. That several of his cantatas are preserved in a large number of widespread manuscripts lends some support to the idea.[168] And of course he himself certainly thought so, as his claim (above) about the popularity of his pieces attests. In any case, Weaver's opinion that "his works show little variation, fitting comfortably into the forms and styles set by Antonio Cesti" must certainly be discarded.[169]

On the other hand, Weaver is right to imply that Atto was not as important to the history of composition as Rossi, Carissimi, and Cesti. But then composition was not as important to Atto. For him, the writing of cantatas appears by and large to have been a means to an end. While the singing of cantatas may have placed Atto in a room with the aristocrats he so pursued, setting these diverting texts allowed him to make his own intellectual and artistic contribution to the conversation. Instead of being called in and dismissed like the vocalist in Guazzo's treatise, Atto's works provided him with a reason (perhaps another reason) to stay. The ability of these works to speak for him even when absent – perhaps sometimes with a veiled personal message – made them even more useful. And for his patrons with developed musical tastes – a group that surely included Mattias, Mazarin, the duke of Mantua, Giulio Rospigliosi, Marie Mancini Colonna, and perhaps Anne of Austria and the duchess of Savoy as well – his musical style proffered the mix of the familiar and novel, the forthright and astonishing, that was highly valued in the atmosphere of the *conversazione*.

As seen in the previous chapter, Atto laid his talents aside when his position as a diplomat became secure: as soon as his musical activities seemed

---

[167] Alessandro Ademollo, who first noted this quotation, implies that Redi is referring to Atto's singing ("Un campanaio e la sua famiglia," *Fanfulla della Domenica*, December 30, 1883, 2). The identification of "Ciecolino" as Antonio Rivani is owed to Robert Lamar Weaver and Norma Wright Weaver, *A Chronology of Music in the Florentine Theater 1590–1750*, Detroit Studies in Music Bibliography, no. 38 (Detroit: Information Coordinators, 1978), 369. Of course, Rivani was an acquaintance of Atto's (see chapter 5).

[168] Atto's most widely dispersed cantatas include *Fileno, idolo mio* (six sources: I Rvat, Chig. Q. IV.18; I Rvat, Barb. lat. 4156; I Nc, 33.4.4; GB Lbl, Harley 1264; GB Lbl, Harley 1863; GB Cfm, 24 F 4); *Filli, per cui mi moro* (six sources: I Rvat, Chig. Q.IV.11; I Nc, 33.5.18; I Bc, V.198; GB Ckc, Rowe 22; F Pc, H.659; US CHH, Music VM2.1 M1); *Occhi miei belli* (six sources: I Fn, Magl. XIX.26; F Pn, Vm^7 18; F Pn, Rés. Vmb. 93; B Bc, 19196; D Mbs, Mus. Ms. 1524; US LAuc, fC 694 M4); *Ove, tra sponde d'oro* (seven sources: I Rvat, Chig. Q.IV.11; I Rc, 2486; I Bc, V.198; I Nc, 33.4.18; I Nc, 33.4.4; F Pn, Vm^7 1; US CHH, Music VM2.1 M1); *Scrivete, occhi dolenti* (six sources: I MOe, Mus. F.1349; I MOe, Mus. E.249; I Nc, 22.2.22; F Pn, Rés. Vmf. 41; B Bc, 15262; D Kl, 2° Mus. 34); and *Tra sponde di smeraldo* (six sources: I Rvat, Chig. Q.IV.11; I MOe, Mus. E.300; F Pn, Rés. Vmf. 14; F Pn, Rés. Vmb. 93; D Kl, 2° Mus. 34; US CHH, Music VM2.1 M1). For full source information on Atto's works, see Atto Melani, *Complete Cantatas*, 97–106.

[169] Robert Lamar Weaver, introduction to *Cantatas by Alessandro Melani 1639–1703, Atto Melani 1626–1714*, vol. XI of *The Italian Cantata in the Seventeenth Century*, ed. Weaver (New York: Garland, 1986), [x].

a social liability, he gave them up. That in 1670 Marino Silvani published Atto's *Scrivete, occhi dolenti* in a collection of *Canzonette per camera* is less likely a sign of Atto's continued involvement in composing, as Weaver hypothesized, than an example of his musical past returning to embarrass him.[170] Atto's abandonment of music – including the writing of it – completes the arc that I have charted throughout this study: his gradual evolution from pure musician to pure diplomat. Throughout, his fixed polestar remained the dream of social advancement. Just as he sang, spied, and carried out negotiations to get ahead in the world, so his composition of cantatas was simply another fruit, if the most delectable one, of his remarkable ambition.

---

[170] Robert Lamar Weaver, "Florentine Comic Operas of the Seventeenth Century" (Ph.D. diss., University of North Carolina, Chapel Hill, 1958), 321.

7 ❧ Completing the portrait: 1671–1714

In 1671, at the age of forty-five, Atto had just passed the midpoint of his life. As we have seen, his years as a musician were over. His correspondence no longer refers to musical activities, and he fails to report even on performances he must have witnessed, including his own brothers' operas in Rome and Lully's works in Paris.[1] To some degree, this total renunciation may be an illusion of the evidence: with the death of Mattias de' Medici in 1667, Atto lost his correspondent most interested in artistic matters; the extant letters after that date are addressed largely to foreign ministers (of France and Tuscany) with narrower concerns. Still, whereas Atto had previously blended music into his political work – indeed had used music as an expedient – he really seems in his mid-forties to have laid the art aside.[2]

I conclude this study, then, not with the kind of detailed account found in previous chapters, but rather with a series of reflections on the remainder of Atto's life. This approach in fact complements the rest of the inquiry. Evidence of Atto's continuing dedication to diplomacy confirms the sincerity of his career change; his activities as a patron – for the Melani as well as a few other Italians – show him capitalizing on his increasing power and wealth; his lifestyle – marked by official honors, elegant living, and the respect of his peers – underscores his arrival as a gentleman of consequence; and his occasional reference to musical issues, which reemerge in late letters to his family, permit both him and us to put his long life into perspective. In short, an overview of Atto's latter forty-three years shows that his strategies of advancement finally pay off and that the trajectory of his life reaches its anticipated conclusion. As a bonus, it also offers his stimulating glimpses of society and culture in the late seventeenth century.

In 1818, the historian Tommaso Trenta published a biography of his fellow Lucchese Cardinal Francesco Buonvisi (1626–1700). Buonvisi had

---

[1] Jacopo Melani's *Il Girello* and Alessandro Melani's *L'empio punito* were written for the Colonna theater for the carnivals of 1668 and 1669 respectively. (On Atto as a possible force behind these commissions, see below.) Atto was present in Paris for the full series of Lully's *tragédies en musique*.

[2] I do not claim to have fully explored the ocean of Atto's late letters, and so an isolated musical observation may yet surface. But with the exception of the letters to his family (see below) my extensive trawling has netted little.

been one of Atto's longtime friends and patrons, and the two exchanged extensive correspondence. Recognizing this connection, Trenta appended to his study a biographical sketch of Atto, emphasizing the diplomatic work of Atto's later years.[3] The sketch is especially important because it draws on documents that at that time were still held by Atto's descendants in Pistoia but now are lost (see below). Although Trenta sometimes misinterpreted his materials, his study stands as a unique and valuable source of information and so serves as the nucleus for much of what follows.

Removal to France

As seen at the end of chapter 5, Atto finished the decade of the 1660s well positioned in papal politics. In addition to his title as "apostolic pronotary," he resided within the Quirinal palace itself, making him a familiar figure at the court of Clement X. At the same time, he corresponded regularly with Louis XIV's foreign ministry and served as a kind of informal French envoy to the Holy See. He was a supreme insider: he had worked hard to forge his many connections, and those connections now gave him a distinctive station in Rome. From all indications, he envisioned that station as his future.

Soon, however, his plan came under threat, as Trenta's synopsis just hints:

> With the death of M. de Lionne, which occurred in 1671, Melani came to miss his most effective protector. Once de Lionne's place in the ministry was taken by [Simon Arnaud, marquis] de Pomponne, [former] ambassador to the court of Sweden, the king directed [François-Michel Le Tellier, marquis] de Louvois to write Melani (who had returned to Rome [after his trip to Paris in 1670]) that he should indeed continue to maintain a correspondence with the new minister as he had always done with the deceased one. But after having assisted in the election of Cardinal [César] d'Estrées, Melani thought it good to return to France to insinuate himself more closely into the good graces of M. de Pomponne.[4]

The situation was rather more complex. Atto indeed wanted to establish a stronger relationship with the new foreign minister, Pomponne; he also looked to resolve issues surrounding his French benefice, which he had not received for some time. But, in reality, Atto's departure from Rome was a barely concealed banishment. For at least two years he had championed one of France's chief projects within the Church: the aforementioned promotion

---

[3] Tommaso Trenta, *Memorie per servire alla storia politica del Cardinale Francesco Buonvisi patrizio lucchese* (Lucca: Francesco Bertini, 1818), I:259–65.

[4] Ibid, I:263. For the original Italian of all excerpts, see appendix E.

of César d'Estrées, bishop of Laon, to the cardinalate. The twin purpose was to reward d'Estrées, the son of a duke and *maréchal* of France, and to strengthen the French party within the college of cardinals. Unfortunately, Atto's typically rash and self-serving approach infuriated leaders on both sides of the matter. On the one hand, he continued to negotiate independently of his French superiors, as he had done in the previous conclave: Louis XIV himself found his behavior "très désagréable."[5] On the other, Atto's zeal for d'Estrées's case – with its overtly French bias – conflicted with the ideal of ecclesiastical independence, an ideal that, as client of the pope, he was supposed to uphold. His enemies within the Church accused him of treason, placed him under surveillance, and in March 1672 even threatened him physically: "they then implied that there would be no safety for me if I continued to exchange letters and reports with the ministers of His Majesty."[6] As usual, Atto himself saw no problem with such divided loyalties: he claimed to use his inside knowledge for the benefit of both parties. But, with the passing of so many long-time protectors, Atto seems to have lost the support that had smoothed things over in the past. Although the crisis eased somewhat in May, when d'Estrées's promotion was finally announced, the powerful Cardinals Altieri and especially Rospigliosi were fed up and wanted Atto out of town. To avoid disgrace, they allowed him officially to maintain his rooms at the Quirinal, but they also made it clear that Atto should leave Rome and not return.[7]

Another less obvious development may also have hastened Atto's departure. His exit coincides almost too coincidentally with the flight of his friend Marie Mancini Colonna from her husband. Tired of what seemed to her the repressive atmosphere of Rome and fearful that her husband might eventually cloister or even murder her, Marie decided to leave, and on May 29, 1672 she secretly fled for France, accompanied by her sister Hortense.[8] Strangely, Atto never mentions these events in his letters, even though they

[5] Notes for a letter from Simon Arnaud, marquis de Pomponne, to César d'Estrées, bishop of Laon, from Paris, March 25, 1672.

[6] Atto to Pomponne, from Rome, March 15, 1672. The tense of the main verb here ("non vi sarebbe stato") would seem imply that the danger had passed ("there *would have been* no safety"), but in fact the remainder of the letter reveals that the cloak-and-dagger activity was at its peak.

[7] This chain of events emerges in the series of Atto's letters from Rome, July 15, 1670 to September 30, 1672 (see appendix A). On the general efforts of the French for Laon's promotion – which actually occurred on August 24, 1671 but was held *in pectore* until May 16, 1672 – see Ludwig Pastor, *The History of the Popes from the Close of the Middle Ages*, trans. Ernest Graf (London: Kegan Paul, Trench, Trubner and Co., 1891–1953), XXXI:473–74. On Atto's position as *pronotario apostolico*, see chapter 5.

[8] Marie Mancini, *La vérité dans son jour*, ed. Patricia Francis Cholakian and Elizabeth C. Goldsmith (Delmar, N.Y.: Scholars' Facsimiles and Reprints, 1998; first published 1677, without place or publisher), 63–64; Claude Dulong, *Marie Mancini: La première passion de Louis XIV* (Paris: Perrin, 1993), 180–87. Dulong's biography is probably the best modern consideration of Marie's melodramatic life.

quickly became an international incident. But as one of Marie's intimates he may well have learned of her plans: it would certainly help explain why about a month before she left he started requesting his own return to France.[9] Unfortunately, the loss of most of Atto and Marie's correspondence makes this scenario pure conjecture, but Atto may well have wanted to follow his powerful friend.

In the event, Atto finally left Rome only in October 1672, and he proceeded directly to Paris. Trenta continues the narrative:

Melani remained in Paris for almost three years, and having patched up his own interests during that period, he returned to Pistoia in 1675. There he was passing his days peacefully when, at the repeated prodding of M. de Gommont, extraordinary envoy to the grand duke, he felt obliged to return with [Gommont] to France in 1679. From then on, he remained [in France] to the end of his life and was employed by the king and [foreign] ministry in weighty and important affairs, so that, with his intervention, various princes settled their issues with that court.[10]

While this outline is helpful, especially as the role of Gommont is otherwise unrecorded, the available evidence again suggests a more involved series of events. In the first place, Atto's initial return to Paris could only have lasted a number of months, not three years. He was certainly back in Pistoia by July 21, 1673, when he addressed a letter to Cardinal Flavio Chigi from there, and he seems to have remained in Tuscany for roughly the next two-and-a-half years.[11] One of Atto's aims during this period "at home" – and perhaps even the principal reason for his return – was his reinsertion into papal politics. In the fall of 1673, Cardinal d'Estrées (in Rome) wrote a long letter to Pomponne about how to deal with Atto's renewed ambitions, which d'Estrées quickly perceived through Atto's feigned apathy:

Since the Abbé Melani returned to Pistoia, he has written me many times about his plans to retire out of world-weariness, and he cites the decline of His Holiness as his

---

[9] The first letter to contain such a request is his to Pomponne, from Rome, April 26, 1672.

[10] Trenta, *Memorie*, I:263. Trenta's study, as well as all of the correspondence I have seen from Atto's later years, contradicts Prunières's assertion that Atto habitually traveled back and forth between Italy and Paris during this period (*L'opéra italien en France avant Lulli*, Bibliothèque de l'Institut Français de Florence [Université de Grenoble], ser. 1, Collection d'histoire et de linguistique française et italienne comparées, no. 3 [Paris: Honoré Champion, 1913], 274). After 1679, Atto seems to have stayed put.

[11] The last certain notice of Atto's presence in France is his letter to his brother Filippo, from Saint-Germain-en-Laye, February 17, 1673. Cardinal d'Estrées addressed a letter to Atto in Florence on October 4, 1674, and Atto registered his first will in Pistoia in 1675. This will is referred to in I Fn, Tordi 133, as cited by Robert Lamar Weaver, "Materiali per le biografie dei fratelli Melani," *Rivista italiana di musicologia* 12 (1977): 264; like Weaver, I was unable to locate an actual copy of this early version.

reason for not coming to Rome for some time. I have understood that he would like me to set aside the order His Majesty had given him to stay away [from Rome] … I do not believe he will carry out his plan to come here after having received my response. If he comes nonetheless, the ambassador and I would need to receive, Sir, His Majesty's orders as to what we should say to him. I see plainly that his presence will be very irksome to Cardinal Rospigliosi and that, if he were to remain here … he would no longer enjoy the same esteem in France as he did [when he visited] last year.[12]

Clearly, the passage of a year had not mollified Rospigliosi's annoyance, and, as d'Estrées puts it, "in a court and with souls so susceptible to alarm and anxiety, things that elsewhere would not be important [here] cause dangerous effects."[13]

In all likelihood, this political roadblock accounts for Atto's eventual and definitive return to Paris. In this light, the requests from M. Gommont look like another attempt to keep Atto away from Rome. Atto left for Paris on October 26, 1675, after signing his first will, and so arrived back in France at least three years before Trenta and all previous studies have placed him there.[14] Apparently, once he saw that Rome was off-limits, he did not tarry long in Tuscany, which offered but a poor arena for his diplomatic skills. Instead, the fifty-year-old returned to serve at the most important and powerful court in Europe, a stage from which he never retired.[15]

Padrone della casa

Throughout his life, but especially in his later years, Atto concerned himself with supporting and advancing the rest of his large family. Although a consideration of his efforts requires some chronological backtracking, the discussion fits well at this point in the study, alongside the other achievements of his maturity. The rise of the *casa* Melani has usually been attributed to the cumulative efforts of the brothers, in Lorenzo Bianconi's words, "to the

---

[12] Cardinal d'Estrées to Pomponne, from Rome, November 8, 1673.   [13] Ibid.

[14] On Atto's departure date, see his letter to Ippolito Bentivoglio, from Pistoia, October 25, 1675. On the widely reported date of 1679, see primarily Weaver, "Materiali," 282, on which all recent dictionary entries are based. Weaver in turn adopted the date from Adelmo Damerini, "La partitura de *L'Ercole in Tebe* di Jacopo Melani (1623–1676)," *Bullettino storico pistoiese* 19 (1917): 63, who depended on Prunières, *L'opéra*, 274.

[15] Evidence for Atto's permanent residence in Paris appears below and, more definitively, in the list of his letters in Appendix A. Among other things, this evidence contradicts the setting of Rita Monaldi and Francesco Sorti's novel *Imprimatur* (Omnibus [Milan: Arnaldo Mondadori, 2002), which, though it claims a historical basis, places Atto in Rome in September 1683.

remarkable success of certain singer and composer members of the family."[16] The family itself propagated this view in its eighteenth-century application for nobility, citing the diplomatic accomplishments of both Atto and his younger brother Alessandro.[17] Instead, it is clear that, by the time Atto withdrew to France, he alone had for years been governing the Melani clan, and that to a great extent his brothers owed their accomplishments – musical and otherwise – to opportunities that Atto orchestrated. Indeed, in much the same way that Mattias patronized Atto (or that Domenico Melani had patronized all his children), Atto now supported his family. Though he could never be a father, Atto's greater wealth and political power made him the *padrone* of the Melani dynasty, and from that position, surprisingly, he may have exercised his greatest influence on the history of music.

Perhaps the most interesting manifestation of Atto's authority appears in the career of Jacopo Melani, Atto's older brother. As the eldest, Jacopo would normally have directed and indeed continued his family. But, by September 26, 1648, when the boys' father Domenico fell from a window and broke his neck, thereby stranding his widow with nine children aged four to twenty-five, Atto already seems to have been leading the clan.[18] It was Atto, not Jacopo, who in the early 1640s had captured the attention of the Medici family and the agents of Mazarin. And although Jacopo accompanied his brother on their two trips to Paris during that decade, Jacopo's invitation was consequent to Atto's, and the young castrato commanded all the attention (see chapter 2).

Atto's rising star thus seems to have governed Jacopo's destiny as well. Within six months of the brothers' return from Paris, i.e., in the fall of 1645, Jacopo was elected organist of the cathedral of Pistoia, having served there as a simple chorister for the previous twelve years.[19] The following year he was chosen as president of a new academy of singers and was admitted into the prestigious Congregazione dei Trentatré, a group of Pistoiese nobility and

---

[16] Lorenzo Bianconi, *Music in the Seventeenth Century*, trans. David Bryant (Cambridge: Cambridge University Press, 1987), 89, originally published as *Il Seicento* (Turin: E.D.T., 1982); Weaver implies much the same thing throughout his "Materiali" article.

[17] Weaver, "Materiali," 261–62n.

[18] The evidence concerning Domenico Melani's death, the precise date of which has not previously been reported, comes from part of the Felice Dondori diary (a general chronicle of activities in Pistoia during this period) found at I PSc, Raccolta Chiappelli, 188, p. 169: "A dì detto [September 26, 1648] Domenico Melani Campanaio della Cattedrale cadde a terra da una Finestra di Casa sua su'l corso, e roppesi 'l collo." On Atto's leadership of the family, see below regarding his purchase in March 1649 of the farm known as "Il Batocchio": note that in this transaction Jacopo served as Atto's agent.

[19] Franco Baggiani, "I maestri di cappella nella cattedrale di Pistoia," *Bollettino storico pistoiese*, 3rd ser., 21 (1986): 53. Baggiani confirms Weaver's observation ("Materiali," 275–59) that Jacopo's election was marred by irregularities in the voting, but Baggiani also clarifies that Jacopo in fact succeeded to the position. Could this controversy be a sign of resistance from other families (including the Fedi, who were also musicians at the cathedral) to the rapid elevation of the Melani?

musicians founded to enrich the music of the cathedral.[20] He scored a real coup in 1655 when he became in effect the official composer to the Florentine Accademia dei Sorgenti, whose aim was to produce theatrical works; the next year he seems to have assumed an analogous position with the similar but more aristocratic Accademia degli Immobili.[21] These positions launched his career as a composer for the stage. That the two academies shared as their "protector" Cardinal Giovan Carlo de' Medici, brother of Atto's patron Mattias, surely helps explain how an obscure organist from Pistoia could have been tapped for work of such prominence.[22]

The real peak of Jacopo's career came about through the support of another prominent family with ties to Atto. For the carnival following the papal election of Giulio Rospigliosi, Marie Mancini Colonna and her husband decided to produce an opera, *Il Girello*, in their palazzo. The Colonnas during these years vied with Queen Christina of Sweden to present the most elaborate entertainments in Rome. Their decision to employ Jacopo as composer, and so bypass a host of competent Romans, again seems explicable only through Atto's influence.[23] That impression is strengthened by their decision the following year to commission Atto's even less-experienced brother Alessandro to write another carnival opera (*L'empio punito*). *Il Girello* turned out to be a hit and became one of the most frequently performed works of the century, helping establish Jacopo, in Robert Weaver's estimation, as "the leading 17th-century composer of comic operas."[24] Jacopo's talent clearly

---

[20] Damerini, "La partitura," 47; Jean Grundy Fanelli, "La musica per la chiesa e l'oratorio di San Prospero nel Sei–Settecento," *Bollettino storico pistoiese*, 3rd ser., 25 (1990): 65.

[21] John Walter Hill, "Le relazioni di Antonio Cesti con la corte e i teatri di Firenze," *Rivista italiana di musicologia* 11 (1976): 28–34. Jacopo's first dramatic effort was apparently the *intermedi* for the *commedia La donna più costante* sponsored by the Sorgenti during the winter of 1655–56. The following year, he produced *Il potestà di Colognole* for the Immobili, the first of a string of works for them. Hill shows that Jacopo was in fact a member of the Sorgenti, although his dues were waived and he received special remuneration. He probably did not belong to the aristocratic Immobili, but merely worked for them.

[22] On the "teamwork" of the four Medici brothers with respect to artistic patronage, see Sara Mamone, "Most Serene Brothers-Princes-Impresarios: Theater in Florence under the Management and Protection of Mattias, Giovan Carlo, and Leopoldo de' Medici," *Journal of Seventeenth-Century Music* 9 (2003), http://sscm-jscm.press.uiuc.edu/jscm/v9/no1/Mamone.html. Jacopo received his greatest sign of prestige in Tuscany in the summer of 1661 with his commission to write *Ercole in Tebe* for the wedding celebrations of Grand Prince Cosimo III and Marguerite-Louise D'Orléans. (On Atto's involvement in the arrangement of this marriage, see chapter 5.)

[23] On the production of *Il Girello*, see Margaret Murata, "Il carnevale a Roma sotto Clemente IX Rospigliosi," *Rivista italiana di musicologia* 12 (1977): 89. Murata (90) implies that Jacopo was given this opportunity because the librettist, Filippo Acciaioli, may have met him during a 1654 production of Cavalli's *Hipermestra* in Florence.

[24] Robert Lamar Weaver, "Melani (1) Jacopo Melani," *Grove Music Online*, ed. Laura Macy, www.grovemusic.com (accessed June 1, 2006). On *Il Girello*, see Robert Lamar Weaver, "*Il Girello*, a 17th-Century Burlesque Opera," *Quadrivium* 12.2 (1971): 141–63; and Murata, "Il carnevale," 89–90, 99.

justified his opportunities. But those opportunities grew so consistently out of Atto's sphere of activity as to imply Atto's patronage, his personal efforts to bring Jacopo to the attention of the powerful. Without Atto, Jacopo might have remained a provincial *maestro di cappella*.

This unconventional hierarchy – with the eldest son reduced to a client of his brother – may have caused humiliation or dispute, for in later life Jacopo distanced himself from his siblings. A financial agreement between Atto and Jacopo dated October 18, 1656 testifies that all financial arrangements between the two had been terminated and that the two "have divided and separated and now live divided and separately."[25] This break is confirmed three years later by a letter in which Atto, begging Mattias for financial assistance, declares that only his brothers Jacinto and Alessandro remain in Pistoia to look after their mother and sisters: "by my luck, [I have] an older brother who has become a priest so as not to be a family man, and to live apart from his relatives so as not to have to think of anyone but himself."[26] Unlike most of his siblings, Jacopo did not name his brother Jacinto – or one of Jacinto's children, i.e., the continuing branch of the family – as sole heir of his estate, and although Jacopo died in Pistoia he chose not to be buried in the family tomb at the church of S. Domenico.[27] Although – or perhaps because – Atto's influence may have launched Jacopo's career, the eldest Melani brother seems eventually to have withdrawn from his family, ceding his position of leadership.

By contrast, the other Melani boys registered few objections to Atto's authority. Indeed, the next younger brother, Francesco Maria, probably owed Atto the better part of his career. Born in 1628, Francesco sang for just three years in the cathedral of Pistoia (1639–41). At some point, presumably in his early adulthood, he entered the Servite order, taking the name Filippo by which he was subsequently known. In the spring of 1654, out of the blue, Cardinal Mazarin began pursuing Filippo's services as a singer, almost certainly at Atto's prodding (see chapter 5). Indeed, the cardinal wrote a letter to his ally Cardinal Antonio Barberini asking the latter's help in procuring Filippo's release from his order (while preserving his standing as a priest). Prunières assumed that the goal was to help Filippo "sortir du

---

[25] I Fas, Notarile moderno, protocollo 14598, f. 80r–v.

[26] Atto to Mattias, from Saint-Jean-de-Luz, August 11, 1659.

[27] Instead, Jacopo left virtually everything to the Congregazione di S. Filippo Neri (Fanelli, "La musica," 66) and was buried in the church of S. Prospero (Robert Lamar Weaver, "Florentine Comic Operas of the Seventeenth Century" [Ph.D. diss., University of North Carolina, Chapel Hill, 1958], 318). On the will, see Weaver, "Materiali," 264n. Although Weaver claims that Jacopo was the only brother not to name Jacinto as the *erede universale*, in fact Alessandro, who spent most of his life in Rome, did likewise (Jean Lionnet, "La musique a Saint-Louis des Français de Rome au XVII° [*sic*] siècle," *Note d'archivio per la storia musicale*, n.s., 4 suppl. [1986]: 155–57).

couvent," so that the singer could come to France, and this interpretation has generally been accepted.[28] More recent investigation has shown that Filippo was not cloistered at all but instead was pursuing a career in church music at various institutions: in 1652, for instance, he joined the *cappella* of San Marco in Venice.[29] Mazarin's entreaty to Barberini, then, aimed not to free Filippo from a monastery, but rather to permit the singer's appearance in operas. Such a career path had a famous precedent, of course: Filippo's fellow Tuscan Antonio Cesti also belonged to a monastic order (Franciscan), began a career in church music, and eventually sought release from his vows upon turning to the stage.[30] As the text of Mazarin's letter reveals, Atto provided the primary stimulus for this brother's discharge:

You yourself know, Your Eminence, how well Atto Melani served in the *Orfeo* that was performed here some years ago. Because afterwards he also has maintained a particular devotion and warm affection toward this crown, he deserves benevolent protection. In one of his letters, he asks me to intercede with Your Eminence to bid you use your authority on behalf of Padre Don Filippo, his brother, so that [Filippo] can receive permission to leave his Servite order while retaining the priest's habit, and so I have happily taken the liberty to keenly entreat this of Your Eminence.[31]

The date of Filippo's eventual release is uncertain. When on May 25, 1654 Antonio Barberini responded to Mazarin's letter, he was not optimistic, although he promised to do his best. But, as Jonathan and Beth Glixon have shown, a "D. Filippo, et suo fratello" sang in the opera *Eupatra* at the Venetian Teatro S. Aponal during carnival 1654–55; the Glixons speculate, quite sensibly, that the singers are Filippo Melani and his brother Bartolomeo.[32] Either the Servites granted Filippo's release very quickly, or – like Cesti – he performed without their consent.

In any case, when Filippo finally left Italy, he proceeded not to Mazarin in Paris, but to Innsbruck, to take up a prestigious post serving at the court of Archduke Sigismund: again, one can sense Atto's hand. The elder brother

---

[28] Prunières, *L'opéra*, 174–77, is the important early source on Filippo's activities. See also Weaver, "Materiali," 256 and 261n.

[29] Beth L. Glixon and Jonathan E. Glixon, *Inventing the Business of Opera: The Impresario and His World in Seventeenth-Century Venice*, AMS Studies in Music (Oxford: Oxford University Press, 2006), 195n.

[30] David L. Burrows, Carl B. Schmidt, and Jennifer Williams Brown, "Cesti, Antonio," *Grove Music Online*, ed. Laura Macy, www.grovemusic.com (accessed June 5, 2006).

[31] Copy of a letter from Mazarin to Cardinal Antonio Barberini, from Paris, April 3, 1654 (published by Prunières, *L'opéra*, 174n).

[32] Antonio Barberini to Mazarin, from Rome, May 25, 1654, quoted in Prunières, *L'opéra*, 175n–76n. Glixon and Glixon, *Inventing*, 195, 198, 328, 346–47; they mistakenly call Bartolomeo "Bortolo."

had solid patronage ties to Innsbruck: that court maintained a close relationship to the Medici through the marriage of Sigismund's brother, Ferdinand
Karl, to Mattias's sister, Anna. And Atto knew everyone personally, having
himself served the court – if not entirely satisfactorily – during his travels
of 1653 (see chapter 3). Especially revealing is the timing of the appointment.
In his fundamental study of music in Innsbruck, Walter Senn reports a pay
record dated March 1655 for "Filippo Mellari [*sic*] und Ludovico Porta …
'Musicanten von Venedig'"; Senn speculates that "Mellari" is a misspelling
of "Melani." [33] That conclusion now seems inescapable, given the Glixons'
evidence of Filippo's Venetian activity in the preceding months. In this
scenario, then, less than a year passed between Mazarin's request to
Antonio Barberini and Filippo's arrival in Innsbruck. Considering the time
needed to arrange both the position itself and the release from Filippo's vows,
Atto may already have been thinking of Innsbruck when he approached
Mazarin for help. In other words, Atto may well have exploited his favor with
Mazarin, as well as the cardinal's need for singers, to open up broader and
more lucrative avenues for his brother.

Of course Mazarin did eventually call Filippo to Paris in 1659, and the
singer soon took part in court entertainments alongside Atto.[34] When these
responsibilities drew to a close, Atto directed Filippo to make a detour to
Florence on his way back to Innsbruck so that the Medici could experience
his talents in person. Atto writes Mattias, "Your Highness will find that
[Filippo] is a skillful *virtuoso* and is better than all those that are here [in
Paris], both for the chamber and the theater; he has developed a contralto
voice of complete perfection, [one] of the most pleasing that has ever been
heard. If the Prince Cardinal Giovan Carlo wishes to employ him in the
celebrations to be undertaken there, my brother will consider himself exceedingly fortunate."[35] When Filippo later lost his post in Innsbruck over the
probably well-founded suspicion of his having spied for Atto (see chapter 5),
Filippo seems to have capitalized on this Florentine introduction, for he
served as a musician to the grand-ducal court from 1672 to 1702, just two

---

[33] Walter Senn, *Musik und Theater am Hof zu Innsbruck: Geschichte der Hofkapelle vom 15.
Jahrhundert bis zu deren Auflösung in Jahre 1748* (Innsbruck: Österreichische Verlagsanstalt
Innsbruck, 1954), 267. Interestingly, Filippo's name appears nowhere else in Senn's study,
presumably because the extant rolls of court musicians preserve only snapshots of the
establishment. The relevant rosters are dated 1653 (before Filippo arrived), 1660 (during his time
in Paris), and October 25, 1665 (the probable year of his departure). Prunières (*L'opéra*, 176–77)
placed Filippo's arrival in Innsbruck in 1657.

[34] Prunières, *L'opéra*, 233, 257, 264, 275.

[35] Atto to Mattias, from Paris, September 3, 1660. The "feste" under discussion are those for the
wedding of Cosimo III and Marguerite-Louise d'Orléans.

years before his death.[36] By touting Filippo to the Medici, Atto again helped orchestrate his brother's future.

The career of Bartolomeo Melani, also a castrato, parallels Filippo's in many ways. Indeed, as Atto was arranging the position for Filippo in Innsbruck, he seems to have found another for Bartolomeo in Munich. Of course, some of the most important diplomatic dealings of Atto's career took place in the summer and autumn of 1657 with the elector of Bavaria and his wife (again, see chapter 5). And so when in September the elector's *maestro di cappella*, Johann Caspar Kerll, granted Bartolomeo a post in the chapel (on excellent financial terms), the move looks very much like a reward of gratitude to Atto.[37] In fact, Bartolomeo's arrival in Munich in December 1657 came just one month after Atto's departure, and the younger Melani appears also to have replaced his brother as secret liaison between Mazarin and the Francophile electress.[38] When less than a year later Bartolomeo was imprisoned for such activities, Atto again came to the rescue and won his release (see chapter 5). By 1660 Bartolomeo had returned to the safety of the cathedral of Pistoia, where eight years later he was named *maestro di cappella*.[39] Franco Baggiani

---

[36] On the suspicions of the archduke, Atto's letter to de Lionne, from Florence, August 24, 1663: "Dopo che D. Filippo mio fratello ritornò da Parigi a Inspruch, l'Arciduca Sigismondo suo Padrone non lo vidde con quella confidenza di prima, et essendo poi divenuto regnante, non faceva altro che addimandare se egli scriveva in Francia." On Filippo's probable dates of return to Innsbruck and later retreat to Italy, see chapter 5, notes 69 and 70. On Filippo's position at the Medici court, see John Walter Hill, "Oratory Music in Florence, II: At San Firenze in the Seventeenth and Eighteenth Centuries," *Acta musicologica* 51 (1979): 260; Weaver, "Materiali," 267; and Warren Kirkendale, *The Court Musicians in Florence During the Principate of the Medici: With a Reconstruction of the Artistic Establishment*, "Historiae musicae cultores" biblioteca, no. 61 (Florence: Olschki, 1993), 412–13. Filippo's precise date of death, which Weaver gave as "*post* 1703" ("Materiali," 256), can now be specified as March 12, 1704 (I PSc, Raccolta Chiappelli, 14, fragment of the Melani family diary).

[37] In Kerll's letter to Bartolomeo Melani, from Munich, September 24, 1657, Kerll accepts the financial terms that Bartolomeo has previously proposed. The letter is published in Adolf Sandberger, introduction to *Ausgewählte Werke des kürfürstlich bayerischen Hofkapellmeisters Johann Kasper Kerll (1627–1693)*, vol. II, part 2 of *Denkmäler der Tonkunst in Bayern*, Denkmäler Deutscher Tonkunst, Folge 2 (Leipzig: Breitkopf & Härtel, 1901), xvii. Prunières attributed the appointment to Kerll's acquaintance with Filippo (*L'opéra*, 177n).

[38] On Bartolomeo's date of entrance into the chapel, Fr[anz] M[ichael] Rudhart, *Geschichte der Oper am Hofe zu München* (Freising: Franz Datterer, 1865), 68. On his activities, [Alessandro] Ademollo, "Un campanaio e la sua famiglia," *Fanfulla della Domenica*, December 30, 1883; also, Atto's letter to Mattias (without date or place, but clearly from this period), I Fas, MdP, filza 5419, f. 940r–v.

[39] The musical life of the cathedral of Pistoia offers its own testimony to Atto's influence. The election of Jacopo as organist in 1645 initiated a 58-year period of the Melani brothers' domination of the posts of *maestro di cappella* or organist. Weaver ("Materiali," 259–60) has suggested that "i Melani … seppero manovrare la cappella come dominio loro proprio," but surely this kind of control would have been impossible without the support of the nobility, either inside or outside the church hierarchy. Although the father, Domenico, had been close to the bishop of Pistoia, it seems more likely that it was Atto's connections to the Medici and, perhaps more importantly, the Rospigliosi, that allowed his brothers to treat the cathedral as "their own dominion."

reports that in November of 1669 Clement IX, for the sake of Bartolomeo's interests, issued the bull "Exigit" that suppressed the convent of S. Girolamo and awarded the revenue to the *maestro di cappella*, organist, and singers of the cathedral of Pistoia: that Atto enjoyed unprecedented access to the pope at this time is surely not coincidental (chapter 5). Bartolomeo remained at the cathedral until his retirement in 1703, just one year before his death.[40]

The career of Atto's youngest brother, Alessandro, echoes remarkably that of Jacopo, and probably for similar reasons. After short stints as *maestro di cappella* at the cathedrals of Orvieto, Ferrara, and finally, upon Jacopo's departure in 1666, Pistoia itself, Alessandro followed Atto to Rome, where he too appears to have profited from his elder brother's familiarity with Clement IX.[41] Only five months after the election, Alessandro was named *maestro di cappella* of S. Maria Maggiore in Rome, a church particularly dear to the pope and in which he was eventually buried.[42] Five years later, upon the specific recommendation of the French ambassador, Alessandro became *maestro* at the French national church in Rome, S. Luigi dei Francesi, an advancement that scholars have already generally conceded to Atto's influence.[43] During carnival 1668, the Rospigliosi looked to Alessandro – a composer with no previous stage experience – to compose *L'Ergenia* for performance in their palace; the next year, the Colonna chose him to follow up Jacopo's *Girello* with an even more opulently produced *L'empio punito*.[44] Atto's support continued even later in life. In 1680, Atto wrote to his family from Paris,

If I have the opportunity to speak with the king, I want to tell him something about the very beautiful *commedia* written by Signor Alessandro, who is today truly the leading man of the world in his art … Greet him and congratulate him in my name for the applause that his efforts have received there, which is one of the greatest satisfactions a *virtuoso* could enjoy. Have the libretto of the poetry sent to me so that I

---

[40] In 1676, for reasons that are unclear, Bartolomeo stepped down as *maestro* and returned to the post of organist. On the history of Bartolomeo's positions at the cathedral, see Weaver, "Materiali," 269, and Baggiani, "I maestri," 55–56. Weaver (256) gives Bartolomeo's date of death as May 29, 1703, based apparently on a letter from I Fas, MdP, filza 5910, f. 169. Baggiani (56n) gives April 20, 1704, based on I PS, Archivio Vescovile, Morti di S. Giovanni Fuorcivitas, a date that is confirmed by the fragment of the Melani family diary at I PSc, Raccolta Chiappelli, 14. Bartolomeo died, then, just one month after his brother Filippo.

[41] Baggiani, "I maestri," 54.

[42] Lionnet, "La musique," n.s., 3 suppl. (1985), 99. Rospigliosi had been canon and later vicar of this church.

[43] Ibid., 99, 117–18; Weaver, "Florentine Comic Operas," 325; Prunières, *L'opéra*, 273.

[44] Weaver, "Materiali," 274–75; and Murata, "Il carnevale," 88–89, 94–95. Also see Nino Pirrotta, *Don Giovanni in musica: Dall'*Empio punito *a Mozart*, Musica Critica, Saggi Marsilio (Venice: Marsilio, 1991), 25–38.

can see whether it is something suitable for this country, in case the king wants to hear it.[45]

The work in question would appear to be *Il Corindo*, a "favola boschereccia" performed that year at the Medici villa in Pratolino. Although a French presentation seems never to have been contemplated, Atto's encouragement is unambiguous.

His greatest act of patronage toward Alessandro came even later. Certainly the accomplishment most often recalled by Alessandro's family was his appointment in 1699 as resident of the king of Poland at the papal court, a promotion that led Weaver to pronounce Alessandro, like his elder brother, "politically shrewd." [46] But again the honor was owed almost entirely to Atto. Only some sort of outside influence can explain how a Roman *maestro di cappella*, with no previous diplomatic experience, could be awarded a post second in rank only to the Polish ambassador. Atto in fact wielded that kind of influence through the person of Cardinal Francesco Buonvisi. In the mid-1670s Buonvisi had been papal nuncio to the king of Poland, and the cardinal maintained his Polish contacts.[47] An entry in the Melani family diary for 1699 further hints at Atto's involvement: "Alessandro received the dispatches, letters, credentials, and patent of His Majesty of Poland by way of Paris, from the abate [i.e., Atto]."[48] And finally, the anonymous "Vita dell'Abbate Atto Melani" preserved in the National Library in Florence states outright that "[Atto] served … King Augustus of Poland in solicitous

---

[45] Atto to Filippo Melani, from Paris, September 27, 1680.

[46] Witness the mention of this position in the family's application for admission to the nobility, reproduced in Weaver, "Materiali," 261–62n. The date of Alessandro's appointment was in fact 1699, not 1700 as reported by Ademollo ("Un campanaio," 2) and repeated by Weaver ("Materiali," 289). The actual patent of appointment, signed by King Augustus II of Poland, is preserved in I PSc, Raccolta Chiappelli, 40.I, and bears the date August 18, 1699. Apparently Prunières (*L'opéra*, 273) was reluctant to believe that Alessandro could actually attain this post, suggesting he only "dreamed" of it. On Weaver's assessment, see his "Florentine Comic Operas," 318.

[47] On Atto's relationship to Buonvisi, see Weaver, "Materiali," 265, as well as many of Atto's letters from Rome, 1669–74, where he proposes Buonvisi for the papacy (see chapter 5). On Buonvisi in Poland, see Sebastiano Ciampi, *Bibliografia critica delle antiche reciproche corrispondenze politiche, ecclesiastiche, scientifiche, letterarie, artistiche dell'Italia colla Russia, colla Polonia ed altre parti settentrionali* (Florence: Guglielmo Piatti, 1839), II:79; and Pastor, *History*, XXXI:455–58 and vol. XXXII *passim*.

[48] I PSc, Raccolta Chiappelli, 188, inserted fascicle with signature "2.do," f. 15v. Three of at least four fascicles of a Melani family diary, covering roughly the years 1697–1711, are preserved; that they were originally conceived as a single document is suggested by the signatures on their first folios (top left recto). The first two fascicles are inserted loosely into I PSc, Raccolta Chiappelli, 188 (the Dondori family diary); the fourth appears as part of the miscellaneous I PSc, Raccolta Chiappelli, 14. The third fascicle, covering roughly late 1700 to late 1703, is missing, and additional fascicles could have existed. The diary appears to have been maintained by Jacinto and then, after his death, his son Luigi.

dealings and arranged that Alessandro his brother be adorned with the title of his minister in Rome to Clement XI."[49]

Atto shared the benefits of his success with all his brothers. By using his connections to advance their (usually) musical careers, Atto himself became a patron of the arts, brokering links – always to his advantage – between those who desired music and those who could provide it. By this mechanism, and particularly by enabling Jacopo's and Alessandro's careers in opera, this castrato may well have made his greatest impact on *Seicento* music not as a virtuoso performer, nor even a composer, but as a conduit of musical patronage.

Along with promoting his brothers' careers, Atto supported his family by managing its resources, and specifically by purchasing real estate. Although in his youth he may have gambled away some of his earnings, he soon began planning more responsibly.[50] To ascend socially, the Melani needed financial independence. For a member of the bourgeoisie, the most common means to this end was investment in land, that is, farms and estates that would render income and free the family from work.[51]

Already in March 1649, as Atto was hiding at Saint-Germain with the French court, he directed Jacopo to make the down-payment on an estate called "Il Batocchio" in Borgo Le Gore. Sold by a certain Giovanni Rinaldi for 3,400 *scudi*, the farm included around eleven fields of vineyard and mulberry trees, a house for the workers, a threshing floor, oven, well, dove-house, stable, cottage, and two vats with the capacity of about one hundred barrels of wine.[52] Almost immediately, Atto acted to increase the profitability of his operation. A letter from a Pistoiese official to Mattias recounts Atto's complaint in the summer of 1650 that the tax collectors at the gates of the city were overcharging the grain tax. Although this official found the allegation

[49] I Fn, Rossi Cassigoli, MS 268, p. 152. Several of the letters to Atto from Cardinal Pietro Ottoboni, from Rome, in 1699–1700 refer to efforts to win this post for Alessandro: Ottoboni was offering both brothers advice on how to proceed.

[50] From the Dondori diary at I PSc, Raccolta Chiappelli, 188, p. 107 (July 26, 1645), as quoted in Jean Grundy Fanelli, "Un animatore della vita musicale pistoiese del Seicento: Monsignore Felice Cancellieri, sopranista," *Bollettino storico pistoiese*, 3rd ser., 24 (1989): 60–61. His gambling may have been an imprudent attempt to mimic the nobility.

[51] On this strategy, see Franco Valsecchi, *L'Italia nel Seicento e nel Settecento*, vol. VI of *Società e costume: Panorama di storia sociale e tecnologica* (Turin: U.T.E.T., 1967), 625; Norbert Elias, *The Court Society*, trans. Edmund Jephcott (New York: Pantheon, 1983), 55, originally published as *Die höfische Gesellschaft* (Darmstadt: Hermann Luchterhand, 1969); James S. Amelang, "The Bourgeois," in *Baroque Personae*, ed. Rosario Villari, trans. Lydia G. Cochrane (Chicago: University of Chicago Press, 1995), 300, originally published as *L'uomo barocco*, Storia e Società (Rome: Laterza, 1991).

[52] Weaver ("Materiali," 263) notes this purchase, which is reported both by the notary who registered the transaction (I Fas, Notarile moderno, protocollo 14591, f. 111r–v) and in the family's collection of important documents (I Fn, Tordi 350, f. 195). Atto paid off his debt on the farm on November 16, 1651 (I Fas, Notarile moderno, protocollo 14594, f. 22).

unlikely, he removed the lieutenant of the tax collectors as a courtesy to Atto, a gesture obviously dependent upon the singer's connections.[53]

Atto in fact continued accumulating property in Tuscany to the end of his life. On January 19, 1663 he purchased a slightly larger estate in the municipality of S. Angiolo from Giovanni Sozzifanti for 6,924 *scudi*.[54] Seven years later he bought two houses on some land in the parish of S. Giovanni Fuorcivitas, for which he paid 1,500 *scudi*.[55] Then in 1699 Atto purchased the Podere della Villa at Castelnuovo, auctioned off by the creditors of the deceased nobleman Giovanni Battista Cellesi, and in 1703 the family acquired the Podere del "Credita Benintendi."[56] With the notice of the purchase at Castelnuovo

---

[53] Lionardo Signorini to Mattias, from Pistoia, July 6, 1650.

[54] Notice of this transaction appears in the Melani papers at I Fn, Tordi 350, f. 204, and in the notarial documents at I Fas, Notarile moderno, protocollo 14603, ff. 56v–66. Weaver ("Materiali," 259) misread the documents surrounding this transaction in Pier Lorenzo Franchi's "Memorie delle famiglie pistoiesi," from which he cites the following entry: "I(de)m la Religione di S. Stefano, et il Cav. Gio: Sozzifanti di consenso di d(ett)a Religione V(alute?) B(ancarie?) p(er) Scudi 6650 a Atto di Domenico Melani 19 Genn(ai)o 1663. roga(tor)e P. Andrea Parisi. 382." Weaver suggests that this entry records a payment made to Atto by the Order of S. Stefano and Cav. Sozzifanti, and he conjectures that Grand Duke Ferdinand II was using the Order and Sozzifanti as clandestine means of supporting Atto during the period of his disgrace in France. But in light of the actual notarial records, which Weaver apparently did not see, this entry must be read in reverse, as the acknowledgment of a *receipt* given to Atto for money he *paid* for the aforementioned property. (The minor difference in price between the two sources is probably attributable to taxes, which Tordi 350 specifically includes.)

Correction can also be offered with respect to Weaver's interpretation of another of these entries from Franchi: "I(de)m Quiet(anz)a di Sc(udi) 200. Atto Melani suo fratello tanti dovutili 18 8bre, 1656. Rog(ator)e P. And(re)a Parisi. 273" ("Materiali," 259). Here, Weaver reads a payment of 200 *scudi* from Jacopo to Atto, positing a link between this transaction and Jacopo's subsequent request for patronage from Mattias, a request that led to Jacopo's composition of works for the Accademia degli Immobili. Implied is that the money was intended (as a bribe?) for Mattias, with Atto as the most convenient courier. (The letter of Jacopo to Mattias, September 25, 1656, is found at I Fas, MdP, filza 5414, ff. 495–96.) Again, however, Weaver has misinterpreted the direction of the payment: the notarial records (I Fas, Notarile moderno, protocollo 14598, f. 80r–v) confirm that, on this date, Atto *paid* the 200 *scudi* to Jacopo to settle an old debt, part of their squaring of accounts noted above. Originally, Atto had borrowed 400 *scudi* from Jacopo on February 14, 1650. The present document acknowledges that Atto has paid back 200 *scudi* in cash, while the other 200 is being invested for the eventual dowry of their sister Cecilia. Atto is to collect the interest on this money to offset the costs of her maintenance, which he has been paying. With this arrangement, Jacopo acknowledges the debt retired.

[55] Maria Vittoria Feri Sguazzoni, "Vita domestica di una famiglia pistoiese: Casa Dondori 1653–1678," *Bollettino storico pistoiese*, 3d ser., 28 (1993): 138. Evidence for this transaction comes only from the Dondori family diary and is not confirmed by the Melani papers at I Fn, Tordi 350, although the property could have been sold before those papers were collected. In Atto's Italian will (see appendix G), this property is not discussed; instead, Atto mentions a house in the parish of S. Paolo in Pistoia.

[56] This purchase of 1699 is reported in both the family papers (I Fn, Tordi 350, f. 209) and their diary fragment (I PSc, Raccolta Chiappelli, 188, inserted fascicle with signature "2.do," f. 14); that of 1703 is mentioned only in the diary, without additional details (I PSc, Raccolta Chiappelli, 14, section G, unbound gathering, f. 35).

comes the telling remark in the Melani diary that, having recognized the need to invest in something secure, Atto had asked his relatives to watch out for promising real estate. Although the comment comes toward the end of Atto's life, it expresses the philosophy of financial planning that he had been practicing all along.[57] Indeed, Atto acquired property for the same reason he supported his brothers: so that he could convert his individual success into permanent advancement for the family.

Music again

In July 1678, the Roman composer Paolo Lorenzani arrived in Versailles and so impressed Louis XIV that – notwithstanding Lully's hostility to Italians – the king installed him as *maître de musique* to the queen. In June of the following year, Louis sent Lorenzani back to Italy with the charge of finding young castrati for the royal chapel, an institution that continued to employ these singers throughout the reign.[58] In that brief interval, Atto sought out this new Italian at court, initiating a relationship that endured through Lorenzani's tenure. The composer's name turns up frequently in Atto's letters to his brother Filippo during the late 1670s and 1680s, and that correspondence sheds new light on several matters, including Lorenzani's trip to Italy, the singers he found there, and the lifestyle of these Italian musicians in France. More importantly, the letters mark the return of music to Atto's recorded thoughts and activities. Now, just as he had promoted his brothers' careers, Atto tried to help the newly arrived Italians. Safely removed from his days as a performer, Atto sought to appear a gentlemanly patron of the art.

Indeed, he seems to have viewed Lorenzani's expedition as a chance to impress the French court with his own influence and taste. Already on February 3, 1679, Atto ordered his family to scout out young castrati:

His Majesty has charged [Lorenzani] to bring back to France as many young castrati as he can find who have the attitude and spirit suited to this [French] manner. He will come to Padre Filippo [in Florence] and to Pistoia to receive notices from all of you about every [prospect] he could engage, not only in Tuscany but also in Lucca and

---

[57] Apparently the Melani family kept acquiring properties after Atto's death. In the inventory of their possessions from 1782, thirteen different holdings are listed (I Fn, Tordi 350, ff. 195–256).

[58] On Lorenzani's career in France, see Henry Prunières, "Paolo Lorenzani à la court de France (1678–1694)," *La revue musicale* 3 (1922): 97–120, a study that has yet to be superseded. On the position of castrati in France in the late seventeenth and eighteenth centuries, and particularly their role in the chapel at Versailles, see Patrick Barbier, *La maison des italiens: Les castrats à Versailles* (Paris: Bernard Grasset, 1998).

other places. I want you to show him every courtesy, especially in Pistoia, and to lodge him and treat him well so that upon his return here he can tell of the favors he received.[59]

When the search did not immediately go well, Atto became sullen, conveying the exaggerated pessimism he often affected when one of his grand schemes was going awry: "I already knew that Signor Lorenzani would not find anything good there [in Tuscany], and the same thing will happen in Rome. I don't even want to talk about what can be hoped for by the fathers of the boys he brings back, because if [the boys] don't please, they will be sent home, and if they please, they will have to agree to a period of study, so as to sing in the French manner."[60]

In fact, though, Lorenzani returned to France with a number of good prospects, whose names were announced publicly in the *Mercure galant*: Antonio Favalli, Giuseppe Nardi, Tommaso Carli, Pietro Ramponi, and Filippo Santoni.[61] Although direct evidence is lacking, Lorenzani seems to have found several of the singers – if not all – through Atto's brothers. While Lorenzani was still in Italy, Atto was already fretting about the composer taking all the credit:

Signor Bartolomeo will do well to speak plainly to Signor Lorenzani, because [Lorenzani] … is a Roman braggart who acts as if he's a blood-brother of the king. He will make a profit on those boys because they will come here just to have an allowance for expenses and clothes, and Signor Lorenzani himself will manage these things for them. I'm not saying that they could not eventually receive the stipend that these other musicians have, which is not much. Since Signor Bartolomeo has endured the strain of teaching [the boys], he should be paid, and that windbag should not come here to brag about his efforts.[62]

The last comment suggests that many of the boys had studied with Bartolomeo, perhaps singing under him at the cathedral of Pistoia. What is known of the boys' birthplaces buttresses the idea. Three came from Tuscany: Santoni (probably) from Pescia, Carli from Siena, and Favalli from near

---

[59] Atto to Filippo, from Paris, February 3, 1679. Although Atto suggests Lorenzani had already departed, the composer was actually delayed until June by his new duties for the queen (Atto to Filippo, from Paris, May 26, 1679).

[60] Atto to Filippo, from Paris, August 4, 1679. (Atto's recognition of a distinctly French style is interesting, if not surprising.)

[61] See Prunières, "Paolo Lorenzani," 101. On the announcement, see Marcelle Benoit, *Versailles et les musiciens du roi 1661–1733: Étude institutionnelle et sociale*, La vie musicale en France sous les rois Bourbons, no. 19 (Paris: A. et J. Picard, 1971), 336–37.

[62] Atto to Filippo, from Fontainebleau, September 22, 1679.

Pistoia itself.[63] Ramponi may just possibly have come from Rome and been one of Alessandro's pupils, for at least later in life the two were linked.[64] Nothing is known of Nardi's origins, but Atto's letters do tell of a previously unknown sixth singer (unnamed) from Bologna, who died not long after his arrival in Paris because (according to Atto) Lorenzani "made them traverse the mountains on horseback through extreme weather so as not to have to spend twenty *doble* on two litters."[65] In light of Atto's familial representatives in Tuscany and Rome and his reference to Bartolomeo's efforts, he and his brothers may well have played a key role in Lorenzani's mission, a role in which Atto certainly took pride.

Not surprisingly, Atto seems to have sympathized with the young castrati, and indeed for many years he informally watched over them. The singer who turns up in Atto's letters most often, and most amusingly, is Favalli. At first, the reports were mostly negative: "Signor Lorenzani complains a great deal about the aforementioned Favalli, who swears like a Turk, and he says that if he had realized the boy's flaws, he would not have brought him here; [Lorenzani also says] the boy drinks too much and further has not read the letters from Signor Bartolomeo. For these reasons I predict a bad future for him, especially on account of the swearing, as the king is very sensitive on that subject."[66] Favalli was clearly a hellion, and the next summer he caused an outright scandal:

[63] Atto twice refers to one of the boys as "il pesciatino," without giving his name (letters to Filippo, from Paris, January 10, February 2, 1680; in the first, Atto comments, "il pesciatino, a me non piace punto."). Benoit (*Versailles*, 270n), however, cites a document of naturalization that describes Santoni as "de Peschia" (an indication Benoit did not understand); it also lists Carli as "de Sienne." Interestingly, a Stefano Carli (tenor) sang under Alessandro Melani at Santa Maria Maggiore in Rome at the turn of the eighteenth century; in fact, the records often refer to him as "Stefano di Melani": see Luca Della Libera, "La musica nella basilica di Santa Maria Maggiore a Roma, 1676–1712: Nuovi documenti su Corelli e sugli organici vocali e strumentali," *Recercare* 7 (1995): 144–54. Perhaps the Carli family, like the Melani, produced a number of singers, and Alessandro encouraged them. As for Favalli, a number of Atto's letters request that Bartolomeo (in Pistoia) pass along a message to Favalli's family directly; also the quotation below from the letter of June 21, 1680 implies that Favalli once lived in Pistoia.

[64] See Atto to Filippo, from Paris, September 20, 1694: at that time, it seems, Ramponi had made a trip to Rome, where he fell ill. Atto writes to his brother, "Sento dalla vostra de 3., il pericoloso stato nel quale si trovava quel povero giovane del Raponi [*sic*], e mi dispiacerebbe grandemente se fosse morto, perché egli è di tutti questi Italiani che sono nella musica del Rè, il più garbato, et il meglio creato, e S.M. le porta affetto particolare. In ogni caso avendo egli li Temperini, e due libre di Tabacco col passaporto, che il signor Alessandro gli ha consegnato in Roma, suppongo che come il putto che doveva venir seco, sarà partito con M. Fucher per passare il mese, gli avrete fatto parlare, accioché mi porti dette cose." Unfortunately, no reference to Ramponi appears in Jean Lionnet's study of the church at which Alessandro long worked ("La musique").

[65] Atto to Filippo, from Paris, February 2, 1680.

[66] Atto to Filippo, from Paris, December 15, 1679. Favalli's exact age at this time is unknown, although Atto consistently refers to him – and to the other young castrati – with the term *putto*.

You can tell the aforementioned Prior [Francesco] Panciatichi [grand prior of Pistoia] that those gentlemen [of Pistoia] were justified in their displeasure at the boy's coming here, for they knew how they had degraded him and that he needed to go to a hospital for healing rather than come to France. It has been necessary to cut out the venereal sores [*creste*] that were in him … to the shame of Tuscany, and Italy. Even the king has learned of it, because his chief surgeon, M. Felise, did the operation and believes that the boy is wracked with *mal francese* [syphilis], which the boy perhaps contributed to. For Favalli said to [Atto's servant] Biagini that he is a great sodomite … I should say that Signor Lorenzani is entirely mortified, and that next time he will first examine the asses of the boys before he hears their voices.[67]

As it turned out, Favalli was not sick with the *mal francese*, and, after a period of about six months convalescing at Saint-Germain, he was back with his cohorts at the royal chapel.[68]

As time passed, Atto came to appreciate better the young singer's talents. Atto's complaints on Favalli's behalf highlight the limitations placed on these castrati in France. In Atto's view, their biggest hurdle was learning the French style: until they did, they would receive but their living expenses. And yet the nature of their service hampered their improvement: "Last week I sent you a letter from Fontainebleau, two rather, given to me by Favalli and by another of these young boys, all of whom are doing well and are in good shape, with their expenses, shoes, and clothes provided for – but no sign of money. What's worse, by always singing in the chorus together with the others, and never *in concerto* [i.e., as a soloist], they will learn this [French] style only with difficulty."[69] Ten years later, Atto saw the situation little changed. When his brothers proposed sending another (unidentified) castrato to Paris, Atto waved them off:

If you have the best interests of that soprano at heart, you should not think about sending him here, because it would be difficult earning enough to live; the example of the others who have come should have made that clear to me. Here no one looks out for them. The king no longer enjoys music, and he only hears it when he goes to mass in his chapel. If Favalli were in Italy, and if he had gone every year to perform in the

[67] Atto to Filippo, from Fontainebleau, June 21, 1680.

[68] On Favalli's continuing illness, Atto's letter to Filippo, from Paris, September 27, 1680: "Il povero Favalli non guarisce, perché è tutto fracide per di dentro, essendo pieno d'ulcere che non si possono spegnere, è è restato a St. Germano solo, onde finché la Corte non anderà in detto luogo, non potrò vederlo, ne saperne altra Nuova." On Favalli's healing, Atto to Filippo, from Paris, February 14, 1681: "Io veddi l'altro giorno il favalli; e gli dimandai perché non scriveva alle sue genti. Mi rispose che aspettava di poter dar loro qualche buona Nuova de' suoi interessi. Egli sta benissimo, come tutti gli altri."

[69] Atto to Filippo, from Paris, August 22, 1681. Atto says much the same thing in his earlier letter to Filippo, from Paris, August 1, 1681: "Vanno Vestiti a spese del Re, e spesati, et imparano a cantare alla moda francese, ma soldo veruno per immaginatione non anno veduto, e non vedranno per un pezzo, onde per i parenti loro questa occasione non è molto favorevole."

operas in Venice, he would have been able to help out his parents. Here [the castrati] have no one who speaks for them; they cannot hope ever to advance beyond what they are now. [Your soprano's] other opportunity in Hannover is a hundred thousand times better, and you are poorly informed if you think that those princes [in Hannover] suffer the damage of the present war when instead they receive money from everywhere and live profligately. But I would send the soprano to the operas in Venice for two years; this would be a good idea for whoever taught him. And since he would acquire there money and reputation, he would then be able to achieve a better condition.[70]

Atto's counsel regarding Venice is particularly interesting given that he himself seems to have performed there for two seasons in his youth (see chapter 1). In any case, court records show that Favalli and the others did eventually secure substantial incomes from positions in both the *chapelle* and the *musique du roi*, as well as from benefices. Favalli was even granted the privilege of hunting on the king's lands.[71] But to Atto such prospects – which still bound the singers to their trade – must have seemed as nothing compared to the social opportunities he had once exploited: branded as musicians, these boys could never hope to be "più di quello che sono."

Atto expressed similar dismay on behalf of his countryman Lorenzani. Notwithstanding their occasional clashes, Atto often praised Lorenzani's skills and seems to have encouraged his career. That career reached a turning point in 1683 during the famous competition held to appoint four new *sous-maîtres* to the royal chapel.[72] Lorenzani entered the contest with thirty-four other candidates, each of whom had a single motet performed for the king during his mass, one each day. The group was then pared to fifteen, who were cloistered while they composed a second motet. In a letter from early May, Atto relates these events (although he still thinks only two *sous-maîtres* would be named) and adds some new information:

Signor Lorenzani has immortalized himself with the motet he has written in competition with all these French *maestri di cappella*; he earned universal applause, so

---

[70] Atto to Filippo, from Paris, April 23, 1691. In his letter to Filippo, from Paris, August 30, 1694, Atto blames the situation not on the king, but on the administrator of the chapel: "il difetto non nasce dal Principe, ma dal Prelato Arcivescovo di Reims che ha la sopraintendenza della Musica della Capella." That archbishop was Charles Maurice Le Tellier, brother of the marquis de Louvois, one of Louis XIV's chief ministers (see Benoit, *Versailles*, 179–80) and well known to Atto (see chapter 5).

[71] On Favalli's income, see Benoit, *Versailles*, 119, 128; also, all of the index entries for Favalli in Marcelle Benoit, *Musiques de cour (1661–1733): Chapelle – chambre – écurie*, La vie musicale en France sous les rois Bourbons, no. 20 (Paris: A. et J. Picard, 1971). Regarding the hunting privilege, see Barbier, *La maison*, 100 (no documentation given).

[72] For a consideration of the contest, see Benoit, *Versailles*, 102–8.

that it is thought he will be one of the two chosen. There were thirty-seven [*sic*] of those *maestri*. The king chose fifteen of them, and they were shut in for a few days. Each of them was given the words of the same psalm, and they had to set it without the help of the harpsichord or other instrument. In the end, Signor Lorenzani wrote a very beautiful motet, and there are a few others that are also very good. Now the king has to choose two of these fifteen *maestri*. I do not doubt that Signor Lorenzani will be pleased [with the king's choice], because in addition to his own merit, he has the queen and the dauphine herself who admire and support him very much, along with Madame de Montespan and various great gentlemen at court, for in fact [Lorenzani] is a good-natured fellow and makes himself loved by all.[73]

Lorenzani was not chosen. In Prunières's view, the king depended heavily on Lully's rather self-serving advice, which explains why some very minor composers (e.g., Guillaume Minoret and Nicolas Goupilliet) were preferred to Lorenzani, whose reputation could threaten Lully.[74] Atto confirms this interpretation and again offers an interesting perspective:

In the end Signor Lorenzani was left out, even though the king chose four *maestri di cappella* and [Lorenzani's] compositions were enjoyed. Briefly put, they no longer want foreigners here, and today they claim that the Italians come to learn music in France. True, he is the *maestro di cappella* of the queen, who is devoted to him, as is also the dauphine. Yet with all that [support], and other notable protectors, he was excluded and done great injustice, for essentially they took two of Battista's [i.e., Lully's] students who barely know counterpoint. But since here everything is done through intrigue, it was poor Lorenzani's fate to be admitted to the contest without winning the prize justly due him, even if his works do not have the spirit and charm that this nation likes.[75]

Other comments about music and the musical life in France appear sporadically throughout Atto's later correspondence. Significantly, all such notices occur in letters to his family, musicians by trade. Atto never raises the subject with his other major correspondent in later years, the Tuscan secretary Carlo Antonio Gondi. Those weekly missives exclusively reflect Atto's continuing work in diplomacy and information-gathering. The familial correspondence thus offers an important counterpoise: having established his standing outside music, Atto did not shrink from patronizing his former art and especially the artists who made it.

---

[73]   Atto to Filippo, from Paris, May 7, 1683.
[74]   Prunières, "Paolo Lorenzani," 111. On the entire contest, see also Marcelle Benoit, *Les événements musicaux sous le régne de Louis XIV: Chronologie*, La vie musicale en France sous les rois Bourbons, no. 33 (Paris: Picard, 2004), 186–87, where the report from the *Mercure galant*, April 1683, is reproduced.
[75]   Atto to Filippo, from Paris, May 21, 1683.

Honors and advancement

Like many aging dignitaries, Atto received a succession of honors and rewards in the last decades of his life, decorations that – for political reasons – his family would later characterize as his greatest achievements. Certainly he exercised his most consistent efforts on behalf of his homeland: the afore-mentioned correspondence with Gondi – full of political reports, accounts of events, and just plain gossip – testifies to Atto's unofficial capacity as an agent of Tuscany in France. His family noted proudly that "Cosimo III, grand duke of Tuscany, honored Atto for seventeen continuous years with weekly letters in his own hand."[76] While virtually all trace of such letters has disappeared, like most of the material addressed to Atto, one need not discount the claim: Atto clearly remained a client of the Medici even after the first generation of his patrons had died off.

But the gaudier honors derived from Atto's work for other governments. Trenta's biographical sketch offers a summary of one important episode:

In 1697, a very animated controversy arose in the court of Tuscany between the extraordinary envoy of France, [Roland] Dupré, and the ambassador of the Republic of Lucca, Lorenzo Cenami, having to do with [official] visits. So the senate [of Lucca] addressed itself to Melani, through whom it hoped to dispel from [Louis XIV's] mind all grounds for displeasure that his minister's malicious reports [might have] formed. The urging that [Melani] received on this matter from Cardinal Francesco Buonvisi [a native of Lucca] obliged [Melani] to take the side of the Republic with fervor. No less than [all] his reputation, shrewdness, and experience were needed to bring this thorny issue to a successful conclusion in a mutually satisfactory arrangement. In this way, the Republic [of Lucca] gained not a little in [the matter of] honorifics, both as regards the titles to be used by French ministers at the court of Florence toward those of the Republic, and as regards the formula used in letters. The government of Lucca wanted to affirm its obligation to Melani, but he could not be induced to receive any sort of demonstration, content just to have been able, through his services, to allow Cardinal Buonvisi to earn merit in the eyes of his fellow citizens.[77]

The incident recalls the historian Gaetano Imbert's comment that, "in the seventeenth century, protocol was more varied, more complicated, and more argued over than it now is. Petty questions of precedence assumed the

---

[76] I Fn, Rossi Cassigoli, MS 268, p. 151.

[77] Trenta, *Memorie*, I:263–64. The Melani family diary (I PSc, Raccolta Chiappelli, 188, loose fascicle beginning "Anno 1697," f. 4v) gives a less detailed version of these events but does reveal that Atto's modesty had more to do with maintaining the king's favor, as any reward from Lucca could have been seen as disloyalty. As a token, Atto did request a quantity of damask.

importance of affairs of state."[78] By this time, it seems, Atto enjoyed a reputation for resolving such squabbles, surely helped by his extensive travels and contacts.

That impression is confirmed by a similar incident that soon followed and led to even greater honors. Again, Trenta's account is valuable:

That same year [1697], the peace treaty between Savoy and France was published, and according to one of its articles, it was agreed that in the future both the ordinary and extraordinary ambassadors of the duke [of Savoy] were to be treated by the ministers of the king [of France] like ambassadors of royalty, accompanied on their first and last audiences by a prince of France instead of a *maréchal*. Cavaliere Niccolò Erizzo, ambassador of the Republic of Venice to Paris, wanted to obtain a similar distinction for his Republic as well. He availed himself of the efforts of Melani, who was very valuable to him in achieving his intent, as one learns from the following paragraph from a letter addressed by Erizzo from Fontainebleau to the [Venetian] Inquisitors of State on October 31, 1698:

> As to how this highly important business with the king and ministers unfolded, I have reported in my countless dispatches to the most excellent senate, to whom this evening I report the conclusion of my fortunate effort. Even more fully, however, must I point out someone who is a confidant of M. de Pomponne and to whom – having been recommended to me – I am entirely indebted for this fine success. Nor can I be excused on this occasion from naming him to Your Excellencies, for I would do an injustice to his merit. With his spirit and prudence he vanquished all the defiant objections in the minds of the monarch and the ministers, wherefore he well deserves the just recognition of the senate. He is Abate Melani, native of Pistoia in Tuscany and subject of the grand duke. In his youth, he went to France and was welcomed into the service of Cardinal Mazarin. So I made use of Melani in this difficult affair, in which he exerted himself with such zeal, efficacy, and love that, through him, I was able to reach a favorable conclusion.

After the departure of Cavaliere Erizzo from the court of France, the Republic, as a gesture of gratitude to Melani, issued a decree with which it declared this Abate Atto, his brother Jacinto, and Jacinto's current and future children and their descendants "original Venetian citizens" [*Cittadini originari Veneti*], to be allowed to share in all the privileges and honors that are enjoyed by the other original citizens. That decree carries the date of April 6, 1700.[79]

---

[78] Gaetano Imbert, *La vita fiorentina nel Seicento secondo memorie sincrone (1644–1670)* (Florence: R. Bemporad e Figlio, 1906), 133. Imbert's observation is echoed by Geoffrey R. R. Treasure, *Seventeenth Century France*, 2nd edn. (London: John Murray, 1981), 290: "The history of the seventeenth century, and especially its diplomacy, cannot be understood unless it is realised how much importance was attached to ceremony and precedence."

[79] Trenta, *Memorie*, I:264–65.

The Melani diary reports that the family knew of the Venetian honors – which Atto had specifically requested – already in August of 1699, and that the nine-month delay after the conclusion of negotiations led to discord with Erizzo.[80] Eventually conferred, the title is further described in one of the family's later petitions:

The Melani family of Pistoia was admitted to noble original Venetian citizenship with a most honorable diploma. This was a tremendous honor to that family, as such citizenship is the first after the nobility [and] precedes all the gentlemen of the *Terraferma* of whatever rank. [Citizens of this status] go forth as secretaries of the Venetian embassy; they are sent as residents of the Republic to Naples, Milan, Florence, England, and other courts; in Venice they dress just like the nobility and also enjoy the privilege of being eligible for election as Grand Chancellors, a leading position in the Republic with the title of Excellency.[81]

These two incidents provide a glimpse of the elderly diplomat at work. Repeating the familiar patterns of his past, he exploited his familiarity with Louis XIV and his ministers (especially the foreign minister, Pomponne) to benefit a wide circle of contacts. With a certain amount of dissimulation, one assumes, he presented his clients' cases in an unremittingly positive light, "dispelling from the king's mind all grounds for displeasure"; the wheels of diplomacy surely felt the grease of his wonted obsequiousness. And, as he helped others, he kept a sharp eye out for himself. He knew his efforts in Lucca would win, if nothing else, the gratitude of Buonvisi, and he made sure to request the specific Venetian honors. Those honors might not seem especially practical for a family based in Tuscany and Paris, but in fact they played a crucial role in the case for advancement. Indeed, one sees all Atto's "reputation, shrewdness, and experience" on display here, the accumulated expertise of his (then) seventy-one years.

The family's continuing social progress can be measured by the various grades of *borse* or stipends awarded them by the Tuscan government and documented in Weaver's careful work. The stipends were a form of patronage aimed at tying ascendant subjects to the rule of the Medici. By 1672, the Melani had already achieved the highest *borsa* available to residents of Pistoia; further progress required Florentine citizenship, which was granted to Jacinto, the head of the continuing Melani line, on November 16, 1678. Twelve years later (December 30, 1692), Jacinto was admitted "to the

---

[80] I PSc, Raccolta Chiappelli, 188, inserted fascicle with signature "2.do," ff. 11v–12, 13v. Atto also discusses the honor in a letter to Filippo, from Paris, August 24, 1699.

[81] I PSc, Raccolta Chiappelli, 64.ii (loose printed folio). On the nature of "cittadinanza originaria," see Gaetano Cozzi and Michael Knapton, *La repubblica di Venezia nell'età moderna: Dalla guerra di Chioggia al 1517*, vol. XII, book 1, of *Storia d'Italia* (Turin: UTET, 1986), 133–34.

enjoyment of all the exemptions and immunities from the tithe and taxes." Eventually, the family began to receive the more prestigious Tuscan *borse*, first the "Borsa de' Quattro" (September 18, 1710) and then the "Borsa dei Proposti (sometime in 1715, just after Atto's death); it was these steps that required the various petitions or *memoriali* that have been preserved. The Melani coveted two more lofty *borse* as well, the "Graduito" and "Gonfaliere," both of which established nobility.[82] In fact, they never seem to have achieved these *borse*, but between 1716 and 1717 Luigi Melani, Jacinto's son, was elected to the Commenda di S. Stefano, the most distinguished knightly order in Tuscany.[83] Although Atto did not quite live to see it, this last honor finally propelled Luigi and his clan into the noble class, giving them the right to the title "Cavaliere" and leading to their inscription in the *libro d'oro* of Pistoia, the registry of aristocrats.[84]

A respected gentleman

Well before this elevation, however, Atto seems to have established himself in an essentially aristocratic lifestyle. While he did not own property in France, he lived there like a gentleman, in a series of plush residences in the Parisian parish of Saint-Eustache.[85] More importantly, his acquaintances – in both Paris and Florence – treated him as such, a respected figure in the halls of power. In 1692, Atto called his nineteen-year-old nephew Leopoldo to join him in Paris, grooming him as a successor. When Leopoldo died prematurely in 1708, he was replaced by his older brother Domenico, whose education in

[82] The above information, much of which was first presented by Weaver based on other sources ("Materiali," 261–62), is confirmed by several Melani family documents collected in I PSc, Raccolta Chiappelli, 14.

[83] Copies of the relevant documents, dated November 11, 1717, are preserved in I Fn, Tordi 350, pp. 276ff. The Melani seem to have attained this honor through a gift of real estate, one of the standard methods for entry. Based on different documents, which I was not able to see, Weaver ("Materiali," 255n and 256) dates the promotion to February 1, 1707. Regarding the order itself, Imbert (*La vita fiorentina*, 178) reports that it was created by Cosimo I in imitation of the knights of Malta. Initially, it had been a similar holy, knightly order, charged with the protection of Florence's naval interests, but by Atto's period it had become an honor "accordato ad alcune famiglie patrizie."

[84] Although the family's first entry into the book is not dated, the first member recorded is Luigi, with the title "cavaliere." Bruno Casini, *I "libri d'oro" delle città di Pistoia, Prato e Pescia*, Biblioteca di "Le Apuane," no. 12 (Massa-Uliveti: Edizioni del Centro Culturale Apuano, 1988), 49–50.

[85] The record is incomplete regarding Atto's residences in Paris during his later years. Here follow the attestations I have found:

"Rue Cocquillère a la Roze blanche près de Saint Eustache" (today, Rue Coquillère): September 27, 1680 (Atto to Filippo, from Paris)

law Atto had supported.[86] Having never met their famous uncle nor experienced the high society in which he moved, the two nephews wrote letters to their family that offer a unique perspective on Atto's way of life. Indeed, they describe – in a way Atto never did – the existence their uncle had achieved for himself in his later years.

On February 23, 1693, Leopoldo wrote a letter that describes Atto's residence in some detail. At that time, Atto was living in an apartment of rooms on the Rue Neuve des Petits Champs (today, Rue des Petits-Champs), between Rue Richelieu and Rue Vivienne; he had moved there sometime after May 1687 and stayed until 1709 or 1710.[87] I reproduce Leopoldo's account at some length for the sense it gives of Atto's material comfort:

To satisfy Uncle Bartolomeo's curiosity to know what Uncle's apartment is like, I must tell him that it is a very beautiful apartment and well decorated. First, I will begin with the lovely view that it has, looking out on the royal garden where on both work days and holidays an endless crowd comes to entertain themselves. To follow the sequence of rooms, I will begin from the room where Uncle spends each day, which is bedecked with green tapestries; the bed where he sleeps is done in green damask; there are many large stools done in a similar green fabric to that in our ground-floor room [in Pistoia], but they are more beautiful. There are two lovely mirrors, with frames made of the same glass; Uncle says that when these come [to Pistoia] he wants to put them in the first room … where Aurora is painted, one on each side over those images of harpies. There is then a desk, on

"Près de la place des Victoires": May 24, 1687 (Cardinal Toussaint de Janson-Forbin to Atto, from Morcy (France); most of the surrounding letters give the more specific address of "Rue des Vieux Augustins," today, Rue Hérold)

"Rue Neuve des Petits Champs" (today, Rue des Petits-Champs): March 8, 1700 (Cardinal d'Estrées to Atto, from Rome); April 2, 1700 (Cardinal de Janson to Atto, from Rome); January 30, 1709; (will; F Pan, Étude XV, 416); April 22, 1709; (lease [*bail*]; F Pan, Étude XV, 417)

"Rue des Vieux Augustins": September 2, 1710 (will; F Pan, Étude XV, 424)

"Rue Plâtrière" (today, Rue Jean-Jacques Rousseau): April 7, 1713 (will; F Pan, Étude XV, 450); May 12, 1713 (lease; F Pan, Étude XV, 451); June 5, 1713 (will; F Pan, Étude XV, 451).

[86] The previous information comes from a number of sources. An entry in the Melani diary for June 15, 1708 (I PSc, Raccolta Chiappelli, 14, loose fascicle) reports Leopoldo's death in Paris and his connection with Atto; a passport for Domenico to France dated March 20, 1709 (Chiappelli, 14 [loose]); a statement in the Melani diary from around 1702 that Atto had sent 50 *louis d'or* to assist in Domenico's legal education in Rome (I PSc, Raccolta Chiappelli, 188, inserted fascicle with signature "2.ᵈᵒ," f. 20v); a series of letters from Carlo Antonio Gondi to Domenico in Paris, dating through June 1716. All of these documents are confirmed by the letters both nephews wrote from Paris back to Italy (see below). A later document (loose in Chiappelli, 14) indicates that Domenico became "Segretario della Consulta di Siena" for a time.

[87] On Atto's series of addresses in Paris, see note 85 above. It has been possible to identify the site described by Leopoldo's letter only because he mentions a view of the "Giardino Reale," a feature also mentioned by the notaries in Atto's will of January 30, 1709, at this address. Indeed, to have the view described, the building must have been located on the short block between Rue Richelieu and Rue Vivienne, on the north side of the street.

which is placed a clock and many other things, two candelabra, and a portrait of Madame de Piennes over the door, and the screen of the desk is done in mirrors. Leaving his room, one enters the drawing room, which is decorated with the same tapestries as Uncle's room, and there are many chairs in green damask that match the bed. There is a very large mirror with a frame in the same glass but violet in color. Then there is a portrait of the king in gouache and another painting of fruit, and an armoire where all the books are kept. There is a day bed like the one M. Foucher has, but not made of the same material: Uncle's is made of red and green brocade. In the room next to the drawing room, there are many stools, and this room too is decorated with tapestries, all with figures. From this room, one enters the cloak room where his clothes and linens are kept, along with the table linens, and next to this is the servant's room. The room where I'm staying is separated from these and is decorated with these Flemish [leather] screens, but they are pretty; the bed is in green cloth with a great deal of gold. There are many geographical maps and three portraits: one of Madame de Pomponne, one of Madame de Nevers, and one of Madame de Châtillon. The carriage that Uncle has is similar to M. Foucher's, but this one is not lined in green velvet but in black, and the bottom is gilded; the horses are similar to [Foucher's]. He has two footmen, a coachman, a serving-woman, who is Roman, and a Savoyard to sweep the rooms. That's as much as I can tell you.[88]

From the time Leopoldo arrived in Paris, Atto worked to introduce him to elegant society. Leopoldo was sent to the opera, both to see the aristocracy and to absorb French style; he likewise attended the Italian *commedie*. Atto also introduced him to salon culture and may even have tried to find him a well-bred wife. In several letters Leopoldo requests to be sent new Italian music – arias and keyboard works – for a *demoiselle* who sang and played such music very well and whose home he visited frequently "for the soirée." Although Atto later complained that his nephew did not show him sufficient respect, Leopoldo seems to have been in awe of his uncle, at least at first, admitting that "every day I am more enchanted by the courtesies that Uncle does me."[89]

Perhaps Atto's biggest "courtesy" was to introduce his nephew to the French court at the palace of Versailles. Leopoldo's description of his

---

[88] Leopoldo Melani to Filippo, from Paris, February 23, 1693. Madame de Piennes is Olympe de Brouilly; Madame de Pomponne, Catherine Ladvocat, marquise de Pomponne and wife of the foreign minister; Madame de Nevers is probably Diane-Gabrielle de Damas, duchess of Nevers; Madame de Châtillon, Marie-Anne de La Trémouille, duchess of Châtillon.

[89] Leopoldo's reports on the opera and the Italian comedies appear in his letters to Filippo, from Paris, February 9, and March 16, 1693; his requests for Italian music, in letters to Filippo, from Paris, April 27, 1695, June 11 and September 3, 1696. For the purpose of illustration, I reproduce here the relevant passage from the June 11 letter: "Già che il Signor Bartolomeo non puol mandarmi alcuna Novità in contracambio di quelle che mi do l'honore di scriverle, vorrei che

one-day, whirlwind tour on May 12, 1693 both communicates the wonder
that the place could inspire and evokes, surprisingly, the modern touristic
experience. Leopoldo sees the king's apartments, the hall of mirrors, the
gardens, the *orangerie*, and like so many others is transfixed by a glance from
the Sun King. More importantly, Leopoldo's account provides the richest
testimony to the esteem that Atto enjoyed, even in the highest court circles:
the elderly Italian castrato was also a privileged French *gentilhomme*. The
quality of Leopoldo's letter again justifies a lengthy quotation:

We left then last Tuesday for Versailles at 6:30 in the morning with beautiful but cool
weather. When we were halfway there, the nice weather changed to rain, which lasted
for half an hour, and then the good weather returned and continued until we arrived
at Versailles, at 8:30. As soon as [we] dismounted, Uncle did me the honor of taking
me up into the antechamber of the palace to wait there until His Majesty arose, so as
to see him dress. We hadn't waited half an hour when the king awoke, and they came
to open the door so that the people might enter to watch him dress. And so we
entered with the others into the rooms of His Majesty, where I had the honor of
seeing the king when he went to say his devotions next to his bed: Uncle had put me
behind him, near the place where the king had to kneel, and when His Majesty stood
up and turned around, he gave me a glance. I cannot express to you with the pen how
beautiful and well formed is this prince, for just upon seeing him one becomes
enchanted. And further, I could not say enough about how much Uncle is favored by
His Majesty and by all the court: [as we pass] through the antechambers one
[courtier] calls him from here and another from there, and everyone shows him
the greatest esteem, and his words are much valued by everyone. Signor Sergio was
also at the *lever* of the king, and when he saw me, he asked Uncle to send me to dine at
his place.

   When the *lever* of the king was over, I went with one of Uncle's footmen to see the
garden, where I stayed until noon, looking at so many fountains and beautiful marble
statues that in the end the beauty and magnitude of that garden are beyond
description. After that, I went to the room of the ambassadors, where Uncle was,
to wait until he did me the honor of taking me with him to the mass of the king, and
an hour after noon he took me to the chapel where His Majesty hears mass. There I
had the opportunity to see the king as much as I wanted, since Uncle put me close to
the kneeling-stool among the abbots, who all kneel at the start of mass, and thus I
remained with a completely clear view. During the mass, the king looked at me three
or four times. When mass was over, I fell in with Abate [Francesco] Averna, a

almeno si compiacesse di favorirmi d'una mezza dozzina d'Ariette, a sua Elezione, che sieno
allegre, non gran cosa lunghe, e parimente che le parole sieno toccanti; Queste devono servire per
una Demoiselle che canta benissimo l'ariette Italiane, et alla quale è un pezzo che gli ho promesso
di fargliene venire, andando spessissimo a Veglia da lei." Atto's complaints about Leopoldo's
attitude appear in his own letter to Filippo, from Paris, August 20, 1696. Leopoldo's statement of
admiration comes in the aforementioned letter of February 9, 1693: "ogni giorno più resto
incantato delle cortesie che mi fa il Signor Zio Abbate."

gentleman from Messina, who also came that morning to dine with Signor Sergio; here I parted from Uncle, as he was going to dine at M. Pomponne's house, where he goes whenever he comes to Versailles.

Before going to lunch, the aforementioned abate took me up into the palace to see the apartments of the king, those of Monsieur the dauphin, and the apartment of the dauphine. There is nothing in the world so beautiful and so magnificent, everything being mirrors, both the galleries and the walls, the floors being all inlaid and incised, and everything gilded. If I had to recount the great and beautiful things that I saw, a ream of paper would not be enough. In short, I will say to you that Versailles is the terrestrial paradise, so that I do not wonder at all that Uncle never gets the urge to come to Italy, because he is in such a beautiful country, esteemed by everyone and revered by everyone, and because he has more friends on a street of Paris than in Florence and Pistoia. Enough! I need not elaborate further on this subject since you gentlemen know better than I.

We left then, after dining with Signor Sergio, who treated us very well, and both his wife, who is always ill, and Don Paolo [Lorenzani?] enjoined me to greet all you gentlemen in their name, and in particular Uncle Bartolomeo. After dining with Signor Sergio and Abate Averna, they took me to see the place where His Majesty keeps all the oranges, which contains thousands and thousands of them and is the most beautiful thing in the world. After that, we returned to see the apartment of Monsieur the dauphin, where we stayed until 6 in the evening, and then I left Abate Averna and Signor Sergio and went to the house where M. de Pomponne lives and where Uncle was, who was just on the point of getting into the carriage. Thus, we returned to Paris, where we arrived at 9 in the evening. So there is the entire trip recounted, and you will excuse me if it is not too well written and if it is short because, as I said, if I had to recount item by item what I saw, a ream of paper would not be nearly enough.[90]

Death and remembrance

Perhaps one of the most remarkable things about Atto Melani is the very length of the life he led. Especially given the era, the years seem to have taken their toll only very slowly. Atto's extant wills between 1709 and 1713 always describe him as "in perfect physical health," an exaggeration,

---

[90] Leopoldo to Filippo, from Paris, May 18, 1693 (paragraphing mine). On the conversion of the times given here (which are in French style), see Michael Talbot, "*Ore italiane*: The Reckoning of the Time of Day in Pre-Napoleonic Italy," *Italian Studies* 40 (1985): 52–53. Because the French system figures hours from the true noon of the sun, and because today noon in Paris on May 12 (in standard time, not daylight savings) occurs at 12:47 p.m., I have added an hour to all times in the letter. As one would expect, then, Atto and his nephew traveled during hours of daylight. I have been unable to identify "Signor Sergio" further.

presumably, that at least suggests a freedom from major illness.[91] The steady fluency of his handwriting through the 1690s – not so different from his style in the 1650s – may hint at the same thing (see plates 12 and 13). From about 1700, though, all his correspondence is penned by a secretary, and Atto's heavy, scrawling signatures on his wills – especially the last ones – betray advancing arthritis or even a mild stroke. Still, only in the final codicil, made less than a month before his death, do the notaries find him "sick in body" and too weak to sign the document, though even then, his mind was sharp.[92]

The end finally came in the new year of 1714, less than two months before his eighty-eighth birthday. By this time, his nephew Domenico had come to replace Leopoldo, and so it is Domenico's letters – written to Gondi, the grand-ducal secretary – that describe the final hours.[93] In a letter begun on New Year's Day, he reports Atto's sorrowful condition:

With this post I bring to Your Most Illustrious Lordship the woeful news of the dangerous state in which the abate my uncle finds himself, already at death's door. Friday morning [i.e., December 29], against everyone's advice, he wanted to get up from bed, saying that he felt he was suffocating, and so we had to put him into a chair to calm him. As soon as he was up, he wanted to take a little walk around the room, supported by two people. But upon starting, he said, "Oh! I can't continue," and he sat down again, after which he seemed to faint. So I immediately had him put back into bed, and, after being wetted with the water of the queen of Hungary [an aromatic], he seemed to return to his senses. Fifteen minutes later the fit happened again, so that his tongue was silenced, having said these last words to me: "My nephew, don't abandon me." Afterwards, he could no longer speak, even with all the remedies that we tried. I don't fail to apply these remedies continuously, assisted frequently by his confessor and other priests, but he is now in a state in which he hears nothing, having completely closed his eyes and lost all movement …

This Tuesday [i.e., January 2] at 7 o'clock, the abate continued without words and motion. He is obviously suffering a great deal, and I fear he will suffer a little while longer, as his pulse is strong.[94]

In fact, Atto held on for two more days. In succeeding letters, Domenico reports that the final illness had lasted three months, with five days of

---

[91] On the wills, see the documents listed in note 85 above: they all use the phrase "parfaite santé de corps," with the exception of the will from April 7, 1713, where he enjoys only "assez bonne santé de corps."

[92] This codicil is recorded – along with the entire final "French" will – in an attachment to the letter from Domenico Melani to Carlo Antonio Gondi, Paris, January 8, 1714.

[93] The Melani diary (I PSc, Raccolta Chiappelli, 14, loose fascicle) tells that Domenico left for Paris on March 25, 1710.

[94] Domenico to Carlo Antonio Gondi, from Paris, January 1, 1714.

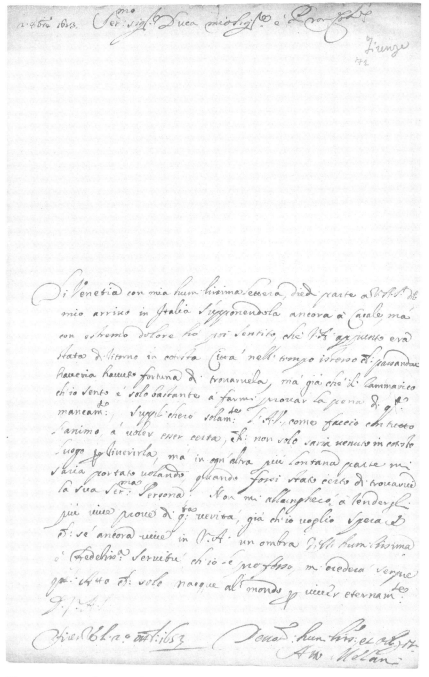

Plate 12 Letter of Atto Melani to Carlo II Gonzaga-Nevers, duke of Mantua, from Florence, October 2, 1653 (I MAas, E.XXVIII.3, busta 1135, diversi–1653, pezzo 5). *Reproduced by permission of the Archivio di Stato di Mantova (Ministero per i Beni e le Attività Culturali).*

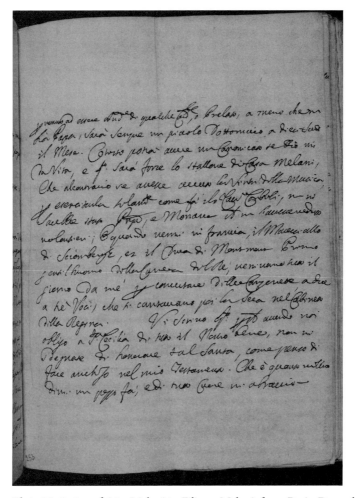

Plate 13 Letter of Atto Melani to Filippo Melani, from Paris, December 1, 1698, conclusion (I Fm, Melani 3, f. 253). *Reproduced by permission of the Biblioteca Marucelliana; any further reproduction, in whole or in part, by any means is prohibited.*

"continual pain" at the end. During those last days, Atto's room had been full of friends, all whom marveled that a man of his age and "delicate complexion" could resist so long. He finally succumbed at around two in the morning on January 4. At least according to Domenico, Atto was widely mourned.[95]

Almost immediately, Atto's nephews launched plans to memorialize their uncle. In Paris, Domenico sought to erect a monument over Atto's tomb. Three days after his death, Atto was buried in the Church of Notre-Dame-des-Victoires, then the Parisian home of the discalced Augustinian order. The Augustinians had authorized the burial only weeks before: the

---

[95] Domenico to Gondi, from Paris, January 8, 1714.

aforementioned codicil, dated December 15, 1713, altered his burial site from the church of the Capuchins in Rue Saint-Honoré, the site in all his previous wills. The reason for the change is unclear: the latter church may simply have carried more prestige once its square was redesigned to honor the king's military triumphs.[96] In any case, less than two weeks later, Domenico reported to Gondi on plans for a memorial in that church:

> Feeling obliged to leave some memory of my uncle in this country, I have decided to build him a funeral monument in the church where he is buried. The fathers have already granted me the site for it in a lateral chapel near the main altar, right in front of the door of the sacristy. So I am sending the design for it to Your Most Illustrious Lordship, and I beg you to show it to His Royal Highness [the grand duke]. It is the work of [Bartolomeo Carlo] Rastrelli, a Florentine sculptor, and already they are beginning to shape the marble and the figures. They promised me that everything would be finished and in place by the end of March.[97]

In the event, the project took longer, and Domenico was finally forced to leave Paris (in May 1714) before seeing Rastrelli's work in place.[98]

The case of this memorial is interesting. Today no remnant remains: if it was indeed installed, it was most likely destroyed during the French Revolution when Notre-Dame-des-Victoires was devastated. Still extant, however, are designs by the artist, Rastrelli, for several other funerary monuments erected in Paris at this time, including one for the marquis de Pomponne (d. 1699), Atto's friend.[99] Remarkably, the architectural historian Nikolai Arkhipov has found evidence that Rastrelli won the commission for Pomponne's tomb on the basis of a recommendation from Atto himself, and indeed in 1703 Atto served as witness to the contract between Rastrelli and Pomponne's widow.[100] Perhaps the Melani

---

[96] Louis XIII had established the church in 1629 as a new home for the discalced Augustinians ("petits pères"); the church was named for Louis XIII's victory over the Huguenots at La Rochelle. The square was redesigned and dedicated to Louis XIV's military victories in 1685–86. (On the codicil to Atto's will, see appendix G.) It is unlikely that the presence in this church of Jean-Baptiste Lully's tomb (along with that of his father-in-law, Michel Lambert) attracted Atto to the place: as suggested above, Atto thought little of Lully.

[97] Domenico to Gondi, from Paris, January 15, 1714. In a later letter (to Gondi, from Paris, April 2, 1714), Domenico includes the inscription for the tomb: "Hic Jacet | Abbas Atto Melani Pistoriensis in Estruria, | Pietate erga Deum | Obsequio erga Regem | Illustris | Obijt Die 4:ᵃ Januarij 1714. | Etatis Sue Octuagesimo octavo [*sic*] | Patruo Dilectissimo | Dominicus Melani Nepos mestissimus posuit." (Here lies Abate Atto Melani, from Pistoia in Tuscany, famous for his piety toward God and his obedience toward the king; he died the fourth day of January 1714, at the age of 88. For a most beloved uncle, Domenico Melani, a very sad nephew, erected this.)

[98] See his letter to Gondi, from Paris, May 7, 1714, where he reveals that he had already paid the sculptor in full, a step he thought would speed the project but that actually ended up slowing it.

[99] See Nikolai Il'ich Arkhipov, *Bartolomeo Karlo Rastrelli: 1675–1744* (Leningrad: Iskusstvo, 1964), 10–15; and Zygmunt Batowski, "B.-C. Rastrelli en France: Le tombeau du marquis de Pomponne," *Gazette des beaux-arts*, series 6, no. 5, part 12 (October 1934): 137–43.

[100] Arkhipov, *Bartolomeo Karlo Rastrelli*, 10–11.

Plate 14 Design for a tomb (Bartolomeo-Carlo Rastrelli, Biblioteka Narodowa, Warsaw). *Reproduced by permission of the Biblioteka Narodowa.*

brothers had first acquainted Atto with the work of this young Florentine sculptor, then still in his mid-twenties; and perhaps, as he had tried to do for Italian musicians in Paris, Atto brokered patronage for his countryman, introducing the artist to a dignitary who needed his services. After several years in

Paris, Rastrelli went on to become a prominent artist in St. Petersburg under Peter the Great, influencing the history of sculpture in Russia. In any case, Atto's personal connections to Rastrelli raise the question of Atto's role in the design of his own tomb. Did the work begin so quickly after Atto's death because the plans were already prepared? Did Atto even help design his own monument?

Whatever the answer, I have begun to believe more may remain of that design than has previously been recognized. One of Rastrelli's extant Parisian drawings has at some point been labeled "project for the tomb of a cardinal" (see plate 14). But a closer inspection of the admittedly rough sketch raises doubts.[101] The crucial element is the coat of arms, located in the lower half of the drawing. The central oval escutcheon (left blank) is surmounted by the wide ecclesiastical hat – common to the arms of all clerics – from which descend two groups of interlaced tassels; above the hat appears a crown (coronet). By tradition, the hat of a cardinal displays thirty tassels, arranged in five rows on either side of the shield, the number of tassels increasing from one to five per row. To my eye, Rastrelli is quite a few tassels short of a cardinal. Indeed, I perceive just three rows, which would make twelve tassels in all, the norm for a bishop or abbot. More problematic, even, is the crown. While some cardinals might represent a coronet *below* the ecclesiastical hat (a sign of their aristocratic origins), a prince of the Church could never show the hat surmounted by a symbol of temporal authority.[102] But that arrangement makes perfect sense for Atto, who was the titular abbot (*abbé-commendataire*) of a royal monastery (Beaubec), that is, a monastery under the king's control. The placement of the crown and the number of tassels thus both correspond to Atto's ecclesiastical rank. One can argue, of course, that Rastrelli's design is too vague for such speculation. But the possibility seems worth considering that this image represents the design for Atto's Parisian monument.

The state of affairs is somewhat clearer in Pistoia. There, the family, led by Domenico's brother Luigi, pursued a monument of its own. In 1702, the family had purchased a simple tomb in the church of S. Domenico: the circular stone in the central aisle near the west entrance still remains, inscribed "38. SEPVLCHRUM MELANÆ FAMIL."[103] But, following Atto's death,

---

[101]   Batowski, "B.-C. Rastrelli," 139, 141–42.

[102]   The information on ecclesiastical heraldry in this discussion is derived from John Woodward, *A Treatise on Ecclesiastical Heraldry* (New York: The Christian Literature Company, 1894), 58–78 (for abbots), 79–107 (bishops), 134–49 (cardinals). On the specific question of the crown, Woodward (138–39) explains that Pope Innocent X expressly forbade the use of the coronet to cardinals but that away from Rome cardinals did employ that symbol if their family or position gave them the right. In those cases, the coronet appeared below the hat.

[103]   Information on the purchase of the tomb comes from I Fn, Tordi 350, p. 305. San Domenico was one of the more prestigious churches in Pistoia at the time, as suggested by the number of Rospigliosi buried there.

the friars of S. Domenico permanently granted the family the use of the first chapel to the right of the altar, called the chapel "of the Name of Jesus" after the fresco in its cupola. By September of 1715, an impressive cenotaph of colored marble was positioned on the north wall of this chapel. Depicted in his ecclesiastical garb and flanked by putti, a bust of the elderly Atto looks out (a bit sourly) over his familial crest (a boar under a fleur-de-lis) and a faux banner engraved with his greatest accomplishments (see plate 15).[104] Unfortunately, Atto's monument has been vandalized in recent years (the putti were torn off), and the family's chapel is in a generally regrettable state.

Even after his death, Atto continued to control the future of his family through his wills. He wrote one testament for his holdings in France, which mostly went to Domenico, and another for those in Italy, bequeathed to Luigi (see appendix G). In truth, Luigi received the greater share by far, since, as noted above, Atto had invested most of his wealth in Tuscan farms and other property. Thus, Atto's wills effectively designated Luigi the new head of the family, or, as Atto put it, "lo stallone di Casa Melani."[105] This disparity led to some bickering and legal action between the nephews, but the clarity and severity of the final Italian will allowed little room for dispute. In fact, Atto's wills are concerned almost exclusively with clarifying the familial succession, arranging for hundreds of requiem masses, and giving away a few token

---

[104] The monument itself was the work of the sculptor Vittorio Barbieri. For a description of the entire chapel (somewhat erroneous in historical details), see Vasco Melani (presumably no relation), *Pistoia*, 2nd edn. (Pistoia: Tellini, 1970), 160–61. The Latin inscription, reproduced also in Ademollo, "Un campanaio," follows: "D.O.M. | Actho Melani | Julii Card. Mazzarrini Servitio Addictus | Adhuc Adolescens Profectus In Galliam | Ludovici Magni Inter Nobiles Cubicularios admissus | Regia Baubacensi Abbatia Decoratus | Cunctis Germaniae, Ac Italiae Principibus Carus | Obiit Parisiis | Anno Reparantis Verbi MDCCXIV. Aetatis Suae LXXXIIX. | Hinc Ne Tanti Viri Memoria Deesset In Patria | Dominicus, Et Aloysius | Patruo Dilectissimo | Posteris Incitamentum Virtutis | Monumentum Hoc In Familiari Sacello Moestissimi posuere | Anno Salutis MDCCXV." (To the glory of Almighty God: Atto Melani, who was a devoted servant of Jules Cardinal Mazarin, who went to France in his youth, who was admitted among Louis the Great's gentlemen of the chamber, who was honored with the royal abbey of Beaubec, and who was dear to all the princes of Germany and Italy, died in Paris in the year of the restored word [i.e., C.E.] 1714, at age 88. Hence, so that the memory of so great a man not fail in his homeland, Domenico and Luigi, in their extreme sorrow, erect this monument to their most beloved uncle in their familial chapel in the year 1715, to incite posterity to virtue.)

One may notice that in this monument only three tassels are visible peeking out at the bottom of each side of the central cartouche. I believe this arrangement implies that the other tassels on each side are hidden behind the cartouche, along with the long cord from which they traditionally hang. Tassels were nearly always arranged in the pyramidal shape: if only three were to be indicated, they would have been arranged one-plus-two. I should also note that Atto's arms are sometimes visible in the wax seals still extant on some of his letters. A particularly fine example appears with his letter to Carlo Antonio Gondi, from Paris, November 28, 1688, in which an unusual *seven* tassels per side are represented, in the usual pyramid of six, plus one single tassel below. I have not been able to discover any significance for this number.

[105] Atto to Filippo, from Paris, December 1, 1698.

Plate 15 Cenotaph for Atto Melani, before and after recent vandalism (Vittorio Barbieri, Church of S. Domenico, Pistoia). *Photo on right courtesy of Massimiliano Sala.*

items to friends and old servants; one learns little about the man himself. At the end, Atto's primary concerns were for his soul and the future of his dynasty.

In the succeeding years, that dynasty seems to have flourished. An inventory of the Melani house in 1782 (excerpted in appendix II) attests to the family's splendid lifestyle, their rooms filled with expensive furnishings and their walls covered in art. As noted, Luigi and his successors entered the ranks of the nobility just after Atto's death, and they maintained their status for close to two hundred years. With the resource of the aforementioned *libro d'oro*, as well as my own digging, I have been able to track the Melani family to the beginning of the twentieth century. Figure 7.1 illustrates the main branch of the family, descending from Luigi (compare to fig. 1.1). I have not been able to go any further, but a letter and postcard from 1906 indicate that an Elena Melani and her daughter Alaide (or Adelaide) were living in

Plate 15 (cont.)

Florence, and that Elena's son Ercolano had moved to Argentina.[106] After that point, the trail vanishes. Today, the surname Melani is so common throughout Tuscany as to make searching for descendants impossible.

The inventory from 1782 also shows that the Melani family preserved its inheritance from its famous uncle. The catalogue of the "Salotto del Abate Melani" – still identified with Atto nearly seventy years after his death – shows that numerous volumes of his papers remained with the family at that time. Numbering over one hundred, these volumes contained Atto's various accounts of political events and especially the letters addressed to him by

---

[106] This results from several documents stuck into I Fn, Tordi 350, between pages 252 and 253. Also mentioned is Elena's sister Vittoria and brother Leone. Elena and her siblings probably only married into the Melani family; unfortunately, her husband's name is not given. According to the postcard, Ercolano was living in Bahia Blanca.

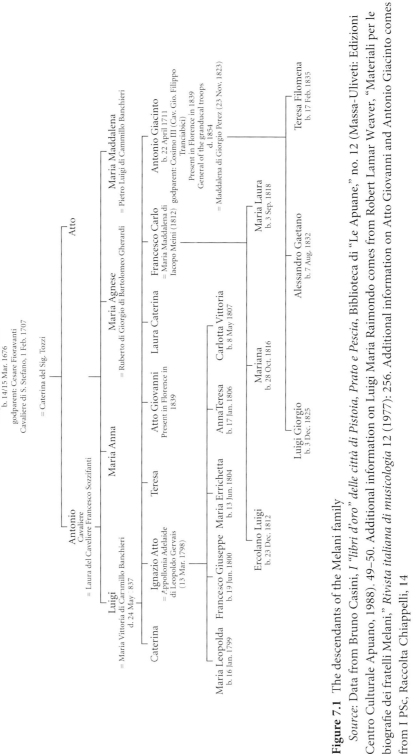

Figure 7.1 The descendants of the Melani family

Source: Data from Bruno Casini, *I "libri d'oro" delle città di Pistoia, Prato e Pescia*, Biblioteca di "Le Apuane," no. 12 (Massa-Uliveti: Edizioni Centro Culturale Apuano, 1988). 49–50. Additional information on Luigi Maria Raimondo comes from Robert Lamar Weaver, "Materiali per le biografie dei fratelli Melani," *Rivista italiana di musicologia* 12 (1977): 256. Additional information on Atto Giovanni and Antonio Giacinto comes from I PSc, Raccolta Chiappelli, 14

others over the years – in other words, the other side of the correspondence that has nourished this study. In the 1880s, when Alessandro Ademollo became interested in the Melani family – the first musicologist to do so – he tried to see these materials. He apparently asked his friend Filippo Rossi Cassigoli to apply for access from the family. The following response, written by the contemporary *capofamiglia* to his cousin (Rossi-Cassigoli's contact), is preserved at the National Library in Florence:

A few days ago, I received your letter, to which I will now reply, saying that at present I cannot at all comply with the request of Signor Cassigoli. I would only be able to do it when my various affairs permit me to linger for a few days in Pistoia. Presently I cannot in any way leave this island [of Elba], nor could I give to others the key to the bureau, as is normal. This is my reply to your letter and that of Signor Cassigoli, to whom I send my distinguished regards as I do also to you and your whole family, while I confirm myself your most affectionate cousin, A. Melani.[107]

Although denied to Ademollo, the documents clearly survived to the end of the nineteenth century, probably in the same cabinet they had occupied since Atto's time.

From the beginning of my research, the pursuit of these volumes has been something of a grail-quest. At first, they seemed as lost as the family who owned them. But in 1995 the Biblioteca Marucelliana in Florence acquired nine codices that correspond to some of the missing materials.[108] Most or all of them were at least temporarily in the possession of a certain Emilia Franceschini, who in 1907 produced an index of their contents and wrote a biographical note. Part of that note tells the fate of the other missing items:

A great number of volumes of memoirs [which Atto] had copied in very beautiful script – documented by the autograph letters of personages with whom he was in correspondence for various reasons – survived until 1906 intact in their lovely original leather bindings. In that year, they were taken by the state, unbound, dispersed and sold to various collectors, together with numerous volumes that

---

[107] A. Melani (Alessandro Gaetano? see figure 7.1) to an unknown recipient ("Caro cugino"), from Portolongone (today Porto Azzuro on the island of Elba), January 14, 1884 (I Fn, Rossi Cassigoli, cassetta 1, pezzo 5).

[108] Monica Maria Angeli, *et al.*, eds., *Dal manoscritto al fumetto: Cinque anni di acquisti in antiquariato 1991–1995* (Florence: Ministero per i Beni Culturali e Ambientali and Biblioteca Marucelliana / Manent, 1995), 19. I am enormously indebted to my colleague James Leve for notifying me of this collection – unattested elsewhere – when he ran across it in his own work. The volumes seem to relate to the 1782 inventory as follows: "Fondo Melani 1–4," containing letters from both Atto and his nephew Leopoldo to their family, must have originated in the fifteen volumes of "Lettere famigliari"; "Melani 5" is certainly the "Lettere di Cardinal d'Estrée"; "Melani 6–8" are the "Lettere del Cardinale Janson Tomi III"; "Melani 9" could well be the "Lettere Curiose, ed utili."

contained thousands of letters written to him by rulers, ministers, ambassadors, nearly all the cardinals, politicians, [and] prominent personages of his time, [all of which] he himself had wanted to leave in France, at the library of the king![109]

Indeed, Atto mentions several times the idea of leaving his materials in the royal library, mostly to boost his own reputation. At his death, though, Domenico sent everything back to Tuscany.[110] The appearance of the nine volumes raises hopes that others may still exist in private collections. I hope that the present investigation will encourage anyone who might possess such materials to make them available for study. Clearly, those missing documents could hold riches for the history of music and culture in the seventeenth century.

Just as Atto's words have been the lifeblood of this study, so they provide its most fitting conclusion. On December 1, 1698, the seventy-two-year-old castrato writes of hearing a nobleman sing at a private gathering, an experience that leads him to some of his most self-reflective comments on the meaning of music in his own life:

Cavaliere [Pompilio] Corboli sang very well, both with much grace and like a real nobleman; what I like most about him is that he doesn't have to be begged at all. All of you in Pistoia were very wrong not to instruct Leopoldo, who would have had a very beautiful voice, because this talent is the most noble ornament that a well-born person can possess. One sees that popes, emperors, princes, and queens do not disdain to profess it for their pleasure and entertainment. No talent introduces one into the private rooms of princes like this one: the beginning of Pope Clement IX's success was poetry, and without music, I would still be in Pistoia staring at the *Leoncino* [a famous ornament on a central well]. None of our nephews will make a big splash in the world because the one in Rome [Domenico] lacks good bearing, and if he becomes a magistrate for some cardinal or prelate, he will always be (unless that man becomes pope) a petty little *dottore* at ten *scudi* a month. If God gives me life, [Domenico] will be able to get a canonicate, and [Leopoldo] will perhaps be the stud of the Melani dynasty. But if, on the other hand, [Leopoldo] had possessed musical skill – to be used only as Cavaliere Corboli does – there would have been no prince or monarch who would not have been happy to give him an audience. When I came to France, [Frédéric-Armand] the maréchal de Schomberg and [Gabriel de Rochechouart] the duke de Mortemart (first gentleman of the king's chamber) came to my home all day long to rehearse canzonettas for two to three voices that

---

[109] I Fm, Melani 1 (unfoliated, at beginning of manuscript). On the basis of her published work, Franceschini herself seems to have been a historian specializing in the arts and was active from the 1910s to the 1930s.

[110] On Atto's desires, see his letter to Filippo, from Paris, July 22, 1686.

were then sung in the evening in the chamber of the queen. Seeing that we are obliged to St. Cecilia for all our good fortune, I write this to you all so that you not disdain to honor that saint, as I too am thinking to do in my will.[111]

For Atto, music is a social vehicle. Its value lies in its matchless ability to further one's career. The only caveat – carefully implied – is that one must perform as a gentleman: one should be trained in music, but one must never become a "musician." Atto thus simultaneously embraces and rejects his past: he recognizes his debt to St. Cecilia, but he reduces her to an effective facilitator, a faithful servant long ago pensioned off. Despite his comments, he decided *not* to honor the saint in his final wills: in fact he removed a provision – present in earlier versions – that provided for the Congregazione di Santa Cecilia in Pistoia.[112]

From Atto's perspective, music was not so much an art, for the entertainment of an audience, as a service, provided to a patron. His career path paralleled that of other courtly servants – from valets to secretaries, and indeed diplomats – more than it did the rising class of free-lance opera stars. If Atto achieved a degree of independence and self-determination, he did so by mastering, not escaping, the traditional patronage system: he and his family excelled at a sophisticated service for which demand was great and supply limited. From this position of strength, Atto's native daring and industry allowed him to accumulate honor and wealth. His life, then, illuminates an older, courtly model of musical patronage as it survived through the seventeenth century, and it does so primarily from the inside, from the unusual vantage point of the musicians themselves. Indeed, Atto's case inverts the customary paradigm: whereas patronage is often studied as a source of musical works and performances, Atto saw such works and performances as an important basis for patronage. What now seem the ends were for Atto the means, with the ultimate goal not of artistry but of dynastic promotion. It is this very human perspective on seventeenth-century music-making – from the other side of the looking glass, so to speak – that Atto's case contributes to the history of this era and that his story so engagingly illustrates.

---

[111] Atto to Filippo, from Paris, December 1, 1698. (See plate 13 for the end of this passage.)

[112] Weaver ("Materiali," 264n) quotes Atto's will of October 13, 1672: in case of the extinction of the Melani family, Atto leaves everything to "la Compagnia, Congregazione e confratelli dei Signori musici di Pistoia sotto il titolo di S. Cecilia," with the obligation that they celebrate her annual feast with special pomp, "per la special protetione che ella ha avuto et ha del Signor testatore e di tutti li suoi fratelli i quali con il mezzo di tal Virtù si sono introdotti nelle prime Corti dei Principi di Europa." This passage does not appear in any of his later wills.

Appendix A: The letters of Atto Melani

The following list gives all of the letters written by Atto Melani known to me; surely more await discovery in the archives and libraries of Europe. Unless otherwise indicated, I have listed all letters individually through 1672; from 1673, I have cited all collections but listed individually only those letters that were of use to this study. Recipients' full names are given at their first appearance and subsequently in shortened form. For the source abbreviations, see either the listing of bibliographic abbreviations at the beginning of this study (for manuscripts) or the bibliography (for published works). In the Source column, all numbers following a slash are folio numbers unless otherwise indicated. Simple numbers refer to *recto* folios; the letter *v* is added for *verso*. Sources followed by (Ma) are transcribed (on the indicated page number) in Mamone, *Serenissimi fratelli*. Sources followed by (Mo) are transcribed (on the indicated page number) in Monaldini, *L'orto dell'Esperidi*. Superscript letters reference notes at the end.

Date	Place	To	Source
Jan. 17, 1644[a]	Florence	Prince Mattias de' Medici	I Fas, MdP, filza 5426/130
Mar. 13, 1644[b]	Florence	Mattias	I Fas, MdP, 5415/218–19
May 22, 1644	Rome	Mattias	I Fas, MdP, 5434/443
Apr. 12, 1644	Rome	Mattias	I Fas, MdP, 5432/190
May 22, 1644	Rome	Mattias	I Fas, MdP, 5434/443
June 4, 1644	Rome	Mattias	I Fas, MdP, 5432/609
Nov. 22, 1644	Paris	Mattias	I Fas, MdP, 5433/240
Dec. 2, 1644	Paris	Mattias	I Fas, MdP, 5433/520
Jan. 13, 1645	Paris	Mattias	I Fas, MdP, 5435/329
Mar. 10, 1645	Paris	Mattias	I Fas, MdP, 5425/221r–v
Mar. 15, 1645	Paris	Mattias	I Fas, MdP, 5425/222–23v
Sep. 26, 1645	Florence	Mattias	I Fas, MdP, 5431/820
Sep. 29, 1645	Pistoia	Mattias	I Fas, MdP, 5472/4
Oct. 6, 1645	Pistoia	Mattias	I Fas, MdP, 5431/1067
Apr. 24, 1646	Florence	Mattias	I Fas, MdP, 5408/260
June 27, 1646	Siena	Annibale Bentivoglio	I FEas, Arch. Bent., 284/732 (Mo 4)
Oct. 6, 1646	Pistoia	A. Bentivoglio	I FEas, Arch. Bent., 286/29 (Mo 7)
Nov. 15, 1646	Pistoia	A. Bentivoglio	I FEas, Arch. Bent., 286/349 (Mo 10)
Nov. 15, 1646	Pistoia	Cornelio Bentivoglio	I FEas, Arch. Bent., 286/353 (Mo 10)
Jan. 12, 1647[c]	Paris	Mattias	I Fas, MdP, 5436/16r–v
Feb. 2, 1647[d]	Paris	Mattias	I Fas, MdP, 5414/259–60v
Mar. 23, 1647	Paris	Mattias	I Fas, MdP, 5413/359–60
July 25, 1647	Amiens	Mattias	I Fas, MdP, 5443/36
Aug. 10, 1647	Paris	A. Bentivoglio	I FEas, Arch. Bent., 291/11r–v (Mo 20)
Oct. 25, 1647	Paris	Mattias	I Fas, MdP, 5443/546–47
Nov. 2, 1647	Paris	Mattias	I Fas, MdP, 5443/751
Nov. 7, 1647	Paris	Mattias	I Fas, MdP, 5443/736r–v
Nov. 8, 1647	Paris	Mattias	I Fas, MdP, 5443/860
Nov. 14, 1647	Paris	Mattias	I Fas, MdP, 5443/854–55
Nov. 22, 1647	Paris	Mattias	I Fas, MdP, 5444/166
Aug. 14, 1648	Paris	Mattias	I Fas, MdP, 5445/61r–v
Aug. 23, 1648	Paris	Mattias	I Fas, MdP, 5445/481
Aug. 27, 1648	Paris	B. Tonti [Florence]	I Fn, Rossi Cassigoli, cassetta 8, inserto I, f. 27
Sep. 2, 1648	Paris	Mattias	I Fas, MdP, 5437/255
Dec. 26, 1648	Paris	Mattias	I Fas, MdP, 5437/822
Jan. 1, 1649	Paris	Mattias	I Fas, MdP, 5414/283
Feb. 8, 1649	Paris	A. Bentivoglio	I FEas, Arch. Bent., 297/41v (Mo 31)
Feb. 27, 1649	Saint-Germain-en-Laye	Mattias	I Fas, MdP, 5408/269–70v
Apr. 3, 1649	Saint-Germain-en-Laye	Mattias	I Fas, MdP, 5492/183r–v
May 22, 1649	Compiègne	A. Bentivoglio	I FEas, Arch. Bent., 297/316 (Mo 32)
June 25, 1649	Amiens	Mattias	I Fas, MdP, 5419/922–24
July 10, 1649	Compiègne	A. Bentivoglio	I FEas, Arch. Bent., 298/59 (Mo 32–33)
Jan. 3, 1650	Pistoia	Mattias	I Fas, MdP, 5419/921r–v

Date	Place	To	Source
July ??, 1650	Florence	Christine Marie of France, duchess of Savoy	I TOas, Lettere particolari, mazzo 33
May 13, 1651	Florence	C. Bentivoglio	I FEas, Arch. Bent., 305/770 (Mo 41–42)
June 12, 1651	Florence	Duke Carlo II Gonzaga-Nevers of Mantua	I MAas, E.XXVIII.3, busta 1135, diversi-1651/pezzo 3
July 12, 1651	Florence	Carlo II of Mantua	I MAas, E.XXVIII.3, busta 1135, diversi-1651/4
Aug. 28, 1651	Florence	Mattias	I Fas, MdP, 5419/915r–v
Sep. 24, 1651	Pistoia	Cardinal Giovan Carlo de' Medici	I Fas, MdP, 5354/682 (Ma 161)
Oct. 12, 1651	Pistoia	Mattias	I Fas, MdP, 5449/691, 692
Nov. 11, 1651	Pistoia	Mattias	I Fas, MdP, 5449/851
Feb. 9, 1652	Mantua	Mattias	I Fas, MdP, 5419/912–13v, 932
Mar. 2, 1652	Mantua	Mattias	I Fas, MdP, 5419/916r–v, (917?)
Mar. 12, 1652	Modena	Carlo II of Mantua	I MAas, E.XXVIII.3, busta 1135, diversi-1652/2
Mar. 16, 1652	Modena	Mattias	I Fas, MdP, 5450/257
Apr. 6, 1652	Modena	Mattias	I Fas, MdP, 5419/910–11
June 16, 1652	Pistoia	C. Bentivoglio	I FEas, Arch. Bent., 310/567 (Mo 56)
Aug. 18, 1652	Pistoia	C. Bentivoglio	I FEas, Arch. Bent., 311/565–66 (Mo 58–59)
Nov. 5, 1652	Pistoia	Mattias	1 Fas, MdP, 5419/918–19
Dec. 23, 1652	Florence	Duke Francesco I d'Este of Modena	I MOas, Cancelleria ducale, particolari, busta 880, Melani
May 9, 1653	Mantua	Mattias	I Fas, MdP, 5454/583
May 25, 1653	Innsbruck	Mattias	I Fas, MdP, 5408/382–83v
May 25, 1653	Innsbruck	Francesco I of Modena	I MOas, Ambasciatori, Germania, busta 99
May 25, 1653	Innsbruck	Francesco I of Modena	I MOas, Amb., Germania, busta 99
May 25, 1653	Innsbruck	Girolamo Graziani [Modena]	I MOas, Amb., Germania, busta 99
May 25, 1653	Innsbruck	Carlo II of Mantua	I MAas, E.VI.3, busta 554, Melani–1653/1
May 30, 1653	Innsbruck	Mattias	I Fas, MdP, 5454/551
May 30, 1653	Innsbruck	Carlo II of Mantua	I MAas, E.VI.3, busta 554, Melani–1653/2
June 2, 1653	Innsbruck	Carlo II of Mantua	I MAas, E.VI.3, busta 554, Melani–1653/3
June 8, 1653	Innsbruck	Carlo II of Mantua	I MAas, E.VI.3, busta 554, Melani–1653/4
June 15, 1653	Innsbruck	Mattias	I Fas, MdP, 5454/807–8v
June 15, 1653	Innsbruck	Carlo II of Mantua	I MAas, E.VI.3, busta 554, Melani–1653/5
June 22, 1653	Innsbruck	Mattias	I Fas, MdP, 5408/379–80v
June 22, 1653	Innsbruck	Graziani	I MOas, Amb., Germania, busta 99
June 29, 1653	Innsbruck	Mattias	I Fas, MdP, 5408/376–78v
July 2, 1653	Innsbruck	Mattias	I Fas, MdP, 5408/384–85v
July 3, 1653	Innsbruck	Mattias	I FEas, MdP, 5407/233
July 7, 1653	Regensburg ("Ratisbon")	Mattias	I Fas, MdP, 5407/211
July 7, 1653	Regensburg	Prince Leopoldo de' Medici	I Fas, MdP, 5561/301
July 14, 1653	Regensburg	Mattias	I Fas, MdP, 5472/27–28v, 30r–v
July 21, 1653	Regensburg	Leopoldo	I Fas, MdP, 5561/764–65v
July 21, 1653	Regensburg	Carlo II of Mantua	I MAas, E.VI.3, busta 554, Melani–1653/6
July 28, 1653	Regensburg	Carlo II of Mantua	I MAas, E.VI.3, busta 554, Melani–1653/7

Date	Place	To	Source
Aug. 4, 1653	Regensburg	Mattias	I Fas, MdP, 5455/227–28
Aug. 11?, 1653	Regensburg	Mattias	I Fas, MdP, 5455/273
Aug. 11, 1653	Regensburg	Mattias	I Fas, MdP, 5455/275–77
Aug. 16, 1653	Regensburg	Mattias	I Fas, MdP, 5455/107–8v
Aug. 22, 1653	Munich	Mattias	I Fas, MdP, 5455/88–89, 90–91v
Sep. 7, 1653	Innsbruck	Mattias	I Fas, MdP, 5414/515–16v, 523–24v, 517
Oct. 2, 1653	Florence	Carlo II of Mantua	I MAas, E.XXVIII.3, busta 1135, diversi-1653/5
Nov. 13, 1653	Florence	Duchess Christine of Savoy	I TOas, Lett. part., mazzo 33
Dec. 23, 1653	Florence	Carlo II of Mantua	I MAas, E.XXVIII.3, busta 1135, diversi-1653/8
Jan. 5, 1654	Florence	Carlo II of Mantua	I MAas, E.XXVIII.3, busta 1135, diversi-1654/1
Sep. 12, 1654	Pistoia	Mattias	I Fas, MdP, 5452/867r–v
Sep. 27, 1654	Florence	Mattias	I Fas, MdP, 5452/747–48
Oct. 2, 1654	Florence	Mattias	I Fas, MdP, 5453/595–96
Oct. 10, 1654	Florence	Mattias	I Fas, MdP, 5453/652–53
Mar. 9, 1655	Florence	Carlo II of Mantua	I MAas, E.XXVIII.3, busta 1135, diversi-1655/1
Mar. 23, 1655	Florence	Carlo II of Mantua	I MAas, E.XXVIII.3, busta 1135, diversi-1655/2
May 1, 1655	Rome	Mattias	I Fas, MdP, 5458/539–40v
May 10, 1655	Rome	Mattias	I Fas, MdP, 5458/547–48v
May 27, 1655	Rome	Mattias	I Fas, MdP, 5458/454–55
June 12, 1655	Rome	Mattias	I Fas, MdP, 5458/748–49v
June 19, 1655	Rome	Mattias	I Fas, MdP, 5419/914r–v
July 3, 1655	Rome	Mattias	I Fas, MdP, 5419/920r–v
July 12, 1655	Rome	Mattias	I Fas, MdP, 5459/140–41
July 26, 1655	Rome	Mattias	I Fas, MdP, 5459/331
July 31, 1655	Rome	Mattias	I Fas, MdP, 5408/458–61
Aug. 4, 1655	Rome	Graziani(?)[1]	I MOas, Canc. duc., part., busta 880, Melani
Aug. 7, 1655	Rome	Mattias	I Fas, MdP, 5459/389
Sep. 24, 1655	Rome	Mattias	I Fas, MdP, 5494/160r–v
Oct. 2, 1655	Rome	Mattias	I Fas, MdP, 5494/669
Oct. 11, 1655	Rome	Mattias	I Fas, MdP, 5494/487
Oct. 23, 1655	Rome	Mattias	I Fas, MdP, 5494/422r–v
Oct. 26, 1655	Rome	Mattias	I Fas, MdP, 5494/441–42
Oct. 29?, 1655	Rome	Mattias	I Fas, MdP, 5494/423–24v
Oct. 30, 1655	Rome	Mattias	I Fas, MdP, 5494/443r–v
Nov. 13, 1655	Rome	Mattias	I Fas, MdP, 5494/743–44
Nov. 20, 1655	Rome	Mattias	I Fas, MdP, 5494/738
Nov. 20, 1655	Rome	Carlo II of Mantua	I MAas, E.XXVIII.3, busta 1135, diversi-1655/5
Dec. 4, 1655	Rome	Mattias	I Fas, MdP, 5459/773
Jan. 8, 1656	Rome	Mattias	I Fas, MdP, 5460/635r–v
Jan. 14, 1656	Rome	Mattias	I Fas, MdP, 5460/636–37v
Apr. 9, 1656	Camucia	Mattias	I Fas, MdP, 5416/546–47

Date	Place	To	Source
Apr. 10, 1656	Figline [Valdarno]	Mattias	I Fas, MdP, 5408/501–2
June 13, 1656	Florence	Carlo II of Mantua	I MAas, E.XXVIII.3, busta 1135, diversi-1656/2
Oct. 14, 1656	Florence	Mattias	I Fas, MdP, 5462/679
Oct. 26, 1656	Parma	Mattias	I Fas, MdP, 5462/738–39v, 748–49v
Nov. 3 or 30, 1656	Moncalieri	Mattias	I Fas, MdP, 5461/240–41v
Dec. 16, 1656	Lyon	Mattias	I Fas, MdP, 5461/482r–v
Jan. 4, 1657	Paris	Mattias	I Fas, MdP, 5463/661–62
Jan. 4, 1657	Paris	Duchess Christine of Savoy	I TOas, Lett. part., mazzo 33
Jan. 11, 1657	Paris	Carlo II of Mantua	I MAas, E.XV.3, busta 685, diversi-1657/2
Jan. 26, 1657	Paris	Mattias	I Fas, MdP, 5411/866–67v
Feb. 2, 1657	Paris	Mattias	I Fas, MdP, 5463/675–76v
Mar. 2, 1657	Paris	Mattias	I Fas, MdP, 5463/749–50
Mar. 16, 1657	Paris	Mattias	I Fas, MdP, 5463/798–800
Mar. 23, 1657	Paris	Duchess Christine of Savoy	I TOas, Lett. part., mazzo 33
Mar. 30, 1657	Paris	Mattias	I Fas, MdP, 5463/719–20
Apr. 14, 1657	Paris	Mattias	I Fas, MdP, 5466/4–5v
Apr. 24, 1657	Paris	Mattias	I Fas, MdP, 5463/704r–v
Apr. 27, 1657	Paris	Duchess Christine of Savoy	I TOas, Lett. part., mazzo 33
May 4, 1657	Paris	Mattias	I Fas, MdP, 5466/157–58
May 11, 1657	Paris	Mattias	I Fas, MdP, 5466/140–41
May 23, 1657	Béville	Mattias	I Fas, MdP, 5466/172
June 7, 1657	La Fère	Mattias	I Fas, MdP, 5466/609–10
June 29, 1657	La Fère	Mattias	I Fas, MdP, 5466/490–91
June 29, 1657	La Fère	Duchess Christine of Savoy	I TOas, Lett. part., mazzo 33
July 6, 1657	La Fère	Duchess Christine of Savoy	I TOas, Lett. part., mazzo 33
July 20, 1657	La Fère	Duchess Christine of Savoy	I TOas, Lett. part., mazzo 33
July 29, 1657	Sedan	Mattias	I Fas, MdP, 5460/278r–v
July 30?, 1657	Sedan	Mattias	I Fas, MdP, 5460/275–77
Aug. 8, 1657	Sedan	Mattias	I Fas, MdP, 5468/171–72
Aug. 16, 1657	Sedan	Mattias	I Fas, MdP, 5468/190r–v
Aug. 28, 1657	La Fère	Duchess Christine of Savoy	I TOas, Lett. part., mazzo 33
Aug. 28, 1657	La Fère	Duke Carlo Emmanuele II of Savoy	I TOas, Lett. part., mazzo 33
Aug. 30, 1657	Péronne	Mattias	I Fas, MdP, 5468/572–73v
[Aug. 30, 1657?][e]	?	Duke Carlo Emmanuele II of Savoy	I TOas, Lett. part., mazzo 33
Oct. 19, 1657	Munich	Mattias	I Fas, MdP, 5408/517–18
Oct. 27, 1657	Munich	Mattias	I Fas, MdP, 5466/742
Nov. 7, 1657	Munich	Cardinal Jules Mazarin	F Pae, CP Bavière 2/ff. 582–83v
Nov. 27, 1657	Frankfurt	Mazarin	F Pae, CP Bavière 2/584–87
Dec. 8, 1657	Frankfurt	Duchess Christine of Savoy	I TOas, Lett. part., mazzo 33
Dec. 14, 1657	Frankfurt	Mazarin	F Pae, CP Bavière 2/594–93v
[early 1658?][f]	[France]	Mattias	I Fas, MdP, 5419/939r–v
[early 1658?][f]	[France]	Mattias	I Fas, MdP, 5419/940r–v
Feb. 15, 1658	Paris	Mattias	I Fas, MdP, 5468/366–67
Apr. 12, 1658	Paris	Mattias	I Fas, MdP, 5469/541–42v

Date	Place	To	Source
June 19, 1658	Calais	Mattias	I Fas, MdP, 5469/483–84v
July 2, 1658	Calais	Mattias	I Fas, MdP, 5469/256r–v
July 10, 1658	Calais	Mattias	I Fas, MdP, 5469/195–96v
July 17, 1658	Calais	Mattias	I Fas, MdP, 5469/246–47
Aug. 2, 1658	Compiègne	Mattias	I Fas, MdP, 5469/820–21
Aug. 16, 1658	Paris	Mattias	I Fas, MdP, 5469/756r–v
Aug. 16, 1658	Paris	Mattias	I Fas, MdP, 5469/757r–v
Aug. 23, 1658	Paris	Mattias	I Fas, MdP, 5470/134
Aug. 27, 1658	Paris	Mattias	I Fas, MdP, 5470/673–74
Aug. 31, 1658	Fontainebleau	Mattias	I Fas, MdP, 5469/653–54v
Sep. 7, 1658	Fontainebleau	Mattias	I Fas, MdP, 5470/188–89v
Sep. 14, 1658	Fontainebleau	Mattias	I Fas, MdP, 5470/209r–v
Sep. 27, 1658	Paris	Mattias	I Fas, MdP, 5470/678r–v
Oct. 11, 1658	Paris	Mattias	I Fas, MdP, 5470/679–80v
Dec. 12, 1658	Lyon	Mattias	I Fas, MdP, 5419/935–37v
Dec. 18, 1658	Lyon	Mattias	I Fas, MdP, 5419/900
Mar. 7, 1659	Paris	Mattias	I Fas, MdP, 5419/933r–v
May 30, 1659	Paris	Orazio Canossa [Mantua]	I MAas, E.XV.3, busta 686, Melani–1659/1bis
June 6, 1659	Paris	Canossa	I MAas, E.XV.3, busta 686, Melani–1659/1
June 20, 1659	Paris	Canossa	I MAas, E.XV.3, busta 686, Melani–1659/2
June 25, 1659	Paris	Canossa	I MAas, E.XV.3, busta 686, Melani–1659/3
July 9, 1659	Châteauneuf	Canossa	I MAas, E.XV.3, busta 686, Melani–1659/4
July 21, 1659	Dax	Mattias	I Fas, MdP, 5490/589–90, 597–600(?)
July 25, 1659	Bayonne	Mattias	I Fas, MdP, 5490/617–18(?)
July 31, 1659	Saint-Jean-de-Luz	Carlo II of Mantua	I MAas, E.XV.3, busta 686, Melani–1659/5
Aug. 4, 1659	Saint-Jean-de-Luz	Mattias	I Fas, MdP, 5408/581–82v, 584–85
Aug. 4, 1659*	Saint-Jean-de-Luz	Mattias	I Fas, MdP, 5408/57–58
Aug. 11, 1659	Saint-Jean-de-Luz	Mattias	I Fas, MdP, 5408/599–600
Aug. 13, 1659	Saint-Jean-de-Luz	Mattias	I Fas, MdP, 5408/578–80
Aug. 14, 1659	Saint-Jean-de-Luz	Mattias	I Fas, MdP, 5408/544–45v
Aug. 19, 1659	Saint-Jean-de-Luz	Mattias	I Fas, MdP, 5408/534–35
Aug. 21, 1659	Saint-Jean-de-Luz	Mattias	I Fas, MdP, 5408/541–43bis
Aug. 28, 1659	Saint-Jean-de-Luz	Mattias	I Fas, MdP, 5408/576–77, 597–98v
Sep. 4, 1659	Saint-Jean-de-Luz	Mattias	I Fas, MdP, 5408/572–75v
Sep. 4, 1659	Saint-Jean-de-Luz	Carlo II of Mantua	I MAas, E.XV.3, busta 686, Melani–1659/6
Sep. 12, 1659	Saint-Jean-de-Luz	Mattias	I Fas, MdP, 5408/561
Sep. 18, 1659	Saint-Jean-de-Luz	Mattias	I Fas, MdP, 5460/590–92v
Sep. 18, 1659	Saint-Jean-de-Luz	Carlo II of Mantua	I MAas, E.XV.3, busta 686, Melani–1659/7
Sep. 25, 1659	Saint-Jean-de-Luz	Mattias	I Fas, MdP, 5408/553–53v, 556–58v
Sep. 25, 1659	Saint-Jean-de-Luz	Carlo II of Mantua	I MAas, E.XV.3, busta 686, Melani–1659/8
Oct. 6, 1659	Saint-Jean-de-Luz	Mattias	I Fas, MdP, 5490/458
Oct. 6?, 1659	Saint-Jean-de-Luz	Mattias	I Fas, MdP, 5408/559–60v
Oct. 13, 1659	Saint-Jean-de-Luz	Mattias	I Fas, MdP, 5408/546–48, 549–50
Feb. 27, 1660	Aix-en-Provence	Mattias	I Fas, MdP, 5409/561–62
Feb. 28, 1660	Aix-en-Provence	Mattias	I Fas, MdP, 5409/559–60v
Mar. 1, 1660	Aix-en-Provence	Mattias	I Fas, MdP, 5409/554–56v

Date	Place	To	Source
July 30, 1660	Paris	Mattias	I Fas, MdP, 5472/5–6v
Aug. 6, 1660	Paris	Mattias	I Fas, MdP, 5474/824–25
Aug. 13, 1660	Paris	Mattias	I Fas, MdP, 5419/902–3v, 901
Aug. 20, 1660	Paris	Mattias	I Fas, MdP, 5474/157–59v
Aug. 27, 1660	Paris	Mattias	I Fas, MdP, 5474/826–27v, 844–45v
Sep. 3, 1660	Paris	Mattias	I Fas, MdP, 5474/869–72
Sep. 10, 1660	Paris	Mattias	I Fas, MdP, 5474/732–33
Sep. 17, 1660	Paris	Mattias	I Fas, MdP, 5474/909–10
Sep. 24, 1660	Paris	Mattias	I Fas, MdP, 5408/630–31
Oct. 1, 1660	Paris	Mattias	I Fas, MdP, 5474/569r–v
Oct. 8, 1660	Paris	Mattias	I Fas, MdP, 5474/552bis,r–v
Oct. 22, 1660	Paris	Mattias	I Fas, MdP, 5409/584–87
Feb. 4, 1661	Paris	Mattias	I Fas, MdP, 5408/681–82
Mar. 25, 1661	Paris	Mattias	Ademollo, *I primi fasti della musica italiana*, pp. 82–83 (excerpt)
Apr. 28, 1661	Fontainebleau	Mattias	Ademollo, *I primi fasti*, 65 (excerpt)
May 25, 1661	Marseille	Anna Maria Gonzaga, Princess Palatine	I MAas, E.XV.3, busta 686, Melani-1661
Aug. 8, 1661	Rome	Hugues de Lionne	F Pae, CP Rome, 141/299–302
Aug. 15, 1661	Rome	De Lionne	F Pae, CP Rome, 141/330–32
Aug. 20, 1661	Rome	Mattias	I Fas, MdP, 5475/608r–v
Aug. 21, 1661	Rome	De Lionne	F Pae, CP Rome, 141/352–53
Aug. 22, 1661	Rome	De Lionne	F Pae, CP Rome, 141/354–55
Aug. 27, 1661	Rome	Mattias	I Fas, MdP, 5475/806–7
Sep. 3, 1661	Rome	Mattias	I Fas, MdP, 5476/281–82v
Sep. 5, 1661	Rome	De Lionne	F Pae, CP Rome, 142/19–20
Sep. 12, 1661	Rome	De Lionne	F Pae, CP Rome, 142/32–34v
Sep. 19, 1661	Rome	De Lionne	F Pae, CP Rome, 142/68–71v
Oct. 1, 1661	Rome	Mattias	I Fas, MdP, 5476/103r–v
Oct. 3, 1661	Rome	De Lionne	F Pae, CP Rome, 142/134–36
Oct. 25, 1661	Rome	De Lionne	F Pae, CP Rome, 142/216–17
Oct. 31, 1661	Rome	De Lionne	F Pae, CP Rome, 142/227–28
Nov. 19, 1661	Florence	Mattias	I Fas, MdP, 5475/632
Apr. 6, 1663[g]	[Florence?]	[De Lionne?]	F Pae, CP Toscane, 8/12–13
Apr. 13, 1663	[Florence?]	De Lionne	F Pae, CP Toscane, 8/18–19v
Apr. 20, 1663	Florence	De Lionne	F Pae, CP Toscane, 8/22–27v
Apr. 20, 1663	Florence	De Lionne	F Pae, CP Toscanc, 8/28–29
Aug. 24, 1663	Florence	De Lionne	F Pae, CP Toscane, 8/109–12
Aug. 24, 1663	Florence	De Lionne	F Pae, CP Toscane, 8/109–12
Oct. 12, 1663	Florence	De Lionne	F Pae, CP Toscane, 8/140–42v
Feb. 16, 1664	Venice	Mattias	I Fas, MdP, 5478/427–28
Feb. 18, 1664	Venice	Mattias	I Fas, MdP, 5478/760r–v
Mar. 12, 1664	Venice	Carlo II of Mantua	I MAas, E.XLX.3, busta 1574, diversi-1664/11
Mar. 26, 1664	Mantua	Marie Mancini Colonna	I SUss, Archivio Colonna, Corrispondenza di Lorenzo Onofrio Colonna, cartella 10 (by date)

Date	Place	To	Source
Apr. 1, 1664	Mantua	Marie Mancini Colonna	"
Apr. 10, 1664	Mantua	Lorenzo Onofrio Colonna	"
Apr. 14, 1664	Ferrara	Carlo II of Mantua	I MAas, E.XXXI.3, busta 1275, diversi-1664/5
Apr. 22, 1664	Florence	Carlo II of Mantua	I MAas, E.XXVIII.3, busta 1135, diversi-1664/1
Apr. 25, 1664	Florence	De Lionne	F Pae, CP Toscane, 8/266r–v
June 7, 1664	Florence	Ippolito Bentivoglio	I FEas, Arch. Bent., 338/462 (Mo 192)
July 15, 1664	Florence	Canossa	I MAas, E.XXVIII.3, busta 1135, diversi-1664/2
Aug. 19, 1664	[Florence]	[I. Bentivoglio?]	I FEas, Arch. Bent., 339/148 (Mo 201)
Aug. 27, 1664	Florence	I. Bentivoglio	I FEas, Arch. Bent., 339/235 (Mo 205)
Sep. 5, 1664	Florence	De Lionne	F Pae, CP Toscane, 8/390–91v
Oct. 31, 1664	Florence	De Lionne	F Pae, CP Toscane, 8/449
Nov. 8, 1664	Florence	I. Bentivoglio	I FEas, Arch. Bent., 339/731r–v (Mo 214)
Jan. 2, 1665	Florence	De Lionne	F Pae, CP Toscane, 9/21r–v
Jan. 30, 1665	Florence	De Lionne	F Pae, CP Toscane, 9/40r–v
Feb. 14, 1665	Florence	Leopoldo de' Medici	I Fas, MdP, 5544/let 26
Feb. 16, 1665	Florence	De Lionne	F Pae, CP Toscane, 9/51–52
Mar. 20, 1665	Florence	De Lionne	F Pae, CP Toscane, 9/68–69
Mar. 27, 1665	Florence	De Lionne	F Pae, CP Toscane, 9/74r–v
Mar. 27, 1665	Florence	I. Bentivoglio	I FEas, Arch. Bent., 340/178r–v (Mo 219)
Apr. 10, 1665	Florence	De Lionne	F Pae, CP Toscane, 9/86r–v
Apr. 17, 1665	Florence	De Lionne	F Pae, CP Toscane, 9/87
May 12, 1665	Florence	Canossa	I MAas, E.XXVIII.3, busta 1135, diversi-1665
July 3, 1665	Florence	De Lionne	F Pae, CP Toscane, 9/118–19v
July 31, 1665	Florence	De Lionne	F Pae, CP Toscane, 9/128–29v
Aug. 14, 1665	Florence	De Lionne	F Pae, CP Toscane, 9/133r–v
Sep. 11, 1665	Florence	De Lionne	F Pae, CP Toscane, 9/140–41
Oct. 16, 1665	Florence	De Lionne	F Pae, CP Toscane, 9/147r–v
Oct. 23, 1665	Florence	De Lionne	F Pae, CP Toscane, 9/152–53
Oct. 30, 1665	Florence	De Lionne	F Pae, CP Toscane, 9/156
Dec. 12, 1665	Florence	De Lionne	F Pae, CP Toscane, 9/175r–v
Dec. 25, 1665	Florence	De Lionne	F Pae, CP Toscane, 9/182–83v
Jan. 1, 1666	Florence	De Lionne	F Pae, CP Toscane, 9/186
Apr. 23, 1666	Florence	De Lionne	F Pae, CP Toscane, 9/203–4
June 25, 1666	Florence	De Lionne	F Pae, CP Toscane, 9/216–17
Sep. 24, 1666	Florence	De Lionne	F Pae, CP Toscane, 9/243–44v
Mar. 18, 1667	Florence	De Lionne	F Pae, CP Toscane, 9/287–88v
Apr. 1, 1667	Florence	De Lionne	F Pae, CP Toscane, 9/293–96
Apr. 15, 1667	Florence	De Lionne	F Pae, CP Toscane, 9/303–6v
Apr. 22, 1667	Florence	De Lionne	F Pae, CP Toscane, 9/312–13v
Apr. 26, 1667	Florence	Canossa	I MAas, E.XXVIII.3, busta 1135, diversi-1667/1
May 3, 1667	Florence	Canossa	I MAas, E.XXVIII.3, busta 1135, diversi-1667/2

Date	Place	To	Source
May 10, 1667	Florence	Canossa	I MAas, E.XXVIII.3, busta 1135, diversi-1667/3
May 20, 1667	Florence	De Lionne	F Pae, CP Toscane, 9/328–29
May 31, 1667[h]	Rome	De Lionne	F Pae, CP Rome, 183/346–49
June 1, 1667	Rome	De Lionne	F Pae, CP Rome, 184/17–18v
June 7, 1667	Rome	De Lionne	F Pae, CP Rome, 184/67–68
June 12, 1667	Rome	De Lionne	F Pae, CP Rome, 184/80–83
June 22, 1667	Rome	De Lionne	F Pae, CP Rome, 184/151r–v
June 22, 1667	Rome	De Lionne	F Pae, CP Rome, 184/152–53v
June 23, 1667	Rome	De Lionne	F Pae, CP Rome, 184/154–58v
June 23, 1667	Rome	De Lionne	F Pae, CP Rome, 184/159–60
June 28, 1667	Rome	De Lionne	F Pae, CP Rome, 184/185–86v
July 5, 1667	Rome	De Lionne	F Pae, CP Rome, 184/228–30v
July 12, 1667	Rome	De Lionne	F Pae, CP Rome, 184/334–37v
July 19, 1667	Rome	De Lionne	F Pae, CP Rome, 185/78–81
July 23, 1667	Rome	Canossa	I MAas, E.XXV.3, busta 1048, Melani–1667/409
July 26, 1667	Rome	De Lionne	F Pae, CP Rome, 185/124–25v
Aug. 2, 1667	Rome	De Lionne	F Pae, CP Rome, 185/158–62v
Aug. 9, 1667	Rome	De Lionne	F Pae, CP Rome, 185/220–26
Aug. 16, 1667	Rome	De Lionne	F Pae, CP Rome, 185/289–91v
Aug. 23, 1667	Rome	De Lionne	F Pae, CP Rome, 185/317–18
Aug. 30, 1667	Rome	De Lionne	F Pae, CP Rome, 185/368–71
Sep. 6, 1667	Rome	De Lionne	F Pae, CP Rome, 186/30–32
Sep. 13, 1667	Rome	De Lionne	F Pae, CP Rome, 186/67–70v
Sep. 20, 1667	Rome	De Lionne	F Pae, CP Rome, 186/109–10v
Sep. 27, 1667	Rome	De Lionne	F Pae, CP Rome, 186/155–58
Sep. 27, 1667	Rome	De Lionne	F Pae, CP Rome, 186/159–60
Oct. 3, 1667	Rome	Canossa	I MAas, E.XXV.3, busta 1048, Melani–1667/410
Oct. 4, 1667	Rome	De Lionne	F Pae, CP Rome, 186/216–28
Oct. 8, 1667	Rome	Canossa	I MAas, E.XXV.3, busta 1048, Melani–1667/411
Oct. 11, 1667	Rome	De Lionne	F Pae, CP Rome, 186/247–48v
Oct. 15, 1667[i]	Rome	Canossa	I MAas, E.XXV.3, busta 1048, Melani–1667/f. 412
Oct. 18, 1667	Rome	De Lionne	F Pae, CP Rome, 186/289–90
Oct. 25, 1667	Rome	De Lionne	F Pae, CP Rome, 186/332–33
Nov. 1, 1667	Rome	De Lionne	F Pae, CP Rome, 187/129–30v
Nov. 15, 1667	Rome	De Lionne	F Pae, CP Rome, 187/128r–v
Nov. 22, 1667	Rome	De Lionne	F Pae, CP Rome, 187/163–64
Nov. 26, 1667	Rome	Canossa	I MAas, E.XXV.3, busta 1048, Melani–1667/413–14
Nov. 28, 1667	Rome	De Lionne	F Pae, CP Rome, 187/173–74
Dec. 13, 1667	Rome	De Lionne	F Pae, CP Rome, 187/279–81v
Dec. 17, 1667	Rome	Canossa	I MAas, E.XXV.3, busta 1048, Melani–1667/415

Date	Place	To	Source
Dec. 18, 1667	Rome	De Lionne	F Pae, CP Rome, 187/312–15
Dec. 20, 1667	Rome	De Lionne	F Pae, CP Rome, 187/335–40
Dec. 27, 1667	Rome	De Lionne	F Pae, CP Rome, 187/365–67v
Dec. 31, 1667	Rome	Canossa	I MAas, E.XXV.3, busta 1048, Melani–1667/ 416r-v
Jan. 3, 1668	Rome	De Lionne	F Pae, CP Rome, 189/39–42
Jan. 7, 1668	Rome	Canossa	I MAas, E.XXV.3, busta 1049, Melani–1668/ 140
Jan. 10, 1668	Rome	De Lionne	F Pae, CP Rome, 189/75–77v
Jan. 14, 1668	Rome	[I. Bentivoglio]	I FEas, Arch. Bent., 342/58 (Mo 230)
Jan. 17, 1668	Rome	De Lionne	F Pae, CP Rome, 189/110–12v
Jan. 24, 1668	Rome	De Lionne	F Pae, CP Rome, 189/139–40
Jan. 25, 1668	Rome	De Lionne	F Pae, CP Rome, 189/143–50v
Jan. 28, 1668	Rome	Canossa	I MAas, E.XXV.3, busta 1049, Melani–1668/ 141-42
Jan. 31, 1668	Rome	De Lionne	F Pae, CP Rome, 189/179–81v
Feb. 4, 1668	Rome	Canossa	I MAas, E.XXV.3, busta 1049, Melani–1668/ 143r-v
Feb. 7, 1668	Rome	De Lionne	F Pae, CP Rome, 189/212–15
Feb. 14, 1668	Rome	De Lionne	F Pae, CP Rome, 189/269–72
Feb. 15, 1668	Rome	De Lionne	F Pae, CP Rome, 189/279–81v
Feb. 18, 1668	Rome	Canossa	I MAas, E.XXV.3, busta 1049, Melani–1668/ 144r-v
Feb. 21, 1668	Rome	De Lionne	F Pae, CP Rome, 189/301–4v
Feb. 21, 1668	Rome	De Lionne	F Pae, CP Rome, 189/305–7v
Feb. 25, 1668	Rome	Canossa	I MAas, E.XXV.3, busta 1049, Melani–1668/ 145
Feb. 28, 1668	Rome	De Lionne	F Pae, CP Rome, 189/363–66
Mar. 3, 1668	Rome	De Lionne	F Pae, CP Rome, 190/11–16
Mar. 6, 1668	Rome	De Lionne	F Pae, CP Rome, 190/56–61
Mar. 13, 1668	Rome	De Lionne	F Pae, CP Rome, 190/85–89v
Mar. 20, 1668	Rome	De Lionne	F Pae, CP Rome, 190/145–55
Mar. 24, 1668	Rome	Canossa	I MAas, E.XXV.3, busta 1049, Melani–1668/ 146r–v
Apr. 10, 1668	Rome	De Lionne	F Pae, CP Rome, 190/231–36v
Apr. 17, 1668	Rome	De Lionne	F Pae, CP Rome, 190/309–13v
Apr. 24, 1668	Rome	De Lionne	F Pae, CP Rome, 190/325–28v
May 2, 1668	Rome	De Lionne	F Pae, CP Rome, 191/28–31
May 2, 1668	Rome	De Lionne	F Pae, CP Rome, 191/32–35
May 2–8?, 1668[j]	Rome	De Lionne	F Pae, CP Rome, 191/84–85v
May 5, 1668	Rome	Canossa	I MAas, E.XXV.3, busta 1049, Melani–1668/ 147
May 8, 1668	Rome	De Lionne	F Pae, CP Rome, 191/102–4v
May 8, 1668	Rome	De Lionne	F Pae, CP Rome, 191/105r–v
May 15, 1668	Rome	De Lionne	F Pae, CP Rome, 191/151–53v
May 29, 1668	Rome	De Lionne	F Pae, CP Rome, 191/212–17v
June 5, 1668	Rome	De Lionne	F Pae, CP Rome, 191/282, 283–84

Date	Place	To	Source
June 12, 1668	Rome	De Lionne	F Pae, CP Rome, 191/309–14
June 15, 1668	Rome	De Lionne	F Pae, CP Rome, 191/325–27
June 26, 1668	Rome	De Lionne	F Pae, CP Rome, 191/419–22
June 30, 1668	Rome	Canossa	I MAas, E.XXV.3, busta 1049, Melani–1668/ 148–49
July 3, 1668	Rome	De Lionne	F Pae, CP Rome, 192/27–30v
July 14, 1668	Rome	De Lionne	F Pae, CP Rome, 192/85–92
July 24, 1668	Rome	De Lionne	F Pae, CP Rome, 192/169–70v
July 24, 1668	Rome	De Lionne	F Pae, CP Rome, 192/171–72v
July 31, 1668	Rome	De Lionne	F Pae, CP Rome, 192/189–92v
Aug. 12, 1668	Rome	De Lionne	F Pae, CP Rome, 192/247–52v
Aug. 14, 1668	Rome	De Lionne	F Pae, CP Rome, 192/289–94
Aug. 21, 1668	Rome	De Lionne	F Pae, CP Rome, 192/326–29
Aug. 28, 1668	Rome	De Lionne	F Pae, CP Rome, 192/375–80
Sep. 1, 1668	Rome	De Lionne	F Pae, CP Rome, 193/14–15v
Sep. 4, 1668	Rome	De Lionne	F Pae, CP Rome, 193/22–23v
Sep. 18, 1668	Rome	De Lionne	F Pae, CP Rome, 193/67–73v
Sep. 18, 1668	Rome	De Lionne	F Pae, CP Rome, 193/305–9
Sep. 25, 1668	Rome	De Lionne	F Pae, CP Rome, 193/172–75
Sep. 28, 1668	Rome	De Lionne	F Pae, CP Rome, 193/184r–v
Oct. 2, 1668	Rome	De Lionne	F Pae, CP Rome, 193/224–27v
Oct. 9, 1668	Rome	De Lionne	F Pae, CP Rome, 193/263–66v
Oct. 16, 1668	Rome	De Lionne	F Pae, CP Rome, 193/295–96
Oct. 23, 1668	Rome	De Lionne	F Pae, CP Rome, 193/346–49v
Oct. 30, 1668	Rome	De Lionne	F Pae, CP Rome, 193/378–81
Nov. 6, 1668	Rome	De Lionne	F Pae, CP Rome, 194/42–45v
Nov. 13, 1668	Rome	De Lionne	F Pae, CP Rome, 194/70–71
Nov. 15, 1668	Rome	De Lionne	F Pae, CP Rome, 194/82–82v
Nov. 21, 1668	Rome	De Lionne	F Pae, CP Rome, 194/110–13
Nov. 27, 1668	Rome	De Lionne	F Pae, CP Rome, 194/159–60
Dec. 4, 1668	Rome	De Lionne	F Pae, CP Rome, 194/201–2
Dec. 11, 1668	Rome	De Lionne	F Pae, CP Rome, 194/252–54v
Dec. 18, 1668	Rome	De Lionne	F Pae, CP Rome, 194/272–73v
Dec. 18, 1668	Rome	De Lionne	F Pae, CP Rome, 194/274–47
Dec. 25, 1668	Rome	De Lionne	F Pae, CP Rome, 194/303–4v
Jan. 1, 1669	Rome	De Lionne	F Pae, CP Rome, 196/29–32v
Jan. 8, 1669	Rome	De Lionne	F Pae, CP Rome, 196/87–89v
Jan. 15, 1669	Rome	De Lionne	F Pae, CP Rome, 196/129–31v
Jan. 29, 1669	Rome	De Lionne	F Pae, CP Rome, 196/221–24
Feb. 5, 1669	Rome	De Lionne	F Pae, CP Rome, 196/272–75
Feb. 12, 1669	Rome	De Lionne	F Pae, CP Rome, 196/325–26v
Feb. 19, 1669	Rome	De Lionne	F Pae, CP Rome, 196/390–93v
Feb. 26, 1669	Rome	De Lionne	F Pae, CP Rome, 196/425–27v
Feb. 26, 1669	Rome	De Lionne	F Pae, CP Rome, 196/428
Mar. 5, 1669	Rome	De Lionne	F Pae, CP Rome, 197/28–29
Mar. 9, 1669	Rome	Canossa	I MAas, E.XXV.3, busta 1049, diversi-1669/ 389–90

Date	Place	To	Source
Mar. 12, 1669	Rome	De Lionne	F Pae, CP Rome, 197/71
Mar. 16, 1669	Rome	Cardinal Leopoldo de' Medici	I Fas, MdP, 5544/letter 46
Mar. 19, 1669	Rome	De Lionne	F Pae, CP Rome, 197/101–2v
Mar. 20, 1669	Rome	De Lionne	F Pae, CP Rome, 197/146–47
Mar. 25, 1669	Rome	De Lionne	F Pae, CP Rome, 197/124–25
Mar. 30, 1669	Rome	Canossa	I MAas, E.XXV.3, busta 1049, diversi-1669/396
Apr. 2, 1669	Rome	De Lionne	F Pae, CP Rome, 197/166–70, 171–73, 175–77
Apr. 2?, 1669	Rome	De Lionne	F Pae, CP Rome, 197/178–83
Apr. 9, 1669	Rome	De Lionne	F Pae, CP Rome, 197/218r–v
Apr. 9, 1669	Rome	De Lionne	F Pae, CP Rome, 197/221–22v
Apr. 10, 1669	Rome	De Lionne	F Pae, CP Rome, 197/236–37
Apr. 16, 1669	Rome	De Lionne	F Pae, CP Rome, 197/272–75
Apr. 23, 1669	Rome	De Lionne	F Pae, CP Rome, 197/294–95v
Apr. 30, 1669	Rome	De Lionne	F Pae, CP Rome, 197/321–22
Apr. 30, 1669	Rome	De Lionne	F Pae, CP Rome, 197/323–25
May 5, 1669	Rome	De Lionne	F Pae, CP Rome, 198/13–15
May 7, 1669	Rome	De Lionne	F Pae, CP Rome, 198/29–30
May 21, 1669	Rome	De Lionne	F Pae, CP Rome, 198/101–3v
May 28, 1669	Rome	De Lionne	F Pae, CP Rome, 198/139–42v
June 4, 1669	Rome	De Lionne	F Pae, CP Rome, 198/193–94
June 11, 1669	Rome	De Lionne	F Pae, CP Rome, 198/224r–v
June 18, 1669	Rome	De Lionne	F Pae, CP Rome, 198/260–61v
June 25, 1669	Rome	De Lionne	F Pae, CP Rome, 198/291–94
July 2, 1669	Rome	De Lionne	F Pae, CP Rome, 199/26–27
July 9, 1669	Rome	De Lionne	F Pae, CP Rome, 199/79–82
July 16, 1669	Rome	De Lionne	F Pae, CP Rome, 199/128
July 19–20, 1669	Rome	De Lionne	F Pae, CP Rome, 199/137–42v, 143–52
July [20–23?], 1669[j]	Rome	Abbé Louis d'Anglur de Bourlemont	F Pae, CP Rome, 199/156r–v
July 23, 1669	Rome	De Lionne	F Pae, CP Rome, 199/177r–v
July 23, 1669	Rome	De Lionne	F Pae, CP Rome, 199/179–81
July 23, 1669	Rome	De Lionne	F Pae, CP Rome, 199/183–86
July 23, 1669	Rome	De Lionne	F Pae, CP Rome, 199/187–90
July 30, 1669	Rome	De Lionne	F Pae, CP Rome, 199/246–49
Aug. 5, 1669	Rome	De Lionne	F Pae, CP Rome, 199/297–98v
Aug. 5, 1669	Rome	De Lionne	F Pae, CP Rome, 199/300r–v
Aug. 6–8, 1669	Rome	De Lionne	F Pae, CP Rome, 199/311–14, 315–16v
Aug. 13, 1669	Rome	De Lionne	F Pae, CP Rome, 199/361–62v
Aug. 20, 1669	Rome	De Lionne	F Pae, CP Rome, 199/393–95v
Aug. 27, 1669	Rome	De Lionne	F Pae, CP Rome, 199/423–24v, 425–26
Aug. 31, 1669	Rome	De Lionne	F Pae, CP Rome, 199/444–45v
Sep. 3, 1669	Rome	De Lionne	F Pae, CP Rome, 200/42–44
Sep. 10, 1669	Rome	De Lionne	F Pae, CP Rome, 200/64–65v
Sep. 17, 1669	Rome	De Lionne	F Pae, CP Rome, 200/99–109

Date	Place	To	Source
Sep. 17, 1669	Rome	De Lionne	F Pae, CP Rome, 200/110r–v
Sep. 24, 1669	Rome	De Lionne	F Pae, CP Rome, 200/137–41v
Oct. 8, 1669	Rome	De Lionne	F Pae, CP Rome, 200/211–14v
Oct. 8, 1669	Rome	De Lionne	F Pae, CP Rome, 201/53–60v
Oct. 10, 1669	Rome	De Lionne	F Pae, CP Rome, 200/215r–v
Oct. 15, 1669	Rome	De Lionne	F Pae, CP Rome, 200/248r–v
Oct. 15, 1669	Rome	De Lionne	F Pae, CP Rome, 200/249–52
Oct. 22, 1669	Rome	De Lionne	F Pae, CP Rome, 200/280–81
Oct. 29, 1669	Rome	De Lionne	F Pae, CP Rome, 200/322–28v
Nov. 5, 1669	Rome	De Lionne	F Pae, CP Rome, 201/31–35v
Nov. 12, 1669	Rome	De Lionne	F Pae, CP Rome, 201/79–82
Nov. 14, 1669	Rome	De Lionne	F Pae, CP Rome, 201/88–90
Nov. 19, 1669	Rome	De Lionne	F Pae, CP Rome, 201/112–18v
Nov. 26, 1669	Rome	De Lionne	F Pae, CP Rome, 201/140–43v
Nov. 29, 1669	Rome	De Lionne	F Pae, CP Rome, 201/163–65v
Nov. 29, 1669	Rome	De Lionne	F Pae, CP Rome, 201/166–67
Dec. 3, 1669	Rome	De Lionne	F Pae, CP Rome, 201/191–93
Dec. 8, 1669	Rome	De Lionne	F Pae, CP Rome, 201/213–14
Dec. 8, 1669	Rome	De Lionne	F Pae, CP Rome, 201/217–24
Dec. 10, 1669	Rome	De Lionne	F Pae, CP Rome, 201/313–15v
Dec. 10, 1669	Rome	De Lionne	F Pae, CP Rome, 201/316–18
Dec. 16, 1669	Rome	De Lionne	F Pae, CP Rome, 201/344–47v
Dec. 17, 1669	Rome	De Lionne	F Pae, CP Rome, 201/382–86
Jan. 7, 1670	Rome	De Lionne	F Pae, CP Rome, 208/36–43
Jan. 7, 1670	Rome	De Lionne	F Pae, CP Rome, 208/44–45v
Jan. 28, 1670	"Dal conclave"	De Lionne	F Pae, CP Rome, 208/130–33v
Feb. 4, 1670	Rome	De Lionne	F Pae, CP Rome, 208/179–84v
Feb. 10, 1670	"Dal conclave"	De Lionne	F Pae, CP Rome, 208/199–208
Feb. 11, 1670	"Dal conclave"	De Lionne	F Pae, CP Rome, 208/223–24
Feb. 16, 1670	"Dal conclave"	De Lionne	F Pae, CP Rome, 208/231–35v
Feb. 18, 1670	Rome	De Lionne	F Pae, CP Rome, 208/257–63v
Feb. [18–25?], 1670[j]	Rome	De Lionne	F Pae, CP Rome, 208/274–76
Feb. 25, 1670	Rome	De Lionne	F Pae, CP Rome, 208/296–98
July 1, 1670	Rome	De Lionne	F Pae, CP Rome, 210/18–22
July 8, 1670	Rome	De Lionne	F Pae, CP Rome, 210/47–48v
July 8, 1670	Rome	De Lionne	F Pae, CP Rome, 210/49–50
July 8, 1670	Rome	De Lionne	F Pae, CP Rome, 210/55–64v
July 15, 1670	Rome	De Lionne	F Pae, CP Rome, 210/95–96v
July 15, 1670	Rome	De Lionne	F Pae, CP Rome, 210/97–98v
July 15, 1670	Rome	De Lionne	F Pae, CP Rome, 210/110r–v
July 22, 1670	Rome	De Lionne	F Pae, CP Rome, 210/150–57
July 22, 1670	Rome	De Lionne	F Pae, CP Rome, 210/158–65v
July 29, 1670	Rome	De Lionne	F Pae, CP Rome, 210/193–99v
July 29, 1670	Rome	De Lionne	F Pae, CP Rome, 210/200–5v
July 29, 1670	Rome	De Lionne	Ciampi, *Bibliografia critica*, 79
Aug. 1, 1670	Rome	De Lionne	F Pae, CP Rome, 210/215–20v

Date	Place	To	Source
Aug. 2, 1670	Rome	De Lionne	F Pae, CP Rome, 210/221–22
Aug. 5, 1670	Rome	De Lionne	F Pae, CP Rome, 210/234–77v
Aug. 12, 1670	Rome	De Lionne	F Pae, CP Rome, 210/271–74v
Aug. 19, 1670	Rome	De Lionne	F Pae, CP Rome, 210/332–33v
Aug. 19, 1670	Rome	De Lionne	F Pae, CP Rome, 210/334–39
Aug. 19, 1670	Rome	De Lionne	F Pae, CP Rome, 210/340–41
Aug. 19, 1670	Rome	De Lionne	Ciampi, *Bibliografia critica*, 82
Aug. 26, 1670	Rome	De Lionne	F Pae, CP Rome, 210/382–87
Aug. 26, 1670	Rome	De Lionne	Ciampi, *Bibliografia critica*, 84
Sep. 12, 1670	Rome	De Lionne	F Pae, CP Rome, 211/89–90
Sep. 13, 1670	Rome	De Lionne	F Pae, CP Rome, 211/108–13v
Sep. 30, 1670	Rome	De Lionne	F Pae, CP Rome, 211/167–71
Oct. 7, 1670	Rome	De Lionne	F Pae, CP Rome, 211/211–16
Oct. 14, 1670	Rome	De Lionne	F Pae, CP Rome, 211/243–46v
Oct. 22, 1670	Florence	De Lionne	F Pae, CP Rome, 211/275–76
Nov. 27, 1670	Paris	Francesco Buonvisi	Trenta, *Memorie*, I:266–70
May 17, 1671	Livorno	Cardinal Gilberto Borromeo	F Pae, CP Rome, 213/206–9v
May 22, 1671	Florence	De Lionne	F Pae, CP Toscane, 10/310–13
May 24, 1671	Florence	De Lionne	F Pae, CP Toscane, 10/316r–v
May 29, 1671	Florence	De Lionne	F Pae, CP Toscane, 10/320–22
June 9, 1671	Rome	De Lionne	F Pae, CP Rome, 214/72–73
June 16, 1671	Rome	De Lionne	F Pae, CP Rome, 214/90–94
June 16, 1671	Rome	De Lionne	F Pae, CP Rome, 214/95–116v
June 23, 1671	Rome	De Lionne	F Pae, CP Rome, 214/148–53
July 21, 1671	Rome	De Lionne	F Pae, CP Rome, 214/224–29
July 21, 1671	Rome	De Lionne	F Pae, CP Rome, 214/230–31v
Sep. 1, 1671	Rome	De Lionne[m]	F Pae, CP Rome, 215/187–89
Oct. 13, 1671	Rome	François-Michel Le Tellier, marquis de Louvois	F Pae, CP Rome, 215/306–9
Oct. 13, 1671	Rome	Louvois	F Pae, CP Rome, 215/310–12v
Nov. 17, 1671	Rome	Simon Arnauld, marquis de Pomponne[n]	F Pae, CP Rome, 216/132–33v
Nov. 17, 1671	Rome	Louvois[m]	F Pae, CP Rome, 216/134–39
Nov. 24, 1671	Rome	Louvois[m]	F Pae, CP Rome, 216/149–55
Dec. 1, 1671	Rome	Louvois[m]	F Pae, CP Rome, 216/223–28
Dec. 8, 1671	Rome	Louvois[m]	F Pae, CP Rome, 216/261–68
Dec. 15, 1671	Rome	Louvois[m]	F Pae, CP Rome, 216/302–9v
Dec. 22, 1671	Rome	Pomponne[m]	F Pae, CP Rome, 216/322–30
Dec. 22, 1671	Rome	Pomponne	F Pae, CP Rome, 216/332–33v
Dec. 30, 1671	Rome	Louvois[m]	F Pae, CP Rome, 216/371–72
Dec. 30, 1671	Rome	Louvois[m]	F Pae, CP Rome, 216/373–80v
Jan. 5, 1672	Rome	Louvois	F Pae, CP Rome, 218/36–39
Jan. 5, 1672	Rome	Louvois	F Pae, CP Rome, 218/40–45
Jan. 9, 1672	Rome	Louvois[m]	F Pae, CP Rome, 218/71–85
Jan. 9, 1672	Rome	Louvois[m]	F Pae, CP Rome, 218/87–88
Jan. 9, 1672	Rome	Pomponne[m]	F Pae, CP Rome, 218/89r–v
Jan. 12, 1672	Rome	Louvois[m]	F Pae, CP Rome, 218/119–22

Date	Place	To	Source
Jan. 19, 1672	Rome	Louvois[m]	F Pae, CP Rome, 218/143–48
Feb. 28, 1672	Rome	Louis XIV	F Pae, CP Rome, supplément 7/125–27v
Mar. 8, 1672	Rome	Pomponne	F Pae, CP Rome, suppl. 7/183–99
Mar. 8, 1672	"Dalle stanze"	César d'Éstrées, bishop of Laon	F Pae, CP Rome, suppl. 7/200r–v
Mar. 15, 1672	Rome	Pomponne	F Pae, CP Rome, suppl. 7/228–51
Mar. 29, 1672	Rome	Pomponne	F Pae, CP Rome, suppl. 7/357–64
Mar. 29, 1672	Rome	Louis XIV	F Pae, CP Rome, suppl. 7/365–66
Apr. 5, 1672	Rome	Pomponne	F Pae, CP Rome, 220/17–28
Apr. 19, 1672	Rome	Pomponne	F Pae, CP Rome, 220/99–105v
Apr. 26, 1672	Rome	Pomponne	F Pae, CP Rome, 220/183–91
May 3, 1672	Rome	Pomponne	F Pae, CP Rome, 220/219–28
May 10, 1672	Rome	Pomponne	F Pae, CP Rome, 220/296–99
May 16, 1672	Rome	Pomponne	F Pae, CP Rome, 221/35–40
May 24, 1672	Rome	Pomponne	F Pae, CP Rome, 221/104–5
May 31, 1672	Rome	Pomponne	F Pae, CP Rome, 221/120–23
June 7, 1672	Rome	Pomponne	F Pae, CP Rome, 221/172–75
June 15, 1672	Rome	Pomponne	F Pae, CP Rome, 221/200r–v
June 16, 1672	Rome	Pomponne	F Pae, CP Rome, 221/212–14v
June 17, 1672	Rome	Pomponne	F Pae, CP Rome, 221/216r–v
June 21, 1672	Rome	Pomponne	F Pae, CP Rome, 221/228–29
June 25, 1672	Rome	Pomponne	F Pae, CP Rome, 221/270–71
June 29, 1672	Rome	Pomponne	F Pae, CP Rome, 221/308–11
June 30, 1672	Rome	Pomponne	F Pae, CP Rome, 221/320–23
July 26, 1672	Rome	Pomponne	F Pae, CP Rome, 222/91–94v
Sep. 20, 1672	Rome	Pomponne	F Pae, CP Rome, 222/298–303

From this point, I do not record all the individual letters that I have found, but only those that have been of use to this study. All the collections are indicated, however.

Date	Place	To	Source
Jan. 13, 1673	Saint-Germain-en-Laye	Filippo Melani	I Fm, Melani 1/ff. 23–24v
Feb. 17, 1673	Saint-Germain-en-Laye	Filippo	I Fm, Melani 1/27–28v
July 21, 1673	Pistoia	Cardinal Flavio Chigi	I Rvat, Archivio Chigi, 34/ff. 29–31v
Feb. 13, 1675	Pistoia	I. Bentivoglio	I FEas, Arch. Bent., 353/269 (Mo 290)
Oct. 22, 1675	Florence	I. Bentivoglio	I FEas, Arch. Bent., 355/655 (Mo 310–11)
Oct. 25, 1675	Pistoia	I. Bentivoglio	I FEas, Arch. Bent., 357/455 (Mo 319)
Sep. 2, 1676	[Paris]	Pomponne	F Pll, MS fond fr., 13054/73–75v
Oct. 15, 1677	Paris	Flavio Chigi	I Rvat, Archivio Chigi, 34/33–34
Dec. 17, 1677	Paris	Filippo	I Fm, Melani 1/99–100v
Jan. 7, 1678	Paris	Cardinal Sigismondo Chigi	I Rvat, Archivio Chigi, 231/195r–v, 208
Jan. 21, 1678	Paris	Sigismondo Chigi	I Rvat, Archivio Chigi, 231/193r–v, 210
Nov. 18, 1678	Paris	Filippo	I Fm, Melani 1/139r–v
Jan. 27, 1679	Paris	Filippo	I Fm, Melani 1/151–52v
Feb. 3, 1679	Paris	Filippo	I Fm, Melani 1/153r–v, 155–56
May 26, 1679	Paris	Filippo	I Fm, Melani 1/165–66v, 167–68
July 20, 1679	Paris	Filippo	I Fm, Melani 1/181r–v
Aug. 4, 1679	Paris	Filippo	I Fm, Melani 1/182–83v

Date	Place	To	Source
Sep. 7, 1679	Paris	Filippo	I Fm, Melani 1/191/92v
Sep. 22, 1679	Fontainebleau	Filippo	I Fm, Melani 1/197–200
Dec. 15, 1679	Paris	Filippo	I Fm, Melani 1/212r–v
Jan. 10, 1680	Paris	Filippo	I Fm, Melani 1/215–16
Feb. 2, 1680	Paris	Filippo	I Fm, Melani 1/222–23v
Mar. 22, 1680	Paris	Filippo	I Fm, Melani 1/230–31
May 24, 1680	Fontainebleau	Filippo	I Fm, Melani 1/240–41v
June 21, 1680	Fontainebleau	Filippo	I Fm, Melani 1/242–43v
Sep. 27, 1680	Paris	Filippo	I Fm, Melani 1/255–56v
Feb. 7, 1681	Paris	Filippo	I Fm, Melani 2/8–9
Feb. 14, 1681	Paris	Filippo	I Fm, Melani 2/10–11
Feb. 21, 1681	Paris	Filippo	I Fm, Melani 2/12–14v
Aug. 1, 1681	Paris	Filippo	I Fm, Melani 2/33–35
Aug. 22, 1681	Paris	Filippo	I Fm, Melani 2/39–40
Sep. 26, 1681	Paris	Filippo	I Fm, Melani 2/41–42
Mar. 20, 1682	Paris	Filippo	I Fm, Melani 2/62r–v
June 5, 1682–June 1714	Paris	Carlo Antonio Gondi (hundreds of letters)	I Fas, MdP, 4801–4813
June 5, 1682	Paris	Filippo	I Fm, Melani 2/71–72v
June 12, 1682	Paris	C.A. Gondi	I Fas, MdP, 4801/(filza ordered by date)
Dec. 11, 1682	Paris	Filippo	I Fm, Melani 2/115–16v
May 7, 1683	Paris	Filippo	I Fm, Melani 2/135–36v
May 14, 1683	Paris	Filippo	I Fm, Melani 2/137–38, 139
May 21, 1683	Paris	Filippo	I Fm, Melani 2/140–43v
Sep. 17, 1683–Oct. 26, 1685	Paris	Duke Francesco II d'Este of Modena & Imperial Prince (many letters)	I MOas, Amb., Francia, busta 147
Feb. 21, 1684	Paris	Filippo	I Fm, Melani 2/204–5
June 30, 1685	Paris	Filippo	I Fm, Melani 2/258–59v
July 22, 1686	Paris	Filippo	I Fm, Melani 2/297–98v
1686–91	Paris	Duke Francesco II of Modena & Imp. Prince (many letters)	I MOas, Amb., Francia, busta 148
May 5, 1687	Paris	Filippo	I Fm, Melani 2/332–33, 334
Aug. 25, 1687	Paris	Filippo	I Fm, Melani 2/347–50
Dec. 6, 1690	Paris	Graziani[l]	I MOas, Canc. duc., part., busta 880, Melani
Apr. 23, 1691	Paris	Filippo	I Fm, Melani 3/19–20
Dec. 14, 1692	Paris	Duke Francesco II of Modena	I MOas, Canc. duc., part., busta 880, Melani
Dec. 24, 1692	Paris	Duke Francesco II of Modena	I MOas, Canc. duc., part., busta 880, Melani
Aug. 23, 1694	Paris	Filippo	I Fm, Melani 3/134–35
Aug. 30, 1694	Paris	Filippo	I Fm, Melani 3/136r–v
Sep. 20, 1694	Paris	Filippo	I Fm, Melani 3/140–41
Oct. 8, 1694	Paris	Duke Francesco II of Modena	I MOas, Canc. duc., part., busta 880, Melani
Dec. 27, 1694	Paris	Filippo	I Fm, Melani 3/148–49
Feb. 14, 1695	Paris	Filippo	I Fm, Melani 3/156–57v
Aug. 15, 1695	Paris	Marchese Luigi Bentivoglio	I MOe, Autografoteca Campori, A. Melani
Aug. 20, 1696	Paris	Filippo	I Fm, Melani 3/208–9v

Date	Place	To	Source
Nov. 19, 1696	Paris	L. Bentivoglio	I MOe, Auto. Campori, A. Melani
Dec. 10, 1696	Paris	L. Bentivoglio	I MOe, Auto. Campori, A. Melani
July 8, 1697	Paris	Filippo	I Fm, Melani 3/226r–v
Sep. 26, 1697	Paris	Pomponne (copy)	I Fm, Melani 9/pp. 291–94
July 14, 1698	Paris	Filippo	I Fm, Melani 3/238–39
Nov. 3, 1698	Paris	Filippo	I Fm, Melani 3/250–51
Dec. 1, 1698	Paris	Filippo	I Fm, Melani 3/252–53
1698–1703	Paris	[Jean-Baptiste Colbert, marquis de Torcy?] and Louis XIV (hundreds of letters)[h]	F Pae, CP Rome, suppl. 10
Aug. 24, 1699	Paris	Filippo	I Fm, Melani 3/260–61
Jan. 18, 1700	Paris	F. Buonvisi	Trenta, *Memorie*, II:260–63
Jan. 24, 1700	[Paris]	F. Buonvisi	Trenta, *Memorie*, II:240
Feb. 15, 1700	[Paris]	F. Buonvisi	Trenta, *Memorie*, II:265–66
Feb. 22, 1700	[Paris]	F. Buonvisi	Trenta, *Memorie*, II:266
Mar. 8, 1700	[Paris]	F. Buonvisi	Trenta, *Memorie*, II:267–68
1704–7	Paris	Louis XIV (many letters)	I PSc, Vetrina Martini 41[1] and 41[2]
1707[k]	Paris	Louis XIV	F Pae, MD France, 307/201–6v

[*] These letters are copies (not in Atto's hand) of the preceding letter on the list.

[a] This letter is clearly dated 1643, but as the month is January and as Florence retained *ab Incarnatione* dating into the seventeenth century, it should probably be attributed to 1644, as Weaver does (Weaver, "Materiali," 253n).

[b] The top of this letter bears the date 1643, written in the hand of a Florentine secretary, whereas Atto has dated it 1644 at the bottom. As the month is still March, the rationale of the previous note again applies, and so the latter date is more likely.

[c] This letter has 1648 written at top, while Atto writes 1647. Thus, it puts the *ab Incarnatione* problem backwards. But the content clearly places the letter at the *beginning* of Atto's time in Paris, so in January of 1647, not 1648. This situation suggests that the hand of the secretary cannot be trusted and may have been added later. In this case, the secretary may have been fooled by Atto's unusual way of writing the numeral 7, which can be mistaken for several other numbers.

[d] Like the previous, this letter has 1648 at top, with Atto writing 1647. Although the heavy political and military content might seem to argue a later date (it presumably being difficult to collect so much information in only a month), see the letter of March 23, 1647, which is also full.

[e] This letter bears no date or location, but based on the content, it must have come at around this time.

[f] These two letters bear no date or location, but by paper type (French), Atto's mention of his being in France, and the content (particularly the incarceration of Bartolomeo Melani), they appear to come from sometime in early 1658.

[g] F Pae, CP Toscane, 8 contains many unsigned letters from Atto between April 6, 1663 and December 19, 1664, all to De Lionne and from Florence. I have listed separately all those that informed this study; although I scanned the rest, I did not have enough time at the archive to record full information.

[h] This letter is identified in the source (in a later hand) as being from Elpidio Benedetti, but the hand of the letter is clearly Atto's.

[i] This letter is clearly not in Atto's hand but, based on the content, still seems to be from him; it is perhaps the work of a secretary.

[j] These letters are undated, but occur in the collection between letters of the dates indicated; their content does not contradict such a placement.

[k] The only date borne by this letter is the year, 1707.

[l] These letters are not addressed to anyone specifically, but the opening salutation uses the same titles ("Illustrissimo signore mio signore e padrone colendissimo") that Atto had used with Graziani before.

[m] In this series of letters, Atto writes to both Pomponne and Louvois but without always designating which he is addressing. The letters in Italian (a language Pomponne understood but apparently Louvois did not) I have tentatively assigned to Pomponne.

[n] The French minister to whom these letters are addressed is not named but may well be the marquis de Torcy, who was at this time the minister of foreign affairs.

Appendix B: Letters addressed to or concerning Atto Melani

The following list gives all of the letters written to Atto Melani or concerning him that are known to me. Unless otherwise indicated, I have listed all letters individually through 1672; from 1673, I have cited all collections but listed individually only those letters that were of use to this study. Senders' and recipients' full names are given at their first appearance and subsequently in shortened form. For the source abbreviations, see either the listing of bibliographic abbreviations at the beginning of this study (for manuscripts) or the bibliography (for published works). In the Source column, all numbers following a slash are folio numbers unless otherwise indicated. Simple numbers refer to *recto* folios; the letter *v* is added for *verso*. Sources followed by (Ma) are transcribed (on the indicated page number) in Mamone, *Serenissimi fratelli*. Sources followed by (Mo) are transcribed (on the indicated page numbers) in Monaldini, *L'orto dell'Esperidi*. Superscript letters reference notes at the end.

Date	From	To	Source
Nov. 23, 1641	Francesco Sacrati	Prince Mattias de' Medici	I Fas, MdP, filza 5421/704
Sep. 27, 1643	Francesco Guicciardini	Mattias	I Fas, MdP, 5430/426r–v
Mar. 2, 1644	Prince Mattias de' Medici	Giovanni Battista Gondi	I Fas, MdP, 5471/313
July 6, 1644	Mattias	Cardinal Giovan Carlo de' Medici	I Fas, MdP, 5296/65 (Ma 113–14)
July 25, 1644	Cardinal Giovan Carlo, Princess Anna, and Prince Leopoldo de' Medici	Mattias	I Fas, MdP, 5392/552 (Ma 114–15)
July 26, 1644	Paolo del Bufalo	Mattias	I Fas, MdP, 5427/683
Aug. 20, 1644	Mattias	Giovan Carlo	I Fas, MdP, 5301/668r–v (Ma 115)
Aug. 20, 1644	Orazio Magalotti (copy)	Bishop Ascanio Piccolomini of Siena	I Fas, MdP, 5301/669r–v (Ma 116)
Sep. 3, 1644	Mattias (*minute*)	Cardinal Jules Mazarin	I Fas, MdP, MdP 5410/112
Sep. 24, 1644	Mattias	Mazarin	I Fas, MdP, MdP 5410/121r–v
Sep. 24, 1644	Mattias	Paolo del Bufalo	I Fas, MdP, 5410/311r–v
Feb. 7/9?, 1645	Mattias (*minute*)	Atto	I Fas, MdP, 5410/389r–v
May 2, 1645	Mattias	G.B. Gondi	I Fas, MdP, 5471/344
May 10, 1645	Cardinal Jules Mazarin	Mattias	Ademollo, *I primi fasti della musica italiana*, 20–21
Sep. 29, 1646	Giovanni Bentivoglio	Cornelio Bentivoglio	I FEas, Arch. Bent., 285/651 r–v (Mo 5–6)
Jan. 4, 1647	Carlo Claudi	C. Bentivoglio	I FEas, Arch. Bent., 287/36–37 (Mo 13–14)
Jan. 11, 1647	Vettor Grimani Calergi	Mattias	I Fas, MdP, 5442/50
May 1, 1647	Mattias	Giovan Carlo	I Fas, MdP, 5346/672 (Ma 136–37)
May 24, 1647	Queen Anne of Austria	Mattias	Ademollo, "Un campanaio," 2
May 27, 1647	Mattias	Giovan Carlo	I Fas, MdP, 5369/222 (Ma 138)
July 10, 1647	Mazarin	Mattias	I Fas, MdP, 5442/927
Aug. 31, 1647	Domenico Melani	Annibale Bentivoglio	I FEas, Arch. Bent., 290/691 (Mo 21)
Nov. 6, 1647	Giovan Carlo	Mattias	I Fas, MdP, 5392/473 (Ma 138)
[1648]	Zongo Ondedei	A. Bentivoglio	I FEas, Arch. Bent., fasc. 1651/73r–v (Mo 41)
Mar. 20, 1648	Lorenzo Guicciardini	Mattias	I Fas, MdP, 5444/222–23
May 8, 1648	C. Claudi	A. Bentivoglio	I FEas, Arch. Bent., 293/291r–v (Mo 28)
Sep. 21, 1649	Mazarin	Mattias	I Fas, MdP, 5408/246
Mar. 20, 1650	C. Bentivoglio	A. Bentivoglio	I FEas, Arch. Bent., 301/560 (Mo 35)
Apr. 25, 1650	Mattias and Leopoldo de' Medici	Grand Duke Ferdinando II de' Medici	I Fas, MdP, 5508/no. 64
July 6, 1650	Lionardo Signorini	Mattias	I Fas, MdP, 5446/351r–v
Oct. 7, 1651	Desiderio Montemagni	Atto	I Fas, MdP, 5449/692
Oct. 23, 1651	Bernardo Castiglioni	Mattias	I Fas, MdP, 5449/616r–v
June 19, 1652	Geronimo Buonvisi	A. Bentivoglio	I FEas, Arch. Bent., 310/591v (Mo 56)
Oct. 5, 1652	Lazzaro Paribeni	C. Bentivoglio	I FEas, Arch. Bent., 312/611v (Mo 60)
Oct? 25, 1652[a]	[Prince Leopoldo de' Medici]	Mattias	I Fas, MdP, 5451/454
Nov. 28, 1652	Paolo Emilio Fantuzzi	Mattias	I Fas, MdP, 5451/608
Dec. 17, 1652	Fantuzzi	Mattias	I Fas, MdP, 5451/770
Apr. 25, 1653	Mazarin	Atto	F Pm, MS 2218/80

Date	From	To	Source
May 9, 1653	Domenico Anglesi	Prince Leopoldo de' Medici	I Fas, MdP, 5561/689
May 31, 1653	Anna de' Medici, archduchess of Innsbruck	Mattias	I Fas, MdP, 5454/554
May 31, 1653	Archduke Ferdinand Karl of Innsbruck	Mattias	I Fas, MdP, 5454/707
June 6, 1653	Archduchess Anna	Mattias	I Fas, MdP, 5454/801r–v
Dec. 2, 1653	Desiderio Montemagni	Atto	I Fas, MdP, 1507/insert 4 (Ma 481)
Apr. 3, 1654	Mazarin	Cardinal Antonio Barberini	F Pae, MD France, 270/113v–14v
May 25, 1654	Cardinal Antonio Barberini	Mazarin	F Pae, CP Rome, 125/185
June 1, 1655	Giovan Carlo	Mattias	I Fas, MdP, 5392/951 (Ma 247–48)
Aug. 30, 1655	Cardinal Stefano Durazzo	Giovan Carlo	I Fas, MdP, 5284/983 (Ma 251)
[summer 1655][b]	Giovan Carlo	Mattias	I Fas, MdP, 5392/842 (Ma 412–13)
Sep. 17, 1655	G. Bentivoglio	A. Bentivoglio	I FEas, Arch. Bent., 319/242 (Mo 100)
Oct. 20, 1655	Mattias	Giovan Carlo	I Fas, MdP, 5375/644 (Ma 254)
Oct. 30, 1655	Giovan Carlo	Mattias	I Fas, MdP, 5494/440r–v
Nov. 3, 1655	Mattias	Giovan Carlo	I Fas, MdP, 5375/699 (Ma 256)
Nov. 6, 1655	Giovan Carlo	Mattias	I Fas, MdP, 5392/892 (Ma 257)
Dec. 15, 1655	Giulio Cittadini	Mattias	I Fas, MdP, 5459/711
Apr. 10, 1656	Mattias (*minute*)	Atto	I Fas, MdP, 5416/689r–v
Jan. 4, 1657	Mazarin	Mattias	I Fas, MdP, 5463/855; copy at F Pae, MD France, 273/282r–v
Mar. 7, 1657	Count Raimondo Montecuccoli	Atto	*Ausgewaehlten Schriften*, IV:369–70
before July 30, 1657	Giovanni Battista Gondi (copy)	Atto	I Fas, MdP, 5460/277
Sep. 2, 1657	Mazarin	Maréchal Antoine III, duke de Gramont	D'Avenel, *Lettres de Mazarin*, VIII:141
Sep. 25, 1657	Mazarin	Atto	F Pae, MD France, 273/439v–40
Oct. 20, 1657	Mazarin	Hugues de Lionne and Gramont	F Pae, MD France, 272/286–89v
Dec. 21, 1657	Mazarin	Atto	F Pae, MD France, 273/485v–86
Dec. 26, 1657	Mattias (*minute*)	Louis XIV	I Fas, MdP, 5416/696
Jan. 17, 1658	Mazarin	De Lionne	D'Avenel, *Lettres de Mazarin*, VIII:268
Feb. 6, 1658	Mazarin	Gramont	D'Avenel, *Lettres de Mazarin*, VIII:296
Mar. 30, 1658	Paolo del Sera	Giovan Carlo	I Fas, MdP, 5330/246r–v (Ma 282)
Sep. 7, 1659	Lionardo Signorini	Mattias	I Fas, MdP, 5419/1027–28
Oct. 13, 1659	Pietro Bonsi	Mattias	I Fas, MdP, 4661 (filza ordered by date)
Oct. 25, 1659	Cardinal Giulio Rospigliosi	Mattias	I Fas, MdP, 5408/535
Oct. 22, 1660	Antonio Rivani	Giovan Carlo	I Fas, MdP, 5336/225 (Ma 346–47)
July 30, 1661	Cardinal Flavio Chigi	Mattias	I Fas, MdP, 5475/539
Aug. 1, 1661	Giulio Rospigliosi	De Lionne	F Pae, CP Rome, 141/270
Sep. 7, 1661	G. Bentivoglio	Giovan Carlo	I Fas, MdP, 5339/210 (Ma 379–80)
Nov. 8, 1661	Elpidio Benedetti	De Lionne	F Pae, CP Rome, 142/250–51

Date	From	To	Source
Jan. 27, 1662	G. Bentivoglio	A. Bentivoglio	I FEas, Arch. Bent., 335/86 (Mo 167)
Mar. 16, 1662	Antonio Rivani	Giovan Carlo	I Fas, MdP, 5340/553–55v (Ma 399–400)
June 10, 1662	Giulio Rospigliosi	De Lionne	F Pae, CP Rome, 145 (Gérin, *Louis XIV*, II:184n)
Oct. 8, 1662	G. Bentivoglio	A. Bentivoglio	I FEas, Arch. Bent., 336/440 (Mo 176)
Jan. 25, 1664	G. Bentivoglio	Atto	I FEas, Arch. Bent., 338/66 (Mo 185)
Apr. 5, 1664	Filippo Melani	Ippolito Bentivoglio	I FEas, Arch. Bent., 338/267 (Mo 189)
June 10, 1664	Filippo	I. Bentivoglio	I FEas, Arch. Bent., 338/480r–v (Mo 193)
Aug. 23, 1664	Filippo	I. Bentivoglio	I FEas, Arch. Bent., 339/192r–v (Mo 203)
Sep. 20, 1664	Filippo	I. Bentivoglio	I FEas, Arch. Bent., 339/383r–v (Mo 208)
Nov. 8, 1664	Filippo	I. Bentivoglio	I FEas, Arch. Bent., 339/737 (Mo 214)
May 24, 1667	Mattias	Prince Don Mario Chigi	I Rvat, Archivio Chigi 3906
[June 1667]	Camillo Rospigliosi	Atto	F Pae, CP Rome, 184/67–68
Jan. 24, 1668	Honoré d'Albert, duke de Chaulnes	De Lionne	F Pae, CP Rome, 189/122–25
Mar. 20, 1668	Augustin Servient	De Lionne	F Pae, CP Rome, 190/142–44v
May 3, 1668	Duke de Chaulnes	De Lionne	F Pae, CP Rome, 191/54–63
May 29, 1668	Cardinal Jacopo Rospigliosi	De Lionne	F Pae, CP Rome, 191/206
Sep. 14, 1668	Hugues de Lionne	Atto	F Pae, CP Rome, 193/85
Jan. 11, 1669	De Lionne	Atto	F Pae, CP Rome, 196/101
Mar. 8, 1669	De Lionne	Atto	F Pae, CP Rome, 197/44–45
Mar. 9, 1669	Giovanni Federighi	Leopoldo de' Medici	I Fas, MdP, 5537/no. 221
Aug. 30, 1669	De Lionne (*minute*)	Atto	F Pae, CP Rome, 199/439–40v
Dec. 17, 1669	Cardinal Rospigliosi	De Lionne	F Pae, CP Rome, 201/351r–v
Feb. 4, 1670	Duke de Chaulnes	De Lionne	F Pae, CP Rome, 208/175–76v
Feb. 11, 1670	Duke de Chaulnes	De Lionne	F Pae, CP Rome, 208/216–17
Feb. 18, 1670	Duke de Chaulnes	De Lionne	F Pae, CP Rome, 208/247–49
Feb. 25–28?, 1670	De Lionne	Duke de Chaulnes	F Pae, CP Rome, 208/305r–v
Mar. 21, 1670	De Lionne	Duke de Chaulnes	F Pae, CP Rome, 209/40–41
July 14, 1670	Cardinal Pauluzzo Pauluzzi Altieri	De Lionne	F Pae, CP Rome, 210/78
Oct. 7, 1670	Cardinal [Flavio or Sigismondo] Chigi	De Lionne	F Pae, CP Rome, 211/181r–v
1670–1702[c]	César d'Éstrées, bishop of Laon (later cardinal)	Atto	I Fm, Melani 5
May 23, 1671	Grand Duke Cosimo III de' Medici	De Lionne	F Pae, CP Toscane, 10/314
Oct. 30, 1671	François-Michel Le Tellier, marquis de Louvois	Atto	F Pae, CP Rome, 216/84
Jan. 1, 1672	Louvois	Atto	F Pae, CP Rome, 218/13
Jan. 26, 1672	Simon Arnauld, marquis de Pomponne	Atto	F Pae, CP Rome, 218/185
Jan. 26, 1672	Pomponne (copy of previous)	Atto	I Fm, Melani 9/pp. 329–30[d]
Feb. 22, 1672	Pomponne	Atto	F Pae, CP Rome, 218/331

Date	From	To	Source
Mar. 8, 1672	César d'Éstrées, bishop of Laon	Simon Arnauld, marquis de Pomponne?	F Pae, CP Rome, supplément 7/170–71
Mar. 25, 1672	Pomponne (*minute*)	César d'Éstrées, bishop of Laon	F Pae, CP Rome, suppl. 7/333–34
May 10, 1672	Bishop of Laon	Pomponne	F Pae, CP Rome, 220/267–73
May 31, 1672	Duke François Hannibal II d'Éstrées	Pomponne	F Pae, CP Rome, 221/110–14v
June 30, 1672	Cardinal César d'Éstrées	Pomponne	F Pae, CP Rome, 221/312–15
July 6, 1672	Cardinal d'Éstrées	Pomponne	F Pae, CP Rome, 222/27–28v
July 23, 1672	Pomponne (*minute*)	Atto	F Pae, CP Rome, 222/68
Aug. 23, 1672	Duke d'Éstrées	Pomponne	F Pae, CP Rome, 222/214r–v
Sep. 2, 1672	Cardinal d'Éstrées	Pomponne	F Pae, CP Rome, 222/242–43
Sep. 16, 1672	Pomponne	Duke François Hannibal II d'Éstrées	F Pae, CP Rome, 222/284–85
Oct. 1, 1672	Cardinal Rospigliosi	Pomponne	F Pae, CP Rome, 223/10
Oct. 12, 1672	Cardinal d'Éstrées	Pomponne	F Pae, CP Rome, 223/57–61v
Feb. 17, 1673	Pomponne	Cardinal César d'Éstrées	F Pae, CP Rome, 225/148r–v
Mar. 14, 1673	Cardinal d'Éstrées	Pomponne	F Pae, CP Rome, 225/228–29
Apr. 7, 1673	Pomponne (*minute*)	Cardinal d'Éstrées	F Pae, CP Rome, 225/279
Oct. 23, 1673	Filippo Melani	I. Bentivoglio	I FEas, Arch. Bent., 350/365 (Mo 280)
Nov. 8, 1673	Cardinal d'Éstrées	Pomponne	F Pae, CP Rome, 228/138–44
Dec. 1, 1673	Pomponne	Cardinal d'Éstrées	F Pae, CP Rome, 228/248r–v
Dec. 14, 1673	Augustin Servient (copy)	Atto	F Pae, CP Rome, 228/286–87
Oct. 4, 1674	Cardinal d'Éstrées	Atto	I Fm, Melani 5/12
Oct. 26, 1675	Filippo	I. Bentivoglio	I FEas, Arch. Bent., 355/695r–v (Mo 311–12)
Nov. 5, 1675	Filippo	I. Bentivoglio	I FEas, Arch. Bent., 356/28 (Mo 312)
Feb. 3, 1676	Cardinal Girolamo Buonvisi	Jacinto Melani	I PSc, Raccolta Chiappelli, 14
Feb. 11, 1676	Filippo	I. Bentivoglio	I FEas, Arch. Bent., 357/312r–v (Mo 318)
Feb. 24, 1676	Cardinal d'Éstrées	Atto	I Fm, Melani 5/60–61
Apr. 14, 1676	Filippo	I. Bentivoglio	I FEas, Arch. Bent., 357/501 (Mo 319)
Sep. 12, 1676	Filippo	I. Bentivoglio	I FEas, Arch. Bent., 358/441 (Mo 324)
Nov. 14, 1676	Filippo	I. Bentivoglio	I FEas, Arch. Bent., 358/571 (Mo 325)
Dec. 12, 1676	Filippo	I. Bentivoglio	I FEas, Arch. Bent., 358/616v (Mo 325)
Nov. 6, 1677	Filippo	I. Bentivoglio	I FEas, Arch. Bent., 360/490v (Mo 334)
Mar. 26, 1678	Filippo	I. Bentivoglio	I FEas, Arch. Bent., 361/448 (Mo 343)
June 11, 1678	Filippo	I. Bentivoglio	I FEas, Arch. Bent., 362/57 (Mo 347)
Sep. 13, 1678	Filippo	I. Bentivoglio	I FEas, Arch. Bent., 362/491 (Mo 348)
June 10, 1679	Filippo	I. Bentivoglio	I FEas, Arch. Bent., 364/135r–v (Mo 392)
Apr. 6, 1680	Filippo	I. Bentivoglio	I FEas, Arch. Bent., 367/311r–v (Mo 424–2!
June 1, 1680	Filippo	I. Bentivoglio	I FEas, Arch. Bent., 367/559r–v (Mo 431)
June 8, 1680	Filippo	I. Bentivoglio	I FEas, Arch. Bent., 367/577 (Mo 432)
Oct. 3, 1682	Filippo	I. Bentivoglio	I FEas, Arch. Bent., 373/229 (Mo 533)
1687–1702	Toussaint de Forbin Janson, bishop of Beauvais (later cardinal; many letters)	Atto	I Fm, Melani 6–8

Date	From	To	Source
Dec. 29, 1688	Filippo	Duke Francesco II d'Este of Modena	I MOas, Cancelleria ducale, particolari, busta 880, Melani
Jan. 25, 1689	Filippo	(unknown, Modena)	I MOas, Canc. duc., part., busta 880, Melani
Feb. 27, 1689	Filippo	(unknown, Modena)	I MOas, Canc. duc., part., busta 880, Melani
Oct. 4, 1691	Beanco Ciardi	Giovanni Domenico Ottonelli (Modena)	I MOas, Canc. duc., part., busta 880, Melani
Dec. 4, 1691	Filippo	Duke Francesco II of Modena	I MOas, Canc. duc., part., busta 880, Melani
Mar. 9, 1699	Niccolò Erizzo (copy)	Gianiacopo Cavallerini	I Fm, Melani 9/pp. 256–58
1699–1702	Cardinals Pietro Ottoboni and Fabrizio Paolucci (many letters)	Atto	GB Lbl, Addl. 62401
Jan. 1, 1714	Domenico Melani	Carlo Antonio Gondi	I Fas, MdP, 4813 (filza ordered by date)
Jan. 8, 1714	Domenico	C. A. Gondi	I Fas, MdP, 4813
Jan. 15, 1714	Domenico	C. A. Gondi	I Fas, MdP, 4813
Jan. 22, 1714	Domenico	C. A. Gondi	I Fas, MdP, 4813
Jan. 29, 1714	Domenico	C. A. Gondi	I Fas, MdP, 4813
Feb. 12, 1714	Domenico	C. A. Gondi	I Fas, MdP, 4813
Feb. 26, 1714	Domenico	C. A. Gondi	I Fas, MdP, 4813
Apr. 2, 1714	Domenico	C. A. Gondi	I Fas, MdP, 4813
May 7, 1714	Domenico	C. A. Gondi	I Fas, MdP, 4813
	Giovan Carlo	Mattias	I Fas, MdP, 5288/842

The date of this letter is very difficult to read: it could also be August.

This letter carries no indication of place or date, but based on the content, it must come from the summer of 1655, from Rome.

I Fm, Melani 5 collects a great number of letters from César d'Éstrées (first, bishop of Laon, then cardinal) to Atto, from 1670 to 1702. A few that were more important for the study are listed individually.

I Fm, Melani 9 is a *copialettere*, containing copies of many letters and documents from the 1670s to *c.* 1700.

Appendix C: Satires

"Sopra Atto Melani Musico"

This poem appears in I Fn, Cl.VII.359, pp. 758–68, a manuscript collection of many different types of contemporary poetry. No author is indicated, nor can one be deduced from the source; the content of the poem, however, would indicate someone well acquainted with Atto.

Sopra Atto Melani Musico
Castrato di Pistoia figliolo d'un Campanaio

Deh pensate al Campanile
quando il Crin v'inpolverate
et allor che vi lisciate
per parer bello, e gentile:
ogni volta che udirete 5
di Campana il suono atroce
dite pur che quella voce
vi richiama al primo stile
  Deh pensate –

So che fate mille mode 10
nelle forme più eccellenti,
e pur dicono le genti,
che attendete a cose sode:
et ogn'un che vi rimira
per le strade andar tirato 15
sa ch'in camera serrato
v'inchinate, e sete humile
  Deh pensate –

Ben si vede ne v'adulo
che seguendo il franco stile 20
la campana e il campanile
e il batocchio havete in culo:
et ad' onta della corda
di cordelle un Milione
vi mettete a strapazzone 25
all'usanza signorile
  Deh pensate –

È bizarro il vostro stato
poi che sete da dovero [*sic*]
in parole cavaliero   30
ed' in fatti cavalcato:
Ma non è però lodato
ch'ogni moda voglia fare
e ogni Principe immitare
un ch'è nato così vile   35
     Deh pensate –

E perché vostro fratello
non amate con affetto?
voi che ogn'or date ricetto
al fratel di questo, e quello?   40
Voi n'andate o poverello
dietro a chi vi vuol d'avante
e sperate in un istante
grossi doni da un sottile   45
     Deh pensate –

Per la vostra voce bella
per il gallico cantare
che fa ogn'un maravigliare
tutti vi offron la Cappella,
ma non è che il vostro muso   50
ricoperto di belletti
ricoprir possa i difetti
e vi renda più gentile
     Deh pensate –

Chi vi sente (senza fallo)   55
si dovrà maravigliare
e dirà come può stare
che un Cappon canti da Gallo?
e di più di rosso, e giallo
v'abbigliate ogn'or la veste   60
e farete ancor le creste
per parer a lui simile
     Deh pensate –

Si può dir che voi cantate
veramente da sirena   65
che cantando si dimena
e le cosce tien slargate.
e perciò molti allettate
a venirvi ad'ascoltare

ne paventano affogare 70
in quel mar fetido e vile
Deh pensate –

È comune oppinione
che quel vostro andar sì male
non proceda da stivale 75
ma più tosto dal Cannone
e per questo vi consiglio
che in riposo lo lasciate
che s'ogn'or l'adoperate
diverrà frusto, e sottile 80
Deh pensate –

Resto ben trasecolato
e stupisce ogni francese
in vedere un Pistolese
tutto in fodero cangiato 85
tanto più resto ammirato
che chi nacque feritore
è ferito a tutte l'ore
ed a ferro non ostile 90
Deh pensate –

Nelle giostre di duello
dove ogn'uno espon la pancia
tutti giostran con la lancia
e voi sempre con l'anello
questo gioco è strano e bello 95
perché solo allor vincete
che da gl'altri vinto sete
ma non è troppo civile
Deh pensate –

Non convien ch'un Marescialle 100
sia poltrone; e pur volete
farvi tal voi che solete
sempre mai voltar le spalle
Se seguite il torto calle
mentre dietro per quant'odo 105
voi l'avete dritto e sodo
vi dirò codardo, e vile
Deh pensate –

Ma però se dritto io guardo
farò dire a ogn'un che m'ode 110

che piacendovi le code
a ragion sete codardo
Per che in dar non sete tardo
dice ogn'un che largo sete
e che sempre vi dolete   115
dello stato poverile
       Deh pensate –

È di già publica fama
che il giocar non vi dispiaccia
e de giochi sol vi piaccia   120
calabrache con la dama.
Meritate per tal brama
già che a Dama non vincete
e a calar primiero sete
nelle chiappe lo staffile   125
       Deh pensate –

Se in giocar non fate motto
per mostrar che flemma havete
fate pur quanto volete
che si sa che sete rotto: 130
e vi son da sette, o otto
che v'han visto di sicuro
con il capo urtar nel muro
spinto forte dalla bile   135
       Deh pensate –

Per che i membri v'abbellite
con le gioie che comprate
voi ch'ogn'or di gioie aurate
gl'altrui membri ne fornite?
Questa gioia poi ne dite   140
mi donò il femmineo sesso
e donate a un tempo stesso
voi medesimo il virile
       Deh pensate –

Con i drappi, e con le sete   145
so che fama v'acquistate
pur che un giorno non moriate
della fame, e della sete
forse forse mi direte
che la spera misurate   150
con le vostre larghe extrate

ma non sempre dura Aprile
    Deh pensate –

Questa è grande che di botto
l'altrui voglie dominate   155
e a Cavallo vi trovate
allor che sete di sotto.
ma se dura questo trotto
io riveggio senza fallo
pria che troppo canti il Gallo   160
essa farvi del focile
    Deh pensate –

Se cantate una Canzona
ad'alcun che voi preghate
che regalo n'aspettate   165
se l'istesso ve la suona?
e per che ciascun vi dona
della vita il primo sangue
e non l'oro che al fin langue
il Regalo non è vile   170
    Deh pensate –

E per dirla fra di noi
voi cantando a queste genti
non sentite con che accenti
esse cantano di voi.   175
S'odon qui le vostre voci
ma se canta forte il Gallo
le sue voci senza fallo
s'udiran da Battro a Tile   180
    Deh pensate –

Morì il Trace Lapidato
da i seguaci di Lieo
voi però Novello Orfeo
morirete sbudellato
lo strumento, se locato   185
fu di lui tra sfere belle
così il vostro ma tra quelle
dove il foco have il sedile
    Deh pensate –

Già che vivo a tutta possa   190
v'abbellite e impolverate
e gran pettini adoprate

vi si scriva nella fossa
Qui son Nervi, polve, ed'ossa
d'un che pria che polve fusse   195
ossa e Nervi è polve strusse
sempre in atto feminile
        Deh pensate –

"Al Signor Atto Melani"

This poem appears in I Rvat, Barb. lat. 3902, f. 281r–v. It may or may not be
by Sebastiano Baldini.

1.
All'hor ch'Atto sta cantando,
Nell'orecchie a gl'Uditori
Mille Gratie, mille Amori
Par che danzin festeggiando,
et i cori   5
fra quei piani, e fra quei forti,
Hora han vite, et hora han morti.

2.
Quelle tremole gorghette,
Che per l'aria impennan l'ali
Nell'orecchie de mortali   10
Son d'amor tante saette.
Trionfali
Egli ha palme a tutte l'hore,
A ogni trillo acquista un core.

3.
Ah' che angelico è quel lusso,   15
C'ho in udir sì nobil canti.
Son quei labbri ciel notanti,
Donde piove un dolce influsso.
Tremolanti
N'escon voci armoniose,   20
Che son stelle in Ciel di rose[.]

Appendix D: Excerpt from the *Recueil des défenses* of Nicolas Fouquet

The following excerpt comes from Nicolas Fouquet, *Suite de la continuation de la production de Mr Fouquet, pour servir de réponse a celle de Mr Talon sur le pretendu crime d'estat*, vol. VIII of *Recueil des defenses de Mr Fouquet* ([Paris?]: n.p., 1666), 167–69.

Atto estoit un Italien de la Musique du Roy, fort bien-voulu de Sa Majesté, & fort affectionné à son service; fort employé du vivant de M. le Cardinal, & tres-familier dans la Maison de Son Eminence. Cet Homme avoit rendu de grands services en Allemagne, pendant la Negociation de Francfort: Il avoit entretenu des liaisons étroites avec M. de Lionne, & donné des avis tres-importans; ensorte qu'on ne pouvoit douter de son industrie, ny de son affection, & de son zele pour la France; & en particulier pour la Famille de Monsieur le Cardinal, logeant actuellement dans le Palais Mazarin.

Aussi-tost que les Ceremonies du Service de M. le Cardinal furent achevées, le trouble se mit dans son Domestique; Madame Colonne fut mariée, & partit mal-contente de son partage; les Heritiers se diviserent; les Domestiques suivirent leurs inclinations, & se separerent chacun de son costé; ceux qui logeoient dans la maison furent congediez …

Mais de toutes les divisions, il n'y en eut point qui fist plus d'éclat, que celle qui parut entre M. le Duc Mazarin & Madame sa femme; on ne doit pas en dire icy le détail; mais le mary dans ses emportemens fit un capital pour son honneur & sa fortune, d'empescher que ceux qui ne luy estoient pas agreables, n'eussent aucun commerce avec Madame sa femme, & dcmanda au Roy qu'Atto sortist non seulement du Palais Mazarin, mais de tout le Royaume, & s'en allast en Italie. Il souhaita cette grace avec tant d'empressement, que le Roy voulut sçavoir la cause de cette haine, & le dissuader de cette entreprise; mais enfin M. Mazarin persistant, le Roy ne voulut pas luy refuser ce qu'il desiroit si ardemment; & fit entendre à Atto qu'il se disposast à sortir, & luy fit esperer que Sa Majesté luy permettroit de revenir quand l'orage seroit calmé.

Cependant Atto avoit recours à M. de Lionne, duquel il demandoit la protection: M. de Lionne estoit témoin des services qu'Atto avoit rendus, &

luy avoit donné tant de bonnes paroles autrefois de la part de M. le Cardinal, qu'Atto vouloit encore l'en rendre garant.

M. le Duc Mazarin en fut averty, & parla tout haut contre M. de Lionne; il dit qu'il feroit roüer de coups de baston Atto, par tout où il le pourroit faire rencontrer; encore qu'Atto se trouva obligé de partir: Mais ne le pouvant faire qu'après quelques jours, dont il avoit besoin pour mettre ordre à ses petites affaires; acheter les choses qui luy estoient necessaires; vendre celles qu'il ne pouvoit emporter; & desirant se mettre à couvert pendant ce temps-là des menaces qu'on faisoit contre luy; dans la peine du choix d'une retraite, il s'adressa à M. de Lionne, lequel l'amena chez moy; me fit entendre son desordre, & me pria de voir ce que je pourrois faire pour luy, me disant qu'il ne vouloit pas le retirer, pource que M. Mazarin ne manqueroit pas de faire observer sa maison, comme suspecte; mais qu'Atto n'estant point connu pour avoir aucune habitude avec moy, il pouvoit passer chez moy les deux ou trois jours qu'il demandoit, sans qu'on s'en pût appercevoir.

M. de Lionne m'exagera ensuite les services qu'Atto avoit rendus; ceux qu'il estoit capable de rendre; les habitudes qu'il avoit; & que c'estoit un homme qu'il faloit conserver pour le service du Roy. Je m'offris de luy donner retraite, pendant la quelle M. de Lionne me dit de prendre un chiffre, & des adresses avec luy pour les nouvelles qu'il voudroit mander, & pour les choses où on voudroit le faire agir.

… M. le Duc Mazarin ne gardoit plus de mesures avec moy; desorte que je ne fis point de difficulté de donner le couvert à un homme de service, qui m'estoit recommandé; qui ne demandoit que d'estre en seureté pendant deux jours, pour éviter une violence; & à dire le vray, je crûs que je rendois service au Roy, & encore un plus grand à Monsieur Mazarin, de luy oster l'occasion de maltraitter un étranger, qui se retiroit avec des témoignages d'affection du Roy.

Le Roy me commanda de faire payer quinze cens livres à Atto; je crois qu'il en receut une partie de cinq cens livres avant son depart, & qu'il pria qu'on luy fist donner les mille livres restans à Rome, quand il y seroit arrivé, pour sauver quelque change, & la risque d'estre volé sur les chemins …

Il partit incontinent après; & depuis ce temps il écrivit au Roy personnellement, & a rendu compte à Sa Majesté de son voyage; le Roy nous en leut les lettres dans le Conseil; il les adressoit à M. de Lionne, & m'a fait quelquefois l'adresse du pacquet de M. de Lionne; Il m'a fait sçavoir diverses choses; il en a mandé d'autres à M. de Lionne avec le même chiffre qu'il m'avoit laissé; & a témoigné grand passion de se rendre utile, & faire quelque chose qui luy pust faire obtenir son retour.

Appendix E: Biographical sketch from Tommaso Trenta's *Memorie*

From Tommaso Trenta, *Memorie per servire alla storia politica del Cardinale Francesco Buonvisi patrizio lucchese* (Lucca: Francesco Bertini, 1818), I:259–65.

La stretta confidenziale amicizia del Melani coi due Buonvisi, e l'aver esso procurato in tutte le occasioni di promuoverne l'inalzamento e i vantaggi, mi assicurano che non sarà riputato esser fuor di proposito il raccogliere qui in pochi tratti le cose più essenziali da lui operate, che si leggono nella vita manuscritta, formatane da un suo nipote, la qual si conserva presso i suoi Eredi.

Nacque l'Abate Atto Melani di onesta e civil famiglia in Pistoja nel mese di Maggio del 1626. Compiuto all'età di 18. anni il corse degli studj, si portò a Parigi ed ebbe la sorte di essere ammesso al servizio del rinomato Cardinal Giulio Mazzarino, che regolava la Monarchia in qualità di primo Ministro. Incontrò il genio di quel grand'Uomo, e sotto la sua direzione apprese la difficile scienze della Politica, e potè esser messo egregiamente al fatto delle cose del Mondo. Passò quindi in Germania, e trovossi [*sic*] a Ratisbona in occasione della Dieta, di dove poi sen venne a Roma. Insinuossi colà nella più intima confidenze del Cardinal Giulio Rospigliosi; e vi conobbe il Sig. di Lionné Ambasciadore Straordinario del Re Cristianissimo ai Principi d'Italia, il quale divenne in appresso uno de' suoi più benevoli e possenti Protettori. Dopo nove mesi di dimora in Roma si trasferì a Firenze, e tanto si adoperò presso il Ministero toscano, che ottennero termine felice i suoi negoziati per concertare i trattamenti da farsi in quella Corte al Sig. di Lionné. Dopo di che fu dal Cardinale Mazzarino richiamato a Parigi, dove ricevette da esso, e dal Re molte onorevoli distinzioni.

Riconosciutolo atto a trattare affari della maggiore importanza e segretezza, fu poi spedito in Baviera per indurre quell'Elettore ad accettare la Corona Imperiale in occasione della Dieta che si teneva in Francfort. Inutili, è vero, riuscirono i maneggi del Melani per la singolar previdenza del Conte Curzio di Fallaya primo Ministro dell'Elettore, e propensissimo verso la Casa Imperiale. Ma non per questo decadde dalla grazia del Re, che anzi restituitosi a Parigi lo dichiarò suo Gentiluomo di Camera con annua pensione di tremila franchi.

Succeduta la celebre rottura fra la Corte di Francia, e quella di Roma per l'insulto che si pretese fatto sotto il Pontifcato di Allessandro VII. all'Ambasciadore Duca di Crequy dai Soldati Corsi, non picciola parte ebbe il Melani nel lungo trattato delle soddisfazioni da darsi al Re, per aver continuata sempre viva la corrispondenza col Sig. di Lionné, il quale a preferenza degli altre Ministri di sua Nazione si valse in questo affare dell'opera sua.

Morto il Cardinale Mazzarino rimase il Melani presso Luigi XIV, e incominciò allora le pratiche per elevare al Pontificato il Cardinal Rospigliosi con metterlo in buona vista al Re e al Sig. di Lionné divenuto primo ministro. Procedette con tanta prosperità nel suo negoziato, che fu da quel Sovrano fatto passare a Roma col pretesto di accompagnare in Toscana la Principessa Margarita Luisa d'Orleans, destinata in consorte al Principe Cosimo de' Medici; ma realmente affinchè potesse dar quelli espedienti che meglio giudicasse per l'esecuzione del suo disegno. Guinto a Roma nel mese d'Ottobre de 1661, tenne subito proposito col Cardinale Rospigliosi delle vedute che aveva la Corte di Francia sopra di lui; ma fermo il Cardinale in non voler dare orecchio a proposizione di sorta alcuna men che onesta, si contenne in guisa che non lasciò traspirare alcuna condescendenza per parte sua.

Il potere, che avea sull'animo del Monarca francese il suo primo Ministro Lionné giovò non poco al Melani per arrivare felicemente al suo scopo di collocare sulla Cattedra Pontificia il Cardinale Rospigliosi, che prese il nome di Clemente IX. Mostrò egli tanta avvedutezza, circospezione, e attività in questa circostanza, che allorquando ritornar dovette in Francia il Duca di Chaunes spedito a Roma col carattere di Ambasciadore straordinario a quel Conclave, si diresse al Melani il Sig. di Lionné in tutti gli affari che trattar dovette in quel Pontificato con la Corte di Roma. Fra gli altri vi fu quello di dover far parti efficaci per portare al Cardinalato il Vescovo di Baziers, il Duca d'Albret, e il Vescovo Duca di Laon.

Venne frattanto a perdere inaspettatamente la grazia del Re il sopraintendente delle Finanze Fouquet, che tirò seco la disgrazia ancor del Melani per esser egli in carteggio con quel Ministro; sebbene le sue lettere non contenessero che semplici espressioni di deferenza a di ossequio. Prese allora il partito di ritirarsi a Firenze presso il suo Principe naturale.

Adunatisi i Cardinali in Conclave dopo la morte di Clemente IX. ebbe l'onore il Melani di servire in qualità di Conclavista il Cardinale di Buglione grande Elemosiniero di Francia, e uno de' tre promossi alla dignità Cardinalizia per opera sua. Rimase cotanto soddisfatto il Re del Melani in quella gelosa congiuntura, che insinuogli il Sig. di Lionné di fare un viaggio a Parigi, e lo assicurò che vi sarebbe stato graziosamente udienza col Re, che gli dette in dono il suo Ritratto contornato di diamanti del valore di Scudi duemila, gli fece pagare cinquecento doppie per le spese di viaggio, e gli conferì la Regia Abbazia di Beaubé in Normandia d'annua rendita di Franchi 18 mila.

La ragion primaria che mosse però il Ministro francese a desiderare un abboccamento col Melani, fu quella di poter restare pienamente informato di tutte le particolarità di quel Conclave, ed in ispecie rispetto all'esclusiva data al Cardinal Girolamo Buonvisi, che sapeva esser suo grande amico, e ch'egli pure stimavalo uno de' più degni soggetti del Sacro Collegio. Com'ebbe il Sig. di Lionné intese dal Melani le cose accadute, prese più vivo interessamento all'esaltazione del Buonvisi, poichè trovandosi già molto avanzato in età Clemente X. era cosa naturale il credere che si dovesse presto dar luogo ad un nuova elezione. Per accertarsi in questo mezzo dell'animo di Francesco nipote del Cardinal Girolamo, commise il Ministro francese al Melani di scrivergli per indagarne le disposizioni, e fu tal la risposta di Francesco, che basta per sè sola a far conoscere quali fossero le religiose massime, e gli onorati sentimenti di questo Prelato.

Con la morte del Sig. di Lionné accaduta nel 1671. venne a mancare al Melani il suo più valido Protettore. Succedutogli nel Ministero il Marchese Arnaldo di Pomponne Ambasciadore alla Corte di Svezia, fece il Re scrivere dal Sig. di Louvois al Melani, il quale già si era restituito a Roma, che continuasse pure a tener carteggio col novello Ministro come avea costumato di fare col defunto. Ma egli dopo aver cooperato all'elezione del Cardinale d'Estrêes stimò bene di ritornare in Francia per insinuarsi più da vicino nella buona grazia del Sig. di Pomponne.

Decaduto questo Ministro, e per dieci anni esiliato dalla Corte con sottentrar nel suo posto il Marchese di Croissy, il solo Melani nol volle abbandonare, sequitando a coltivarne l'amicizia e a servirlo con risico proprio. Tanto colpì l'animo riconoscente del Sig. di Pomponne il generoso affetto del Melani, che scopertosi finalmente il vero, e ritornato nell'auge di sua fortuna lo riguardò sempre con parzialità di benevolenza, e di amicizia.

Si trattenne il Melani quasi tre anni a Parigi, e avendovi in questo mentre aggiustati i proprii interessi, si restituì a Pistoja nel 1675. Conduceva colà tranquillamente i suoi giorni, quando ai reiterati impulsi del Sig. di Gommont Inviato Straordinario presso il Gran Duca dovette prender la risoluzione di ritornare seco in Francia il 1679. D'allora in poi vi rimase finchè visse, e venne adoperato frequentemente dal Re e dal Ministero in gravi e rilevanti affari, di maniera che con la interposizione sua varj Principi accomodarono le cose loro in quella Corte.

Suscitatasi nel 1697. una controversia molto animata alla Corte di Toscana tra l'Inviato straordinario di Francia Duprès, e l'Ambasciadore della Repubblica di Lucca Lorenzo Cenami a cagione di visite, si indirizzò il Senato al Melani, onde volesse dileguar dall'animo del Re ogni apprese ragion di disgusto per le sinistre informazioni dategli dal suo Ministro. La raccomandazione che ne ricevette dal Cardinal Francesco Buonvisi lo impegnò a prender con calore le parti della Repubblica; nè ci volea meno del credito, dell'accortezza, e dell'esperienze sua per condurre a termine con buon successo questo spinoso affare per mezzo di un temperamento di reciproca soddisfazione. Di modo che ve guadagnò non poco la Repubblica nell'onorifico, tanto rispetto ai trattamenti da praticarsi dai Ministri francesi alla Corte di Firenze verso quelli della Repubblica, quanto circa il cerimoniale in occasione di lettere. Avrebbe voluto il Governo lucchese attestare al Melani la sua obbligazione; ma non gli fu possibile d'indurlo a riceverne dimostrazione di sorta alcuna, contento solo di aver potuto co' suoi servizj dar campo al Cardinal Buonvisi di farsene un merito con i suoi Concittadini.

Nell'anno stesso si pubblicò il trattato di pace tra la Savoja e la Francia, ed in vigore d'uno degli articoli del medesimo rimase convenuto, che per l'avvenire tanto gli Ambasciardori ordinarj che straordinarj del Duca dovessero essere trattati dai Ministri del Re, come quelli delle Corone, i quali si accompagnavano alla prima ed ultima Udienza da un Principe invece di un Maresciallo di Francia. Il Cavaliero Niccolò Erizzo Ambasciadore della Repubblica di Venezia a Parigi volle ottenere una simile onorificenza anche per la sua Repubblica. Si prevalse pertanto dell'opera del Melani, che molto gli fu utile a conseguire l'intento, come si rileva dal seguente paragrafo di lettera indirizzata dall'Erizzo agli Inquisitori di Stato in data de' 31. Ottobre 1698. da Fontaneblò.

"Quanto nella serie di questo importantissimo affare è passato col Re e coi Ministri, lo rappresentai in più mani de' miei dispacci all'Eccellentissimo Senato, a cui questa sera porto il fine del mio fortunato maneggio. In più numeri però mi è convenuto far cenno di persona confidente del Sig. di Pomponne, a cui essendomi raccomandato, debbo tutto l'obbligo del buon successo, nè posso in questa occasione dispensarmi dal nominarlo alle VV. EE. perchè farei ingiustizia al di lui merito, mentre col suo spirito e con la sua prudenza ha vinto tutte le opposizioni insorte nell'animo del Monarca e dei Ministri, onde ben se gli deve la giusta riconoscenza del Senato. Questo è l'Abate Melani nativo di Pistoja in Toscana, e suddito del Gran Duca, il quale negli anni suoi giovanili venne in Francia e fu accolto al servizio del Cardinal Mazzarino. Del Melani adunque io mi sono servito nell'arduo affare, in cui si è adoperato con tanto zelo, efficacia, ed amore, che col suo mezzo ho potuto condurlo a buon fine."

Dopo la partenza del Cavaliero Erizzo dalla Corte di Francia, trasmise la Repubblica in segno di gratitudine al Melani un Decreto col quale dichiarò Cittadini originarj Veneti il medesimo Abate Atto, il fratello Giacinto, e i suoi figli nati e che nasceranno e loro discendenti per essere ammessi a participare di tutti quei Privilegj, ed onori che sono goduti dagli altri Cittadini originarj. Il qual Decreto porta la data de' 6. Aprile 1700.

Appendix F: The texts of Atto Melani's cantatas, with analyses and translations

Below are the texts of each of Atto's cantatas, along with English translations. The Italian texts are given in a format similar to the published poetry of the period, where the lyrical canzonettas were often indented.* The translations attempt to balance literalness and readability, with a general tendency toward the former. In most cases, the translation appears on the same line as the Italian, but sometimes that procedure has not been possible. The central column shows the rhyme and metrical schemes of the poems, with refrain lines in boldface. All lines are assumed to have a *piano* ending unless marked *s* for *sdrucciolo* or *t* for *tronco*.

1 A più sventure ancora

A più sventure ancora,		a	7	"In the face of still more misfortunes
Serberò questa vita; e la fortuna		b	11	I will continue my life; and Fortune,
Lieta calpesterà le mie rovine.		c	11	happy, will trample my remains.
Forse l'empia padrona		d	7	Perhaps this pitiless mistress [Fortune]
Versa i suoi mali, e contro me l'aduna;	[5]	b	11	pours out her evils and assembles them against me
Perché tutte le pene abbia vicine.		c	11	so that I will have all my sorrows nearby.
Ahi, che Fileno al fine,		c	7	Ah, for Fileno, in the end,
Filen, volgendo il piede in altra parte;		e	11	Fileno, setting off for somewhere else,
Quel traditor Fileno, oh Dio, si parte!		e	11	that traitor Fileno, oh God, departs.
Non si parli più di vita.	[10]	**F**	**8**	"Let us talk no more of life:
Voglio andarmene alla morte,		g	8	I wish to go off to death,
Già che vuol fortuna, e sorte,		g	8	since Fortune and Fate require
Che 'l perfido amator faccia partita.		f	11	the faithless lover to depart.
Non si parli più di vita.		**F**	**8**	Let us talk no more of life.
Numi, cieli, sfere, stelle;	[15]	h	8	"Gods, heavens, spheres, stars,
Ch'a miei danni risplendete:		i	8	you who shine [down] on my wrongs:
A quel'anima piovete		i	8	rain on that soul
Influenze sì rubelle.		h	8	forces just as intractable.
Io son misera, che si pretende:		j	10	I am a miserable woman who begs this:
Sono amante; si può penar più?	[20]	k	10t	I am a lover; can one suffer more?
Cieco Amor, tu dillo, tu,		k	8t	Blind Cupid, you tell him, you,
Quali del mio dolor sien le vicende;		j	11	what the circumstances of my pain are,

* (For further information on the editing of the poetry, see Atto Melani, *Complete Cantatas*, 96–97.)

E quant'oggi riman l'alma atterita!		f 11	and how terrified my soul remains today!
Non si parli più di vita.		**F 8**	Let us talk no more of life."
Disse, e partir vedea la disperata	[25]	l 11	She spoke, and the desperate lady watched
Dal Tebro il cavalier, dal petto il core;		m 11	the knight leave the Tiber, [and] the heart [leave] her breast,
E spinta dal dolore		m 7	and driven by pain,
Su la vicina sabbia,		n 7	on the nearby sand,
S'era in braccio alla morte, abbandonata.		l 11	she was in the embrace of death, abandoned;
Ma poiché nel crudel gl'occhi rivolse,	[30]	o 11	but when she turned her eyes to the cruel man,
Gli venne tanta rabbia;		n 7	so much rage arose in her
Che per dispetto suo morir non volse.		o 11	that, out of spite, she did not turn to her death.
Imparate, alme costanti,		p 8	Learn, constant souls,
A lasciar chi v'abbandona.		q 8	to leave whoever abandons you.
V'è l'insegna, che si dona	[35]	q 8	This is the motto that one gives
A novello amatore in mezzo ai pianti:		p 11	to a new lover in the midst of tears:
Che nel mondo non v'è follia maggiore,		m 11	that in the world there is no greater folly
Che morir o per rabbia o per amore.		m 11	than dying, either through rage or through love.
L'innamorata gente		r 7	People in love
Dice voler morir, ma poi si pente.	[40]	r 11	say they want to die, but then they repent.

2 Fileno, idolo mio

Fileno, idolo mio,		a 7	Fileno, my idol,
Ove lungi da me ti stai mio bene;		b 11	where are you keeping yourself, so far from me, my love,
Che tu non riedi a questo seno, oh Dio?		a 11	that you do not return to this breast, oh God?
Già la vezzosa Aurora		c 7	Already the lovely Aurora
Sorge dal Gange a sprigionar gli albori.	[5]	d 11	rises from the Ganges to release the dawn.
Io sol de' tuoi splendori		d 7	I alone do not behold the sun of your splendors:
Non miro il sol; è per me notte ancora.		c 11	for me it is still night.
Vieni sol, che sol'adoro;		e 8	Come sun that I alone adore:
Vieni, vieni a questo seno:		f 8	come, come to this breast,
A portar pace, e ristoro	[10]	e 8	to bring peace and relief,
Ad un'alma, che si more.		g 8	to a soul that dies.
Vieni mio sol, sì, sì,		h 7t	Come my sun, yes, yes:
A questo afflitto sen riporta il dì.		h 11t	to this afflicted breast bring back the day.
Ahi, che tardi Fileno?		i 7	Ah, why do you delay, Fileno?
T'aspetta questo seno,	[15]	i 7	This breast awaits you,
Che ti prepara ogn'or vezzi, e contenti;		j 11	which constantly prepares for you charms and pleasures;
Vieni, e su labri miei gusta, o mio core,		k 11	come, and taste on my lips, O my heart,
Dentro coppa di rose il miel d'amore.		k 11	the honey of love in a cup of roses.
Or dell'alba i vaghi rai		l 8	Now the beautiful rays of the dawn
Già de' mont'il crin indorano,	[20]	m 8s	already gild the shaggy head of the mountains;
E col dolce cant'omai		l 8	and now with sweet song
Gl'augeletti il giorno onorano;		m 8s	the little birds honor the day.
Sol'indarno il mio cor si lagna, e duole:		n 11	Only in vain my heart complains and suffers
Che è nato il dì, e non rimira il sole.		n 11	that the day is born and [yet] [my heart] does not gaze upon the sun.

3 Filli, per cui mi moro

Filli, per cui mi moro,		a 7	Phyllis, for whom I die,
Disprezza il pianto mio;		b 7	despises my weeping;
E sempre cruda, oh Dio,		b 7	and always cruel, O God,
M'abborrisce; mi sdegna: et io l'adoro!		a 11	she abhors me, disdains me: and [still] I love her!
Anzi, se del mio seno	[5]	c 7	Moreover, although sometimes I reveal to her
Gli paleso talor l'aspra ferita,		d 11	the harsh wound of my breast,
Delle luci turbando il bel sereno;		c 11	disturbing the beautiful clear sky of her eyes,
L'empia omicida mia mi nega aita.		d 11	my murderous, cruel lady denies me help.
Così tra doglie, e pene,		e 7	Thus among pains and woes,
Fatto bersaglio al suo rigore eterno;	[10]	f 11	made a target for her eternal harshness,
Provo come diviene		e 7	I experience how
Adorata beltà nume d'inferno.		f 11	beauty adored becomes a goddess of hell.
Vilipesa mia fede,		g 7	O scorned faith,
È questo il premio, è questo:		h 7	is this the reward, is it this,
Ch'a tuoi lunghi martir amor concede	[15]	g 11	that to your long torments love concedes
Misero guiderdon, premio funesto?		h 11	the miserable reward, the evil prize?
Qual mai s'udì nel amoroso regno		i 11	Who has ever heard in the realm of love
Più fiero orgoglio, o crudeltà più ria?		j 11	more haughty pride, or more wicked cruelty?
Filli si prende a sdegno,		i 7	Phyllis disdains
Che languisca per lei l'anima mia.	[20]	j 11	that my spirit languishes for her.
Lumi rei del mio morire,		k 8	Eyes, guilty of my death,
Che spirate ira et amore;		l 8	you that inspire anger and love:
Dite, crudi, e come un core		k 8	tell, cruel ones, how a heart
Può mirarvi, e non languire.		l 8	can gaze on you and not languish.
Dunque, armatevi pur di ferità;	[25]	m 11t	So arm yourselves [eyes] still for cruelty,
Congiurate a miei danni:		n 7	conspire for my injuries:
Ché la vostra beltà		m 7t	for your beauty,
Amo, benché sdegnata, occhi tiranni.		n 11	although scorned, I love, tyrannous eyes.
Nel mar del duolo mio,		b 7	In the sea of my sorrow,
Scoglio di fé son'io;	[30]	b 7	a rock of faith am I:
E, se ver me spietati		o 7	and if towards me you are pitiless,
Sete, cieli adirati;		o 7	angry heavens,
Non pavento, costante, il vostro orgoglio:		p 11	I, constant, do not fear your pride:
Ch'i furori del ciel non teme un scoglio.		p 11	for a rock does not fear the furies of the heavens.

4 Il tacer non fa per me

Il tacer non fa per me;		**A 8t**	Being silent is not for me:
Ch'un incendio, ch'è celato,		**b 8**	for a fire that is hidden
Porta fiamme in ogni lato		**b 8**	incites flames everywhere
Con il rapido suo piè:		**a 8t**	with its rapid movement.
Il tacer non fa per me.	[5]	**A 8t**	Being silent is not for me.
Nacque nel seno mio picciol favilla		c 11	In my breast was born a little spark
D'amoroso contento;		d 7	of amorous pleasure,
Ma crebbe in un momento,		d 7	but [the flame] increased in a moment

Sol perché tacqui a danni miei la fiamma;		e	11	only because I was silent about my injuries;
Onde ben racconterò	[10]	f	8t	Wherefore I will clearly recount
Le mie pene, il mio martoro,		g	8	my pains, my torment,
A colei, che mi piagò:		f	8t	to her who wounded me:
Ché non s'offende un nume a dir t'adoro.		g	11	for one does not offend a god by saying "I adore you."

Su voci veloci;		h	6	Come forth, swift words:
Palesate d'amor l'anticha fé,	[15]	a	11t	reveal the ancient creed of love,
Ch'amante senza ardir già mai godè.		a	11t	that [no] lover ever found pleasure without burning.

Dal core all'ardore		i	6	To [that] burning from the heart
Rimedio si dia, si cerchi mercé;		a	11t	let a remedy be granted, let mercy be sought;
Per chi copre il suo mal cura non v'è.		a	11t	there is no cure for him who covers his wound.

Il tacer non fa per me;	[20]	**A**	**8t**	Being silent is not for me:
Ch'un incendio, ch'è celato,		**b**	**8**	for a fire that is hidden
Porta fiamme in ogni lato		**b**	**8**	incites flames everywhere
Con il rapido suo piè:		**a**	**8t**	with its rapid movement.
Il tacer non fa per me.		**A**	**8t**	Being silent is not for me.

5 Io voglio esser infelice

Io voglio esser infelice		**A**	**8**	I want to be unhappy
Per saziare i miei tormenti,		**b**	**8**	in order to satiate my torments,
Ché sperar mai più contenti		**b**	**8**	since hoping for more pleasures
Ad un misero non lice:		**a**	**8**	is never permitted to a wretch.
Io voglio esser infelice.	[5]	**A**	**8**	I want to be unhappy.

La certezza del mio male		c	8	The certainty of my illness
Disporrà l'alma alla morte,		d	8	will prepare my soul for death,
Consolando la sua sorte		d	8	its fate being cheered
Col saper, ch'ella è fatale;		c	8	by the knowledge that [death] is inevitable.
E la piaga, ch'è mortale,	[10]	c	8	And the wound, which is mortal,
Sentirà meno il dolore;		e	8	will feel the pain less
S'io potrò dire ad Amore,		e	8	if I can say to Cupid
Che non posso esser felice.		a	8	that I cannot be happy.

Io voglio esser infelice		**A**	**8**	I want to be unhappy
Per saziare i miei tormenti,	[15]	**b**	**8**	in order to satiate my torments,
Ché sperar mai più contenti		**b**	**8**	since hoping for more pleasures
Ad un misero non lice:		**a**	**8**	is never permitted to a wretch.
Io voglio esser infelice.		**A**	**8**	I want to be unhappy.

Ah, speranze bugiarde:		f	7	Ah, lying hopes,
Come toglieste a me la mia quiete?	[20]	g	11	how did you take from me my peace?
Come, come voi siete		g	7	How, how is it that you are
Sì veloci alle pene, al ben sì tarde?		f	11	so quick to pain [but] to pleasure so slow?
Io già più non vi credo,		h	7	Already I no longer believe you,
Mentre, lasso, m'avvedo,		h	7	for, alas, I realize

Che nel mar del mio pianto	[25]	i	7	that in the sea of my tears,
Siete sirene, allettatrici infide;		j	11	you are sirens, unfaithful seducers,
E che ben spesso uccide		j	7	and that quite often
La dolcezza crudel del vostro canto:		i	11	the cruel sweetness of your song kills:
Ond'altro non m'avanza,		k	7	wherefore I am left with nothing
Che lo sperar di non aver speranza!	[30]	k	11	but the hope of not having hope!

Pensieri, sì, sì:		l	6t	Thoughts, yes, yes
Lasciate la spene;		m	6	leave hope behind:
Talvolta così		l	6t	sometimes thus
Finiscon le pene.		n	6	the suffering ends.

Del cor le catene,	[35]	n	6	The chains of the heart,
I lacci dell'alma,		o	6	the snares of the soul:
Con inclita palma		o	6	with glorious triumph,
Sol frange chi dice:		a	6	[these] are broken only by he who says,

Io voglio esser infelice		**A**	8	I want to be unhappy
Per saziare i miei tormenti,	[40]	**b**	8	in order to satiate my torments:
Ché sperar mai più contenti		**b**	8	for hoping for more pleasures
Ad un misero non lice:		**a**	8	is never permitted to a wretch.
Io voglio esser infelice.		**A**	8	I want to be unhappy.

6a La più dolente, e misera, che viva

La più dolente, e misera, che viva		**A**	11	The most afflicted and miserable [woman] who lives
Nel grembo della terra,		b	7	on the face of the earth,
D'ogni pietà, d'ogni conforto priva;		a	11	lacking every pity and comfort,
Che, dovunque si volga, ha sempre guerra:		b	11	who, anywhere she turns, finds always strife,
Quella a cui non dan riposo i cieli, oh Dio;	[5]	c	12?	she, to whom the heavens do not give rest, O God,
Quell'infelice, sì, quella son'io!		c	11	that unhappy woman, yes, that one, am I.

Da chi spero aver pietà		d	8t	From whom do I hope to have relief
Di sì barbari tormenti,		e	8	for such barbarous torments
Se congiuran gli elementi	[10]	e	8	if the elements conspire
Per usarmi crudeltà?		d	8t	to treat me with cruelty?
Viver sì sventurato il cor non cura;		f	11	My heart does not mind a life so wretched:
Perdasi con la vita ogni sventura.		f	11	may every misfortune perish with my life.

Oh, che strana servitù		g	8t	Oh what strange servitude
Vuol da me l'empia fortuna?	[15]	h	8	does cruel Fortune want from me?
Tante pene insieme aduna,		h	8	So many pains gather together
Che non può crescerne più.		g	8t	that [Fortune] can increase them no further.
Ah, perfida, ah, crudel nemica sorte!		i	11	Ah treacherous, ah cruel, hostile fate:
Dove, per minor mal, dov'è la morte?		i	11	where, for less suffering, where is death?

No, no, che non curo aita;	[20]	j	7	No, no! I do not care for help;
Un, che misero sia, sprezza la vita.		j	11	One who is miserable despises life.

E che v'ho fatto, o stelle,		k	7	And what have I done to you, O stars,

Che sete contro me tanto adirate;	l	11	that you are so enraged against me,
Così crude, e rubelle,	k	7	so cruel and contrary,
Così fiere, e spietate? [25]	l	7	so haughty and pitiless?
Non è, non è gran vanto	m	7	It is no great glory
Veder dagli occhi miei piover'il pianto.	m	11	to see the tears rain down from my eyes:
Il piangere a me lice:	n	7	weeping is permitted to me.
Ben'è ragion, che pianga un infelice.	n	11	An unfortunate who weeps has good reason.
Qual vanto fia, se a lagrimare arriva [30]	a	11	What glory will it be if she begins to cry,
La più dolente, e misera, che viva?	**A**	**11**	the most afflicted and miserable woman who lives?
Io veggio, o veder parmi,	o	7	I see, or it seems to me that I see,
Armarsi a danni miei tutto l'abisso.	p	11	the whole abyss being armed for my injury.
Furie, a che le vostr'armi?	o	7	Furies, what is the point of your arms?
Altro tormento a me trovo prefisso; [35]	p	11	I find another torment appointed for me;
Del vostro è assai maggiore:	q	7	it is much greater than yours:
Quel, che chiudo nel sen, porto nel core.	q	11	[it is] one that I enclose in my breast, [that] I carry in my heart.
Io credea, che doppo tant'anni	r	9	I believed that after so many years
Si stancassero i miei martiri;	s	9	my tortures had wearied,
Che cedessero questi affanni [40]	r	9	that these pains of many lustra[a] had yielded
Di più lustri ai rapidi giri:	s	9	to the rapid turnings [of Fortune's wheel]:
Ma provo, che sempre	t	6	but it seems that forever
Fra rigide tempre	t	6	among harsh furors
La vita trarrò;	u	6t	I will lead my life;
E sento ch'ogn'ora [45]	v	6	and I feel that,
Vie più s'addolora,	v	6	if before I was suffering,
Se dianzi penò.	u	6t	I will [now] be all the more afflicted.
Tizio, Sisifo, Tantalo, Issione:	w	11	Tityus, Sisyphus, Tantalus, Ixion:[b]
Ahi, capaci non son di paragone,	w	11	ah, I am not as worthy of comparison [to these figures];
Come lo stato suo fia, che descriva	a	11	as will be the condition of whoever tells the tale of
La più dolente, e misera, che viva! [50]	**A**	**11**	the most afflicted and miserable woman who lives.

Sebastiano Baldini

[a] Lustrum (pl., lustra): a period of five years.

[b] All of these figures received special punishments in the underworld. Tityus was a giant, the son of Zeus and Elara, whom Hera incited to attack Zeus's lover Leto; killed by Apollo and Artemis (Leto's children), Tityus was punished by having vultures peck continuously at his heart. Sisyphus was a cruel man who offended the gods and was punished by being forced for all eternity to push a stone block up a steep hill, only to have it roll back down on him each time as he neared the top. Tantalus was a son of Zeus who angered the gods by inviting them to a banquet at which he served the body of his own son; he was condemned to stand forever in a pool of water that drained away each time he tried to get a drink and underneath a fruit tree whose branches moved beyond his grasp when he reached for them. Ixion was admitted by Zeus to Olympus but abused that privilege by trying to seduce Hera; his punishment was to be bound on a fiery wheel that rolled unceasingly.

6b La più dolente, e misera, che viva (from the papers of Sebastiano Baldini: I Rvat, Chig. L.VI.187, ff. 28–29v)

La Sventurata	*The Wretched Lady*

Una Bellissima Dama essendo molto travagliata da varij accidenti ha dato materia del seguente recitativo	*A very beautiful lady, being much distressed by various mishaps, gave voice to the following* recitativo

Recitativo malinconico	*Melancholy recitative*

La più dolente, e misera, che viva		**A** **11**	"The most afflicted and miserable woman who lives
Nel grembo della terra;		b 7	on the face of the earth,
D'ogni pietà, d'ogni conforto priva,		a 11	lacking every pity and comfort,
Che dovunque si volge, ha eterna guerra:		b 11	who, anywhere she turns, finds eternal strife,
Quella, a cui non da pace il cielo, oh Dio,	[5]	c 11	she, to whom heaven gives no peace, O God,
Quell'infelice, sì, quella son'io.		c 11	that unhappy woman, yes, that one am I.

Aria			*Aria*
Da chi spero aver pietà		d 8t	"From whom do I hope to have relief
Di sì barbari tormenti,		e 8	from such barbarous torments,
Se congiuran gli elementi		e 8	if the elements conspire
Per usarmi crudeltà?	[10]	d 8t	to treat me with cruelty?
Viver sì sventurato il cor non cura.		f 11	My heart does not mind a life so wretched:
Perdasi con la vita ogni sventura.		f 11	may every misfortune perish with my life.

A che strana servitù		g 8t	"To what strange servitude
Mi riduce empia fortuna?		h 8	does cruel Fortune reduce me?
Tante pene insieme aduna,	[15]	h 8	So many pains gather together
Che non può crescerne più.		g 8t	that [Fortune] can increase them no further.
Crudelissima sorte,		i 11	Most cruel fate:
E dove a scapa mia, dove è la morte?		i 11	where, for my escape, where is death?
Sì che voglio morir; non chieggio aita:		j 7	Thus I want to die; I do not ask for help:
Un che misero sia sprezza la vita.	[20]	j 11	One who is miserable despises life.

E che vi feci o stelle,		k 7	"And what have I done to you, O stars
Che siete contro me tanto adirate;		l 11	that you are so enraged against me,
Così crude e rubelle,		k 7	so cruel and contrary,
Così fiere e spietate?		l 7	so haughty and pitiless?
Ah no non è gran vanto	[25]	m 7	Ah no, it is no great glory
Trarre dagli occhi miei fiumi [di] pianto.		m 11	to draw from my eyes rivers of tears.
Ché il piangere a me lice,		n 7	For weeping is permitted to me.
Ben'è ragion che pianga un infelice;		n 11	An unfortunate who weeps has good reason.
Qual vanto è poi se a lagrimare arriva		a 11	What glory is it then if she begins to cry,
La più dolente, e misera che viva?	[30]	**A** **11**	the most afflicted and miserable woman who lives?"

Recit.			*Recitative*
Io veggio, o veder parmi,		o 7	"I see, or it seems to me that I see,
Armarsi a danni miei tutto l'abisso:		p 11	the whole abyss being armed for my injury.
Furie a che le vostr'armi,		o 7	Furies, what is the point of your arms?
Maggior tormento a me trovo prefisso;		p 11	I find a greater torment appointed for me;
De' vostri è assai peggiore:	[35]	q 7	it is much greater than your [torments]:
Quel che chiudo nel sen porto nel core.		q 11	[it is] one that I enclose in my breast, [that] I carry in my heart."

Aria

Io credea, che doppo tant'anni		r	9
Si stancassero i [miei] martiri		s	8
Che cedessero questi affanni		r	9
Di più lustri ai rapidi giri:	[40]	s	9
Ma veggo, che sempre		t	6
Fra barbare tempre		t	6
La vita trarrò;		u	6t
Provando ch'ogn'ora		v	6
Vie più si addolora,	[45]	v	6
Se dianzi penò.		u	6t

Tizio, Sisifo, Tantalo, Issione:		w	11
Ma capace io non son di paragone:		w	11
Come lo stato suo fia che descriva		a	11
La più dolente, e misera, che viva.	[50]	A	11
Così disse una ninfa, anzi una dea,		x	11
Una dea, che qual Psiche		y	7
Per invidia, cred'io, di Citerea		x	11
Viveva afflitta in questo paese, e in quella,		z	11
Perché sendo mortal, troppo era bella.	[55]	z	11

Sebastiano Baldini

Aria

"I believed that after so many years
my tortures had wearied,
that these pains of many lustra had yielded
to the rapid turnings [of Fortune's wheel]:
but I see that forever
among barbarous furors
I will lead my life;
feeling that
if before I was suffering,
I will [now] be all the more afflicted.

"Tityus, Sisyphus, Tantalus, Ixion:
but I am not as worthy of comparison
as will be the condition of whoever tells the tale of
the most afflicted and miserable woman who lives."
Thus spoke a nymph, rather, a goddess,
a goddess who, like Psyche,
because of Venus's jealousy, I think,
lived afflicted in this town and that [one]
because she was too beautiful for a mortal woman.

7 M'abbandona la sorte

M'abbandona la sorte,		a	7
E sdegnate le stelle;		b	7
Vibran fatte rubelle		b	7
Contro l'inerme sen strali di morte;		a	11
Pieno d'ira,	[5]	c	4
Il mio ciel fulmini spira:		c	8
E pure abbandonata,		d	7
Colpevol non son'io, ma sventurata.		d	11

Giri la ruota errante		e	7
Contro me cieca dea;	[10]	f	7
Non potrà far la rea,		f	7
Che innocente io non sia, non sia costante;		e	11
Importuna,		g	4
Pur m'opprima empia fortuna:		g	8
Ch'afflitta, abbandonata,	[15]	d	7
Colpevol non sarò, ma sventurata.		d	11

Fate abandons me
and the stars [are] angered:
made hostile, they hurl arrows of death
against my unarmed breast.
Full of anger,
my heaven breathes thunderbolts,
and truly abandoned,
I am not guilty, but unfortunate.

Let the blind goddess turn the errant wheel
    against me:

that evil [goddess] will not be able to make
me less innocent, less constant.
Unyielding,
let pitiless Fortune oppress me,
[so] that afflicted, abandoned,
I will not be guilty, but unfortunate.

8 Occhi miei belli

Occhi miei belli,		a	5	My beautiful eyes,
Occhi adorati,		b	5	adored eyes,
Occhi beati,		b	5	blessed eyes,
Che furon quelli;		a	5	that were those
Che mi feron nel sen piaga sì gradita:	[5]	c	12	that made in my breast a wound so welcome
Che è felice il morir per te mia vita.		c	11	that it is a happy thing to die for you, my love.

Labri divini,		d	5	Divine lips,
Labri amorosi,		e	5	loving lips,
Labri gioiosi,		e	5	joyous lips,
Vivi i rubbini;	[10]	d	5	living rubies
Che d'esser fedeli mi giuraste un dì:		f	12t	that once swore to me to be faithful,
Quando fiero destin ci dipartì.		f	11t	when proud destiny parted us.

Cari miei lacci,		g	5	My dear bonds,
Care cattene,		h	5	dear chains,
Care mie pene,	[15]	h	5	my dear pains,
Amati impacci;		g	5	beloved troubles:
Sempre portarvi vo' con gran costanza:		i	11	I desire always to bear [you] with great constancy,
Poiché viva è la fede,		j	7	since faith is alive
Se morta è la speranza.		i	7	[even] if hope is dead.

9 O quanto si dolea

O quanto si dolea		a	7	Oh, how much he complained
Dell'invida fortuna,		b	7	about envious Fortune,
Chi lungi dal bel Tebro ardeva amante!		c	11	he who, far from the lovely Tiber, burned with love:

Giurò, che non potea		a	7	he swore that no distance could
Fargli perder già mai distanza alcuna	[5]	b	11	ever make him lose
Il titolo di fido, e di costanza.		d	11	his claim to faithfulness and constancy.
Quindi ver lontananza,		d	7	And so against Distance,
Che le piaghe d'amor sanar gli volse,		e	11	which endeavored to heal his wounds of love,
Dispettoso così la lingua sciolse.		e	11	he, spiteful, thus loosed his tongue:

Lascia pur le piaghe intatte	[10]	f	8	"Leave untouched the wounds
Per cui l'anima vien meno;		g	8	through which my soul dissipates:
Chi le aperse nel mio seno		g	8	she who opened them in my breast
Insanabili l'ha fatte.		f	8	made them incurable.
È vano il tuo rimedio, il tuo conforto:		h	11	It is vain, your remedy, your comfort:
La feritrice mia nel core io porto.	[15]	h	11	I carry in my heart the one who injures me.

Se di Lete il cieco oblio		i	8	"If the blind oblivion of Lethe
Vuoi destar contro di me,		j	8t	you think to arouse against me;
Se d'amor la pura fé		j	8t	if the pure faith of love
Vuoi scacciar dal petto mio;		i	8	you think to drive from my chest;
Del mio sen la costanza, ah, non intendi	[20]	k	11	ah, [then] you do not understand the constancy of my breast;

Sin l'acque dell'oblio cangian in incendi;	k	11	it turns even the waters of oblivion into flames.
E sa le forze tue schernire Amore:	l	11	"And Love knows how to scorn your powers:
Ché quando parte il piè, non parte il core.	**L**	**11**	for when the foot departs, the heart does not.

Sieno pur tuoi rimedi	m	7	"Although your tactics be
Sciogliere un rivo, e diramare un fonte, [25]	n	11	to let loose a stream, issue a spring,
Stender un lago, e dilatare un fiume:	o	11	extend a lake, enlarge a river;
Provedi, pur provedi	m	7	although you present, indeed present [before me]
Alpestri vie d'inaccessibil monte,	n	11	the alpine paths of an inaccessible mountain
Ove arrivar non san d'augel le piume.	o	11	to which [even] the wings of birds cannot come;
Spandi l'orride spume [30]	o	7	although you spread the horrid foam
D'un mar più tempestoso, e più severo:	q	11	of an ever more stormy and severe sea:
Puoi trattenermi il piè, non il pensiero.	q	11	you can hold back my foot, [but] not my thought.

Il pensier dispiega il volo,	r	8	"The thought spreads [its wings in] flight
E trapassa rivi, fonti,	s	8	and crosses brooks, springs,
Laghi, fiumi, mari, monti; [35]	s	8	lakes, rivers, seas, mountains,
Ogni clima, ed ogni polo.	r	8	every climate and each pole;
Press'a lui tard'il lampo, e tardo il vento:	t	11	compared to it, lightning and wind are slow;
Basta raggiunger Filli un sol momento.	t	11	only a moment is needed to reach Phyllis.

Io so, che ben tu puoi,	u	7	"I know that you can easily,
Co' gl'ostacoli tuoi, [40]	u	7	with your obstacles,
In lontani ricetti	v	7	in distant abodes
I corpi separar, ma non gl'affetti.	v	11	separate the bodies, but not the affections.
Non fia, che ceda alle tue forze Amore:	l	11	Love will [never] succumb to your powers:
Ché quando parte il piè, non parte il core.	**L**	**11**	when the step departs, the heart does not.

Se, col tempo insuberabile, [45]	w	8s	"If with insurmountable Time
Pensi renderti invincibile;	x	8s	you think to make yourself invincible,
Quanto più ti fai terribile,	x	8s	the more you make yourself terrible,
Tanto men sei formidabile.	w	8s	the less you are formidable.
Il tempo in van per me cangia vicende;	y	11	Time in vain changes my circumstances;
Con l'ali sue le mie faville accende. [50]	y	11	with its wings[a] my sparks catch fire.

Non avrà l'istessa morte,	z	8	"This destiny [of mine] will not have
Questa sorte;	z	4	a typical death:
Quando il punto,	aa	4	when the moment
Sarà giunto,	aa	4	arrives
Ch'io dovrò ceder al fato; [55]	bb	8	at which I must surrender to Fate,
Dal mio petto innamorato,	bb	8	from my enamored breast,
Che tal bellezza idolatrar si vede,	cc	11	which you see worshiping such beauty,
Lo spirto uscir vedrai, ma non la fede.	cc	11	you will see the spirit leaving, but not the faith;

E dirai, se ver me volgi le piante:	c	11	"and you will say, if you come to me:
È morto, è ver; ma, benché morto, è amante. [60]	c	11	he is dead, it is true; but although dead, he is a lover."

Sebastiano Baldini

[a] The reference here is to depictions of Time as a winged figure, an image that emphasizes time's rapid passage and that goes back to the Greek god Kronos.

10 Ove, tra sponde d'oro

Ove, tra sponde d'oro,	a	7	Where, between banks of gold,
L'indico Gange imprigionò l'arena;	b	11	the sand imprisoned the Ganges of India,
Stretta la bianca mano	c	7	having grasped the white hand
Della vezzosa Clori,	d	7	of charming Clori,
Seco fermolla consigliero amante; [5]	e	11	the loving sailor held her there with him;
E mostrando nel volto aspro dolore,	f	11	and showing harsh pain in his face,
Disse sui labri suoi, parlando il core.	f	11	he said, his heart speaking through his lips:
Vedi la bella Aurora,	g	7	"See the beautiful Aurora,
Che del vecchio Titon lascia le piume;	h	11	who leaves the mattress of old Tithonus:
Fuga le stelle, e intanto al nuovo sole [10]	i	11	she puts the stars to flight, while for the new sun
Fanno cuna i ligustri, e le viole.	i	11	the privets and violets make a cradle.
Passan l'ombre così:	j	7t	Thus the shadows disappear:
Doppo la notte al fin rinasce il dì.	j	11t	after the night, the day is finally reborn.
Ma dal tuo viso adorno	k	7	But if from your beautiful face
Se parte un dì, mai più ritorna il giorno. [15]	k	11	the day one day departs, it will never again return.
Deh, lascia, severa,	**l**	**6**	"Oh, cease – severe,
Superba et altera,	**l**	**6**	proud, and haughty woman –
Cotanto rigore:	**f**	**6**	such harshness:
Non è eterno il tuo bel, né 'l mio dolore!	**f**	**11**	your beauty is not eternal, nor is my pain.
Tra l'umane vicende, [20]	m	7	"Among the human traits
Nei giardin di Fortuna;	n	7	in the gardens of Fortune,
È rosa la bellezza:	o	7	beauty is [the] rose:
Ma sol di pianto, oh Dio, beve ruggiade!	p	11	but it drinks only the dewdrops of tears, O God!
E quando al sol s'appressa, allora cade.	p	11	And when it draws nearer to the sun, then it falls.
Sfioriscono gl'anni [25]	q	6	"The years fade
Coi gigli del seno;	r	6	with the lilies of your breast:
Verranno ben meno	r	6	your beauty will greatly dwindle,
A te bellezza, et a chi t'ama affanni.	q	11	as will the pains of the man who loves you.
Così con alta legge il tempo impera.	l	11	"Thus with [this] great law Time rules.
Deh, lascia, severa, [30]	**l**	**6**	"Oh, cease – severe,
Superba et altera,	**l**	**6**	proud, and haughty woman –
Cotanto rigore:	**f**	**6**	such harshness:
Non è eterno il tuo bel, né 'l mio dolore!	**f**	**11**	your beauty is not eternal, nor is my pain."

11 Scrivete, occhi dolenti

Scrivete, occhi dolenti,	a	7	Write, aching eyes,
Con inchiostro di pianto	b	7	with ink of tears
Sul foglio del mio volto, i vostri affanni.	c	11	on the page of my face your pains:
Narrate i miei tormenti,	a	7	relate my torments,
Registrate i miei danni; [5]	c	7	register my injuries,
E dite a chi no' l' crede,	d	7	and tell whoever does not believe it
Ch'amar tacendo ogni martire eccede.	d	11	that to love in silence exceeds every martyrdom.
Per un ciglio amoroso,	e	7	For a loving brow
Che piace ma saetta;	f	7	that pleases, but shoots arrows;

Per un labro vezzoso,	[10]	e	7	for a graceful lip
Ch'uccide ma dilletta;		f	7	that kills, but delights;
Per un seno di neve,		g	7	for a breast of snow
Che mirar non si può senza adorarlo:		h	11	that one cannot see without adoring:
Ardo, piango, sospiro; e pur non parlo.		h	11	I burn, I weep, I sigh, and yet I do not speak.
Sì, sì, tacia la lingua;	[15]	i	7	Yes, yes, let the tongue be silent,
Ma favellino i lumi.		j	7	but let the eyes speak:
Dolor, tu detta i carmi; Amor, coreggi;		k	11	pain, may you dictate the poems; love, correct;
Occhi, scrivete: e tu mia vita, leggi.		k	11	eyes, write; and you, my life, read.

Se il mio cor non sa ridire		l	8	If my heart cannot repeat
La caggion, che l'arde tanto;	[20]	m	8	the reason it burns so much:
A caratteri di pianto		m	8	[then] in characters of tears,
Farò noto il mio morire.		l	8	I will record my death.

Segnarò per tutti i lidi		n	8	I will note down for all shores
La beltà, che m'inamora;		o	8	the beauty that enamors me:
E sapran l'arene ancora,	[25]	o	8	and the sands too will know
Che tu sol, bella, m'uccidi.		n	8	that you alone, beautiful one, kill me.

Ogni amante leggerà		p	8t	Every lover will read
Quest'epilogo d'amore,		q	8	this epilogue of love:
Ch'io sospiro a tutte l'ore		q	8	that I sigh continuously for
La perduta libertà.	[30]	p	8t	my lost liberty.

E perché mia vita langue,		r	8	And because my life ebbs away,
Chiudo il foglio sventurato;		s	8	I close the wretched page:
Sottoscritto dal mio fato,		s	8	signed by my fate,
Sigillato col mio sangue.		r	8	sealed with my blood.

Leggi, deh leggi, o bella,	[35]	t	7	Read, pray read, O beautiful lady
Le note a te dirette;		u	7	the notes directed to you:
E se qualche pietà nel seno ascondi,		v	11	and if some pity hides in your breast,
Con un muto rescritto		w	7	with a mute reply
O di vita o di morte almen rispondi!		v	11	at least answer, "life" or "death"!

Francesco Melosio

12 S'io sapessi dipingere

S'io sapessi dipingere,		a	7s	If I knew how to paint,
Belle cose farei		b	7	I would create beautiful things
Pria te, bella cagion de' dolor miei;		b	11	[and] you first, O beautiful cause of my sorrows;
In una vaga tela vorrei fingere		a	11s	on a lovely canvas, I would like to simulate
Ciò ch'ha di bel il ciel tutto raccolto	[5]	c	11	the splendors of the heavens, all collected,
Ritrarvi nel bel volto;		c	7	to portray your beautiful face.
Ma non hanno i colori		d	7	But the pigments do not have
Così vivi splendori:		d	7	such lively brilliance:
No, no; solo le stelle		e	7	no, no; only the stars
Ponno ritrar la sù forme sì belle.	[10]	e	11	can depict up above forms so beautiful.

Ma poiché non poss'io,		f	7	But since I cannot [paint you],
Se pur voi lo volete;		g	7	although you want me to,

Aprite, o bella Filli, il petto mio:		f	11	open my breast, O beautiful Phyllis,
Ch'ivi per man d'Amor scolpita sete!		g	11	for there you are sculpted by the hand of Cupid.
L'opra fu del suo strale; altro che Amore	[15]	h	11	The work was of his arrow; nothing but Cupid/ Love
Non travaglia il mio core;		h	7	afflicts/shapes my heart;
E di sì bella immago		i	7	and with such a beautiful image
Vivo contento, e pago:		i	7	I live content and satisfied:
Sì, sì; forza è di stella		j	7	yes, yes; it is by means of a star
Idolatrando Amor cosa sì bella.	[20]	j	11	that Cupid/Love makes an idol of/worships something so beautiful.

13 Sola tra le sue pene

Sola tra le sue pene,		a	7	Alone with her suffering,
L'addolorata Lusinda;		b	7	the anguished Lucinda –
Lungi dal proprio bene,		a	7	far from her beloved,
Che muove altrove solitario il passo;		c	11	who wanders elsewhere alone –
Temprando coi sospiri	[5]	d	7	tempering her innocent torments
Del cor innamorato		e	7	with the sighs
Inocenti martiri:		d	7	of an enamored heart,
Sovra corde sonore,		f	7	to sonorous chords
Sfogava in mesti accenti il suo dolore.		f	11	poured out her pain in sad words:
Spiega i vanni, o mio pensiero,	[10]	g	8	"Unfold your wings, O my thought,
Messaggiero di mia fé;		h	8t	messenger of my faith:
Presto vola, e la t'invia		i	8	quickly fly and dispatch yourself there
Dove ogn'or raggira il piè!		h	8t	where [his] step ceaselessly rambles.
Il mio cor, l'anima mia;		i	8	My heart, my spirit:
Digli tosto, che per me;	[15]	h	8t	tell him at once that for me
Lungi dagli occhi suoi luce non è.		h	11t	there is no light apart from his eyes.
Digli pur, ch'a tanto ardore,		f	8	"Tell him too that I can no longer endure
Più resister io non so;		j	8t	so much emotion:
E quest'alma, e questo core,		f	8	both this soul and this heart
Senza lui viver non può:	[20]	j	8t	cannot live without him;
Ma che sol vive nel seno		k	8	but that there only lives in my breast
L'immagine di lui, che mai vien meno.		k	11	the image of him that never fades.
Ah, che sospiro invano, e spargo ai venti		l	11	"Ah, I sigh in vain and throw to the winds
Le mie voci dolenti!		l	7	my sad words/notes;
Misera è, che già mai	[25]	m	7	if it is only a thought that can give me comfort,
Provò stato sì fiero;		g	7	then wretched is she who has never
Se conforto mi da solo un pensiero.		g	11	experienced a condition so severe.
Vieni, torna in questo seno,		k	8	"Come, return to this breast,
Fido porto ai tuoi contenti;		l	8	faithful portal to your pleasures:
Splenda ormai quel dì sereno,	[30]	k	8	let shine at last that serene day
Che dia fine a miei tormenti:		l	8	that brings an end to my torments,
E lontananza avara		n	7	and let stingy distance
Non tolga agli occhi miei luce sì cara.		n	11	not deprive my eyes of so precious a light."

14 Tra sponde di smeraldo

Tra sponde di smeraldo,	a	7	Between banks of emerald
Correa, con piè d'argento,	b	7	was running, with silvery foot,
Figlio d'annosa rupe, un rio sonante;	c	11	a noisy brook, sprung from an old rock,
Ove tradito amante	c	7	where a betrayed lover
Spiegò l'aspro lamento:	[5] b	7	poured out his harsh lament;
E mentre ei parla intanto,	d	7	and as he speaks,
Turba l'onde di lui col proprio pianto.	d	11	he agitates the brook's waters with his own weeping:
Filli non è più mia.	**E**	**7**	"Phyllis is no longer mine!
Alla candida fede,	f	7	To pure faith,
Empia questa mercede?	[10] f	7	this cruel reward?
Al mio sincero core,	g	7	To my sincere heart,
Tradimento, e dolore?	g	7	betrayal and pain?
Occhi mestissimi,	h	5s	[O my] eyes, so sad,
Spiegate in lagrime,	i	5s	explain in tears
Ch'il mio lungo servir oggi s'oblia:	[15] e	11	that my long service has today been forgotten:
Filli fatt'è d'altrui; non è più mia.	**E′**	**11**	Phyllis belongs to another; she is no longer mine.
Amanti, voi, ch'al saettar severo	j	11	Lovers, you who [once] made your breast a target
Del cieco dio festi bersaglio il seno;	k	11	for the harsh arrows of the blind god:
Ogni vostro tormento	b	7	let your every torment
Dal mio grave martir prenda ristoro.	[20] l	11	take solace from my solemn martyrdom.
No, no, che non si può	m	7t	No, no, for one cannot
Soffrir del mio dolor pena più ria:	e	11	suffer pain more cruel than my anguish:
Filli fatt'è d'altrui; non è più mia.	**E′**	**11**	Phyllis belongs to another; she is no longer mine.
Ma, se vuol crudo destino,	n	8	"But if cruel destiny decrees
Ch'io per lei vivendo speri;	[25] o	8	that, living, I [continue to] hope for her,
Sian di Filli i modi alteri	o	8	may the proud ways of Phyllis be [also]
Il tenor della mia sorte:	p	8	the character of my fate:
Filli non è più mia; son della morte.	**p**	**11**	Phyllis is no longer mine; I belong to death."
Quindi di speme fuori,	q	7	So, without hope,
Volea, per entro all'onde,	[30] r	7	he wanted, by entering the waves,
Estinguer con la vita i propri ardori;	s	11	to extinguish his passions with his life:
Ma rimirando l'acque,	t	7	but gazing at the waters,
Sospeso alquanto, tacque;	t	7	somewhat uncertain, he fell silent.
Gli sembrò, che dicesse il vago rio:	u	11	It seemed to him that the lovely brook spoke:
Ferma! ogni donna amante,	[35] c	7	"Stop! Every mistress,
Al par dell'onde mie, vive incostante.	c	11	like my waves, is inconstant."

15 Anima, che di foco (duet)

Anima, che di foco	a	7	My soul, you who feed on the fire
Ti nutri entro il mio seno,	b	7	within my breast,
Fuggi; o mi guida almeno	b	7	flee! Or at least guide me
Tra i popoli d'Averno,	c	7	among the peoples of Hades,
Già dalle Parche uccisi;	[5] d	7	already slain by the Fates,
Che gli abissi per me saranno Elisi.	d	11	so that the abysses will be Elysium for me.

Quando un cor si trova oppresso	e	8	When a heart finds itself oppressed
Da quel dio, che vibra strali;	f	8	by that god who shoots arrows,
Non conosce in tutti mali	f	8	it knows not in all its pain
Altro inferno, che se stesso. [10]	e	8	another hell than itself.
Stuolo rio di mostri fieri	g	8	A cruel throng of fierce monsters
Sferza ogn'or l'ombre penanti;	h	8	constantly whips the suffering shades:
Ma per crucio degli amanti,	h	8	but for the vexation of lovers,
Bastan solo i lor pensieri.	g	8	their thoughts alone suffice.
S'un ardor d'eterne tempre [15]	i	8	Just as a fire of eternal vigor
L'alme abbrugia, e mai risplende;	j	8	scorches the souls [of hell] but never shines,
Anco amore ignoto offende:	j	8	so also unfamiliar love causes pain:
Arde i cori, e dura sempre.	i	8	it burns hearts and lasts forever.
Gelo, che mai si strugge;	k	7	Ice that never melts,
Fiamma, che non consuma: [20]	l	7	flame that never consumes:
Sirti son di chi fugge	k	7	these are quicksands for whoever flees
Calma di libertà, sopra la spuma	l	11	the calm of liberty over the foam
Del vasto Egeo d'amore.	m	7	of the vast Aegean of love.
E chi, senza dolore	m	7	And whoever, without the pain
D'una giurata e poi mentita fede, [25]	n	11	of a promised and then betrayed faith,
Solca del cieco dio il golfo immenso;	o	11	sails the immense gulf of the blind god,
O non arde, o non crede, o non ha senso/core.	o	11	either does not burn, does not believe, or has no feeling/heart.

Appendix G: The wills

At his death, Atto left two final wills: one covering his holdings in France and the other those in Italy. For details on the division, see chapter 7. Here, I reproduce the two versions.

The Italian will

(from a copy included in the volume of official family papers preserved at I Fn, Tordi 350, pp. 264–72)

Avanti Pauolo Ballin, e Matteo Antonio Gaillardie Consiglieri del Re Notari Guardanote, e Guarda Sigilli di Sua Maestà nel Castelletto di Parigi sottoscritti, fu presente il Sig. Atto Melani Abbate di Beaubec abitante in Parigi nella Via de Vecchi Agostiniani Parrocchia S. Eustachio, Italiano di Nazione Naturalizzato Francese, per la Dio Grazia in perfetta salute di Corpo, e sano di mente, memoria, et intendimento, come è apparso a Notari sottoscritti per le sue parole, e facciamo fede averlo trovato nella sua camera in un'appartamento distaccato dal corpo dell'appartamento a sinistra nell'entrare di un Palazzo, che sta nella detta strada de' Vecchi Agostiniani appartenente al Sig. Montelon Uffizziale de' Moschettieri del Re, quale nella Reflessione della Morte, della quale l'ora è incerta, ha fatto, decretato, e nominato quello suo Testamento, et Ordinanza di ultima volontà a i Notari sottoscritti a riguardo de' Beni a lui spettanti situati, e stabiliti in Italia, secondo che segue. Primieramente ha raccomandato l'Anima sua a Dio Creatore del Cielo, e della Terra pregandolo per i meriti infiniti della Morte, e Passione di Nostro Signor Gesù Cristo a volergli perdonare le sue offese, e quando sarà la sua anima separata dal corpo, collocarla nel Luogo de' Beati.

Vuole, et ordina che se ha qualche debito in Italia, che i suoi Debiti siano pagati sopra i Beni d'Italia per i suoi Esecutori Testamentarj, qui sotto nominati; Egli dona e lassa al Signor Luigi Melani suo Nipote abitante in Pistoja nello stato del serenissimo Gran Duca di Toscana un Palazzo, e Dependenze di quello situato nella detta città di Pistoja al Corso, ed al medesimo tutti gli mobili, argenterie, et altre compreso ancora le gioje, quali il detto Signor Testatore ha voluto lassare l'uso alla moglie del detto Signor Melani suo Nipote. Un'altra casa, e dependenze, che risiede nel medesimo luogo dirimpetto alla sopraddetta, che serve di rimessa, stalla, e granaro, et alloggio della servitù.

Un'altra casa situata nella detta Città nella Parrocchia di San Pauolo, dove abita attualmente la sorella del detto Signor Testatore, della quale Ella ne ha l'uso per la sua Vita durante; come ancora le dependenze, e circostanze di quella.

Un Gran Podere con casa, e Terre, e Fabbriche, ed appartenenze possedute avanti dal Signor Cavalier Sozzifanti, situate tra Pistoja, e Fiorenza.

Un'altra Possessione, che si chiama Batocchio vicino alla detta Città di Pistoja, Terre, e Fabbriche, e Dependenze.

Una Terra chiamata Castel Nuovo situata vicino alla Città di Pistoja, Casa, Terre, Boschi, Eredità, e Dependenze di Essa, tutti gli Mobili, e Bestiami, che vi si trovavano attualmente.

Tutti gli luoghi di Monte Comprati, e costituiti dal Serenissimo Gran Duca sopra i Monti del Sale di Firenze, e generalmente tutti gli altri Beni mobili, et immobili, che possono, e potessero appartenere al detto Signor Testatore in Italia al giorno della sua Morte; il tutto proveniente dall'Acquisto, che ne ha fatto de' suoi Denari, quali dona, e lasso il detto Signor Testatore al detto Signor Luigi Melani suo Nipote a condizione però, che non possa in nessuna maniera ne vendere, ne impegnare, ne alicnare alcuno de' suddetti Beni Mobili, ed Immobili, che dovranno stare, come un Fondo Stabile, come il Signor Testatore stabilisce, e vuole per il presente suo Testamento ai Figliuoli Maschi da nascere di legittimo Matrimonio del detto Luigi Melani, uno succedendo all'altro, le Femmine essendo escluse; Volendo che l'Usufrutto sia riservato al detto Signor Luigi Melani sua vita durante solamente, ed in mancanza de' suoi Figli Maschi, il detto Signor Testatore vuole, et ordina, che la detta sostituzione passi a profitto del detto Domenico Melani fratello del detto Signor Luigi Melani, e morendo questo a benefizio de' Figliuoli Maschi di detto Domenico Melani, così l'uno succeda all'altro; ad effetto della qual sostituzione, e per la sicurtà di quella il detto Signor Testatore vuole, et intende, che immediatamente dopo la sua Morte, se non fosse stato fatto avanti, che sia fatto in presenza di detto Signor Domenico Melani un buono, e fedele Inventario di tutti questi Beni Mobili, ct Immobili appartenenti al detto Signor Testatore, situati, e stabiliti in Italia, delli quali il detto Signor Luigi Melani sarà tenuto d'incaricarsi del tutto per renderne conto alla detta sostituzione, senza che ne possa dissipare cosa alcuna; e per levare tutta le difficoltà, che potessero succedere al sopraddetto della Denunzia fatta per il Signor Domenico Melani avanti il [illeg.] Notaro della Città di Pistoja li 18 Novembre 1705 Et altri Atti, che potessero essere stati fatti da lui, e a fine, che il detto Signor Domenico Melani possa godere pacificamente tanto degli Effetti della detta sostituzione, che degli altri Beni situati in Francia, quali il detto Signor Testatore ha disposto a favore del detto Signor Domenico Melani per un'altro Testamento particolare passato avanti gli Notari sottoscritti questo giorno, del quale ne avrà La Minuta Gaillardie, uno di quelli, che il detto Signor Testatore conferma tanto che bisogno sia, o sarà, e per prevenire tutte le Contestazioni, il detto Signor Testatore vuole, et intende, che il detto Signor Domenico Melani sia ristabilito in tutti i suoi Dritti, Nomi, Ragioni, et Azioni non ostante la detta rinonziazione, come avrebbe potuto fare avanti di quella a condizione espressa, che il detto Signor Luigi Melani sarà tenuto d'astenersene, come s'è detta. Renonzia non fosse stata fatta, ne ammessa, istituendo il detto Signor Luigi Melani per il detto Signor Testatore a Carico e condizione, come sopra suo Erede Universale di tutti i suddetti Beni d'Italia senza altra eccezione, e riserva, che cinque cento scudi moneta di Roma, che il detto Signor Testatore ha sborsato de' suoi proprj Denari per terminare il Prezzo della Libreria, della quale gode presentemente il detto Signor Domenico Melani; la qual somma di Scudi Cinquecento Moneta di Roma il detto Signor Testatore dona, e lassa al detto Signor Domenico Melani. Sarà tenuto il detto Signor Luigi Melani dall'istante della Morte di detto Signor Testatore, e che il presente Testamento sarà venuto in sua cognizione di far dire, e celebrare in tale quale Chiesa, che desidera della detta Città di Pistoja il numero di Cinque Cento Messe Basse di Requiem all'Intenzione, e per il riposo dell'Anima di detto Signor Testatore.

Succedendo, che il detto Signor Luigi Melani contrastasse, e dibattesse le condizioni del presente Testamento, o alcuno di quelli, o non l'esequisse in tutto, il detto Signor Testatore vuole, et intende, che resti privato, et escluso di tutti li Beni, mobili, et Immobili sopraddetti lassatigli, e che tutti gli detti Beni Mobili, et Immobili passino in testa, ed a profitto, e Benefizio di detto Signor Domenico Melani suo Fratello istituito dal detto Signor Testatore in detto caso suo Erede Universale di tutti gli suddetti Beni d'Italia, a condizione sempre detta sostituzione in favore de' Figliuoli Maschi, come è stato qui sopra spiegato.

Et accadendo la mancanza dei Figli Maschi dell'uno, e dell'altro Signori Luigi, e Domenico Melani, gli detti Beni apparterranno alle loro Figlie per l'Usufrutto solamente, riservando il Fondo agli Figli, che nasceranno da quelle di legittimo Matrimonio, dovendosi sempre principiare dai Maschi all'esclusione delle Femmine; e per mancanza de' Figlj maschi alle Femmine colle medesime condizioni come sopra, et in mancanza di Linea del Signori Luigi e Domenico Melani, e de' loro Figlj, al giorno della loro morte li suddetti Beni saranno amministrati dalla Congregazione di S. Atto di Pistoja a perpetuità per le Rendite di tutti i suddetti Beni doppo la Riparazione, e spese pagate, e piacerà sopra di questi essere impiegati per gli detti amministratori della detta Congregazione i frutti di detti Beni serviranno per dotarsi povere Fanciulle del detto luogo, e città di Pistoja per maritarsi, o monacarsi da dargli Cinquanta scudi Moneta Fiorentina per ciascuna Dote, al quale effetto le suddette Povere Fanciulle, che vorranno presentarsi per ottenere questa Dote si faranno scrivere sopra il Registro di detta Congregazione, allorché si troverà un Fondo sufficiente della detta Entrata per fare dette Doti di Cinquanto scudi moneta Fiorentina per ciascheduna di quelle; al Prete, che averà celebrato la Messa della detta congregazione il giorno, e Festa di Sant'Atto tirerà a sorte il numero di dette povere Fanciulle, descritte sopra il detto Registro per sapere quelle Prime, che averanno la sorte di dette Doti fino alla somma dell'Entrate, che vi saranno.

E per esequire, e terminare il presente Testamento, e per augumentare piuttosto che diminuire, il detto Signor Testatore ha nominato, e dichiarato il Signor Abbate Gondi Ministro, e Segretario di Stato del Serenissimo Gran Duca di Toscana, et il Signor Gran Priore Del Bene Maestro di Camera di S. A. il Serenissimo Gran Duca di Toscana, e uno dei due in mancanza dell'uno, e dell'altro, pregandogli di prendersi l'incomodo, e di dargli questo ultimo contrassegno del loro Affetto. Revocandosi per detto Signor Testatore tutti gli altri Testamenti, e Codicilli, che Egli potesse aver fatto avanti di questo concernenti la disposizione de' suoi Beni situati in Italia, e particolarmente il Testamento autenticato avanti da Lui fatto secondo l'Uso di Firenze, che deve trovarsi nell'Archivio Pubblico di Firenze, qualsisia causa derogatoria da derogarsi, volendo, et ordinando, che il presente Testamento per la disposizione de' suoi Beni d'Italia sia esequito secondo la sua forma, e tenore di questa sua ultima volontà, et Istituzione.

Questo fu fatto, dettato, e Nominato dal detto Sig. Testatore a detti Notari sottoscritti a lui l'Uno, e l'altro presenti letto, e riletto, attestando averlo bene inteso, e vi ha persistito nella Camera sopraddetta, che risponde sul Cortile, e su le Rimesse delle Carrozze l'anno 1710 li due di settembre alle 10 ore della mattina, et ha sottoscritto il presente, e la minuta di questo essendo appresso il Signor Gaillardie l'Uno di detti Notari sottoscritti.

Atto Melani
Ballin Gaillardie

The French will

(from a copy included in the letter from Domenico Melani to Carlo Antonio Gondi, from Paris, January 8, 1714)

Pardevant M.rs Paul Ballin et Mathieu Antoine Gaillardie Conseilleurs du Roy nottaires au Chatelet de Paris soussignez fut présent M.r Atto Melani cy devant Abbé de Beaubec demeurant à Paris rue plastrière parroisse Sainte-Eustache Italien de Nation naturalisé François par la grâce de Dieu en parfaite santé de Corps, d'ailleurs sain d'esprit, mémoire et entendement, comme il est apparu aux nottaires soussignez par ses paroles et maintient, trouvé dans sa chambre au premier appartement ayant veüe d'un costé sur ladite rue platrière et de l'autre costé sur la Court: habillé et assis dans son fauteuil: lequel dans la veüe de la mort dont l'heure est incertaine, a fait, dicté, nommé son testament et ordonnance de dernière volonté aux nottaires soussignez pour le regard des biens à luy appartenant scituez et deus dans le Royaume de France selon et ainsy qu'il ensuit Premièrement a Recommandé son âme à Dieu Créateur du Ciel et de la Terre le priant par les mérites infinis de la mort et Passion de Notre Seigneur Jésus Christ luy pardonner ses fautes et offences, et lorsque son âme sera séparée de son Corps la colloquer au rang des bienheureux. Veut et ordonne ses dettes être payées et torts faits si aucun y a réparez et amendez par son Exécuteur Testamentaire cy après nommé.

Item veut et ordonne son corps mort être Inhumé et enterré sans aucune pompe et avec le plus de simplicité que faire se pourra dans l'Église des Révérends Pères Capucins de la vie Saint-Honoré de dette ville de Paris suivant la permission qui luy en a été accordée par écrit le 21 Juillet mil six cent soixante et quatorze par le Révérend Père Bonnaventure Revannatty [*sic*] pour lors Procureur et Commissaire général de l'ordre de Saint-François Capucin les priant d'agréer ce témoignage d'affection envers leurs ordre et de vouloir bien prier Dieu pour le repos de son âme voulant et ordonnant qu'il leur soit fais une aumône de la somme de cent livres une fois payée pour l'ouverture de la fosse et qu'il leur soit donné pareille somme de cent livres une fois payée saurois cinquante livres pour une grande messe le lendemain de son inhumation et les autres cinquante livres pour la rétribution de cent messes basses de Requiem qui seront dittes en leur Église à son intention et pour le repos de son âme le plustost que faire le pourra.

Item veut et ordonne qu'il soit dit et célébré en l'Église des R. P. Théatins de cette Ville le nombre ce cent messes Basses de Requiem à son intention et pour le repos de son âme pour la rétribution des quelles sera payé la somme de cinquante livres.

Item veut et ordonne qu'il soit dit et célébré en L'Église des R. P. Augustins déchaussez de la place des Victoires pareil nombre de cent messes basses de Requiem pour le repos de son âme pour la rétribution desquelles Il sera payé pareille somme de cinquante livres.

Item veut et ordonne qu'il soit dit et celebré en l'Eglise des RR. PP. Augustins du Grand Couvent de Paris pareil nombre de cent messes basses de Requiem pour le repos de son âme pour la retribution des quelles sera payé pareille somme de cinquante livrcs.

Item veut et ordonne qu'il soit dit et célébré dans l'Église des Cordeliers du Grand Couvent de Paris pareil nombre de cent messes basses de Requiem à pareille intention que dessus pourquoy sera payé semblable somme de cinquante livres. Item veut et ordonne qu'il soit dit et célébré en L'Église des Saints Péres Jacobins de la rüe Saint-Honoré le nombre de cinquante messes basses de Requiem à même intention que dessus pourquoy sera payé vingtcinq livres.

Item veut et ordonne qu'il soit dit en l'Église des Feuillans de la rüe Sainte-Honoré pareil nombre de cinquante messes basses de Requiem à même intention que dessus pourquoy sera payé pareille somme de vingtcinq livres. Item veut et ordonne qu'il soit manuellement délivré et distribué par le sieur son Éxecuteur Testimentaire cy après nommé le jour de son enterrement ou le plutost que faire se pourra à cinq cens pauvres la valleur de quatre sols à chacun d'eux, dans laquelle distribution, sera observé de la faire particulièrement aux femmes qui ont de pauvres petits enfants.

Item donne et lègue au nommé Champigny son valet de chambre en cas qu'il soit à son service lors de son décèds deux cent livres de rentes et pension viagère par chacun an la vie durant seulement du Sieur Champigny laquelle rente aura cours à compter du jour du Décèds du Sieur Testateur sans être obligé d'en faire demande en justice, à l'avoir et prendre généralement sur tous et chacuns les biens qui se trouveront appartenir au Sieur Testateur au jour et heure de son décèds scituez et deus en France, Ou la somme de mil livres une fois payée au choix du Sieur Champigny le tous outre les gages qui se trouveront luy être deüs au jour du décèds du Sieur Testateur, Et si le Sieur Champigny fait choix de ladite pension viagère au lieu de ladite somme de mil livres une fois payée, en ce cas le fond et propriété desdits deux cent livres de rente après le décèds du sieur Champigny demeurera réunis au fond et propriété des biens compris au Legs Universel cy après des biens appartenants audit Sieur Testateur scituez et deus dans le Royaume de France.

Item donne et lègue à sa Cuisinière qui se trouvera à son service lors de son décèds la somme de cinquante livres une fois payée outre les gages qui se trouveron luy être deus. Déclare le dit Sieur Testateur qu'il possède des biens de différentes natures les uns scituez dans l'État de Florence en Italie et les autres en France; Qu'à l'égard de eux scituez en Italie Il en a disposé par un testament particulier receu par les nottaires soussignez le 2.e Septembre 1710 dont il y a minutte vers Gaillardie l'un d'iceux en faveur de Louis Melani son neveu aux charges et conditions y portées, lequel Testament pour le regard desdits biens d'Italie le dit sieur Testateur veut et entend être exécuté selon sa forme et teneur, le conformant d'abondant par celuy cy, et par ce moyen il ne luy reste plus à disposer que du surplus de ses biens scituez et deus en France après le présent testament accomply, lesquels biens consistent en plusieurs parties de rente sur l'hôtel de cette ville de Paris, en deniers comptants Voinselle [?] d'argent, meubles meublans, batterie de Cuisinne linge de Table et de six chevaux de carosse et autres effets mobiliers, et d'autant qu'il a plu à Sa Majesté par une grâce particulière d'accorder au sieur Louis Melani et à Dominique Melani ses deux neveux des lettres de Naturalité avec dispense de résidence dans le Royaume de France, Et que par lesdites lettres Sa M.té leur a permis de recueillir la succession du dit Sieur Testateur leur oncle, a ces causes iceluy Sieur Testateur ayant comme dit est disposé en faveur du sieur Louis Melani de ses biens d'Italie, Il a par le présent son Testament, donné et légué, donne et lègue audit Dominique Melani son autre Neveu avocat et secrétaire de la consulte de Sienne natif de la Ville de Pistoye en Italie, le surplus de tous ses biens meubles et immeubles appartenants au Sieur Testateur et qui se troveront appartenir au jour et heure de son décèds scituez et deus en France après le présent Testament accomply sans aucune exception ni réserve a quoy que le tout puisse monter concister et valoir, l'institnant [*sic*] pour cet effect son légataire universel en tous sesdits biens meubles et immeubles scituez et deus en France pour en disposer par luy sieur Dominique Melani en toute propriété et comme de chose luy appartenant, Et sans donner aucune atteinte ni préjudicier à la substitution faite en sa faveur des biens scituez en Italie par le susdit Testament du deux Septembre 1710 fautes d'enfens masles du dit Sieur Louis Melani, Et pour exécuter et accomplir le présent testament iceluy augmenter plutost que de diminuer, le dit Sieur Testateur a nommé et esleu la personne de Monsieur Prailly premier commis de Monseigneur le Marquis de Torcy Ministre et Sécrétaire d'État le priant de luy fait par son présent Testament de son Crucifix d'Ivoir qui est auprès du liet du Sieur Testateur, Révoquant par le dit Sieur Testateur tous autres testamens et codiciles qu'il pourroit avoir faits pour la disposition de sesdits biens scituez en France avant le présent auquel seul il s'arrête comme étant sa dernier volonté et intention Ce fut fait dicté et nommé par le dit Sieur Testateur auxdits nottaires soussignez et a luy part l'un d'eux l'autre présent leu et réleu qu'il a dit avoir bien entendu et y a persisté en la chambre sus désignée l'an 1713 le 5.e de Juin sur les unzes du matin et a signé la minutte des présentes demeurées a Gaillardie nottaire, Signé Ballin et Gaillardie avec paraphe et Scitté.

   [Codicil]

Et le quinzième jour de décembre audit an mil sept cens treinze sur les deux heures de relevée au mandement et réquisition du dit Sieur Melani les Conseillers du Roy nottaires au Châtelet de Paris soussignez se son transporté en la maison où demeure le dit Sieur Melani susdite vie platrière au même lieu et appartement désignez au dit testament, trouvé au liet malade de corps toutefois sain d'esprit mémoire et entendement, ainsy qu'il est apparu aux nottaires soussignez par ses paroles et maintient, lequel a requis les dits nottaires soussignez de luy faire lecture de son dit testament, ce qu'ayant été fait dicté et nommé aux dits nottaires ce qui suit. C'est à savoir qu'au lieu de ce qu'il a ordonné par le dit testament son corps mort être inhumé et enterré en L'Église des RR.PP. Capucins de la rüe Saint-Honoré de cette Ville Il veut et ordonne que son dit Corps soit inhumé et enterré en l'Église des RR.PP. Augustins déschaussez de la place des Victoires de cette ditte ville, Et que les deux cens livres qu'il avoit ordonné d'être payé audit Couvent des Capucins pour les causes énoncées audit Legs porté par les dits Déschaussez Révoquant a cet effet le don et legs qui en aura été fait aux dits Reverends PP. Capucins, et au surplus confirme son dit testament des autres parts qu'il veut et entend être exécuté de point en point selon sa forme et teneur; Ce fut ainsy fait dicté et nommé par les Codicillians aux dits Nottaires Soussignez et à luy par l'un d'eux l'autre présent leu et releu qu'il a dit avoir bien entendre et y a persisté en la chambre où il est comme dit est [*sic*] assisté les jour et an que dessus et a déclaré ne pouvoir quant a présent écrire ni signer de ce enquis suivant l'ordonnance à cause de sa foiblesse, de saveüe causée par la maladie dont il est atteint par son grand âge ainsy qu'il est dit en la minutte des présentes étant au pied du dit Testament des autres parts le tous demeuré au dit Monsieur Gaillardie Nottaire Signé Balin et Gaillardie aux paraphe et Scitté.

Appendix H: The cabinet in the "Salotto dell'Abbate Melani," from the inventory of 1782

The following is taken from a detailed inventory of the Melani household conducted in 1782 (and preserved in I Fn, Tordi 350). Each of the rooms and its contents is described in turn. One room was still at that time referred to as the "Parlor of Abate Melani" (described on pp. 59–64). Many of its contents seem to date to Atto's lifetime, as if the room were left mostly untouched. Of particular interest is the listing of the contents of the cabinet containing the volumes of Atto's correspondence, a record of the materials once held by the family and now mostly lost (see chapter 7). I reproduce that part of the inventory here.

Catalogo di Numero Cento Dieci Libri Manoscritti, che si conservano nello scaffale chiuso con sportelli di Vetro, de' quali molti furono stampati in Francese senza nome dell'Autore.

> I. Palco
>
> Relazione del Pontificato di Clemente IX
>
> Ministero del Cardinale Mazzarrino
>
> Dieta di Francfort
>
> Promozione de' Cardinali di Buglione, d'Estrees, e Bonsi Tomi III
>
> Corte di Roma dall'Anno 1670 al 1688
>
> Progetto di Pace tra l'Imperatore, ed il Re di Francia
>
> Prerogativa ottenuta dall'Ambasciator di Venezia alla Corte di Francia
>
> Ministero del Marchese di Torcy Tomi VI
>
> Affari di Baviera Tomi due
>
> Pace de' Pirenei
>
> Pretenzioni della Duchessa d'Orleans contro l'Elettor Palatino
>
> Differenze del Principe di Monaco in Roma
>
> Affari del Duca di Modana Tomi II
>
> Lettere del Cardinal Litta Tomi II

Testamento Politico del Cardinale de Richelieu Tomi II

Descrizione di Quattro Conclavi

Elezione del Pontefice

Lettere del Cardinal Delfino

Lettere dell'Ambasciatore Erizzo

Lettere del Cardinale Ottoboni

Pontificato d'Innocenzo XI

Pontificato di Clemente IX

Non può esser Papa, chi non è Cardinale

II. Palco

Lettere dell'Ab. Gondi Ministro di Stato del Gran Duca di Toscana Tomi XIV

Lettere del Gran Duca di Toscana Cosimo III. Tomi IV

Minute di Lettere dell'Ab. Melani al Gran Duca di Toscana, e suo Ministro Tomi X

Lettere Diverse

Memorie Curiose, e belle

Lettere di Cardinali

Memorie dall'anno 1683 fino all'anno 1707 Tomi VI

III. Palco

Lettere Famigliari dell'Ab. Melani Tomi XV

Lettere Curiose, ed utili

Viaggio di Baviera Tomi II

Lettere del Cardinale di Janson Tomi III

Lettere del Cardinale di Estrees

Lettere di Diversi Cardinali

Lettere di M.ʳ Pomponne

Lettere di Varj Ambasciatori

Lettere di Personaggi Distinti

Lettere del Cardinale Bonvisi

Lettere del Cardinale Francesco Bonvisi Tomi IV

Lettere del Monsig. Tanara

Lettere del Cavaliere Erizzo

Lettere del Cardinale Delfino

Promozioni de' Cardinali d'Estrees, e Bonsy

Promozioni de' Suddetti Tomi II

Works cited

Published, secondary

Accorsi, Maria Grazia, introduction to *Scherzi e favole per musica*, by Francesco De Lemene, ed. Maria Grazia Accorsi, Il lapazio: Collezione di letteratura italiana moderna, no. 10 (Bologna: Mucchi, 1992).

Acton, Harold, *The Last Medici* (London: Faber and Faber, 1932).

Ademollo, A[lessandro], "Un campanaio e la sua famiglia," *Fanfulla della Domenica*, December 30, 1883.

  I primi fasti della musica italiana a Parigi (1642–1662) (Milan: Ricordi, [1884]).

Adler, Guido, ed., *Musikalische Werke der Kaiser Ferdinand III., Leopold I. und Joseph I*, 2 vols. (Vienna: Artaria, [1892]).

  "Umfang, Methode und Ziel der Musikwissenschaft" in *Music in European Thought, 1851–1912*, ed. Bojan Bujić, trans. Martin Cooper, Cambridge Readings in the Literature of Music (Cambridge: Cambridge University Press, 1988), 348–55, originally published in *Vierteljahrsschrift für Musikwissenschaft* 1 (1885): 5–8, 15–20.

Ambros, August Wilhelm, *Geschichte der Musik*, vol. IV, [ed. G. Nottebohm] (Leipzig: Leuckart, 1878).

Amelang, James S., "The Bourgeois," in *Baroque Personae*, ed. Rosario Villari, trans. Lydia G. Cochrane (Chicago: University of Chicago Press, 1995), 314–33, originally published as *L'uomo barocco*, Storia e Società (Rome: Laterza, 1991).

Angeli, Monica Maria, *et al.*, eds., *Dal manoscritto al fumetto: Cinque anni di acquisti in antiquariato 1991–1995* (Florence: Ministero per i Beni Culturali e Ambientali and Biblioteca Marucelliana / Manent, 1995).

Annibaldi, Claudio, "Introduzione" to *La musica e il mondo: Mecenatismo e committenza musicale in Italia tra Quattro e Settecento*, ed. Claudio Annibaldi, Polifonie: Musica e spettacolo nella storia (Bologna: Società Editrice il Mulino, 1993), 9–43.

  "Towards a Theory of Musical Patronage in the Renaissance and Baroque: The Perspective from Anthropology and Semiotics," *Recercare* 10 (1998): 173–82.

Ariès, Philippe, introduction to *A History of Private Life*, vol. III, *Passions of the Renaissance*, ed. Roger Chartier, trans. Arthur Goldhammer (Cambridge, Mass., and London: Harvard University Press/Belknap Press, 1989).

Arkhipov, Nikolai Il'ich, *Bartolomeo Karlo Rastrelli: 1675–1744* (Leningrad: Iskusstvo, 1964).

Asor Rosa, Alberto, *La lirica del Seicento*, Letteratura italiana Laterza, no. 28 (Rome: Laterza, 1975).

Austern, Linda Phyllis, "'Alluring the Auditorie to Effiminacie': Music and the Idea of the Feminine in Early Modern England," *Music and Letters* 74 (1993): 343–54.

Baggiani, Franco, "I maestri di cappella nella cattedrale di Pistoia," *Bollettino storico pistoiese* 3rd ser., 21 (1986): 41–81.

Bangen, Johann Heinrich, *Die römische Curie, ihre gegenwärtige Zusammensetzung un ihr Geschäftsgang* (Münster: Aschendorffschen Buchhandlung, 1854).

Barbagli, Marzio, *Sotto lo stesso tetto: Mutamenti della famiglia in Italia dal XV al XX secolo*, Saggi, no. 267 (Bologna: Il Mulino, 1984).

Barbier, Patrick, *La maison des italiens: Les castrats à Versailles* (Paris: Bernard Grasset, 1998).

Barkan, Leonard, *Transuming Passion: Ganymede and the Erotics of Humanism* (Stanford: Stanford University Press, 1991).

Barnett, Gregory, "Modal Theory, Church Keys, and the Sonata at the End of the Seventeenth Century," *Journal of the American Musicological Society* 51 (1998): 245–81.

Batowski, Zygmunt, "B.-C. Rastrelli en France: Le tombeau du marquis de Pomponne," *Gazette des beaux-arts*, series 6, no. 5, part 12 (October 1934): 137–43.

Battaglia, Salvatore, ed., *Grande Dizionario della lingua italiana* (Turin: U.T.E.T., 1988).

Beani, Gaetano, ed., *La chiesa pistoiese dalla sua origine ai tempi nostri: Appunti storici* (Pistoia: Fratelli Bracali, 1883).

Beaussant, Philippe, *Lully, ou, Le musicien du soleil* (Paris: Gallimard/ Théâtre des Champs-Elysées, 1992).

Bély, Lucien, *Espions et ambassadeurs au temps de Louis XIV* ([Paris]: Fayard, 1990).

Benoit, Marcelle, *Les événements musicaux sous le régne de Louis XIV: Chronologie*, La vie musicale en France sous les rois Bourbons, no. 33 (Paris: Picard, 2004).

Musiques de cour (1661–1733): Chapelle – chambre – écurie, La vie musicale en France sous les roi Bourbons, no. 20 (Paris: A. et J. Picard, 1971).

Versailles et les musiciens du roi 1661–1733: Étude institutionnelle et sociale, La vie musicale en France sous les rois Bourbons, no. 19 (Paris: A. et J. Picard, 1971).

Bérenger, Jean, *A History of the Habsburg Empire 1273–1700*, trans. C. A. Simpson (London: Longman, 1994), originally published as *Histoire de l'empire des Habsbourg* (Paris: Fayard, 1990).

Besutti, Paola, "Produzione e trasmissione di cantate romane nel mezzo del Seicento," in *La musica a Roma attraverso le fonti d'archivio*, ed. Bianca Maria Antolini, Arnaldo Morelli, and Vera Vita Spagnuolo, Strumenti della ricerca musicale, no. 2 (Lucca: Libreria Musicale Italiana, in association with the Archivio di Stato di Roma and the Società Italiana di Musicologia, 1994), 137–66.

Bevan, Bryan, *The Duchess Hortense: Cardinal Mazarin's Wanton Niece* (London: Rubicon Press, 1987).

Bianchi, Fulvio, and Paolo Russo, eds., *La scelta della misura: Gabriello Chiabrera, L'altro fuoco del barocco italiano* (Genoa: Costa & Nolan, 1993).

Bianconi, Lorenzo, "Il Cinquecento e il Seicento," in *Letteratura italiana*, vol. VI, *Teatro, musica, tradizione dei classici*, ed. Roberto Antonelli, Angelo Cicchetti, and Giorgio Inglese (Turin: Giulio Einaudi, 1986), 319–63.

    Music in the Seventeenth Century, trans. David Bryant (Cambridge: Cambridge University Press, 1987), originally published as *Il Seicento* (Turin: E.D.T., 1982).

Bianconi, Lorenzo, and Thomas Walker, "Dalla *Finta pazza* alla *Veremonda*: Storie di Febiarmonici," *Rivista italiana di musicologia* 10 (1975): 379–454.

Bielert, C.F., "The Effects of Early Castration and Testosterone Propionate Treatment on the Development and Display of Behavior Patterns by Male Rhesus Monkeys" (Ph.D. diss., Michigan State University, 1974).

Binni, W[alter], *L'Arcadia e il Metastasio* (Florence: La Nuova Italia, 1963).

Boggione, Valter, and Giovanni Casalegno, *Dizionario storico del lessico erotico italiano: Metafore, eufemismi, oscenità, doppi sensi, parole dotte e parole basse in otto secoli di letteratura italiana*, Teadue, no. 762 (Milan: Tascabili degli Editori Associati, 1999).

Bossy, John, "Godparenthood: The Fortunes of a Social Institution in Early Modern Christianity," in *Religion and Society in Early Modern Europe 1500–1800*, ed. Kaspar von Greyerz (London: The German Historical Institute / George Allen & Unwin, 1984), 194–201.

Bridges, David Merrell, "The Social Setting of *musica da camera* in Rome: 1667–1700" (Ph.D. diss., George Peabody College for Teachers, 1976).

Brinton, Selwyn, *The Gonzaga – Lords of Mantua* (London: Methuen and Co., 1927).

Browe, Peter, *Zur Geschichte der Entmannung: Eine religions- und rechts-geschichtliche Studie* (Breslau: Müller und Seiffert, 1936).

Brown, Peter, *The Body and Society: Men, Women, and Sexual Renunciation in Early Christianity* (New York: Columbia University Press, 1988).

Bruno, Silvia, "Musici e pittori tra Firenze e Roma nel secondo quarto del Seicento," *Studi secenteschi* 49 (2008): 185–207.

Bullough, Vern L., *Sexual Variance in Society and History* (New York: John Wiley and Sons, 1976).

Burke, Peter, *The Italian Renaissance: Culture and Society in Italy*, 2nd edn. (Princeton: Princeton University Press, 1987).

Burrows, David L., "The Cantatas of Antonio Cesti" (Ph.D. diss., Brandeis University, 1961).

Bush, M[ichael] L[accohee], *Rich Noble, Poor Noble*, vol. 2 of *The European Nobility* (Manchester and New York: Manchester University Press, 1988).

Bussi, Francesco, "I teatri d'opera a Piacenza prima della costruzione del Teatro Municipale (1804)," *Nuova rivista musicale italiana* 24 (1990): 457–64.

Calcaterra, Carlo, "La melica italiana della seconda metà del Cinquecento al Rolli e al Metastasio," in his *Poesia e canto: Studi sulla poesia melica italiana e sulla favola per musica* (Bologna: Nicola Zanichelli, 1951), 99–189.

Caluori, Eleanor, *The Cantatas of Luigi Rossi: Analysis and Thematic Index*, 2 vols., Studies in Musicology, no. 41 (Ann Arbor, Mich.: University Microfilms, 1981).

Campardon, Émile, *Les comédiens du roi de la troupe italienne pendant les deux derniers siècles: Documents inédits recueillis aux Archives Nationales*, 2 vols. (Paris: Berger-Levrault, 1880).

Campbell, Malcolm, *Pietro da Cortona at the Pitti Palace: A Study of the Planetary Rooms and Related Projects*, Princeton Monographs in Art and Archaeology, no. 41 (Princeton: Princeton University Press, 1977).

Canonica, Elvezio, introduction to *Raccolta di cantate a voce sola*, by Francesco De Lemene, ed. Elvezio Canonica, Biblioteca di scrittori italiani (Parma: Fondazione Pietro Bembo/Ugo Guanda, 1996).

Capponi, Pier Maria, "L'educazione di una virtuosa nel secolo XVII," *Lo spettatore musicale* 3 (1968): 12–15.

Capponi, V[ittorio], *Biografia pistoiese. . .* (Pistoia: Rossetti, 1878).

Carboni, Fabio, *Incipitario della lirica italiana dei secoli XV–XX*, 12 vols., Studi e testi, nos. 297–99, 321, 330, 334–35, 349–50, 370–72 (Rome: Biblioteca Apostolica Vaticana, 1982–94).

Cardinale, Flavia, introduction to *Sebastiano Baldini (1615–1685): Le poesie per musica nei codici della Biblioteca Apostolica Vaticana*, ed. Giorgio Morelli, Studi, Cataloghi e Sussidi Istituto di Bibliografia Musicale, no. 5, Progetti di ricerca bibliografica-musicale dell'IBIMUS, no. 5 (Rome: Istituto di Bibliografia Musicale, 2000).

Chafe, Eric, *Monteverdi's Tonal Language* (New York: Schirmer, 1992).

Chard, Chloe, "Effeminacy, Pleasure and the Classical Body," in *Feminity and Masculinity in Eighteenth-Century Art and Culture*, ed. Gill Perry and Michael Rossington (Manchester: Manchester University Press, 1994), 142–61.

Chéruel, A[dolphe], *Histoire de France sous le ministère de Mazarin (1651–1661)*, 3 vols. (Paris: Hachette, 1882).

Christout, Marie-Françoise, *Le ballet de cour de Louis XIV 1643–1672: Mises en scène*, La vie musicale en France sous les rois Bourbons, no. 12 (Paris: A. et J. Picard, 1967).

Cialdea, Basilio, *Gli stati italiani e la pace dei Pirenei: Saggio sulla diplomazia seicentesca*, Istituto di studi storico-politici, Università di Roma–Facoltà di scienze politiche, no. 8 (Milan: A. Giuffrè, 1961).

Ciampi, Sebastiano, *Bibliografia critica delle antiche reciproche corrispondenze politiche, ecclesiastiche, scientifiche, letterarie, artistiche dell'Italia colla Russia, colla Polonia ed altre parti settentrionali*, 3 vols. (Florence: Guglielmo Piatti, 1839).

Cochrane, Eric W., *Florence in the Forgotten Centuries 1527–1800: A History of Florence and the Florentines in the Age of the Grand Dukes* (Chicago: University of Chicago Press, 1973).

Tradition and Enlightenment in the Tuscan Academies 1690–1800 (Chicago: University of Chicago Press, 1961).

Coci, Laura, introduction to *L'Alcibiade fanciullo a scola*, by Antonio Rocco, ed. Laura Coci, 2nd edn., Faville, no. 22 (Rome: Salerno, 2003).

Colvin, Sarah, *The Rhetorical Feminine: Gender and Orient on the German Stage, 1647–1742*, Oxford Modern Languages and Literature Monographs (Oxford: Clarendon Press, 1999).

Covell, Roger, "Voice Register as an Index of Age and Status in Opera Seria," in *Opera and Vivaldi*, ed. Michael Collins and Elise K. Kirk (Austin: University of Texas Press, 1984), 193–210.

Cozzi, Gaetano, and Michael Knapton, *La repubblica di Venezia nell'età moderna: Dalla guerra di Chioggia al 1517*, vol. XII, book 1, of *Storia d'Italia* (Turin: UTET, 1986).

Crane, Thomas Frederick, *Italian Social Customs of the Sixteenth Century and Their Effect on the Literatures of Europe*, Cornell Studies in English (New Haven, Conn.: Yale University Press, 1920).

Cusick, Suzanne G., "Gendering Modern Music: Thoughts on the Monteverdi–Artusi Controversy," *Journal of the American Musicological Society* 46 (1993): 1–25.

Damerini, Adelmo, "La partitura de L'*Ercole in Tebe* di Jacopo Melani (1623–1676)," *Bullettino storico pistoiese* 19 (1917): 45–66.

Datson, Lorraine, and Katharine Park, "The Hermaphrodite and the Orders of Nature: Sexual Ambiguity in Early Modern France," in *Premodern Sexualities*, ed. Louise Fradenburg and Carla Freccero (New York: Routledge, 1996), 117–36.

Da Vinha, Mathieu, *Les valets de chambre de Louis XIV* (Paris: Perrin, 2004).

Della Libera, Luca, "La musica nella basilica di Santa Maria Maggiore a Roma, 1676–1712: Nuovi documenti su Corelli e sugli organici vocali e strumentali," *Recercare* 7 (1995): 87–161.

Della Seta, Fabrizio, "I Borghese (1691–1731): La musica di una generazione," *Note d'archivio per la storia musicale*, n.s., 1 (1983): 139–208.

Dent, Edward J., *Alessandro Scarlatti: His Life and Works*, 2nd edn. (London: Edward Arnold, 1960).

Dethan, Georges, *The Young Mazarin*, trans. Stanley Baron (London: Thames and Hudson, 1977), originally published as *Mazarin et ses amis* (Paris: Berger-Levrault, 1968).

Dixson, A.F., "Sexual and Aggressive Behaviour of Adult Male Marmosets (*Callithrix jacchus*) Castrated Neonatally, Prepubertally, or in Adulthood," *Physiology and Behaviour* 54 (1993): 301–7.

Dulong, Claude, *Marie Mancini: La première passion de Louis XIV* (Paris: Perrin, 1993).

Durante, Sergio, "Il cantante," in *Il sistema produttivo e le sue competenze*, vol. IV of *Storia dell'opera italiana*, ed. Lorenzo Bianconi and Giorgio Pestelli, Biblioteca di cultura musicale (Turin: E.D.T. Musica, 1987), 347–415.

   "The Opera Singer," in *Opera Production and Its Resources*, ed. Lorenzo Bianconi and Giorgio Pestelli, trans. Lydia G. Cochrane, The History of Italian Opera, part 2, "Systems," vol. 4 (Chicago and London: University of Chicago Press, 1998), 345–415.

Eisley, Irving Robert, "The Secular Cantatas of Mario Savioni (1608–85)" (Ph.D. diss., University of California, Los Angeles, 1964).

Elias, Norbert, *The Court Society*, trans. Edmund Jephcott (New York: Pantheon, 1983), originally published as *Die höfische Gesellschaft* (Darmstadt: Hermann Luchterhand, 1969).

Elwert, W. Theodor, *La poesia lirica italiana del Seicento: Studio sullo stile barocco*, Saggi di "Lettere italiane," no. 10 (Florence: Leo S. Olschki, 1967).

Versificazione italiana dalle origini ai giorni nostri (Florence: Felice Le Monnier, 1973).

Enggass, Robert, foreword to *The Life of Bernini*, by Filippo Baldinucci, trans. Catherine Enggass (University Park, Penn.: Pennsylvania State University Press, 1966), originally published as *Vita del Cavaliere Gio. Lorenzo Bernini* (Florence: V. Vangelisti, 1682).

Erspamer, Francesco, "Il primo Seicento" and "L'età del barocco," in *Manuale di letteratura italiana: Storia per generi e problemi*, vol. II, *Dal Cinquecento alla metà del Settecento*, ed. Franco Brioschi and Costanzo Di Girolamo (Turin: Bollati Boringhieri, 1994), 225–36 and 237–49.

Fabbri, Paolo, "Inediti monteverdiana," *Rivista italiana di musicologia* 15 (1980): 71–86.

Fanelli, Jean Grundy, "Un animatore della vita musicale pistoiese del Seicento: Monsignore Felice Cancellieri, sopranista," *Bollettino storico pistoiese*, 3rd ser., 24 (1989): 53–62.

"Castrato Singers from Pistoia, 1575–1660," *Civiltà musicale*, no. 40 (May–August 2000): 47–53.

A Chronology of Operas, Oratorios, Operettas, Cantatas and Miscellaneous Stage Works with Music Performed in Pistoia: 1606–1943 (Bologna: Edizioni Pendragon, 1998).

"Famiglie di cantanti pistoiesi nel secolo XVII," *Bullettino storico pistoiese*, 3rd ser., 34 (1999): 103–116.

"La musica patrocinata dai Rospigliosi: Il Collegio dei Nobili," *Bullettino storico pistoiese*, 3rd ser., 31 (1996): 113–28.

"La musica per la chiesa e l'oratorio di San Prospero nel Sei–Settecento," *Bollettino storico pistoiese*, 3rd ser., 25 (1990): 113–28.

Feldman, Martha, "Magic Mirrors and the *Seria* Stage: Thoughts toward a Ritual View," *Journal of the American Musicological Society* 48 (1995): 423–84.

Folena, Gianfranco, *L'italiano in Europa: Esperienze linguistiche del Settecento*, Einaudi Paperbacks, no. 139 (Turin: Giulio Einaudi, 1983).

Folman, Y., and R. Volcani, "Copulatory Behaviour of the Prepubertally Castrated Bull," *Animal Behavior* 14 (1966): 572–73.

Foresti, Fabio, "Il lessico della campana e del suono 'alla bolognese,'" in *Campanili e campane di Bologna e del Bolognese*, ed. Mario Fanti (Bologna: Grafis Edizioni, 1992), 257–74.

Fortune, Nigel, "Italian Secular Monody from 1600 to 1635: An Introductory Survey," *Musical Quarterly* 39 (1953): 171–95.

Frandsen, Mary E., "*Eunuchi conjugium*: The Marriage of a Castrato in Early Modern Germany," *Early Music History* 24 (2005): 53–124.

Frare, Pierantonio, "Antitesi, metafora e argutezza tra Marino e Tesauro," in *The Sense of Marino: Literature, Fine Arts and Music of the Italian Baroque*, ed. Francesco Guardiani, Literary Criticism Series, no. 5 (New York: Legas, 1994), 299–321.

Freitas, Roger, "*Un Atto d'ingegno*: A Castrato in the Seventeenth Century" (Ph.D. diss., Yale Univ., 1998).

"The Eroticism of Emasculation: Confronting the Baroque Body of the Castrato," *Journal of Musicology* 20 (2003): 196–249.

"Singing and Playing: The Italian Cantata and the Rage for Wit," *Music and Letters* 82 (2001): 509–42.

Fritz, Hans, *Kastratengesang: Hormonelle, konstitutionelle und pädagogische Aspekte*, Musikethnologische Sammelbände, vol. 13 (Tutzing: Hans Schneider, 1994).

Galluzzi, Riguccio, *Istoria del Granducato di Toscana sotto il governo della Casa Medici*, vol. VII (Florence: Gaetano Cambiagi, 1781).

Gambassi, Osvaldo, *"Pueri cantores" nelle cattedrali d'Italia tra medioevo e età moderna: Le scuole eugeniane: Scuole di canto annesse alle cappelle musicali*, "Historiae Musicae Cultores" Biblioteca, no. 80 (Florence: Leo S. Olschki, 1997).

Gandini, Alessandro, *Cronistoria dei teatri di Modena dal 1539 al 1871* (Modena: Tipografia Sociale, 1873).

Gerbino, Giuseppe, "The Quest for the Castrato Voice: Castrati in Renaissance Italy," *Studi musicali* 33 (2004): 303–57.

Gérin, Charles, *Louis XIV et le Saint-Siège*, 2 vols. (Paris: Victoire Lecoffre, 1894).

Gialdroni, Teresa M., "Bibliografia della cantata da camera italiana (1620–1740 ca.)," *Le fonti musicali in Italia: Studi e ricerche* 4 (1990): 31–131.

Gianturco, Carolyn, "The Italian Seventeenth-Century Cantata: A Textual Approach," in *The Well-Enchanting Skill: Music, Poetry, and Drama in the Culture of the Renaissance: Essays in Honour of F. W. Sternfeld*, ed. John Caldwell, Edward Olleson, and Susan Wollenberg (Oxford: Clarendon Press, 1990), 41–51.

Giazotto, Remo, "Nel CCC anno della morte di Antonio Cesti: Ventidue lettere ritrovate nell' Archivio di Stato di Venezia," *Nuova rivista musicale italiana* 3 (1969): 496–512.

Gilman, Todd S., "The Italian (Castrato) in London," in *The Work of Opera: Genre, Nationhood, and Sexual Difference*, ed. Richard Dellamora and Daniel Fischlin (New York: Columbia University Press, 1997), 49–70.

Glixon, Beth L., "New Light on the Life and Career of Barbara Strozzi," *Musical Quarterly* 81 (1997): 311–35.

"Recitative in Seventeenth-Century Venetian Opera: Its Dramatic Function and Musical Language" (Ph.D. diss., Rutgers Univ., 1985).

Glixon, Beth L., and Jonathan E. Glixon, *Inventing the Business of Opera: The Impresario and His World in Seventeenth-Century Venice*, AMS Studies in Music (Oxford: Oxford University Press, 2006).

Goldberg, Edward L., *Patterns in Late Medici Art Patronage* (Princeton: Princeton University Press, 1983).

After Vasari: History, Art, and Patronage in Late Medici Florence (Princeton: Princeton University Press, 1988).

Goldsmith, Elizabeth C., *"Exclusive Conversations": The Art of Interaction in Seventeenth-Century France* (Philadelphia: University of Philadelphia Press, 1988).

Greenblatt, Stephen, *Shakespearean Negotiations: The Circulation of Social Energy in Renaissance England*, The New Historicism: Studies in Cultural Poetics, vol. 4 (Berkeley: University of California Press, 1988).

Haar, James, "On Musical Games in the 16th Century," *Journal of the American Musicological Society* 15 (1962): 22–34.

Haas, Louis, *The Renaissance Man and His Children: Childbirth and Early Childhood in Florence 1300–1600* (New York: St. Martin's Press, 1998).

Hammond, Frederick, *Girolamo Frescobaldi: A Guide to Research*, Garland Composer Resource Manuals, vol. 9, Garland Reference Library of the Humanities, vol. 672 (New York: Garland, 1988).

Music and Spectacle in Baroque Rome (New Haven, Conn.: Yale University Press, 1994).

Heller, Wendy, *Emblems of Eloquence: Opera and Women's Voices in Seventeenth-Century Venice* (Berkeley: University of California Press, 2003).

"Reforming Achilles: Gender, *Opera seria* and the Rhetoric of the Enlightened Hero," *Early Music* 26 (1998): 562–81.

Heriot, Angus, *The Castrati in Opera* (1956; repr., New York: Da Capo Paperback, 1975).

Herlihy, David, *Medieval and Renaissance Pistoia: The Social History of an Italian Town, 1200–1430* (New Haven, Conn.: Yale University Press, 1967).

Hill, John Walter, "Oratory Music in Florence, II: At San Firenze in the Seventeenth and Eighteenth Centuries," *Acta musicologica* 51 (1979): 246–67.

"Oratory Music in Florence, III: The Confraternities from 1655 to 1785," *Acta musicologica* 58 (1986): 129–79.

"Le relazioni di Antonio Cesti con la corte e i teatri di Firenze," *Rivista italiana di musicologia* 11 (1976): 27–47.

Roman Monody, Cantata, and Opera from the Circles around Cardinal Montalto, 2 vols., Oxford Monographs on Music (Oxford: Clarendon Press, 1997).

Holford-Strevens, Leofranc, "'Her Eyes Became Two Spouts': Classical Antecedents of Renaissance Laments," *Early Music* 27 (1999): 379–93.

Holmes, William Carl, "*Orontea*: A Study of Change and Development in the Libretto and the Music of Mid-Seventeenth-Century Italian Opera" (Ph.D. diss., Columbia Univ., 1968).

Holzer, Robert Rau, "Music and Poetry in Seventeenth-Century Rome: Settings of the Canzonetta and Cantata Texts of Francesco Balducci, Domenico Benigni, Francesco Melosio, and Antonio Abati," 2 vols. (Ph.D. diss., University of Pennsylvania, 1990).

Hurteau, Pierre, "Catholic Moral Discourse on Male Sodomy and Masturbation in the Seventeenth and Eighteenth Centuries," *Journal of the History of Sexuality* 4 (1993): 1–26.

Imbert, Gaetano, *La vita fiorentina nel Seicento secondo memorie sincrone (1644–1670)* (Florence: R. Bemporad e Figlio, 1906).

Ingrao, Charles W., *The Habsburg Monarchy 1618–1815*, New Approaches to European History, 2nd edn. (Cambridge: Cambridge University Press, 2000).

International Dictionary of Medicine and Biology (New York: John Wiley and Sons, 1986).

Jander, Owen, "The Cantata in Accademia: Music for the *Accademia de' Dissonanti* and Their Duke, Francesco II d'Este," *Rivista italiana di musicologia* 10 (1975): 519–44.

Jannaco, Carmine, and Martino Capucci, *Il Seicento*, vol. VIII of *Storia letteraria d'Italia*, ed. A. Balduino, 3rd rev. edn. (Padua: Dr. Francesco Vallardi; Piccin Nuova Libraria, 1986).

Jarrard, Alice Grier, "Theaters of Power: Francesco I d'Este and the Spectacle of Court Life in Modena" (Ph.D. diss., Columbia Univ., 1993).

Jones, Ann Rosalind, and Peter Stallybrass, "Fetishizing Gender: Constructing the Hermaphrodite in Renaissance Europe," in *Body Guards: The Cultural Politics of Gender Ambiguity*, ed. Julia Epstein and Kristina Straub (New York: Routledge, 1991), 80–111.

Kamen, Henry, "The Statesman," in *Baroque Personae*, ed. Rosario Villari, trans. Lydia G. Cochrane (Chicago: University of Chicago Press, 1995), 9–31, originally published as *L'uomo barocco*, Storia e Società (Rome: Laterza, 1991).

Kettering, Sharon, "Gift-Giving and Patronage in Early Modern France," *French History* 2 (1988): 131–51.

Patrons, Brokers, and Clients in Seventeenth-Century France (New York: Oxford University Press, 1986).

Kirkendale, Warren, *The Court Musicians in Florence During the Principate of the Medici: With a Reconstruction of the Artistic Establishment*, "Historiae musicae cultores" biblioteca, no. 61 (Florence: Olschki, 1993).

Klapisch-Zuber, Christiane, "Parenti, amici, vicini: Il territorio urbano d'una famiglia mercantile nel XV secolo," *Quaderni storici* 33 (1976): 953–82.

Kleinman, Ruth, *Anne of Austria: Queen of France* (Columbus, Ohio: Ohio State University Press, 1985).

Kowaleski-Wallace, Beth, "Shunning the Bearded Kiss: Castrati and the Definition of Female Sexuality," *Prose Studies* 15 (1992): 153–70.

Laqueur, Thomas, *Making Sex: Body and Gender from the Greeks to Freud* (Cambridge, Mass.: Harvard University Press, 1990).

Laurain-Portemer, Madeleine, "La politique artistique de Mazarin," in *Il Cardinale Mazzarino in Francia: Colloquio italo–francese (Roma, 16–17 Maggio 1977)*, Atti dei Convegni Lincei, vol. 35 (Rome: Accademia Nazionale dei Lincei, 1977), 41–76.

Le Boeuf, Burney J., "Copulatory and Aggressive Behavior in the Prepubertally Castrated Dog," *Hormones and Behavior* 1 (1970): 127–36.

Leopold, Silke, "Al modo d'Orfeo: Dichtung und Musik im italienischen Sologesang des frühen 17. Jahrhunderts," *Analecta musicologica* 29 (1995): all (2 vols.).

  "Chiabrera und die Monodie: Die Entwicklung der Arie," *Studi musicali* 10 (1981): 75–106.

  "'Not Sex but Pitch': Kastraten als Liebhaber – einmal *über* der Gürtellinie betrachtet," in *Provokation und Tradition: Erfahrung mit der Alten Musik*, ed. Hans-Martin Linde and Regula Rapp (Stuttgart and Weimar: Verlag J.B. Metzler, 2000), 219–40.

Lescourret, Marie-Anne, *Rubens: A Double Life*, trans. Elfreda Powell (Chicago: Ivan R. Dee, 1993), originally published as *Rubens* ([Paris]: J.C. Lattès, 1990).

Levine, Laura, *Men in Women's Clothing: Anti-Theatricality and Effeminization, 1579–1642*, Cambridge Studies in Renaissance Literature and Culture, no. 5 (Cambridge: Cambridge University Press, 1994).

Line, Scott W., Benjamin L. Hart, and Linda Sanders, "Effect of Prepubertal Versus Postpubertal Castration on Sexual and Aggressive Behavior in Male Horses," *Journal of the American Veterinary Medical Association* 186 (1985): 249–51.

Lionnet, Jean, "La musique a Saint-Louis des Français de Rome au XVIIᵒ [*sic*] siècle," *Note d'archivio per la storia musicale*, n.s., 3 (1985): supplement; n.s., 4 (1986): supplement.

Lipschütz, Alexander, *The Internal Secretions of the Sex Glands: The Problem of the "Puberty Gland"* (Cambridge: W. Heffer and Sons, 1924).

Liuzzi, Fernando, *I musicisti in Francia*, vol. I, *Dalle origini al secolo XVII*, L'opera del genio italiano all'estero, second series (Rome: Edizioni d'arte Danesi, 1946).

Lorenzetti, Stefano, "'Per animare agli esercizi nobili': Esperienza musicale e identità nobiliare nei collegi di educazione," *Quaderni storici*, vol. 32, no. 95 (August 1997): 435–60.

Loschelder, Josef, "Neue Beiträge zu einer Biographie Giacomo Carissimis," *Archiv für Musikforschung* 5 (1940): 220–29.

Loy, James, *et al.*, *The Behavior of Gonadectomized Rhesus Monkeys*, Contributions to Primatology, no. 20 (Basel: Karger, 1984).

Macy, Laura W., "The Italian Madrigal and Renaissance Games" (paper presented at the annual meeting of the American Musicological Society, Minneapolis, October 1994).

Mamone, Sara, "Most Serene Brothers-Princes-Impresarios: Theater in Florence under the Management and Protection of Mattias, Giovan Carlo, and Leopoldo de' Medici," *Journal of Seventeenth-Century Music* 9 (2003), http://sscm-jscm.press.uiuc.edu/jscm/v9/no1/Mamone.html.

Mamone, Sara, ed., *Serenissimi fratelli principi impresari: Notizie di spettacolo nei carteggi medicei: Carteggi di Giovan Carlo de' Medici e di Desiderio Montemagni suo segretario (1628–1664)*, Storia dello spettacolo: Fonti, no. 3 (Florence: Le Lettere, 2003).

Maravall, José Antonio, *Culture of the Baroque: Analysis of a Historical Structure*, trans. Terry Cochran, Theory and History of Literature, vol. 25 (Minneapolis: University of Minnesota Press, 1986), originally published as *La cultura del barroco: Un análisis de una estructura histórica*, Letras e ideas, maior, vol. 7 (Esplugues de Llobregat [Spain]: Editorial Ariel, 1975).

Marcello, Luciano, "Società maschile e sodomia: Dal declino della 'polis' al principato," *Archivio storico italiano* 150 (1992): 137–71.

Martini, Gabriele, *Il "vitio nefando" nella Venezia del Seicento: Aspetti sociali e repressione di giustizia*, Collana della Facoltà di Lettere e Filosofia dell'Università di Venezia *in San Sebastiano*, sezione di studi storici 2; Materiali e Ricerche, n.s., 4 (Rome: Jouvence, 1988).

Masetti Zannini, G.L., "Virtù e crudezza: Scolari di canto e famiglie tra rinascimento e barocco," *Strenna dei romanisti* 41 (1980): 332–41.

Massip, Catherine, *La vie des musiciens de Paris au temps de Mazarin (1643–1661): Essai d'étude sociale*, La vie musicale en France sous les rois Bourbons, no. 24 (Paris: A. et J. Picard, 1976).

Masson, Giorgina, *Queen Christina* (New York: Farrar, Straus and Giroux, 1968).

Mazzoldi, Leonardo, Renato Giusti, and Rinaldo Salvadori, eds., *Mantova: La storia*, vol. III, *Da Guglielmo III Duca alla fine della seconda guerra mondiale*, Mantova: La storia, le lettere, le arti (Mantua: Istituto Carlo D'Arco per la storia di Mantova, 1963).

McClary, Susan, "Constructions of Gender in Monteverdi's Dramatic Music," in *Feminine Endings: Music, Gender, and Sexuality* (Minneapolis: University of Minnesota Press, 1991), 35–52.

Melani, Vasco, *Pistoia*, 2nd edn. (Pistoia: Tellini, 1970).

Melicow, Meyer M., "Castrati Singers and the Lost 'Cords,'" *Bulletin of the New York Academy of Medicine* 59 (1983): 749–54.

Merrick, Jeffrey, and Bryant T. Ragan, Jr., eds., *Homosexuality in Early Modern France: A Documentary Collection* (New York and Oxford: Oxford University Press, 2001).

Meyer, Jean, "Le cas Fouquet: Faut-il réhabiliter Fouquet?," in *Les années Fouquet: Politique, société, vie artistique et culturelle dans les années 1650*, ed. Chantal Grell and Klaus Malettke, Forschungen zur Geschichte der Neuzeit: Marburger Beiträge, vol. 2 (Münster: LIT, 2001), 11–33.

Middleton, W. E. Knowles, "A Cardinalate for Prince Leopoldo de' Medici," *Studi secenteschi* 11 (1970): 167–80.

Milner, Anthony, "The Sacred Capons," *Musical Times* 114 (1973): 250–52.

Mioli, Piero, "Per uno studio sulla cantata italiana del '600: L'opera di Cesti e di Stradella," in *Alessandro Stradella e Modena*, ed. Carolyn Gianturco (Modena: Teatro Comunale, 1985), 65–76.

Monaldi, Rita, and Francesco Sorti, *Imprimatur*, Omnibus (Milan: Arnaldo Mondadori, 2002).

    Secretum (Amsterdam: De Bezige Bij, Cargo, 2005).

Monaldi, Rita, and Francesco Sorti, eds., *Los secretos del cónclave* (Barcelona: Ediciones Salamandra, 2005).

Monaldini, Sergio, ed., *L'orto dell'Esperidi: Musici, attori e artisti nel patrocinio della famiglia Bentivoglio (1646–1685)*, ConNotazioni, no. 5 (Lucca: Libreria Musicale Italiana, 2000).

Mongredien, Georges, *L'affaire Foucquet* ([Paris]: Hachette, 1956).

Morelli, Arnaldo, "La musica a Roma nella seconda metà del Seicento attraverso l'archivio Cartari-Febei," in *La musica a Roma attraverso le fonti d'archivio*, ed. Bianca Maria Antolini, Arnaldo Morelli, and Vera Vita Spagnuolo, Strumenti della ricerca musicale, no. 2 (Lucca: Libreria Musicale Italiana in association with the Archivio di Stato di Roma and Società Italiana di Musicologia, 1994), 107–36.

Morelli, Giorgio, ed., *Sebastiano Baldini (1615–1685): Le poesie per musica nei codici della Biblioteca Apostolica Vaticana*, intro. Flavia Cardinale, Studi, Cataloghi e Sussidi Istituto di Bibliografia Musicale, no. 5,

Progetti di ricerca bibliografica-musicale dell'IBIMUS, no. 5 (Rome: Istituto di Bibliografia Musicale, 2000).

Müller, Wolfgang, *et al.*, *The Church in the Age of Absolutism and Enlightenment*, trans. Gunther J. Holst, vol. 6 of *History of the Church* (New York: Crossroad, 1981), originally published as *Die Kirche im Zeitalter des Absolutismus und der Aufklärung* (Freiburg: Herder, 1970).

Murata, Margaret, "Il carnevale a Roma sotto Clemente IX Rospigliosi," *Rivista italiana di musicologia* 12 (1977): 83–99.

Operas for the Papal Court 1631–1668, Studies in Musicology, no. 39 (Ann Arbor, Mich.: UMI Research Press, 1981).

"The Recitative Soliloquy," *Journal of the American Musicological Society* 32 (1979): 45–73

"Roman Cantata Scores as Traces of Musical Culture and Signs of Its Place in Society," in *Atti del XIV congresso della Società Internazionale di Musicologia: Trasmissione e recezione delle forme di cultura musicale*, vol. I, *Round Tables*, ed. Angelo Pompilio *et al.* (Turin: EDT, 1990), 272–84.

"Scylla and Charybdis, or Steering between Form and Social Context in the Seventeenth Century," in *Explorations in Music, the Arts, and Ideas: Essays in Honor of Leonard B. Meyer*, ed. Eugene Narmour and Ruth A. Solie, Festschrift Series, no. 7 (Stuyvesant, N.Y.: Pendragon Press, 1988), 67–85.

"Why the First Opera Given in Paris Wasn't Roman," *Cambridge Opera Journal* 7 (1995): 87–105.

Namias, Angelo, ed., *Storia di Modena* (1894; repr., Bologna: Atesa, 1987).

Nello Vetro, Gaspare, *Dizionario della musica e dei musicisti dei territori del Ducato di Parma e Piacenza*, Istituzione Casa della Musica, http://biblioteche2.comune.parma.it/dm/449.htm.

Newcomb, Anthony, *The Madrigal at Ferrara 1579–1597*, 2 vols., Princeton Studies in Music, no. 7 (Princeton: Princeton University Press, 1980).

"Secular Polyphony in the 16th Century," in *Performance Practice: Music before 1600*, ed. Howard Mayer Brown and Stanley Sadie, The Norton/Grove Handbooks of Music (New York and London: W. W. Norton, 1989), 222–39.

Pacini, Alfredo, ed., *La chiesa pistoiese e la sua cattedrale nel tempo: Repertorio di documenti*, 10 vols. (Pistoia: Editrice CRT, 1994).

Palisca, Claude V., "Marco Scacchi's Defense of Modern Music (1649)," in *Words and Music, the Scholar's View: A Medley of Problems and Solutions Compiled in Honor of A. Tillman Merritt by Sundry Hands*, ed. Laurence Berman ([Cambridge, Mass.]: Harvard University Department of Music, 1972), 189–235.

Pastor, Ludwig, *The History of the Popes from the Close of the Middle Ages*, trans. Ernest Graf, 40 vols. (London: Kegan Paul, Trench, Trubner and Co., 1891–1953).

Pekacz, Jolanta T., "Memory, History and Meaning: Musical Biography and Its Discontents," *Journal of Musicological Research* 23 (2004): 39–80.

Pelous, Jean-Michel, *Amour précieux, amour galant (1654–1675): Essai sur la réprésentation de l'amour dans la littérature et la société mondaines*, Bibliothèque française et romane, ser. C, vol. 77 (Paris: Librairie Klincksieck, 1980).

Pennington, D[onald] H., *Europe in the Seventeenth Century*, A General History of Europe, 2nd edn. (London: Longman, 1989).

Peschel, Enid Rhodes, and Richard E. Peschel, "Medical Insights into the Castrati in Opera," *American Scientist* 75 (1987): 578–83.

   "Medicine and Music: The Castrati in Opera," *Opera Quarterly* 4, no. 4 (1987): 21–38.

Pirrotta, Nino, *Don Giovanni in musica: Dall'*Empio punito *a Mozart*, Musica Critica, Saggi Marsilio (Venice: Marsilio, 1991).

Prunières, Henry, "The Italian Cantata of the XVII Century," *Music and Letters* 7 (1926): 38–48, 120–32.

   "Les musiciens du Cardinal Antonio Barberini," in *Mélanges de musicologie offerts a M. Lionel de la Laurencie*, Publications de la Société Française de Musicologie, ser. 2, vols. 3–4 (Paris: La Société Française de Musicologie / E. Droz, 1933), 117–22.

   L'opéra italien en France avant Lulli, Bibliothèque de l'Institut Français de Florence (Université de Grenoble), ser. 1, Collection d'histoire et de linguistique française et italienne comparées, no. 3 (Paris: Honoré Champion, 1913).

   "Paolo Lorenzani à la court de France (1678–1694)," *La revue musicale* 3 (1922): 97–120.

Quazza, Romolo, *Mantova attraverso i secoli* (Mantua: Tipografia editoriale de "La voce di Mantova," 1933).

Quondam, Amadeo, introduction to *La civil conversazione*, by Stefano Guazzo, ed. Amadeo Quondam, 2 vols., Testi: Istituto di Studi Rinascimentali Ferrara (Bologna: Franco Cosimo Panini, 1993).

Ranke-Heinemann, Uta, *Eunuchs for the Kingdom of Heaven: Women, Sexuality and the Catholic Church*, trans. Peter Heinegg (New York: Doubleday, 1990), originally published as *Eunuchen für das Himmelreich: Katholische Kirche und Sexualität* (Hamburg: Hoffmann und Campe, 1988).

Rapaport, Ionel Florian, *La castration rituelle: L'état mental des Skoptzy* (Paris: Lipschutz, 1937).

Revel, Jacques, "The Uses of Civility," in *A History of Private Life*, vol. III, *Passions of the Renaissance*, ed. Roger Chartier, trans. Arthur Goldhammer (Cambridge, Mass., and London: Harvard University Press / Belknap Press, 1989), 167–205.

Rey, Michael, "Parisian Homosexuals Create a Lifestyle, 1700–1750: The Police Archives," trans. Robert A. Day and Robert Welch, in *'Tis Nature's Fault: Unauthorized Sexuality during the Enlightenment*, ed. Robert Purks Maccubbin (Cambridge: Cambridge University Press, 1985), 179–91.

Ricci, Corrado, *I teatri di Bologna nei secoli XVII e XVIII: Storia aneddotica* (1888; repr. Bologna: Arnaldo Forni, 1965).

Robertson, Jennifer, *Takarazuka: Sexual Politics and Popular Culture in Modern Japan* (Berkeley: University of California Press, 1998).

Rocke, Michael, *Forbidden Friendships: Homosexuality and Male Culture in Renaissance Florence*, Studies in the History of Sexuality (New York: Oxford University Press, 1996).

Rodocanachi, E[mmanuel], *Les infortunes d'une petite-fille d'Henri IV: Marguerite d'Orléans Grande-Duchesse de Toscanne* (1645–1727) (Paris: Ernst Flammarion, [1902?]).

Rosand, Ellen, "The Descending Tetrachord: An Emblem of Lament," *Musical Quarterly* 55 (1979): 346–59.

Opera in Seventeenth-Century Venice: The Creation of a Genre, A Centennial Book (Berkeley: University of California Press, 1991).

Rose, Gloria, "The Cantatas of Carissimi" (Ph.D. diss., Yale University, 1959).

"The Cantatas of Giacomo Carissimi," *Musical Quarterly* 48 (1962): 204–15.

"The Italian Cantata of the Baroque Period," in *Gattungen der Musik in Einzeldarstellungen: Gedenkschrift Leo Schrade*, ed. Wulf Arlt, Ernst Lichtenhahn, and Hans Oesch (Bern: Francke, 1973), 655–77.

Rose, Gloria, compil., *Giacomo Carissimi (1605–1674)*, The Wellesley Cantata Index Series, fasc. 5 ([Wellesley, Mass.]: Wellesley College, 1966).

Rosselli, John, "The Castrati as a Professional Group and a Social Phenomenon, 1550–1850," *Acta musicologica* 60 (1988): 143–79.

"From Princely Service to the Open Market: Singers of Italian Opera and Their Patrons, 1600–1850," *Cambridge Opera Journal* 1 (1989): 1–32.

Rudhart, Fr[anz] M[ichael], *Geschichte der Oper am Hofe zu München* (Freising: Franz Datterer, 1865).

Rudolph, Stella, "A Medici General, Prince Mattias, and His Battlefield Painter, Il Borgognone," *Studi secenteschi* 13 (1972): 183–91.

Sandberger, Adolf, introduction to *Ausgewählte Werke des kürfürstlich bayerischen Hofkapellmeisters Johann Kasper Kerll (1627–1693)*, vol. II, part 2, of *Denkmäler der Tonkunst in Bayern*, Denkmäler Deutscher Tonkunst, Folge 2 (Leipzig: Breitkopf & Härtel, 1901).

Sartori, Claudio, *I libretti italiani a stampa dalle origini al 1800: Catalogo analitico con 16 indici*, 7 vols. (Turin: Bertola e Locatelli Musica, 1993).

"La prima diva della lirica italiana: Anna Renzi," *Nuova rivista musicale italiana* 2 (1968): 430–52.

Schleiner, Winfried, "Cross-Dressing, Gender Errors, and Sexual Taboos in Renaissance Literature," in *Gender Reversals and Gender Cultures: Anthropological and Historical Perspectives*, ed. Sabrina Petra Ramet (London: Routledge, 1996), 92–104.

"Male Cross-Dressing and Transvestism in Renaissance Romances," *Sixteenth Century Journal* 19 (1988): 605–19.

Schmitz, Eugen, *Geschichte der weltlichen Solokantate* [2nd edn.] (Leipzig: Breitkopf & Härtel, 1955).

Seifert, Herbert, "Cesti and His Opera Troupe in Innsbruck and Vienna, with New Informations [*sic*] about His Last Year and His Oeuvre," in *La figura e l'opera di Antonio Cesti nel Seicento europeo: Convegno internazionale di studio, Arezzo, 26–27 aprile 2002*, ed. Mariateresa Dellaborra, Quaderni della Rivista Italiana di Musicologia, Società Italiana di Musicologia, no. 37 (Florence: Leo S. Olschki, 2003), 15–61.

Seifert, Lewis C., "Masculinity and Satires of 'Sodomites' in France, 1660–1715," *Journal of Homosexuality* 41 (2001): 37–52.

Senn, Walter, *Musik und Theater am Hof zu Innsbruck: Geschichte der Hofkapelle vom 15. Jahrhundert bis zu deren Auflösung in Jahre 1748* (Innsbruck: Österreichische Verlagsanstalt Innsbruck, 1954).

Sguazzoni, Maria Vittoria Feri, "Vita domestica di una famiglia pistoiese: Casa Dondori 1653–1678," *Bollettino storico pistoiese*, 3rd ser., 28 (1993): 131–42.

Simon, Roger, "Mazarin, la cour et l'influence italienne," in *La France et l'Italie au temps de Mazarin*, ed. Jean Serroy (Grenoble: Presses Universitaires de Grenoble, 1986), 33–39.

Skrine, Peter N., *The Baroque: Literature and Culture in Seventeenth-Century Europe* (New York: Holmes and Meier, 1978).

Solie, Ruth, "Changing the Subject," *Current Musicology* 53 (1993): 55–65.

Solomon, Maynard, "Thoughts on Biography," in *Beethoven Essays* (Cambridge, Mass., and London: Harvard University Press, 1988), 101–15.

Southorn, Janet, *Power and Display in the Seventeenth Century: The Arts and Their Patrons in Modena and Ferrara*, Cambridge Studies in the History of Art (Cambridge: Cambridge University Press, 1988).

Talbot, Michael, "*Ore italiane*: The Reckoning of the Time of Day in Pre-Napoleonic Italy," *Italian Studies* 40 (1985): 51–62.

Tandler, Julius, and Siegfried Grosz, "Über den Einfluß der Kastration auf den Organismus, II., Die Skopzen," *Archiv für Entwicklungsmechanik der Organismen* 30 (1910): 236–53.

Timms, Colin, "Brigida Bianchi's *Poesie musicali* and Their Settings," *I quaderni della civica scuola di musica* 9, nos. 19–20 (December 1990): 19–37.

"The Italian Cantata since 1945: Progress and Prospects," in *Cinquant'anni di produzioni e consumi della musica dell'età di Vivaldi 1947–1997*, ed. Francesco Fanna and Michael Talbot, Fondazione Giorgio Cini, Istituto Italiano Antonio Vivaldi; Studi di Musica Veneta, Quaderni Vivaldiani, no. 10 (Florence: Leo S. Olschki, 1998), 75–94.

Tomassini, Luciano, *Raimondo Montecuccoli: Capitano e scrittore* (Rome: Stato Maggiore dell'Esercito, Ufficio Storico, 1978).

Treasure, Geoffrey R.R., *Mazarin: The Crisis of Absolutism in France* (London and New York: Routledge, 1995).

Seventeenth Century France, 2nd edn. (London: John Murray, 1981).

Trenta, Tommaso, *Memorie per servire alla storia politica del Cardinale Francesco Buonvisi patrizio lucchese*, 2 vols. (Lucca: Francesco Bertini, 1818).

Tribby, Jay, "Cooking (with) Clio and Cleo: Eloquence and Experiment in Seventeenth-Century Florence," *Journal of the History of Ideas* 52 (1991): 417–39.

Trumbach, Randolph, "Sex, Gender, and Sexual Identity in Modern Culture: Male Sodomy and Female Prostitution in Enlightenment London," *Journal of the History of Sexuality* 2 (1991): 186–203.

Valsecchi, Franco, *L'Italia nel Seicento e nel Settecento*, vol. VI of *Società e costume: Panorama di storia sociale e tecnologica* (Turin: U.T.E.T., 1967).

Waddington, Raymond B., "The Bisexual Portrait of Francis I: Fontainebleau, Castiglione, and the Tone of Courtly Mythology," in *Playing with Gender: A Renaissance Pursuit*, ed. Jean R. Brink, Maryanne C. Horowitz, and Allison P. Coudert (Urbana: University of Illinois Press, 1991), 105–22.

Weaver, Andrew Hudsco, "Piety, Politics, and Patronage: Motets at the Habsburg Court in Vienna during the Reign of Ferdinand III (1637–1657)" (Ph.D. diss., Yale Univ., 2002).

Weaver, Robert Lamar, "Florentine Comic Operas of the Seventeenth Century" (Ph.D. diss., University of North Carolina, Chapel Hill, 1958).

"*Il Girello*, a 17th-Century Burlesque Opera," *Quadrivium* 12 (1971): 141–63.

"Materiali per le biografie dei fratelli Melani," *Rivista italiana di musicologia* 12 (1977): 252–95.

Weaver, Robert Lamar, ed., *Alessandro Melani (1639–1703), Atto Melani (1626–1714)*, The Wellesley Edition Cantata Index Series, fasc. 8–9 ([Wellesley, Mass.:] Wellesley College, 1972).

Cantatas by Alessandro Melani 1639–1703, Atto Melani 1627–1714, vol. XI of *The Italian Cantata in the Seventeenth Century* (New York: Garland, 1986).

Weaver, Robert Lamar, and Norma Wright Weaver, *A Chronology of Music in the Florentine Theater 1590–1750*, Detroit Studies in Music Bibliography, no. 38 (Detroit: Information Coordinators, 1978).

Weissman, Ronald, "Taking Patronage Seriously: Mediterranean Values and Renaissance Society," in *Patronage, Art, and Society in Renaissance Italy*, ed. F.W. Kent and Patricia Simons (Canberra [Australia]: Humanities Research Centre; Oxford: Clarendon Press, 1987), 25–45.

Whigham, Frank, "Interpretation at Court: Courtesy and the Performance–Audience Dialectic," *New Literary History: A Journal of Theory and Interpretation* 14 (1983): 623–39.

Wistreich, Richard, *Warrior, Courtier, Singer: Giulio Cesare Brancaccio and the Performance of Identity in the Late Renaissance* (Aldershot, Eng., and Burlington, Vt.: Ashgate: 2007).

Woodward, John, *A Treatise on Ecclesiastical Heraldry* (New York: The Christian Literature Company, 1894).

Wright, A[nthony] D[avid], *The Early Modern Papacy: From the Council of Trent to the French Revolution, 1564–1789*, Longman History of the Papacy (Harlow: Pearson Education, Longman, 2000).

Young-Bruehl, Elisabeth, "The Writing of Biography," in *Mind and the Body Politic* (New York and London: Routledge, Chapman and Hall / Routledge, 1989), 125–37.

Zaslaw, Neal, "The First Opera in Paris: A Study in the Politics of Art," in *Jean-Baptiste Lully and the Music of the French Baroque: Essays in Honor of James R. Anthony*, ed. John Hadju Heyer, in collaboration with Catherine Massip, Carl B. Schmidt, and Herbert Schneider (Cambridge and New York: Cambridge University Press, 1989), 7–23.

Zoller, Franz Karl, *Geschichte und Denkwürdigkeiten der Stadt Innsbruck*, vol. I (Innsbruck: Wagner, 1816).

Published, primary

[Ancillon, Charles], *Eunuchism Display'd* (London: E. Curll, 1718), originally published as (and slightly altered from) *Traité des eunuques* (Paris: n.p., 1707).

Arrest contre les chastrez (Paris: n.p., 1619).

Baldinucci, Filippo, "Vita di Jacopo Cortesi," in *Notizie de' professori del disegno* . . . , vol. XIX (Florence: G.B. Stecchi, 1773).

Bandello, Matteo, *Novelle*, 4 vols. (Lucca: Il Busdrago, 1554–73).

Bargagli, Girolamo, *Dialogo de' giuochi che nelle vegghie sanesi si usano da fare*, ed. Patrizia D'Incalci Ermini, Accademia Senese degli Intronati: Monografie di storia e letteratura senese, no. 9 (Siena: Industria Grafica Pistolesi, 1982; first published, Siena: Luca Bonetti, 1572).

Benserade, [Isaac de], *Ballets pour Louis XIV*, ed. Marie-Claude Canova-Green, 2 vols., Collection de rééditions de textes du XVIIe siècle (Toulouse: Société de Littératures Classiques; Paris: Éditions Klincksieck, 1997).

Bontempi, Giovanni Andrea Angelini, *Historia musica* (Perugia: Costantini, 1695).

Bullarum, diplomatum et privilegiorum sanctorum romanorum . . . , vol. VIII (Turin: Seb. Franco and Enrico Dalmazzo, 1863).

Il cannocchiale per la finta pazza, dilineato da M[aolino] B[isaccioni] C[onte] di G[enova] (Venice: Giovanni Battista Surian, 1641).

Capitoli della magnifica città di Parma (Parma: Seth de Viothis, 1555).

Carissimi, Giacomo, *Cantatas by Giacomo Carissimi 1605–1674*, vol. II of *The Italian Cantata in the Seventeenth Century*, ed. Günther Massenkeil (New York: Garland, 1986).

Casanova, [Giacomo], *Mémoires*, ed. Robert Abirached, 3 vols., Biblothèque de la Pléiade ([Paris]: Gallimard, 1958–60)

Casini, Bruno, *I "libri d'oro" delle città di Pistoia, Prato e Pescia*, Biblioteca di "Le Apuane," no. 12 (Massa-Uliveti: Edizioni del Centro Culturale Apuano, 1988).

Castiglione, Baldassare, *The Courtyer of Count Baldessar Castilio*, trans. Thomas Hoby (London: Wyllyam Seres, 1561).

   Il libro del cortegiano, ed. Giulio Preti, I millenni, no. 49 (Turin: G. Einaudi, 1960; first published, Venice: Aldo Romano e Andrea d'Asola, 1528).

Chiabrera, Gabriello, "Il Geri: Dialogo della tessitura delle canzoni," in *Opere di Gabriello Chiabrera e lirici non marinisti*, ed. Marcello Turchi, 2nd edn. (Turin: Unione Tipografico-Editrice Torinese, 1973), 548–70.

   Maniere, scherzi e canzonette morali, ed. Giulia Raboni, Biblioteca di scrittori italiani (Parma: Fondazione Pietro Bembo and Ugo Guanda, 1998).

Crescimbeni, Giovanni Maria, *Commentarj . . . intorno alla sua Istoria della volgar poesia* (Venice: Lorenzo Basegio, 1731).

Del Colle, Giulio, "Descrittione de gli Apparati," in *Il Bellerofonte: Drama Musicale*, by Vincenzo Nolfi ([Venice]: n.p., 1642).

Delphinus, Hieronymus (pseud.) (ed.), *Eunuchi conjugium: Die Capaunen-Heirath* . . . , 3rd edn. (Halle: n.p., 1718).

Le Dictionnaire de l'Académie Française (Paris: Jean Baptiste Coignard, 1694).

Fielding, Henry, *The Historical Register for the Year 1736* and *Eurydice Hissed*, ed. William W. Appleton (Lincoln, Neb.: University of Nebraska Press, 1967).

Fortini, Pietro, *Le giornate delle novelle de' novizi*, ed. Adriana Mauriello, 2 vols., I novellieri italiani, no. 28 (Rome: Salerno, 1988).

  Le piacevoli et amorose notti de' novizi, ed. Adriana Mauriello, 2 vols., I novellieri italiani, no. 28–2 (Rome: Salerno, 1995).

Fouquet, Nicolas, *Recueil des defenses de Mr Fouquet*, vol. VIII, *Suite de la continuation de la production de Mr Fouquet, pour servir de réponse a celle de Mr Talon sur le pretendu crime d'estat* ([Paris?]: n.p., 1666).

Garzoni, Tomaso, *La piazza universale di tutte le professioni del mondo*, ed. Giovanni Battista Bronzini, Biblioteca di "Lares," monographs, 2 vols., n.s. vol. 49 (Florence: Leo S. Olschki, 1996; based on the edition from Venice: G.B. Somasco, 1589).

Graziani, Girolamo, *La gara delle stagione [sic], Torneo a cavallo rappresentato in Modana nel passaggio de' serenissimi arciduchi Ferdinando Carlo, Sigismondo Francesco d'Austria et Arciduchessa Anna di Toscana* (Modana: Soliani, 1652).

  La gara delle stagioni: Torneo a cavallo, in *Varie poesie, e prose* (Modena: Soliani, 1662), 139–91.

Gualdo Priorato, Galeazzo, *Historia della Sacra Real Maestà di Christina Alessandra Regina di Svetia, &c.* (Rome: Stamperia della Rev. Camera Apost., 1656).

Guazzo, Stefano, *La civil conversazione*, ed. Amadeo Quondam, 2 vols., Testi: Istituto di Studi Rinascimentali Ferrara (Bologna: Franco Cosimo Panini, 1993; first published, Venice: Enea de Alaris, 1574).

Herberay, Nicolas de, *Le huitiesme livre d'Amadis de Gaule* (Lyon: Benoist Rigaud, 1575).

Leti, Gregorio, *The Loves of Charles, Duke of Mantua, and of Margaret, Countess of Rovera* (Savoy: Henry Herringman, 1669), originally published as Giulio Capocoda [Gregorio Leti], *L'amore di Carlo Gonzaga, duca di Mantova, e della Contessa Margarita della Rovere* (Ragusa [Geneva]: Fabio Fabi, 1666).

Liberati, Francesco, *Il perfetto maestro di casa*, 3 vols., rev. edn. (Rome: Bernabò, 1668).

Machiavelli, Niccolò, *Istorie fiorentine*, in *Tutte le opere*, [ed. Mario Martelli] ([Florence]: Sansoni, 1971; Intratext CT, 2007), book 4, section 12, www.intratext.com/IXT/ITA1109/_P8Y.HTM.

Mancini, Hortense, *Les illustres aventurières ou Mémoires d'Hortense et de Marie Mancini*, ed. G. Doscot, Les hommes, les faits et les moeurs (Paris: Henri Jonquières, 1929), 45–46, originally published as *Mémoires de M. L. D. M. A.* (Cologne: Pierre de Marteau, 1676).

Mancini, Marie, *La vérité dans son jour*, ed. Patricia Francis Cholakian and Elizabeth C. Goldsmith (Delmar, N.Y.: Scholars' Facsimiles and Reprints, 1998; first published 1677, without place or publisher).

Marino, Giambattista, *Adonis: Selections from* L'Adone *of Giambattista Marino*, trans. and intro. Harold Martin Priest (Ithaca, N.Y.: Cornell University Press, 1967).

Epistolario, seguito da lettere di altri scrittori del Seicento, ed. Angelo Borzelli and Fausto Nicolini, 2 vols. (Bari: Gius. Laterza & Figli, 1911–12).

La Murtoleide (Nuremberg: Joseph Stampier, 1619).

Mazarin, Jules, *Lettres du Cardinal Mazarin pendant son ministère*, ed. G. D'Avenel, 9 vols. (Paris: Imprimerie Nationale, 1894).

Melani, Atto, *Complete Cantatas*, ed. Roger Freitas, Collegium Musicum: Yale University, ser. 2, vol. 15 (Middleton, Wis.: A-R Editions, 2006).

Memmo, Giovanni Maria, *Dialogo nel quale dopo alcune filosofiche dispute, si forma un perfetto prencipe, et una perfetta repubblica, e parimente un senatore, un cittadino, un soldato, et un mercatante* (Venice: Gabriele Giolito de' Ferrari, 1659).

Metastasio, Pietro, *Tutte le opere di Pietro Metastasio*, ed. Bruno Brunelli, vol. I, I Classici Mondadori, Fondazione Borletti (Milan: A. Mondadori, 1943).

Montecuccoli, Raimund, *Ausgewaehlte Schriften*, vol. IV, *Miscellen, Correspondenz*, ed. Alois Veltzé (Vienna: Wilhelm Braumüller, 1900).

Moreau, C[élestin], ed., *Choix de Mazarinades*, 2 vols. (Paris: Jules Renouard, 1853).

Morley, Thomas, *A Plaine and Easie Introduction to Practicall Musicke* (London: P. Short, 1597).

Muratori, Lodovico Antonio, *Della perfetta poesia italiana spiegata* (Modena: Soliani, 1706).

11ᵉ livre d'Amadis de Gaule (Lyon, 1577).

Paré, Ambroise, *The Workes of Ambrose Parey*, trans. Thomas Johnson (London, 1634).

Penna, Lorenzo, *Li primi albori musicali*, Bibliotheca musica bononiensis, sezione 2, no. 38 (1684; repr., Bologna: Arnaldo Forni, 1996).

Les privileges et fidelitez des chastrez (Paris: n.p., 1619).

[Raguenet, François], *Paralele des Italiens et des François, en ce qui regarde la musique et les opera* (1702; repr., Geneva: Minkoff Reprint, 1976).

Redi, Francesco, *Osservazioni intorno alle vipere* (Florence: All'Insegna della Stella, 1664).

Ricciardi, G[iovanni] B[attista], *Rime burlesche*, ed. Ettore Toci (Livorno: Francesco Vigo, 1881).

Ringhieri, Innocentio, *Cento giuochi liberali, et d'ingegno* (Bologna: Anselmo Giaccarelli, 1551).

Rocco, Antonio, *L'Alcibiade fanciullo a scola*, ed. and intro. Laura Coci, 2nd edn., Faville, no. 22 (Rome: Salerno, 2003).

Romagnesi, Marc-Antonio, *Poesie liriche . . . divise in quattro parti* (Paris: Denys Langlois, 1673).

Rosa, Salvator, "La musica," in *Poesie e lettere edite e inedite di Salvator Rosa*, ed. G. A. Cesareo (Naples: R. Accademia di Archeologia, Lettere e Belle Arti, 1892), I:163–87.

Rossi, Luigi, *Cantatas by Luigi Rossi c. 1597–1653*, vol. I of *The Italian Cantata in the Seventeenth Century*, ed. Francesco Luisi (New York: Garland, 1986).

Saint-Évremond, [Charles Marguetel de Saint Denis, Seigneur de], *Lettres*, ed. René Ternois, Société des Textes Français Modernes, 2 vols. (Paris: Librairie Marcel Didier, 1968).

Scudéry, Madeleine de, *Clélie*, 10 vols. (Paris: A. Courbé, 1654–60).

Shakespeare, William, *Venus and Adonis*, in *The Poems*, ed. F.T. Prince, 3rd edn., The Arden Edition of the Works of William Shakespeare (London: Methuen & Co.; Cambridge, Mass.: Harvard University Press, 1960), 1–62.

Siri, Vittorio, *Memorie recondite dall'anno 1601 sino al 1640*, 8 vols. (Ronco: n.p., 1677–79).

   Il Mercurio, ovvero, Historia de' correnti tempi, 15 vols. (Casale: Christoforo della Casa, 1644–82).

Straparola, Giovan Francesco, *Le piacevoli notti*, ed. Donato Pirovano, 2 vols., I novellieri italiani, no. 29 (Rome: Salerno, 2000).

Stubbes, Philip, *The Anatomy of Abuses* (London: Richard Iones, 1583).

Tesauro, Emanuele, *Il cannocchiale aristotelico* (Turin: Gio. Sinibaldo, 1654).

Tosi, Pietro Francesco, *Observations on the Florid Song, or Sentiments on the Ancient and Modern Singers*, trans. [Johann Ernst] Galliard, 2nd edn. (1743; repr., with a preface by Paul Henry Lang, New York: Harcourt Brace Jovanovich, Johnson Reprint Corporation, 1968), originally published as *Opinioni de' cantori antichi e moderni o sieno Osservazioni sopra il canto figurato* (Bologna: Lelio dalla Volpe, 1723).

[Turenne, Henri de la Tour d'Auvergne, vicomte de], *Lettres de Turenne extraites des Archives Rohan-Bouillon*, ed. Suzanne d'Huart, Archives Nationales, Inventaires et Documents (Ministère des Affaires Culturelles, Direction des Archives de France) (Paris: S.E.V.P.E.N., 1971).

"Vita di Ferdinando II, quinto Granduca di Toscana" (printed with two other works in an otherwise untitled book), ed. F. Orlando and G. Baccini, Bibliotechina Grassoccia, Capricci e curiosità letterarie inedite o rare (Florence: Il "Giornale di Erudizione," 1886), I:5–36.

Vocabolario degli Accademici della Crusca (Venice: Giovanni Alberti, 1612).

Wollstonecraft, Mary, *A Vindication of the Rights of Women* (1792; repr., Harmondsworth: Penguin, 1985).

Zeno, Apostolo, *Lettere*, 2nd edn. (Venice: Sansoni, 1785).

Manuscripts

Individually cited works

[Baldini, Sebastiano?], "Al Signor Atto Melani," I Rvat, Barb. lat. 3902, f. 281r–v.

Caramelli, Tommaso, "Alberi genealogici delle famiglie nobili e civili della città di Pistoia," I Fn.

Franchi, Pier Lorenzo, "Memorie delle famiglie pistoiesi," I PSas, MSS 1–35.

"Per la partenza di un castrato amato dalla Sig.ra Anna Maria N. [backwards] Cortigiana, e cantatrice romana detta Campaspe per haver recitata quella parte con grande applauso in una commedia in musica nella città di Firenze," I Fn, Magl.VII.364, ff. 289–95v.

"Sopra Atto Melani, musico, castrato di Pistoia, figliolo d'un campanaio," I Fn, Cl.VII.359, pp. 758–59.

"Sopra il giuoco del Cocconetto," I Fn, Magl.VII.364, ff. 300v–302.

"Vita dell'Abate Melani," in "Memorie antiche," I Fn, Rossi Cassigoli, MS 268, pp. 151–52.

Collections

B Bc, 15262	F Pae, CP Rome, 185
B Bc, 19196	F Pae, CP Rome, 186
D Kl, 2° Mus. 34	F Pae, CP Rome, 187
D Mbs, Mus. Ms. 1524	F Pae, CP Rome, 189
F Pae, CP Bavière, 2	F Pae, CP Rome, 190
F Pae, CP Rome, 125	F Pae, CP Rome, 191
F Pae, CP Rome, 141	F Pae, CP Rome, 192
F Pae, CP Rome, 142	F Pae, CP Rome, 193
F Pae, CP Rome, 145	F Pae, CP Rome, 194
F Pae, CP Rome, 183	F Pae, CP Rome, 196
F Pae, CP Rome, 184	F Pae, CP Rome, 197

F Pae, CP Rome, 198

F Pae, CP Rome, 199

F Pae, CP Rome, 200

F Pae, CP Rome, 201

F Pae, CP Rome, 208

F Pae, CP Rome, 209

F Pae, CP Rome, 210

F Pae, CP Rome, 211

F Pae, CP Rome, 213

F Pae, CP Rome, 214

F Pae, CP Rome, 215

F Pae, CP Rome, 216

F Pae, CP Rome, 218

F Pae, CP Rome, 220

F Pae, CP Rome, 221

F Pae, CP Rome, 222

F Pae, CP Rome, 223

F Pae, CP Rome, 225

F Pae, CP Rome, 228

F Pae, CP Rome, suppl. 7

F Pae, CP Rome, suppl. 10

F Pae, CP Toscane, 8

F Pae, CP Toscane, 9

F Pae, CP Toscane, 10

F Pae, MD France, 270

F Pae, MD France, 272

F Pae, MD France, 273

F Pae, MD France, 307

F Pae, MD France, 855

F Pae, MD France, 933

F Pan, Étude XV (Gaillardie)

F Pan, O^1 15

F Pc, H.659

F Pm, MS 2218

F Pn, MS fond français, 13054

F Pn, Rés. Vmb. 93

F Pn, Rés. Vmf. 14

F Pn, Rés. Vmf. 41

F Pn, Vm^7 1

F Pn, Vm^7 18

GB Cfm, 24 F 4

GB Ckc, Rowe 22

GB Lbl, Addl. 62401

GB Lbl, Harley 1264

GB Lbl, Harley 1863

I Bc, V.198

I Fas, MdP, filza 1507

I Fas, MdP, filza 1509

I Fas, MdP, filza 4661

I Fas, MdP, filza 4801

I Fas, MdP, filza 4802

I Fas, MdP, filza 4803

I Fas, MdP, filza 4804

I Fas, MdP, filza 4805

I Fas, MdP, filza 4806

I Fas, MdP, filza 4807

I Fas, MdP, filza 4808

I Fas, MdP, filza 4809

I Fas, MdP, filza 4810

I Fas, MdP, filza 4811

I Fas, MdP, filza 4812

I Fas, MdP, filza 4813

I Fas, MdP, filza 5284

I Fas, MdP, filza 5288

I Fas, MdP, filza 5296

I Fas, MdP, filza 5301

I Fas, MdP, filza 5322

I Fas, MdP, filza 5326

I Fas, MdP, filza 5330

I Fas, MdP, filza 5336

I Fas, MdP, filza 5339

I Fas, MdP, filza 5340

I Fas, MdP, filza 5345

I Fas, MdP, filza 5346

I Fas, MdP, filza 5354

I Fas, MdP, filza 5369

I Fas, MdP, filza 5375

I Fas, MdP, filza 5392

I Fas, MdP, filza 5407

I Fas, MdP, filza 5408

I Fas, MdP, filza 5409

I Fas, MdP, filza 5410

I Fas, MdP, filza 5411

I Fas, MdP, filza 5413

I Fas, MdP, filza 5414

I Fas, MdP, filza 5415

I Fas, MdP, filza 5416

I Fas, MdP, filza 5419

I Fas, MdP, filza 5421

I Fas, MdP, filza 5425

I Fas, MdP, filza 5426

I Fas, MdP, filza 5427

I Fas, MdP, filza 5430

I Fas, MdP, filza 5431

I Fas, MdP, filza 5432

I Fas, MdP, filza 5433

I Fas, MdP, filza 5434

I Fas, MdP, filza 5435

I Fas, MdP, filza 5436

I Fas, MdP, filza 5437

I Fas, MdP, filza 5442

I Fas, MdP, filza 5443

I Fas, MdP, filza 5444

I Fas, MdP, filza 5445

I Fas, MdP, filza 5446

I Fas, MdP, filza 5449

I Fas, MdP, filza 5450

I Fas, MdP, filza 5451

I Fas, MdP, filza 5452

I Fas, MdP, filza 5453

I Fas, MdP, filza 5454

I Fas, MdP, filza 5455

I Fas, MdP, filza 5458

I Fas, MdP, filza 5459

I Fas, MdP, filza 5460

I Fas, MdP, filza 5461

I Fas, MdP, filza 5462

I Fas, MdP, filza 5463

I Fas, MdP, filza 5466

I Fas, MdP, filza 5468

I Fas, MdP, filza 5469

I Fas, MdP, filza 5470

I Fas, MdP, filza 5471

I Fas, MdP, filza 5472

I Fas, MdP, filza 5474

I Fas, MdP, filza 5475

I Fas, MdP, filza 5476

I Fas, MdP, filza 5478

I Fas, MdP, filza 5490

I Fas, MdP, filza 5492

I Fas, MdP, filza 5494

I Fas, MdP, filza 5537

I Fas, MdP, filza 5544

I Fas, MdP, filza 5561

I Fas, MdP, filza 5910

I Fas, Misc. Med. 94

I Fas, Notarile moderno, protocollo 14591

I Fas, Notarile moderno, protocollo 14594

I Fas, Notarile moderno, protocollo 14596

I Fas, Notarile moderno, protocollo 14598

I Fas, Notarile moderno, protocollo 14603

I FEas, Arch. Bent., 284

I FEas, Arch. Bent., 285

I FEas, Arch. Bent., 286

I FEas, Arch. Bent., 287

I FEas, Arch. Bent., 290

I FEas, Arch. Bent., 291

I FEas, Arch. Bent., 293

I FEas, Arch. Bent., 297

I FEas, Arch. Bent., 298

I FEas, Arch. Bent., 301

I FEas, Arch. Bent., 305

I FEas, Arch. Bent., 310

I FEas, Arch. Bent., 311

I FEas, Arch. Bent., 312

I FEas, Arch. Bent., 319

I FEas, Arch. Bent., 335

I FEas, Arch. Bent., 336

I FEas, Arch. Bent., 338

I FEas, Arch. Bent., 339

I FEas, Arch. Bent., 340

I FEas, Arch. Bent., 342

I FEas, Arch. Bent., 350

I FEas, Arch. Bent., 353

I FEas, Arch. Bent., 355

I FEas, Arch. Bent., 356

I FEas, Arch. Bent., 357

I FEas, Arch. Bent., 358

I FEas, Arch. Bent., 360

I FEas, Arch. Bent., 361

I FEas, Arch. Bent., 362

I FEas, Arch. Bent., 364

I FEas, Arch. Bent., 367

I FEas, Arch. Bent., 373

I FEas, Arch. Bent., fasc. 1651

I Fm, Melani 1

I Fm, Melani 2

I Fm, Melani 3

I Fm, Melani 4

I Fm, Melani 5

I Fm, Melani 6

I Fm, Melani 7

I Fm, Melani 8

I Fm, Melani 9

I Fn, Cl.VII.359

I Fn, Magl.VII.364

I Fn, Magl.XIX.26

I Fn, Rossi Cassigoli, cassetta 1

I Fn, Rossi Cassigoli, cassetta 8

I Fn, Rossi Cassigoli, MS 268

I Fn, Tordi 133

I Fn, Tordi 350

I MAas, E.VI.3, busta 554

I MAas, E.XV.3, busta 685

I MAas, E.XV.3, busta 686

I MAas, E.XXV.3, busta 1048

I MAas, E.XXV.3, busta 1049

I MAas, E.XXVIII.3, busta 1135

I MAas, E.XXXI.3, busta 1275

I MAas, E.XLII.3, busta 1574

I MOas, Ambasciatori, Ferrara, busta 28

I MOas, Ambasciatori, Francia, busta 147

I MOas, Ambasciatori, Francia, busta 148

I MOas, Ambasciatori, Germania, busta 99

I MOas, Cancelleria ducale, particolari, busta 880, Melani

I MOe, Autografoteca Campori, A. Melani

I MOe, Mus. E.249

I MOe, Mus. E.300

I MOe, Mus. F.1349

I Nc, 22.2.22

I Nc, 33.4.4

I Nc, 33.4.18

I Nc, 33.5.18

I PS, A/1-18

I PS, Archivio Vescovile, Morti di S. Giovanni Fuorcivitas

I PS, C-50

I PS, H-263

I PS, L-25 (M-49)

I PS, L-35 (M-61)

I PS, L-68

I PS, L-75

I PSc, Raccolta Chiappelli, 14

I PSc, Raccolta Chiappelli, 40.I

I PSc, Raccolta Chiappelli, 64.ii

I PSc, Raccolta Chiappelli, 188

I PSc, Vetrina Martini 41[1]

I PSc, Vetrina Martini 41[2]

I Rc, 2486

I Rvat, Archivio Chigi 34

I Rvat, Archivio Chigi 231

I Rvat, Archivio Chigi 3906

I Rvat, Barb. lat. 3902

I Rvat, Barb. lat. 4156

I Rvat, Barb. lat. 6407

I Rvat, Chig. L.IV.94
I Rvat, Chig. L.V.153B
I Rvat, Chig. L.VI.187
I Rvat, Chig. L.VI.197
I Rvat, Chig. Q.IV.11
I Rvat, Chig. Q.IV.18
I Rvat, Vat. lat. 13363

I SUss, Archivio Colonna,
    Corrispondenza di Lorenzo
    Onofrio Colonna, cartella 10
I TOas, Lettere particolari,
    mazzo 33
US CHH, Music VM2.1 M1
US LAuc, fC 694 M4

Index

Page numbers in italics refer to tables, figures, and plates. Page numbers in parentheses refer to material in appendices.